International organisations, non-State actors, and the formation of customary international law

MANCHESTER
1824
Manchester University Press

Melland Schill Perspectives on International Law

MELLAND SCHILL *Perspectives on* INTERNATIONAL LAW

Building on the history of Melland Schill Classics and Melland Schill Studies at Manchester University Press, Melland Schill Perspectives on International Law was established to reflect the diversity of international legal scholarship worldwide. This inclusive, accessible series aims to offer a platform for scholars from different regions who adopt innovative approaches to new and old topics.

Melland Schill Perspectives on International Law is founded on the idea that every international legal issue should be debated from various and, at times, incommensurable perspectives. Though there is a great deal of diversity in international legal debates and practice, this diversity is often obfuscated by prevailing Euro-centric and positivist narratives, which not only creates difficulties for non-Western scholars to be heard but hinders the development of different approaches.

International organisations, non-State actors, and the formation of customary international law

Edited by Sufyan Droubi and Jean d'Aspremont

Manchester University Press

Published by Manchester University Press
Altrincham Street, Manchester M1 7JA
www.manchesteruniversitypress.co.uk

British Library Cataloguing-in-Publication Data
A catalogue record for this book is available from the British Library

ISBN 978 1 5261 3415 8 hardback

First published 2020

Typeset by Newgen Publishing UK

Contents

Figures

Tables

Contributors

Valentina Azarova is an international legal practitioner and scholar with fifteen years of experience working with and advising non-governmental organisations, focusing on questions of economic and social global inequality including as they result from armed conflict. She is Legal Advisor to the Global Legal Action Network (GLAN). She is also Research Fellow at the Manchester International Law Centre, University of Manchester and Visiting Fellow at the Institute for International Law of Peace and Armed Conflict, Ruhr University, Bochum. Her contribution to this volume is based on her work with civil society in the Middle East and North Africa where she has lived and held academic posts for over a decade, including in Palestine, Lebanon, and Turkey.

Antal Berkes is lecturer in law at Brunel University London. In 2019, he was a postdoctoral research fellow at the SARChI Professorship on International Constitutional Law (Prof Erika de Wet) at the University of Pretoria, where he wrote his book entitled *International Human Rights Law in Areas out of the Effective Control of the State* (forthcoming). He is visiting scholar at the Manchester International Law Centre, University of Manchester.

Veronika Bílková is an associate professor in International Law at the Faculty of Law of the Charles University in Prague and the head of the Centre for International Law of the Institute of International Relations, Prague. Since 2010, she has represented the Czech Republic in the Venice Commission of the Council of Europe. Since 2018, she has been the Secretary-General of the European Society of International Law (ESIL). Having a background in both law and political science, she combines theoretical research with a more policy-oriented approach. She was the final rapporteur of the ILA Committee on Non-State Actors.

Contributors

Catherine Brölmann is Associate Professor of International Law at the University of Amsterdam. She is co-editor-in-chief of Oxford International Organizations and an editor on the board of International Community Law Review. She is a member of the Advisory Committee for Public International Law of the Netherlands Government.

Fabian Cardenas is Professor of International Law at the University of Bogota Jorge Tadeo Lozano. He directs the LLM programmes in environmental law and teaches public international law, international legal theory, and international environmental law. He is founder and board member of the Colombian Academy of International Law; member of the interest group on international responsibility and the environment of the Latin American Society of International Law. His books and academic articles primarily concern the theory of the sources of international law, international environmental law, as well as the law of the sea and the operation of the International Criminal Court with regards to Colombia and Latin America. With fifteen years of academic experience, he has also worked as a diplomat and international legal advisor of Colombia and some international organisations.

Jean d'Aspremont is Professor of International Law at Sciences Po School of Law. He also holds a chair of Public International Law at the University of Manchester where he founded the Manchester International Law Centre (MILC). He is General Editor of the Cambridge Studies in International and Comparative Law and Director of Oxford International Organizations (OXIO). He is a member of the Scientific Advisory Board of the European Journal of International Law and series editor of the Melland Schill Studies in International Law.

Rossana Deplano is Lecturer in Law at the University of Leicester. Her main research interests lie in the field of public international law, with a focus on United Nations law, international legal theory, and international legal research. In 2017, her monograph entitled *The Strategic Use of International Law by the United Nations Security Council: An Empirical Study* (Springer 2015) was noted as one of the five most influential books of the year by the President of the European Society of International Law. She is currently writing a monograph for Cambridge University Press entitled *Empirical and Theoretical Approaches to International Law: How States Use the United Nations General Assembly to Create International Obligations*. She is also the co-editor of the first *Handbook on Research Methods in International Law* (Elgar, forthcoming 2020).

Contributors

Sufyan Droubi is Lecturer in Law within the School of Social Sciences, University of Dundee. Previously, Sufyan was a Research Fellow at the University of São Paulo and at the University of Manchester, sponsored by a FAPESP Postdoctoral Fellowship. He holds a PhD in Law from the University of Essex. A fully qualified lawyer in Brazil since 1996, he spent fifteen years in practice before turning to the academia. He is one of the editors of the Melland Shill Perspectives to International Law; and one of the coordinators of the Interest Group on International Organisations of the European Society of International Law.

Lorenzo Gasbarri is research fellow in international law and visiting lecturer at Bocconi University. He has studied at the University of Florence, Milan and at the Graduate Institute in Geneva. Lorenzo has held research positions at University College London and at the University of Helsinki and has been visiting fellow at the University of Copenhagen and at the Max Planck Institute in Heidelberg. He is junior editor of the Oxford database on international organisations and convener of the interest group on the law of international organisations of the European Society of International Law.

Kasey McCall-Smith is a Senior Lecturer in Public International Law and the Programme Director of the LLM in Human Rights at the University of Edinburgh Law School. She researches and publishes predominantly in the areas of treaty law, corporate social responsibility relating to modern slavery, treaty body jurisprudence, and the domestic incorporation and implementation of human rights treaties. She is currently the Chair of the Association of Human Rights Institutes.

Maiko Meguro is a PhD research fellow of the Amsterdam Centre for International Law, University of Amsterdam. Her research focus is mainly on international lawmaking, particularly on the way decision-making processes at domestic and international levels interact. She also works as a legal officer for DG CNECT (the European Commission) and Ministry of Economy, Trade and Industry of Japan.

Jean-Baptiste Merlin is an associate member of the Centre de droit international de Nanterre (CEDIN) and a consultant in public international law. From October 2015 to the completion of the topic in 2018 he was an assistant of the Special Rapporteur of the United Nations International Law Commission on the topic 'Identification of customary international law'. A graduate from the Institut d'Etudes Politiques of Aix-en-Provence, France (2010), he holds a PhD in public law from the University of Paris Nanterre (2015). His experience as an international lawyer also includes practice as Counsel representing States in cases before international jurisdictions, including the International Court of Justice and the International Tribunal for the Law of the Sea. He also serves as arbitrator's collaborator in cases before the International Centre for Settlement of Investment Disputes.

Iris Müller, Legal Adviser, Legal Division, International Committee of the Red Cross.

Luíza Leão Soares Pereira is Lecturer in International Law at the University of Sheffield, UK. She has studied at the University of Cambridge, UK, and at Universidade Federal do Rio Grande do Sul, Brazil. Her research is on the role of individual international lawyers in lawmaking and the functioning of the international legal profession.

Maruša T. Veber is a teaching assistant and a PhD candidate at the Department of International Law at the Faculty of Law, University of Ljubljana. She is pursuing her PhD in collaboration with the Manchester International Law Centre on the topic of sanctions adopted by international organisations in the defence of the general interest. Previously she was a junior visiting fellow at the Graduate Institute of International and Development Studies in Geneva, a visiting scholar at the University of Hull Law School and a researcher at the United Nations University Institute on Comparative Regional Integration Studies (UNU-CRIS) in Bruges. She is a member of Geneva International Sanctions Network and a member of Slovene branch of International Law Association.

Nikolaos Voulgaris is a law lecturer at the European Law & Governance School in Athens and a post-doctoral Fellow at the Athens Public International Law Center. He studied law in Athens (National and Kapodistrian University) and London (King's College London). He is also teaching assistant at the National and Kapodistrian University and is a non-practising member of the Athens bar.

Michael Wood, 20 Essex Street Chambers, Member of the International Law Commission (Special Rapporteur for *Identification of customary international law* between 2012 and 2018).

William Thomas Worster is Senior Lecturer in International Law at The Hague University of Applied Sciences where he has taught public international law, international organisations, and international migration and refugee law for more than ten years. Prior to teaching, he served at the International Criminal Tribunal for the former Yugoslavia, and also worked in various countries in private firms, NGOs, and government. He is the author of more than forty articles and book chapters in his fields of expertise, and has also spoken at more than fifty universities and international conferences worldwide.

Tomoko Yamashita is Associate Professor of International Law at Aichi Prefectural University, Japan. She obtained PhD (2015), LLM (2009), and LLB (2007) from Kobe University and Master Complémentaire en droit international (2012) from Université libre de Bruxelles.

Introduction: stories about international organisations, non-State actors, and the formation of customary international law

Sufyan Droubi and Jean d'Aspremont

International lawyers relish telling stories about customary law, its contents, and its modes of ascertainment. There is hardly a question of international law that has continuously attracted as much passionate story-telling as customary international law. The present volume contributes to such scholarly self-indulgence. Yet, it does so by presupposing that there exists an approach to custom-forming that is adverse to the central role of international organisations and non-State actors and which it calls the dominant orthodoxy. According to this projected dominant orthodoxy, the formation of customary international law is reduced to a process through which international actors with full lawmaking capacity – States – adopt practices with the conviction that such practices are required in international law.[1] In such image, international organisations are reduced to agents of States; and their main

1 Institut de Droit International, 'The Elaboration of General Multilateral Conventions and of Non-Contractual Instruments Having a Normative Function or Objective' (1987) Session of Cairo, notably Conclusion 22 ('[a] Resolution may contribute to the consolidation of State practice, or to the formation of the *opinio juris communis*'); International Committee of the Red Cross, 'Study on Customary International Humanitarian Law' (2007) 2007 30IC/07/8.3 xxxviii ('the existence of a rule of customary international law requires the presence of two elements, namely State practice (*usus*) and a belief that such practice is required, prohibited or allowed, depending on the nature of the rule, as a matter of law (*opinio juris sive necessitates*)'); United Nations General Assembly Resolution 203 (73rd Sess) (11 January 2019) 'Identification of customary international law' A/RES/73/203 and Annex 'Identification of customary international law', Conclusion 2 ('[t]o determine the existence and content of a rule of customary international law, it is necessary to ascertain whether there is a general practice that is accepted as law (*opinio juris*)'). Even the nuanced approach that the International Law Association adopts speaks of the two elements: *see* International Law Association, 'Final Report of the Committee on Formation

contribution comes in the form of resolutions, which are relevant to the extent that they reflect practice or *opinio juris* of States.[2] International organisations "as such", i.e. as autonomous actors, are often taken to have very restricted formal participation in the formation of customary international law – which is often the result of a generally held perception that in most issues international organisations lack *volonté distincte*.[3] At best, this image holds that international organisations and non-State actors may *influence* the conduct and *opinio juris* of States, but this only

of Customary (General) International Law: Statement of Principles Applicable to the Formation of General Customary International Law', Principle 16 Commentary (c) ('It may well be true (though trivial) to observe that States will usually or always hold an *opinio juris* about an established rule of law … where it can be shown that an *opinio juris* exists about a practice, that will be sufficient').

2 *See* Institut de Droit International (n 1) Conclusion 6 (a) ('intent and expectation of States') (d) ('extent of support for the Resolution'); Conclusion 8 ('it is desirable that States particularly interested in the matter be enabled to take part in the deliberations of the organ and in the elaboration of the draft'); Conclusion 14 ('In situations where a rule of customary law is emerging from State practice or where there is still doubt whether a rule, though already applied by an international organ or by some States, is a rule of law, a Resolution adopted without negative vote or abstention may consolidate a custom or remove doubts that might have existed'). International Law Association 2000 (n 1) Principle 11 Commentary (b) ('Organs of international organizations, and notably the United Nations General Assembly, also from time to time adopt resolutions containing statements about customary international law. Formally, since the decision is recorded as a resolution of (the organ of the) organization, its adoption is a piece of practice by the organization; and some writers treat it in this way. However, in the context of the formation of customary international law, it is probably best regarded as a series of verbal acts by the individual member States participating in that organ. If so, it would add little or nothing to the weight of such practice by the member States themselves to treat the resolution itself (as distinct from voting for it) as a further piece of practice, this time on the part of the organization'); *also* Principles 31 and 32 and their Commentary (resolutions of the United Nations General Assembly). cf with International Law Commission, 'Identification of Customary International Law, Text of the Draft Conclusions and commentaries thereto' [2018] Report of the International Law Commission Seventieth session (30 April–1 June and 2 July–10 August 2018) International Law Commission Report, A/73/10, 2018, chap V, para 66, Conclusion 4 Commentary (7) ('As a general rule, the more directly a practice of an international organization is carried out on behalf of its member States or endorsed by them, and the larger the number of such member States, the greater weight it may have in relation to the formation, or expression, of rules of customary international law').

3 *See*, for all, International Law Commission 2018 (n 2) Conclusion 4 Commentary para 4–6 (suggesting the *opnio juris* of international organisations are relevant in respect to matters upon which States have accorded them either exclusive competence or specific powers). For insightful accounts of this point, *see* Chapters 2 and 3 in this volume.

means that their participation is instrumental or merely accidental.[4] In some variants of this image, the role of non-State actors in custom-formation is even denied on grounds that they lack lawmaking capacity.[5]

Whether such adversity towards international organisations and non-State actors in the formation of customary law constitutes an empirical actuality in the international legal scholarship as a whole is not relevant here. In fact, it does not matter whether most international lawyers actually defend such restricted role of international organisations and non-State actors in the formation of custom. This image and its depiction as the dominant orthodoxy offer a convenient starting point for this discussion attempted in this volume. In particular, this projected dominant orthodoxy provides a sounding board for reflecting anew on the possible ways in which international organisations and non-State actors contribute to the formation of customary law and providing new perspectives to the *formation* of customary international law. For instance, the presupposed orthodoxy described above is what allows many contributions in this volume to suggest that the process of formation of customary international law should be placed beyond the static, formal rule-making framework – and appreciated in all its full dynamism and complexity. This presupposed orthodoxy also provides the background story against which the following chapters offer a wide range of refreshing and new stories about the role of non-State actors and international organisations in the formation of customary international law.

1 The International Law Commission as the starting point of contemporary stories about customary international law

Although customary international law has continuously been on the agenda of international legal scholars, it seems uncontested that debates and storytelling on custom have been reinvigorated by the work of the International Law Commission on the topic. Indeed, under the rapporteurship of Sir Michael Wood, the work of the International Law Commission has fueled much interest for the

4 International Law Association 2000 (n 1) Principle 7 Commentary; Draft Conclusion with Commentary (n 2) Conclusion 4.3 and Commentary (9) and (10).

5 *See* International Law Association 2000 (n 1) Principle 7 ('Acts of individuals, corporations etc. do not count as State practice, unless carried out on behalf of the State or adopted ("ratified") by it'); Resolution A/RES/73/2–3 (n 1) Conclusion 4(3) ('Conduct of other actors is not practice that contributes to the formation, or expression, of rules of customary international law, but may be relevant when assessing the practice referred to in paragraphs 1 and 2').

question within and outside academic circles. It is noteworthy that Sir Michael has personally encouraged input from academics over the years, and has made ample use of the academic commentary.[6] As is well-known, the objective of the International Law Commission has always been to produce a set of Conclusions and Commentaries thereto to 'offer practical guidance on how the existence of rules of customary international law, and their content, are to be determined'.[7] In the view of the International Law Commission:

> This is not only of concern to specialists in public international law: others, including those involved with national courts, are increasingly called upon to identify rules of customary international law. In each case, a structured and careful process of legal analysis and evaluation is required to ensure that a rule of customary international law is properly identified, thus promoting the credibility of the particular determination as well as that of customary international law more broadly.[8]

Whether the Conclusions and Commentaries will succeed in enhancing the 'process of legal analysis and evaluation', which a multitude of academics and professionals carry out routinely, so that the identification of a rule of customary international law be 'properly' made, is unknown. However, the International Law Commission codification process encapsulates a powerful story,[9] which has already been affecting the story-telling activities that international lawyers articulate – and one should expect that the Conclusions and Commentaries will have a significant impact on international lawyers' story-telling. To substantiate this assertion, it is enough to recall that the General Assembly of the United Nations has recently adopted Resolution 203 in which the General Assembly, inter alia:

6 As the bibliography that he had amassed and submitted as part of his last reports confirms. cf 'Fourth report on identification of customary international law by Michael Wood, Special Rapporteur. Addendum. Annex II. Identification of customary international law: bibliography' (2016) International Law Commission Sixty-eighth session, UN Doc A/CN.4/695/Add.1 (25 May 2016); and 'Fifth report on identification of customary international law by Michael Wood, Special Rapporteur. Addendum. Annex II. Identification of customary international law: revised bibliography' (2018) International Law Commission Seventieth session, UN Doc A/CN.4/717/Add.1 (6 June 2018).

7 International Law Commission (n 2), General Commentary 2.

8 ibid.

9 *Note* the unfolding of the story throughout the reports submitted by Sir Michael Wood to the International Law Commission and the records of the debates held by the International Law Commission in 'Analytical Guide to the Work of the International Law Commission: Identification of Customary International Law' http://legal.un.org/ilc/guide/1_13.shtml accessed 23 February 2019.

> *Welcomes* the conclusion of the work of the International Law Commission on identification of customary international law and its adoption of the draft conclusions and commentaries thereto;
>
> ... *Also takes note* of the conclusions on identification of customary international law, the text of which is annexed to the present resolution, with the commentaries thereto, brings them to the attention of States and all who may be called upon to identify rules of customary international law, and encourages their widest possible dissemination.[10]

And, taking forward an important recommendation put forward by Sir Michael and the International Law Commission,[11] the General Assembly, in the same Resolution 203:

> *Acknowledges* the utility of published digests and surveys of practice relating to international law, including those that make legislative, executive and judicial practice widely available, and encourages States to make every effort to support existing publications and libraries specialized in international law.[12]

In these paragraphs, with these simple but significant actions – welcoming, taking note, and acknowledging – the General Assembly not only strengthened the story that encapsulates the Conclusions and Commentaries – but also made a call for States to continue to tell this story.

This having been said, it is undeniable that the work that Sir Michael and the International Law Commission carried out *has already* significantly, positively contributed in terms of offering opportunities for international lawyers to reflect upon both the orthodox (proper?) and unorthodox (improper?) approaches to the process of formation and expression of rules of customary international law. Of this, the present volume is evidence enough. On the topics that mostly interest us in this volume – formation of customary international law and the weight to be ascribed to international organisations and non-State actors – the work that Sir Michael and the International Law Commission conducted has shed light on a number of controversies that will be taken up in the following chapters. It suffices here to mention a few of them.

First, the International Law Commission codification enterprise appears to have been affected by differing perceptions by members of the International Law Commission in respect to how much the latter could delve into *formation* of customary international law *without* going beyond the scope of its mandate and surrendering to academic exercises.[13] For his part, Sir Michael was not fully convinced

10 General Assembly Resolution 203 (n 1), operative paras 1 and 4.

11 International Law Commission 2018 (n 2), para 63.

12 General Assembly Resolution 203 (n 1), operative para 5.

13 *See* e.g. International Law Commission, 'Sixty-Fourth Session (Second Part) Provisional Summary Record of the 3150th Meeting' [2012] UN Doc n A/CN.4/SR.3150, 11 (statement

as to the need to address formation in an express manner.[14] Second, these three topics – formation, international organisations, and non-State actors – proved contentious *within* the International Law Commission. As far as these matters are concerned, the Conclusions and Commentaries only reflect the extent of the agreement that members of the International Law Commission were able to reach.[15]

by Mr Forteau, who 'did not see how the formation of custom fell within the Commission's mandate and thought the focus should be on the much more practical matter of identifying customary international law, meaning the specific evidence of custom'); and International Law Commission, 'Sixty-Fourth Session (Second Part) Provisional Summary Record of the 3151st Meeting' [2013] UN Doc n A/CN 4/SR 3151, 13 (statement by Mr Nolte, who 'did not … subscribe to the idea that a clarification of the "formation" of customary international law would be less important and would be merely an academic exercise. States and practitioners … also wanted to know how to explain to their national courts and other bodies why and under which circumstances those means led to the conclusion that a particular rule was or was not a rule of customary international law. Of course, in trying to explain the formation of customary international law, the Commission ran the risk of becoming involved in a discussion of certain general questions of principle, but that was inevitable in the current exercise. If the Commission did not deal with such issues, it would not meet the expectations of States and the international community at large, and the result of its work might be called into question too easily').

14 International Law Commission, 'Identification of Customary International Law' [2014] Report of the International Law Commission Sixty-sixth session (5 May–6 June and 7 July–8 August 2014) 74, para 172.

15 On formation, *see*, above, n 13. On the weight of international organisations, *see* International Law Commission 2014 (n 14), 74 para 159 ('Some members of the Commission were of the view that the use of the word "primarily" was misguided as it suggested that the practice of entities other than the State could be relevant. Those members were of the view that the practice of international organizations was not to be taken into account in the process of identification of rules of customary international law. Other members considered that the practice of international organizations was only pertinent to the extent it reflected the practice of States. Some other members, however, agreed with the Special Rapporteur that the practice of international organizations as such could be relevant to the establishment of customary rules, particularly in regards to certain fields of activity within the mandates of those organizations'). *See* International Law Commission, 'Identification of Customary International Law' [2015] Report of the International Law Commission Sixty-seventh session (4 May–5 June and 6 July–7 August 2015) 38 paras 83–4 and 89. On non-State actors, *see* ibid para 90 ('The draft conclusion proposed by the Special Rapporteur that the conduct of other non-State actors was not practice for the purposes of the formation or identification was supported by several members of the Commission … Some members of the Commission considered the proposal to be too strict, in particular in the light of the importance of the practice of certain non-State actors, such as the International Committee of the Red Cross, as well as in view of the importance of activities involving both States and non-State actors').

This explains why the International Law Commission did not prove very innovative in respect to such topics, and did not do justice to the different processes and actors that operate in the formation and identification of customary international law and which has long been acknowledged in parts of the scholarship and the international argumentative practice of certain States.[16] This is why, for the sake of this volume, the work of the International Law Commission and of Sir Michael are deemed to represent the orthodoxy which this volume takes as its starting point.[17] Within the strict limits of academic rigour, the following chapters at times support and at times challenge this orthodoxy – as well as the standards of 'proper' identification of rules of customary international law that this orthodoxy encapsulates in a coherent and well-told story. This is why the work of the International Law Commission on the formation of customary international law – and the project of dominant orthodoxy that serves as the starting point of this volume – must be sketched out in more detail.

We must begin by recalling that the International Law Commission reaffirms the two-element approach, defining customary international law in terms of 'general practice accepted as law (*opinio juris*)'.[18] It attempts to photograph moments in the advanced stages of the processes of formation of customary legal rules, and then to offer the pictures as proofs against which the existence of putative norms may be assessed. This photographing strips the socio-political processes of formation of customary international law of much of their dynamism. For instance,

16 This is not to say that the International Law Commission, and Sir Michael in particular, have not been aware of these debates. In fact, Sir Michael and the International Law Commission have engaged in an extensive dialogue with different actors, including academics. E.g. Stephen Mathias, 'Editorial Comment: The Work of the International Law Commission on Identification of Customary International Law: A View from the Perspective of the Office of Legal Affairs' (2016) Chinese Journal of International Law 17; Sienho Yee, 'Report on the International Law Commission Project on "Identification of Customary International Law"' (2015) Chinese Journal of International Law 375. *See also* Niels Blokker, 'International Organizations and Customary International Law' (2017) 14 International Organizations Law Review 1; George Rodrigo Bandeira Galindo and César Yip, 'Customary International Law and the Third World: Do Not Step on the Grass' (2017) 16 Chinese Journal of International Law 251; Noora Arajärvi, 'The Requisite Rigour in the Identification of Customary International Law' (2017) 19 International Community Law Review 9.

17 *See*, generally, the contributions in this volume. For an insightful account of the practical limitations that scholars and practitioners, including within the International Law Commission, face when attempting to break free from mainstream approaches, *see* Chapters 6 and 7 in this volume.

18 General Assembly Resolution 203 (n 1), Conclusion 2.

it narrows 'practice', which has a dynamic component of continuity or repetition, down to 'conduct', which is often related to a particular situation and place.[19] It attempts to clearly distinguish between *lex lata* and *lege ferenda*: treaties and resolutions of international organisations, for instance, may either reflect customary international law or contribute to the development of new customary international law,[20] avoiding the debate of whether *emergent* custom in its more mature stage really fits within either category.

Whether or not the position of the International Law Commission will withstand the reality of the process of emergence and identification of customary international law is to be seen. At this stage, it should not be difficult to understand why some of the following chapters contend that the Conclusions and Commentary fail to capture the dynamics of the socio-political processes of formation of customary international law. For these scholars, the Conclusions might fail to address important implications that these processes have in international law. They might fail in providing guidance as to the identification of certain rules of customary international law, and in offering help in the weighting of the role that actors other than the State play in the formation of customary international law. Let us look at these two aspects in turn.

The Conclusions and Commentaries might fail in providing guidance as to the proper identification of new rules of customary international law – rules which have not been clearly affirmed as such in the international practice and which not rarely are identified as 'emerging' rules of custom.[21] What is the weight of an 'emerging' rule? Who decides when it has fully 'crystallised'? When does it 'crystallise'? Is it really possible to ascertain the 'crystallisation' of a rule of customary international law? The metaphor of crystallisation encapsulates the challenges in providing formal standards for the identification of a new rule of customary international law and differentiating it from an emerging custom in its more mature stage. It is curious that the International Law Commission decided to keep the metaphor of 'crystallisation',[22] *after* the International Law Association

19 ibid Conclusion 5 ('State practice consists of conduct of the State, whether in the exercise of its executive, legislative, judicial or other functions').

20 ibid Conclusion 11(1) and Conclusion 12(2).

21 *See*, for instance, *Legality of the Threat or Use of Nuclear Weapons*, Advisory Opinion, ICJ Reports 1996, 226, 555, 579 ('the Court should have given due consideration and weight to the statements of the overwhelming majority of States together with the resolutions adopted by various international organizations on the use of nuclear weapons, as evidence of the emergence of an opinio juris'). On this point, *see* Chapter 3, this volume.

22 General Assembly Resolution 203 (n 1) Conclusion 11(1) (b); International Law Commission 2018 (n 2) Conclusion 11(1) (b) Commentary (6).

cautioned, though timidly, against it.[23] In its attempt to explain 'crystallisation', the Commentary becomes circular:

> Subparagraph (b) concerns the case where it is established that a general practice that is accepted as law (accompanied by *opinio juris*) has crystallized around a treaty rule elaborated on the basis of only a limited amount of State practice. In other words, the treaty rule has consolidated and given further definition to a rule of customary international law that was only emerging at the time when the treaty was being drawn up, thereby later becoming reflective of it. Here, too, establishing that this is indeed the case requires an evaluation of whether the treaty formulation has been accepted as law and does in fact find support in a general practice.[24]

Interestingly, a very similar criticism was anticipated in the debates within the International Law Commission. In 2012 Shinya Murase noted that the word 'evidence', which had been part of the title of the Conclusions, 'was static and premised on the idea that the law was made up of a body of rules' and that it 'meant stopping the clock and trying to ascertain the applicable law at a given moment'.[25] In contradistinction, he argued, 'formation was a dynamic concept which ... suggested a sociological process whereby a customary rule was created over a period of time'.[26] Murase contended that 'it was impossible to talk simultaneously of formation and evidence without causing some methodological confusion'.[27] Ultimately, the word 'formation', initially part of the title, was dropped altogether.[28] That said, the Conclusions are less concerned with the formation and more concerned with the identification of customary international law.[29] Nevertheless, whether a framework that is developed to identify customary international law *should be applied also* to ascertain its formation, an aspect that becomes more relevant the younger

23 International Law Association 2000 (n 1), Principle 26 Commentary footnote 128 ('it is questionable whether the metaphor of the formation of crystals is in fact entirely apt: in chemistry, the beginning of crystallization can be located fairly precisely in time, whereas it is not normally possible (or necessary) to be so precise about the emergence of a customary rule').

24 International Law Commission 2018 (n 2), Conclusion 11(1) (b) Commentary (6).

25 International Law Commission, 'Provisional Summary Record of the 3148th Meeting. Held at the Palais Des Nations, Geneva, on Tuesday, 24 July 2012, at 10 Am A/CN.4/SR.3148' 6.

26 ibid.

27 ibid.

28 International Law Commission, 'Chapter VII – Formation and Evidence of Customary International Law' [2012] Report of the International Law Commission Sixty-fifth session 2(6 May–7 June and 8 July–9 August 2013) 108, para 76.

29 ibid, para 77.

the rule is, is a point that is open to discussion.[30] Notwithstanding the obvious fact that formation and identification remain deeply interlinked, some contributions in this volume clearly suggest that not only it is possible to differentiate between them, but that they should be differentiated so as to grasp their different legal implications.[31]

It should also be recalled here how difficult the specific debates on the very role of international organisations and non-State actors in the formation of customary international law turned out within the International Law Commission.[32] According to the approach favoured by the Commission, it is 'primarily … the practice of States that contributes to the formation, or expression of rules of customary international law'.[33] In respect to international organisations, the most relevant contributions that the Conclusions make consist in the affirmation that '[i]n certain cases, the practice of international organisations also contributes to the formation, or expression, of rules of customary international law'.[34] As one reads the Commentary, one notes that the expression 'in certain cases' is critical:

> The practice of international organizations in international relations (when accompanied by *opinio juris*) may count as practice that gives rise or attests to rules of customary international law, but only those rules (a) whose subject matter falls within the mandate of the organizations, and/or (b) that are addressed specifically to them (such as those on their international responsibility or relating to treaties to which international organizations may be parties). The words 'in certain cases' in paragraph 2 indeed serve to indicate that the practice of international organizations will not be relevant to the identification of all rules of customary international law, and further that it may be the practice of only some, not all, international organizations that is relevant.[35]

30 cf e.g. International Law Association (n 1) Principle 16 Commentary (c): 'But this tells us nothing about the necessity of this subjective state for the formation of a new rule of customary law … And in fact, it is hard to see how a State, if properly advised, could entertain the belief that its conduct is permitted (or required) by existing law when that conduct is, by definition, a departure from it. States actively engaged in the creation of a new customary rule may well wish or accept that the practice in question will give rise to a legal rule, but it is logically impossible for them to have an *opinio juris* in the literal and traditional sense, that is, a belief that the practice is already legally permissible or obligatory. This is true both individually and collectively.'

31 *See* Chapters 3 and 19, this volume.

32 *See* n 15 above and accompanying text.

33 General Assembly Resolution 203 (n 1), Conclusion 4(1).

34 ibid Conclusion 4(2).

35 International Law Commission 2018 (n 2) Conclusion 4 Commentary (5); *see* also Commentary (6).

The principal-agency theory, implicit in the extract above, becomes clear in other parts:

> International organizations are not States [!] They are entities established and empowered by States (or by States and/or other international organizations) to carry out certain functions, and to that end have international legal personality, that is, they have their own rights and obligations under international law.
>
> … As a general rule, the more directly a practice of an international organization is carried out on behalf of its member States or endorsed by them, and the larger the number of such member States, the greater weight it may have in relation to the formation, or expression, of rules of customary international law.[36]

Within this framework, it should be expected that the International Law Commission would, as it in fact did, largely ignore the issue concerning the *opinio juris* of international organisations, which is mentioned *en passant* in the Commentary to Conclusion 4(2).[37]

As the Institute of International Lawyers and the International Law Association have done before, the International Law Commission places particular emphasis on resolutions of international organisations, clearly affirming that resolutions 'may provide evidence for determining the existence and content of a rule of customary international law, or contribute to its development'.[38] Even on this point, however, there is a strong caveat to the effect that 'a provision in a resolution … may reflect a rule of customary international law if it is established that the provision corresponds to a general practice that is accepted as law (*opinio juris*)'.[39]

Interestingly, and unfortunately, the International Law Commission refrained from providing any Conclusion defining its own role in the process of formation and identification of customary international law. The point is however briefly mentioned in the Commentary to Conclusion 10 where it is contended that 'a determination by the Commission affirming the existence and content of a rule of customary international law may have particular value' because of the Commission's 'unique mandate', the 'thoroughness of its procedures' and its 'close relationship with the General Assembly and States' – even in these circumstances, however, the significance of its determinations depends on 'various factors, including sources relied upon by the

36 ibid Conclusion 4 Commentary 5 and 7. cf with Chapter 1 in this volume.

37 *Contrast* Conclusion 4 with Conclusion 9 in General Assembly Resolution 203 (n 1). *See* Chapters 2 and 3 in this volume.

38 General Assembly Resolution 203 (n 1) Conclusion 12(2). For good accounts of this point, *see* Chapters 9, 11, and 12, this volume.

39 General Assembly Resolution 203 (n 1) Conclusion 12(3); *see* Conclusion 12(1).

Commission, the stage reached in its work and above all upon States' reception of its output'.[40]

As far as non-State actors are concerned, the Conclusions clearly affirm that their conduct 'is not practice that contributes to the formation, or expression of' customary international law, but acknowledge that their 'conduct may be relevant when assessing the practice' of States and international organisations.[41] In Commentary to Conclusion 4(3), it is clearly stated, in respect to non-governmental organisations, non-State armed groups, transnational corporations, and private individuals, that their conduct does not qualify as 'direct (primary) evidence of the existence and content of' rules of customary international law, but their 'conduct may have an indirect role in the identification of customary international law, by stimulating or recording the practice and acceptance as law (opinio juris) of States and international organisations'.[42] The International Committee of the Red Cross is also mentioned, in a separate and brief paragraph, as capable of playing 'an important role in shaping the practice of States'; while its 'activities may thus contribute to the development and determination of customary international law; but they are not practice as such'.[43] The question that arises is whether one paragraph can summarise the many stories about formation and identification of customary international law, in which non-State actors have been playing increasingly important roles. Several chapters in this volume suggest it does not.

2 The stories of this volume

The work of the International Law Commission, as it has been depicted, has promoted most scholarly debates in the last years, and constitutes the presupposed dominant orthodoxy which most of the following chapters take issue with. These contributions do not only engage with the International Law Commission Conclusions and Commentary but also with the numerous reports and debates produced on this occasion with a view to furthering the academic discussion on the three above-mentioned topics, namely, formation of customary international law and the weight to be ascribed to international organisations and non-State actors. These contributions are organised in two main groups, which form the two parts of this volume. A first group of contributions provides innovative theoretical and conceptual perspectives on the role of international organisations and non-State actors

40 ibid Conclusion 10 Commentary (2). *See* Chapter 10, this volume.
41 ibid Conclusion 4(3). *See* Chapter 9, this volume.
42 International Law Commission 2018 (n 2) Conclusion 4(3) Commentary (8).
43 ibid para (10). cf in this volume, Chapter 14.

on the formation of customary law. A second group of contributions offer field perspectives and case studies.

The volume begins with a chapter by Voulgaris, who aims at understanding the reasons behind the lack of consensus within International Law Commission on the weight of international organisations in the formation of customary international law and how this has affected outcomes of International Law Commission work. With a careful enquiry into the debates of the International Law Commission he lays bare some of the shortcomings of the International Law Commission's approach to the topic. The main point of his analysis is whether international organisations play a role in their own name and not as agents of States in the production of rules of customary international law. He articulates a principled approach to the relation between international organisations and custom based on the notion of autonomy. He argues that autonomy constitutes an inherent element of international legal personality. On this basis, he argues that international law confers lawmaking power on both States and international organisations. By critically approaching the work of the International Law Commission, Voulgaris engages in a broader reflection on the lawmaking capacity of international organisations.

The volume continues with two contributions addressing *opinio juris*. Brölmann looks at the role of the juridical will of legal actors, and international organisations in particular, in the formation of customary international law. She addresses two main aspects, the *volonté distincte* and *intentional state*. Brölmann's point is that the difficulties in defining the juridical will of international organisations likely result from the mechanistic, functionalist view of international organisations. She concludes that while the modest role of international organisations as independent lawmakers in the Conclusions may be justified, ultimately it will be untenable in the light of international organisations' full-fledged participation in international law. In turn, Droubi looks into whether international organisations, which knowingly have many instruments to shape the behaviour of States, are also capable of shaping the *opinio juris* of States. For instance, would an international organisation such as the United Nations be able to promote, or at least influence, the formation of *opinio juris* that is consistent with findings and recommendations of the Intergovernmental Panel on Climate Change? He argues that, although international organisations have a wide array of instruments to affect and even shape the collective behaviour of States, they face almost unsurmountable challenges when it comes to shaping the *opinio juris* of States in a desired form – including pursuant to scientific standards. He develops the argument by revisiting the concept of *opinio juris*, which leads him to define *opinio juris* as an institutional object. This permits the unveiling of the various manners in which international organisations might interfere in the process of formation of *opinio juris*. He then turns to the ability of international organisations to promote *opinio juris* with a desired content. Droubi concludes by playing down the possibility that international organisations are able to coordinate international processes in a manner to shape *opinio juris* pursuant to desired standards.

Gasbarri puts forward a theoretical framework for the role of international organisations in the formation of customary international law that aims at reconciling their traditional, conflicting conceptualisations as either agents of States or autonomous actors. Through the discussion of three case studies concerning what he identifies as 'anomalies' in the development of so-called 'objective regimes', he articulates a theoretical framework on the role of international organisations in the formation of customary international law that acknowledges their dual nature.

Meguro seeks to clarify the role of non-State actors in custom-making processes by shouldering aside the dominant two-element understanding of *opinio juris* and practice. She demonstrates that the mainstream approaches are incognisant to the role of non-State actors because of constructions that are highly questionable. Maiko unveils the shortcomings of the prevalent approach to *opinio juris* by emphasising its reliance on an anthropomorphic concept of *opinio juris*. Turning to practice, she emphasises the role of domestic non-State actors in the creation of international norms that shape State practice. She concludes with some remarks about the general implications of her approach to the doctrine of customary law as a whole.

Cardenas argues that non-State actors play an important role in the formation of customary international law. After recalling that the two-element approach to customary international law is just one possible perspective to the study of the topic, Cardenas opts for a social perspective of customary international law, which allows him to argue that the community of international lawyers can possibly give weight to non-State actors' positions in the formation of customary international law. Indeed, he approaches international law as socially constructed argumentative practice to claim that customary international law is the product of successful argumentative campaigns undertaken by international lawyers. While the latter often work for States, they may also represent the interests of non-State actors. On this ground, he posits that, in ascertaining customary international law, although the views of State lawyers tend to be prioritised, those of lawyers working for non-State actors are often taken into due consideration.

D'Aspremont returns to the last decade of scholarly reflections on the question of non-State actors and customary international law and revisits some of the specific argumentative constructions and presuppositions that have informed – and continue to inform – discourses on the contribution of non-State actors and international law. His chapter is specifically premised on the idea that international legal thought and practice on non-State actors and customary international law have remained chained by certain modes of reasoning and category of thoughts which have been precluding any renewal of scholarly reflection on the matter. It is submitted in this chapter that, in order to make a chance of novelty and creative thinking, any new wave of scholarly reflections on the contribution of non-State actors to custom-forming processes – including this very volume – must reinvent the very categories around which international legal discourses are currently articulated.

The second part of the volume begins with Sir Michael Wood's chapter. With an emphasis on the role of international organisations and non-State actors to the formation of customary international law, this chapter recalls some of the key choices made by the International Law Commission in its work on the identification of customary international law. In doing so, this chapter offers some reactions to a number of criticisms made by international legal scholars, including some of the contributors to this volume.

Bílková critically engages the view on non-State actors that the Conclusions adopt. She gives an impressive account of the history of the drafting process that led to the adoption of the Conclusions – which in itself is a valuable source of information for any student of the topic. Then, Bílková challenges the International Law Commission approach to the role of non-State actors in the process of emergence of customary international law, and puts forward a strong case in that the International Law Commission fails to do justice to the plurality of roles that non-State actors currently play in the formation and identification of customary international law.

Pereira addresses a specific aspect of International Law Commission work that resulted in the Conclusions, namely, the manner in which the International Law Commission defines its own output vis-à-vis the formation of customary international law. While the International Law Commission specifically addresses 'teachings of publicists' and judgments, it has chosen to simply mention the relevance of its own work – which it did in the commentary opening Part V. Pereira argues that the Commission was right in not including its work under the 'teachings of publicists' heading.

Deplano examines the role of resolutions adopted by intergovernmental organisations in the Conclusions. Through a careful empirical study, Deplano shows that over time resolutions of the General Assembly have acquired a systemic character. Therefore, she claims that these resolutions do not exist in isolation from each other. In developing her argument, Deplano shows that a rule of customary international law, which resolutions may generate, lays *outside* the text of the resolutions. Rather, the resolutions trigger the rule in question. On these grounds, she argues that, insofar as the purpose of the International Law Commission is to provide a methodology for identifying a customary rule, then the Commission has set out an impossible task for itself in what respects the role of resolutions in the formation of customary international law.

Merlin's chapter, which looks at the role of the United Nations in the formation and identification of customary international law, argues that it can be described as a 'specificity within a specificity'. He emphasises that the contribution of the United Nations to the formation and identification of rules of customary international law is not uniform; rather, it varies from organ to organ. In his chapter, Merlin is mostly concerned with the Secretariat and Secretary-General. He argues that the universal character of the United Nations places it in a better position relative to other international organisations to contribute, at various levels, in various ways and often involving the combined conduct of several organs, to the formation and expression of general rules of customary international law. Looking at the Secretariat, Merlin recalls that it interacts, e.g. with the Security Council and the General Assembly as well as the International Law Commission, which typically is vested with the double mandate of promoting the development of international law and its codification.

Veber seeks to demonstrate an increasingly important role of international organisations in relation to the formation of customary international law rules by virtue of the sanctions they adopt in response to violations of *erga omnes* obligations. She argues that through the adoption of sanctions to uphold rules of international law, international organisations can contribute to these rules acquiring the status of customary international law. However, she posits that the contribution of sanctions to the formation of custom varies significantly on a case-by-case basis. Contrasting cases in which the underlying rules have *erga omnes* character with cases in which they do not have, Veber concludes that the potential for customary lawmaking is greater when the *erga omnes* status of the underlying rule is not confirmed yet.

Müller looks at the ten-year effort that the International Committee of the Red Cross carried out to complete its study on customary international humanitarian law, which was published in 2005. The study identified 161 rules of customary international humanitarian law and presented the material collected in their determination. Müller explains that the International Committee of the Red Cross needed to consider many of the methodological questions that the International Law Commission faces today in its work on the identification of customary international law. Like the International Law Commission's draft conclusions on that topic adopted at first reading in 2016, the study is based on the fundamental requirement of two elements: a general practice that is accepted as law (*opinio juris*). Among the issues arising from this approach that the study, like the International Law Commission, had to address were the questions whose practice it is that forms rules of customary international law and whether actors other than States could be relevant in this context.

McCall-Smith looks at human rights treaty bodies to argue that the responses by States to human rights treaty body interpretations warrants the conclusion that treaty bodies can, and do, contribute to the development of customary international law, albeit in often subtle ways and through their relationships with States parties.

Worster addresses international territorial administrations. He argues that when an international organisation becomes entangled with a State government, the normal participation in the formation of customary international law becomes confused. He provides a survey of practice citing to the acts of international territorial administrations to show that it is possible for these governance arrangements to contribute to customary international law in the same manner as States, even though those acts are formally undertaken by by an international organisation.

Berkes argues that the activities of *de facto* regimes can be considered as properly speaking 'practice' that contributes to the formation, or expression, of rules of customary international law under two scenarios. Firstly, the custom-creating or custom-strengthening conduct of the *de facto* regime can be attributed to a State, usually to an occupying power or a State supporting in various means the *de facto* regime by exercising effective control or at least decisive influence over it. Berkes explains that in this first scenario the conduct of *de facto* regimes can be regarded as 'practice' for the identification of customary international law. He also argues that, *lege ferenda*, even without attributing the conduct of a *de facto* regime to a State, its conduct should be taken into account as strengthening the practice forming customary international law at least in subject matters governing the rights and obligations of the *de facto* regime itself. Although both scenarios may raise various theoretical and practical objections, Berkes explains that in areas under-regulated by international law, the conduct of *de facto* regimes may be relevant as 'practice' revealing a State's (usually the territorial or an outside State's) practice.

Yamashita argues that investors have emerged as the most powerful claimants who certainly influence the clarification of customary international law rules through investor–State dispute settlement on the international sphere. Her objective is to answer the question of how and to what extent references to customary international law in investor–State dispute settlement may influence the formation of customary international law. She proposes to answer these questions through the combination of two concepts – namely, 'framing' and 'spilling-over effect'. Investors who raise questions of customary international law have a significant ability to frame the debates that lead to a final award. These arguments have a spill-over effect, i.e. their impact can be felt beyond the immediate realities of the case at hand. Through a well-developed case study, she ascertains the impact of these arguments.

In her chapter, Azarova offers a constructivist account of the proliferating roles of non-governmental organisations in the making of customary international law. While these roles are largely informal, and non-governmental organisations' influence on the content and interpretation of customary international law norms is primarily indirect, non-governmental organisations contribute to the formation of customary international law through an increasingly diverse set of activities, which has been particularly influential when implemented in a strategic and concerted manner. Non-governmental organisations' documentation, litigation, lobbying, and other forms of advocacy have contributed to treaty-making and ratification; to the domestication and internalisation of international norms and processes, including domestic accountability and remedies; and to codifying the obligations of, and stimulating practice by, non-State actors such as business and armed groups. Despite a broad acknowledgement of the increasing involvement of non-governmental organisations in global governance by scholars and practitioners, their role in customary international lawmaking remains under-appreciated. To understand the increased influence of non-governmental organisations on the identification, formation, and application of customary international law rules, the chapter offers a differentiated, effects-based account of non-governmental organisations' participation in customary international lawmaking.

On a final note, this volume results from a 2017 conference hosted by the Manchester International Law Centre, University of Manchester, with the support of the University of Manchester, the Interest Group on International Organizations of the European Society of International Law, and of the São Paulo Research Foundation, and which counted with academics and practitioners from different parts of the world and with the kind participation of Sir Michael Wood. May all those who made this volume and the preceding conference possible be thanked. Their efforts and generosity allow international lawyers' story-telling about customary international law to continue.

Part I

Theoretical and conceptual perspectives

Chapter 1

International organisations as autonomous actors

Nikolaos Voulgaris

International organisations have emerged in the United Nations era, alongside States, as some of the most prominent actors in international law. Within a very limited time-span they have grown considerably in number but also in size. There remains nevertheless, until today, a certain ambivalence as to their lawmaking capacity in the international legal order, especially with respect to customary international law.[1] The argument has been made long ago that such institutions provide 'shortcuts to finding custom'.[2] Decision-making procedures within such institutions expose the practice and *opinio juris* of States and in this way, the argument runs, they have revolutionised the procedure for the generation of customary international law. What is more, it has been suggested more recently that the functioning of international organisations changed the formation of custom in another way;[3] when examining whether such a rule has been formed, one should look not only at 'what States actually do and seek to understand whether they recognise an obligation or a right to act in that way',[4] but extend this inquiry to international organisations too. Both propositions are by no means settled law and the role of international organisations in the formation of custom remains the subject of considerable controversy among commentators.

1 It is generally accepted that international organisations possess, explicitly or otherwise, the power to conclude treaties, J Klabbers, *An Introduction to International Organizations Law* (Cambridge University Press 2015) ch 12; *see* also *Vienna Convention of the Law of Treaties between States and International Organizations, or between International Organizations*, 1986, UN Doc A/CONF.129/15, Article 6.

2 J Alvarez, *International Organizations as Law Makers* (Oxford University Press 2005) 594.

3 St Mathias, 'The Work of the International Law Commission on Identification of Customary International Law: A View from the Perspective of the Office of Legal Affairs' (2016) 15 *Chinese Journal of International Law* 17–31.

4 Report of the International Law Commission 2016, Sixty-Eight Session, UN Doc A/71/10, 100.

In the context of the project on the identification of customary international law, the International Law Commission has dealt extensively since 2013 with the role of international organisations in the formation of custom. Despite the long debates between the members and the reports undertaken by the Special Rapporteur Sir Michael Wood, the issue remains controversial after the second and final reading of the Conclusions.[5] Several entrenched positions were adopted by the International Law Commission members during the discussions and the International Law Commission leaves questions unanswered as to the exact role of international organisations in the formation of custom. Therefore, Conclusion 4(2) that addresses the issue is of weak normative value and of limited usefulness to the consumers of the Commission's work.

This chapter aims to understand the reasons behind this lack of *consensus* and how this has affected the end-product of the International Law Commission's work; that is the Conclusions incorporated in the International Law Commission's 2018 Report. Such an enquiry is, I believe, the key to addressing the shortcomings of the International Law Commission's approach and to understanding whether the relevant Conclusion bears a strong normative claim to hardening into *lex lata*. To this end, the chapter is divided in four sections. The first one delimits the issue *rationae personae* and *materiae*. The chapter deals with the most controversial aspect of international organisation contribution to the production of custom: whether international organisations have a role to play in their own name and not as a cover of States in the production of rules that do not pertain to the internal sphere of the organisation. The second section attempts a chronology of the International Law Commission discussions on this issue that lead to the final reading of the Conclusions in the latest 2018 Report. As will be demonstrated, certain questions were left open-ended by the International Law Commission and thus expose a limited understanding of the lawmaking capacity of international organisations in international law and of their exact position in the international legal order, especially when compared to that of States. The next section argues for a way to remedy those defects. The International Law Commission should have adopted an alternative juristic methodology when inferring rules that reflect the progressive development of the law such as Conclusion 4(2). It is essential to put forward a principled understanding of the connection between international organisations and custom as the basis for legal discussion in order to account for the lawmaking power of international organisations. The final section proposes such an understanding of

5 Report of the International Law Commission 2018, Seventieth Session, UN Doc A/73/10, 130–31, [4]–[7].

principle based on the notion of autonomy. Being inherent in the concept of international legal personality, autonomy is, I believe, the reason why international law confers lawmaking power on both States and international organisations.

So, while the chapter criticises the approach utilised by the International Law Commission, it also makes a normative proposition on the lawmaking capacity of international organisations. In this sense, the argument is not focused solely on the International Law Commission and its methodology when inferring international law's progressive development. It rather seeks to put the International Law Commission project in perspective and understand the normative underpinnings of international organisation contribution in the production of international law and customary international law in particular.

1 Delimiting the issue

1.1 Rationae personae: *international organisations as international legal persons and not as the aggregate of their member States*

In the past, the relevant discussion was permeated by a purely State-centric view of international lawmaking. Scholars have debated whether international organisation resolutions may be constitutive of State practice or *opinio juris*.[6] The debate was sparked by the jurisprudence of the International Court of Justice and mainly the *Military and Paramilitary Activities in and Against Nicaragua (Nicaragua v United States)* judgment[7] and the *Legality of the Threat or Use of Nuclear Weapons* advisory opinion.[8] In the former case, the Court held that: '*opinio juris* may, though

6 SM Schwebel, 'The Effect of Resolutions of the UN General Assembly on Customary International Law' (1979) 73 *Proceedings of the Annual Meeting (American Society of International Law)* 304; G Tunkin, 'The Role of Resolutions of International Organizations in Creating Norms of International Law' in W Butler (ed), *International Law and the International System* (Martinus Nijhoff 1987) 11–15; KR Skubizewski, 'Resolutions of the U.N. General Assembly and Evidence of Custom', in Università di Genova, Istituto di Diritto Internazionale e della Navigazione della Facoltà di Giurisprudenza (ed), *Le Droit International a l' heure de sa codification-etudes en l' honneur de Roberto Ago*, vol I (Giuffrè 1987) 503; MD Oberg, 'The Legal Effects of Resolutions of the UN Security Council and General Assembly in the Jurisprudence of the International Court of Justice' (2006) 16 *European Journal of International Law* 879.

7 *Military and Paramilitary Activities in and Against Nicaragua (Nicaragua v United States)*, Merits, Judgment, ICJ Reports 1986, [188]–[207].

8 *Legality of the Threat or Use of Nuclear Weapons*, Advisory Opinion, ICJ Reports 1996, [70]–[73].

with all due caution, be deduced from, inter alia [...] the attitude of States towards certain General Assembly resolutions'.[9] The subsequent International Court of Justice opinion was more cryptic when it suggested that '[United Nations General Assembly resolutions] can, in certain circumstances provide evidence important for establishing the existence of a rule or the emergence of an *opinio juris*'.[10] The issue that went largely unnoticed at the time and was left unresolved from the International Court of Justice's *dicta* was to what extent the relevant resolutions were understood as the product of the member States or of the international organisation itself.[11] Despite the disagreement on the interpretation of the aforementioned statements, the whole debate revolved around whether United Nations General Assembly resolutions reflect the *opinio juris* and practice of States and thus contribute to the formation of custom.

The view that international organisations provide shortcuts to finding custom has been accepted by most commentators and the International Law Commission. Notwithstanding claims to the opposite,[12] decision-making procedures within such institutions effectively expose State practice and *opinio juris* and thus, the argument runs, they have revolutionised the procedure for the generation of customary international law.[13] Conclusion 12 (2) of the International Law Commission's Articles endorses this view by stating that:

> A resolution adopted by an international organization or at an intergovernmental conference may provide evidence for establishing the existence and content of a rule of customary international law, or contribute to its development.[14]

In the same vein, the commentaries to this provision clarify that 'what is relevant is that they [international organisation resolutions] may reflect the collective expression of the views of such States'.[15] Without undermining the importance of such statement, I argue that it addresses only one of the ways in which international organisations can contribute to the formation of custom.

9 *Nicaragua* (n 7) [191].
10 *Nuclear Weapons* (n 8) [70].
11 A Pellet, 'La formation du droit international dans le cadre des Nations Unies' (1995) 6 *European Journal of International Law* 416 [20].
12 J Wouters and P De Man, 'International Organizations as Law Makers' in J Klabbers and A Wallendahl (eds), *Research Handbook on the Law of International Organizations* (Edward Elgar 2011) 190–224.
13 Alvarez (n 2) 591–95; T Treves, 'Customary International Law' *Max Planck Encyclopaedia of Public International Law* (2006) [25]; Mathias (n 3) 24–25.
14 International Law Commission Report 2018, 147.
15 ibid [3].

Given the views taken by the International Law Commission on the way international organisations operate and customary law is formed, such institutions may have another role to play in the formation of custom. First, according to the International Law Commission, international organisations possess 'international legal personality' which means that 'they may have their *own* rights and obligations under international law' (emphasis added).[16] Without making a value judgment on whether the International Law Commission holds the correct view on the conceptualisation of international organisations,[17] this view necessarily entails that such institutions enjoy a separate existence and are not merely 'vehicles' for their member States. Second, according to Conclusion 2 'it is necessary to ascertain whether there is a general practice that is accepted as law (*opinio juris*)' in order to infer the existence of an international customary rule.[18] This language, that reflects Article 38 paragraph 1(b) of the International Court of Justice Statute, is broad enough to encompass both the practice and the *opinio juris* of entities other than States. By taking into consideration the International Law Commission's definitions of 'international organisations' and 'international customary law' there is ample room to consider whether international organisations can contribute *in their own name* to the formation of such law. Since custom incorporates two elements the debate revolves around two propositions; on the one hand, that international organisation practice *per se* – not as a cover of State practice – can contribute to the formation of customary law. Second, that international organisations can have a say as to whether certain practice has been undertaken with a sense of legal right or obligation (*opinio juris*).

1.2 Rationae materiae: *the production of internal custom*

The fact that international organisations possess international legal personality distinct from that of their members does not necessitate that international organisation practice and *opinio juris* with respect to any subject-matter may establish customary rules of an international nature. Article 38 1(b) refers to 'international custom', as opposed to internal custom, so of relevance is the formation of those rules established by the international organisations in their capacity as

16 ibid 131 [5]. The Commission follows the definition adopted in its Articles on the Responsibility of International Organizations, Article 2(a), International Law Commission Report 2011, Un Doc A/66/10, 52.

17 For more on the two main competing theories on the conceptualisation of international organisations *see* K Daugirdas, 'How and Why International Law Binds International Organizations' (2016) 57 *Harvard International Law Review* 327.

18 International Law Commission Report 2018, 119.

international actors. According to Article 2(j) of the Draft Articles on the Law of Treaties Between States and International Organizations or Between International Organizations '"rules of the organization" means, in particular, the constituent instruments, relevant decisions and resolutions, *and established practice of the organization*' (emphasis added). The Commentary to this provision does not specify the exact legal nature of such practice however it is widely accepted that within the context of an international organisation, the latter's organs through their practice establish 'a kind of customary law of the organization'.[19] The most prominent example of such practice pertains to the effect of abstentions by permanent members of the Security Council in the voting procedure in that organ.[20] Such rules constitute a source of law for the internal sphere of the international organisation, are purely for internal consumption and are not applicable outside the framework of the organisation. Admittedly then, they do not form part of customary international law and thus fall outside the remit of the International Law Commission's project.[21]

2 Chronology of the International Law Commission's approach: an ideological debate

2.1 Practice of international organisations

The Special Rapporteur's second report was the first attempt to address this issue. From the outset, Sir Michael Wood adopted the term 'general practice' in order to refer to the objective/material element of custom.[22] Conscious of the inherent limitation of the 'State practice' formulation generally invoked, the Special Rapporteur opted for language that reflects Article 38 paragraph 1(b) of the International Court of Justice Statute, which is broad enough to encompass the practice of entities other than States such as international organisations. Despite the recognition that international organisation practice could, from a legal point of view, play a role in the

19 C Peters, 'Subsequent Practice and Established Practice of International Organizations' (2011) 3 *Göttingen Journal of International Law* 631; C Ahlborn, 'The Rules of the International Organization and the Law of International Responsibility' (2011) 8 *International Organizations Law Review* 424.

20 *Legal Consequences for States of the Continued Presence of South Africa in Namibia (South West Africa)*, Advisory Opinion, ICJ Reports 1971 [22].

21 M Wood, *Third Report on the Identification of Customary International Law* UN Doc A/CN.4/682, 49–50.

22 M Wood, *Second Report on Identification of Customary International Law* UN Doc A/CN.4/672 [32]–[34].

formation of custom,[23] the Special Rapporteur's proposals did not put it on a par with State practice. Conclusion 5 at the time reflected the International Court of Justice's view from the *Continental Shelf (Libyan Arab Jamahiriya v. Malta)* case[24] and read:

> The requirement, as an element of customary international law, of a general practice means that it is *primarily* the practice of States that contributes to the creation, or expression, of rules of customary international law.[25]

The members of the Commission received with mixed feelings these proposals; international organisation practice was considered completely irrelevant by some, pertinent to the extent it reflected the practice of States by others or relevant for the establishment of customary rules in regards to their fields of activity by another group of members.[26] There was general *consensus* however that further clarification was necessary in order to indicate precisely whose practice is relevant to determining the existence of a general practice so the matter was left open for reconsideration in the next Special Rapporteur's report.

Right after the adoption of the International Law Commission 2014 Report the proposals were reverted for the fifth time to the Drafting Committee for consideration. The latter failed to arrive at 'any firm conclusion on the issues relating to the role of international organization practice'.[27] Nevertheless, it provisionally adopted what was about to be the final wording of Conclusion 4(2): 'In certain cases, the practice of international organizations also contributes to the formation, or expression, of rules of customary international law.'[28] International organisation practice then, though secondary to State practice, should not be overlooked. The limitation of international organisation contribution to 'certain cases' was inserted to express the idea that certain conditions should be fulfilled before that contribution was taken into account.[29] This statement was the product of a gut feeling rather, and not

23 International Law Commission Report 2014, Sixty-Sixth Session, UN Doc A/69/10, 240 fn 829 Conclusion 7 [4].

24 ICJ Reports 1985 [27]: '[i]t is of course axiomatic that the material of customary international law is to be looked for primarily in the actual practice and *opinio juris* of States'.

25 International Law Commission Report 2014, 239 fn 829.

26 ibid [159].

27 *Statement of the Chairman of the Drafting Committee, Mr Gilberto Saboia 7 August 2014*, available at: http://legal.un.org/docs/?path=../ilc/sessions/66/pdfs/english/dc_chairman_statement_identification_of_custom.pdf&lang=E, all electronic sources last accessed 11 February 2019, 8.

28 ibid 18.

29 ibid 9.

of an overview of existing international organisation practice, which the Committee admittedly could not undertake for 'practical difficulties'.[30] Also, it is not a statement of principle since the Committee does not identify the conditions that render international organisation practice pertinent and one cannot understand whether such practice is relevant by default or, for example, as a reflection of State practice. Being the outcome of intuition and not of a systematic legal inquiry, the Drafting Committee's observations are of questionable legal validity.

It fell upon the third report of the Special Rapporteur to provide the necessary guidance for a legal pronouncement on the issue. The report failed to deliver such guidance as the Special Rapporteur was caught in between two positions that point to different directions. He attributes from the outset weight to the difference in nature between States and international organisations; States create, control, and empower international organisations to function as separate legal persons.[31] This justifies a disparity, he believes, between the two categories of subjects in the formation of custom. Thus, without taking his syllogism further he seems hesitant to attribute 'autonomous law-making power' to international organisations whatever that signifies.[32] On the other hand, he puts forward his belief that generally international organisation practice *may* be relevant, especially in cases when it pertains to activities akin to those undertaken by States, and when States have assigned competence to the international organisation.[33] The aforementioned proposal of the Drafting Committee encapsulates in its generality these ideas and so he proposes no amendments to it.

The Commission members received the third report in a similar way to the second. Several members had doubts as to whether the report takes account of the members' comments on how to deal with international organisation practice in the first place.[34] Escobar Hernández and Saboia thought that the analysis was not sufficiently clear and to the point.[35] Murphy, Kittichaisaree, and Hmoud disagreed in principle with the Rapporteur's approach; only State practice was of relevance and contributory to the formation of custom.[36] Wisnumurti[37] and

30 ibid.

31 Wood, *Third Report* [69]–[70].

32 ibid [70]. In section 3, I argue that the lack of a definition of this concept is a major defect in the International Law Commission's project.

33 ibid [76]–[77]; M Wood, 'International Organizations and Customary International Law' (2015) 48 *Vanderbilt Journal of Transnational Law* 617.

34 UN Doc A/CN.4/SR.3254, 11.

35 UN Doc A/CN.4/SR.3252, 9–10 (Escobar Hernández), 12–13 (Saboia).

36 UN Doc A/CN.4/SR.3251, 3–4 (Murphy), 8 (Kittichaisaree), 11 (Hmoud).

37 UN Doc A/CN.4/SR.3252, 7–8.

Gómez-Robledo[38] held no definite position on the matter. Finally, the majority of the members that expressed an opinion (Hassouna,[39] Šturma,[40] Forteau,[41] Al-Marri,[42] Jacobsson,[43] Kolodkin,[44] Singh,[45] Nolte,[46]) found the Special Rapporteur's arguments convincing at least to some extent. It is evident that Sir Michael's effort to curb the differences amongst the members and unite the International Law Commission on this issue did not bear fruit.

In view of this lack of *consensus* no further survey was undertaken by the Special Rapporteur on this issue and the matter has been left since *in limbo*, stalemated. The whole debate was becoming, according to Sir Michael, almost ideological, so he decided to proceed cautiously.[47] His fourth report reiterates all arguments, acknowledges that the issue is controversial and thus reverts the matter for reconsideration after States have had an opportunity to react on the first reading of the Conclusions.[48] So, Conclusion 4 and its commentary as incorporated in the 2016 International Law Commission Report reflect a compromise of the opinions expressed during the debates. The Commission suggests that international organisation practice is of relevance 'in certain cases' but fails to clearly delimit which exactly those cases are.[49] They certainly pertain to practice that derives from EU-like institutions but they could possibly extend to cases where States have conferred powers upon the international organisation equivalent to State powers or with respect to customary rules that are addressed specifically to them. The Commission finally held that reference to State practice within the report should be read as encompassing international organisation practice too '*where it is relevant*' (emphasis added).[50] The International Law Commission made no further inferences from this, so it is not clear how this equation plays out with respect to Conclusions 5 entitled 'Conduct of the State as State practice', 6 'Forms of practice', and 7 'Assessing a State's practice'. Blokker

38 UN Doc A/CN.4/SR.3254, 8.
39 UN Doc A/CN.4/SR.3252, 6.
40 ibid 13.
41 UN Doc A/CN.4/SR.3251, 6.
42 ibid 12.
43 UN Doc A/CN.4/SR.3254, 3.
44 ibid 6.
45 ibid 9.
46 UN Doc A/CN.4/SR.3339, 4.
47 UN Doc A/CN.4/SR.3303, 8.
48 M Wood, *Fourth Report on the Identification of Customary Law* UN Doc A/CN.4/695 [19]–[20].
49 International Law Commission Report 2016, 107 [5]–[8].
50 ibid 106 [3].

suggests similarly that this 'cosmetic sentence, hidden in the commentary, cannot remedy the deficiency of ambivalence in the main text of the Conclusions themselves'.[51] All in all, due to the entrenched positions adopted by the International Law Commission members the 2016 International Law Commission report in its ambiguity leaves questions unanswered as to the exact role of international organisation practice in the formation of custom.

In his fifth and final report, the Special Rapporteur tried to identify the scope of disagreement concerning the possible role of the practice of international organisations. He begins his analysis with a *tour d' horizon* of the different positions adopted by States (paras 36–39) and suggests that the heart of their disagreement lies as to whether international organisation practice merely shows what the member States do in or through the relevant international organisation, or whether it is international organisation practice as such. In paragraph 44 he answers unequivocally: 'international organizations do act on the behalf of their members States; but in so doing they are actors in their own right'. The suggestions he sets out in paragraphs 42–44 support the view that the powers of international organisations to contribute to the formation of customary rules should be better acknowledged in the Conclusions, nevertheless the improvements to the wording of Conclusion 4(2) he suggests, put forward a more restrictive formulation.[52] This antiphasis in the Special Rapporteur's report did not go unnoticed and was not well received by the members of the Commission.[53]

The downgrading of the role of international organisations attempted with the Special Rapporteur's fifth report in an effort to curb the differences in legal opinions and put forward a commonly accepted formulation did not make its way into the final wording of the Conclusions. Thus, the Commission's final report adopts the same approach as the previous one. What has changed though, is the reference to international organisation practice within the International Law Commission's latest report. The Commission holds that State practice within

51 N Blokker, 'International Organizations and Customary International Law: Is the International Law Commission Taking International Organizations Seriously?' (2017) 14 *International Organizations Law Review* 5.

52 The improvements suggested were: (a) addition of the word 'may' to emphasise that caution is needed and (b) the reference to 'rules of customary international law' should be made in the singular, to better indicate that the practice of international organisation would not always be relevant, M Wood, *Fifth Report on the Identification of Customary International Law*, UN Doc A/CN.4/717, [46].

53 International Law Commission, Provisional summary record of the 3397th meeting, UN Doc A/CN.4/SR.3397, 11 (Galvao Treves).

the report should be read as encompassing international organisation practice *mutatis mutandis* in relevant cases[54] and this appears also in the commentary to Article 6.[55] While no further inference or elaboration follows from this, it seems that the *per analogiam* statement resulted from the examination of the establishment of the *opinio juris* of international organisations in the 2018 report for the first time.[56]

2.2 Opinio juris *of international organisations*

While the presence of both elements – practice and *opinio juris* – is indispensable for the production of a customary rule (practice without acceptance as law can be no more than a non-binding usage, while a belief that something is – or ought to be – the law unsupported by practice is mere aspiration),[57] two separate inquiries pertain to the existence of each one.[58] Thus, *opinio juris*[59] should not be automatically inferred merely from practice and is to be sought with respect not only to those taking part in such practice but also to those in a position to react to it.[60] The contribution of international organisations in their own name in the formation of the subjective element of custom is a question addressed by the International Law Commission in the 2018 report.

The Commission has said hardly anything to provide guidance with respect to this issue up to that time and thus it has been criticised by Commission members,[61] States,[62] and commentators.[63] The International Law Commission did not make any relevant reference in its 2016 report leaving in this way the matter open to various interpretations. The Chapeau of the relevant Part Four seemingly

54 International Law Commission Report 2018, 130 [4].

55 International Law Commission Report 2018, 134 [7]. Note that same understanding is not found to the Commentary of Articles 5 and 7 that also pertain to State practice.

56 *See* next section.

57 International Law Commission Report 2016, 101 [3]–[4] and accompanying footnotes.

58 ibid 105 [8].

59 *See* also Chapter 2 in this volume.

60 *North Sea Continental Shelf (Federal Republic of Germany v Denmark/ Federal Republic of Germany v Netherlands)*, Judgment, ICJ Reports 1969 [76].

61 E.g. Vazquez-Bermudez and Aurescu *see* International Law Commission, Summary record of the 3402nd meeting, UN Doc A/CN.4/SR.3402, 6.

62 International Law Commission, Comments and observations received from Governments, UN Doc A/CN.4/716, 38 (Austria) and 41 (Netherlands).

63 J Odermatt, 'The Development of Customary International Law by International Organizations' (2017) 66 *International and Comparative Law Quarterly* 493.

limited the enquiry to States,[64] while Conclusions 9 and 10 and the commentary thereto did not explicitly exclude international organisations but did not take them under consideration either. The issue was not addressed during the debates in the International Law Commission either and hence a member of the Commission wondered whether international organisation practice could 'contribute only to practice but not to *opinio juris*?'[65] So, a series of questions was left unaddressed: do international organisations possess such a belief in the first place? If they do, the Commission makes no reference to it because it doesn't contribute to the formation of custom or because it is covered by the aforementioned caveat that reference to State practice within the report should be read as encompassing international organisation practice too?

The final report of the Special Rapporteur takes into the account such criticisms, addresses the point, and puts the discussion to bed. In paragraph 45 he holds that the issue 'does not seem to raise special difficulties' and thus a *mutatis mutandis* approach with the *opinio juris* of States is in order. Statements of senior officials of international organisations can contribute to the establishment of *opinio juris* in the same way as statements by State officials. This suggestion did not meet opposition within the Commission and found its way into paragraph 7 of the Commentary to Article 10 in the latest International Law Commission Report. Once this proposition had been accepted, for reasons of consistency it was only logical that the same approach should be followed with respect to international organisation practice as demonstrated above. Nevertheless, the reason for the inclusion of such inferences in the International Law Commission Report was their persuasiveness as a matter of logical necessity and not their foundation in legal argumentation.

A careful reading of the latest International Law Commission Report as a whole suggests that the reference to international organisations is not entirely consistent throughout. The unprincipled way in which international organisations have been dealt with in the context of this project reveals a limited understanding of the law-making capacity of international organisations in international law. What is more, the approach adopted by the Commission demonstrates that it is uncertain as to the exact position of international organisations in the international legal order, especially when compared to that of States. This is also evident from other projects of the International Law Commission where the Commission has chosen either to address separately States and international organisations (e.g. Law of Treaties,

64 '[I]n each case, it is also necessary to be satisfied that there exists among States an acceptance as law (*opinio juris*) as to the binding character of the practice in question', International Law Commission Report 2018, 138, Chapeau of Part Four.

65 UN Doc A/CN.4/SR.3251, 4 (Murphy).

Law of International Responsibility) or to treat both subjects in the context of the same work (e.g. Guide to Reservations to Treaties).[66] The main argument running through this chapter is that convincing answers to all pending issues are possible. The International Law Commission could have arrived at a normatively solid outcome had it dealt with the defects of its project in turn. First, the Commission should put forward a comprehensive and principled understanding of how international organisations partake in the international lawmaking process and then attempt to draft a coherent set of conclusions.

3 The defect of the International Law Commission's approach

There are two intertwined reasons why the International Law Commission has not arrived at a satisfactory conclusion regarding the role of international organisations in the formation of custom. Conclusion 4(2) is not the product of a clear legal syllogism and this is why, I believe, International Law Commission members and the Special Rapporteur himself remain unconvinced as to whether it represents the progressive development of the law.[67] The methodology employed by the Special Rapporteur failed to account for the lawmaking power of international organisations as a basis of the ensuing legal debate.[68] And since his reports set the tone for the discussion within the Commission, the latter unfolded in an 'ideological' debate that lacked a *minimum* consensual starting point.

Given the divergence of views expressed and the ensuing lack of *consensus* among International Law Commission members, any pronouncement on the role of international organisations in the formation of custom clearly does not codify existing law, but is rather an attempt to infer its progressive development.[69] The Statute of the Commission defines progressive development as the 'preparation of draft conventions

66 Odermatt (n 63) 493–94.

67 The Special Rapporteur himself does not think that the conclusion 'could reasonably be described as *lex ferenda*' so arguably the International Law Commission may be stepping beyond its mandate here, UN Doc A/CN.4/SR.3303, 8.

68 Methodology is here used as 'juristic methodology' as in BG Ramcharan, *The International Law Commission: Its Approach to the Codification and Progressive Development of Interenational Law* (Martinus Nijhoff 1977) ch 4. Koskenniemi points out in a similar vein that: '[i]t is often the point of the international legal method to articulate and justify a position in a legal controversy', M Koskenniemi, 'Methodology of International Law' *Max Planck Encyclopedia of Public International Law* (2007) [12].

69 Statute of the International Law Commission, GA Resolution 174 (II), 1947, Article 1[1]. It must be recalled that the International Law Commission proceeds 'on the basis of a composite idea of "codification and progressive development"', and thus very seldom

on subjects which have not yet been regulated by international law or in regard to which the law has not yet been sufficiently developed in the practice of *States* [*sic*]'.[70] Given the lack of guidance from its Statute on this respect, the International Law Commission does not follow systematically a juristic methodology in order to infer the progressive development of the law.

A sector of doctrine describes the work of the International Law Commission as searching technically and with some empiricism for the general points of agreement between States.[71] In this sense, the Commission employs a combination of empiricism with inductive and policy-oriented approach.[72] Nevertheless, the empirical and inductive methods are of limited usefulness in this matter as existing practice is scant and inconclusive,[73] case law is inexistent and commentators are divided.[74] Thus, a methodological question automatically arises: how to infer the progressive development of the law when resort to empiricism and induction does not point to a specific direction? It would seem that the way to go is to attribute weight mainly to policy-oriented argumentation.

Naturally, the reports of the Special Rapporteur reflect a certain unease in this respect. The inferences are drawn mainly by academic literature which is surveyed extensively – occasionally to the point of exhaustion, and by the practice of the European Union to which he attributes much weight. So, Sir Michael doesn't resort to policy argumentation to support his thesis. But mindful of the few authoritative sources he had in hand to support his position, he concedes that the role of international organisations as reflected in the conclusions reflects reality but not necessarily the progressive development of the law or *lex ferenda*.[75]

For a rule to reflect such development though, it cannot run counter to existing law. The drafting of rules that do not codify *lex lata* but rather aim to depict the progression of the law in the future should not contradict the law as it stands at present. The law does not develop against itself but rather seek coherence. This

does it explain whether a particular provision falls under the rubric of 'customary law' or that of the 'progressive development of the law', *Yearbook of the International Law Commission* (1996) Vol II, pt 2 [156]–[57].

70 ibid Article 15.

71 S Sur, *L'interprétation en droit international public* (Librairie générale de droit et de jurisprudence 1974) 71.

72 Ramcharan (n 68) 86ff, 103.

73 The European Union was the only international organisation, whose role was undeniably relevant for the formation of customary rules, M Wood, *Fourth Report* [20].

74 M Wood, *Third Report* [70] and accompanying footnotes.

75 UN Doc A/CN.4/SR.3303, 8.

tendency is clearly reflected in the Al-Jedda judgment of the European Court of Human Rights.[76] The Court held that Security Council-imposed obligations are presumed to be *prima facie* in accordance with existing international obligations, such as those deriving from the European Convention on Human Rights.[77] Thus, the International Law Commission cannot develop rules that set to the side the legal *status* of international organisations as international legal persons for this has been recognised as *lex lata* by the Commission.[78] If the identifiable characteristic of international organisations – and the only one that puts them on a par with States – is their possession of international legal personality, the Special Rapporteur should have elaborated on the ramifications of this personality and in particular whether it is somehow attached to – what the International Law Commission termed – 'autonomous law-making power'. In a matter so broad as the formation of customary rules, I believe it is essential to understand the limited existing practice and the vast literature in the legal context in which they are placed. To the extent that the International Law Commission addresses the role of other non-State actors in the formation of custom, the same question pertains to them too.

Thus, the International Law Commission should have taken one step back and pondered on the fundamental question of the relationship between subjects and custom in international law. One does not clearly understand whether international organisations matter *in principle* in the formation of customary rules since the International Law Commission did not provide a legal reasoning to this respect as a throat-clearing exercise.[79] Such an approach would have added legal consistency to the

76 ECtHR, *Al-Jedda v The United Kingdom*, App. No 27021/08, 7 July 2011.

77 ibid [102].

78 *See* (n 16) and accompanying text. Deplano holds that '[t]he combined interpretation of Conclusions 4(2) and 12(2) suggests that international organisations do not possess a distinctive normative identity as subjects of international law', R Deplano, 'Assessing the Role of Resolutions in the International Law Commission Draft Conclusions on Identification of Customary International Law: Substantinve and Methodological Issues' (2017) 14 *International Organizations Law Review* 229. Similar point by Odermatt (n 63) 495.

79 Forteau proposed to add the words 'in principle' to paragraph 3 of Conclusion 4 that reads: 'Conduct of other actors is not practice that contributes to the formation, or expression, of rules of customary international law, but may be relevant when assessing the practice referred to in paragraphs 1 and 2', UN Doc A/CN.4/SR.3251, 6. Because the members of the International Law Commission agreed that by default the practice of those actors is not relevant, with wide consensus they also agreed upon the exception to the rule. Essentially, my proposition would be equivalent to that of Forteau's but with respect to paragraph 2.

International Law Commission's project and would have further facilitated the drafting of rules – and of commentaries thereto – since existing practice would have been understood under a certain perspective. The Commission should have resolved first and foremost whether international organisations, as autonomous subjects of international law detached from their member States, can *in principle* play a role in the formation of custom and then under this prism employ any methodology they see fit. As noted perceptively by the Netherlands in its latest written comments:

> If it is the separate international legal personality of an international organization that determines whether that organization can play a role in the formation and identification of international law, it is unclear why this role should be limited to these two cases. The legal basis for such a limitation remains unclear.[80]

This lack of a principled basis for discussion was evident in both the arguments evoked during the ensuing debates and the entrenched positions adopted. The argumentation employed by those unfavourable to the Special Rapporteur's position was based on two axes: first, to diminish the authoritative weight of the evidence used by Sir Michael to substantiate his thesis (e.g. does not find support in existing international law, has not been substantiated by any references to international case law, is a product of theorising).[81] This line of argumentation, even if it has some merit, does not prove that the opposite thesis is correct. Second, to focus on the primacy of States in the international legal order and thus conclude that the role of international organisations is subsidiary or indirect to the formation of custom.[82] This argument, based on a truism, confuses legal with political primacy and thus constitutes a *non sequitur*. The question that must be answered to substantiate this thesis is: why is the practice and *opinio juris* of international organisations considered to have less normative value than that of States since both possess legal personality? This requires a principled statement on the relationship between subjects and custom that the proponents of this position never put forward. Nevertheless, such a convincing principled statement was not advanced by those holding the opposite view either so the whole debate ended in a stalemate.

80 International Law Commission, Comments and observations received from Governments, UN Doc A/CN.4/716, 16. The two cases referred to are taken from the commentaries and concern (a) conferral of exclusive competences to the international organisation or (b) conferral of powers upon the international organisation functionally equivalent to those exercised by States.

81 *See* UN Doc A/CN.4/SR.3301, 16 (Murphy).

82 *See* UN Doc A/CN.4/SR.3251, 11 (Hmoud).

4 The importance of autonomy

This last section offers some thoughts on what can be the minimum consensual starting point for a fruitful debate on the issue that has been left *in limbo*. As mentioned above, the Commission should have made a principled statement on the connection between subjects and customary law in the international order. This connection could be established from two different points of departure.

First, from the nature of custom as a source of law with a communitarian basis. Klabbers for instance holds that customary law constitutes 'the aggregate of activities of the members of a political community'.[83] When a customary rule is established then, it is applicable to the legal order in its entirety, that is, to all the subjects that are members of the community.[84] The definitive factor then is not statehood, but membership in a community.[85] Such membership carries with it both the duty to submit to the existing body of such rules, and the right to contribute to their modification or development in accordance with the prevailing rules for such processes.[86] Since international organisations *are* bound by rules of general international law,[87] then perforce they are members of such a community and hence can contribute to the creation of custom.[88] This line of argumentation is attractive because it is based upon a logical connection: if international organisations are bound by customary rules, shouldn't they also be in a position to take part in the formation of such rules? However, it does not rest upon a legal definition of custom and is thus of limited legal value.

The second plausible argument is based on the nature of the subjects of international law. International organisations have a role to play in the formation of custom because their legal nature is akin to that of States. And the latter admittedly can contribute in this formative process. This argument does not rest upon

83 J Klabbers, 'The Sources of International Organizations Law: Reflections on Accountability' in J d'Aspremont and S Besson (eds), *The Oxford Handbook on Sources of International Law* (Oxford University Press 2018).

84 *North Sea Continental Shelf* (n 60) [63]: 'general or customary law rules and obligations [...] by their very nature, must have equal force for all members of the international community, and cannot therefore be the subject of any right of unilateral exclusion exercisable at will by any one of them in its own favour'.

85 D Murray, *Human Rights Obligations of Non-State Armed Groups* (Hart 2016) 84.

86 Sir A Jennings and D Watts, *Oppenheim's International Law*, vol I (Oxford University Press 1992) 14.

87 *Interpretation of the Agreement of 25 March 1951 between the WHO and Egypt*, Advisory Opinion, ICJ Reports 1980 [37].

88 Similar argument by Blokker (n 51) 10.

analogical reasoning in the sense that analogy *constitutes* the reason why international organisations contribute to the formation of customary international law. The role of international organisations in the formative process is in principle the same as that of States *because* both subjects possess international legal personality which in turn constitutes the reason behind the attribution of lawmaking power in international law.

But why do these two categories of subjects possess the same legal nature? It is considerations of autonomy that dictate the answer to this question. Autonomy, as the expression of separate juridical will,[89] exists in a dialectic relationship with separate legal personality; without autonomy, international legal personality is not conceivable and vice versa.[90] In the *Certain Phosphate Lands in Nauru* case, the International Court of Justice denied to attribute international legal personality to the tripartite Administering Authority for Nauru on the justification that the Administrator 'was at all times appointed by the Australian Government and was accordingly under the instructions of that Government' and that his acts 'were subject to confirmation or rejection by the Governor-General of Australia'.[91] The Court concluded that the Administering Authority did not possess a distinct will and therefore an international legal personality distinct from those of the States that comprised it.[92] It is thus the expression of a separate will with respect to certain competence and not the conferral of competence as such, that bestows legal personality upon the international organisation.[93] The GATT, for example, in its early stages was refused international organisation status because it did not possess such *volonté distincte*.[94] Two different types of autonomy are germane to the present

89 P Reuter, *Institutions internationales* (Paris Presses Universitaires 1955) 195: 'En tant qu' organisation il ne peut que s'agir d'un groupe susceptible de manifester d'une manière permanente une *volonté juridiquement distincte* de celle de ces membres' (emphasis added).

90 HG Schermers and NM Blokker, *International Institutional Law: Unity Within Diversity* (Martinus Nijhoff 2011) 34–35; P Sands and P Klein, *Bowett's Law of International Institutions* (Sweet and Maxwell 2001) 16; G Verdirame, *The UN and Human Rights: Who Guards the Guardians?* (Cambridge University Press 2011) 59–60. Autonomy derives from the Greek word αυτονομία that literally means the 'freedom to use one's own laws', HG Liddell and R Scott, *An Intermediate Greek-English Lexicon* (Clarendon Press 1889).

91 *Nauru v Australia*, Judgment, ICJ Reports 1992, 257.

92 ibid 258.

93 The International Court of Justice referred to international organisations as 'subjects of law endowed with a certain autonomy', *Nuclear Weapons* (n 8) [19]; Ahlborn (n 19) 416.

94 Schermers and Blokker (n 90) 35. White suggests that the G7 is denied legal personality because of the lack of a separate will, N. White, *The Law of International Organizations* (Manchester University Press 2005) 31.

context: the autonomy international organisations enjoy from member States and conversely the autonomy member States enjoy from the international organisation.

As far as the first one is concerned, autonomy of an international organisation is defined by the constituent instrument of that organisation, and hence the rules that are enacted in accordance with this instrument. When drafting the constituent instrument, members intend to bestow legal personality upon the organisation and consequently every decision of the international organisation adopted in accordance with its rules is necessarily an expression of the separate juridical will of that organisation.[95] To uphold the opposite would be tantamount to suggesting that such institutions can have legal personality without possessing autonomy at the same time. This is why, it cannot be upheld that international organisations lose their autonomy when member States operate in accordance with the rules of the international organisation.[96] For example, in the *Application of the Interim Accord of 13 September 1995* case,[97] NATO's decision not to invite the Federal Yugoslav Republic Of Macedonia to join the international organisation, was rendered autonomously by NATO, albeit Greece's *de facto* veto was the catalyst to the international organisation's stance. Therefore, the formation of the separate will of the international organisation, through the processes envisioned in its rules, cannot undermine the autonomy of that institution.

Being so closely tied to the formation of a separate juridical will through specific processes which are different in every international organisation, autonomy, when attached to international organisations, is a relative concept without a fixed meaning. This is why it is an elusive trait to establish and in general writers have not elaborated on how it should be identified.[98] However, the fact that an international

95 Ahlborn (n 19) 403 and 415.

96 J d'Aspremont argues in a similar vein that no abuse of the international organisation's legal personality occurs in such instances, J d'Aspremont, 'Abuse of the Legal Personality of International Organizations and the Responsibility of Member States' (2007) 4 *International Organizations Law Review* 110. Sarooshi suggests that international organisations cannot be considered as agents of member States when the latter exercise control within the confines of the decision-making processes of the international organisation, D Sarooshi, *International Organizations and Their Exercise of Sovereign Powers* (Oxford University Press 2007) 45. Neither of them however explains in normative terms why this is so. *See* also, T Gazzini, 'The Relationship between International Legal Personality and Autonomy' in ND White and R Collins (eds), *International Organisations and the Idea of Autonomy* (Cavendish-Routledge 2010) 199ff.

97 *The Former Yugoslav Republic of Macedonia v Greece*, Judgment, ICJ Reports 2011, 644.

98 White has offered some indicia of existence of a separate will, N White, 'Discerning Separate Will' in W Heere (ed), *From Government to Governance: The Growing Impact of Non-State Actors on the International and European Legal System* (Proceedings of the 2004 Hague Joint ASIL/NVIR Conference 2004) 31–38.

organisation will enjoy autonomy from members with respect to the processes covered by its rules, does not render autonomy a quantitative value.[99] No such thing as 'a large measure' of autonomy is conceivable when it comes to conferring competence to an international organisation.[100] Because, as said earlier, such a proposition suggests that no personality is conferred to the organisation with respect to specific competence which is clearly not the intention of the members.

When it comes to autonomy of member States from the international organisation, if the outcome of a process is an expression of the organisation's autonomy, the same outcome (for example a decision or a resolution) cannot be the expression of the *separate* juridical will of member States at the same time. Since a process pertains to the exercise of certain competence, when the international organisation exercises autonomously this competence, member States necessarily lose their autonomy with respect to the said competence and hence the separateness of their legal personality.[101] Member States *are* the international organisation in such instances. This however does not mean that States lose their legal personality altogether; this will be the case only to the extent that their conduct is not an autonomous exercise of certain competence.

The understanding of autonomy is only functional and thus legal subjects can at the same time be autonomous with respect to certain competence but not with respect to others. The existence of different types of autonomy (territorial, cultural, etc.) corroborates this functional understanding of the notion.[102] During the *interbellum* for example, Estonia implemented the Cultural Autonomy Law which vested certain ethnic groups with autonomy only in the fields of education, culture, sports, and youth affairs.[103] Similarly, in the context of the *Request for Interpretation of the Judgment of 31 March 2004 in the Case concerning Avena and Other Mexican Nationals* case the United States argued that individual states hold a degree of autonomy in 'matters relating to criminal justice'.[104] Since autonomy is attached to legal personality, when States limit their autonomy by merging with the international

99 *Contra* Gazzini (n 96) 200.

100 Alvarez (n 2) 129; A Cassese, *International Law* (Oxford University Press 2005) 137.

101 Geslin suggests that it is the international organisation that loses its autonomy when member States control its actions, A Geslin, 'Réflexions sur la Répartition de la Responsabilité entre l'Organisation Internationale et ses Etats Membres' (2005) 109 *Revue générale de droit international public* 564.

102 HZ Heintze, 'On the Legal Understanding of Autonomy' in M Suksi (ed), *Autonomy: Applications and Implications* (Kluwer Law International 1998) 17–24.

103 ibid 21.

104 *Mexico v United States of America*, Provisional Measures, Order of 16 July 2008, ICJ Reports 2008 [33].

organisation, this impacts their capacity to invoke separate international personality with respect to matters covered by international organisation competences.

The characteristic that derives from international legal personality then is the autonomy to express a separate will with respect to certain competence. This is something States and international organisations have in common. The fact that States possess the totality of competences while international organisations only a portion does not alter their common legal nature. Therefore, there exists no good reason why these two subjects should have different legal powers with respect to the competences they possess. If autonomous lawmaking power is an exercise of such powers it should not be a prerogative of States. Since it is attributed to them by virtue of their legal nature, international organisations should be entitled to contribute too in the formation of international law to the extent that it pertains to their competences.

5 Concluding remarks

The International Law Commission's work on the Identification of Customary International Law project is done. The Conclusions and the Commentaries are in the hands of the General Assembly now, which is in charge of the final form the Conclusions will take and how they will be disseminated.[105]

International organisations' participation in the formation of custom is one of those stalemated issues that the Special Rapporteur hoped to resolve with authority in the context of this project. Despite his commendable efforts to find common ground, the differences in the entrenched positions adopted within the Commission and by States and international organisations in their comments were not reconcilable. Thus, Conclusion 4(2) remains of questionable legal validity. This chapter suggests that a possible way to unite Commission members in this issue is by providing a principled exegesis of the legal connection between international organisations and customary international law. No matter which approach was adopted by the International Law Commission, such an understanding of principle will provide a consensual starting point for future debates. Lastly, by offering some tentative thoughts as to the relationship between subjects and sources of international law, the chapter suggests there are good legal grounds why the International Law Commission should leave behind a State-centric view of the sources of international law and recognise the autonomous lawmaking power of international organisations.

105 For the recommendations of the International Law Commission to the General Assembly in this respect *see* International Law Commission, Provisional Summary Record of the 3444th Meeting, UN Doc A/CN.4/SR.3444 (12 October 2018), 3.

Chapter 2
Capturing the juridical will

Catherine Brölmann

The *Conclusions on Identification of Customary International Law* (hereafter 'the Conclusions') as adopted by the International Law Commission on second reading[1] are an important resource in a thorny area of international law. A stated primary aim is to offer guidance to practitioners,[2] which accounts for the focus on systematisation of positive international law and practice.

The Conclusions are brief on the position of international organisations as *independent* actors in the formation of customary international law. This modest role could seem remarkable, given that international organisations participate ever more fully in international-legal affairs. The present chapter argues that one – generally under-studied – factor in explaining the apparently modest role of international organisations as independent actors in the formation of custom is the hesitation of international law to attribute a 'juridical will' to international organisations.

The construct of the juridical will plays a key role in legal actors' creation of law and legal relations in any legal system. This also holds for international law, and includes the process of the formation of custom. The ascription of a juridical will to States has been – especially since the nineteenth century – generally unproblematic. For international organisations, however, this is different. It seems international law has not been at ease with the construal of a 'mental state' for organisations, even when and where their status as independent legal actors was uncontested. Still, this tension is inconspicuous where a sign is agreed to communicate a legally relevant mental state, such as 'signature' for 'approval' or 'assent'.[3] The same holds for cases

1 International Law Commission Report 2018, Ch V, Draft Conclusions on Identification of Customary International Law, with commentaries (UN Doc A/73/10).

2 ibid 122 para 2.

3 In reality this does not quite capture the different layers at stake. E.g. (leaving aside the signified and the signifier of the legal terms) in treaty-making at least three levels exist (the physical act of signing, which signifies the legal act of signing, which in turn signifies consent to be bound (or any other intention).

in which international law accepts a fact in social reality – for example the sending of a military mission or the issuance of a Resolution – as a result of, in a legal sense, *willed* conduct and thus an expression of juridical will.

There are on the other hand situations in which juridical will must be ascertained without the help of agreed signs, as with the determination of *opinio juris*. To discern 'intention' or 'opinion' in States for the purpose of establishing customary international law is a nebulous process,[4] but when it comes to international organisations it is more problematic still, as in general the international organisation is not recognised as a sentient legal person in the way of states. A detailed tracing of the position of international organisations as independent actors in the Conclusions is carried out in another chapter of this volume.[5] The point which the present chapter aims to make is that the work of the International Law Commission confirms a general hesitation on the part of international law in attributing to international organisations a juridical will. This in turn can be linked to the mechanistic, functionalist view of international organisations that has persisted even when international organisations came to be recognised as independent actors.

This chapter is structured as follows. It briefly addresses the place of international organisations in the *Conclusions on the Identification of Customary International Law* (1), and recalls the role of the juridical will in the formation of customary international law on the part of legal actors in general (2). It then turns to the development of international organisations as legal actors (3), after which it zooms in on two facets of the concommitant feature of juridical will that are relevant to the formation and identification of custom (4): the *opinion* of organisations and the proverbial *volonté distincte* (that is, distinct from the will of the member States). The chapter addresses one implication, which is the asymmetry of international organisations not contributing to the formation of the customary law by which they are bound (5), followed by some concluding remarks (6).

1 International organisations in the Conclusions

In the Conclusions international organisations appear in two ways: as a platform for the (legal) acts of States, and as an independent international-legal actor. As to the latter, Conclusion 4 (*Requirement of practice*) para 2, refers to the practice of international organisations in their own right, as a possible contribution to 'the

4 The endeavour of the Conclusions to establish signs for *opinio juris* – for States – bears this out; Conclusion 10 and commentary (UN Doc A/73/10) 140–42.

5 *See* Chapter 1, this volume.

formation, or expression, of rules of customary international law'. This is most likely to occur, according to the commentary, when States have transferred exclusive competences to an international organisation, or 'conferred powers upon the international organization that are functionally equivalent to the powers exercised by States'.[6] More generally the commentary points to a key role for states: '[a]s a general rule, the more directly a practice of an international organisation is carried out on behalf of its member States or endorsed by them, and the larger the number of such member States, the greater weight it may have in relation to the formation, or expression, of rules of customary international law'.[7] Otherwise, Conclusion 6 (*Forms of practice*) para 2; Conclusion 10 (*Forms of evidence of acceptance as law (opinio juris)*) para 2; and Conclusion 12 (*Resolutions of international organisations and intergovernmental conferences*) are explicitly concerned with the practice and *opinio juris* of States in the context of international organisations.[8]

In short, the Conclusions give a relatively prominent part to organisations as a framework for customary international law formation by States, but they are brief about an independent role of international organisations in the identification and by implication formation of customary international law. While the *practice* of international organisations as such comes up in aforementioned Conclusion 4(2) ('in certain cases …'), Conclusion 10 makes no mention of the *opinio juris* of international organisations, and also its commentary speaks only of States.[9] International organisations thus figure predominantly as vehicles for State action, which in turn may bespeak *opinio juris* or relevant practice on the part of the State. In terminology introduced elsewhere: organisations are presented with a *transparent* institutional veil.[10] The emphasis on States is borne out by the Commentary to Conclusion 12: 'Although resolutions of organs of international organizations […] emanate, strictly speaking, not from the States members but from the organization, […] they may reflect the collective expression of the views of such States'.[11]

6 UN Doc A/73/10, 131 paras 5–6; *see* also Chapter 12 in this volume regarding the discussions leading up to Conclusion 4(2).

7 UN Doc A/73/10, 132, para 8.

8 cf R Deplano, 'Assessing the Role of Resolutions in the ILC Draft Conclusions on Identification of Customary International Law' (2017) 14 International Organizations Law Review 227, 229. This is set out in more detail in Chapter 1 of this volume.

9 UN Doc A/73/10, 138–42, Conclusions 9 and 10 and commentaries; *see* also Michael Wood, 'International Organizations and Customary International Law (2014 Jonathan J Charney Distinguished Lecture in Public International Law)' (2015) 48 Vanderbilt Journal of Transnational Law 609.

10 C Brölmann, *The Institutional Veil in Public International Law* (Hart 2007).

11 UN Doc A/71/10, 147 para 3.

That said, the Commentary to Conclusion 4 indicates that in principle international organisations *can* display their own relevant practice and *opinio juris*.[12] This idea gains additional weight as international organisations are set apart from 'other actors' by paragraph 3 of Conclusion 4, which articulates that the practice of other non-State actors does not have that potential. In this the Conclusions follow the reports by the Special Rapporteur, which – generally – give evidence of a more open approach to international organisations' independent role in customary international law formation.[13]

The 2018 Conclusions then recognise the possibility of an independent role for international organisations, but they do not elaborate; and some key questions are left pending. One is how the *opinio juris* of an organisation is to be established. Another is how to determine *when* we are dealing with practice (or *opinio juris*) of the organisation as such, and when with the practice of member States. It is worth noting the layered and more elaborate conceptualisation of '[subsequent] practice of the organisation' found in the International Law Commission's *Conclusions on subsequent agreements and subsequent practice in relation to the interpretation of treaties*, also adopted in 2018.[14] In the context of interpretation of constitutive treaties these envisage 'subsequent practice of the parties [… that …] *may arise from, or be expressed in*, the practice of an international organization' (Conclusion 12 (2) – emphasis added), as well as independent '[p]ractice of an international organization in the application of its constituent instrument' (Conclusion 12 (3)), both with abundant examples from practice.[15] The commentary also points out how the

12 cf the Commentary to Conclusion 4 (UN Doc A/73/10, 131 para 5): 'The practice of international organizations in international relations (when accompanied by *opinio juris*) may count as practice that gives rise or attests to rules of customary international law'.

13 International Law Commission, First report on formation and evidence of customary international law (Sir Michael Wood, Special Rapporteur) (2013) UN Doc A/CN.4/663; International Law Commission, Second report on identification of customary international law (2014) UN Doc A/CN.4/672; International Law Commission, Third report on identification of customary international law (2015) UN Doc A/CN.4/682; International Law Commission, Fourth report on identification of customary international law (2016) UN Doc A/CN.4/695. cf especially the Third Report, UN Doc A/CN.4/682, paras 68–79; *see* also Michael Wood, 'International Organizations and Customary International Law (2014 Jonathan J Charney Distinguished Lecture in Public International Law)' (2015) 48 Vanderbilt Journal of Transnational Law 609, 616–20.

14 Conclusions on *Subsequent agreements and subsequent practice in relation to the interpretation of treaties* (International Law Commission Report 2018 (UN Doc A/73/10), Chapter IV).

15 ibid 93–106.

authorship of legally relevant 'practice' might be even shared by the organisation and the (member) states, as was suggested by the International Court of Justice in the *Wall Case* when it subtly referred to 'the *accepted* practice of the General Assembly'.[16] This said, it is fair to assume that the disconnect between the two descriptions of 'practice' in relation to international organisations is more contextual than conceptual;[17] that issue, however, lies outside the scope of the present chapter.

2 The juridical will in public international law

The juridical will, that elusive legal attribute, has a key role in the creation of law and legal relations in any legal order. The concept of 'juridical will' is taken here to denote a broad category of mental states on the part of a legal actor that have an effect in law (and may thus translate into both legal acts and legal facts). We may think for example of assent, acquiescence, intention, opinion, aim, and good or bad faith. These are states of mind or, to borrow a helpful term from theory of agency, 'intentional states',[18] ascribed to recognised participants in any legal order. As a construct the juridical will operationalises legal agency, which is why it is also a key component of 'legal personality'.

Leaving aside the development in natural persons of the link between the psychological (theological) will on the one hand and the juridical will on the other, it is fair to say that by the eighteenth century in international law the idea of a juridical will had been successfully transposed to the State[19] as a component in the creation of law and – especially, in the contractual vision of that time – legal obligations. In the nineteenth century then, the 'natural' view of actorhood, or 'personality' in

16 *Legal Consequences of the Construction of a Wall in the Occupied Palestinian Territory*, Advisory Opinion, ICJ Reports 2004 136, 150 (emphasis added).

17 As constitutive treaty interpretation is a more diffuse and 'inward-turned' exercise than the identification of a rule of customary international law, it may require less stringent parameters for the determination of practice; this is not unlike the way attribution of conduct with the consequence of rendering applicable a particular field of law seemed to allow for a lower threshold than attribution of conduct with the consequence of making a State legally responsible – something which famously led to divergent concepts of 'control' in the ICTY and the ICJ.

18 P Pettit, *A Theory of Freedom: From the Psychology to the Politics of Agency* (Polity Press 2001) 104, 115.

19 cf the different forms of consent identified by Emmerich De Vattel (*Le Droit des gens* (1758), *The Law of Nations* (from the Classics of International Law series by J Brown Scott (ed), the Carnegie Institute of Washington 1916) 9. This time also saw a move away from natural law, to some extent, and towards *voluntarism* in international relations.

doctrinal terms, in international law gained prominence. The only candidate for that role on the international plane was the State, described by Hegel as 'completely autonomous totalities in themselves' and as 'the absolute power on earth … in which the world spirit unfolds itself'.[20] By then the State's corporate and fictional nature had largely disappeared from view,[21] which in turn facilitated the incorporation in international law of domestic law analogies and the accommodation of a 'natural person', to whom a particular intentional state could be attributed.

The anthropomorphic view of the State, and of its international-legal 'personality', was to some extent dismantled by interbellum scholars such as Kelsen, Brierly, and Nekam,[22] and has been the object of contestation ever since. It has been pointed out that '[o]rthodox international law proceeds from the assumption that States have a legal conscience, [even if] it has no workable or operational way to explain how this is supposed to work',[23] 'as if governments, let alone states, had determinable states of mind'.[24] At the same time, the fiction of the intentional state is locked in in systems of law; it is needed to operationalise legal agency on the part of recognised actors.[25] And in truth international law has remained discretely at ease with ascribing a legally relevant 'state of mind' to States. One example is the weight traditionally given to the State's 'intention' in the interpretation of treaties or in the determination of the *juridical* character of an agreement. Another example is precisely the doctrine of States' *opinio juris* as a component of customary international law.

References to psychological agency and the attribution of will to legal actors are, in the same way as in domestic (private) law, common in international law, witness classic references such as '[t]he signed text is … the most recent expression of the common will of the parties'.[26] For the twentieth century the ability to *think* has

20 GF Hegel, *Grundlinien der Philosophie des Rechts* (Knox translation of 1821) (Suhrkamp 1986) paras 330 and 331.
21 cf M Koskenniemi, 'The Wonderful Artificiality of States' (1995) 89 Proceedings of the Annual Meeting of the American Society of International Law 22.
22 Brölmann (n 10) ch 4.
23 A Carty, 'Doctrine versus State Practice' in Bardo Fassbender and Anne Peters (eds), *The Oxford Handbook of the History of International Law* (Oxford University Press 2012) 972, 976.
24 P Allott, 'The Concept of International Law' (1999) 10 European Journal of International Law 31, 39.
25 *See* also Chapter 5 in this volume (while I disagree with the construal of *opinio juris* as 'unintentional … acceptance', I concur with the author's observation that the intentional state of 'will' is especially relevant in the 'positivist theory of lawmaking').
26 International Law Commission Special Rapporteur Sir Humphrey Waldock, ILC Ybk 1964 II 56; ILC Ybk 1966 II 220.

been linked to the doctrine of 'fundamental' rights of States, which is taken as an anthropomorphic construction.[27] Generally however, the subjective, mental dimension of the juridical will, and especially its construction for non-human legal actors, seems under-theorised.

At this point it must be recalled that this chapter is concerned with the ascription of a juridical will *within* the law. Seen from an immanent perspective this depends not only on particular features which may turn an entity into a legal actor, but foremost on the legal framework, and the legal imagery, within which the legal actor finds itself. It is true that political theory and political philosophy have brought to light how group agents are distinct from the sum of their component parts because of a particular decision-making structure,[28] and how by the ability to formulate a separate, collective will, they would become susceptible to bearing responsibility.[29] Philosophy of language can explicate how (groups of) human individuals may impose intentionality on governments and international organisations, and how *opinio juris* in fact may amount to an institutional object, brought about by speech acts that express beliefs and intentions.[30] From these perspectives the construction of a 'willful state of mind' for one composite (i.e. non-individual human) actor does not require more effort than for another.

However *within* the law intentional states are projections used by the system, necessary for it to function. The prime question is therefore whether a legal environment ascribes legally relevant intentional states to an actor. This mostly coincides with the recognition by the system of (a degree of) legal personhood – but not always, as in the case of international organisations, which, as set out below, in the imagery of international law have a seemingly subservient role.

The process is easiest when an agreed sign in external reality exists for a legally relevant state of mind on the part of a legal actor, such as 'signature' for 'assent', or the 'passing of 30 days' for 'acquiescence'. In these cases there is a presumption of juridical will, without the need for its ascertainment. When no agreed sign exists, it is a more intricate process to establish juridical will and its orientation. Yet, this

27 J d'Aspremont, 'The Doctrine of Fundamental Rights of States and Anthropomorphic Thinking in International Law' (2015) 4 Cambridge Journal of International and Comparative Law 501, esp 515ff.

28 P Pettit, 'Collective Persons and Powers' (2002) 8 Legal Theory 443; also F Johns (ed) *International Legal Personality* (Ashgate 2010) xi–xxix, and fn 87.

29 From the angle of international relations scholarschip *see* e.g. T Erskine, 'Assigning Responsibilities to Institutional Moral Agents: The Case of States and 'Quasi-States' in T Erskine (ed), *Can Institutions Have Responsibilities?* (Palgrave Macmillan 2003) 19, 20.

30 *See* Chapter 3 in this volume.

process can be fluid and flexible when an actor's capacity to have an intentional state as such is uncontested, as with States. The search for a subjective, mental state is typically at issue in the ascertainment of *opinio juris*, as can be seen from the range of expressions used by the International Court of Justice to render the notion, collected in the Second Report, which include 'feeling', 'belief', 'deliberate intention', 'awareness', 'conviction', 'general feeling', and 'actual consciousness'.[31] The next sections consider the 'legal will' of organisations, first as part of the image of organisations as legal persons (4) and then with a focus on two aspects that are specifically important for the formation of custom (5).

3 The thin legal personality of international organisations

This section aims to trace the development of organizations as international legal actors, which includes the facet of juridical will, since their entry on the scene. As argued above, this development is closely connected to the role that organisations are allowed to play in international law, more than to their particular institutional features in social reality. International organisations often are taken to represent the essential non-State actors' success story. The received narrative is that international organisations in the course of more than a century have come to act on a par with States as actors in international law. But the newfound legal agency of organisations can be unpacked further.

The development of international organisations as legal actors has been steep. As I have argued elsewhere,[32] after a 'functional' phase in which organisations acted as mere platforms for State action, international organisations have come to participate in international life also as independent legal actors, an independence that became prominent in the United Nations era. Organisations came to conclude treaties and send envoys, and to participate in international political and legal relations at an unprecedented scale. The conceptualisation of international organisations' legal independence (that is, the external aspect of their institutional autonomy) was couched first of all in the doctrinal terms of 'legal personality'. Here it is important to recall that international organisations, unlike states, in their history of conceptual and doctrinal development, never passed a stage in which they counted as a

31 Second Report of the Special Rapporteur, 66th session of the International Law Commission (2014) (UN Doc A/CN.4/672) para 67.

32 C Brölmann, 'Het constitutionele perspectief en de coming of age van internationale organisaties' [The constitutional perspective and the coming of age of international organisations], in JH Reestman et al (eds) *De Regels en het Spel: Opstellen over Recht, Filosofie, Literatuur en Geschiedenis* (TMC Asser Press 2011) 73.

'natural' form of political organisation with ensuing 'natural' international legal personality. If this had been the case, the image of the international organisation would arguably have been a different one today.

The possibility of international legal personality for international organisations had been a topic of debate among scholars in the interbellum, and had been left unresolved. Still, in practice the question whether organisations could, and did, have international legal personality was brought to a head immediately after the creation of the United Nations and was decided essentially for all international organisations with the 1949 International Court of Justice *Reparation* Opinion.[33] Later on, international legal personality would be boldly mentioned in the constitutive treaties of some new organisations (even if technically speaking the enjoyment of legal personality would not depend on a decision of the constituting states), such as the Rome Statute (Article 4(1)) and the Treaty on the European Union (Article 47). With the independent activity of organisations rapidly increasing, one response of the system was the codification of applicable rules of international law in specific substantive areas, such as privileges and immunities,[34] the law of treaties,[35] and the law of international responsibility.[36] At the same time, the mechanistic and partly transparent image of the international organisation remained.[37]

States kept a close and critical eye on the rapidly expanding independent activity of international organisations, but many scholars and commentators applauded the rise of international organisations.[38] Undoubtedly this enthusiasm was tied to an image of the autonomous international organisation as an a-political and spiritless mechanism.[39] In that vision international organisations embodied neutrality and were not susceptible to the political snares and conflicts of interest that so often were seen to hamper the effectiveness of international law when States were involved. For its part this view fitted in the post-war progress narrative on international law: the more international power and authority would be organised along

33 Brölmann (n 10) 65–96.

34 1946 Convention on the Privileges and Immunities of the United Nations, 1 UNTS 15.

35 1986 Vienna Convention on the Law of Treaties between States and International Organizations or between International Organizations (UN Doc A/CONF.129/15).

36 UN Doc. A/66/10, 9 December 2011.

37 Brölmann (n 10) 245–47.

38 J Klabbers, 'The Changing Image of International Organisations' in JM Coicaud and V Heiskanen (eds), *The Legitimacy of International Organisations* (United Nations University 2001) 221, 226–27.

39 *See* also Chapter 1 in this volume.

functional lines rather than on the basis of State sovereignty,[40] the more compliance and *rule of law* – and hence safety and wellbeing of people – would improve. Another dimension of this was of course a confirmation of the State as the dominant form of political organisation and power. The functionalist, a-moral vision of international organisations was not about an 'unmoral organisation' in the way of Allott's 'unmoral state'[41] – which posits that only human individuals can be responsible behind the screen of corporate legal persons. Rather, it was about (member) States as the ultimate political, moral, and juridical agents.

This vision in turn strengthened a particular conceptualisation of organisations in which they were independent legal persons, but in a 'thin version'. One could say that organisations were accommodated as legal persons but not *willful* legal persons or *personnes morales*.[42] The codification process of the 1986 *Vienna Convention on the Law of Treaties between States and International Organisations or between International Organisations* ('1986 Convention'), which lasted from 1971 until 1986, gives evidence of that. From the text, the commentaries and the *travaux* in general emerges, next to a State's concern about the possibility of independent action of organisations, primarily a 'technical', a-political view of the autonomy of international organisations. To be sure, according to the regime of the 1986 Convention, international organisations can engage in treaty-making, especially if they can produce an agreed sign of a legal will expressed to this effect, such as the formal 'expression of consent to be bound by a treaty'. At the same time international organisations as such are not ascribed the moral and political 'considerations' and 'intentions' that are part of the legal persona ascribed to States. Thus, the 1986 Convention envisages the possibility of error or fraud in the conclusion of a treaty on the part of an organisation, but in order to ascertain that this is the case, the claimant must resort to the internal institutional order of the international organisation, or – in other words – to the member States (Articles 48 and 49 of the 1986 Convention).[43] The Convention provides that states 'acquiesce in the validity of the treaty', while

40 The work of eminent institutional law scholars such as Schermers and Seidl-Hohenveldern provides a clear example of this optimism in relation to international organisations.

41 P Allott, 'State Responsibility and the Unmaking of International Law' (1988) 29 Harvard Journal of International Law 1.

42 On 'moral personality' in the civil law tradition *see* e.g. FW Maitland, 'Moral Personality and Legal Personality' (1905) 6 Journal of Comparative Legislation and International Law 192; E Pisier-Kouchner, 'La notion de personne morale dans l'oeuvre de Léon Duguit' (1974) 11/12 Quaderni fiorentini per la storia del pensiero giuridico moderno 667.

43 Yearbook Of The International Law Commission 1982 Vol II (Part Two) 5 para 2 (re Art 48(2)).

organisations must be seen to have '*renounced* the right to invoke that ground' based on the passing of a certain stretch of time.[44] The reluctance to ascribe juridical will, or a specific intentional state, to international organisations is also reflected in the longtime idea of impossibility of an international organisation's 'wrongdoing' ('[i]s it really conceivable that … organisations may … employ, the threat or use of force …?').[45] In relation to an early version of the Draft Articles on State Responsibility the International Law Commission had stated that 'it must not be forgotten that, by their very nature, international organizations normally behave in such a manner as not to commit internationally wrongful acts'.[46]

In the past two decades the neutral, mechanistic view of organisations has lost much of its appeal, arguably due to a disenchantment and sobering of expectations regarding international organisations, triggered for example by information about misconduct of United Nations military missions[47] and self-enrichment of United Nations staff members.[48] Already there were longtime misgivings about the manifestation of, especially universal, international organisations as a Western-hegemonic project.[49] Meanwhile circles of legal theory and sociology critiqued the presumed move from a territorial to a functional basis for power and authority[50] in international affairs, because of the risks that come with *single issue* agenda. It is safe to say that in our time the independent actorship of international organisations no longer raises only institutional and formal-juridical questions, or concerns on the role of member States as *Herren der Verträge* (Masters of the Treaties). Issues of legitimacy and ethics arise, both inside the organisation and in the context of general international law. A cynical thought experiment has described how in a traditional institutional law context an imaginary 'International Torture Organisation' operates entirely in accordance with the 'law of international organisations' (which

44 Articles 45(1)(b) and 45(2)(b) respectively.

45 Yearbook Of The International Law Commission 1982 Vol II (Part Two) 55 para 2.

46 Yearbook Of The International Law Commission 1975 Vol II para 3 87 (emphasis added); both the article and the commentary were adopted in an unaltered version in 1996.

47 C Lutz, M Gutmann and K Brown, 'Conduct and Discipline in UN Peacekeeping Operations: Culture, Political Economy and Gender' 2009 Watson Institute for International Studies Research Paper, http://dx.doi.org/10.2139/ssrn.2323758.

48 SA Notar, 'The Oil-for-Food Program and the Need for Oversight Entities to Monitor UN Sanctions Regimes' (2007) 101 Proceedings of the Annual Meeting of the American Society of International Law 163.

49 B Chimni, 'International Institutions Today: An Imperial Global State in the Making' (2004) 15 European Journal of International Law 1, 23–24.

50 G Teubner, 'Globale Zivilverfassungen: Alternativen zur staatszentrierten Verfassungstheorie' (2003) 63 Zeitschrift für ausländisches öffentliches Recht und Völkerrecht 1.

after all leaves quite some room for individual institutional arrangements) and practices its monopolistic right to torture (since torture is prohibited for States) without the possibility of calling the 'International Torture Organisation' to account.[51] An expression of the changing perspective on international organisations is that the notorious gap in individual legal protection vis-à-vis international organisations (if perhaps not in case of torture) that is created by a coinciding of attribution of conduct on the one hand and immunity on the other, or attribution of conduct on the one hand and a (lack of) *locus standi* on the other, increasingly has come to be considered unacceptable. With the increased activity of international organisations on the international scene, also in fields of *high politics* such as peace operations and other engagements which touch upon the internal affairs of States, the call for accountability of international organisations has grown accordingly. This has sparked interest in formal responsibility mechanisms[52] as well as non-legal accountability processes of international organisations;[53] it has created space for a concern about the compatibility of international organisation international conduct with human rights,[54] and ultimately questions as to whether international organisations are and should be bound by general international law.[55]

4 International organisations' juridical will and the formation of custom

As with States, the notion of a juridical will is key to the independent contribution of organisations to the formation ofcustomary international law.

Two facets of the juridical will of international organisations then are especially relevant for the formation of customary international law: the subjective and psychological dimension of the international organisation's juridical will, to

51 M Parish, 'An Essay on the Accountability of International Organisations' (2010) 7 International Organisations Law Review 277.

52 C Ahlborn, 'The Rules of International Organisations and the Law of International Responsibility' (2011) 8 International Organisations Law Review 397.

53 ILA Committee on *Accountability of International Organisations* (final report of 2002 New Delhi (70th) Conference).

54 cf J Wouters et al (eds), *Accountability for Human Rights Violations by International Organisations* (Intersentia 2010) – who incidentally also refer to the mechanistic view of organisations in the book's introduction: 'Some may consider the theme … far-fetched. How could one imagine international organisations violating human rights?' (at 2).

55 K Daugirdas, 'How and Why International Law Binds International Organizations' (2016) 57 Harvard International Law Journal 325.

be identified as a 'pure' intentional state, and second, the *distinctness* of the international organisation's juridical will.

4.1 Opinion

It appears that international law can handle the juridical will on the part of an organisation when this turns on agreed signs, both internally ('majority decision-making') and internationally ('signature' as expression of the 'intention to be legally bound'). When no such signs are available (while also no concrete action can be determined from which to infer juridical will), it is necessary to ascertain a 'pure' intentional state with.

Whether international organisations can 'have an opinion' in a legally relevant sense appears to be a pending question in the 2018 Conclusions. The attention for international organisations as independent actors is geared to *practice* (albeit there is rarely agreement on its status)[56] rather than *opinio juris*. It is fair to say that this silence is an adequate reflection of the law and doctrine as it currently stands, and fitting the general context as set out above.

An earlier reflection of this position vis-à-vis international organisations, with an openly political dimension, is in the 1986 Convention the direct denial to organisations of the possibility to contribute to the formation of (customary) *jus cogens*. Articles 53 and 64 envision States but not international organisations to be part of the proverbial 'international community' that is empowered to establish which norms are part of *jus cogens*.[57] This case of direct political exclusion reflected in law may be compared to the doctrinal barrier to participation of non-governmental organisations in international legal relations.

4.2 Volonté distincte

The *volonté distincte* of international organisations is another facet of what has been described as the juridical will. The term specifically points to the *separateness* of the will of the organisation from that of the member States, and has come to be a term of art used only in that context. The *distinctness* of the international organisation's

56 *See* J Odermatt, 'The Development of Customary International Law by International Organizations' (2017) 66 International and Comparative Law Quarterly 491; *see* also Chapter 1 in this volume.

57 On the commentary by the International Law Commission on this point Brölmann (n 10) 241–43.

juridical will then can be at issue in concrete cases in which it is unclear to whom the relevant practice needs to be attributed; again this would require the ascertainment of a 'pure' intentional state, since practice does not per se convey *to whom* the objectivised intention should be attributed.

From the early days of international organisation doctrine the institutional feature of 'autonomy' has served as a foundation for the attribution of an *external* separate legal identity of sorts – formalised as 'legal personality' – to the extent that these have been, erroneously, assimilated (confusion may arise when some definitions of 'organisation' – with the aim to identify a category for the application of a particular regime, rather than to make a legal-ontological claim about international organisations – include 'legal personality' as a definitional element).[58]

The *volonté distincte* is admittedly of a fictional character, and how it should be identified is not generally elaborated upon by authors,[59] although it is of old the key element in the factual definition of 'international organisation'.[60] The *volonté distincte* is construed from, and translated into, objective institutional traits, and inferred from a particular institutional architecture in which ('at least one permanent organ' of) the organisation displays a degree of autonomy vis-à-vis the member states, as shown mainly in decision-making.[61] In technical terms the autonomy or *volonté distincte* of the organisation takes precedence – if only to a minimal extent – over the sovereignty of the individual states. This is part also of more sophisticated analyses of international organisations' 'autonomy'.[62]

58 As for example in the Conclusions (UN Doc A/73/10 131 para 5).

59 Schermers and Blokker do not elaborate. cf Jan Klabbers, 'The Changing Image of International Organisations' in Jean Marc Coicaud and Veijo Heiskanen (eds), *The Legitimacy of International Organisations* (United Nations University 2001) 221, 226ff; *see* Brölmann (n 10) 35–55 on the concept of the 'will' of international organisations in nineteenth- and early twentieth-century legal writing.

60 cf P Reuter, *Institutions internationales* (Presses Universitaires de France 1954), 195: 'En tant qu'*organisation* il ne peut que s'agir d'un groupe susceptible de manifester d'une manière permanente une volonté juridiquement distincte de celle de ces membres.'

61 HG Schermers and NM Blokker, *International Institutional Law: Unity Within Diversity* (Martinus Nijhoff 2011), paras 44 and 44A; N White, *The Law of International Organisations* (Manchester University Press 2017) at 9; R Collins and N White (eds), *International Organisations and the Idea of Autonomy* (Routledge 2011).

62 J d'Aspremont, 'The Multifaceted Concept of the Autonomy of International Organisations and International Legal Discourse' in R Collins and N White (eds), *International Organisations and the Idea of Autonomy* (Routledge 2011) 63 – identifies four types of 'autonomy'.

But *volonté distincte* is not just another word for institutional autonomy (although the latter is used as an indicator for the former) – as a concept it has a subjective, intentional aspect, which is left consistently undiscussed. It does explain why the *volonté distincte* has always remained a vague notion. The difficulty in discerning the international organisation's independent will, other than by looking at institutional voting rules, bears this out.[63]

Objectively verifiable conduct or 'practice' then may raise an additional question when it comes to international organisations: *willed* by whom – by the member States or the organisation? In concrete cases in which particular 'practice' for the formation of customary international law would need to be attributed to an organisation, the *distinctness* of the underlying will, ascribable to the organisation rather than to its member States, may be contested. The Commentary mentions the independent relevance of the practice of the EU and also of the UN, as an organisation without exclusive competences.[64] Still, indeterminacy remains and leaves space, for example, for the as yet unresolved discrepancy between the rule in Article 7 of the Articles on the Responsibility of International Organisations (which uses 'effective control' for attribution of conduct to the international organisation) and the United Nations internal rule and practice (which uses 'command and control' for attribution of conduct to the international organisation).[65]

5 The coming of age of international organisations: creating the law that binds you

A cursory view of signs from positive law and practice specifically in the law of treaties and the law of international responsibility, indeed suggest that notwithstanding organisations' independent participation in international legal affairs on

63 One of the few authors to have addressed this systematically is N White ('Discerning Separate Will', in W Heere (ed), *From Government to Governance: The Growing Impact of Non-State Actors on the International and European Legal System* (Proceedings of the 2004 ASIL/NVIR Conference), 2004, 31–38), who distinguishes the extent of such autonomy, which will, for example, be dependent on whether the organisation has contractual or constitutional foundations.

64 International Law Commission Report 2018 (UN Doc A/73/10) Ch V, 131 para 6; cf Odermatt (n 56) 491, who illustrates the relevance for customary international law of practice by international organisations as such by EU external acts.

65 Comments and Observations [to the Articles on the Responsibility of International Organisations] received from the United Nations (17 Feb 2011, UN Doc A/CN.4/637/Add.1 10).

the point of creation of obligations, accountability, and, in more recent times, expectations to international organisations of 'moral behaviour', international law seems is reluctant to project onto international organisations a fully fledged juridical will. This is one factor in explaining how for the establishment of customary international law, as set out in the previous section, both the element of practice and the element of *opinio juris* can pose a challenge when these are to be ascertained in an international organisation – precisely because the conceptual components of *opinio juris* and *distinctly willed* practice are not communicated by agreed signs.

With the technical, mechanistic vision of international organisations losing appeal, and with the growing attention to international organisations' accountability and responsibility, and to their being bound by international law, the image of an actor with thin legal personality, unsusceptible to the intentional states that are a habitual construct in the operationalisation of legal agency, also becomes less easy to accommodate. This is brought to the fore by the work on the formation of customary international law.

What then is the origin of this hesitation on the part of international law? It is likely to be a mixture of factors: (historical development of) international law doctrine; limitations to our legal imagination; the idea that a subjective, intentional state *should* not be ascribed to international organisations for philosophical reasons (e.g. an international organisation is not a 'natural' political community; or an international organisation is less suited for protecting everyone's interests); or for *legal* reasons (e.g. an international organisation is ultimately too transparent as a legal structure, and the member States are too independently present); or for *political* reasons (e.g. States do not wish to share their power). When the possibility of international organisations' independent legal agency is addressed, this is generally done – as may be gleaned from earlier International Law Commission materials – in terms of *political viability*. To be sure, the degree to which the States in this world *want* international organisations to have an independent role in lawmaking, is a major determining factor for any legal construction in regard of organisations. That account however excludes the conceptual aspect and the constraints both consciously and unconsciously posed upon the notion of 'juridical will' of international organisations in the imagery of international law.

The result may be problematic on different counts. This chapter mentions one, which as a topic has garnered renewed attention – possibly in the wake of the International Law Commission's engagement with custom. The debate spurred by developments in the field of human rights law, the proposition of international organisations being fully bound by relevant customary law in the field of human rights is arguably since at least a decade no longer controversial.[66] Likewise it seems to be generally accepted that multilateral development banks, as international organisations with international legal personality, are bound by customary rules developed in international environmental law or international humanitarian law where these are practically relevant.[67] This raises the recurring question of symmetry: when international organisations are taken to be bound to customary international law, the setup of the system would suggest that international organisations are also able to create customary international law.[68] However, as to an overall symmetry scholars and commentators seem undecided.[69]

The view that international organisations are in many cases unable to generate legally relevant practice is connected at a deep level with the hesitation to project the intentional state associated with *opinio juris* onto an organisation. The implication is that organisations cannot fully contribute to international lawmaking, which means that customary rules *binding upon* organisations would be incidental and unaccounted for by the voluntarist systématique of international law. Even if we accept a 'constitutional turn' in international (institutional) law and the concomitant idea of an independent communal acquis to which legal participants unwittingly become privy, in this case the fact that international organisations may not contribute to the law that binds them may well be difficult in the long run, as it does not sit well with the idea of full-fledged actorship. It is true that 'international legal personality' has become an ex post predicate, designating the apparent ability to perform *some* juridical act, but it is undeniable that the international legal personality of organisations – with their broad spectrum of activity and their use of

66 cf O De Schutter, 'Human Rights and the Rise of International Organisations: the Logic of Sliding Scales in the Law of International Responsibility', in Jan Wouters et al (eds), *Accountability for Human Rights Violations by International Organisations* (Intersentia 2010) 51, 56.

67 LB de Chazournes, 'The Bretton Woods Institutions and Human Rights: Converging Tendencies', in Wolfgang Benedek et al (eds), *Economic Globalization and Human Rights* (Cambridge University Press 2007) 210–42.

68 J Von Bernstorff, 'Procedures of Decision Making and the Role of Law in International Organizations' in A von Bogdandy et al (eds), *The Exercise of Public Authority by International Institutions* (Springer 2010) 777.

69 J Klabbers, 'Sources of International Organizations' Law: Reflections on Accountability' in J d'Aspremont and Samantha Besson (eds), *The Oxford Handbook of the Sources of International Law* (Oxford University Press 2017) 987; and A Reinisch, 'Sources of International Organizations' Law: Why Custom and General Principles are Crucial' in J d'Aspremont and S Besson (eds), *The Oxford Handbook of the Sources of International Law* (Oxford University Press 2017) 1007.

the *Kompetenz Kompetenz* – captures a kind of actorhood different from that of individuals in international law. Neither is the analogy proposed for example by Reinisch,[70] between international organisations and the Newly Independent States emerging from colonial structures and becoming bound by custom to which they never agreed, quite convincing. At stake are not organisations that have newly come into being. Most of them have been in existence for a long time and have long entered the international system. Learned comments[71] and the current scantiness of signs in legal practice (no International Court of Justice Advisory Opinions come to mind in which the *intention* of an organisation is at issue, as opposed to decisions in which the *intention* of a State plays a role) notwithstanding: if organisations remain the active participants in international affairs that they are, in the long run the State-centric perspective on the formation of customary international law could be untenable.

On customary lawmaking, the position of international organisations is arguably somewhat 'under-analysed',[72] and notably the 'principle of speciality'[73] is under-explored. No theoretical reason or systemic obstacle exists that would preclude the principle of speciality from serving as a foundational tenet more broadly than with regard to the traditional question of an international organisation's 'powers'. It makes good sense that within the parameters of its competences, which set the 'constitutional limitation' of the organisation, the organisation would be able to contribute to customary international law also by holding *opinio juris*. The Commentary to the Conclusions cautions that '[i]nternational organisations vary greatly, not just in their powers, but also in their membership and functions',[74] but – taken from the one-dimensional perspective of general international law – the variety among organisations does not exceed the variety among States. The speciality principle does figure in the Commentary to the Conclusions, but primarily in support of the

70 Reinisch (n 69) 1007, 1017.

71 cf in the Second Report of the Special Rapporteur (UN Doc A/CN.4/672) fn 121, examples of authors predominantly seeing the international organisation – in Higgins' words – as 'a very clear, very concentrated, focal point for state practice'.

72 But see Third report on identification of customary international law (2015) UN Doc A/CN.4/682.

73 International Court of Justice, *Legality of the Use by a State of Nuclear Weapons in Armed Conflict*, Advisory Opinion, 1996, para 25.

74 *See* also Third Report, on identification of customary international law (2015) UN Doc A/CN.4/682, 50 para 73: 'The fact that there is a great variety of international organizations calls for particular caution in assessing their practice and the weight to be attributed to it.'

comment that 'international organisations are not States',[75] and of a reiteration of the functional character of organisations as legal creatures.

Still, arguably clear cases exist of emerging customary law – in any case *opinio juris* – generated by an organisation (*in casu* the United Nations), rather than by its member States. Here 'Responsibility to Protect' (R2P) and 'The Rule of Law at the National and International Levels' are prime examples. We can leave aside here whether utterances on these themes would count as expressions of *opinio juris*, or as practice. Also the latter reading – as indicator of a to-be-determined *distinct* will on the part of the international organisation – serves to support the point which this chapter aims to make.

6 Concluding remarks

The Conclusions bring to light that contemporary international law offers little ground for elaborating on the contribution to customary international law by international organisations as independent actors. This is a noteworthy fact, as international organisations tend to be taken as full-fledged participants in international law and international life, such moreover within the parameters of classic public international law. In nearly all fields of human collaboration one or more international organisations exist, in total approx. 275 international organisations[76] versus approximately 194 States. Major procedural areas of international law – not least the law of treaties and the law of international responsibility – have been the subject of codification projects aimed at specifically including international organisations in the pertinent legal regimes.

This chapter explains the modest role of international organisations in the practice of international custom formation, and in the Conclusions, by a hesitation on the part of international lawyers and policy-makers and thus a limitation of the imagery of international law, when it comes to the attribution to international organisations of an independent 'juridical will'. The term is used as a shorthand for various 'states of mind' or 'intentional states', such as intention, opinion, acquiescence. Systems of law project onto participants such 'states of mind' in order to operationalise legal agency. International law seems to have had no problem

75 International Law Commission Report 2018 (UN Doc A/73/10) Ch V 131 para 5 and fn 693.

76 Based on a conservative calculation. *See* Union of International Associations, 'The Yearbook of International Organizations' (20th Online Edition Brill 2020) www.uia.org/yearbook, accessed 30 November 2019.

accommodating States in this respect, but shows signs of hesitation in ascribing legally relevant 'states of mind' to international organisations. This can be linked to organisations' functional, mechanistic identity in international law – in all its political and theoretical facets – which has persisted even after organisations came to appear as increasingly prominent independent legal actors. The 'thin legal personality' of international organisations comes to the fore especially where agreed signs in social reality for intentional states (such as 'signature' for 'consent to be bound') are absent. It is one reason why the ascertainment of *opinio juris* or of an international organisation's *distinct* will to steer the attribution of a particular practice, may pose a challenge. The chapter finally proposes that in light of their current role in global affairs, international organisations would need to assume a role in the formation of custom insofar as relevant for their work. More generally, organisations must come of age as actors in international law and assume full legal personality, which includes the full susceptibility to projection of intentional states for the purpose of legal agency. This in turn will facilitate international organisations' participation, among other things, in the formation of customary international law.

Chapter 3

Opinio juris: between mental states and institutional objects

*Sufyan Droubi**

> Certes, il existe des coutumes sages qui sont lentement dégagées des fait immémoriaux, établis sur une tradition mentale, mais on voit aussi récemment, des coutumes sauvages dont l'excroissance soudaine puise sa racine plus dans les volontés alertées que dans des esprits assoupis par une longue habitude.
>
> [...]
>
> [La règle] assume une mission que la coutume sage ne peut remplir en raison de sa somptueuse lenteur; elle agit comme la coutume sauvage, avec la même ardeur, mais ele réagit contre la barbarie du monde technologique et industriel; elle puise sa sagesse dans la science qui a dénoncé les péril, son dynamisme dans la necessite de fair vite. Elle est tout à la fois coutume savante et alertante.[1]

In a well-known 1974 piece, from which the words above have been extracted, René-Jean Dupuy sheds light on many aspects of importance for the present discussion about the role of international organisations in the formation of customary international law, specifically, in the formation of *opinio juris*, in the present times. Dupuy starts by affirming a tension between fact and mind, and by highlighting the role of *consciousness* in the formation of international custom.[2] His now famous distinction between wise and wild custom arises from the different roles that, he argues, *consciousness* plays in the formation of customary international law. Wise custom arises slowly from immemorial facts and is established by a *mental tradition*,[3]

* The research in connection with this chapter was funded by the São Paulo Research Foundation - FAPESP (grant 2015/24219-7) and was partly carried out at the School of Law, University of São Paulo, and at the Manchester International Law Centre, School of Law, University of Manchester. I would like to thank Jean d'Aspremont for his invaluable comments. All mistakes are mine. Contact: seldroubi@dundee.ac.uk. ORCID: 0000-0001-9749-6388.

1 René-Jean Dupuy, 'Coutume sage et coutume sauvage' (1974) La communauté internationale Mélanges offerts à Charles Rousseau 75, 76, 86 ('Coutume Sage').

2 ibid 75.

3 ibid 76.

and wild custom arises in Bergsonian time,[4] out of the *vigilant will* of the States.[5] Dupuy claims that modern custom is both wild and wise – developing quickly and drawing wisdom from *science*.[6] Dupuy does not explicitly refer to *natural* sciences, but the context in which the term appears – pollution – suggests that he has natural sciences in mind.[7] (Even if this is not the case – in the present chapter, the word 'science' and derivatives refer to 'natural sciences' unless explained otherwise.) What is more, Dupuy suggests that international organisations may promote collective consciousness about present-day problems – and pursuant to the values that reflect their own ethics.[8] Likewise, Dupuy claims that international organisations can coordinate processes that lead to the crystallisation of new custom.[9]

The claims that Dupuy make should be critically placed against the background of the literature on the topic. For instance, does *coutume sage* ascribe too much importance to *consciousness* in the formation of custom? Is it not the case that States 'awake' too late, when custom has already crystallised? Recall that, in *Normative Dilemma*, Alain Pellet argues that this is exactly the case.[10] Further, Pellet argues that only practice is constitutive of customary international law and that *opinio juris* appears much later.[11] Moreover, Pellet is sceptical about the role that Dupuy ascribes to international organisations in the formation of custom.[12]

Be that as it may, even if we accept Dupuy's claims in respect to the roles of consciousness and international organisations in the formation of custom, the question that I want to raise is whether international organisations are able to activate consciousness and coordinate processes of formation of custom in manners that the custom in question be consistent with any given standards – and to simplify the discussion I place focus on scientific standards. The idea of *shaping* rules of customary international law in a desired form is not new – having been contemplated, e.g. in the field of law of armed conflicts.[13] Given the historic moment we live in,

4 ibid 85.
5 ibid 76.
6 ibid 86–87.
7 ibid 86.
8 ibid 80.
9 ibid 84.
10 Alain Pellet, 'The Normative Dilemma: Will and Consent in International Law-Making' (1989) 12 Australian Yearbook of International Law 22 ('The Normative Dilemma').
11 ibid.
12 ibid 36.
13 Sufyan Droubi, 'Institutionalisation of Emerging Norms of Customary International Law through Resolutions and Operational Activities of the Political and Subsidiary Organs of the United Nations' (2017) 14 International Organizations Law Review 276.

the question gains importance. One just needs to phrase it in respect to, e.g. climate change, to realise its relevance – would an international organisation such as the United Nations be able to promote, or at least influence, the formation of custom that is consistent with findings and recommendations of the Intergovernmental Panel on Climate Change? *Coutume sauvage* would probably justify an optimistic answer to this question.

With some caveats, I agree with many of Dupuy's assertions: that modern custom might be promoted by the vigilant will of States – in other words, that States' consciousness of problems might eventually force them to adapt their behaviour to tackle such problems; that time should be accounted for also in terms of quality – though not necessarily through a Bergsonian perspective; that modern custom reflects the needs and expectations of a society undergoing deep transformations – but at a much higher pace than Dupuy could have imagined in 1974; that international organisations might activate collective consciousness and promote the emergence of rules of customary international law – but that they have very restricted control (if they have any control at all) of these processes. In other words, I do not share Dupuy's optimism.

Elsewhere, I argued that a rule of customary law can be seen as an advanced stage in the life cycle of an international norm.[14] This chapter looks into some of the challenges that are involved in the transition into this more advanced stage. In the present chapter, I am mostly concerned with *opinio juris*. I argue that, although international organisations have a wide array of instruments to affect and even shape the collective behaviour of States, they face almost unsurmountable challenges when it comes to shaping the *opinio juris* of States in a desired form – notably, in a form that is consistent with scientific standards. To develop my argument, I organise the chapter in two main parts – a study into the concept of *opinio juris*, and a study into the ability of international organisations to promote *opinio juris* with a desired content. I depart from the framework provided by the work of Dupuy and Pellet to articulate a working understanding of *opinio juris* (1), and place this understanding within a broader context (2). Against this background, I distinguish, now drawing on the work of John Searle,[15] between *opinio juris*, which I define as an institutional object, and the *underlying mental states* which support it (3) – the endpoint being that international organisations intervene in the formation of both.

14 Sufyan Droubi, 'The Role of the United Nations in the Formation of Customary International Law in the Field of Human Rights' (2017) 19.1 International Community Law Review 68.

15 Notably but not solely, JR Searle, *Making the Social World* (Oxford University Press 2011).

Section 4 launches the second part of the chapter; and it discusses the dynamics of the formation of custom, accounting for the impact that free will, timeframes, and the complexity of certain events have in the consciousness of decision-makers and lawyers; and laying bare the challenges that international organisations face in affecting the *opinio juris* of States (4). The chapter ends with some concluding remarks (5).

1 *Coutume sage* and *the normative dilemma*: consciousness and conscience in modern times

In what reminds us of the old debate between materialism and idealism, Dupuy identifies a constant tension between *fact* and *consciousness* in the formation of customary international law.[16] Dupuy attributes this tension to the dynamic character of international custom and the different functions that, arguably, it plays.[17] On the one hand, wise custom plays a creative function through continued evolution, and it becomes backward-looking and conservative; not only is this typical of a homogeneous society – Dupuy claims – but it is also expressive of the latter's common ethics.[18] On the other hand, Dupuy identifies what he calls the revisionist and, further still, revolutionary character of international custom: its capacity to challenge the established order. Accordingly, he argues that at the time of his writing (1970s) the main challenge was put up by new States, on grounds of self-determination, against universal customs.[19] Accordingly, Dupuy argues that this type of *contre-coutume* is typical of an increasingly heterogeneous society.[20] Further, he claims that this custom is articulated through unilateral acts, declarations, domestic legislative measures, in coordination among domestic and international organisations.[21]

Against wild custom, one may invoke the brevity of the precedents which support it.[22] However, Dupuy argues that this challenge is relative.[23] While the passage of a short span of time becomes an argument of resistance of non-conforming States,[24] States supporting this wild form of custom, explains

16 Dupuy (n 1) 79.
17 ibid.
18 ibid 79–80.
19 ibid 83.
20 ibid 83.
21 ibid 83.
22 ibid 84.
23 ibid 84.
24 ibid 85.

Dupuy, see time in Bergsonian terms.[25] Essentially, Bergson's contribution to the topic,[26] which Dupuy probably had in mind, consists in rejecting the identification of time mechanical movement: Bergson differentiates time as a magnitude, the clock time, and time as quality, conscious time, or duration.[27] On the one hand, there is what Bergson defines as concrete duration, i.e. duration as *quality*, and the feeling it produces in consciousness; on the other hand, there is the abstract, mechanical concept of time used by mathematicians and physicists.[28] Whether Dupuy, in referencing Bergson, means much more than suggesting that some States are more concerned with the quality, and less with the amount of, time elapsed – is not clear.[29] In any case, Dupuy argues that the structure of international custom is altered to the benefit of the volitive element: *the idea precedes the facts*. In wild custom, there is a factual projection of the politico-legal idea.[30]

Dupuy argues that wild custom arises on 'other fronts' like environmental law.[31] He exemplifies with the emerging rule of customary international law that makes States responsible for the pollution they cause. He argues that this rule had been hidden behind soft law, arising out of the work of experts within international conferences under the aegis of the United Nations, of declarations and international conventions, many of which still lacking ratification.[32] This is a consequential

25 ibid 85 ('ils ont conscience d'assumer une misère ou une pauvreté que confère à leur temps psychologique plus de valeur et de poids qu'un temps historique que la plupart d'entre eux ne vivent que depuis une independence encore recente').

26 Henri Bergson, *Creative Evolution* (Arthur Mitchell tr, Henry Holt and Company 1911); Henri Bergson, *Matter and Memory* (Nancy Margaret Paul and W Scott Palmer trs, The Macmillan Company 1929); Henri Bergson, *Time and Free Will* (FL Pogson tr, First, George Allen & Unwin Ltd 1950).

27 Bergson, *Time and Free Will* (n 26).

28 ibid.

29 *See* V Jankélévitch, *Henri Bergson* (Alexandre Lefebvre and Nils F Schott eds, Nils F Schott tr, English tr, Duke University Press 2015); G Deleuze, *Bergsonism* (Zone Books 1991). The Bergsonian theory of time lost steam after the fateful debate between Bergson and Einstein. *See* the interesting account provided in J Canales, *The Physicist and The Philosopher: Einstein, Bergson, and the Debate that Changed Our Understanding of Time* (Princeton University Press 2016) and J Canales, 'Einstein, Bergson, and the Experiment that Failed: Intellectual cooperation at the League of Nations' (2005) 120 Modern Language Notes 1168–91. However, there have been recent attempts to revive the 'Bergsonian time' (by which it is often meant time as quality), for instance, in respect to time on the Web (e.g. M Vafopoulos, 'Being, Space, and Time on the Web' (2012) 43 Metaphilosophy 405–25).

30 Dupuy (n 1) 84.

31 ibid 86.

32 ibid 86.

point: Dupuy suggests that international organisations might coordinate processes that trigger the emergence of rules of customary international law because, inter alia, international organisations benefit from the work of experts, within which I include scientists, to articulate, e.g. in their resolutions, norms which might provide content to rules of customary law.[33]

However, there remains the need of States adapting their behaviour and attitude in accordance with the norms that a resolution articulates. Dupuy is not very clear about this move. Apparently, resolutions would trigger States' *consciousness* (awareness) of a given problem and shape their *conscience* (sense of right or wrong) about their behaviour and attitude. It is their *conscience of the danger* of environmental pollution that forces States to accept the rule in question,[34] and that *imposes* the rule on pollution into the *opinio necessitatis* of the world.[35] So it seems that after becoming conscious of the dangers of pollution, States cannot but adopt the rule. But the devil is in the detail, and Dupuy does not explain how exactly the move from *consciousness* and *conscience* to *intention* to *behaviour* occurs – as if one's intention could not clash with one's awareness of a danger and one's sense of right and wrong. Be that as it may, for Dupuy, wild custom works as a *continued S.O.S alert.* It assumes a function that *wise custom cannot display* because of the latter's characteristic slowness. Dupuy claims that wild custom is a reaction to the barbarity of the technological and industrial world,[36] *that it draws its wisdom from science.*[37] I note the subtle tension that Dupuy describes between technology and science – something to which I revert later in the chapter.[38] Ultimately, Dupuy says that modern custom is at once wise and wild – which allows it to respond spontaneously to the contradictory needs of the international society.[39]

While Dupuy emphasises the role of *intention* in the formation of customary international law, at the other end of the spectrum, Alain Pellet affirms that in the modern world the traditional threshold of international law – namely, State *will* (i.e. intention) – has in fact *disappeared.*[40] Looking at the wording of Article 38 of the Statute of the International Court of Justice, Pellet argues that 'acceptance … is, by no means, achieved by the expression of will of individual States, but a general, communal

33 I have addressed this role of international organisations in Droubi 'Institutionalisation of Emerging Norms' (n 13).

34 Dupuy (n 1) 86.

35 ibid 86.

36 ibid 86.

37 ibid 86.

38 *See* n 194 and accompanying text.

39 Dupuy (n 1) 87.

40 Pellet (n 10) 45ff.

acceptance of some more or less openly expressed conviction by States or by international bodies'.[41] This prompts Pellet to emphasise the material element of customary international law and to reduce the importance of the will of the State. Pellet lays bare many of the shortcomings of the voluntarist approach to the formation of law and, what is of more interest, the formation of international custom.[42] Hence, he affirms that practice and *opinio juris* are not 'on the same footing' and '*it is only practice which is "constitutive"*, *opinio juris* can only appear after the event'.[43] He underlines the wording used by the International Court of Justice in *North Sea Continental Shelf* to assert: 'a "feeling" that an obligation exists is a very different thing from a will'[44] – and he notes, citing Jimenez de Arechaga, that the International Court of Justice had 'not required strict proof of the specific acceptance of the defendant State, thus rejecting the voluntarist approach to custom'.[45] Interestingly, Pellet does not identify this feeling with belief – and we are left without a clear explanation of what exactly this 'feeling' entails. For the present purpose, I define it as a degree of belief.[46]

Pellet also addresses *consciousness*, and submits that 'in most cases, States do not care; *practice develops without them being aware of the process*' and concludes: 'when they "awake", that is, when the time of *opinio juris* has arrived, it is too late – the evil is done and the rule does exist'.[47] Correctly, Pellet differentiates between the individual and collective consciousness and highlights that the latter is not the sum of the wills of the individual States.[48] Importantly for what ensues, this reminds us of Émile Durkheim, who explains that 'the totality of beliefs and sentiments common to the average members of a society forms a determinate system with a life of its own. It can be termed the collective or creative consciousness'.[49] Finally, Pellet rejects 'wild custom' as customary international law. Although he sees merit in Dupuy's concept of *coutume sauvage*, Pellet argues that 'it has more to do with resolutions than with customs, and, in any case, it relates more to the "mental" or "psychological" element

41 ibid 41 (for the difference between will and consent), 46 and 47 (role of consent in modern times). Also, *see* A Pellet, 'Article 38' in Andreas Zimmermann et al (eds), *The Statute of the International Court of Justice: A Commentary* (Second Edition, Oxford University Press 2012).
42 Pellet (n 10) 41
43 ibid 41. Emphasis added.
44 ibid 41.
45 ibid 37.
46 *See* n 108 below.
47 Pellet (n 10) 37. Emphasis added.
48 ibid 37.
49 E Durkheim, 'From mechanical to organic solidarity' (2010) 2 Sociology: Introductory Readings 25. *Cf.* n 116 and accompanying text.

of custom than to practice'.[50] But, interestingly, he clearly reaffirms the importance of resolutions in terms of soft law, and ascribes to the latter a much higher standing than the mainstream literature often assigns to it.[51]

This discussion gives us a working definition of *opinio juris*. Whether intention or belief, *opinio juris* arises as a *mental* state. This discussion also brings to light the role that consciousness and time play in the process of emergence of this mental state. For Dupuy, consciousness and conscience shapes intention, which is crucial in the formation of modern custom, because it allows the latter to develop quickly in response to present-day problems. Pellet argues that States become aware only too late – and that the material element is constitutive of custom.

2 Consent, belief, statement: what is *opinio juris*?

Note that the difference between Dupuy's and Pellet's approaches to the subjective element is not ontological – they both speak of *mental* states.[52] Their difference respects the *type* of mental state and the *relevance* they ascribe to it. Dupuy emphasises intention and Pellet emphasises acceptance (belief). Dupuy clearly ascribes to both mental states more relevance than Pellet does. This clash of opinions reflects an old debate that is worth recalling.

Walden provides a good mapping of the different approaches to the psychological element.[53] He distinguishes between *consent* theories, which emphasise the role of intention, and whose purpose is that of explaining how the norm comes to being; and *declaratory* theories, which emphasise belief, and whose purpose is that of explaining the difference between customary international law and non-law (morality, comity, etc.).[54] In this regard, Walden identifies two major schools. The *classical* school, represented by for instance Rachel (1628–91), Vattel (1714–67), and Triepel (1868–1946), affirms that the consent of the State is a necessary requirement for the formation of customary international law. The *historical* school, represented inter alia by Blackstone (1723–80), Rivier (1835–98), and Gény (1861–1959), challenges the idea that law is a conscious product of human will. For this school, law is a spontaneous product of the *Volksgeist*. On Walden's account, the historical school was responsible

50 Pellet (n 10) 36.

51 ibid 47.

52 ibid 749 (explaining that *opinio juris* is often referred to as psychological, intellectual or subjective element) and 753 (adopting the 'psychological element' terminology).

53 RM Walden, 'The Subjective Element in the Formation of Customary International Law' (1977) 12 Israel Law Review 344.

54 ibid 357 *et seq.*

for articulating the concept of *opinio juris* as *belief*.[55] Walden notes that, since its first articulation, probably by Alphonse Rivier,[56] different publicists came to define the *opinio juris* in different manners – conviction that a practice is binding, conviction that it is binding as law, binding as social necessity, binding on natural law grounds.[57]

On his part, Walden challenges the historical school on the account that it is necessary to go beyond the declaratory theory *without* mixing *opinio juris* with consent.[58] He draws on Herbert Hart's work to define *opinio juris* in terms of *internal point of view*.[59] Then, Walden differentiates between fact-created custom and law-created custom.[60] Although this differentiation looks artificial in some points, it does offer an insight into the need to attend to the context in which *opinio juris* is expressed, and into the *fluidity* of the mental state. It begins by arguing that, in certain circumstances ('law-created' custom), a secondary rule 'stipulates how and under what conditions a rule of customary law comes to being'.[61] That is, 'the conduct of the subjects of a legal system is only recognised as generating customary law, if … the practice is treated as standard of *legal* behaviour'.[62] Consequently, 'those who follow the practice, and treat it as a legal standard of behaviour, *may be doing so with deliberate legislative intention*'.[63] Based on this, Walden elegantly brings to light the fluidity of *opinio juris* – 'what starts as an *intention to create law* ultimately *becomes a belief* that the law in question *exists*'.[64] This description, which I adopt with several qualifications,[65] offers an important insight into the dynamics of the formation of *opinio juris* for the present purposes.[66]

55 ibid 358.
56 ibid 358. Mendelson shares this understanding, but Crawford claims that Franz von Liszt was the first to use the term in 1898. cf M Mendelson, 'The Subjective Element in Customary International Law' (1996) 66 The British Year Book of International Law 177, 194; J Crawford, *Chance, Order, Change: The Course of International Law* (Ail-Pocket 2014) 62–65. D'Amato attributes the concept to Gény; *see* A D'Amato, *The Concept of Custom in International Law* (Cornell University Press 1971) 48–49.
57 Walden (n 53) 362–3.
58 Walden (n 53) 363–64.
59 RM Walden, 'Customary Interantional Law: A Jurisprudential Analysis' (1978) 13 Israel Law Review 86, 98.
60 ibid 90–91, 96–97.
61 ibid 97.
62 ibid 97.
63 ibid 97. Emphasis added.
64 ibid 98. Emphasis added. Similarly, JF Williams, *Aspects of Modern International Law: An Essay* (Oxford University Press 1939) 44–46, as quoted in CW Jenks, 'Fischer Williams: The Practitioner as Reformer' (1964) 40 British Yearbook of International Law 233, 245.
65 *See* n 176 and accompanying text.
66 Sender and Wood explain that the framework which Walden articulates is compatible with the approach that the International Law Commission adopts in the Conclusions.

Moreover, Walden also looks at the relationship between *opinio juris* and the normative *language* to submit that, although '*opinio juris* is evinced by the use of normative language, it is *not identical* with it, and may be held by a State, even if that State has never expressed it in words'.[67] With this, Walden rejects a *third* approach to *opinio juris*, which defines the latter as *statements* and, hence, which ascribes to it a different ontology – an approach developed, to an extent, by D'Amato (theory of promulgative articulation),[68] and by Akehurst (*opinio juris* as statements).[69] In a telling passage, D'Amato explains:

> Of course a practice based on comity or expediency might become a rule of customary law, this is what allegedly occurred in the case of the Paquete Habana. But a necessary ingredient of change is the *articulation* of the practice *as an issue of international law*. Simple repetition is insufficient.[70]

I have already addressed aspects of D'Amato's theory elsewhere and I will not come back to them here.[71] The crux of the matter, in my view, is that, for D'Amato, *opinio juris* derives from a mental state (in the case, intention) that is necessarily *manifested*, *articulated*, and *communicated*.[72] I should also emphasise that both articulation and communication might occur verbally or through certain behaviours. On this point, recall that D'Amato draws on Lon Fuller's approach to promulgation,[73] – and on McDougal's concept of promulgative communication.[74] It is interesting to see how both authors deal with rituals in the context of customary law:

> I would assert … that a significant function of ritual is precisely that of communication, of labelling acts so that there can be no mistake as to their meaning.[75]

See O Sender and M Wood, 'A Mystery No Longer? Opinio Juris and Other Theoretical Controversies Associated with Customary International Law' (2017) 50 Israel Law Review 299.

67 Walden (n 59) 99. Emphasis added.

68 *See* D'Amato (n 56). cf Walden (n 59) 99.

69 M Akehurst, 'Custom as a Source of International Law' (1976) 1974–75 The British Yearbook of International Law 1.

70 D'Amato (n 56) 78.

71 Droubi, 'Institutionalisation of Emerging Norms' (n 13) 272.

72 *See* e.g. A D'Amato, 'Manifest Intent and the Generation by Treaty of Customary Rules of International Law' (1970) 64 The American Journal of International Law 892.

73 *See* LL Fuller, 'Human Interaction and the Law' (1969) 14 American Journal of Jurisprudence 1; and LL Fuller, *The Morality of Law* (Yale University Press 1969) 45–49. Note the close relationship between communication and promulgation.

74 MS McDougal, HD Lasswell, and WM Reisman, 'The World Constitutive Process of Authoritative Decision' (1966) 19 Journal of Legal Education 253, 426.

75 Fuller, 'Human Interaction and the Law' (n 73) 6.

> … when a constitutive process is thoroughly established, its strategies tend to combine rational persuasion with ritualized acceptance … Promulgative strategies may comprise the ritual of a judicial decision, the signature and ratification of an international agreement, a parliamentary vote, and so on. Many of these acts, in addition to publicizing the communication, impart a degree of authority to it.[76]

In other words, *opinio juris* is a mental state that is not only articulated and communicated – rather, it is a mental state that is articulated and communicated in specific contexts that allow for the mental state in question to be understood as having legal relevance.[77]

But it is Akehurst, more than D'Amato, who develops the third approach to its fullest extent. Akehurst acknowledges the importance of D'Amato's work for recognising that 'what matters are statements, not beliefs'.[78] However, Akehurst goes on to affirm that 'a statement by a State about the content of customary law should be taken as *opinio juris* even if the State does not believe in the truth of the statement'.[79] Now, acquiescence by other States – already relevant in D'Amato's work[80] – will play a definitive and crucial role: the 'true' mental state – true belief, true will – of the State making a statement *is irrelevant* – 'if other States acquiesce, a new rule of customary law comes into being'.[81] (The important role of acquiescence had already been affirmed by many authors,[82] and recently also by the International Law Commission, notably on the importance of ascertaining States' reaction to the practice of international organisations.[83])

Hence, in ascertaining *opinio juris*, this third approach de-emphasises the importance of the 'true' or 'subjective' mental state. Rather, it emphasises the

76 McDougal, Lasswell, and Reisman (n 74) 407, 426.
77 This aspect complements what I describe in Droubi 'Institutionalisation of Emerging Norms' (n 13).
78 Akehurst (n 69) 36.
79 ibid 37. cf n. 125–28 below.
80 D'Amato (n 56) 82.
81 Akehurst (n 69) 37.
82 For instance, IC MacGibbon, 'Customary International Law and Acquiescence' (1957) 33 The British Yearbook of International Law 115.
83 UNGA Res 203 (73rd Sess) (11 January 2019) 'Identification of customary international law' A/RES/73/2–3, Annex Conclusion 10(3). *Also,* International Law Commission, 'Identification of Customary International Law, Text of the Draft Conclusions and commentaries thereto' [2018] Report of the International Law Commission Seventieth session (30 April–1 June and 2 July–10 August 2018) International Law Commission Report, A/73/10, 2018, chap V, para 66 ('Conclusions and Commentaries'), Conclusion 10(3) and its commentary.

importance of the manifestation of the mental state in the form of statements or (in the case of nonverbal manifestation) of what can be expressed through statements. Moreover, in ascertaining the existence of *opinio juris*, this approach looks at statements in the specific contexts in which they are expressed. By doing all this, this approach inadvertently introduces the concept of *opinio juris* as an *institutional object*. Nevertheless, the concept is very incipient because the third approach fails to look at the institutional roles that *opinio juris* plays in the formation of custom.

More recently, other scholars have drawn on this third approach. Roberts, in a well-received piece, expressly adopted 'D'Amato's distinction between action (state practice) and statements (*opinio juris*)'.[84] Roberts distinguishes between traditional and modern custom. Roberts draws on the work of Kirgis and Tasioulas (custom on a sliding scale) and Dworkin (law as interpretation) to define traditional custom as based on a descriptive approach to custom and the modern custom, on a normative approach to custom.[85] The former 'focuses primarily on state practice in the form of interstate interaction and acquiescence' and it places *opinio juris* in a secondary place – its objective is solely to distinguish between law and non-law.[86] For Roberts, traditional custom 'is identified through an inductive process in which a general custom is derived from specific instances of state practice'.[87] *Modern* custom, in contradistinction, is 'derived by a deductive process that begins with general statements of rules rather than particular instances of practices'.[88] For Roberts, this approach 'emphasises *opinio juris* … because it relies on statements rather than actions'.[89] Crucially, Roberts claims – similarly to what Dupuy submits in respect to wild custom – 'this process can develop quickly because it is deduced from multilateral treaties and declarations by international organs such as the General

84 AE Roberts, 'Traditional and Modern Approaches to Customary International Law: A Reconciliation' (2001) 95 The American Journal of International Law 757, 757 ('action can form custom only if accompanied by an *articulation* of the legality of the action' [Emphasis added]).

85 ibid 757–60 and 764 ('practice is descriptive, while *opinio juris* can be descriptive or normative').

86 ibid 758.

87 ibid 758. cf with B Simma and P Alston, 'The Sources of Human Rights Law: Custom, Jus Cogens, and General Principles' (1989) 12 The Australian Yearbook of International Law 82.

88 Roberts (n 84) 758 and 762–63 ('traditional custom is closely associated with descriptive accuracy because norms are constructed primarily from state practice – working from practice to theory' and 'modern custom derives norms primarily from abstract statements of *opinio juris* – working from theory to practice').

89 ibid 758.

Assembly'.[90] Again, we have the idea of international organisations operating as co ordinators and promoters of the process. After identifying the limits of both approaches, Roberts makes the very important submission that neither is 'completely descriptive or normative, because both recognize the importance of state practice and *opinio juris* to varying degrees'.[91]

It is important to note that Roberts articulates a *reflective interpretive approach* to the exercise of identifying custom. I believe that this approach helps understanding the *process of* ascertaining customary international law and the significant discretion that lawyers enjoy in it, a point to which I come back later. Roberts proposes to *first* define the relevant data (preinterpretation);[92] *second*, to interpret this data accurately in view of past practice (dimension of fit);[93] *third*, to ascertain whether the 'content of custom is substantively moral and whether it is derived by a legitimate process' (dimension of substance);[94] and, *then*, to balance fit and substance in a coherent manner, and decide between the resulting interpretations in a process similar to Rawls' mediation between intuitions and moral principles.[95] Note that this account, and the third stage in particular, coheres with Walden's account on the relevant behaviour that triggers customary international law;[96] and that it brings to light the significant role that lawyers play in the establishment of customary international law.[97] After applying her approach to some cases, Roberts concludes that the 'best balance between fit and substance varies according to the relative strength of the practice and principles involved' so that 'strong substantive considerations may compensate for a relatively weak fit, while equivocal substantive considerations will require a finer balance between fit and substance'.[98] Furthermore, Roberts submits that custom is a 'fluid source of law', which can 'change and harden over time'.[99] In Hart's terminology, it would be a 'primitive source of law because it lacks clear rules of change'.[100] Finally, Roberts emphasises the process through which customs are formed – optional conduct becoming habitual, then obligatory, then decaying through deviations.

90 ibid.
91 ibid 767.
92 ibid 774.
93 ibid 775.
94 ibid 778.
95 ibid 779.
96 *See* n 61–64 above.
97 *See* n 151ff and accompanying text.
98 Roberts (n 84) 783.
99 ibid 784.
100 ibid 784.

With this background, I propose to distinguish between the underlying mental state (belief or will) and *opinio juris* as an institutional object and to pay close attention to the process of affirming and ascertaining *opinio juris*.

3 *Opinio juris*: from mental state to institutional object

The theories described in the prior sections operate against the background of the old dualism between mind and body, seemingly presupposing that a tension marks their relationship. Because they also anthropomorphise the State, they lead to a sharp tension between the subjective and the material elements of custom: some theories say that mind precedes bodily movement and others say the opposite. I start by rejecting this dualism (as well as the anthropomorphisation of the State,[101] a topic that is beyond the present work) on grounds that it is artificial and that it makes it difficult to understand certain aspects of the emergence of *opinio juris*. John Searle shows the impossibility of separating mind from body, or mental from physical states, and cogently demonstrates that they are better understood as different levels of a system.[102] If this is the case, then *opinio juris* cannot be, or cannot only be, about mental states.

As Searle explains, mental processes trigger consciousness and intentionality,[103] which are part of the human biology – brain, consciousness, and intentionality are part of the same system.[104] Intentionality consists in the capacity of the mind to represent objects and states in the world.[105] Intentional states are literally *states*, which are caused by neurophysiological processes, i.e. they are 'caused and realised in the brain'.[106] At the most fundamental level, these states are triggered by primordial forms of intentionality, namely, perception and action.[107] Beliefs and desires are 'etiolated forms of more primordial experiences in perceiving and doing'.[108] Henceforth, I refer to both beliefs and intentions as primary intentional states. It is a characteristic of

101 For a critique of the anthropomorphisation of the State, *see* Chapter 5 in this volume.
102 JR Searle, *Intentionality: An Essay in the Philosophy of Mind* (Cambridge University Press 1983) ch 10.
103 ibid 3.
104 ibid ix.
105 ibid 1, 4.
106 ibid 15. Governments and international organisations have derived intentionality (n 118 below).
107 ibid 36, 75.
108 ibid 36. I adopt Searle's broad definition of beliefs and desires so as to encompass degrees of conviction and degrees of desire. ibid 29.

beliefs that they are supposed to match an independent reality, and they may be true or false depending on whether they succeed or fail to match it.[109] In contradistinction, intentions are supposed to change the reality, and they may succeed insofar as the reality effectively changes.[110] Intentions rest on the desire to change a state of affairs and on the belief that this change is possible.[111] Given that intentional states never come in isolation;[112] notably, given the close relationship between beliefs and intentions, I will not attempt to isolate one from the other. So the first point to make is that the separation between intention and belief is a theoretical and rather artificial exercise.

Intentional states may not be conscious, but they are always accessible through consciousness.[113] Consciousness can be defined as sentience or awareness.[114] Both consciousness and intentionality are typical of humans and certain animals. It is through cooperation, through *collective* intentionality, that human beings ascribe intentionality to objects and that they create *institutional* objects.[115] It is the '*we*-intend', rather than the '*I*-intend', which creates institutions.[116] Hence, it is collective rather individual intentionality that is of relevance here.

Indeed, for their capacity to *symbolise* and *cooperate*, humans may ascribe intentionality to entities that are not 'intrinsically intentional'.[117] This is what Searle defines as *derived* intentionality.[118] Through cooperation, humans can impose intentionality on sounds and visual objects – e.g. they create language.[119] Not only it is the case that intentional states can be expressed through language, but it is also the case that some intentional states *require* language – there are intentional states that can only be expressed through propositions.[120] This can be better understood by means

109 ibid 6–8.
110 ibid 6–8.
111 ibid 34
112 *See* the discussion below (n 169–71).
113 ibid 2.
114 JR Searle, *Consciousness and Language* (Cambridge University Press 2002) 7 ('Subjective states of sentience or awareness that begin when one awakes in the morning … and continue throughout the day until one goes to sleep at night').
115 Searle, *Making the Social World* (n 15) 43 and ch 5.
116 Note that collective intentionality is not necessarily a sum of individual intentionalities: the form 'we-intend' *might occur* to an individual *irrespectively* of occuring to others of the collective. ibid 47 *et seq*. and 50 *et seq*. cf n 49 and accompanying text.
117 Searle, *Intentionality* (n 102) viii.
118 JR Searle, 'Insight and Error in Wittgenstein' (2016) 46 Philosophy of the Social Sciences 527.
119 Searle, *Making the Social World* (n 15) ch 5.
120 Searle, *Intentionality* (n 102) 6, 7.

of a simple example. Imagine that the foreign secretary of a particular country utters the following words: *humanitarian intervention without United Nations Security Council authorisation is lawful in certain circumstances.* The content is the proposition 'humanitarian intervention without Security Council authorisation is lawful in certain circumstances' – and the object is the reality, the state of affairs that the proposition represents. The psychological mode may be either the *belief* that it is the case that *humanitarian intervention is lawful* or the *intention* that *humanitarian intervention be lawful.* This introduces us to the relationship between intentional states and *speech acts.*[121] Essentially, there are five types of speech acts, namely, assertives (expressed in statements), which correspond to beliefs; directives (orders), which correspond to desires; commissives, i.e. promises, which correspond to intentions; expressives, i.e. apologies, thanks, etc., which correspond to feelings; and declarations (statements), which correspond *to both beliefs and intentions.*[122] Not only speech acts express intentional states; they also *carry the psychological mode* of the intentional state they express.

To facilitate the analysis, I will deal solely with one class of speech acts, *declarations*, which often materialise in *statements*, because they have a crucial role in the formation of institutional objects,[123] e.g. they explain how certain groups of human beings can impose intentionality on governments and international organisations, and how certain other groups of human beings can establish *opinio juris*. Indeed, declarations are often the realm of individuals who enjoy a special status in their society: authorities who are capable of declaring a state of affairs. As mentioned, it is a characteristic of declarations that they express *both* a belief and an intention:

> since the illocutionary point of the declaration is to bring about some new state of affairs solely by virtue of the utterance, declarations [express belief and intention]. For this to work the speech act must be performed within some extra-linguistic institution where the speaker is appropriately empowered to bring about new institutional facts solely by the appropriate performance of speech acts … all declarations bring about institutional facts, facts which exist only within systems of constitutive rules, and which are, therefore, facts by virtue of human agreement.[124]

Moreover, speech acts carry the presupposition that the speaker in fact meant what he or she uttered.[125] Evidently, it is possible that the speaker has a different intentional

121 JR Searle, *Speech Acts: An Essay in the Philosophy of Language* (Cambridge University Press 1969).

122 For a summary of the argument, Searle, *Making the Social World* (n 15) 69.

123 ibid 12, 13.

124 Searle, *Intentionality* (n 102), 171–72.

125 ibid 9, 10, 164.

state than that which he or she expresses.[126] Besides the possibility of lying, an individual may dissociate him or herself from their speech acts and this is often what occurs with, e.g. State representatives – they express the belief/intention of their respective States. Thus, the individual's real intention in uttering the declaration (e.g. the intention to deceive, or to speak 'on behalf of') is different from the intentional state that the declaration carries with it. The individual who intends to utter certain sounds and utters them, satisfies the object of his or her real intention. However, by uttering certain sounds in a public language, the individual cannot escape the fact that these sounds carry publicly held meanings (this is sincerity condition).[127] Note that a person does not publicly commit him/herself to anything just by having intentional mental states like beliefs/intentions, but a person commits him/herself by expressing these and other states in words of a public language.[128] This insight is crucial for the understanding of how an institutional object comes to be: through *speech acts*.[129]

In analytical terms, institutional objects are established by the operation of declarations which have the form 'X in circumstances C counts as Y' or 'it is the case that Y status function exists in circumstances C'.[130] In the first case, institutional objects derive from the collective attribution of deontic status and function (therein the expression *status function*) to other objects; which can be either brute facts, which exist independently of the human mind; or which can be social objects (to which a new status function is attached). With the imposition of a certain status on an object, it acquires a function that otherwise it does not have.[131] So, the original object is *represented* as being something else.[132] In the second case, a status function can be established where no prior object exists (this case is often referred as free standing Y term).[133] In both cases, collective *acceptance* is required for the maintaining of the new status function. In both cases, the representation (Y) carries a deontology – e.g. it gives individuals desire-independent reasons for action.[134] In general, 'there is no

126 ibid 9, 10.
127 ibid 9, 10.
128 Searle, *Making the Social World* (n 15) 87–88.
129 ibid 100, 101.
130 ibid 97–100.
131 ibid 59–60, 94.
132 ibid 95.
133 JR Searle, 'Language and Social Ontology' (2008) 37 Theory and Society 443, http://link.springer.com/10.1007/s11186-008-9068-y, accessed 2 December 2019.
134 Searle, *Making the Social World* (n 15) ch 5. *See* F Kratochwil, *Rules, Norms, and Decisions: On the Conditions of Practical and Legal Reasoning in International Relations and Domestic Affairs* (Cambridge University Press 1991).

specific moment at which there is a specific act of Declaring, but there must be some speech act or set of speech acts and other sort of representation that constitute representing' the new object.[135] To be clear – a set of different speech acts may serve as an informal declaration. Still, the context – or the non-linguistic institution – in which the speech acts occur remain important.[136] However, and crucially, there are circumstances in which declarations must comply to some formal requirements so that they can constitute a new reality. This occurs, e.g. when declarations must conform to prior declarations, the so-called standing declarations, which establish

> into the indefinite future that anything that satisfies the X condition counts as having the Y status function. Thus, for example, getting a majority of votes in the Electoral College counts as winning the presidency of the United States. And anyone who wins and is subsequently sworn in counts as the president of the United States. This is why you do not need separate acts of acceptance for each individual case. By accepting the constitutive rules you're committed to accepting the cases that fall under those rules … Once you have accepted the constitutive rules the facts of the case determine whether it has the appropriate institutional status and your commitment to the rules commits you to accepting that status.[137]

Standing declarations allow individuals to *speak on behalf of an institution*. Consequently, by making a declaration on behalf of an institution, e.g. a government or an international organisation, individuals impose intentionality on said government or international organisation. In fact, standing declarations might allow individuals to impose intentionality on governments and international organisations through means other than declaration – other speech acts or *even actions that serve as* speech acts. Consequently, governments, as well as international organisations, have a form of *derived* intentionality, but intentionality it is. It is often the case that an international organisation's *intentionality* is denied on the basis of not being 'really' autonomous or independent vis-à-vis the member States.[138] However, subordinate intentionality continues to be intentionality – and let us not forget that governments also have intentionality that is derived from human intentionality. Thus, international organisations have intentionality – whether manifestations of their intentionality should qualify as *opinio juris* constitutes an entirely different question, as I hope to clarify. With these aspects in mind, let us give a more realistic gloss to our example.

135 Searle, *Making the Social World* (n 15) 96.
136 On this point, cf with n 61 (above), D'Amato drawing on Fuller and McDougal (n 75 and 76) and Roberts (n 91ff).
137 Searle, 'Language and Social Ontology' (n 133).
138 *See* Chapters 1, 2, and 4 in this volume.

> As set out in the note of the [United Kingdom] government's legal position published on 29 August 2013 in connection with possible United Kingdom military action against Syria, if action in the Security Council is blocked, the position of the government is that it is permitted under international law to take exceptional measures in order to avert a humanitarian catastrophe.[139]

And:

> I believe that we must embrace the responsibility to protect, and, when necessary, we must act on it … if national authorities are unable or unwilling to protect their citizens, then the responsibility shifts to the international community to use diplomatic, humanitarian and other methods to help protect the human rights and well-being of civilian populations. When such methods appear insufficient, the Security Council may out of necessity decide to take action under the Charter of the United Nations, including enforcement action, if so required.[140]

The picture that arises is different from mere utterance of words. The United Kingdom Minister formally *declares* the position (on behalf) of the United Kingdom government in respect to humanitarian intervention. The declaration is uttered by the Minister in his official capacity. Irrespective of the *sincerity* of the Minister towards the object of the declaration, the latter carries the psychological modes (i.e. belief and intention), as well as the sincerity condition, that define it as, and make it identifiable as, a declaration. Moreover, the Minister makes a declaration in circumstances and in a manner in which the declaration indeed *becomes* a declaration by the United Kingdom government.[141] Consequently, the mental states the declaration expresses are ascribed to the United Kingdom government.

139 United Kingdom Foreign and Commonwealth Office, 'Further Supplementary Written Evidence from the Rt Hon Hugh Robertson MP, Minister of State, Foreign and Commonwealth Office: Humanitarian Intervention and the Responsibility to Protect (USA 19)' (*Just Security*, 2014) (hereinafter UKFCO 2014) http://justsecurity.org/wp-content/uploads/2014/01/Letter-from-UK-Foreign-Commonwealth-Office-to-the-House-of-Commons-Foreign-Affairs-Committee-on-Humanitarian-Intervention-and-the-Responsibility-to-Protect.pdf, accessed 9 February 2019.

140 United Nations Secretary General, 'In Larger Freedom: Towards Development, Security and Human Rights for All' (2005) A/59/2005 (*In Larger Freedom*), 135. To be clear, unless the case is that of an *imminent* threat that falls within the scope of Article 51 of the United Nations Charter (*see In Larger Freedom* para 124), it is for the Security Council, and not for States without a Security Council mandate, to adopt enforcement action (*In Larger Freedom* para 126).

141 For a different, interesting approach that also emphasises the actors behind the State, *see* Chapter 5 in this volume.

Something similar happens with the United Nations Secretary-General[142] – with the difference that Kofi Annan apparently *does not dissociate himself* from the declaration, as he assumed the role of norm entrepreneur in respect to the promotion of the responsibility to protect or simply responsibility to protect principle.[143] I call derived intentional states that speech acts like these express and impose on institutions *underlying intentional states* – and, to be clear, I differentiate them, on the one hand, from primary, non-derived intentional states that occur to individuals and, on the other, of the speech acts that express them. As it happens with primary intentional states, it seems rather difficult to isolate an underlying intentional state.

Opinio juris is neither the primary intentional states that occur, not in isolation but in profusion, to decision-makers; nor the underlying intentional states, many times ambiguous or conflicting, expressed through speech acts; nor the speech acts themselves. Rather, *opinio juris* constitutes an institutional object, a complex status function which – (a) is imposed on speech acts, which carry underlying intentional states (beliefs or intentions), and which are uttered by specific classes of individuals in specific circumstances – and (b) has the purpose of promoting the emergence or facilitating the identification of customary international law. Analytically, *opinio juris* is established through a declaration:

X in circumstances C counts as Y

Where:

X = speech acts that carry certain underlying intentional states;
C = uttered by certain individuals in certain circumstances
Y = *opinio juris*.

The *function* of this status is that of *promoting* the emergence or *facilitating* the identification of customary international law (Z). Note that we can distinguish a standing declaration that establishes that in all cases where speech acts in certain circumstances constitute *opinio juris*, from declarations that establish individual occurrences of *opinio juris*. Henceforth, I differentiate between *opinio juris* as an institution as opposed to individual occurrences – or *tokens* of occurrences – of *opinio juris*. In individual occurrences, 'x' (e.g. speech acts carrying the intention/belief that humanitarian intervention be/is lawful without Security Council

142 For a precise account of the implications and the influence that a declaration by the United Nations Secretary-General can have, *see* Chapter 12 in this volume.

143 *See* I Johnstone, 'The Role of the UN Secretary-General: The Power of Persuasion Based on Law' (2003) 9 Global Governance 441; Droubi 'The Role of the United Nations' (n 14). (Both address, inter alia, the role of the Secretary-General as norm entrepreneur).

authorisation) in circumstances 'c' (uttered by Foreign Ministers etc.) counts as 'y' (*opinio juris* that humanitarian intervention be/is lawful without Security Council authorisation). The function of 'y' is to promote/facilitate the emergence/identification of 'z', a rule of customary international law that authorises humanitarian intervention without Security Council authorisation. Evidently, the expression *opinio juris* may be replaced by *acceptance as law* and similar formulations – the process remains the same.

But this is only part of the story. Because *opinio juris* is not sufficiently regulated, the standing declaration (X in circumstances C counts as Y) is not strong enough to dispense with specific acts of declaration and of *acceptance* of each individual occurrence. Let us go back to our two examples. They might suggest that we have individual occurrences of *opinio juris*: in the case of the United Kingdom, *opinio juris* that humanitarian intervention without Security Council authorisation be/is lawful, and in the case of the United Nations, *opinio juris* that Security Council authorisation is required. However, I do not think this is the case – on their own, the examples offer instances of underlying mental states. The *establishment* of an occurrence of *opinio juris* escapes the *sole* authority of an individual State or international organisation – because there needs be acts that serve as declaration that an occurrence is present, and because there needs be continuous acceptance that this is indeed the case. *Opinio juris*, by definition, is created by, and it serves, the collective which it addresses. Let us recall that the collective of States *may not accept* that all those who participate in it enjoy the same level of lawmaking capacity. Evidently, for the United Kingdom and all clearly recognised States, the question of lawmaking capacity does not arise – but for international organisations, States that do not count with general recognition and other entities,[144] the question may and does arise. The question even arises in respect to the concept of 'specially affected States', i.e. 'States that are particularly involved in the relevant activity or are most likely to be concerned with the alleged rule'.[145]

Besides, occurrences of *opinio juris* should be established on grounds of speech acts that express *somewhat stable shared* beliefs/intentions. By stable I mean that the same psychological modes about certain propositions are distinguishable in different speech acts. By shared, I mean collective intentional states. In order to clearly differentiate between the collective and individual intentional state, let us see how the United Kingdom looks at the responsibility to protect. In the excerpt below, we see that the United Kingdom government *shares* the United Nations collective

144 *See* e.g. Chapters 16 and 17 in this volume.

145 International Law Commission Conclusions (n 83) Conclusion 8, Commentary para 4.

belief/intention in the responsibility to protect principle, which forces it to *justify* its own belief/intention in the legality of humanitarian intervention without the Security Council authorisation.

> The Summit's adoption of the 'Responsibility to Protect' was politically significant, and one that the *Government welcomed and has continued to promote*. But the 'Responsibility to Protect' … *does not* address the question of unilateral State action in the face of an overwhelming humanitarian catastrophe to which the Security Council *has not* responded.[146]

Ultimately, there might be a very weak line separating individual from collective beliefs/intentions, and speech acts may simply reflect this ambiguity. To summarise the argument so far: there must be continuous acceptance of each occurrence of *opinio juris*, which is established on the basis of speech acts that carry *shared* underlying intentional states.

The practice of identifying *opinio juris* supports the argument above. Lawyers often remark that it is impossible to know the 'real' beliefs of a State.[147] Consequently, lawyers turn to written and unwritten materials and, at times, behaviours – in order to ascertain which 'beliefs' they evince.[148] From the available material, lawyers infer the belief of a State – notable in this respect is the possibility to infer a 'belief' from failure to react to a certain practice.[149] They need not concern with all States. Then, on the basis of the evidence, lawyers are able to affirm occurrences of *opinio juris* and, on its basis, they are able to affirm customary international law.[150] If we stick to the

146 UKFCO 2014 (n 139).

147 International Law Association, 'Final Report of the Committee on Formation of Customary (General) International Law: Statement of Principles Applicable to the Formation of General Customary International Law' ('ILA London Statement') 33, Principle 16 Commentary (b) ('it is not so much a question of what a State really believes (which is often undiscoverable, especially since a State is a composite entity involving many persons with possibly different beliefs), but rather a matter of what it says it believes, or what can reasonably be implied from its conduct')

148 International Law Commission (n 83) Conclusion 10.

149 ibid Conclusion 10(2) and commentary. Interestingly, the word 'deduce' was present in the 2016 version of the Conclusions and Commentary. cf International Law Commission, 'Identification of Customary International Law, Text of the draft conclusions and commentaries thereto' [2016] Report of the International Law Commission Sixty-eighth session (2 May–10 June and 4 July–12 August 2016) International Law Commission Report, A/71/10, 2016, ch V, para 63, Conclusion 10, Commentary 1 ('Draft conclusion 10 concerns the evidence from which acceptance of a given practice as law (opinio juris) may be *deduced*' – emphasis added).

150 International Law Commission (n 83), Conclusion 9.

traditional definition of *opinio juris*, namely, a *primary* intentional state, then, at different moments, the exercise looks artificial: how exactly does the lawyer isolate a belief from an intention; how exactly does the lawyer navigate from individual to collective intentionality; how can belief or acceptance, as mental states, be inferred from lack of action? The artificiality breaks down if we look at *opinio juris* as an institutional artefact – now, 'belief' or 'acceptance' and even 'intention' acquire another meaning, with a different ontology than mental states or speech acts: 'belief' or 'acceptance' or 'intention' qua *opinio juris* is that what lawyers establish in each case, on the basis of speech acts serving as evidence, for the specific purpose of ascertaining a rule of custom.

Henceforth, for analytical purposes only, I differentiate between the collective of individuals who mostly contribute to the formation of the *underlying* beliefs, like policy-makers and norm-entrepreneurs;[151] and those who mostly contribute to the establishment of *opinio juris*, namely, international lawyers broadly defined, including those working in Foreign Offices and in Secretariats and other organs and procedures of international organisations, or as judges and arbiters in international courts and tribunals. In a certain manner, a token of *opinio juris* is that what international lawyers say it is. Clearly, there is a self-referentiality in the concept;[152] but there is no circularity because the expression '*opinio juris*' is, paraphrasing Searle, a 'node in a whole network of practices', and it functions as 'a placeholder for the linguistic articulation of all these practices'.[153] These are the practices, we should not forget, of ascertaining customary international law. As an institutional artefact, *opinio juris* only makes sense in the ascertaining of customary international law and individual occurrences of *opinio juris* will only make sense in the ascertaining of rules of customary international law. This may explain an oft-noted fact: not every affirmation of a rule of customary international law – by, say, the International Court of Justice – rests on a prior affirmation of *opinio juris*.[154] The reason for this may be that if international lawyers, should they be able to establish, in any given case, the existence of a rule of customary international law without getting enmeshed in the

151 *See* Chapter 12 in this volume (arguing that the United Nations Secretariat and Secretary-General, given their independence as per United Nations Charter, Article 100, can contribute to customary international law).

152 Drawing on Tuomela, it could be argued that it depends on the *continued* acting of the collective on the agreement that it is *opinio juris*. *See* R Tuomela, *The Philosophy of Social Practices: A Collective Acceptance View* (Cambridge University Press 2002).

153 JR Searle, *The Construction of Social Reality* (Penguin 1996) [ebook].

154 For all, *see* N Petersen, 'The International Court of Justice and the Judicial Politics of Identifying Customary International Law' (2017) 28 European Journal of International Law 357.

intricacies of discussing *opinio juris*, they may simply avoid the latter. This does not necessarily mean that, in such cases, there is no *opinio juris* – it may be that international lawyers have internalised the rules of the game to an extent that they use *opinio juris* in an unconscious manner.

Moreover, the activity of ascertaining *opinio juris*, which the international lawyer undertakes, is a *politico-legal* activity. Its outcome has politico-*legal* value. Let us look at it more closely. Technically, the international lawyer should only affirm an occurrence of *opinio juris* on grounds of speech acts that evince shared intentional states. Insofar as the United Kingdom belief in the lawfulness of humanitarian intervention without Security Council authorisation remains the individual belief of the United Kingdom government[155] – it should not qualify as an occurrence of *opinio juris*. At the moment other States come to share the belief/intention, the situation changes. However, the activity which the lawyers carry out is a politico-legal, and not a scientific activity, which is mostly uncodified and full of inconsistencies. Consequently, it seems possible that international lawyers establish an occurrence of *opinio juris* on grounds of speech acts which, under close scrutiny, express only individual beliefs/intentions.[156] In fact, it may be impossible for the lawyer to distinguish, from the available evidence, individual and collective mental states. In any case, the 'premature' or 'improper' affirmation of an occurrence of *opinio juris* might be either rejected or accepted by other lawyers – which, in turn, might either undermine or strengthen the underlying speech acts. The effects of a premature or improper affirmation of *opinio juris* depends on different factors, such as the degree of legitimacy and authority of the lawyers in question; or the presence of active norm-entrepreneurship in promoting the underlying beliefs/intentions.

With this background, Section 4 turns to the dynamics of the formation of tokens of *opinio juris* – with the objective of understanding the extent to which emergence of *opinio juris* might be considered the outcome of processes that individuals carry out consciously; and of understanding how international organisations might influence these processes.

155 Note that from a United Kingdom domestic perspective, it necessarily constitutes the belief of a collective. However, at the international plane, which interests us here, it should be treated as an individual belief. What goes beyond the present scope is the manner that a belief shared by a collective within one country can dissipate to collectives in other countries. As I tried to show elsewhere, international organisations seem to play an important role in this respect. *See* Droubi 'Institutionalisation of Emerging Norms' (n 13).

156 In practical terms, an international lawyer may be tempted to qualify as collective *opinio juris* the individual belief of his or her own State or international organisation. *See* e.g. the discussion in Chapter 12 of this volume.

4 International organisations and *opinio juris*: between politics and science

A good exercise is to look at the formation of a new rule of customary international law that transforms settled law. As the International Law Association notes, 'it is hard to see how a State, if properly advised, could entertain the belief that its conduct is permitted (or required) by existing law when that conduct is, by definition, a departure from it'.[157] Indeed, decision-makers tend to be very cautious when making statements or acting on behalf of their respective institutions; in fact, it is often the case that only certain individuals are authorised to speak on behalf of governments and international organisations in matters that have an international dimension. The acts of parliaments and the decisions of domestic courts, which may also amount to evidence of *opinio juris*, are also the outcome of detailed politico-legal processes. In turn, international lawyers, diplomats, and professionals dealing with issues of international law tend to be careful when dealing with these materials for the purpose of ascertaining *opinio juris*. These professionals have mastered and internalised the 'rules of the game' – e.g. the international legal concepts such as responsibility, precedence, unilateral acts, acquiescence, and estoppel – to a point that makes them naturally very cautious in these matters. Let us say that all these factors form part of a background.[158]

Therefore, it can be hypothesised that, by the time the processes through which speech acts start being used to ground the establishment of an occurrence of opinio juris, it is already clear to all involved that these processes are in movement. Apparently, decision-makers and, notably, lawyers are conscious of these processes and time seems to be in their favour – giving them opportunity for reflection.[159] However, if there is opportunity for reflection, the argument that Dupuy makes – that international organisations might be able to trigger consciousness and coordinate these processes – seems pertinent. Indeed, as a substantial constructivist literature in international relations shows, international organisations are able to trigger collective consciousness; to promote the diffusion of norms across jurisdictions and to influence State behaviour.

157 ILA London Statement (n 147) 1, 33, Principle 16 Commentary (c).

158 I am using the term background to refer to background 'of capacities, dispositions, tendencies, practices, and so on that enable the intentionality to function' as well as to the network of 'beliefs, attitudes, desires, and so on that enable specific intentional states to function'. Searle, *Making the Social World* (n 15) 155.

159 Indeed, in most cases in which States refer to customary international law in, say, the United Nations Security Council, they do so to *deny* that the norm is question has this character. *See* Droubi 'Institutionalisation of Emerging Norms' (n 13).

However, the picture above is incomplete – it does not distinguish between the promotion and diffusion of international norms, which might or might not be accompanied by a change of behaviour to comply with the norm, and the promotion and diffusion of an *opinio juris* to the effect that a norm is customary international law; it does not account for the role that *free will* plays in the process of establishing and ascertaining *opinio juris*; it does not account for the effect that different timeframes – and certain categories of events – have on consciousness and, consequently, on underlying intentional states. I will deal with these factors in turn.

It is uncontested that international organisations are capable of promoting the diffusion of international norms across States, for instance as rules of domestic law,[160] and that they are capable of affecting State behaviour.[161] However, this does not necessarily mean that international organisations can affect the content of the *opinio juris* of States on any given matter in a significant manner.[162]

International organisations can function as *neutral parties* to promote worldviews, within which they define problems and the manner to address them.[163] International organisations can lead the way in defining problems, identifying the actors responsible for creating and for addressing such problems; can articulate new prescriptions of behaviour to tackle behaviours that trigger or accentuate these problems; can adopt resolutions that introduce these prescriptions as norms to the international society; can persuade States to adopt these norms; can oversee compliance with the latter, aid States that lack the necessary resources to comply with these norms, administer sanctions on States that refuse to comply with them.[164] We can say that, in these processes, individuals working in the international organisations, often experts in their fields, 'quietly inject their thought or take the initiative

160 M Finnemore, 'International Organizations as Teachers of Norms: The United Nations Educational, Scientific, and Cutural Organization and Science Policy' (1993) 47 International Organization 565; G Porter and JW Brown, 'The Emergence of Global Environmental Politics' (1996) 615 Global Environmental Politics 1; SE Davies, A Kamradt-Scott, and S Rushton, *Disease Diplomacy: International Norms and Global Health Security* (Johns Hopkins University Press 2015).

161 For instance, R Goodman and D Jinks, *Socializing States: Promoting Human Rights through International Law* (Oxford University Press 2013).

162 Note e.g. that the Conclusions list 'legislative and administrative acts' as evidence of State practice – but not of evidence of *opinio juris*. cf UNGA RES 73/203 (2019) (n 83) Conclusions 5, 6.2 and 10.2.

163 The notion and role of neutral parts can be found in F Parisi, 'Spontaneous Emergence of Law: Customary Law' (1999) Encyclopedia of Law and Economics 608.

164 Droubi, 'The Role of the United Nations' (n 14); Droubi, 'Institutionalisation of Emerging Norms' (n 13).

in offering government representatives ideas and data for mapping an altered or, for that matter, unchanged course'.[165] Moreover, international organisations often provide favourable environments to norm-entrepreneurs to act globally in the promotion of these worldviews, definitions of problems, and forms of addressing them. These entrepreneurs, who rely on a network of experts from different States, other international organisations, and non-governmental organisations, often trigger collective alertness.[166]

Throughout these processes, decision-makers in different governments might learn to see the world through certain prisms; they might become convinced (i.e. come to believe) that the problems, the solutions, and norms that international organisations present to them make sense, are warranted; they might imprint such norms onto official policies. In contradistinction, decision-makers *might remain unconvinced* that the problems, solutions, and norms are warranted and, nonetheless, they might, for whatever practical or material reasons, imprint such norms onto official legislation and policies (i.e. they give in to social pressure or positive or negative sanctions). It should appear that this latter situation would be covered by the discussion on the sincerity condition.[167] However, it is not. This is so because of one aspect that so far remains under-developed. In theory, *opinio juris* requires speech acts that carry an underlying intentional state with a *specific* propositional content, which has the format 'international norm "α" is or should be customary in character'. Again, we should account for the inconsistencies of the practice, so it should be expected that tokens of *opinio juris* might be established even when speech acts do not carry an intentional state with said propositional content.

In more precise terms, the move (a) from successfully triggering collective consciousness about a given problem 'μ' and from successfully disseminating a given norm 'α' to tackle problem 'μ' as rule of law in different jurisdictions, and even affecting States behaviour to comply with norm 'α'; – towards (b) the establishment of *opinio juris* to the effect that norm 'α' is custom, is not automatic. Even if States adapt their behaviour to norm 'α' this does not mean that there is *opinio juris* to the effect that norm 'α' is custom. Considering that *opinio juris* requires continuous reaffirmation lest it decays, it seems that international organisations have different tasks if the objective is to coordinate processes to shape *opinio juris*: they need to promote the belief that 'μ' is indeed a problem (cf climate change); they need to promote the belief that norm 'α' as an effective or at least a proper instrument to tackle

165 L Gordenker, *The UN Secretary-General and Secretariat* (Routledge 2013).

166 Droubi, 'The Role of the United Nations' (n 14).

167 *See* n 127 and 141 and accompanying text.

problem 'μ' (cf reduction of carbon emissions), and the belief or intention that norm 'α' is or should be customary. It is by no means clear that strategies developed for the promotion and diffusion of norms and management of compliance are *effective* for the promotion and diffusion of *opinio juris*. For the present purpose, for lack of better strategies, let us assume these strategies can be effective at least to a certain extent. Even then, there remain serious challenges.

Continuing with the example above, even if norm 'α' is repeatedly affirmed in resolutions of an international organ; even if it becomes inserted as a rule of law into the domestic legislation of different countries, even in face of mounting social pressure for complying with norm 'α', decision-makers and lawyers have much room to operate to jeopardise the processes that would lead to the affirmation of norm 'α' as custom. This is how Searle describes the 'causal gap' or 'free will':

> we have a special kind of consciousness in which we have a sense of making decisions that are not forced, the kind of consciousness where we choose one thing but we have a sense that we could have chosen something else. In such cases we sense a causal gap between the reasons for our decisions and actions [and here Searle is speaking of rules including legal rules as reasons for decisions and actions]. Though we do act on reasons, the reasons do not normally set causally sufficient conditions for our decisions and actions, and in that sense there is a gap between the causes and the effects.[168]

This gap is, obviously, only a gap between *reasons* and *actions* – it is not a gap in mental states: in fact, the gap allows a human being to *sense* something else, to *believe in* and to *intend to bring about*, a new state of affairs.

Belief and intentions – i.e. the primary intentional states of belief and intention – do not occur in isolation,[169] and they do not simply appear by fiat.[170] These intentional states are necessarily embedded in unique backgrounds.[171] Among the factors that trigger primary mental states are memory, experience, and perception.[172] Indeed, successes and failures that the decision-makers and their society *experienced*, and the *memory of* such experiences, affect the manner in which they perceive the present and form their beliefs and intentions. In a simplistic account, the memories, experiences, perceptions, inter alia, of an individual trigger his or her intentional states. Social processes allow the individual to share their experiences and memories, their beliefs and intentions with their peers. In these social processes, some factors (like norm-entrepreneurs) trigger individual and collective

168 Searle, *Making the Social World* (n 15) 133.
169 ibid 31.
170 ibid 31.
171 ibid 31–32.
172 ibid.

consciousness. Conscious actors rely on their individual and shared background to test beliefs and question intentions. Decision-making processes, which ground much of the exercise of ascribing intentional states to governments, serve to purge unwarranted beliefs and intentions.[173] In a manner, decision-making processes stabilise collective beliefs and intentions. However, these processes can only go so far.

Indeed, individuals in a government may entertain all sorts of beliefs and intentions. Whenever a collective of individuals come to share the belief that an official policy of their government should change, even if this means going against settled law, they have in their favour a variegated range of mechanisms, many of which are very subtle, to work on their *intention* to change the policy in question.[174] The classic use that judges make of legal argumentation as a form of civil resistance for the undermining of extant law illustrates the point.[175] Moreover, let us not forget that the object of intentional states, the state of affairs in the world to which they refer, might change. By formally expressing intentions/beliefs that conflict with settled rule of customary international law, decision-makers might work towards the transformation of the rule in question.

This allows us to revisit the argument Walden articulates.[176] The *primary* intention, which certain human beings might share, to change a rule of customary intentional law already comes enveloped in a network of primary intentional states in which it finds support. The primary intention to change a rule is necessarily grounded on the belief that a change of the rule is possible; it might be grounded on the belief that the rule should be changed, which may be grounded on the belief that circumstances changed, or interests changed, and these intentional states are intimately related to many others. The intentionality that is ultimately imposed on a government is the outcome of ferociously dynamic singular and collective *psychological* processes, as well as of live *social* interactions through which individuals

173 *See* the developments in the debate in the United Kingdom on the topic of responsibility to protect and humanitarian intervention: United Kingdom House of Commons, Common Affairs Committee 'Global Britain: The Responsibility to Protect and Humanitarian Intervention' Twelfth Report of Session 2017–19 HC 1005 (10 September 2018).

174 *See* e.g. S Droubi, *Resisting United Nations Security Council Resolutions* (Routledge, 2014) 15 *et seq.*

175 *See* e.g. J Dugard, 'Should Judges Resign? A Reply to Professor Wacks' (1984) 101 South African Law Journal 286; MJ Osiel, 'Dialogue with Dictators: Judicial Resistance in Argentina and Brazil' (1995) 20 Law & Social Inquiry – Journal of the American Bar Foundation 481.

176 *See* n 64–65 and accompanying text.

come to share their beliefs and intentions, and, through special categories of speech acts, come to impose certain beliefs/intentions on their governments. All things being equal, it should be expected that certain beliefs/intentions resonate, more than others do, with individuals in other governments. It is by no means clear that international organisations can *coordinate* these processes that shape *opinio juris*, which occur often simultaneously at the domestic, transnational, and international levels. In fact, in the face of events like Brexit and the United States' official approach to climate change,[177] it seems that international organisations have no means of coordinating processes with this wingspan.

Likewise, when collecting and ascertaining evidence about putative occurrences of *opinio juris*, international lawyers are affected by a multitude of primary intentions/beliefs, which are triggered by their own experiences, memories, and perceptions. They certainly express some of them through formal speech acts. Take Judge Koroma's dissenting opinion in *Threat or Use of Nuclear Weapons*: does he not start by recalling the tragedy of Hiroshima to build a powerful argument to affirm, inter alia, his own belief in the *emergence* of *opinio juris* whose propositional content is the prohibition of the use of nuclear weapons?[178] By '*emergence* of an *opinio juris*' (emphasis added), does he not suggest, perhaps unconsciously, that he sees intention *and* belief on the part of the States? This example shows us that it is in the *process* of affirming a token of *opinio juris* where lawyers express, in carefully articulated speech acts, their own belief/intention that the token in the case exists. It also evinces the high level of discretion that lawyers enjoy.

But for an occurrence of *opinio juris* to be established, there needs be agreement among a collective of lawyers (recall, I am not only speaking of judges here) that it is, indeed, the case that it exists. In the example above, when Judge Koroma affirms the existence of tokens of an emerging *opinio juris* to the effect that the use of nuclear arms is prohibited, is Judge Koroma *describing* a real state of affairs or engaging, even if incidentally, in wishful thinking? But, then, again, are lawyers properly equipped to *describe* the state of affairs that tokens of *opinio juris* express? Or, alternatively, are they always engaging in wishful thinking – and, then promoting or demoting the state of affairs in question? As I explained above, I believe that lawyers *establish* occurrences of *opinio juris*. But they do so on the basis of speech acts that evince certain, stable, shared underlying intentional states – their power *is* constrained. However, in borderline, ambiguous cases, their power seems to increase: a lawyer

177 *See* e.g. CM Brölmann et al, 'Exiting International Institutions: A Brief Introduction' (2018) 15 International Organizations Law Review.

178 *Legality of the Threat or Use of Nuclear Weapons*, Advisory Opinion 226, 555, 579.

may simply emphasise *emergence* of an *opinio juris* to describe a state of affairs that is not fully developed; and by so doing a lawyer may promote the development of the state of affairs. The question that arises is – how international organisations would coordinate these processes? At most, it seems that international organisations may provide the frameworks within which lawyers work.

The picture becomes more complex once we bring time to the analysis. It is not possible to do away with the requisite of time by simply arguing that States experience time in a Bergsonian way. A Bergsonian approach would need to go much further than Dupuy does. A central feature in Bergson's theory is the relationship between time and *free will.*[179] In what interests us here, Bergson builds a critique of the classic schematics of *voluntary* act, which identify a moment for deliberation and following moments for decision and action.[180] Bergson suggests that experience is contemporaneous to action; that the individual *deliberates* after he or she acts to justify the decision they had already made; that, consequently, deliberation generates a circle of justification in which the individual loses him or herself. As Jankélévitch explains, to act *freely*, the individual needs to acquire a direct perception of the world (a 'learned naivety'), i.e. a perception cleared of theories, opinions, and perspectives – cleared of deliberation.[181] In other words, the individual can break the vicious circle though action – but he or she needs to act upon intuition, a type of intuition ('duration intuition') that emanates from a 'higher system', which allows the individual to experience the *instant* 'from within' and directly.[182] With this, we reach the fundamental idea that the instant when the individual becomes aware of the state of affairs in the world, is irreversible, implying a precise past and future (essentially, this is the idea of 'duration'). It does not take much to see that, whatever the time in which States operate or operated at the time Dupuy wrote *Coutume Sauvage*, this is not it. In fact, a Bergsonian approach seems to offer material enough to counter any claim that States act 'freely'.

Nevertheless, the above invites us to think about the intricacies of understanding the world at the instant one becomes aware of it – the intricacies of understanding the formation of intentional states about world affairs at the instant one becomes aware of the affairs. To help in this analysis, I bring Ruggie's work on timeframes and decision-making.[183] Ruggie differentiates between three temporal forms, namely,

179 Bergson, *Time and Free Will* (n 25); Bergson, *Matter and Memory* (n 25).

180 Jankélévitch (n 29).

181 ibid.

182 ibid.

183 JG Ruggie, 'Social Time and Ecodemographic Contexts', *Constructing the World Polity: Essays on International Institutionalization* (Routledge 1998).

incremental, conjunctural, and epochal.[184] In the three timeframes, decision-makers bring their own knowledge and worldviews to the analysis of information, to the debate and decision-making.[185] In doing so, they *simplify* available information about the phenomena they *define* as socially relevant – they make the information manageable, *usable*.[186] Pursuant to Ruggie, each temporal form frames the 'social perceptions' of phenomena.[187] Critically, Ruggie carefully explains the types of *problems* that actors define through these timeframes, and he concludes that these problems differ not only in substance but also *epistemologically*.[188]

Incremental timeframes present the world in a more *familiar* or *knowable* way than conjunctural and epochal timeframes.[189] In incremental timeframes, information and evidence necessary for decision-making are available, and policy-makers will likely adopt a benefits–costs rationale to define problems and policies.[190] However, epochal and, to a certain degree, conjunctural timeframes, respect long-wave processes about which information may be insufficient and evidence may be unconvincing or simply lacking.[191] Ruggie submits that, in such cases, conventional problem-solving rationale – 'wherein doing nothing is favoured on burden-of-proof grounds' – can give way to a risk-averting approach – 'wherein prudent contingency measures would be undertaken to avoid risks that we would rather not face … much as we do in the realm of *national security*'.[192]

I argue that incremental and, to a degree, conjunctural timeframes are *familiar* because the memory of past experience is strong. In long-wave events, memory is weak if existent. In the first case, individuals *recognise* present states of affairs, their past experience (successes, failures) and the memory it left causes certain beliefs and intentions – e.g. it is the unique memories and experiences and perceptions of certain individuals in the United Kingdom that frame the debate on the lawfulness of humanitarian intervention without Security Council authorisation.[193] In

184 ibid.

185 ibid.

186 ibid.

187 ibid.

188 ibid.

189 ibid.

190 ibid.

191 Ruggie does not use the expression long-wave event, which I borrowed from T Barnett and Gwyn Prins, 'HIV/AIDS and Security: Fact, Fiction and Evidence—a Report to UNAIDS' (2006) 82.2 International Affairs 361.

192 Ruggie (n 183). Emphasis added.

193 Note the development of the debate by contrasting the document in n 139 with the document in n 173.

long-term events, however, individuals *do not* recognise the state of affairs – factors in the background like fears, ideologies, biases, might weigh more heavily in the generation of underlying intentional states.

It would seem that the main problem constitutes long-wave events; however, let us look at the potential effects of the Internet and the Web on 'incremental timeframes'. For Hassan, the digital environment generates and sustains its own temporality (*realtimeness*), displacing temporal relationships that have *traditionally* defined human lives.[194] Notably, he claims that the digital environment *destroys old forms of knowledge*, and favours the production of new knowledge that reflects the needs and imperatives of efficiency. Hassan claims that the digital environment emphasises the production of technical knowledge, and jeopardises the production of *critical* knowledge.[195] Consequently, the individual fails to understand the world, which becomes out of control.[196] Hassan argues that, in the name of efficiency, even those 'in control' (decision-makers) are out of control because their timeframes for action *are set in the present and near future* ('actions spiral out into an unknown eternity').[197] In contradistinction, Kitchin offers what might be an even darker picture. Responding to the literature that claims that realtimeness 'overemphasises the present at the expense of learning from the past and planning for the future' and that posits that temporal dissonance should be recovered – Kitchin claims that people are 'enmeshed in several competing temporalities simultaneously', which force them to negotiate 'a complex "chronotopia" of varying pace, tempos, rhythms, scheduling, temporal relations and modalities, and these are contingent for different people in different places'.[198] Kitchin argues that the implications of this to individuals and to governance are not fully clear, but that the critique should attack the *maintenance* rather than the *recovery* of asynchronous time.[199] Perhaps it is the point that these approaches have in common – the *unfamiliarity* of the state of affairs – which offers a reasonable ground for arguing that individuals might not recognise many present-day state of affairs. If so, Ruggie's approach to incremental timeframes might be jeopardised – which is relevant insofar as the Internet and the Web have clear impact on decision-makers and lawyers.

194 R Hassan, 'Network Time and the New Knowledge Epoch' (2003) 12 Time & Society 226.
195 ibid.
196 ibid.
197 ibid.
198 R Kitchin, 'The Realtimeness of Smart Cities' (2017) 8 Tecnoscienza: Italian Journal of Science & Technology Studies 19 www.tecnoscienza.net, accessed 6 July 2020.
199 ibid.

On this note, it could be argued that scientific knowledge could counterbalance the lack of familiarity, offering grounds for actors like international organisations to promote sound beliefs/intentions respecting state of affairs that are not familiar to decision-makers. Indeed, international organisations may facilitate the diffusion of scientific knowledge to States and other actors.[200] Scientific knowledge is indisputably a relevant factor in the background; however, in the present times, it is hard to affirm that it weighs more than other factors in the formation of primary beliefs and intentions of the population at large and of decision-makers and, consequently, in the formation of underlying intentional states. Moreover, problems such as the global financial crisis or climate change deeply challenge the scientific community. There is not a strong agreement in the specialised literature about, e.g. the causes of the global financial crisis,[201] or about the implications, if any, of climate change on violent conflicts or international security.[202] Consequently, decision-makers are left with contradictory narratives. The belief that more financial regulation might prevent another crisis is no stronger than the belief that it makes access to money more difficult for those who might be in most need of it.[203] The belief that reliance of fossil fuels should be significantly reduced is no stronger than the belief that such a reduction causes people to lose their jobs and negatively affects economies.[204]

200 For instance, *see* the United Nations actions and processes in respect to climate change, United Nations, 'Climate Change' (2018) www.un.org/en/sections/issues-depth/climate-change/, accessed 6 October 2018.

201 'Ten Years after Lehman: Has Finance Been Fixed?' [2018] *The Economist*; M Phillips and K Russel, 'The Next Financial Calamity Is Coming: Here's What to Watch' *The New York Times*, 12 September 2018; G Tett, 'Have We Learnt the Lessons of the Financial Crisis?' *Financial Times*, 31 August 2018; A Tooze, 'The Forgotten History of the Financial Crisis' [2018] Foreign Affairs www.foreignaffairs.com/articles/world/2018–08–13/forgotten-history-financial-crisis, accessed 6 October 2018.

202 WN Adger et al, 'Human Security' in CB Field et al (eds), *Climate Change 2014: Impacts, Adaptation, and Vulnerability. Part A: Global and Sectoral Aspects. Contribution of Working Group II to the Fifth Assessment Report of the Intergovernmental Panel on Climate Change* (Cambridge University Press 2014).

203 Contrast e.g. GB White, 'Trump Begins to Chip Away at Banking Regulations' [2017] *The Atlantic*; with Kamal Ahmed, 'Bank Warns "Lax Financial Rules" Are a Route to Failure', *BBC News*, 2018, www.bbc.co.uk/news/business-38913306, accessed 29 September 2018.

204 *See* e.g. P Karp, 'Australian Government Backs Coal in Defiance of IPCC Climate Warning', *The Guardian*, 8 October 2018, www.theguardian.com/australia-news/2018/oct/09/australian-government-backs-coal-defiance-ipcc-climate-warning, accessed 6 July 2020.

Whether, in this complex scenario, international organisations may *successfully* promote primary and underlying beliefs/intentions that are consistent with scientific (or other) standards is questionable to say the least. Because of the need of constant reaffirmation, the formation of *opinio juris* is a continuous process, which might be jeopardised even if it is in a mature stage if decision-makers begin to resist the process – and they might resist the process because they do not share the same beliefs and intentions of their predecessors – or, simply, because their own beliefs and intentions fluctuate and change. Indeed, for different reasons which go beyond the scope of the present chapter, multitudes of individuals across the globe now view international organisations with deep suspicion.[205] Worse, many *resist* the worldviews, narratives, beliefs, and intentions that international organisations espouse and actively promote.[206] In this environment, international organisations are seen not as neutral, but as *interested* parties in the different debates. As they lose the mantle of neutral parties, their ability to promote certain beliefs and intention is jeopardised. All in all, in the face of lack of agreement in the scientific community, in an environment that demotes critical knowledge and places the individual in unfamiliar space-times – fears, biases, ideologies might weigh in in the formation of false beliefs and unwarranted intentions – which compete and not rarely prevail over beliefs and intentions that cohere with scientific findings and recommendations. The extent to which international organisations are able to neutralise these factors, and successfully promote beliefs/intentions that make any sense from any scientific viewpoint, is by no means clear. In fact, this constitutes a hypothesis that cannot be dealt with anecdotally and that deserves proper empirical study.

Furthermore, international organisations affect the manner international lawyers carry out the activity of ascertaining *opinio juris*. For instance, more than simply setting parameters for international lawyers, decisions of the International Court of Justice and other courts and tribunals, and the work of the International Law Commission, play a crucial role in developing ontological understandings

205 Brölmann et al (n 177).

206 For instance, M Howard and R Aikens, 'The EU's Court Is Picking Apart Our Laws', *The Telegraph* (online), 22 June 2016, www.telegraph.co.uk/news/2016/06/22/the-eus-court-is-picking-apart-our-laws/, accessed 6 July 2020 (reflecting popular dissatisfaction in the United Kingdom towards the European Court of Human Rights). Also, M Simiti, 'Rage and Protest' (2015) 3 Contention 33; N Sotirakopoulos and G Sotiropoulos, '"Direct Democracy Now!": The Greek Indignados and the Present Cycle of Struggles' (2013) 61 Current Sociology 443 (describing popular frustration towards the troika formed by European Central Bank, European Commission, and the International Monetary Fund).

and epistemological approaches to the identification of *opinio juris*, which become part of a lawyer's background. In *North Sea*, for instance, the International Court of Justice defined *opinio juris* as a 'belief that this practice is rendered obligatory by the existence of a rule of law requiring it',[207] defining *opinio juris* as a mental state. In the same judgment, the International Court of Justice gave the well-known verdict about the passage of time,[208] apparently rejecting the constraints of mechanical time. The International Court of Justice has done more by ascribing, although timidly, normative force to the 'belief' in question.[209] The real extent to which lawyers, in the stricter sense of the term, and scholars have internalised these understandings, and the influence of these particular decisions in the process of internalisation, are unknown. At least *prima facie*, it seems that these decisions have been crucial in placing these understandings in the individual and collective background of lawyers and scholars.

Moreover, the manner that the International Court of Justice, and other international courts and tribunals, use *opinio juris* affects the way international lawyers understand and identify *opinio juris*.[210] If the International Court of Justice fails to make a systematic and coherent use of *opinio juris* when identifying customary international law, lawyers and academics might ultimately reflect the confusion in their work.[211] Indeed, there are instances of authoritative affirmation of customary international law essentially on the basis of *opinio juris*, and there are instances of affirmation of customary international law without any regard to *opinio juris*. Consequently, there are scholarly works that strongly affirm the

207 North sea continental shelf cases (Federal Republic of Germany/Denmark; Federal Republic of Germany/Netherlands) (Judgment) [1969] ICJ Reports 76–77.

208 ibid.

209 Case concerning Right of Passage over Indian Territory (Merits), Judgment (1960) 1960 ICJ Reports 6, 42–43 ('nothing to short that grant of permission was incumbent … as an obligation'). North sea continental shelf cases (Federal Republic of Germany/Denmark; Federal Republic of Germany/Netherlands) (n 207) 74 ('general recognition that a rule of law … is involved'). Jurisdictional Immunities of the State (Germany v Italy; Greece intervening) [2010] ICJ Reports 1, 55 ('the grant of immunity is not accompanied by the requisite opinio juris').

210 cf D'Amato reaction to *Nicaragua* in A D'Amato, 'Trashing Customary International Law' (1987) 81 The American Journal of International Law 101.

211 Which might explain the phenomenon described by J d'Aspremont, 'Customary International Law as a Dance Floor: Part I' (*EJIL: Talk!*, 2014), www.ejiltalk.org/customary-international-law-as-a-dance-floor-part-i/, accessed 6 August 2018; J d'Aspremont, 'Customary International Law as a Dance Floor: Part II' (*EJIL: Talk!*, 2014), www.ejiltalk.org/customary-international-law-as-a-dance-floor-part-ii/, accessed 6 August 2018.

preponderance of *opinio juris*;[212] there are others who affirm the preponderance of behaviour;[213] there is the brilliant sliding scale approach negotiating between them;[214] and there are some, perhaps more sensate, qualifying the whole situation as a mess.[215] In his second report to the International Law Commission on the topic of identification of customary international law, Wood touches on the deep academic divergences on the concept of *opinio juris* – but just to dismiss them on the argument 'the theoretical torment which may accompany it in the books has rarely impeded its application in practice'.[216] However, is it not the inconsistencies in the practice that trigger the academic torment? Wood acknowledges the existence of 'different approaches' not only in the academia but also in *practice* – but he does not take the latter aspect forward.[217]

While the perception of a state of affairs is affected by the lawyer's own background, the fact remains that lawyers and their narratives enjoy different levels of authority within the invisible college. The work of the International Law Commission emerges in a different light because – as the work of the International Committee of the Red Cross and the International Law Association before – it amasses, organises, and studies a huge literature and case-law, and offers a systematic approach to the ascertaining of *opinio juris* in the Conclusions. While these bodies have *authority*, it is incontestable that the International Law Commission has a different level of authority, which arises from it being *the* organ of the United Nations with a mandate on the codification and progressive development of international law. In other words, the Conclusions have a great potential to become a natural part of the collective and individual background of international lawyers – a background that affects their perception of the reality up to the establishment of tokens of *opinio juris*. This potential seems greatly accentuated by the fact that the International Law Commission offers its Conclusions *now*, in a time where the Web and the Internet promote certain views – and demote others.

Indeed, the work of the International Law Commission is likely to have a huge impact on the academic work on the subject. The number of scholarly works citing or dealing with *opinio juris* since the International Law Commission has taken the topic

212 Dupuy (n 1).
213 Pellet (n 10).
214 FL Kirgis, 'Custom on a Sliding Scale' (1987) 81 American Journal of International Law 146.
215 AT Guzman, 'Saving Customary International Law' (2005) 115 SSRN Electronic Journal 116, 117, www.ssrn.com/abstract=708721, accessed 13 June 2019.
216 M Wood, *Second Report on Identification of Customary International Law* (2014) para 66.
217 ibid 27–28.

and has affirmed *opinio juris* as a necessary element of customary international law, surpasses the number in the previous twelve years, which is greater than the number of the prior six decades.[218] Let us not forget that it was in the 1990s and 2000s that the International Committee of the Red Cross's and International Law Association's efforts also affirmed *opinio juris* as a requirement of customary international law. Where there seems to be correlation between these facts, further research is needed to establish any causation. Should there be any causation we may be witnessing the strengthening of one approach to customary international law and to *opinio juris* in particular to the prejudice of others. If there is indeed causation, the future might bring uniformity and synchronicity, i.e. the adoption by scholars of the same ontological and epistemological approaches on *opinio juris*. However, the question arises, would dissonance serve the cause, of understanding what *opinio juris* is, better?

In reality, the process of synchronisation might be accelerated by the effects of the imposition of a 'market logic' on academia.[219] Paraphrasing Weiler, consciously and subconsciously, this market logic affects the research agenda on the topic: why would someone explore 'somewhat esoteric' approaches to *opinio juris* which 'will generate less citations, less "impact"? Or reduce the chances of winning a grant, of getting "time off" '.[220]

Indeed, what the International Law Commission Conclusions do not and, given the ethos and scope of the exercise it undertook on this topic, what they certainly could not show is the ontological and epistemological idiosyncrasies that affect the mainstream approaches to *opinio juris*: how exactly can a mental *state*, i.e. a state that is caused by neurophysiological processes and triggered by a range of factors, be isolated, kept fixed, and be ascribed normative force? How exactly does one move from the singular mental state to that of the collective? If the relevant mental state is that of the collective – how to differentiate them in practice? What is the role that lawyers have – i.e. when they agree and affirm the presence of a token of *opinio juris*, do they simply say

218 The data derives from a Google Scholar search 'opinio juris' conducted in December 2018, which returned 8,040 results for the period 2012–present; 7,950 results for the period 2000–2012; 1,660 for 1990–2000, and 1,320 for 1950–1990. The meaning of a Google Scholar search of this type is very restricted; it is used here for illustrative purposes only. Nevertheless, it helps emphasising that properly designed empirical research is necessary on this particular aspect.

219 J Weiler, 'Publish and Perish: A Plea to Deans, Faculty Chairpersons, University Authorities' (*EJIL: Talk! – Publish and Perish: A Plea to Deans, Faculty Chairpersons, University Authorities*, 2018), www.ejiltalk.org/publish-and-perish-a-plea-to-deans-faculty-chairpersons-university-authorities/, accessed 8 November 2018.

220 Weiler (n 219).

what law is or do they create law? Should we not openly acknowledge that any affirmation of a token of *opinio juris* always has a constitutive character of the *opinio juris* in question? If there is any possibility that affirmations of occurrences of *opinio juris* are having constitutive force, should we not clearly aim at studying this phenomenon and distinguishing the role that certain categories of international lawyers – e.g. those serving as judges in international courts and tribunals; those sitting in the International Law Commission – play in it? It seems that research on the topic is relevant beyond the limits of the legal research and scholarship – because it can throw light on aspects of collective intentionality and collective action. Let us not forget that the theory that Searle articulates, and on which I draw, remains contentious in many respects.[221]

5 Concluding remarks

In articulating a framework for the understanding of the role of international organisations in the formation of *opinio juris*, this work plays down the possibility that international organisations might be able to coordinate international processes in a manner to shape custom pursuant to desired standards. It seems clear that the challenges involved in the shaping of the *opinio juris* of the States are much greater than that those involved in the shaping their behaviour (which are complex in their own account). Throughout the work, submissions were made and points were raised which require further research. There are, however, three aspects that deserve being revisited albeit briefly – whether it is really the case that international organisations *should* have lawmaking capacity;[222] the *power* lawyers, notably those siting in organs of international organisations, have in ascertaining *opinio juris*;[223] and whether scholars themselves *are unconsciously* affected by certain worldviews and beliefs that international organisations help disseminate.[224]

An arm's-length approach seems to require caution as to the *formal* role that international organisations *should have* in the formation of *opinio juris*. Naïve assumptions about international organisations shaping *opinio juris* must be dealt with sceptically and submitted to proper, empirical validation. Especially as they lose, for different reasons, the appearance of 'neutral parties', it is far from clear the extension to which international organisations may offer any relief in shaping *opinio juris* in any form,

221 For all, *see* R Tuomela, 'Searle's New Construction of Social Reality' (2011) 71 Analysis Reviews 706.
222 *See* n 145 and accompanying text.
223 *See* n 210–18 and accompanying text.
224 *See* n 219–21 and accompanying text.

including pursuant to scientific models. A good question to start with is the extent to which a full-fledged lawmaking capacity would prove counterproductive to its intended objectives. International organisations play a role – this is undeniable. However, whether this role deserves being elevated to its fullest extent, as a lawmaking role, is far from clear – and it involves questions that go beyond international law. The affirmation that international organisations have the capacity to formally contribute to *opinio juris* is always an affirmation of power. There is a clear need for studies that openly question this power and subject it to in-depth analyses of its diverse implications.

Lawyers that occupy positions in international organisations enjoy a privileged position vis-à-vis their peers in States insofar as they benefit from the authority and legitimacy that the international organisation in question provides to address a varied range of subject-matters. In fact, their work – as judge or otherwise – deeply affects the ontological and epistemological approaches to *opinio juris*. There is a clear need to understand the depth of the processes that affect the emergence, within the scholarship, of ontological and epistemological understandings of *opinio juris*. Likewise, lawyers serving in international organisations have a higher degree of authority to establish occurrences of *opinio juris*. It appears that, although on very defendable grounds, the International Law Commission missed an important opportunity to address the role of lawyers in the process of affirmation of *opinio juris*.

Finally, there is the role that international organisations play in affecting the academic work on the topic. Study after study addresses both the theory and the practice of establishing and ascertaining *opinio juris* and its individual manifestations. How significantly are academic works on *opinio juris* affected by the lawyers that work within or under the umbrella of an international organisation? How deeply do the factors I describe above affect this academic activity? How much power do legal academics draw when articulating their approaches to *opinio juris*? How much power do they draw when affirming the existence of occurrences of *opinio juris*? In contradistinction, how much power do they renounce when accommodating what more authoritative voices, too often lawyers in international organisations, say? This latter question is particularly problematic – notably in a time when 'the teachings of the most highly qualified publicists of the various nations' seem to have lost much of the authority they once had. Operating in an environment that increasingly emphasises *efficiency*, be it in terms of number of publications, be it in terms of 'impact beyond the academia' – which is ascertained, to too great an extent, by the manner in which a scholarly work is taken over by *authorities* in the field – slowly, unconsciously and uncritically, legal scholars might be internalising misconceptions about the topic, and synchronising their voices towards uniform understandings of some fundamental aspects of *opinio juris* which, rather, require questioning.

Chapter 4

Beyond the either-or paradigm

*Lorenzo Gasbarri**

This chapter proposes a theoretical framework for the role of international organizations in the formation of customary international law that rejects their traditional conceptualization as double-faced entities. This debate, and the law of international organizations in general, is affected by the adoption of either a State-centric perspective or an organization-centric perspective.[1] Under the former, organizations are only forum for the development of the practice and the *opinio juris* of States; under the latter, the independence of the new entity reflects its capacity to autonomously contribute to the formation of customary international law. The aim of the following pages will be to describe an alternative framework able to reconcile these two faces of the same coin.

Consider this paradox: while certain institutional organs play a major part in the identification and application of customary law, they refuse to acknowledge the role of their organization. For instance, the International Court of Justice actively contributes to the identification of customary law while avoiding taking a stance on the role of the United Nations.[2] Similarly, the 2018 International Law Commission's conclusions on the identification of customary international law mention the contribution of the Commission itself only in the commentaries and privilege a

* The author would like to thank Jed Odermatt and Ralph Wilde for very valuable comments on the first draft of this chapter.

1 For instance, compare the organization-centric perspective adopted in this volume and the criticism it conveys against the State-centric perspective privileged by the International Law Commission. The two concepts of international organizations are analysed in Jan Klabbers, 'Two Concepts of International Organization' (2005) 2 International Organizations Law Review 277.

2 J Klabbers, 'International Organizations in the Formation of Customary International Law' in E Cannizzaro and P Palchetti (eds), *Customary International Law On the Use of Force* (Brill 2005). The case law of the International Court of Justice will be examined in section 2.

State-centric perspective.[3] Curiously, organs that actively engage in this relevant activity deny the same capacity to themselves and to their own institution.

The friction between the traditional role of States and the growing role of international organizations in the international community contributes to this paradox. Either organizations are considered as vehicles for member States, or they are considered as autonomous entities. This chapter analyses anomalies associated with the either-or paradigm in order to show the relevance of a third variable, concerning the characteristics of the rules of international organizations. The focus on the rules instead that on the subjects shows that is not convenient to distinguish between the practice of member states within the organization and the practice of the organization as such. The functioning of so-called 'objective regimes' will foster this perspective and finally describe the dual nature of international organizations and their role in the formation of customary international law.

The next section will first describe the either-or paradigm and its alternative in order to read, from this perspective, the work of the International Law Commission and of the International Court of Justice (1). Subsequently, the chapter will describe three 'anomalies' of this paradigm, concerning the development of so-called 'objective regimes' (2). Finally, the last section will propose a theoretical framework on the role of international organizations in the formation of customary international law that acknowledges their dual nature (3). The chapter ends with a few concluding remarks.

1 Setting the scene: the International Law Commission and the International Court of Justice

Upon the guidance of Special Rapporteur Sir Michael Wood, the International Law Commission adopted sixteen conclusions during its 70th session.[4] International organizations are involved on the basis of three variables. Two of them reflect the distinction between the State-centric and the organization-centric perspective,

3 International Law Commission, 'Identification of customary international law' (Report of the International Law Commission on the Work of its Seventieth Session, 2018) UN Doc A/73/10, 121–156, at 142. The International Law Commission decided not to include a conclusion on the role of its own output in the formation of customary international law. *See* International Law Commission, 'Identification of customary international law' (Report of the International Law Commission on the Work of its sixty-eighth Session, 2016) UN Doc A/71/10, 101. On the status of International Law Commission materials, *see* Chapter 10 in this volume.

4 International Law Commission, Identification of customary international law (n 3).

while the third one gives prevalence to the differences among organizations and among relevant instruments.[5]

Conclusions 6 (2), 10 (2), and 12 are founded on a conception of international organization limited by a State-centric perspective.[6] Under this conception, international organizations are transparent entities, within which member States act in an open international forum. For example, under conclusion 12 resolutions do not constitute the international practices of the organization but they are 'aggregates of expression of the volition of States'.[7] The State-centric perspective is used when the International Court of Justice decides only on the basis of the practice of member States within the organization and applying only external (international) limits of validity. In the first opinion on *Admissions* the Court described the United Nations Charter as a multilateral treaty,[8] while in 1950 it stated that the existence of an 'administrative practice' within the organization is not a decisive factor in ascertaining the rights and obligations of States deriving from a convention drafted and adopted by the General Assembly.[9] In one of the foundational decisions on

5 Similarly, under the project on subsequent agreements and subsequent practice in relation to the interpretation of treaties, the International Law Commission distinguished between the subsequent practice of the parties to constituent instruments of international organizations, the practice of organs of an international organization and a combination of practice of organs of the international organization of subsequent practice of the parties. *See* Georg Nolte, 'Third Report on subsequent agreements and subsequent practice in relation to the interpretation of treaties' (2015) UN Doc A/CN.4/683.

6 Conclusion 6(2): 'Forms of State practice include, but are not limited to: [...] conduct in connection with resolutions adopted by an international organization [...]'; 10(2): 'Forms of evidence of acceptance as law (*opinio juris*) include, but are not limited to: [...] conduct in connection with resolutions adopted by an international organization or at an intergovernmental conference'; 12: '1. A resolution adopted by an international organization or at an intergovernmental conference cannot, of itself, create a rule of customary international law. 2. A resolution adopted by an international organization or at an intergovernmental conference may provide evidence for establishing the existence and content of a rule of customary international law, or contribute to its development. 3. A provision in a resolution adopted by an international organization or at an intergovernmental conference may reflect a rule of customary international law if it is established that the provision corresponds to a general practice that is accepted as law (*opinio juris*)'.

7 B Conforti and A Labella, *An Introduction to International Law* (Martinus Nijhoff 2012) 42, 43. Quoted by Wood, 'Second report on identification of customary international law' (2014) UN Doc A/CN.4/672, 27.

8 Conditions of Admission of a State to Membership in the United Nations (Article 4 of the Charter) (Advisory Opinion) [1948] ICJ Rep 57 at 61.

9 *Reservations to the Convention on Genocide* (Advisory Opinion) [1951] ICJ Rep 15 at 25.

the formation of customary international law, *Military and Paramilitary Activities in and Against Nicaragua*, the Court adopted a State-centric approach in dealing with the role of resolutions in the formation of customary law.[10] Moreover, in *Legality of the Threat or Use of Nuclear Weapons* the Court considered that resolutions have value in providing evidence of emerging law.[11] More recently, in the *Whaling* case the Court considered that only resolutions 'adopted by consensus or by a unanimous vote … may be relevant for the interpretation of the Convention or its Schedule'.[12]

Conversely, conclusion 4(2) is based on a conception of international organization limited by an organization-centric perspective.[13] Under this view, organizations are not open international fora but autonomous actors. However, their role is considered by the International Law Commission as radically different from the one of States. First, the Commission did not include a specular provision for what concerns the forms of evidence of *opinio juris*, limiting the role of organizations in the formation of customary law to express practice. Second, it is conditioned to 'certain cases', implying that only some organizations or only some acts can partially contribute to the formation of customary law. The organization-centric perspective is used when the International Court of Justice decides only on the basis of the practice of institutional organs and applying only intra-systemic limits of validity. For instance, it is employed in the second opinion on *Admissions* in which the Court gave relevance to the consistent interpretation made by institutional organs.[14] The opinion on *Certain Expenses* adopts a clear organization-centric perspective, in which the Court recognized the special characteristics of the treaty establishing the United Nations, gave relevance to the 'practice of the Organization throughout its history' and established that 'each organ must, in the first place at least, determine its own jurisdiction'.[15] More

10 Military and Paramilitary Activities in and against Nicaragua (Nicaragua v United States of America) (Merits) [1986] ICJ Rep 14.

11 Legality of the Use by a State of Nuclear Weapons in Armed Conflict (Advisory Opinion) [1996] ICJ Rep 66 at para 70.

12 Whaling in the Antarctic (Australia v Japan: New Zealand intervening) (Merits) [2014] ICJ Rep 226 at para 46 e 83.

13 It reads '2. In certain cases, the practice of international organizations also contributes to the formation, or expression, of rules of customary international law'.

14 Competence of Assembly regarding admission to the United Nations (Advisory Opinion) [1950] ICJ Rep 4 at 9.

15 Certain Expenses of the United Nations (Article 17, paragraph 2 of the Charter) (Advisory Opinion) [1962] ICJ Rep 151 at 165 and 168.

recently, the importance of the 'accepted practice' of international organizations has been recognized in the *Wall* Opinion.[16]

The third variable that characterizes the role of international organizations in the formation of customary law deals with the differences in kind of organizations and in kind of practices. Indeed, conclusion 4(2) distinguishes 'certain cases' by reason of the variety of international organizations.[17] More concretely, the International Law Commission contends that it is only due to the supranational nature of the European Union that would allow it to contribute to the formation of customary law due to the attribution of exclusive competences that makes it similar to a State.[18] Moreover, conclusions 12 and 13 isolate particular acts, dealing with resolutions and decisions of international courts.[19] This is the perspective that will be adopted in the following pages, looking at the nature of the rules of international organizations and rebutting the either/or paradigm and its correlate necessity to focus only on some rules and on some organizations.

The 'rules' perspective is used by the International Court of Justice when it considers the dual nature of international organizations. Under this framework, the Court does not uphold the either-or paradigm, mixing the two points of view while focusing on the nature of the rule itself. When the rule is considered, the International Court of Justice does not clearly distinguish between the practice of member States within the organization and the practice of the organization as such. The advisory opinion on *Reparations* depicts the United Nations as an entity founded by a treaty, but possessing 'objective international personality'.[20] In its 1959 advisory opinion, the Court considered the practice followed by the Inter-Governmental Maritime Consultative Organization in carrying out the functions enshrined in the Inter-Governmental Maritime Consultative Organization's Constitution, but

16 Legal Consequences of the Construction of a Wall in the Occupied Palestinian Territory (Advisory Opinion) [2004] ICJ Rep 136 at 150, para 28.

17 M Wood, 'Third report on identification of customary international law' (2015) UN Doc A/CN.4/682, para 77.

18 J Odermatt, 'The Development of Customary International Law by International Organizations' (2017) 66 International and Comparative Law Quarterly 491.

19 'Conclusion 13: Decisions of courts and tribunals 1. Decisions of international courts and tribunals, in particular of the International Court of Justice, concerning the existence and content of rules of customary international law are a subsidiary means for the determination of such rules. 2. Regard may be had, as appropriate, to decisions of national courts concerning the existence and content of rules of customary international law, as a subsidiary means for the determination of such rules'.

20 Reparation for Injuries Suffered in the Service of the United Nations (Advisory Opinion) [1949] ICJ Rep 174 at 185.

it relied on the rules of treaty interpretation to declare the adopted decision as 'unconstitutional'.[21] Wording that implies the capacity of international organizations to contribute to the formation of customary law have been used in the 1971 advisory opinion on *Namibia*, in which the Court explicitly combined the practice of member States with the practice of the organization in order to rebut the thesis that abstention by a permanent member of the Security Council forms an obstacle to the adoption of a resolution: 'This procedure followed by the Security Council, which has continued unchanged after the amendment in 1965 of Article 27 of the Charter, has been generally accepted by Members of the United Nations and evidences a general practice of that Organization.'[22] In a similar vein, the Court discussed at more length, but also more cryptically, the relationship that organizations have with customary law in the opinion on the *WHO Headquarter Agreement*. Here it stated that organizations are bound by customary law, and, summarizing its findings, considered that the answer has been given considering general international law, treaty law, and the rules of the organization.[23] An explicit reference to the dual nature of international organizations is found in the two advisory opinions on *Nuclear Weapons*. In *Legality of the Use by a State of Nuclear Weapons in Armed Conflict*, the International Court of Justice described the WHO Constitution as being 'conventional and at the same time institutional', giving fundamental importance to the practice of the organization, and considering 'that the WHO, as a subject of international law, should be led to apply the rules of international law or concern itself with their development is in no way surprising'.[24] In *Legality of the Threat or Use of Nuclear Weapons*, moreover, General Assembly Resolutions are not treated as the product of member States alone.[25] While the formation of customary law is considered to be a matter of States' concerns, resolutions may provide evidence of the formation of customary law, both due to their content and the conditions of their adoption. In the *Kosovo* advisory opinion, the Court considers that Security

21 Constitution of the Maritime Safety Committee of the Inter-Governmental Maritime Consultative Organization (Advisory Opinion) [1960] ICJ Rep 150 at 169.

22 Legal Consequences for States of the Contitiued Presence of South Africa in Namibia (South West Africa) notwithstanding Security Council Resolution 276 (1970) (Advisory Opinion) [1971] ICJ Rep 16 at 22.

23 Interpretation of the Agreement of 25 March 1951 between the WHO and Egypt (Advisory Opinion) [1980] ICJ Rep 73 at para 48.

24 *Legality of the Use by a State of Nuclear Weapons in Armed Conflict* (n 11) at para 19 and 27.

25 *Legality of the Threat or Use of Nuclear Weapons* (Advisory Opinion) [1996] ICJ Rep 226, para 68–73.

Council Resolutions possess a dual nature, being international and constituting a territorial administration at the same time.[26]

To sum up, the International Law Commission conclusions distinguish three effects that international organizations have in the formation of customary law. From the State-centric perspective, what happens within international organizations is relevant insofar it can be recognized as State practice accepted as law. From the organization-centric perspective, some 'exceptional' organizations may provide practice (but not *opinio juris*) for the formation or expression of customary law. From the practice perspective, some acts and some organizations have a particular function in the formation of customary law. The following pages will adopt the third perspective, relying on the dual nature of the rules of international organizations, being at the same time internal and international.[27] In order to develop a theoretical framework on the role of international organizations in the formation of customary law focused on the law they produce, the next sections will first present 'anomalies' to the either/or paradigm. They will then introduce the concept of so-called 'objective regimes'.

2 Anomalies in international lawmaking

The will to formalize the mechanism in which customary international law is formed represents the need for stability of the international community.[28] Notwithstanding the best possible outcome of this effort, there will continue to be circumstances that do not clearly fit within the box. Anomalies play a fundamental role in the development of theoretical thought and produce constant changes.[29]

26 *Accordance with International Law of the Unilateral Declaration of Independence in Respect of Kosovo* (Advisory Opinion) [2010] ICJ Rep 403 at p 442, para 94. *See* also Hugh Thirlway, 'The Law and Procedure of the International Court of Justice 1960–1989: Part Eight' (1996) 67 British Yearbook of International Law 1 at 29; Michael Wood, 'The Interpretation of Security Council Resolutions' (1998) Max Planck Yearbook of United Nations Law 85.

27 L Gasbarri, 'The Dual Legality of the Rules of International Organizations' (2017) 14 International Organizations Law Review 87.

28 M Wood, 'First report on identification of customary international law' (2013) UN Doc A/CN.4/663 at para 16: 'The Special Rapporteur is of the opinion that the Commission should aim to describe the current state of international law on the formation and evidence of rules of customary international law, without prejudice to developments that might occur in the future.'

29 The term 'Anomaly' recalls its use in TS Kuhn, *The Structure of Scientific Revolutions* (4th edn, University of Chicago Press 2012).

One of the main reasons to create an international organization is to produce normative standards that apply to member States. Yet, activities of international organizations frequently expand in areas not covered by the consent to the founding treaty.[30] The theoretical dispute between the theory of the attributed/implied powers and the theory of inherent powers is a consequence of the two concepts of international organizations.[31] Similarly, many organizations tend to expand their powers in order to have normative force on third parties. The power to create rules binding third parties can be considered as deriving from the will of member States or from the independent will of the organization. When international organizations deal with non-member States, they can do so presenting themselves as autonomous entities or as instruments of member States. In both cases, there are circumstances in which third parties cannot do anything else than recognize the existence of new obligations and comply with them. The double nature of international organizations create these anomalies, constituting so-called 'objective regimes' that seek to adopt universal rules issued by permanent collective organs.[32] Objective regimes are presented as anomalous forms of lawmaking, useful to shed light on the relation that organizations have with customary international law.

At the outset, three examples will be presented: one concerning objective regimes created for the necessity of a geographical space; a second one concerning objective regimes created by the particular quality of an organization's source of law; and, finally, a third one concerning objective regimes created by the particular quality of an organization. Thus, section 4 will conceptualize the 'objective' nature of international organizations.

2.1 International Civil Aviation Organization binding over the high seas[33]

The first example concerns the competence of the International Civil Aviation Organization to regulate air traffic over the high seas.[34] The reason why this

30 C Tomuschat, 'Obligations Arising for States Without or Against Their Will (Volume 241)' in The Hague Academy of International Law (ed), *Collected Courses of the Hague Academy of International Law* (Publications of the Hague Academy of International Law, Brill 1993).
31 J Klabbers, *An Introduction to International Organizations Law* (3rd edn, Cambridge University Press 2015) 50.
32 F Salerno, 'Treaties Establishing Objective Regimes' in E Cannizzaro (ed), *The Law of Treaties Beyond the Vienna Convention* (Oxford University Press 2011).
33 I own this example to my very first meeting with Professor Jan Klabbers.
34 M Milde, *International Air Law and ICAO*, vol 4 (Eleven International Publishing 2008); Ludwig Weber, *International Civil Aviation Organization* (Wolters Kluwer 2007).

organization seeks to establish an objective regime comes from the particular status of the geographical space concerned.

The practical exigency of a uniform set of rules shared by members and non-members of the International Civil Aviation Organization Convention is self-evident and it is codified in Article 12 of the Chicago Convention, stating: 'over the high seas, the rules in force shall be those established under this Convention'.[35] Due to the absence of sovereignty over the high seas and for safety considerations, it is indispensable that all States conform to the same regulations without exceptions. This peculiar power to prescribe rules of civil conduct has been defined as 'meaningful' lawmaking.[36] It is the lawmaking power of the International Civil Aviation Organization Council to determine the international standards relating to the flights over the high seas. This competence derives from the will of the founding States that adopted the International Civil Aviation Organization Convention. In these circumstances, the need for a universal lawmaker was evident. Even if Article 12 of the Chicago Convention does not contain an explicit rule on the power to bind third parties, it intends to regulate a space which is not under the sovereignty of any party or non-party.

In 1944 the Chicago Convention was signed by fifty-two States, and, shortly after, scholars debated the legal basis of its peculiar lawmaking power.[37] The question was how a non-universal organization could regulate air traffic over waters not subjected to claims of sovereignty and under the freedom of overflight established by what today is article 87 United Nations Convention on the Law of the Sea. The main explanation relied on the objective existence of the organization as elaborated by the International Court of Justice in the *Reparation* advisory opinion, claiming that third States would be inclined to observe these rules for safety considerations.[38] However, there is an important theoretical difference between considering that an injured organization can present a claim against a non-member State and claiming that an organization can regulate the conduct of non-member States.

Rules of international organizations such as International Civil Aviation Organization regulations do not become opposable to third parties as general practice accepted as law. They are not instant custom. However, the power enshrined

35 E Yemin, *Legislative Powers in the United Nations and Specialized Agencies* (AW Sijthoff 1969) 146.

36 R Abeyratne, 'Law Making and Decision Making Powers of the ICAO Council: A Critical Analysis' (1992) 41 Zeitschrift fur Luft-und Weltraumrecht 387.

37 J Carroz, 'International Legislation on Air Navigation over the High Seas' (1959) 26 Journal of Air Law and Commerce 158.

38 *Reparation for Injuries Suffered in the Service of the United Nations* (above n 20) at 185.

in Article 12 could become customary law itself by the means of general practice accepted as law by international organizations as much as by States. It is article 12 of the Chicago Convention that could develop in a rule of customary law.

This example illustrates how the two concepts of international organizations interact. The International Civil Aviation Organization contributes to the formation of customary law both as an entity created by member States and by developing a kind of objective regime that derives from a rule of customary law. There is no distinction between the practice and the *opinio juris* of the member States within the organization and the practice of the organization itself. Today, the quasi-universal membership of the International Civil Aviation Organization demonstrates how costly it can be to remain outside the center of norms production.

2.2 The Security Council of the United Nations binding international organizations

The United Nations Charter contains a rule to deal with non-member States. Article 2(6) states: 'The Organization shall ensure that States which are not Members of the United Nations act in accordance with these Principles so far as may be necessary for the maintenance of international peace and security.' Furthermore, Article 39 attributes to the Security Council the power to decide the measures to maintain and restore international peace and security without distinguishing between members and non-members.[39] In this situation, the necessity to establish an objective regime does not derive from the needs of the territory concerned, but from the particular quality of the rules issued by the organization. The organization seeks to produce rules with universal effects in order to carry out its aims and principles.

The *travaux préparatoires* show that there was an intention to explicitly endow the organization with the power to take measures in regard to third parties.[40] The first circumstance in which the Security Council dealt with a third State was in 1946, in order to be ready to take all necessary measures concerning the situation in Spain.[41] In the case regarding the measures against Southern Rhodesia, Resolution 232(1966) 'urged' third States to act in accordance with the embargo, while Resolution 418(1977) against South Africa called 'all States' to adopt the measures. The expression entered

39 Art 39 United Nations Charter: 'The Security Council shall determine the existence of any threat to the peace, breach of the peace, or act of aggression and shall make recommendations, or decide what measures shall be taken in accordance with Articles 41 and 42, to maintain or restore international peace and security.'

40 United Nations Conference on International Organization 6, 722.

41 United Nations Security Council, *The Spanish Question*, 26 June 1946, S/RES/7 (1946).

the vocabulary of the Security Council and has been repeated consistently ever since, for example in the cases concerning Iraq,[42] Yugoslavia,[43] Serbia and Montenegro,[44] and Liberia.[45] Today, the expression 'all States' is justified by the rapid expansion of United Nations membership and it can be easily understood as a contraction of 'all member States'. However, until recently there were States, such as Switzerland, that adopted resolutions based only on their own will.[46]

In the development of practice, the Security Council started to refer to international organizations without facing any opposition and despite the absence of a reference in Article 2(6) of the United Nations Charter. The entire practice of the Security Council resolutions seeking to bind international organizations cannot be recalled here, and we will refer only to some examples extracted from its anti-terrorism agenda. Resolution 1333(2000) 'calls upon all States and all international and regional organizations, including the United Nations and its specialized agencies, to act strictly in accordance with the provisions of this resolution, notwithstanding the existence of any rights or obligations conferred or imposed by any international agreement or any contract entered into or any licence or permit granted prior to the date of coming into force of the measures imposed'.[47] Indeed, this resolution seeks to impose certain rules on third entities, and further establishes its hierarchical superiority over contrasting obligations, as Article 103 does for member States. Since then, similar provisions are constantly reiterated with different degrees of binding vocabulary. Often, but not always, the Council 'urges all States and encourages regional organizations', distinguishing between the two entities.[48]

Again, the legal bases that have been invoked to bind non-member entities derive from the two concepts of organization. If organizations are international fora, the conduct of member States is what really matters. Among the unexpected consequences of this conceptualization there is the fact that even if the European Union is

42 United Nations Security Council, *The Situation Between Iraq and Kuwait*, 2 August 1990, S/RES/661 (1990); United Nations Security Council, *The Situation Between Iraq and Kuwait*, 25 September 1990, S/RES/670(1990).

43 United Nations Security Council, *Socialist Federal Republic of Yugoslavia*, 25 September 1991, S/RES/713(1991).

44 United Nations Security Council, *Bosnia and Herzegovina*, 30 May 1992, S/RES/757(1992).

45 United Nations Security Council, *Liberia*, 19 November 1992, S/RES/788(1992).

46 Tomuschat (n 30) 256.

47 United Nations Security Council, *Measures Against the Taliban*, 19 December 2000, S/RES/1333 (2000).

48 United Nations Security Council, *On Strengthening Measures Against Al-Qaida*, 30 January 2004, S/RES/1526 (2004).

not formally bound by Security Council resolutions, the obligations of its member States could be claimed to be 'transferred' to the organization.[49] Conversely, if organizations are considered independent actors, they can only be bound by the development of a United Nations power to impose obligations to third entities. Indeed, it is the autonomous nature of the European Union legal system that can prevent the implementation of United Nations resolutions.[50] These two legal constructs are not acceptable if taken separately. On the one hand, member States cannot transfer their treaty obligations to the organization for the same reason that organizations cannot transfer their treaty obligations to their member States.[51] On the other hand, every organization could claim to be an order separate from international law for the purpose of enacting a different set of internal standards. Clashes between legal systems would not have a solution and they would only feed discussions on fragmentation.

The United Nations power to bind third entities in certain matters derives from a rule developed as general practice accepted as law. In order to bind third parties, the United Nations Charter (and not the resolution) must develop a rule of customary law. In general terms, the United Nations contributes to the formation of customary law due to this dual peculiarity of being founded by member States and at the same time being an entity with a legal basis in custom. The dual nature of international organizations focuses on the law they produce in order to overcome the either/or paradigm.

2.3 The European Union binding third parties

The last circumstance that will be described concerns the so-called 'supranational' nature of the European Union. The need for an objective regime is justified by the exceptional nature of the organization. Indeed, to claim exceptionalism in the law of international organizations is a way to deal with the existence of the two concepts. In short, exceptionalism means that only a few organizations (e.g. the EU) can be properly identified as independent actors of international law, while other organizations are fora for the conducts of member States.[52] The assumption is that

49 M Hirsch, *The Responsibility of International Organizations toward Third Parties: Some Basic Principles* (Martinus Nijhoff 1995) 49.

50 Joined Cases C-402–05 P and C- 415/05 P, Yassin Abdullah Kadi and Al Barakaat International Foundation [2008] ECR I-6351.

51 C Tomuschat, 'International Organizations as Third Parties under the Law of International Treaties' in E Cannizzaro (ed), *The Law of Treaties Beyond the Vienna Convention* (Oxford University Press 2011).

52 M Ličková, 'European Exceptionalism in International Law' (2008) 19 European Journal of International Law 463.

international organizations are all different, and when member States confer exclusive competences, organizations assume part of their sovereignty and they tend to become more similar to States in the exercise of those competences. However, this thesis on the existence of different kind, or different degrees of 'organizationhood', has unexpected consequences that affect third parties.

During the work of the International Law Commission on the project on the responsibility of international organizations, the European Commission repeatedly claimed the special status of the EU.[53] In particular, it demanded a special rule on the attribution of conduct that would reflect the fact that member States are quasi-organs in the exercise of EU exclusive competences. Consequently, the conduct of member States is claimed to be the conduct of the organization when implementing Union law. After a long debate, the International Law Commission rejected the need to codify this rule, leaving space to the *lex specialis* envisaged in the rules of each organization. One of the main reasons to refuse the codification of a rule on exclusive competences was that injured third parties cannot be affected by rules to which they are not party. Indeed, EU exclusive competences are not a black or white matter and there is a risk that responsibility for a wrongful act would be diluted in the different internal shades. If the conduct was attributed following internal rules, the EU would have the power to apportion its responsibility with a decision that would bind injured third parties.

If the EU is to be considered an international forum, the *pacta tertiis* rule would prevent the formation of a *lex specialis* for the attribution of conduct based on internal competences. Third parties could then claim their externality to the rules of the organization, unless they established so in an agreement. For example, the United Nations Convention on the Law of the Sea specifically considers that EU responsibility is attributed on the basis of its competences.[54] In this case, the *lex specialis* derives from the regime in which the organization and the third party operate, and not from the internal rules of the organization. Conversely, if the EU is considered an independent actor, it will act in the international community as a federal State. There is no need to rely on the *pacta tertiis* rule or on the *lex specialis* argument since internal rules that confer competences belong to a legal system which is no longer international.

53 International Law Commission, Responsibility of International Organizations, Comments and observations received from international organizations, UN Doc A/CN.4/545, A/CN.4/556, A/CN.4/568 and Add.1, A/CN.4/637.

54 T Treves, 'The European Community and the Law of the Sea Convention: New Developments' in E Cannizzaro, P Palchetti, and R Wessel (eds), *International Law as Law of the European Union* (Nijhoff 2002).

Again, both solutions are not satisfactory. The first one would prevent non-contractual damages to be repaired; the second one does not reflect the actual status of the organization. However, they can be both rebutted considering the dual nature of the organization and its interaction with customary law. In order to be an objective regime opposable to third parties, international organizations must rely on a customary rule. This customary rule could have different content depending on the organization and on the circumstances. The EU could claim that third parties are subjected to legal effects from its internal division of competences only if a norm of customary law emerged. This norm would be applicable to all states (save persistent objectors) and not only for those in a contractual relationship with the Union.

The European Union contributes to the formation of customary law as much as other international organizations, sharing with them the same dual nature. If the legal nature of international organizations is the same, there is no reason to consider its exceptional qualities as requiring a special power to provide for practice in the formation of customary international law.

To sum up, three examples have been provided in which the either/or paradigm does not explain the role that international organizations have in the formation of customary international law. By the means of three cases concerning the International Civil Aviation Organization's regulations, United Nations Security Council's resolutions, and European Union's competences, it has been shown that international organizations are at the same time the product of member States and of customary law itself. The next section will deal with the notion of objective regimes in order to assess the complex nature of international organizations.

3 Objective regimes of international organizations and why they matter

The intriguing relation between treaties, customs, and the rules of international organizations is the reason to deal with the controversial notion of objective regimes. The discussion will develop on the complex nature of international organizations in order to define their role in the formation of customary law.

The International Law Commission's Conclusion 12 (1) rejects the existence of so-called 'instant custom', stating that 'A resolution adopted by an international organization or at an intergovernmental conference cannot, of itself, create a rule of customary international law'.[55] While this is a relatively uncontested position, there are certain circumstances in which organizations seek to bind non-member entities.

55 International Law Commission, 'Identification of customary international law' (n 3) at 147.

Focusing on anomalies, this chapter rethinks the paradigm over which organizations are commonly studied.

Objective regimes are traditionally considered exceptions to Article 34 of the 1969 Vienna Convention on the Law of Treaties, codifying the maxima *pacta tertiis neque nocent neque prosunt*.[56] The main characteristic of objective regimes is their capacity to create 'situations' before which third parties do not have any other possibility than acknowledging their existence and to comply with their obligations. Before the codification of the law of treaties there was an active debate on the existence of this rule, often seen as a dangerous exception to the sovereign equality of States.[57] To mention only a few, Rousseau, Monaco, and McNair affirmed the existence of treaties with universal effects by reason of their fundamental and general importance in the creation of new institutions giving a particular status to territories.[58]

In the context of the International Law Commission, Sir Humphrey Waldock proposed to include the rule in the project on the law of treaties.[59] In order to be

56 Art 34 Vienna Convention on the Law of Treaties: 'A treaty does not create either obligations or rights for a third State without its consent.'

57 Malgosia Fitzmaurice, 'Third Parties and the Law of Treaties' (2002) 6 Max Planck Yearbook of United Nations Law 37.

58 Charles Rousseau, *Principles Generaux du Droit International Public* 2 (Pedone 1944) 452–84; AD McNair, *The Law of Treaties* (Oxford University Press 1961) 311.

59 Humphrey Waldock, 'Third Report on the law of treaties' (Yearbook of the International Law Commission Part II, 1964) UN Doc A/CN.4/167 and Add.1–3 at p 26: '1. A treaty establishes an objective regime when it appears from its terms and from the circumstances of its conclusion that the intention of the parties is to create in the general interest general obligations and rights relating to a particular region, State, territory, locality, river, waterway, or to a particular area of sea, sea-bed, or air-space; provided that the parties include among their number any State having territorial competence with reference to the subject-matter of the treaty, or that any such State has consented to the provision in question. 2. (a) A State not a party to the treaty, which expressly or impliedly consents to the creation or to the application of an objective regime, shall be considered to have accepted it. (b) A State not a party to the treaty, which does not protest against or otherwise manifest its opposition to the regime within a period of X years of the registration of the treaty with the Secretary-General of the United Nations, shall be considered to have impliedly accepted the regime. 3. A State which has accepted a regime of the kind referred to in paragraph 1 shall be — (a) bound by any general obligations which it contains; and (b) entitled to invoke the provisions of the regime and to exercise any general right which it may confer, subject to the terms and conditions of the treaty. 4. Unless the treaty otherwise provides, a regime of the kind referred to in paragraph 1 may be amended or revoked by the parties to the treaty only with the concurrence of those States which have expressly or impliedly accepted the regime and have a substantial interest in its functioning.'

'objective', a regime must fulfil three requisites: to be the intention of the parties; to concern territorial, maritime, or air space; and to fall in the territorial competence of one of the parties.[60] The existence of objective regimes has always been debated, either relying on the necessary consent of third parties,[61] or to its colonial legacy.[62] The International Law Commission rejected Waldock's proposal, but international practice showed the development of the phenomena in unexpected directions.

The particular relevance of treaties establishing boundaries or 'other territorial regimes' was considered in the 1978 Convention on Succession of States in Respect of Treaties.[63] Another frequent example is the international regime of 'the Area', subjected to the international sea-bed authority by the 1982 Montego Bay Convention as modified by the 1994 agreement.[64] Francesco Salerno compiled an exhaustive list of agreements dealing with an objective nature.[65] Examples of the notion have been considered in the context of the 1995 Agreement for the Conservation and Management of Straddling Fish Stocks and Highly Migratory Fish Stocks,[66] to

60 C De Casadevante Romani, 'Objective Regime' (2010) Max Planck Encyclopedia of Public International Law.

61 P Cahier, 'Le problème des effets des traités à l'égard des états tiers (Volume 143)' in The Hague Academy of International Law (ed), *Collected Courses of the Hague Academy of International Law* (Publications of the Hague Academy of International Law, Brill 1974) 589.

62 C Chinkin, *Third Parties in International Law* (Oxford University Press 1993).

63 Art 11: 'A succession of States does not as such affect: (a) a boundary established by a treaty; or (b) obligations and rights established by a treaty and relating to the regime of a boundary'; Art 12: '1. A succession of States does not as such affect: (a) obligations relating to the use of any territory, or to restrictions upon its use, established by a treaty for the benefit of any territory of a foreign State and considered as attaching to the territories in question; (b) rights established by a treaty for the benefit of any territory and relating to the use, or to restrictions upon the use, of any territory of a foreign State and considered as attaching to the territories in question. 2.A succession of States does not as such affect: (a) obligations relating to the use of any territory, or to restrictions upon its use, established by a treaty for the benefit of a group of States or of all States and considered as attaching to that territory; (b) rights established by a treaty for the benefit of a group of States or of all States and relating to the use of any territory, or to restrictions upon its use, and considered as attaching to that territory. 3.The provisions of the present article do not apply to treaty obligations of the predecessor State providing for the establishment of foreign military bases on the territory to which the succession of States relates'.

64 H Mosler, 'The International Society as a Legal Community (Volume 140)' in The Hague Academy of International Law (ed), *Collected Courses of the Hague Academy of International Law* (Publications of the Hague Academy of International Law, Brill 1980) 252.

65 Salerno (n 32).

66 JA de Yturriaga, *The International Regime of Fisheries: From UNCLOS 1982 to the Presential Sea*, vol 30 (Martinus Nijhoff 1997) 164.

protect certain species of fauna[67] or the environment,[68] to ensure international peace or disarmament,[69] to address drug trafficking,[70] to regulate international communications,[71] to define the status of the so-called maritime cemeteries,[72] and in the context of human rights treaties.[73]

Several theses have been proposed in order to describe the legal basis of objective regimes.[74] Simma, discussing the Antarctic treaty system, considered three main positions.[75] The first is based on a treaty law approach, considering objective regimes as an exception to the *pacta tertiis* rule. He disregarded this theory on the basis of the primacy of State's consent, and on the fact that silence of third parties cannot be taken as assent. The second possible legal basis was the 'public law theory', founded on the quasi-legislative power of certain States to develop a regime binding third States. Simma disregarded this theory in seven points, mainly concerning sovereign equality and incompatible circumstances surrounding the Antarctica treaty. Third and lastly, he described the 'subsequent practice approach', according to which the process of customary law, recognition, estoppel, and acquiescence can transform a contractual regime into an objective regime. He discarded this theory, and finally contested the objective nature of the regime as incompatible with the Antarctica treaty. On the theoretical background, there is the undisputed and unsurmountable thesis that the rules of international organizations do not create instant custom.

67 For example, the International Convention for the Regulation of Whaling of 2 December 1946; CL Carr and GL Scott, 'Multilateral Treaties and the Environment: A Case Study in the Formation of Customary International Law' (1998) 27 Denver Journal of International Law and Policy 313.

68 DM Ong, 'International Environmental Law's Customary Dilemma: Between General Principles and Treaty Rules' (2006) 1 Irish Yearbook of International Law 3.

69 T Schweisfurth, 'International Treaties and Third States' (1985) 45 Zeitschrift für ausländisches öffentliches Recht und Völkerrecht 653.

70 Cahier (n 62) 654–55.

71 JF Prevost, Les effets des traités conclus entre Etats à l'égard des Etats tiers (Dphil thesis, Paris, 1973), 424 *et seq.*

72 J Klabbers, 'Les cimetières marins sont-ils établis comme des régimes objectifs? A propos de l'accord sur l'épave de M/S Estonia' (1997) Espaces et Resources Maritimes 121.

73 MN Shaw, *International Law* (6th edn, Cambridge University Press 2008) 981.

74 SP Subedi, 'The Doctrine of Objective Regimes in International Law and the Competence of the United Nations to Impose Territorial or Peace Settlements on States' (1994) 37 German Yearbook of International Law 162 at 174.

75 B Simma, 'The Antarctic Treaty as a Treaty Providing for an Objective Regime' (1986) 19 Cornell International Law Journal 189.

The interactions between treaty law and custom make this last theory relevant for the purposes of this chapter. Article 38 of the 1969 Vienna Convention states that a rule set forth in a treaty may become binding upon a third State as custom.[76] It is a saving clause that seeks to avoid any conclusions on the formation of customary law.[77] Thus, it clearly differentiates the rule binding States parties to a treaty from the rule binding third parties as customary law, and it only concerns customary rules that are created after the stipulation of the treaty. Article 38 does not codify a process of formation of new customary law. It states that the development of custom is not excluded by the existence of a treaty.[78] Mark Villiger considered that objective regimes do not derive from conventional rules because treaties do not produce legal effects for non-parties. First, the non-party conforms to the rule due to its persuasiveness and, with the formation of customary law, 'the process of a written rule generating customary law is the closest approximation to true legislation offered by international law'.[79] Again, international organizations do not produce instant custom, but customary law could develop independently from it. This is the position of the International Law Commission, stating that resolutions may provide evidence for establishing the existence and the content of customary law.[80]

The complex nature of international organizations can be appreciated at this point after this brief description of the relation of objective regimes with the law of treaties and customary law. Indeed, a notion similar to objective regime was used by the International Court of Justice in its advisory opinion on *Reparations* in order to allow the United Nations to bring a claim against a non-member State. It considered that 'fifty States, representing the vast majority of the members of the international community, had the power, in conformity with international law, to bring into being an entity possessing objective international personality, and not merely personality recognized by them alone, together with capacity to bring international claims'.[81] Evidently, international organizations do not create objective

76 Art 38: 'Nothing in articles 34 to 37 precludes a rule set forth in a treaty from becoming binding upon a third State as a customary rule of international law, recognized as such.'

77 G Gaja, 'Article 38' in O Corten and P Klein (eds), *The Vienna Conventions on the Law of Treaties: A Commentary* (Oxford University Press 2011) 949.

78 ME Villiger, *Customary International Law and Treaties: A Study of Their Interactions and Interrelations, with Special Consideration of the 1969 Vienna Convention on the Law of Treaties* (Brill 1985) 183.

79 ibid 197.

80 International Law Commission, 'Identification of customary international law' (n 4) Conclusion 12(2).

81 *Reparation for Injuries Suffered in the Service of the United Nations* (n 20) at 185.

regimes in the sense considered by Special Rapporteur Waldock. However, there is an important similarity in the fact that third parties cannot easily deny the existence of a new entity. They are subjected to legal effects emanating from a treaty to which they are not party.

The interaction between the two concepts of international organizations explains how rules of international organizations do not form instant custom but they are opposable to third parties in certain circumstances. The State-centric concept applies insofar resolutions and other rules derive from the will of member States enshrined in the institutional treaty. Complementary, the organization-centric concept explains how the institutional treaty may develop a customary power to bind third parties by the means of its rules. International organizations contribute to the formation of customary law being entities that are founded on the will of member States and, at the same time, on customary international law itself. Finn Seyersted contended that if a law common to every organization exists, it must be found in customary international law.[82] However, his differentiation between internal and external law does not reflect the complex relation that organizations have with members and third States. It reproduces the dynamic of ambivalence, either focusing on what is internal from a State-centric perspective or on what is external for an organization-centric perspective. Conversely, the present focus on anomalies to this binary mindset exposes the nature of international organizations as dual entities.

4 Concluding remarks

The International Law Commission project on the formation of customary law has been described as a measure to contrast the fragmentation of international law.[83] Special Rapporteur Wood accords a fundamental role to the unity of the international legal system, relying on the assumption that 'it is neither helpful nor in accordance with principle ... to break the law up into separate specialist fields' and therefore 'the same basic approach to the formation and identification of customary international law applies regardless of the field of law under consideration'.[84] Yet, the International Law Commission project clearly differentiates between different subjects of international law and between different acts. If the Commission is looking for 'the same

82 F Seyersted, *Common Law of International Organizations* (Martinus Nijhoff 2008) 21.

83 L Gradoni, 'La Commissione del diritto internazionale riflette sulla rivelazione della consuetudine' (2014) 97 Rivista di diritto internazionale 667.

84 M Wood, 'Formation and evidence of customary international law' (2012) UN Doc A/CN.4/653, 5, para 22.

basic approach', the mechanism for the formation of customary law should be the same, even if the materials are disparate and coming from different subjects. The quality of an act that contributes to the formation of customary law should not be confused with the mechanism of its identification. Conclusion 6(3) states that 'there is no predetermined hierarchy among the various forms of practice', while the commentary recognizes that 'it may be that different forms (or instances) of practice ought to be given different weight when they are assessed in context'. The capacity to contribute to the formation of customary law is different even within the same category of acts: not many United Nations General Assembly resolutions had the same value of the Universal Declaration of Human Rights or the Declaration on Friendly Relations among States.[85] This does not mean that different resolutions should be subjected to different methods. Broadening the perspective, in the quest for the same basic approach different instruments should not be subjected to different methods. The risk is to confuse the variety of international subjects with the variety of materials that concur to the formation of customary law.

Jan Klabbers considered that the 'open-ended and intensely political nature of customary law doctrine in conjunction with the ambivalent position of international organizations' makes their role in the formation of customary international law a political battlefield.[86] Indeed, politics is the reason why institutional organs such as the International Court of Justice and the International Law Commission actively contribute to the formation of customary international law without acknowledging the role of their organization. Instead, this chapter focused on the dual nature of international organizations with the purpose of reconciling the doctrinal distinction between the State-centric and the organization-centric approaches.

The controversial notion of objective regimes was the starting point from which this chapter analyzed the relationship that organizations have with customary international law. International organizations are as much founded on customary international law as on treaty law, and this dual nature affects the law they produce. Every rule of every international organization is both the product of the conduct of member States and of the organization. The rulings of the International Court

85 Universal Declaration of Human Rights, UNGA Resolution 217A(III); Declaration on Principles of International Law Concerning Friendly Relations and Cooperation among States in accordance with the Charter of the United Nations, United Nations General Assembly Resolution 2625(XXV). *See* Rossana Deplano, 'Assessing the Role of Resolutions in the International Law Commission Draft Conclusions on Identification of Customary International Law' (2017) 14 International Organizations Law Review 227.

86 Klabbers, 'International Organizations in the Formation of Customary International Law' (n 3) at 195.

of Justice confirmed the dual quality of constitutive instruments and resolutions, showing how the Court does not privilege one of the two concepts of organizations, modifying their nature throughout its case law. Even in *Military and Paramilitary Activities in and Against Nicaragua*, the Court adopted a State-centric approach while stating that the United Nations Charter refers to pre-existing customary law, which continues to exist and it is not 'subsumed and supervened'.[87] Moreover, the Court states that customary law could have developed under the influence of the Charter, stressing that 'The essential consideration is that both the Charter and the customary international law flow from a common fundamental principle outlawing the use of force in international relations'.[88] International organizations are founded on treaty law and on customary law, with the consequence that the conditions posed by the Charter have to be respected even when the conduct is in breach of both customary law and the Charter.[89]

In conclusion, if the same basic approach to the formation of customary law is foreseeable, the dual nature of international organizations has to be acknowledged, rebutting special mechanisms for the practice of a particular organization or for certain rules within an organization. In practical terms, the role of international organizations in the formation of customary law can be described by a simplified framework. Rebutting the either-or paradigm means to rely on one conclusion only. The International Law Commission should have focused on the notion of 'rules of international organizations' and acknowledging that it is not convenient to distinguish between the practice and *opinio juris* of member States within organizations and the practice and *opinio juris* of organizations as such.

87 Military and Paramilitary Activities in and against Nicaragua (Nicaragua v United States of America) (n 10) para 176.

88 ibid para 181.

89 ibid para 200.

Chapter 5

Between anthropomorphism and artificial unity

Maiko Meguro

This chapter seeks to shed light on the role of non-State actors in custom-making processes. It does so by repudiating the dominant understanding of *opinio juris* and practice as they are found in the two-element variant of the doctrine of customary law that has informed practice and scholarship since the 1920s. It shows that dominant approaches to *opinio juris* and practice are indifferent to the role of non-State actors by virtue of constructions that are highly questionable.

Section 1 sketches out the dominant understanding of two elements of customary international law (1). Section 2 discusses the limitations of the dominant understanding of opinio juris by showing the extent to which the anthropomorphic concept of *opinio juris* fails to perform the functions assigned to it and denies any role to non-State actors (2). In section 3, the attention turns to practice which is the object of a much greater variety of approaches. This section particularly emphasizes the role of *domestic* non-State actors in the creation of international norms that shapes State practice. (3). This chapter ends with a few concluding remarks about the general implications of the approach promoted here for the doctrine of customary law as a whole (4).

Before proceeding with the arguments above, a caveat must be made. The purpose of this chapter is neither to solve all the problems commonly associated with identification of customary international law nor to repudiate the doctrine customary international law. Instead, this chapter, by shedding light to the role of domestic actors in making of international customary law and its consequences, extends an invitation for the readers to recognize the malfunctioning of the dominant approach of custom as a 'source' of international law, and suggests avenues to refresh international lawyers' reflections on customary international law.

1 *Opinio juris* and State practice in the dominant approach to customary international law

Despite the widespread scholarly inclination to extract the two-element variant of the doctrine of customary law from Article 38 of the Statute of the Permanent

Court of International Justice and the International Court of Justice, it can be defended that the two elements of custom, namely, practice and *opinio juris* are not a product of Article 38 but creation of the Permanent Court of International Justice.[1] Article 38(2) of the Statute of the Permanent Court of International Justice list custom merely as law applicable by the Permanent Court of International Justice under the terms of 'International custom, as evidence of a general practice accepted as law'. While the wording of 'a general practice accepted as law' allows an interpretation that 'a general practice' and 'acceptance as law' exist as separate elements,[2] the drafting process of Article 38 does not suggest there was discussion on what is meant by 'custom' nor attempt to distinguish between the two elements in accordance under the monolithic understanding of that time.[3] Instead, it was the Permanent Court of International Justice that first established the necessity of the two separate elements of custom in finding 'evidence of a general practice accepted as law'.[4] In particular, the Permanent Court of International Justice in the Lotus case in 1927 held that in identifying international custom, not only there is the practice of States (abstention) but also the practice must be 'based on their being conscious of having a duty to abstain'.[5] It is well-known that this two-element approach was perpetuated by the International Court of Justice.[6] According to this approach, and notwithstanding divergent scholarly positions on what is exactly meant by each element, there seems to be general agreement that State practice refers to the regularity of conduct by States with uniformity and generality[7] while *opinio juris* – the subjective element – is the recognition on the side of States that its conduct is in accordance with a sense of legal obligation. The two-elements approach has also been upheld by the International Law Commission in its work on the 'identification of customary international law' under the guidance of Sir

1 Jean d'Aspremont, 'The Decay of Modern Customary International Law in Spite of Scholarly Heroism' (2015) Global Community: Yearbook of International Law and Jurisprudence 8–10; James Crawford, 'The Identification and Development of Customary International Law (Keynote Speech at the ILA British Branch Annual meeting)' (2014) 3.

2 *See* for example, O Sender and M Wood, 'The Emergence of Customary International Law: Between Theory and Practice', *Research Handbook on the Theory and Practice of International Lawmaking* (Elgar 2016).

3 Christian Tams, 'Meta-Custom and the Court: A Study in Judicial Law-Making', *The Law & Practice of International Courts and Tribunals* (Brill, Nijhoff 2015). Also *see* d'Aspremont (n 1) 9.

4 SS 'Lotus' case, 1927 PCIJ (ser A) No 10, 18, 29; SS Wimbledon, 1923 PCIJ (ser A) No 1, 25.

5 SS 'Lotus' 28.

6 North Sea Continental Shelf case, 1969 ICJ Judgement, para 77.

7 For example, North Sea Continental case, and SS 'Lotus' case. Also Crawford (n 1) 5–6.

Michael Wood since 2012.[8] A few remarks on each of these two elements are warranted.

As far as the objective element ('State practice') is concerned, it must first be acknowledged that there is ambiguity in usage of term 'State practice', namely duplicative use of the term to describe the repetition of State conducts and the norm that shapes the repetition of State conducts. Behind the traditional dichotomy between State practice as physical acts and State practice as verbal acts, this fundamental distinction exists in the meaning of State practice. In this regard, the International Law Commission Conclusion states that State practice 'consists of conduct of the State, whether in the exercise of its executive, legislative, judicial or other functions',[9] and includes 'both physical and verbal acts'.[10] The same line of argument is also found in the International Law Association report on the formation of customary international law.[11] However, neither organization clearly defines what it means by 'State practice'.[12]

Another remark about State practice is in order. If identification of custom is a normative evaluation, what constitutes State practice as a component of custom should not be the repetition of conducts itself but the subjective reasoning that underlies the repetition. As will be discussed in section 3, the standard of identification could vary depending on which understanding courts and tribunals take with regards to State practice. This chapter will come back to this point.

As far as the subjective element (*opinio juris*) is concerned,[13] it should preliminarily be stressed that there are different understandings on the subjective element that leads to different theoretical and practical consequences to the question. First of all, the subjective element which the International Court of Justice, in the North Sea Continental Shelf case, construed as 'a belief' (or 'sense of legal duty') by States

8 International Law Commission, 'Identification of Customary International Law: text of the Conclusions: A/CN.4/L.872' (UN 2016). Conclusions: 2(3). 'Two constituent elements. To determine the existence and content of a rule of customary international law, it is necessary to ascertain whether there is a general practice that is accepted as law (*opinio juris*)'.

9 ibid Conclusion 5.

10 ibid Conclusion 6.

11 International Law Association, Committee on the Formation of Rules of Customary International Law, Final Report of the Committee: Statement of Principles Applicable to the Formation of General Customary International Law (2000) 14–15.

12 The proposed amendment in 2016 to Conclusion 4 ('Requirement of Practice') can be understood to put forward the practice as 'the norm'. *See* the Forth Report (2016), Annex, A/CN.4/695 and this formula is maintained in the amendment in 2018. *See* the Fifth Report (2018), Annex, A/CN.4/717.

13 *See* also Chapters 1 and 2 in this volume.

that 'this practice is rendered obligatory by the existence of a rule of law requiring it'.[14] Under this narrative, States can be considered to recognize that the legal obligation 'had already existed' at the certain time in the past before the conduct at issue.[15] Whereas this understanding of 'pre-existing law' has been criticized by the scholars such Hans Kelsen[16] and D'Amato,[17] the narrative remained as dominant. Under this narrative, the question 'how the customary legal obligation came into being' remains unsolved. Secondly, the subjective element is sometimes, albeit more marginally, understood as consent. Indeed, some scholars construe the subjective element as implicit agreement which transforms a rule of conduct into a legally binding norm of customary international law.[18] In the second understanding, contrary to the first understanding, the subjective element is construed as equivalent to legal identification of the customary norms. However, this position has been criticized for its artificiality in inferring consent from silent States since it fails to reconcile with the fact that the majority of States neither protect nor support the emergence of customary legal norms clearly. For instance, Mendelson rejects the 'consent' narrative as '(t)o say that all States gave their consent, in any normal sense of the word "consent", is simply untrue'.[19] While construction of *opinio juris* as consent is theoretically designed to provide a way to address the issue of legal identification, the reliance on the construction of tacit consent – in other words, 'acquiescence'[20] reinforces the narrative whereby 'States had come to accept' and thus the idea of *opinio juris* as a belief. Equating non-participation to giving a consent implicitly 'reduces general

14 North Sea Continental Shelf case, para 77.
15 Hans Kelsen, in Charles Leben and Doctrine Juridique (eds), *Hans Kelsen: Ecrits français de droit international* (Presses Universitaires de France 2001) 72; Raphael M Walden, 'The Subjective Element in the Formation of Customary International Law' (1977) 12 Israel Law Review 344, 357–59; Anthony D'Amato, *Concept of Custom in International Law* (Cornell University Press 1971) 47–48; Michael Akehurst, 'Custom as a Source of International Law' (1976) 47 British Yearbook of International Law 1, 32; Michael Byers, *Custom, Power and the Power of Rules: International Relations and Customary International Law* (Cambridge University Press 1998), 131.
16 Kelsen (n 15), especially 72–73.
17 D'Amato (n 15). D'Amato rejoins Kelsen while he recognizes rejecting the approach is 'difficulty of imagining all states', 263ff.
18 Gennady M Danilenko, 'The Theory of International Customary Law' (1988) 31 German Yearbook of International Law 9, 11; Walden (n 15).
19 Maurice Mendelson, 'The Subjective Element in Customary International Law' (1996) 66 British Yearbook of International Law 177, 185.
20 IC MacGibbon, 'Customary International Law and Acquiescence' (1957) 33 British Year Book of International Law 115.

acceptance to an obvious fiction, since the conclusion is presumed rather than proven'.[21] Lastly, the subjective element is sometimes equated to a community value to maintain orderly co-existence.[22] In this respect, some scholars argue that the reference to 'sive necessitatis' indicates that *opinio juris* includes the cases where practice is rendered necessary by the common popular sentiment.[23]

It is noteworthy that the International Law Commission did not clearly take any clear position and fell short to embrace any of the abovementioned understandings of *opinio juris*. Instead, the International Law Commission rephrased the old formula of 'the general practice be accepted as law (*opinio juris*)' in the context of two-element approach.[24] Being aware of the theoretical ambiguity and constrains in every position, the Special Rapporteur seems to have chosen a more pragmatic (and supposedly prudent) approach rather than going for an attempt to join the theoretical controversy by establishing an inclusive understanding of the subjective element as '(b)elief, acquiescence, tacit recognition, consent have one thing in common – they all express subjective attitude of States either to their own behavior or to the behavior of other states in the light of international law'.[25] In referring to the inclusive understanding of subjective element, Special Rapporteur Wood stated that '(w)hile the term *opinio juris* has undoubtedly become established in referring to this element, it is suggested that "accepted as law maybe the better term" '.[26] In the fifth report, he recognizes that there is still ongoing debate about whether 'the law' only concerns the sense of legal obligation or both legal obligation and legal rights.[27]

According to the author of this chapter, however, the International Law Commission's pragmatic approach to *opinio juris* is perplexing, particularly in the light of the purpose of the current work of the International Law Commission, 'identification of customary international law'. The International Law Commission's phrasing of Article 38 is not self-explanatory at all in this regard. For example, the

21 J Patrick Kelly, 'The Twilight of Customary International Law' (2000) 40 Virginia Journal of International Law, 473.

22 P Allott, 'The Concept of International Law' (1999) 10 European Journal of International Law 3; D'Amato (n 15) 71–72 (referring to scholars such as Raman and Cheng).

23 ibid 47–48 (referring to scholars such as Puchata and Savigny), 71–72 (referring to Sorenson and Kopelmanas).

24 The International Law Commission (n 8) Conclusion 9.

25 The Second Report on Identification of Customary International Law by Michael Wood, Special Rapporteur A/CN.4/672, ICL Sixty-sixth session (2014) para 67.

26 The Second Report (n 25) para 68.

27 The Fifth Report on Identification of Customary International Law by Michael Wood, Special Rapporteur A/CN.4/717, para 73, 76–77.

International Law Commission Special Rapporteur contends the term under Article 38 'goes a large way towards overcoming the *opinio juris* "paradox"'.[28] This *opinio juris* paradox is at the heart of the dominant approach whereby *opinio juris* is construed as the belief that the legal obligation 'had existed' at the time of State conduct. This construction has commonly been considered problematic. For instance, Kelsen famously contended it is redundant to have the second criteria of *opinio juris* since the States had already believed in the legal obligation when the conduct was made.[29] D'Amato described this redundancy as a tautology since customary international law that is created by State practice which must be preceded by the legal obligation.[30] What is more, this chronologically paradoxical relationship between State conducts and the legal obligation may cause a real problem when the customary norm emerges in a violation of existing customary norm.[31] The 'belief' approach would lead to the conclusion that customary international law cannot be modified once it is established, for any new norm emerges in violation of existing customary law.[32]

It is submitted here that the abovementioned paradox appears on the assumption that customary international law is produced spontaneously at an intangible point in the past. Given this uncertainty about the moment of crystallization, one cannot distinguish between the repetition of State conducts tied to emerging customary norms that should take place before the legal identification and the repetition of State conduct as implementation of customary international law in identification of customary international law. In regard to the crystallization, the International Law Commission approach seems to be equally avoiding the question of legal identification of customary international law as the dominant approach of *opinio juris*.

As already stated above, the scholarly construction on subjective element as a belief – and as a consent – are based on totally different understandings on identification of customary international law. Turning to the wordings of Article 38, 'accepted as law' is not at all self-explanatory on the issue of legal identification. Under Article 38's approach, the legal obligation remains presupposed as 'had been accepted' at the certain point of the past, thus there is no guidance on how norms of customary international law are identified. Under this approach, it is argued here that the question of legal identification of customary international law is treated as 'a black box' in the sense that emergence of new legal norms is completely circumvented by the narrative that States came to recognize the legal obligation to which they accord their conducts.

28 *Supra* note 25.

29 Hans Kelsen, 'Théorie du droit international coutumier', in Kelsen (n 15) 72.

30 D'Amato (n 15) 66, 73.

31 The Second Report (n 25) para 66.

32 For example, Byers (n 15) 130–33.

This chapter is not the place to continue to revisit the traditional criticisms of each of the two constitutive elements of customary international law. Nor is it the place to repudiate the doctrine of customary international law as a whole because of all the problems mentioned in this section. Abandoning the two-element variant of the doctrine of customary international law would be unrealistic let alone non-desirable.[33] Indeed, notwithstanding all these problems, customary international law continues to be central tool of functioning of international law.[34] As has been discussed elsewhere, custom has been considered as the primary source of international law in the early stage of international law for its 'universality' in application[35] while the treaty law could only bind the contracting States.

Instead, the next section focuses on one aspect of the discussion carried out in this section, namely what has been called the 'black box approach' to identification of custom by questioning its anthropomorphic foundation that informs the dominant understanding thereof. In articulating such a criticism, the next section revisits the dominant approach adopted by the International Court of Justice and the International Law Commission which both espouse the narrative of 'belief' or that of 'a general practice accepted as law'. It is submitted in the next section that a 'belief' or 'the general practice accepted as law' is a porous fiction created by some anthropomorphism that could undermine the entire international legal order by giving courts and tribunals immense power to create customary international law as needed. In doing so, it draws on the idea that the lawmaking process constitutes a consciously coordinated process within each a State by casting the light to the various actors behind the 'statehood'. It will be particularly shown that States' decisions to support the creation of certain legal norms are the result of domestic coordination among different actors at domestic level.

33 D'Amato who is known for his extensive research on the theories on customary international law, still could not entirely refute the concept of *opinio juris* despite all the theoretical problems including *opinio juris* paradox. He states 'in so far as the identification of existing customary law is concerned. Here, *opinio juris* is at worst a harmless tautology'. *See* D'Amato (n 15) 73. Also, Special Rapporteur Wood refers to the statement by Briggs regarding the problems of the subjective element as 'creates more difficulty in theory than practice' in his second report to the International Law Commission. *See* The Second Report, para 66.

34 D'Aspremont (n 1) 22.

35 H Lauterpacht (ed), *Oppenheim's International Law: Volume 1 Peace* (8th edn, Oxford University Press 1955) 6. The emphasis of universality is weakened in Robert Jennings and Arthur Watts KCMG QC (eds), *Oppenheim's International Law: Volume 1 Peace* (9th edn, Oxford University Press 2008) 4.

2 Anthropomorphism and the limitations of the dominant approach to *opinio juris*

This section takes issue with the anthropomorphism informing the dominant approach to *opinio juris*. Under the dominant approach, customary international law is construed as a product of a spontaneous form of law-ascertainment in contrast to the treaty making. Whereas the dominant proposition has been criticized by the wide range of scholars including those who tried to construe the subjective element as 'consent',[36] it has been found in the case-law of the International Court of Justice[37] as well as the current work of the International Law Commission. Under this position, the lack of formal legal identification is compensated by the concept of 'belief' or 'acceptance' that the conduct is according to the legal obligation.[38] It is submitted here that *opinio juris* understood as the subjective element or the psychological element[39] manifests an anthropomorphic pattern of legal thought.

Debates on anthropomorphism in international legal thought are not new.[40] While some scholarly debate exists about the scope and function of anthropomorphism in international law, there is general agreement that anthropomorphism is necessary in the practice of international law since the concepts such as 'will' of States constitute the very core of the dominant positivist theory of lawmaking. In this sense, a State is treated as a unitary personality – a normative being in the light of international lawmaking.[41] This been said, criticisms of anthropomorphism in

36 For example, Danilenko pointed out deficiency of Article 38 in the light of ascertainment under customary international law is 'largely caused by natural law theories' *see* Danilenko (n 18) 10.

37 Meldelson argues that the Permanent Court of International Justice and the International Court of Justice has not been clear about the nature of opinion juris – namely, consent or belief. *See* Mendelson (n 19) 180.

38 The argument of acquiescence also adopts the narrative 'States had come to accept' although it is understood as a variation of 'consent'. *See* section 1.

39 Mendelson (n 19) 177; S Talmon, 'Determining Customary International Law: The International Court of Justice's Methodology between Induction, Deduction and Assertion' (2015) 26 European Journal of International Law 433.

40 Jean d'Aspremont, 'The Doctrine of Fundamental Rights of States and Anthropomorphic Thinking in International Law' (2015) 4 Cambridge Journal of International and Comparative Law 516.

41 For example, Kelsen claims the concept of State as purely normative one, stating 'the state is not a visible or tangible body', Hans Kelsen, 'General Theory of Law and the State', translated by Anders Wedberg (Harvard University Press 1949) 191. In this comment, Kelsen had Jellineck's sociological concept of statehood in his mind. For Jellineck,

customary law are not unheard of. For instance, D'Amato[42] and Akehurst[43] advocate the position that States do not have minds of their own like natural persons since States are institutions consisting of various organs and actors. However, these criticisms overlook the role of fiction in international legal practice. This section takes issue with the anthropomorphism of the doctrine of customary international law, and more specifically the fiction this anthropomorphic pattern is built on. This is the fiction according to which States may have positions which can be described as 'thoughts' or 'intention'. In doing so, this section will show how such legal fiction impacts the recognition of the role of non-State actors in customary lawmaking.

In taking issue with the usage of fiction of anthropomorphism in customary international law, the notion of fiction must be spelled out first. Fiction in general is a legal device whose use is unavoidable in the legal system since the legal system cannot be perfect – there is always a possibility of a situation that existing legal rules do not cover. In other words, fiction could treat an existing fact as if a different fact followed by the different legal effect. An example of legal fiction[44] under international law is diplomatic protection where injury suffered by an individual is treated 'as if' injury to the individual's national State.[45] While there is some debate on possible scope and function of fiction, it is widely accepted that fiction provides harmless simplification or transformation of the facts to fit into the existing legal system rather than announcing a vacuum of law.[46] In the context of international lawmaking, whilst the respective decision by the constituents

this sociological concept co-exist with the legal concept 'a State as a legal person (Körperschaft)' (G Jellineck, *Allgemeine Staatslehre* (O Häring 1900) 173 and 183).

42 D'Amato (n 15) 35–39.

43 Akehurst (n 15) 36–37.

44 In the context of domestic law, inheritance by an unborn child is often referred to as an example. While legal capacity is only given to the child at the moment of birth, an unborn child is treated as if the child has already been born with regard to inheritance in many legal systems. Without legal fiction, the child who is not born at the time of inheritance cannot be an inheritor since he or she lacks legal capacity to do so.

45 A Vermeer-Künzli, 'As If: The Legal Fiction in Diplomatic Protection' (2007) 18 European Journal of International Law 37.

46 In general, *see* J Salmon, 'The Device of Fiction in Public International Law' (1974) 4 Georgia Journal of International and Comparative Law; LL Fuller, 'Legal Fictions' (1930) 25 Illinois Law Review 363. The issue of legal personality bears a controversy between 'a fiction' or 'a conceptual fact' – however, for the sake of this chapter, the term 'fiction' is understood in the wider sense to the issue of legal personality. As to this controversy, Fuller states that it is as a matter of terminology, 372–73. Also *see* Bryant Smith, 'Legal Personality' (1928) 37 The Yale Law Journal 283, 292–93.

of a State does not fit in the State-centred international legal framework, if these decisions are treated collectively, the device of fiction can make it possible to be treated as if it is a decision by a unitary personality of State – a subject of international law. While the usage of fiction is widely accepted among legal practice and scholarship, the important thing to note here is fiction cannot generate legal effect out of 'nothing'. In the abovementioned example of diplomatic protection, for a State to exercise the right of diplomatic protection, the corresponding fact that their national was injured must be established. In the same vein, for a State to be perceived as having a 'will' through the fiction of anthropomorphism, there must be a corresponding outcome of decision-making participated by the State organs and entities. In other words, the State will cannot exist where the decision-making among the State organs and entities does not take place. As a general statement, the fiction of anthropomorphism is based on the above premise.

According to the argument made here, the mainstream understanding of *opinio juris* can be considered to be based on a fiction. In constructing *opinio juris* as 'belief' or 'unintentional recognition', courts and tribunals, for instance, have presupposed that the belief by States amounts to 'a position' on the international scene, possibly originating in a domestic political process. In other words, the very fiction at work behind the subjective element pertains to the question of the formation of *opinio juris*, that whether a State can form a position 'unintentionally'. By virtue of the idea that a State has come to recognize a legal obligation without formal acceptance, the fiction boils down to the idea that State position to accept a legal obligation is possibly formed spontaneously. The fictitious character of this construction is confirmed by the fact that not much scholarly attention has been paid to formation of such 'subjective element'. It is argued here that paying more attention to the formation of *opinio juris* allows one to show that the fiction of *opinio juris*, as is commonly understood, lacks the very premise required for the fiction of anthropomorphism.

To articulate the claim that *opinio juris* is a fiction built on a wrong premise, it is necessary to recall the variables that can possibly shape the formation of State positions in international relationship. Scholars of international relations (hereafter, IR) and political studies have put forward two main models to explain the behaviours of States: (i) the traditional normative *statehood* model and (ii) the *social actor* model.

The normative model of the State, which construes a State as an independent and unitary person, constitutes the basis of the mainstream understanding of consent in international legal scholarship. This model views 'international or external forces' (i.e. balance of powers, international reputation, membership to the community etc.) as the key variables to explain State positions. However, as has been widely pointed out, this model relies heavily on the fiction of anthropomorphism as States are institutions consisting of various organs and actors.[47] While some scholarly debate exists about the scope and function of anthropomorphism in international law, there is general agreement that anthropomorphism is necessary in the practice of international law since the concepts such as 'will' of States constitute the very core of the dominant positivist theory of lawmaking.[48] This anthropomorphism is sustained by a fiction – according to which States have positions which can be described as 'thoughts' or 'intention' by States in international legal practice.

In contrast, the social actor model has its primary focus on the individuals and private groups that are behind the 'veil of the state', which has been created by the fiction of anthropomorphism discussed here. For the social actor model, the preferences and interests of these actors is the crucial variable while international/external forces are subordinated.[49] This model is the core framework of the liberal IR theory as the primacy of demands by domestic actors for formation of a State position is the basic premise in explaining international relations. This liberal theory rests on the view that the demands of individuals and societal groups at domestic level has more significance than the influence of the international environment in the decision-making by States. This argument will even be pushed further by virtue of the concept of 'audience cost'[50] – the penalty imposed by the domestic public in cases where the political leaders fail to meet their demands (i.e. likelihood of facing

47 From this perspective, D'Amato and Akehurst criticized the personalization of statehood that states do not have mind of their own like natural persons. Anthony D'Amato, *Concept of Custom in International Law* (Cornell University Press 1971), 35–39; M Akehurst, 'Custom as a Source of International Law' (1976) 47 British Yearbook of International Law 1, 36–37.

48 J d'Aspremont, 'The Doctrine of Fundamental Rights of States and Anthropomorphic Thinking in International Law' (2015) 4 Cambridge Journal of International and Comparative Law 516.

49 For liberalism thinking, *see* e.g. A Moravcsik, 'Taking Preferences Seriously: A Liberal Theory of International Politics' (1997) 51 International Organization 549; F Hoffman, F Hoffman, and A Oxford, 'International Legalism and International Politics', *The Oxford Handbook of the Theory of International Law* (2016); J Ruggie, 'International Regimes, Transactions, and Change: Embedded Liberalism in the Postwar Economic Order' (1982) 36 International Organization 379.

50 The concept of 'audience cost' is originally developed by Fearon in the context of threat. *See* JD Fearon, 'Domestic Political Audiences and the Escalation of International Disputes' (1994) 88 The American Political Science Review 577. For the empirical studies from the institutional perspectives, *see* G Tsebelis, 'Decision Making in Political Systems: Veto Players in Presidentialism, Parliamentarism, Multicameralism and Multipartyism' (1995) 25 British Journal of Political Science 289; BB de Mesquita et al, *The Logic of Political Survival* (The MIT Press 2004).

electoral consequences,[51] losing the necessary support to stay in power[52] etc.) in a wide range of political regimes[53] is indicated by various political studies. The threat of audience costs suggests various domestic actors come to influence the determination of international legal bindingness regardless of the formal authority of decision-making under the domestic law. The abovementioned social actor model is crucial in understanding the collective characteristic of the consent by States in international lawmaking. This perspective posits that creation of legal bindingness is possibly conducted in such ways that could be explained by the social network of organs and actors connected by interest. This assumption is not totally alien to the international legal scholarship. In tandem with the development of the argument on expanding subjects of international law,[54] the international legal scholarship came to focus on the liberal State–society relationship where social actors bargain, negotiate, and fight in making, applying, and verifying particular international legal rules.[55]

Yet, there is a strong limitation to the social actor model. The existing studies on the social actor model remain to spell out their argument from the dichotomy between 'the State' and 'the society', which creates a sort of black box effect on the

51 Earlier in 1980s, the rational choice theory was also built upon the nature of legislators to avoid conflicts with the potential voters under the desire to be re-elected. *See* J Buchanan, 'Politics Without Romance: A Sketch of Positive Public Choice Theory and Its Normative Implications' in J Buchanan and R Tollison (eds), *The Theory of Public Choice – II* (University of Michigan Press 1984) 11–13; RD Tollison, 'Public Choice and Legislation' (1988) 74 Virginia Law Review 33, 341–44; Also in general, D Farber, 'A Public Choice Theory and Legal Institutions' (Social Science Research Network 2014) UC Berkeley Public Law Research Paper No 2396056, http://ssrn.com/abstract=2396056.

52 G Tsebelis, *Veto Players: How Political Institutions Work* (Princeton University Press 2002), also Tsebelis (n 50). These arguments were also tested against the authoritarian regime where the political authority is dominated by the state leader *see* JL Weeks, 'Autocratic Audience Costs: Regime Type and Signaling Resolve' (2008) 62 International Organization 35; O Chyzh, 'Can You Trust a Dictator: A Strategic Model of Authoritarian Regimes' Signing and Compliance with International Treaties' (2014) 31 Conflict Management and Peace Science 3.

53 For example, Weeks (n 53); Chyzh (n 53).

54 For example, J Alvarez, *International Organizations as Law-Makers* (Oxford University Press, 2005), K Raustiala, 'States, NGOs, and International Environmental Institutions' (1997) 41 International Studies Quarterly 719.

55 *See* for example, MS McDougal, 'Law as a Process of Decision: A Policy Oriented Approach to Legal Study' [1956] Faculty Scholarship Series Paper 2464. Also, the recent attempt to illustrate the non-State actors between 'law-maker' and 'law-taker', *see* M Noortmann and C Ryngaert (eds), *Non-State Actor Dynamics in International Law: From Law-Takers to Law-Makers* (Routledge 2013).

concept of 'the State'.[56] On the other hand, the 'State' also consists of various actors with different interests such as the political parties or the ministries. These governmental actors are largely influenced by the elements such as balance of powers, international reputation, membership of the community apparent in the *normative* statehood model.

The perspective given by the above models suggests that formation of a State position should be construed as a consciously coordinated process among relevant domestic actors rather than belief ('spontaneously come to be bound'). The social actor model enables to shift the focus to the process behind the veil of the State – the process in which the interests of domestic actors motivate the State to accept or reject the legal bindingness of international norms. Meanwhile, it must be acknowledged that the State is not only motivated by the domestic interests – the State entities are also influenced by the various factors in international relations such as diplomatic reputations or external pressures as has been informed by the normative model of the State based on traditional IR studies. The decision-making on the creation of legal bindingness must be construed as interaction between international and domestic levels which involves different motivating factors for the State entities as a focal point of this interaction. What seems a State position is a result of internal negotiations among the governmental actors with different interests – or raison d'être, and the large part of political decisions by such governmental actors is closely worked out with various social actors.

Since acceptance of international legal obligation influences the interests of the various domestic actors, the argument here is that a State cannot spontaneously come to be bound by a legal obligation without pre-coordination among the different interests, otherwise such legal obligation cannot be implemented or the political leaders are punished by domestic actors (the audience cost).

In coordinating different interests, the domestic actors in the process are at least conscious with respect to what interest they may gain or lose as a result of creating a new international legal obligation. Acceptance of legal obligation through *opinio juris* should instead be construed as the result of careful political coordination among domestic actors. A State would not come to accept a legal obligation and secure the support by domestic actors if it cannot be specified when and how the State is bound by a legal obligation.

A useful illustration of the foregoing can be provided here. The domestic control over the State decision in international lawmaking is increasing as the substance of international law has come to cover the issues which directly influence the interests of domestic actors such as environment, trade and investment, control of chemical

56 *See* general i.e. Moravcsik (n 50).

substances, food safety. In terms of treaty making, when the pre-existing coordination does not reach a compromise, it is very difficult to conclude a treaty for procedural difficulty (i.e. Parliament approval), and substantial domestic punishment (i.e. audience cost). For example, the Clinton administration faced bipartisan opposition to the ratification of the Kyoto Protocol when President Clinton signed the Protocol at COP3. Before COP3 started, it was clear that the Senate opposed a treaty that would create a competitive burden on the US economy because such a treaty allowed developing countries not to commit to binding targets.[57] Whilst the Clinton administration and the environmental interest groups such as non-governmental organisations seem to have believed they could use the outcome of international negotiations to persuade Congress into ratification in future,[58] this estimate proved to be wrong. The Bush administration formally withdrew from the Protocol in 2001 because domestic support needed for its ratification depended on the participation of developing countries which could not be achieved under the Kyoto Protocol.[59]

According to the argument developed in this section, the common narrative of 'unintentional' or 'spontaneous' acceptance of legal obligation by States – which has been recalled in section 1 – should thus give way to a new understanding, namely the *consciously coordinated* process among relevant domestic actors. While the anthropomorphism is a necessary fiction in international law, the function of fiction is only to treat something that fits ill with the existing legal framework as if it were 'something' that fits well in the existing legal framework. It cannot generate 'something' out of nothing. In the specific case of custom making, a State would not 'accept' the creation of a legal obligation without the actors at domestic level recognizing such creation. Thus, the fiction of *opinio juris* as a belief – or as an unintentional, unconscious, or even inferred acceptance – rests on a wrong premise.

3 Artificial unity and the limitations of the dominant approach to practice

As was argued in the previous section, the formation of a State position in the international lawmaking processes should be construed as the outcome of a *consciously*

57 *See* Byrd-Hagel Resolution, Senate Resolution 98, 105th Congress (1997) (Passing the resolution 95–0).

58 David Hunter, 'International Climate Negotiations: Opportunities and Challenges for the Obama Administration' (2009) 19 Duke Environmental Law & Policy Forum 255.

59 Press Release by White House, President Bush Discusses Global Climate Change (11 June 2001) available at https://georgewbush-whitehouse.archives.gov/news/releases/2001/06/20010611-2.html, accessed 28 May 2017.

coordinated process among relevant domestic actors. Hence, it was submitted in the previous section that the dominant approach to construe the emergence of customary international law as being based on an unconscious and spontaneous form of law identification is a fiction built on wrong premises. This section turns to the other element of customary international law, namely State practice. It is argued in this section that the emergence of international organizations and instruments strengthen the role of domestic actors in creating international norms that shape State practice. In doing so, this section plays down the common criticisms – referred to in section 1 – as to the artificial unity built around unconnected State conducts by virtue of deductive reasoning.[60]

Contemporary channels of norm-making at the international level helps illustrate the point that the criticisms pertaining to artificial unity may be overblown. In particular, international organizations and other institutional instruments – which are now active with respect to most issues of international relations – play a crucial role in the making of the norms that can potentially shape State practice,[61] especially by collecting information and offering a common ground for State acts which used to exist in disparity, through the decision-making process of resolutions, issuance of guidelines, and other policies to promote convergence of State acts. In many international organizations, decision-making bodies such as committees under the United Nations or Conference of Parties under multilateral environmental treaties (hereafter MEAs) are core instruments in accelerating the emergence of new international norms. In this process, these instruments act as focal points of various actors including member States, experts, and, if needed, representatives of the civil society in exchanging information, enhancing mutual understanding, and standard-setting in the fields. These arenas of cooperation transformed international norm creation from zero-sum collision of different practices to an institutionalized and continuous process that enables to form and modify the norms flexibly according to the fast-developing international situations and constant feedback from the participating actors.

The consequences for custom-making are dramatic. Under these instruments and institutional arrangements international norms that shape the State practice are continuously nourished by formal instruments such as resolutions, decisions, or

60 For example, Robert Kolb, 'Selected Problems in the Theory of Customary International Law' (2003) 50 Netherlands International Law Review 119. *See* also Chapter 7 in this volume.

61 The formalization and institutionalization of international norm making by IO is also discussed by S Droubi in 'The Role of the United Nations in the Formation of Customary International Law in the Field of Human Rights' (2017) International Community Law Review 19, 70.

guidelines. This formalization of norm creation by international instruments, despite the growing visibility of non-State actors at the international level, enabled member States to keep the grips on shaping and accepting international norms by their formal decision-making power at the organizations and the instruments, and arguably contributed to reinforcing the influence of the domestic actors behind statehood curtains. It is in this sense that it can be contended that the margin of possible artificial unity in identification of State practice (international norms) by courts and tribunals is increasingly diminished in contemporary identification of customary international law. Hence, the common criticisms about artificial unity come to be overblown.

An illustration of the contribution of such institutions and instruments to the creation of norms that shape State practice must now be provided. This contribution is especially salient in the field of environment. As has been discussed elsewhere, the increasing participation of international non-governmental organizations contributes to enriching the content of norms by providing technical information, assisting the process of negotiations, or improving State compliance by surveillance under environmental legal regime.[62] Also, the emergence of international norms often starts with the introduction of established domestic practice. For example, the principle of 'precautionary action' which was originally administrative law concept in countries like Germany, was not known at the international level until it was introduced by the German representatives as a 'requirement for a successful environmental policy for the North Sea ecosystem'[63] during the North Sea Conference. It is reconfirmed under the United Nations Environment Program with regard to marine pollution,[64] and even in the wider context, i.e. air pollution by the preamble

62 Raustiala (n 55), Also Raustiala, 'States, NGOs, and International Environmental Institutions' (1997) 41 International Studies Quarterly 719; W Schoener, 'Non-Governmental Organizations and Global Activism: Legal and Informal Approaches' (1997) 4 Indiana Journal of Global Legal Studies 537; E Enge and R Malkenes, 'Non-Governmental Organizations at UNCED: Another Successful Failure' (1993) 25 Green Globe Yearbook of International Co-operation on Environment and Development; K Raustiala, 'Nonstate Actors in the Global Climate Regime' in Luterbacher and Sprinz (eds), *International Relations and Global Climate Change* (MIT Press 2001); PJ Sands, 'Environment, Community and International Law, The' (1989) 30 Harvard International Law Journal 393.

63 Lothar Gundling, 'The Status in International Law of the Principle of Precautionary Action The North Sea: Perspective on Regional Environmental Co-Operation: Part 1: The International North Sea Conferences in Perspective' (1990) 5 International Journal of Estuarine and Coastal Law 23, 23–24.

64 As to the negotiation process under the UNEP and North Sea Conference, *see* James Cameron and Juli Abouchar, 'The Precautionary Principle: A Fundamental Principle of

of Montreal Protocol in 1987 and United Nation Convention on Climate Change in 1992 as a general principle. While uncertainty remains as to the status of the precautionary approach under the international law,[65] emergence of the above process accelerated international recognition of the precautionary approach as a norm of international environmental cooperation.

The foregoing bears another important consequence. Emphasizing the role of domestic actors through the central role of States in international norm making matters a great deal because the informality of identification strengthens the discretion of courts and tribunals in finding the elements of customary international law as discussed in section 2. Whereas there is general agreement that international norm making has undergone pluralization in actors and arenas, non-State actors have not yet fully obtained a grip over formal norm making since non-governmental organizations are often only observers without voting rights to the formal decision-making in the instruments of international organizations.[66] The general tendency of international lawyers to empower non-governmental organizations bears the risk of obscuring the locus of power in the creation of international law. This being said, the informality in norm identification has provided a flexibility that has been instrumental in the success of the customary international law in the international legal order. However, this flexibility, in the end, functions to delegate the norm creating power to courts and tribunals by creating 'artificial unity' among unlinked State

Law and Policy for the Protection of the Global Environment' (1991) 14 Boston College International and Comparative Law Review 1; Gundling (n 64).

65 There are authors who see the approach as customary international law or general principle of law while others define them as international principles of environmental policies. For the former position, *see* O McIntyre and T Mosedale, 'The Precautionary Principle as a Norm of Customary International Law' (1997) 9 Journal of Environmental Law 221; the latter view is Cameron and Abouchar (n 65).

66 For example, the United Nations Framework Convention on Climate Change limits the right to vote is only for State parties. Observers do not have the right to vote unless at least one-third of the parties present at the session object. (*See* The draft rules of procedure (FCCC/CP/1996/2), Rule 7). Scholars also pointed out the retained States' grip on international lawmaking – *see* Duncan Hollis, 'Why State Consent Still Matters – Non-State Actors, Treaties, and the Changing Sources of International Law' (2005) 23 Berkeley Journal of International Law 137; J d'Aspremont, 'Non-State Actors in International Law: Oscillating between Concepts and Dynamics'; GB Goff, 'NGO's Perspective on Non-State Actors' in J d'Aspremont (ed), *Participants in the International Legal System: Multiple Perspectives on Non-State Actors in International Law* (Routledge 2011). *See* also the reports of the International Law Association Committee on Non-State Actors (2005–2016), www.ila-hq.org/index.php/committees.

activities.[67] In this regard, the emergence of international organizations is transforming the formation of State practice to more transparent and conscious processes by systemising interaction between the decision-making at the international level and the domestic level.

In these processes, these actors continuously interact, bargain, coordinate, and negotiate in shaping and verifying the norms at the heart of State practice through resolutions, decisions, guidelines, and various political recommendations. What must be noted here is that the role of international organization on state practice, or international norm making, should not be mixed with the questions pertaining to conferral of legal bindingness,[68] which has been treated in section 2.

4 Concluding remarks

The previous sections have challenged the dominant approaches to *opinio juris* and State practice, and the constructions by virtue of which the role of non-State actors in custom-making is obfuscated. At this final stage, it is submitted that the criticisms voiced here also bear more wide-ranging consequences for the doctrine of customary international law as a whole. Three general implications of the arguments developed in this chapter should be mentioned. It is hoped that the realization of the following implications will help refresh international lawyers' reflections on customary international law.

First of all, the discussion above has helped elucidate the deception that accompanies the notion of *opinio juris*, and the underlying assumption of unintentional acceptance of legal obligation by States. The concept of *opinio juris* is at the core of identification of customary international law. Contrary to treaty law, which is only binding among contracting States, customary international law is to be applied to a wider number of States without formal announcement of intention to be bound. This informal form of customary law identification was necessary especially at the beginning of formation of international legal order, to provide overarching structure among partial contractual agreements among a small number of States. As mentioned in the previous sections, the International Law Commission maintained the traditional informality of identification despite acknowledging the theoretical leakiness. However, such construction of the subjective element as 'a belief' or 'acceptance as law' that the legal obligation 'existed' at the time of State conducts is rather unconvincing. The 'unconscious' 'spontaneous' construction is

67 *See* Chapter 7 in this volume.

68 d'Aspremont, 'Non-State Actors in International Law' (n 67) 468.

contradicted by strong empirical arguments regarding the formation of a State position. Clarification of the deception in the dominant narrative of *opinio juris* invites the lawyers and legal practitioners to rethink the design of identification of customary international law. For customary international law to perform the functions assigned to it and to remain a central tool of functioning international legal order, it is necessary to move beyond the current usage of legal fiction that accompanies *opinio juris*.

Second, the perspective adopted here bears important consequences in relation to the central role of courts and tribunals in customary international lawmaking. The *opinio juris* construction, by deploying a fiction built on wrong premises, enables court and tribunals to affirm the existence of legal norms in circumstances in which there was no sense of obligation within States. As already indicated, unconscious acceptance of legal obligation as presupposed by the traditional *opinio juris* narrative cannot be established. This vacuum provides courts and tribunals unverifiable power to create law through the narrative that courts and tribunals identify customary international law which States recognized without knowing themselves. The International Law Commission and its Special Rapporteur, by reconfirming this 'unconscious acceptance' approach, reinforce the suspicion of 'judicial legislation' through customary international law.

Last but not least, the discussion conducted here has shown that 'custom' may even not constitute a source of international law properly so called. 'Custom' can be a source of international norms but this still is short of a convincing system of law-ascertainment. There is little indication that such international norms are necessarily recognized as having an obligatory nature. These norms still need to be ascertained as law. Yet, as has already been argued in the previous sections, such system of law-ascertainment proves frail in the case of customary international law. While there seems to be a consensus about increasing convergence of State conducts in various areas of international law, this idea of convergence of conducts provides only a scaffold but falls short of elevating international norms around which State practice is articulated into a proper source of international law. In order to make sense of 'custom' as a source of international law, a system of law-identification must be designed as to recognize the essential role of domestic actors in the formation of a State position in custom-making.

Chapter 6

Custom as the product of successful argumentative campaigns

Fabian Cardenas

The influence of non-State actors in international law is almost uncontested.[1] It is commonly recognized that non-State actors have definitely revolutionized the traditional State-centric perspective of international law as they have permeated multiple international legal dynamics and institutions.[2] Accordingly, non-State actors are nowadays addressees of rights and obligations contained in international treaties[3] and customary law,[4] they have appeared before international courts,[5] they have promoted massive international summits that have led to the adoption of influential treaties[6] and declarations that have promoted customary principles,[7]

1 *See* e.g. International Law Association, 'Sofia Conference – Non State Actors' (2012).

2 *See* e.g. art 4(1) (i) of the United Nations Framework Convention on Climate Change or Art Vol (2) of the Agreement Establishing the World Trade Organization.

3 *See* e.g. D Murray, 'How International Humanitarian Law Treaties Bind Non-State Armed Groups' (2015) 20 J Conflict Sec L 101; A Clapham, *Human Rights Obligations of Non-State Actors* (Oxford University Press 2006).

4 J Marshall, 'Torture Committed by Non-State Actors: The Developing Jurisprudence from the Ad Hoc Tribunals' (2005) 5 Non-State Actors & Intl L 171.

5 *See* e.g. S Baughen, 'Customary International Law and Its Horizontal Effect? Human Rights Litigation Between Non-State Actors' (2015) 67 Rutgers U L Rev 96.

6 *See* e.g. the ICRC and other six NGOs involved in anti-mine campaigns united to form the International Campaign to Ban Landmines (ICBL), which led to The Convention on the Prohibition of the Use, Stockpiling, Production and Transfer of Anti-Personnel Mines and on their Destruction, known informally as the Ottawa Treaty. MA Cameron, BW Tomlin, and RJ Lawson (eds), *To Walk Without Fear: The Global Movement to Ban Landmines* (Oxford University Press 1998).

7 *See* e.g. the Declaration on the Elimination on the Discrimination Against Woman and its drafting committee. J Connors, 'NGOs and the Human Rights of Women in the United Nations' in P Willetts (ed), *'The Conscience of the World': The Influence of Non-Governmental Organisations in the UN System* (Brooking Institution 1996); BK Woodward, *Global Civil Society in International Lawmaking and Global Governance: Theory and Practice* (Martinus Nijhoff 2010).

they have triggered unilateral actions of States,[8] and their conduct can sometimes be attributed to States in terms of international responsibility.[9]

And yet, there is no consensus as to whether non-State actors can actually make or contribute to the making of customary international law. It is the aim of this chapter to shed some light on the matter by showing that, by nature, it would not be possible to provide a precise answer to those questions from traditional perspectives.[10] Indeed, this chapter is predicated on the idea that the contribution of non-State actors in the making of customary international law will always depend on the theoretical standpoint of the observer. This is why this chapter consciously introduces a social perspective in order to situate the argument. It is from this perspective that this chapter argues that customary international law is not the outcome of practice and *opinio juris* but the product of successful argumentative campaigns finally accepted by the community of international lawyers.

In order to develop the argument, non-State actors will initially be contextualized within the orthodox perspective of customary international law which essentially claims for exclusion (1). Special regard will be given to the conclusions of the International Law Commission, considering that nowadays it has one of the leading voices on the matter (2). Subsequently, and with the purpose to relativize the orthodox two-element approach as reused by the International Law Commission, an inclusive perspective regarding the role of non-State actors in customary international law will be presented in order to show how a specific outcome would always be perspective dependent; this reflection aims to detach the discussion from a sense of correctness in international law in order to shift to a discourse of perspectives (3). While exposing some inadequacies of the foregoing perspectives, this chapter finally proposes an alternative perspective that instead of focusing on *opinio juris* and practice (either excluding or including the contributions of non-State actors), sees customary international law as the

8 *See* e.g. regarding terrorism SC Res 1624, UN Doc S/RES/1624 (2005) [Threats to international peace and security (Security Council Summit 2005)] or the adoptions of various anti-terrorism conventions. N Gal-Or, *International Cooperation To Suppress Terrorism* (Croom Helm 1985).

9 *See* e.g. Arts 8 and 9 of the Articles on Responsibility of States for Internationally Wrongful Acts YB of the ILC (2001) Vol II, Part 2.

10 In words of d'Aspremont, it would be necessary to 'unlearn some common tropes'. *See* Chapter 7 in this volume. In this particular regard Hollis states: 'the international lawyer cannot yet dispense with the question of what makes international law "law" and where one looks to find it'. D Hollis, 'Why State Consent Still Matters: Non-State Actors, Treaties, and the Changing Sources of International Law' (2005) 23 Berk J Intl L 137.

product of successful argumentative campaigns, possibly including the views of non-State actors, according to the acceptance made by the community of international lawyers, who in its turn, is the final ascertainer of the source and the one who determines whether to include non-State actors' input on a case by case basis (4).

1 Customary international law's orthodox perspective and the place of non-State actors in it

The orthodox perspective of customary international law[11] would not only prioritize the two-element approach[12] but it would also circumscribe practice and *opinio juris* exclusively to that of States,[13] anchored in a classic view of international law as a juridical order regulating the relations (only) between States.[14] Although the referential clause contained in Art. 38 1 (b) of the International Court of Justice Statute does not specify whose practice and whose acceptance as law is to be looked upon, the Court's jurisprudence and dominant scholarship has interpreted it as being limited to the practice and opinio of States.[15] The International Court of Justice has affirmed on this regard that 'it is of course axiomatic that the material of customary international law

11 Although this is referred as the 'dominant understanding' by Meguro in Chapter 5, I agree that the two-element characterization or any other conceptualization of customary international law at the end is just a discourse, an approach, and a construction out of many possible. Therefore, it would not be possible by definition to find the right criteria of customary international law identification. It explains why I will be referring to Art. 38 definition just as a 'perspective'. On this regard, *see* Chapter 5 in this volume.

12 M Shaw, *International Law* (7th edn, Cambridge University Press 2014) 51. An opposite view of the two-element approached has been presented by P Haggenmacher, 'La Doctrine des Deux Éléments du Droit Coutumier dans la Jurisprudence de la Cour International' (1986) 90 Revue Générale du Droit International Public 5.

13 Contemporary reflections based on State-centric perspectives are still popular. This is the approach given later in this book by Antal Berkes, 'De facto regimes in the formation of custom', at Chapter 17, where the author defends the incidence of those actors in the making of customary international law not because of their own capacity but because, in particular circumstances, their conduct could be considered State practice.

14 M Wood, 'Second Report on Identification of Customary International Law', UN International Law Commission (2014) para 33. *See* also C Walter, 'Subjects of International Law', *MPEPIL* (2007).

15 An account of the orthodoxy is found in J Klabbers, '(I Can't Get No) Recognition: Subjects Doctrine and the Emergence of Non- State Actors' in J Petman and J Klabbers (eds), *Nordic Cosmopolitanism: Essays in International Law for Martti Koskenniemi* (Brill 2003).

is to be looked for primarily in *the actual practice and opinio juris of States*';[16] and that 'the Court must satisfy itself that the existence of the rule in *the opinion juris of States* is confirmed by practice'.[17] The Court has in fact emphatically assured that it is '*State practice from which customary international law is derived*'.[18] Therefore, according to this widespread view although the role of non-State actors in international law may be influential as a whole, the lawmaking capacities, as far as customary international law is concerned, is exclusively bestowed in the State.[19] In any case, it should be kept in mind that this view is anchored in the traditional approach developed by the Court jurisprudence that interprets Art. 38 1 (b) of the Statute, which is highly controversial, being the source of biases to the role of non-State actors within customary international law lawmaking.[20] Both the wrong assumption that customary international law departs from Art. 38 of the International Court of Justice Statute and the artificiality of the two-element approach are discussed more extensively in this book.[21]

On the other hand, more recent perspectives, rooted in the orthodoxy, have stuck to the priority role of the State on the identification of customary international law but without denying the impact that non-State actors may have.[22] These approaches

16 *Continental Shelf Case* (Libyan Arab Jamahiriya v. Malta), Merits, Judgment, ICJ Rep 1985, 29–30, para 27. (Emphasis added).

17 Military and Paramilitary Activities in and against Nicaragua (Nicaragua v United States of America), Merits, Judgment, ICJ Rep. 1986 (June 27), p 14, para 184. (Emphasis added).

18 Jurisdictional Immunities of the State (Germany v Italy: Greece Intervening), Judgment, ICJ Reports, 2012. p 99, para 101. (Emphasis added).

19 International Law Association, 'London Conference – Statement of Principles Applicable to the Formation of General Customary International Law' 16; GM Danilenko, *Law-Making in the International Community* (Martinus Nijhoff 1993) 84; K Wolfke, *Custom in Present International Law* (2nd edn, Martinus Nijhoff 1993); AC Arend, *Legal Rules and International Society* (Oxford University Press 1999) 176; J d'Aspremont, 'Conclusion: Inclusive Law-Making and Law-Enforcement Processes for an Exclusive International Legal System' in J d'Aspremont (ed), *Participants in the International Legal System* (Routledge 2011) 425, 430.

20 Absolute reliance on the International Court of Justice Statute as regards customary international law is disputable. Among others it could be said that: the two-element approach is not present in the clause but it was developed by the Court's jurisprudence; its only purpose is to regulate inter-State relations, particularly of the signatories; it is wrongly worded as it should be rather 'general practice accepted as law' the evidence of customary international law and not the other way around; it suffers from a chronological paradox because the acceptance as law cannot appear until custom has already developed; the clause is so vague that it also suffers from evidentiary problems.

21 In the same vein *see*, among others, Chapters 3, 4, 5, and 7 in this volume.

22 T Buergenthal and S Murphy, *Public International Law in a Nutshell* (5th edn, West 2013) 75.

believe that although the lawmaking capacity will always finally remain in the State, non-State actors may indirectly influence, promote, or shape the will and action of the State 'through inspiration and pressure, or formally when empowered by States'.[23] So, although the input that non-State actors could have is not disregarded, its influence will always depend on the validation by the State.[24] In other words, non-State actors could matter for the identification of customary international law but solely 'through State approval or adoption'.[25] Thus, non-State actors can contribute to the formation of any of the two elements of customary international law, because they boosted practice or helped the State achieve acceptance. However, it is the State which decides whether to be influenced by non-State actors, considering that 'there is no general right of non-State participation in the formation of international law'.[26]

To illustrate, it could be said that non-State actors promoted the adoption of the International Criminal Court Statute which nowadays contains some rules that may be descriptive of customary international law,[27] notwithstanding they were influential just because States decided it so. In the same vein, there is no doubt that the 1992 Rio Declaration –which was prompted by non-State actors– contains principles of environmental law that are currently considered customary international law,[28] nonetheless such principles emerged as customary international law just because States

23 This argument is sustained along this volume. *See* for instance Chapters 15, 18, and 19 in this volume. *See* also J d'Aspremont, 'International Law-Making by Non-State Actors: Changing the Model or Putting the Phenomenon into Perspective?' in M Noortmann and C Ryngaert (eds), *Non-State Actor Dynamics in International Law: From Law-Takers to Law-Makers* (Routledge 2010); N Carrillo-Santarelli, 'The Possibilities and Legitimacy of Non-State Participation in the Formation of Customary Law' (2017) 19 Intl Comm L Rev 98.

24 For example, one can see Carrillo-Santarelli's main thesis 'argued, a) some actors, namely international organizations, can contribute in the shaping of custom in connection with their functions; b) States can *ad hoc* empower non-State actors without the capacity to do so to participate in the formation of custom; c) States can make non-State conduct as theirs in the formation of custom; and d) because non-State actors can have a relevant indirect influence in custom'. ibid 103. *See* also: M Wood, 'Second Report' (n 15) para 45.

25 International Law Association Sofia Report (n 1) 5.

26 Carrillo-Santarelli (n 23) 103.

27 For instance, the ICRC has recognized some of its content as part of customary international law regarding IHL J-M Henckaerts and L Doswald-beck, *Customary International Humanitarian Law – Vol I Rules* (2009). Rule 90.

28 F Cardenas, 'Customary International Law as an Argumentative Framework: An Alternative Theoretical Approach in International Environmental Law' (PhD thesis, Pontificia Universidad Javeriana 2016) 347.

considered the proposal acceptable and decided to back them up with State practice and *opinio juris*.[29] Despite how large the non-State actor's influence may be, from this view, it is the State as a primary subject of international law which has the final say.

2 The International Law Commission's orthodoxy

The International Law Commission, led by Special Rapporteur on the Identification of Customary International Law, Sir Michael Wood, in one of the most contemporary and influential studies on customary international law, has decided to stay aligned with the orthodoxy. Thereby, and despite scholarly criticisms,[30] the International Law Commission not only decided to repeat and reuse the two-element approach to customary international law as recognized in the early jurisprudence of the Court and described in the most traditional textbooks of international law, but kept the State-centric approach to customary international law, arguing the impossibility for non-State actors to take part in the formation of customary international law. Within its initial conceptualization along the conclusions, the International Law Commission seemed to have decided to leave the matter open by concluding that 'to determine the existence and content of a rule of customary international law, it is necessary to ascertain whether there is a general practice that is accepted as law',[31] without specifying whose practice and whose acceptance.

Notwithstanding, in conclusion four, it was detailed that 'the requirement of a general practice, as a constituent element of customary international law, refers *primarily to the practice of States* that contributes to the formation, or expression, of rules of customary international law'.[32] One could wonder whether the International Law Commission intended to leave the matter unresolved when it decided not to specify that it was exclusively the practice of State rather than 'primarily' the practice of States. However, the discussion was set when it was specified that this window

29 Carrillo-Santarelli (n 23) 108. 'NSAs can not only influence practice, but also opinio juris, when inspiring, prompting or pressurizing States to come up with certain discourses and to convince them that a given practice is or ought to be mandatory.'

30 Just to mention one example, note that with a few exceptions, almost all the academic contributions made in this book present critic approaches to the International Law Commission Conclusions.

31 Conclusions on identification of customary international law, with commentaries, International Law Commission, seventieth session, in Yearbook of the International Law Commission, Vol II, Part Two, 2018. At Conclusion 2.

32 ibid Conclusion 4, para 1; Wood 'Second Report' (n 15) para 33 (Emphasis added).

of opportunity was left only for the sake of international organizations (IOs) under particular circumstances,[33] when it was affirmed that 'in certain cases, the practice of international organizations also contributes to the formation, or expression, of rules of customary international law',[34] accentuating that '*conduct of other actors is not practice that contributes to the formation, or expression, of rules of customary international law*, but may be relevant when assessing the practice referred to in paragraphs 1 and 2'.[35]

This conclusion admits that, for the International Law Commission, non-State actors may be influential in international law as a whole and in customary international law though indirectly, but categorically denies their probable participation in the making or expression of customary international law. In fact, the commentaries to this conclusion are emphatic when it is declared that:

> [T]he conduct of entities other than States and international organizations – for example, NGOs, non-State armed groups, transnational corporations and private individuals – is neither creative nor expressive of customary international law. As such, their conduct does not serve as direct (primary) evidence of the existence and content of rules of customary international law. The paragraph recognizes, however, that such conduct may have an important indirect role in the identification of customary international law, by stimulating or recording practice and acceptance as law (opinio juris) by States and international organizations. For example, the acts of private individuals may sometimes be relevant to the formation or expression of rules of customary international law, but only to the extent that States have endorsed or reacted to them.[36]

As for the requirement of *opinio juris*, it should be noted that the International Law Commission's conclusions express that 'the practice in question must be undertaken with a sense of legal right or obligation',[37] so considering that it is linked to the previous requisite of practice, it could be inferred that it refers 'primarily' to the *opinio juris* of States as well.[38] This is later reiterated when further conclusions on *opinio juris* are exclusively concerned with States.[39]

33 Commentaries to draft Conclusion 4 include more detailed explanations of what is meant by IOs and under which circumstances their practice may be relevant for the identification of customary international law, which denotes that international organisations' acceptance remains in any case exceptional. International Law Commission 'Identification' (n 32) Conclusion 4 and Commentaries.
34 ibid Conclusion 4, para 2. (Emphasis added).
35 ibid para 3. (Emphasis added).
36 ibid Conclusion 4 and Commentaries, para 8.
37 ibid Conclusion 9.
38 ibid Conclusion 15. 'Persistent Objector' is also related to the objection of State.
39 ibid Conclusion 10 and 15.

Therefore, without giving much surprise it could be summarized that the International Law Commission has simply stuck to the orthodoxy both on the conception of customary international law and the participation of non-State actors. According to this view the role of non-State actors remain secondary and their participation in customary international law may be only exceptionally useful when backed up by the State, who remains the supreme and formal lawmaker of international law. In fact, the International Law Commission's conclusions seem to be a reiteration of what the International Law Association had earlier concluded in this regard in the 2012 Sofia Conference when it settled that non-State actors:

> [C]an contribute *indirectly* to the formation of customary international law. Although unlike the *direct, formal* role played by governmental practice (that is, States through their organs and instrumentalities, and to a lesser extent, IGOs), NSA practice does not count in the formation of customary international law, it can constitute material, historical or indirect 'sources' for rules of international law.[40]

In its turn, it should be stressed that the findings of the International Law Association were not completely new either but they had been already influenced by some previous scholarly developments that had already proposed a rethinking of the classic State-centred approach giving due regard to the undeniable expansion *ratione personae* of international law but without granting them lawmaking powers. In this vein, it is worth quoting what d'Aspremont had argued in 2010 when he affirmed that:

> There is no doubt that, whatever the influence of these non-State actors may be, States remain the exclusive international law-makers. The upstream influence wielded by some non-State actors can help ignite new law-making initiative or orientate ongoing law-making undertakings but this is insufficient to elevate these actors to the status of law-makers. Indeed, no formal international law-making powers have been bestowed upon these actors and States always retain the final word.[41]

It would be enough so far to highlight that the importance of describing what the most standing perspective on customary international law and non-State actors purports, lies not only in the need to establish a conceptual point of departure but in the fact that it pretty much remains – with minor turns – the most accepted discourse, although nowadays this orthodoxy does not necessarily remain the mainstream which is being doctrinally superseded by alternative views. This scenario of theoretical reflexion can be evidenced not only in the most recent work of the International Law Commission but also within the discussions contained in this volume.

40 International Law Association (n 1) 6.

41 J d'Aspremont, 'International Law-Making by Non-State Actors' (n 23) 178.

3 The contestation of the orthodoxy: inclusive approaches to non-State actors' contribution to customary international law

Despite of what the orthodox perspective sustains, this section shows that there can also be divergent approaches that not only deny the appropriateness of the two-element approach as a whole,[42] but also that challenge the State-centrism of customary international law.[43] Hence, just as the foregoing exclusive perspectives reject the participation of non-State actors as customary lawmakers, there are inclusive perspectives that contend quite the opposite. This section thus demonstrates that views like the International Law Commission's remain just possible – not necessarily correct – discourses.

According to inclusive views, usually formulated from empirical groundings,[44] the influence of non-State actors should be somehow taken into consideration, as it could constitute a direct component in the identification process of customary international law. The reasons behind such consideration vary, but they are usually based on the transformation of the concept of subjectivity in international law, the practical consequences derived from the allocation of rights and obligations, the need for coherence, the strengthening of legitimacy, or simply because realities demand.

On the one hand, it could be affirmed that these perspectives did not appear spontaneously, but they have been doctrinally developed as a result of the subjecthood diversification in international law.[45] Thus, as it is increasingly accepted that international law can no longer be defined as a juridical order regulating the relations (exclusively) between States,[46] but rather, as a juridical order regulating the relations between its subjects – as a more embracing gender – these views deem it necessary to expand the spectrum beyond the State, in order to consider the inevitable role of IOs and other 'State-empowered bodies' as well

42 Haggenmacher (n 12); CJ Tams, 'Meta-Custom and the Court: A Study in Judicial Law-Making' (2015) 14 L & Prac Intl Courts & Trib 51. There are diverse challenges to the two-element approach in this volume. *See* Chapters 3, 5, and 7 in this volume.

43 Other chapters of this volume depart from the inadequacy of a strict State-centric approach, *see* e.g. Chapters 1, 2, 9, 18, and 19 in this volume.

44 From an effect-based approach *see* Chapter 19 in this volume.

45 'I argue further that customary acceptance of the international legal personality of MNEs has also developed into international law, as a result of the vast number of investment treaties to this effect now in force.' RF Hansen, 'The International Legal Personality of Multinational Enterprises: Treaty, Custom and the Governance Gap' (2010) 10 Global Jurist 1.

46 MN Schmitt and S Watts, 'Beyond State-Centrism: International Law & Non-State actors in Cyberspace' (2016) 21 J Conflict & Sec L 595.

as non-State actors *in strictu sensu*, like non-governmental organizations, multinational enterprises, armed non-State actors, individuals, and so on and so forth.[47]

The other way around, it could be also argued, that non-State actors have acquired international legal personality, precisely because they have been increasingly granted with rights and obligations under international law.[48] Which came first, non-State actors' rights and obligations or their legal personality? This is also a matter of perspective, however they are usually seen as a direct consequence one from the other; this is why it is usually agreed that 'an entity of a type recognized by customary law as *capable* of possessing rights and duties and of bringing international claims, and having these capacities conferred upon it, is a legal person'.[49] From this point of view, should we move from non-State actors to non-State subjects? Are we therefore 'relativizing the subjects or subjectivizing the actors?'[50]

In this regard, inclusive views submit that considering the growing recognition of non-State actors' subjectivity, evidenced by their increasing activity in international law that has already located them as addressees of rights and obligations, including customary international law itself, it would be contradictory not to allow them to take part in the lawmaking of international law. From this view, non-State actors are no longer objects of international law, like the environment, the high seas, or the Antarctic, but they should be treated as subjects, bearers of rights and obligations but also bestowed with the capability of making law; that would include the possibility of producing relevant practice and *opinio juris* (in case the two-element approach is taken for granted) for the sake of customary international law.[51] However, such approach, I agree, would be a matter of doable normative choice rather than an interpretative exercise.[52]

It should be noted that inclusive views are often defended for the sake of clarity and coherence and not because international subjectivity legally demands the

47 A Roberts and S Sivakumaran, 'Lawmaking by Nonstate Actors: Engaging Armed Groups in the Creation of International Humanitarian Law' (2012) 37 Yale J Intl L 107. *See* also Chapters 18 and 19 in this volume.

48 Contrary to this line of analysis Gasbarri believes that the debate should not focus on the subjects but rather on the rules produced, in this regard *see* Chapter 4 in this volume.

49 I Brownlie, 'International Law at the Fiftieth Anniversary of the United Nations: General Course on Public International Law' (1995) 255 Hague Academy of Intl L Collected Courses 58.

50 A Bianchi, 'Introduction: Relativizing the Subjects or Subjectivizing the Actors: Is That the Question?' in A Bianchi (ed), *Non-State Actors and International Law* (Routledge 2009).

51 Roberts and Sivakumaran (n 47) 109.

52 This is in fact one of the conclusions presented by Jean d'Aspremont in Chapter 7 in this volume.

granting of lawmaking powers. This explains why it has been claimed that although non-State actors undeniably can be 'law-consumers' of international law – as they are addressees of international rights and obligations – they ought not necessarily to be permitted to make the law, which remains an exclusive faculty of States.[53] Therefore, in spite of the fact that views that promote the recognition of lawmaking capacities to non-State actors usually build their arguments from the pluralization *ratione personae* of international law, lawmaking and legal personality should be conceptually distinguished.[54]

Inclusive perspectives also come from the aspiration of strengthening legitimacy in international law. In accordance with this view, it is convenient to allow subjects to participate in the creating process of the very rules that will regulate their behaviour precisely because such involvement will integrate their opinions and will make them feel more committed to the rules, so their conduct will be effectively shaped by international law.[55] The louder their voice resounds the faster the subfield evolves and the higher the compliance.

In this vein, and encouraged by arguments like McCorquodale's that emphasize the need to enlarge participation in international law by allowing non-State actors to play a part in the making of customary law,[56] Roberts and Sivakumaran wonder if 'it is time to reconsider whether it is possible and desirable for non-State actors to play a role in the making of international law'.[57] However, such inclusive perspectives are based on the premise that participation should not be unrestricted like the State's, but should be limited to certain fields where non-State actors' interest are more evident, like non-State combatants with regards to international humanitarian law,[58] individuals with regard to human rights,[59] or MNEs in relation to human rights and environmental standards which may be applicable to them,[60] among others. Having in mind that the lawmaking capacities of non-State actors

53 J d'Aspremont, 'International Law-Making by Non-State Actors' (n 23).

54 *See* E Kassoti, 'The Normative Statute of Unilateral Ad Hoc Commitments by Non-State Armed Actors in Internal Armed Conflicts: International Legal Personality and Law-Making Capacity Distinguished' (2017) 22 J Conflict & Sec L 67.

55 Klabbers (n 15).

56 R McCorquodale, 'An Inclusive International Legal System' (2004) 17 Leiden J Intl L 477.

57 Roberts and Sivakumaran (n 47).

58 ibid 109.

59 C Ochoa, 'The Individual and Customary International Law Formation' (2007) 48 Va J Intl L 119.

60 E Morgera, *Corporate Accountability in International Environmental Law* (Oxford University Press 2009).

should be limited to their specific sphere of action, this proposal will need to work the other way around as well. Therefore, e.g. non-State combatants practice and acceptance of law could not be relevant for the sake of customary law regarding corporate responsibility. Neither could the practice of multinational enterprises matter in the identification process of customary international humanitarian law.

On the other hand, there are also approaches based on the real circumstances in which some non-State actors participate in the international arena, giving attention to their factual capabilities due to their budget, size, and power; that is the actual effect that they may cause in international law despite formalism.[61] These views enhance, e.g. the fact that multinational enterprises constantly increase their share of the world's exports, that they hold the majority of the foreign direct investment in the world or that many of them are economically stronger than many States.[62] For instance, it is not surprising any more that 'the revenues of top corporations exceed by far the GDP of the majority of States',[63] that 'of the largest one hundred concentrations of wealth in the world, 51 per cent are owned by multinational companies and 49 per cent by States' or that 'the 15 largest multinationals each have a budget that exceeds the GPD of more than 120 countries'.[64] Thus, considering that they already have economic power, holding the strings of politics and economics, should not their lawmaking muscles also be recognized?

Although arguments are diverse, it is worth noting that even those who claim a non-State actor participation in the formation of customary law acknowledge the current priority of the aforementioned State-centred orthodox perspective.[65] Thus, their open account of customary international law is usually presented as a proposal, or what may be called *lege ferenda*, and not as the description of the state of art on customary international law or *lex lata*.[66] Hence, it is worth noting that even divergent views agree that nowadays customary international law is exclusively formed out of State practice and acceptance as law, where non-State actor contribution could influence only through State's manifestations of will and action.[67]

61 E.g. J Alvarez, *International Organizations as Law-Makers* (Oxford University Press 2010). This is for instance the perspective defended by Tomoko Yamashita in Chapter 18 in this volume.
62 Morgera (n 60).
63 ibid.
64 ibid 4–5.
65 Roberts and Sivakumaran (n 47).
66 This same distinction is later made by Veronika Bílková in Chapter 9 in this volume.
67 ibid.

Nevertheless, considering that in the end an inclusive perspective will remain a call for change, should this call be taken? Moreover, who is entitled to take it anyway? Only the State? Should this change be carried out in light of the anachronic two-element approach? That would bring us of course back to the orthodox perspective. Alternatively, could this pressure permit also non-State actor participation in the decision? In other words, could non-State actors decide whether their practice and acceptance as law could matter in the formation process of customary international law?[68] Those are questions which are not fully settled with the conceptual tools of orthodox views but which may need to be faced, keeping in mind that whether non-State actor participation in customary international law matters will always be a matter of perspective, and that any divergent understanding, such as the one that claims for inclusiveness, will require a higher degree of persuasion. Using the conceptual tools developed by d'Aspremont in Chapter 7 in this volume, we could argue that we will need to get rid of the 'common tropes' that are currently impairing the development of new thinking and new perspectives, such as the presumption that customary international law emerges from Art. 38 of the International Court of Justice Statute, that it necessarily contains the two-element approach, and that legal discussion concerning the relation between customary international law and non-State actors can be solved by interpreting the existing secondary rule that governs customary international law.[69] I therefore agree that whether non-State actors take part in the making of customary international law is not something we can conclude after a hermeneutic exercise around Art. 38 or any other so-called secondary rule governing the source, but it is the result of conscious (or unconscious) political choices that precede the legal argument.[70] At the end, any position, even the orthodox one refurbished by the International Law Commission, will be the product of a prior choice, which is later strengthened through argumentative processes that are always theory dependent.

In this vein, it could be said that whereas a scholar more akin to positivism and formalism would cling to the orthodoxy and affirm that non-State actors do not have lawmaking capacity at all, though they could indirectly influence formal lawmakers (the State), a perspective more lean on empiricism and informality would be probably enhance what non-State actors are actually doing (effect-based approach),[71] and despite formalism, just conclude that non-State actors are truly

68 This argument is made by Jean d'Aspremont. *See* Chapter 7 in this volume.

69 This is one of the main arguments developed by Jean d'Aspremont. *See* Chapter 7 in this volume.

70 ibid.

71 This is the approach given by V Azarova in Chapter 19 of this volume.

making customary international law.[72] Accordingly, there is no doubt that people working for certain non-State actors – like non-governmental organizations or multinational enterprises – put pressure on the people working for States, when they provide technical information, lobby for a particular agenda, promote diplomatic conferences or write drafts of treaties or soft law instruments, or simply when they write and disseminate studies and proposals that aim to promote international legal initiatives;[73] the issue at stake is how to interpret those facts.

So, while formalists will always argue that despite the influence made by non-State actors, States will have the final say and will therefore remain the only and supreme lawmakers of international law, observers taking any sort of empiric perspective will focus on the tangible acts of influence, measuring the size of the pressure and its final outcome, in order to conclude that despite the formalistic discussion, non-State actors are actually creating law when they managed to make States and other subjects support the emergence of certain customary rule. From effect-based approaches, what makes non-State actors lawmakers is not the label that international law (or rather, international lawyers) grant them, but the fact that their action and their agendas, somehow, finally became law in spite of the State having the final and formal say.

Positions are the result of how facts are read, and the way of processing available information is essentially shaped by further theoretical preconceptions possessed by the observer;[74] in this case considerations regarding the lawmaking capacities of non-State actors and the place of non-State actors in international law as a whole definitely inform (though do not necessarily determine) the direction that a perspective on non-State actors and customary international law will take. Possible perspectives on the matter will always appear as a response of the theoretical grounds we decide to take, however all of them could be included in both exclusive and inclusive views.

Hence, I would argue that the foregoing panorama reiterates the lack of correctness with regards to the formation of customary international law. It also relativizes the orthodox perspective on the role of non-State actors in customary international law by describing it simply as one possible perspective towards the matter.[75] It is within

72 Regarding informality in the sources of international law I have elsewhere made a reflection, F Cardenas, 'A Call for Rethinking the Sources of International Law: Soft Law and the Other Side of the Coin' (2013) 13 Anuario Mexicano de Derecho Internacional 355.

73 *See* Chapter 19 in this volume.

74 J d'Aspremont, 'Non-State Actors and the Social Practice of International Law' in Math Noortmann, August Reinishch, and Cedric Ryngaert (eds), *Non-State Actors in International Law* (Hart 2015) 11.

75 This seems to be also the perspective of Maiko Meguro in Chapter 5 in this volume.

this context that an alternative perspective is postulated, that no longer sees customary international law as the outcome of practice and *opinio juris* in which non-State actors may not be present, but that sees customary international law rather as the product of successful argumentative campaigns where non-State actors could take part.

4 Customary international law as successful argumentative campaigns

The idea of conceiving customary international law as the product of practice and *opinio juris*, regardless whether it includes the practice and acceptance of non-State actors, will always have difficulties,[76] precisely due to the fact that it is not only the product of an imposed view developed by the jurisprudence of the two Courts rather than by the Statute itself – in spite of the International Law Commission's efforts[77] – but also because such definition is grounded on a rule-based approach to international law,[78] which is also imbedded within the confines of positivism; the latter, I insist, is just one possible approach out of many. This perspective will always have a limited sphere of action precisely because it will always search for a secondary rule governing customary international law.[79] Hence, those perspectives will always be static, either including or excluding the practice and acceptance of non-State actors in addition to other factors, but without being able to provide any sort of concreteness or even the ability to adapt itself to dynamic and changing realities. The orthodox rule-based perspective of customary international law will remain a sophism of formalism.

Likewise, I agree that the fact is that such a secondary rule governing customary international law does not even exist.[80] In the absence of a universal treaty, clearly

76 We have explored them already in F Cardenas and O Casallas, 'Una Gran Medida de "Opinio Juris" y Práctica Estatal al Gusto: ¿ la Receta de la Costumbre Internacional Contemporánea?' (2015) 8 Anuario Colombiano de Derecho Internacional 87. Positions challenging the two-element approach are also well developed in different manners along this volume. *See* Chapters 3, 5, and 7 in this volume.

77 A critic perspective to the two-element approach has been also presented by Maiko Meguro in Chapter 5 of this volume.

78 A Peters, L Koechlin, and GF Zinkernagel, 'Non-State Actors as Standard Setters: Framing the Issue in an Interdisciplinary Fashion', *Non-State Actors as Standard Setters* (Cambridge University Press 2009) 1–32.

79 D Bodansky, 'Customary (and Not So Customary) International Environmental Law' (1996) 3 Global Legal Studies 105.

80 This is one of the core arguments in J d'Aspremont, *International Law as a Belief System* (Cambridge University Press 2017).

establishing and regulating customary international law, what we have instead are efforts to accommodate the little that has been written – in the literal sense of Article 38 1 (b) of the International Court of Justice Statute – to construct perspectives and versions of what the supposed secondary rule governing customary international law would demand.[81] In this vein, both orthodox perspectives and inclusive perspectives on the role of non-State actors in customary international law – which had been presented by way of example – are also theoretical approaches, none of them correct or incorrect, in spite of the orthodoxy imposing – so far – the view that non-State actors' practice and acceptance do not have a (direct) incidence in the formation of customary international law.

Hence, I think that the difficulties faced by the theory of customary international law are rooted in the fact that the object of study has been approached as if it were 'a natural phenomenon like the phenomena studied in physics, chemistry and biology'[82] when what we face is a social phenomenon.

In some aspects of natural sciences, it is more common to see how observers often describe what it already is, however, those natural laws were there even before a scientist described them. Moreover, they cannot be easily changed, not even by the unanimous decision of the scientific community. Nonetheless, in social sciences, it is more evident to see how things aren't so but they are rather socially constructed, produced by society through social arrangements. From this view, I believe, e.g. that the secondary rule governing customary international law and whether it takes direct account of non-State actor practice and acceptance cannot be found, because it does not exist before it is defined. Customary international law is constructed when it is described, precisely because customary international law is essentially social and is therefore a construction.[83] In this regard, Berger and Luckmann's assertions are worth quoting:

> Man is biologically predestined to construct and to inhabit a world with others. This world becomes for him the mainstream and definite reality. Its limits are set by nature, but once constructed, this world acts back upon nature. In the dialectic between nature and the socially constructed world the human organism itself is transformed. In this same dialectic man produces reality and thereby produces himself.[84]

81 The argument has been elaborated in Cardenas, 'Customary International Law as an Argumentative Framework' (n 28).

82 J Searle, *Making the Social World: The Structure of Human Civilization* (Oxford University Press 2010) 201.

83 A discourse of 'constructions' regarding the role of non-State actors in customary international law can be also found in Chapter 5 in this volume.

84 PL Berger and T Luckmann, *The Social Construction of Reality: A Treatise in the Sociology of Knowledge* (Doubleday/Anchor Books 1966), 183.

Similarly, Focarelli in his 'International Law as a Social Construct' stresses that:

> Law is law not because this or that academic has distilled the 'correct' notion of law which should serve as a paradigm. Law is law because it works among its addressees in their own perception. It is a social construct, not a scientific enterprise.[85]

Hence, as a construct, I agree that there is no such thing as the correct law, but only the accepted law in a particular moment in history. In addition, I think that although nowadays the orthodox perspective maintains that non-State actors do not have a (direct) impact in the formation of customary international law, it does not mean that they cannot eventually acquire a position of influence when their actual contribution is formally recognized. Nothing is more illustrative than all the normative developments of contemporary international legal fields like international environmental law or cyberspace law which did not even exist a few decades ago but which nevertheless emerged once it was decided that they should be created as autonomous fields.[86]

In this vein, I believe that the idea according to which customary international law is the product of *opinio juris* and practice, and that such practice only encompasses States and international organizations, is in itself a construction; a discourse definitely not made by the International Law Commission but nevertheless strengthened by its work. An argumentative enterprise that usually creates the illusion of having a large support, with the purpose of positioning its perspective as if it were a purely objective exercise of codification and development of what international law says on the matter, when it is not. Notwithstanding, the International Law Commission celebrates the adoption of its Conclusions on the identification of customary international law and its orthodoxy as if such discussions on customary international law were settled, when they aren't. They only purport a unified discourse of the orthodox – not necessarily mainstream – perspective, so they can still be challenged. However, how can a perspective be positioned in the orthodoxy, or how can a divergent perspective overthrow the orthodox one? I believe we have the answer in the legal Latin aphorism *peristi quae fiunt*, which literally means that in law things can be unmade just as they were made. Hence, perspectives emerge and position themselves through argumentative struggles also; as Focarelli would say: 'The law of today is the result of past struggles and the law of tomorrow will be the result of the struggles to be engaged today.'[87] In this regard, Koskenniemi has also well pointed out:

85 C Focarelli, *International Law as Social Construct: The Struggle for Global Justice* (Oxford University Press 2012).

86 P Sands, *Principles of International Environmental Law* (3rd edn, Cambridge University Press 2012) 111; Schmitt and Watts (n 46).

87 Focarelli (n 85).

> International law is an argumentative practice. It is about persuading target audiences such as courts, colleagues, politicians, and reads of legal texts about the legal correctness – lawfulness, legitimacy, justice, permissibility, validity, etc. – of the position one defends.[88]

Hence, I think that just as international law is an argumentative practice, the formation of customary international law depends on successful argumentative campaigns.[89] In turn, this success depends on the possibility of convincing the right audience. So, for instance, whereas an international treaty is finally signed and ratified after all parties were convinced to support the draft text, customary international law is also the result of persuading the emergence of a particular rule, though the act of being convinced is not formalized in a written document.

However, I deem that the ways of convincing are not unlimited but they are regulated by the dynamic practice of the community of international lawyers who construct social arrangements that orientate the way in which an emerging customary rule can be argued. That would include, among others, the use of a technical legal language that takes into account the orthodox discourse on the sources of international law, preferably (and ironically) including the orthodox two-element approach of practice and *opinio juris*; reference to the rule being the product of State consent or acquiesce as well as arguments trying to prove its present;[90] as well as harmony between the novel rule and the standing legal order – including of course compliance with current jus cogens norms.[91] It is interesting to note, that although arguments supposedly complying with the requirements of *opinio juris* and practice may toughen the campaign, such practice and *opinio juris* is not always substantially required.[92] It is well known, e.g. how some human rights and environmental customary rules have emerged even against contrary practice and solely via deduction,[93]

88 M Koskenniemi, 'Methodology of International Law', *MPEPIL2* (2007).

89 J d'Aspremont, *Epistemic Forces in International Law* (Edward Elgar 2015) 1–32.

90 R Lesaffer, 'Siege Warfare and the Customary Laws of War' in A P-Saussine and JB Murphy (eds), *The Nature of Customary International Law: Legal, Historical and Philosophical Perspectives* (Cambridge University Press 2007). 'Customs were based on consent. In consequence, they were solely binding upon those who had consented to them.'

91 A Bianchi, 'Human Rights and the Magic of Jus Cogens' (2008) 19 Eur J Intl L 491.

92 S Talmon, 'Determining Customary International Law: The ICJ's Methodology between Induction, Deduction and Assertion' (2015) 26 Eur J Int L.

93 Regarding the identification of customary international environmental law *see* e.g. F Cardenas, 'La Obligacion de Protección Ambiental en la Jurisprudencia de la Corte Internacional de Justicia' in R Prieto and A Moreira (eds), *La Responsabilidad Internacional del Estado y el Medio Ambiente* (Pontificia Universidad Javeriana, Biblioteca Jurídica Diké 2016) 143. Tams (n 42). We have elsewhere discussed how international

or how the International Court of Justice has managed to position customary rules simply by asserting their existence.[94]

Consequently, having in mind that customary international law is rather the product of successful argumentative campaigns, it turns out to be relevant to discuss the way in which such arguments are campaigned. It will require both a select group of people (such as the International Law Commission's members) spreading the arguments as well as specific channels through which those arguments are spread, so the said customary rule can be prompted and eventually come into existence.[95]

Hence, in most cases, I believe, contemporary customary rules could emerge when an argument sustaining it grows thanks to the dissemination made by respected and well-known members of the community of international lawyers. Meanwhile, the argument is campaigned through accepted channels, like an international judgment, a memorial sent on behalf of a State before an international tribunal, an official speech before a large international organization – namely the United Nations – a report coming from a group of recognized experts of an international organisation – namely the very International Law Commission – or even a recognized research book or an academic article published by a prestigious publisher or academic institution, preferably from the Western world. While the most influential members of the community of international lawyers, like International Court of Justice judges through their rulings, can easily succeed in positioning new customary rules, less known members will need to be better (argumentatively) armed, counting on the subsequent support of other influential members.

However, who can integrate this community of international lawyers? It can be essentially comprised of individuals, lawyers that either exercise or study international law and who have recognition within the same community.[96] That would include lawyers working for States, international organizations, universities and research centres,

environmental law has 'defiled' classic international legal institutions at many levels, F Cardenas and F Cadena, 'Desafios Impuestos por el Derecho Internacional Ambiental al Derecho Internacional Púbico Clásico' (2009) 2 Anuario Colombiano de Derecho Internacional 141.

94 Talmon (n 92). Cardenas, 'La Obligacion de Protección Ambiental en la Jurisprudencia de la Corte Internacional de Justicia' (n 93).

95 Cardenas 'Customary International Law as an Argumentative Framework' (n 28).

96 Carrillo-Santarelli (n 23) 107. 'In that regard, it must be borne in mind that States and international organizations are collective actors that operate through agents, who are ultimately individuals. Therefore, to understand why States agents shape or react to a nascent custom, it is convenient to examine their conduct and motivations in a disaggregated manner.'

and of course international lawyers working for non-State actors.[97] Additionally, it is believed that with regards to some fields it could be possible for non-lawyers to integrate the community whenever their input remains essential for the development of the field, e.g. hard scientists in the development of international environmental law.[98]

Likewise, once international law is considered an argumentative practice and customary international law as the product of argumentative campaigns promoted, regulated, and validated by members of the community of international lawyers, it would be possible to conclude that non-State actors could play a role in the formation of customary international law. This involvement in customary international law could be feasible if people working for non-State actors and belonging to the community of international lawyers end up contributing in one of those successful argumentative campaigns. Nonetheless, non-State actors lawyers' involvement would not be effective unless their initiatives or considerations are backed up by other members of the community, in which the lawyers of States and State-empowered actors[99] remain highly influential. However, note that the result does not depend on legal personality or source interpretation but it is a question of social influence and recognition.

Consequently, non-State actors' lawyers can play a role in the formation of customary international law when they write and disseminate highly influential reports that create awareness of the need to develop a new customary rule.[100] They do so by convincing State lawyers, international organizations' lawyers, and legal scholars to support the emergence of such novel rules. To illustrate, it can be evoked how the diplomatic efforts of the 1992 Rio Conference, primarily campaigned by non-governmental organizations' lawyers, initiated the spark that ended up with the emergence of the most fundamental customary rules of international environmental law, which succeeded despite States' reluctance to sign an universal treaty on the environment.[101] Likewise, non-State actors' lawyers can institute or take part in proceedings before international tribunals where customary rules can be evolved or supported by the

97 Cardenas, 'Customary International Law as an Argumentative Framework' (n 28).

98 P-M Dupuy, 'Formation of Customary International Law and General Principles' in D Bodansky, J Brunnée, and E Hey (eds), *Oxford Handbook of International Environmental Law* (Oxford University Press 2008).

99 S Sivakumaran, 'Beyond States and Non-States Actors: The Role of State-Empowered Entities in the Making and Shaping of International Law' (2016) 55 Colum J of Transnat'l L 343.

100 This is how the outcome of the International Law Commission can have a lawmaking value in its own despite of the uncertainties.

101 C Fuchs, 'Environment, Role of Non-Governmental Organizations', *MPEPIL* (2009).

lawyers working for those tribunals.[102] Moreover, non-State actors lawyers can join private and/or public international initiatives in which standards applicable to them are developed and reinforced, which after being supported by other members of the community can begin to be considered emerging customary international law;[103] such initiatives could be also possibly disseminated through unilateral acts or declarations that depending on their intensity could be assumed by others as acceptance of customary rules regulating their conduct. Additionally, non-State actors' lawyers could take advantage of their status as observers within different international organizations, namely the United Nations, the European Union, the World Trade Organization, the International Labour Organization, inter alia, in order to present or support argumentative campaigns leading to the emergence of new customary rules.[104]

Although the range of possibilities could be extensive and would require a further research, the point is that although State lawyers' views tend to be prioritized when identifying customary international law, considerations of lawyers working for non-State actors could be taken into account, so they can surely be in a position to contribute to the formation of customary international law even despite the reluctance of the orthodox to formally accept the incidence of non-State actors.

Likewise, it should be pointed out that considering that there is still debate on which kind of actors could be labelled as non-State actors, whether including or excluding international organizations or State-empowered actors and whether it goes beyond non-governmental organizations, multinational enterprises, and some types of armed non-State actors,[105] there will be also debate on the influence that international lawyers working for such actors may have. In the end, it will not formally depend on the institutional affiliation of the lawyer, but on how influential or how able to position successful argumentative campaigns he can be. Therefore, the role of lawyers working for already largely recognized non-governmental organizations or multinational enterprises would certainly be more effective than that of lawyers working for unknown non-State actors.

5 Conclusion

Contrary to what the orthodox perspective of customary international law argues – as supported by the International Law Commission's Conclusions – I think that it is

102 International Law Association, 'Sofia Conference – Non State Actors' (n 1) 19–25.

103 E.g. United Nations Global Compact, www.unglobalcompact.org/, accessed 4 December 2018.

104 International Law Association, 'Sofia Conference – Non State Actors' (n 1).

105 *See* e.g. Roberts and Sivakumaran (n 48); M Wagner, 'Non-State Actors', *MPEPIL* (2017).

still possible to recognize the participation of non-State actors in the making of customary international law. This influence is noticeable when customary international law is rather conceived as the product of successful argumentative campaigns in which non-State actors' lawyers can play a role. In fact, it is undeniable that people working for non-State actors are influential in the formation of certain customary rules; so, theories, and whether non-State actors matter for the formation of customary international law remains a matter of perspective.

In this vein it is also possible to locate the work of the International Law Commission into perspective and loosen its disproportionate influence in international legal scholarship. Thus, the International Law Commission's Conclusions on the identification of customary international law should be approached moderately, and solely as one out of many possible perspectives to customary international law and not as the – never wanted – codex on customary international law. Actually, as made evident in the second part of this chapter, I believe that the International Law Commission does not have its 'own' approach to customary international law; and that it does not have its 'own' approach to the role of non-state actors in the formation of customary international law. The International Law Commission merely sums up and assembles what the orthodoxy has been saying for decades as constantly repeated in the most traditional international legal doctrine. As a matter of fact, I believe that it exposes how disappointing has been the outcome of the International Law Commission on this regard. While it is entrusted with the duty to make studies to encourage the progressive development of international law and its codification, the latest results on customary international law are simply refurbished versions of the most traditional perspectives. What we knew about customary international law before the work of the International Law Commission started is the same as we know after the Conclusions were finally adopted. Whereas it is undeniable that existing reports are careful to acknowledge alternative and modern theories, it does so only to reiterate the orthodox view, which remains inconclusive and scarce of pragmatism. A body like the International Law Commission is expected to produce innovative developments on international law, leading old traditions into the newest realities and not a room to celebrate academic anachronisms. The International Law Commission should be a place to make international law useful and practical and not just another place for mere theoretical reflexion and repetition. Needless to stress that this is not the case of all the topics under the consideration of the International Law Commission although it is the fate of the latest products on customary international law.

Moreover, it should be highlighted that this very experience within the International Law Commission regarding customary international law illustrates why we refer to argumentative campaigns. While a Rapporteur is only the person who organizes the views and who drafts them in a structured document, the argument does not come exclusively by his own personal initiative, but he is unavoidably limited both by his former and present colleagues and by what State lawyers and other recognized members of the community of international lawyers write in their commentaries, communications, or scholarly pieces. With this in mind, I believe that not even the most progressive international lawyer would write without consequences, in such capacity, something different from the orthodox perspective, due to the fact that he would always be tied to the pressures put by influential members of the community of international lawyers. Nowadays, it is clear that the current successful campaign is interested in maintaining the status quo on customary international law with all its flaws, uncertainties, and difficulties. That remains of course very convenient for those States holding the dominant position.[106]

In line of the foregoing, and after accepting d'Aspremont's invitation to 'unlearn some common tropes'[107] such as the presumption that discussions on customary international law can only be made within the limits of the discourse created around Art. 38 of the International Court of Justice Statute, I believe that approaching customary international law as successful argumentative campaigns will provide international law with more transparency because it will detach customary international law from a misguided sense of correctness. Once it is accepted that there is not an objective secondary rule governing customary international law which provides 'the truth' about the emergence of non-written international legally binding norms, but rather the open possibility to campaign through a technical legal argumentation for the emergence of new legal norms, it becomes clear that it is for different actors to play their role fighting for their respective agendas, in the promotion of such norms. No matter if these actors play to the apology of State sovereignty in its most restrictive way on the one hand, or whether they play to promote supranational objectives. The latter would work for the benefit of global concerns like peace, development, or the environment, inter alia, which are usually eluded by (the most powerful) States, as they tend to avoid accepting hard, serious, and specific commitments on such regards. With this in mind, I believe that approaching customary international law as the product of argumentative campaigns would also accelerate the emergence and consolidation of awaited customary rules concerning the environment and some other human rights belonging to the third generation.

106 *See* Chapter 3 in this volume.

107 *See* Chapter 7 in this volume.

Thereby, describing customary international law as the product of successful argumentative campaigns, will also transform the making of international law in a more democratic process. While from orthodox approaches the strings of international law can only be pulled by States' lawyers, an alternative approach that sees customary international law as the product of argumentative campaigns would consciously acknowledge the interests of those no represented by the dominant views of the State, namely, indigenous people, tribes, third world views, environmentalists, and so on. The fact is that while the orthodox view does not allow international law to be actually international and public, being just the private law of those imposing a so-called truth, a social perspective that recognizes how customary international law is argumentatively campaigned would make public participation more accessible where not only the agendas of a few powerful stakeholders are pleaded.

It should be reiterated that this position does not suggest that international legal doctrines should be discarded, quite the contrary, it is the technicality offered by international law which provides how customary international law could be campaigned. Therefore, describing customary international law from this perspective would not impair the field. This does not imply that the profession of international lawyers should be diminished either. On the contrary, it claims that it should be rather strengthened considering that international lawyers are particularly the ones capable of bringing an argumentative campaign as it is the community of those very same lawyers who regulate the process and decide whether a particular campaign for a customary rule succeeded or not. So the profession would not lose its consistency, quite the contrary, it will gain even more value.

The posture here proposed finally corroborates the importance of maintaining the topic of the sources of international law and that of customary international law as one of the most important issues in international legal studies. Thus, it is important to keep in mind that even if the International Law Association concluded its work on customary international law in 2000 and the International Law Commission did so in 2018 – to mention a couple of examples – that does not mean that the matter is settled. On the contrary, continuing progress should be made in order to conceptualize how the argumentative campaigns for customary international law are carried out, no matter whether they are called secondary rules, principles, or Conclusions.

Chapter 7

Unlearning some common tropes

*Jean d'Aspremont**

The question of the role of non-State actors in custom-forming processes has recently resurfaced in international lawyers' discourses. We have been here before. In fact, the contribution of non-State actors to international customary law – that is to behaviourally self-generated law – has already been the object of innumerable discussions and scholarly exchanges over the last decade.[1] Previously, scholarly interest for the question had been kindled by the International Committee of the Red Cross's study on customary humanitarian law and, especially by some of the International Committee of the Red Cross's ambiguous positions on the matter.[2] This time – and as if scholarly research agendas were determined outside academic circles – it is the provisional adoption by the International Law Commission of a specific draft conclusion on the matter that ignited this new fervour.[3] This renewed scholarly excitement for the oft-discussed question of non-State actors' participation in custom-forming processes – and which this volume is certainly complicit in — remains in need of justifications as to whether, from the perspective of international

* The author wishes to thank GC McBain for his assistance.

1 *See* e.g. the reports of the ILA Committee on Non-State Actors (2005–2016), and especially the first and second reports, available at www.ila-hq.org/index.php/committees.

2 *See*, generally, J-M Henckaerts, 'Study on Customary International Humanitarian Law: A Contribution to the Understanding and Respect for the Rule of Law in Armed Conflict' (2005) 87 International review of the Red Cross 175; *see* the critique of A Boyle and C Chinkin, *The Making of International Law* (Oxford University Press 2007), 36; *see* also the critique expressed by JB Bellinger and WJ Haynes, 'A US Government Response to the International Committee of the Red Cross's Customary International Humanitarian Law Study' (2007) 46 *International Law Materials* 514; *see* the remarks of C Ryngaert, 'Non-State Actors in International Humanitarian Law' in J d'Aspremont (ed), *Participants in the International Legal System* (Routledge 2011) 284–94.

3 *See* the Conclusions adopted by the International Law Commission at International Law Commission, 'Draft report: Chapter V – Identification of customary international law', 68th session (2016), UN Doc A/CN.4/L.883/Add.1.

legal scholarship, something can still be assimilated, cognised, or simply said about non-State actors' contribution to customary international law. This demand is certainly not unwarranted. After all the sophisticated studies produced in the last ten years, one may legitimately wonder what there still is to be added to the debate.

This chapter returns to the last decade of scholarly reflections on the question of non-State actors and customary international law and revisits some of the specific argumentative constructions and presuppositions that have informed – and continue to inform – discourses on the contribution of non-State actors and international law. This chapter is specifically premised on the idea that international legal thought and practice on non-State actors and customary international law have remained chained by certain modes of reasoning and category of thoughts which have been precluding any renewal of scholarly reflection on the matter. It is submitted in this chapter that, in order to make a chance of novelty and creative thinking, any new wave of scholarly reflections on the contribution of non-State actors to custom-forming processes – including this very volume – must reinvent the very categories around which international legal discourses are currently articulated.

It is argued here that three tropes have been mechanically repeated in previous rounds of scholarly debates on non-State actors and customary law and must be confronted for scholarly reflections to have any potential to generate new insights. These constructions can be summarised as follows:

1. The idea that the two-element variant of the doctrine of customary international law originates in Article 38 of the Statute of the Permanent Court of International Justice.
2. The continuous attachment of international lawyers – including the International Law Commission – to the distinction between practice and *opinio juris*.
3. The understanding of the concept of non-State actors as a plain and innocent descriptive category.

This chapter gainsays these three abovementioned presuppositions. By challenging these three contentions, this chapter attempts to unchain international lawyers from some of the categories of legal thought informing their latest discourses on non-State actors and customary international law with a view to renewing legal thinking on the question. According to the following discussion, challenging these three common contentions allows one to understand that venturing into the scholarly debates about non-State actors' contribution to custom-forming processes is not about any mechanical alteration of Article 38 of the Permanent Court of International Justice Statute and the two-element doctrine that comes with it. As is ultimately argued here, engaging with the question of non-State actors' contributions to custom-forming processes is, instead, about making the definitional choices that shapes the politics of international lawmaking.

This chapter is structured as follows. It discusses the three abovementioned dominant constructions one after the other and makes, on that occasion, three distinct separate claims: the doctrine of customary international law is built on an imaginary genealogy (1); the two-element doctrine has long disappeared in international legal thought and practice (2); the concept of non-State actors is a managerialist device of both inclusion and exclusion (3); and the last section of this chapter sheds light on the renewal of scholarly discourses made possible once the three mainstream constructions have been debunked (4).

One important caveat is necessary before developing these claims further. It must be acknowledged that key argumentative moves and contentions other than the three abovementioned constructions have informed discourses over non-State actors and international law. Two of them must be mentioned here; yet, they do not draw significant attention here because their contentious character seems, in the eyes of the author of this chapter, rather overblown. The first construction is the very principle that non-State actors contribute to the formation of custom. Since the inception of international law, they have been playing a crucial role in the making of norms, including customary norms.[4] Whilst such a role has never been captured by the modern categories of the doctrine of the sources of international law, there seems to be no reason why recognising their cardinal (albeit informal or indirect) contribution to the custom-making process ought to prove so contentious. This does not seem to be further questioned. Second, there equally seems to be nothing extravagant in the idea that non-State actors can generate practice and *opinio juris* for the formation of customary norms specifically binding on non-State actors themselves. Indeed, if one understands custom as a behaviourally self-generated norm-forming process, which constitutes the dominant approach since the abandonment of voluntaristic understandings of custom at the end of the nineteenth century,[5] there does not seem to be any conceptual obstacle

4 *See* also Chapter 5 in this volume.

5 On the conventional foundations of customary law, *see* H Triepel, *Völkerrecht und Landesrecht* (Scientia Verlag 1899); K Strupp, *Elements du droit international public* (Rousseau & Co 1927); T Lawrence, *The Principles of International Law* (5th edn, Macmillan, 1910); John Westlake, *International Law* (Cambridge University Press 1904) 14; D Anzilotti, *Scritti di diritto internazionale pubblico* (Cedan Padova, 1956–7) 1, 38, 95ff; GI Tunkin, *Theory of International Law* (Harvard University Press 1974) 124; C Chaumont, 'Cours général de droit international public' (1970) 129 *Collected Courses* 333, 440; for an attempt to modernise the consensual conception of customary international law, *see* A

against the recognition that non-State actors can generate customary rules for themselves.[6]

1 Custom and Article 38: the imaginary genealogy of customary international law

Custom is known to most legal systems where it refers to an unwritten process whereby normativity is behaviourally generated short of any written instrument. It is well known that, in international law, custom has been systematised through a two-tier process. This is the so-called 'two-element doctrine' of customary international law, which distinguishes between practice and *opinio juris*.[7] This two-element variant of custom has been elevated to one of the fundamental modes of identification of international legal rules as well as a central mode of lawmaking by virtue of a narrative that derives this two-element doctrine not from the practice of international courts and tribunals, but from the Statute of the Permanent Court of International Justice. Said differently, in contemporary international legal discourses, the dominant modes of legal reasoning to determine the existence and content of a rule of customary international law are articulated around the establishment of two distinct facts, i.e. practice and *opinio juris* (acceptance as law). Despite some continuous emancipatory and fragmentary forces,[8] this understanding of customary international law has

Orakhelashvili, *The Interpretation of Acts and Rules in Public International Law* (Oxford University Press 2008) 70–107; A D'Amato 'Treaties as a Source of General Rules of International Law' (1962) 3 *Harvard International Law Journal* 1; for some classic criticisms of such a convention-based approach to customary law, *see* H Lauterpacht, 'Decisions of Municipal Courts as a Source of International Law' (1929) 10 *British Yearbook of International Law* 65, 83; J Brierly, *The Law of Nations: An Introduction to the International Law of Peace* (Clarendon Press 1955) 52; J Kunz, 'The Nature of Customary International Law' (1953) 47 *American Journal of International Law* 662, 664.

6 Much more controversial is obviously the claim that State practice and *opinio juris* can be conducive to the crystallisation of customary norms that equally binds non-State actors but this is a question alien to the matter revisited here.

7 *See* P Haggenmacher, 'La doctrine des deux éléments en droit coutumier dans la pratique de la Cour international' (1986) 90 *Revue Générale de Droit International Public* 5.

8 J d'Aspremont, 'An Autonomous Regime of Identification of Customary International Humanitarian Law: Do Not Say What You Do or Do Not Do What You Say?' in R van Steenberghe (ed), *Droit International Humanitaire: Un Régime Spécial de Droit International?* (Bruylant 2013) 72–101; SH Choi, and M Gulati, 'Customary International Law: How Do Courts Do it?' 9 February 2015, available at SSRN: https://papers.ssrn.com/sol3/papers.cfm?abstract_id=2561900; R Kolb, 'Selected Problems in the Theory of Customary International Law' (2003) 50 *Netherlands International Law Review* 119, 128.

dominated contemporary legal argumentation about customary international law in the twentieth century.[9] The recent work of the International Law Commission has confirmed that the two-element approach continues to be the dominant articulation of the modes of legal reasoning related to the determination of the existence and content of customary rules in the twenty-first century.[10]

The abovementioned two-element approach is riven with conceptual and practical problems that have been extensively discussed in the literature.[11] This is not a discussion that ought to be rehashed here. What matters for the discussion carried out here is that the two-element approach is, in mainstream international legal

9 On the rise of the two-element doctrine, *see* also P Haggenmacher, 'La doctrine des deux éléments en droit coutumier dans la pratique de la Cour internationale' (1986) 90 *Revue Générale de Droit International Public* 5.

10 *See* the text of the draft conclusions on identification of customary international law adopted by the Commission on first reading, International Law Commission, 'Draft report: Chapter V – Identification of customary international law', 68th session (2016), UN Doc A/CN.4/L.883/Add.1; *see* also International Law Commission, 'Third report on the identification of customary international law by the Special Rapporteur Sir Michael Wood', 67th Session (2015), UN Doc A/CN.4/682, para 15; the claim of a fragmentation of the doctrine of customary law has been rejected by the International Law Commission which has continued to see unity in the practice – International Law Commission, 'First Report of the Special Rapporteur, Sir Michael Wood', 65th session, A/CN.4/663, para 19; as well argued there exists only a difference in interpretation and application, *see* also International Law Commission, 'Second Report on Identification of Customary International Law by the Special Rapporteur Sir Michael Wood', 66th Session (2014), UN Doc A/CN.4/672, 22 May 2014, para 28.

11 J Kammerhofer, 'Uncertainty in the Formal Sources of International Law: Customary International Law and Some of Its Problems' (2004) 15 *European Journal of International Law* 523; V Tzevelekos, 'Juris dicere: Custom as Matrix, Custom as a Norm, and the Role of Judges of (Their) Ideology in Custom Making' in N Rajkovic, T Aalberts, and T Gammeltoft-Hansen (eds), *Power of Legality: Practices of International Law and their Politics* (Cambridge University Press 2016) 188–208; S Yee, 'Article 38 of the ICJ Statute and Applicable Law: Selected Issues in Recent Cases' (2016) 7 *Journal of International Dispute Settlement* 472, 479–87; JP Kelly, 'The Twilight of Customary International Law' (2000) 40 *Virginia Journal of International Law* 449; C Bradley, 'A State Preferences Account of Customary International Law Adjudication', 10 October 2014, available at http://ssrn.com/abstract=2508298; Lazlo Blutman, 'Conceptual and Methodological Deficiencies: Some Ways that Theories on Customary International Law Fail' (2014) 25 *European Journal of International Law* 529; *see* the famous contradiction highlighted by M Sørensen, 'Principes de droit international public' (1960-III) 101 *Collected Courses of the Hague Academy on International Law* 1, 50; on the same sense, *see* A D'Amato, *The Concept of Custom in International Law* (Cornell University Press 1971) 7; on this paradox, *see* the comments of Kolb (n 8) 137; M Byers, *Custom, Power and the Power of Rules: International Relations and*

discourses, held as being derived from Article 38 of the Statute of the Permanent Court of International Justice. Indeed, this provision is continuously invoked as the repository of the two-element variant of the fundamental doctrine of custom.[12] Yet, it is argued here that, although the two elements were not absent from international legal thought in the nineteenth century and early twentieth century,[13] this genealogical narrative whereby international lawyers root their two-element doctrine is contestable.[14] Indeed, a scant review of the *travaux préparatoires* of the drafting of this provision indicates that, in 1920, there was little discussion on the very notion of customary international law in the debates in the Advisory Committee of Jurists, and, subsequently, in the Council or Assembly of the League.[15] Most discussions related to the sources of international law revolved around the need for a provision on the sources,[16] the necessity to address *non liquet*, and general

Customary International Law (Cambridge University Press 1999) 129–46; M Koskenniemi, *From Apology to Utopia: The Structure of International Legal Argument* (Cambridge University Press 2006) 388–473; J Klabbers, 'The Curious Condition of Custom' (2002) 8 *International Legal Theory* 29; James Crawford, *Chance, Order, Change: The Course of International Law: General Course on Public International Law* (Brill 2013) 82–84; for a criticism from general legal theory perspective, *see* e.g. A. Somek, 'Defective Law', University of Iowa Legal Studies Research Paper No 10–33, December 2010.

12 *See* e.g. DJ Bederman, *Custom as a Source of Law* (Cambridge University Press 2010) 135, 137, 166, 137ff. He writes that custom 'involves a searching analysis of what has been taken as a canonical set of elements for the proof of any customary international law norm: International Court of Justice Statute Article 38's requirements of a "general practice" of states, which is "accepted as law"'; in the same vein, A Pellet, 'Article 38' in A Zimmermann, C Tomuschat, and K Oellers-Frahm (eds), *The Statute of the International Court of Justice* (Oxford University Press 2012) 813; for some examples, MH Mendelson, 'The Formation of Customary International Law' (1998) 272 *Collected Courses* 159, 187; I Brownlie, *Principles of Public International Law* (Oxford University Press 2003) 6; A Cassese, *International Law* (Oxford University Press 2005) 156.

13 Alphonse Rivier is credited with the first use of the modern concept of *opinio juris* as an essential element of custom, *see* A Rivier, *Principles du droit des Gens* (A Rousseau 1896) 35; for a recognition of such paternity, A Carty, *Philosophy of International Law* (Edinburgh University Press 2007) 50.

14 In the same vein, CJ Tams, 'Meta-Custom and the Court: A Study in Judicial Law-Making' (2015) 14 *Law and Practice of International Courts and Tribunals* 51, 54–57.

15 Ole Spiermann, '"Who attempts too much does nothing well": The 1920 Advisory Committee of Jurists and the Statute of the Permanent Court of International Justice' (2002) 73 British Yearbook of International Law 187, 212–18; in the same vein, *see* Bederman (n 12) 141; *see* also International Law Commission, 'First report' (n 10) para 30.

16 Permanent Court of International Justice, Advisory Committee of Jurists, Procès-Verbaux of the Proceedings of the Committee, 16 June–24 July 1920 (Reprint 2006) 286ff and 293ff.

principles.[17] The drafting history of Article 38 even shows that the drafters did not seriously discuss what was meant by customary international law and certainly not the need to distinguish between practice and *opinio juris*.[18] They simply 'had no very clear idea as to what constituted international custom'.[19] In other words, they 'did not have in mind a splitting-up of the definition of custom into two distinct elements'.[20] In that sense, the *travaux préparatoires* of Article 38 are, as far as the two-element variant of the doctrine of customary international law is concerned, rather inconsequential.[21] This is certainly not surprising as the purpose of including a provision on the applicable law by the Permanent Court of International Justice was not to define each source mentioned therein but rather to provide the new court with some guidance.[22] This being said, it is still the case that grounding the two-element doctrine of custom in a provision that was not meant to carry any specific understanding of customary law only reinforces the imaginariness of the genealogical link established with the Statute of the Court.[23]

The idea that the two-element variant of the doctrine of custom can be derived from Article 38 by virtue of such imaginary genealogy can even turn more idiosyncratic when approached from a purely textual perspective. It is hardly contested that the very text of Article 38,[24] provided it can be construed in an intelligible way,[25] does not lend any support to the dominant two-element doctrine of custom embraced by international lawyers.[26] Interestingly, international lawyers usually explain the

17 ibid, 311–12, 331–38.

18 In the same vein, *see* Haggenmacher (n 9) 30–31; Tams (n 12) 59; Pellet (n 12) 813.

19 'Summary records of the second session 5 June-29 July 1950' (1950) 1 Yearbook of the International Law Commission 6, para 45.

20 Pellet (n 12) 813.

21 This was confirmed by the report of D Hammarskjöld (Report of 2 July 1920), Hammarskjöl Arkivet, 480, cited in Spielmann (n 15) 216–17.

22 L Ferrari, 'Méthodes de recherche de la coutume internationale dans la pratique des etats' (1965) 192 Collected Courses of the Hague Academy on International Law 243; Spielmann (n 15) 212–18; Pellet (n 12) 813.

23 I have elaborated on the history of the doctrine of custom and the fluctuations in the modes of argumentation on custom elsewhere. *See* J d'Aspremont, 'The Four Lives of Customary International Law' (2019) 21.3–4 International Community Law Review 229.

24 The original Root-Philimoore formulation read 'international custom, as evidence of a common practice in use between nations and accepted by them as law' before being slightly amended to read 'international custom, as evidence of a general practice accepted as law', *see* Procès-Verbaux (n 16) 306, Annex no 3.

25 For a recent criticism, *see* Crawford (n 11) 84; *see* also Tams (n 12) 52.

26 Pellet (n 12) 813; Bradley (n 11); JL Kunz, 'The Nature of Customary International Law' (1953) 47 American Journal of International Law 662, 664.

discrepancy between their genealogical claim and the text of Article 38 by virtue of an argument of poor drafting.[27] Like the incongruence of the *travaux préparatoires*, the discrepancy with the text does not prevent them from continuing to assert that Article 38 provides for the foundations of the two-element doctrine of customary international law.[28] With Article 38, customary international law is provided with a formal repository and is able to prescribe the modes of legal reasoning pertaining to the determination of the existence and content of those international legal rules that behaviourally generated it.

It is argued here that discourses about custom, including discourses on the contribution of non-State actors to the formation of custom, have been dramatically restricted because of this imaginary genealogy that traces back the two-element doctrine to Article 38 and have fallen short of appreciating the intervention of the Permanent Court of International Justice in designing this doctrine. Engaging with the role of non-State actors and the formation of custom ought not to be confined to the realm of Article 38.

2 The two elements of custom: the collapse of a modern dichotomy

Besides emancipating discourses on the contribution of non-State actors to customary law-forming processes from Article 38, as was vindicated in the previous section, it also seems possible to question the dogmatic attachment to the two-element variant of the doctrine of customary law found in the literature and practice. This section argues that, in debates over custom in the last decades, international lawyers have come to embrace 'argumentative shortcuts'[29] that strip the two-element variant of the doctrine of custom of its nucleus: the distinction between practice and *opinio juris*.

This move away from the two-element version of the doctrine of customary international law originally started with a seemingly harmless move: finding practice. Both judges and international legal scholars quickly found out that practice was not easier to find than *opinio juris*.[30] As the Nicaragua decision famously taught them,[31] how can one possibly ascertain the unascertainable, that is, how can one establish an intangible practice of abstention? Since the great majority of rules of international

27 *See* e.g. Bederman (n 12) 142–43.

28 Pellet (n 12) 813.

29 The expression is from Christian Tams, *see* Tams (n 14) 66.

30 *See* also Chapters 2 and 5 in this volume.

31 *Military and Paramilitary Activities in and against Nicaragua (Nicaragua v United States of America) (Merits)*, Judgment [1986] ICJ Reports 14.

law are of a prohibitive character, the establishment of customary international law very often requires a speculative venture into nothingness. Confronted with this overdue realisation that practice – especially with respect to prohibitive rules – was not more easily captured inductively than *opinio juris*, international lawyers have been forced to resort to all sorts of new nets and traps to hunt and capture practice where there was none.

The stratagems and ploys which are being used to 'discover' practice are numerous and well known. Two of them are mentioned here, the second one deserving most of the attention. One of the ruses deployed by international lawyers to discover practice has involved a move away from the self-generating character of customary international law. According to that stratagem, customary rules are no longer emerging by virtue of the behaviour and beliefs of those actors to whom those rules are meant to apply. This means, for instance, that the practice of international organisations or that of non-State actors is said to be instrumental in the crystallisation of purely inter-State rules. In that sense, third-party practice becomes a source of practice for the sake of customary international law. This is so even if the practice of that third party is purely virtual. Indeed, it is sometimes argued that, even if international organisations have no territory, they generate practice relevant for the establishment of inter-State obligations pertaining to how a territory is used. In the same vein, non-State actors who are not engaged as belligerent in armed conflicts are sometimes said to generate practice for customary rules prescribing how States should behave as belligerent on the battlefield.[32]

The abovementioned stratagem, albeit in the light of the traditional self-generative character of custom, is, however, benign. It alters but does not jeopardise the core structure of the doctrine of custom. More devastating is probably the mainstream tendency to turn declarative processes whereby custom is identified into constitutive ones. This is the common contention according to which what is said about a given behaviour is constitutive of that behaviour. By this account, written materials can be constitutive of attitude,[33] while verbal acts can simultaneously be

32 For a discussion of this question, *see* van Steenberghe (n 8); d'Aspremont (n 8) 72–101.

33 J Crawford, 'The Identification and Development of Customary International Law', Spring Conference of the ILA British Branch – Foundations and Futures of International Law, Kings College London, 23–24 May 2014, available at www.youtube.com/watch?v=oXBcoZjMVSM; cf R Higgins, *Problems and Process: International Law and How We Use it* (Clarendon Press 1995) 28.

constitutive of practice.[34] Accordingly, the declarative and the constitutive ought not to be distinguished anymore and the possible evidence of a behaviour thus becomes the behaviour itself. A variant of this stratagem derives behavioural practice from interpretive practice. According to this variant, what is said about an existing rule feeds into the behavioural practice supporting the customary rule. This means, for instance, that qualifications made by certain international actors of given situations (e.g. the Security Council acting in the framework of Chapter VII) generate behavioural practice for the sake of the customary law applicable to that situation.

It is true that warnings against such destructive conflation are not unheard of, as concerns have long been vented about the so-called 'double-counting'.[35] Yet such reprimands – and the reminders that verbal acts can only count as practice as far as customs of making such declarations are concerned and not customs of the conduct described in the content of the verbal acts – have not sufficed to rein in the embrace of such a construction.[36] Indeed, this understanding of custom whereby the constitutive and the declarative collapse in one argumentative maelstrom is rife within the literature.[37] It has even been endorsed by the International Law Association and, notwithstanding some awareness for the problem,[38] the

34 International Law Association, Final Report of the Committee on Formation of Customary (General) International Law (2000), available at www.law.umich.edu/facultyhome/drwcasebook/Documents/Documents/ILA%20Report%20on%20Formation%20of%20Customary%20International%20Law.pdf, 14.

35 The expression is probably from Mendelson (n 12) 206–207, 283–93; *see* also D'Amato (n 11) 88: 'A claim is not act … claims themselves, although they may articulate a legal norm, cannot constitute the material component of custom'; Kammerhofer (n 11) 527; ME Villiger, *Customary International Law and Treaties: A Manual on the Theory and Practice of the Interrelation of Sources* (2nd edn Martinus Nijhoff 1997) 50; K Wolfke, *Custom in Present International Law* (2nd edn, Springer Netherlands 1993); according to Crawford (ILA above n 33) 2.

36 Wolfke (n 35).

37 This understanding dominates all field of international law. For an account *see* J d'Aspremont, 'Customary International Law as a Dance Floor – Part 1' (2014) *EJIL Talk*, available at www.ejiltalk.org/customary-international-law-as-a-dance-floor-part-i/ and 'Customary International Law as a Dance Floor – Part' 2 (2014) *EJIL Talk*, available at www.ejiltalk.org/customary-international-law-as-a-dance-floor-part-ii/; for a similar account with respect to international investment law, *see* J d'Aspremont, 'International Customary Investment Law: Story of a Paradox' in E de Brabandere and T Gazzini (eds), *Sources of International Investment Law* (Brill 2012) 5–47.

38 'Acceptance as law should generally not be evidenced by the very practice alleged to be prescribed by customary international law', *see* International Law Commission, Second Report (n 10) para 74

International Law Commission.[39] It is also found in the practice of international courts and tribunals.[40]

It is argued here that, in their hunt for practice, international lawyers have thus espoused lethal all-embracing construction whereby practice and *opinio juris*, behavioural practice and interpretative practice, and declarative and constitutive processes are two elements of the same dialectical process, if not two faces of the same coin. This conflation between the declarative, the constitutive, and the interpretative can only be fatal for the two-element doctrine of customary law in international legal theory and practice. By allowing the constitutive, the declarative, and the interpretative to overlap and by accepting that the practice be constitutive of the *opinio juris* and the *opinio juris* be constitutive of practice, international lawyers are simply tearing down the two-element construction which they had been so painstakingly and patiently tried to build and improve.[41]

If international legal thought and practice, as has been argued in this section, denotes a great nonchalance with respect to the two-element doctrine, there is greater room for more innovative discourses on non-State actors' contribution to customary international law. In fact, the collapse of the distinction between practice and *opinio juris* facilitates a renewal of scholarly reflections on the matter.

39 Drawing on the claim that such a distinction is artificial, the International Law Commission decided to avoid distinction between constitutive acts and evidence of constitutive acts, *see* International Law Commission, Second Report (n 10) para 38. Although the second report of the Special Rapporteur takes pains to distinguish between the establishment of customary law and the evidence of the two elements (*see* the report's draft conclusion 4 and draft conclusion 10), the two processes remain conflated in some provisions (*see* the 2nd report's draft conclusion 2). While unflinchingly adhering to the two-element approach, the second report occasionally nurtures some conflation between the two elements. For instance, some acts can indeed be constitutive (and/or declarative) of both practice and *opinio juris* (*see* report's draft conclusion 7 and draft conclusion 11); *see* also the list of acts that can be constitutive of practice in para 41–42 and para 48 (draft conclusion 7) and para 76–77 and para 80 (draft conclusion 11) of the report; *see*, however, the more nuanced approach in the third report (n 10) para 15.

40 For J Crawford, the Gulf of Maine case constitutes a case where the International Court of Justice conflated the two elements, *see* Crawford (n 33) 8; for an example of association of declaration of States with State practice in the practice of investment tribunals, *see Glamis Gold Ltd v United States*, Award of 8 June 2009, UNCITRAL, para 602.

41 CJ Tams makes a similar albeit slightly different argument. He argues that 'the actual application of the meta-law of custom has moved away from direct inquiries into State conduct' and that the 'link between practice and custom is much, and further, attenuated, to the point where custom ends up being a bypoduct of other processes of normative clarification', *see* Tams (n 12) 76–77.

3 Non-State actors: an exclusive and inclusive category of thought

The third and last presupposition on which discourses on non-State actors and customary international law are built pertains to the very notion of non-State actors. Indeed, the notion has been deployed in denial of its managerial dimensions, and especially its inclusive and exclusive nature.

Although belligerency and international organisations have been discussed by international lawyers for more than a century,[42] the very notion of non-State actors was sparsely used in international legal scholarship prior to 1990.[43] Even with the development of the concept of armed conflict of a non-international character after the Second World War,[44] the notion of non-State actor only became a big hit – and the object of a prolific body of international legal literature – in the post-Cold War era. Indeed, a quick inquiry though the search engine of the most comprehensive catalogues of international law suffices to show that, although the term had been occasionally used prior to 1990,[45] it is not until 1990 that one witnessed its dramatic mushrooming in international law works.[46] Although the notion may no longer have the lustre and the appeal it had in the post-Cold War scholarship, it remains a very popular category in international lawyers' common parlance.[47]

42 On belligerency, *see* e.g. Institut de Droit International, 'Droits et devoirs des Puissances étrangères, au cas de mouvement insurrectionnel, envers les gouvernements établis et reconnus qui sont aux prises avec l'insurrection' (8 September 1900), Neuchâtel Resolution, available at www.idi-iil.org/fr/sessions/neuchatel-1900/?post_type=publication; for an interesting study with historical insights on the legal scholarship devoted to the law of international organisations, *see* DJ Bederman, 'The Souls of International Organizations: Legal Personality and the Lighthouse at Cape Spartel' (2006) 36 Virginia Journal of International Law 275.

43 This is not exclusive of the notion being commonly used in other disciplines. This is a point I owe to an exchange with Eyal Benvenisti.

44 *See* e.g. G Abi Saab, 'Cours général de droit international' (1987) 207 Collected Courses 81, 96.

45 *See* e.g. DC Turack, 'Passports Issued on Behalf of Non-State Entities' (1970) 16 *New York Law Forum* 625; Tiyanjana Maluwa, 'The Treaty-Making Capacity of the Holy See in Theory and Practice: A Study of the *jus tractum* of a Non-State Entity' (1987) 20 The Comparative and International Law Journal of Southern Africa 155; JK Bleimaier, 'The Legal Status of the Free City of Danzig 1920–1939: Lessons to be Derived from the Experiences of a Non-State Entity in the International Community' (1989) 2 Hague Yearbook of International Law 69.

46 The Peace Palace Library engine generates 633 occurrences of the notions of non-State actors and non-State entities.

47 For a recent set of studies, *see* M Noortmann, A Reinisch, and C Ryngaert (eds), *Non-State Actors in International Law* (Hart 2015).

In this context, it is argued in this section that the very notion of non-State actors carries two managerial dimensions, one inclusive and one exclusive. Indeed, on the one hand, the concept of non-State actors feeds into a general quest for cosmopolitanism. This is what is called here the *inclusiveness* character of the notion of non-State actors whereby actors are made subject to the rules and institutions of international law and contributors to their making and functioning. On the other hand, the concept of non-State actors expresses the idea of a rational consensus on the foundations and mode of operation of international law by creating an *otherness* and thereby creating an image of international law as a space of peace and order that protects those subdued to its rules from the chaos and conflicts of the outside world.

To understand the inclusive character of the non-State actor category, it is necessary to recall that there was a time when international law was defined mainly though its subjects.[48] Subjects were then the main definitional category to describe international law, its origins and its goals. It is no coincidence in this respect that the appellation 'international law' directly refers to its main 'fabricants', for, as is well known, it is this reference to nation States as the makers of international law that prodded Bentham's *An Introduction to the Principles of Morals and Legislation* to coin the expression 'international law'.[49] Such construction was made possible by virtue of, among others, an analogy between the State and the individual of the liberal doctrine of politics.[50] This move gave rise to what has been called classical

48 For a historical account of the concept of subject, *see* the fascinating work of J Nijman, *The Concept of International Legal Personality: An Inquiry into the History and Theory of International Law* (Cambridge University Press 2004).

49 J Bentham, *An Introduction to the Principles of Morals and Legislation* (first published 1781, Kessinger Publishing Co 2005) 326.

50 After Hobbes and Spinoza paved the way for a human analogy, Pufendorf ascribed an intellect to the State and created anthropomorphic vocabularies and images about the main institution of international law, i.e. the State. Such anthropomorphism was later taken over by Vattel – not without adjustment – and subsequently translated itself in the classical positivist doctrine of fundamental rights of states that contributed to the consolidation of modern international law in the nineteenth century. On this point, *see* M Nutkiewicz, 'Samuel Pufendorf: Obligation as the Basis of the State' (1983) 21 Journal of the History of Philosophy 15; F Palladini, 'Pufendorf Disciple of Hobbes: The Nature of Man and the State of Nature: The Doctrine of Socialitas' (2008) 34 History of European Ideas 26; for a criticism of the analogy, *see* EDW Dickinson, 'The Analogy Between Natural Persons and International Persons in the Law of Nations' (1917) 26 Yale Law Journal 564; *see* the discussion of this analogy in J d'Aspremont, 'The Doctrine of Fundamental Rights of States and Anthropomorphic Thinking in International Law' (2005) 4 Cambridge Journal of International and Comparative Law 501; or T Carty, *The Decay of International Law* (Manchester University Press 1986) 44–46.

international legal thought.[51] According to this approach, the makers of international law were deemed originally the sole subjects of international law in that they enjoyed legal personality. There was thus a correlation between states as the makers of international law and subject-hood. In this sense, 'International Law (was) conceived of as horizontal law, in which the subjects of the law are also the makers of the law'.[52] The kinship so established between prominence in lawmaking and subject-hood constituted a conceptual premise that permeated legal scholarship and practice for more than a century. Even with the advent of the modern doctrine of sources as the main definitional mechanism of international law and the shift from a State-based to a source-based definition of international law in the nineteenth century, the correlation between subject-hood and the makers of the international law remained. As a result, an entity not qualifying as a subject could not claim to be participating in lawmaking and vice versa. Interestingly, it is this kinship between the prominent lawmaking role of states and subject-hood that long barred the recognition of an international legal personality to international organisations and other actors.[53] Such kinship was discontinued by the 1949 International Court of Justice advisory opinion on the *Reparation for Injuries Suffered in the Service of the United Nations* (hereafter *Reparation*).[54] This opinion can be understood as constituting a 'constitutionalising' breaking point whereby lawmaking and subject-hood came to be severed from one another, for, in the case of international organisation, subject-hood was no longer derived from its lawmaking role but rather, as is well known, from its functions (the so-called objective school) or the will of its creators (the so-called subjective school).

The severance between centrality in lawmaking and subject-hood operated in the mid-twentieth century bore two main consequences for international legal discourses. These consequences ought to be sketched out here for the sake of the argument made here. First, as a result of the disconnection of legal personality from lawmaking, the question of subject-hood came to potentially arise with respect to all kind of other actors who do not directly or formally participate in lawmaking. Besides internationally personified international organisations, it became possible to recognise other international legal persons, although this has been less construed as the outcome of a direct conferral of international legal personality upon

51 Koskenniemi (n 11) 106.

52 P Allott, 'The True Function of Law in the International Community' (1997–98) 5 Global Legal Studies Journal 391, 404.

53 Bederman (n 12).

54 *Reparations For Injuries Suffered In The Service Of The United Nations*, Advisory Opinion of 11 April 1949 [1949 ICJ Reports 174].

non-State actors than an indirect consequence stemming from them having rights and duties.[55] The severance between legal personality and lawmaking thus allowed the recognition of a legal personality to actors deprived of any major lawmaking powers. The second consequence of the mid-twentieth century dissociation between lawmaking and subject-hood pertains to the possibility that a lawmaking role was recognised for a new range of actors not necessarily endowed with legal personality. In that sense, in the post-*Reparation* era, participation in lawmaking does not turn the actor concerned into a new legal subjects,[56] thereby making possible to rethink international lawmaking, State-centricism, participation, and pluralism irrespective of debates on legal personality.

The foregoing should suffice to figure out the extent to which the 1949 severance between lawmaking and subject-hood promotes a more cosmopolitan international legal order whereby other actors are recognised as contributing to lawmaking. It is noteworthy that the liberal potential of the 1949 Advisory Opinion on Reparations remained unexploited by international lawyers for several decades. In fact, it is not until the 1990s that international lawyers came to make use of the space created by the severance between lawmaking and subject-hood in international legal thought. In this respect, it is no coincidence that it is only in the 1990s that the very notion of non-State actors grew to become central in the discourses of international lawyers. It is submitted here that the emergence of the concept of non-State actors in the 1990s is what materialised the potential of the 1949 Advisory Opinion as it allowed international lawyers to project a pluralised image of international law and repudiate the State-centric representation(s) of international law that had been dominating legal thought until then. By virtue of the notion of non-State actors, international lawyers have been able to impose the view that, in practice, international law and its making have witnessed a growing pluralisation *ratione personae*. The notion thus allows the

55 *See* generally, C Dominicé, 'La personnalité juridique internationale du CICR' in C Swinarski (ed), *Etudes et essais sur le droit international humanitaire et sur les principes de la Croix-Rouge en l'honneur de Jean Pictet* (CICR 1984) 663; in the context of the debate about the responsibility of transnational corporations, *see* O de Schutter (ed), *Transnational Corporations and Human Rights* (Hart 2006); this has led scholars to deem that the question of international legal personality was described as 'circular', 'sterile', and boiling down to an 'intellectual prison', *see* A Reinisch, 'The Changing International Legal Framework for Dealing with Non-State Actors' in P Alston (ed), *Non-State Actors and Human Rights* (Oxford University Press 2005) 37, 69–72.

56 On this point, J d'Aspremont, 'Cognitive Conflicts and the Making of International Law: From Empirical Concord to Conceptual Discord in Legal Scholarship' (2013) 46 Vanderbilt Journal of Transnational Law 1119.

projection of an image where states have ceased to be (perceived as) the only actors in charge of international law. As a result of this image, normative authority is seen as being no longer exercised by a closed circle of high-ranking officials acting on behalf of states, but has instead turned into an aggregation of complex procedures involving non-State actors.[57] Such pluralisation has been articulated through notions like 'standard-setters',[58] 'law-takers',[59] or 'participants'.[60] It also manifested itself through the more contested[61] recognition of some possible role of non-State actors in the formation of customary international law.[62] It is noteworthy that to sustain this image of a pluralised international law, an important body of empirical evidence has been produced.[63]

It is in this context that it can be contended that the very notion of non-State actors came to function as the concept through which international lawyers have

57 This has sometimes been called 'verticalization', *see* J Klabbers, 'Setting the Scene' in J Klabbers, A Peters, and G Ulfstein (eds), *The Constitutionalization of International Law* (Oxford University Press 2009) 14.

58 Anne Peters et al (eds), *Non-State Actors as Standard Setters* (Cambridge University Press 2009).

59 M Noortmann and C Ryngaert (eds), *Non-State Actor Dynamics in International Law: From Law-Takers to Law-Makers* (Ashgate 2010).

60 J d'Aspremont (ed), *Participants in the International Legal System* (Routledge 2010).

61 This view has been contested by the International Law Commission Special Rapporteur in International Law Commission, Second Report (n 10) 32–33.

62 J Henckaerts and L Doswald-Beck (eds), *Customary International Humanitarian Law, Volume I: Rules* (ICRC/Cambridge University Press, 2005) xlii: the ICRC seems to give it significance despite claiming that 'while such practice may contain evidence of the acceptance of certain rules in noninternational armed conflicts, its legal significance is unclear'; J Bohoslavsky, Y Li, and M Sudreau, 'Emerging Customary International Law in Sovereign Debt Governance?' (2014) 9(1) *Capital Markets Law Journal* 55, 63.

63 Non-State actors are said to have been expending their say in international lawmaking processes and that they also wield some influence in the review and amendments procedures of conventional instruments. To buttress that contention, reference is made to how their formal presence and participation in international lawmaking processes has swollen, as is demonstrated by their (potential) involvement within the framework of the UN Economic and Social Council (ECOSOC), the UN Global Compact, the UN Human Rights Council, the UN Security Council (to a very limited extent), the World Trade Organization (WTO) and within the cooperation policies of the European Community with the Group of African, Caribbean and Pacific Countries (ACP countries). Mention is moreover made of some notorious recent convention-making conferences having also weathered a renewed NGO involvement as is illustrated by the conferences leading to the adoption of the 1997 Convention on the Prohibition of the Use, Stockpiling, Production and Transfer or Anti-Personnel Mines and on Their Destruction, the 2008 Convention on

made use of the cosmopolitan space created by the 1949 Advisory Opinion.[64] This means that the notion of non-State actors can be considered an inclusive tool feeding the quest for cosmopolitanism. This being said, it is important to emphasise that the inclusiveness that came with the 1949 severance between lawmaking and subject-hood and which was materialised through the notion of non-State actors has another facet. Indeed, inclusiveness that accompanies the notion of non-State actors does not only pertain to the configuration of international of lawmaking processes but is simultaneously articulated in terms of binding-ness and liability. Said differently, according to this aspect of inclusiveness, the concept of non-State actors has been used in international legal thought and practice, not only to enhance the cosmopolitanism of the international legal order, but also to expend the outreach of international law and subdue new actors and subject them to the rules and

Cluster Munitions or the well-known examples of the processes leading to the adoption of 1984 Torture Convention, the 1990 Convention on the Rights of the Child, and the 1999 Rome Statute of the International Criminal Court. It is said that, in these situations, it can hardly be denied that non-State actors, through their formal role, have left their imprint in the substance of the rules finally adopted. The same allegedly holds with respect to the International Law Commission (ILC) which has engaged in regular consultations with NGOs, as is illustrated its work on the Protection of Persons in the Event of Disaster.

64 The use of the notion of non-State actors to project an image of a pluralised international law, while being dominant, is not exempt from criticisms. Indeed, it could be contended that international law has always been pluralised. For instance, it could be said that non-governmental organisations (NGOs) have been involved in international lawmaking for more than 200 years. It is also often recalled that NGOs have aroused the initiative or have been granted a formal participatory role in various international lawmaking conferences since as early as the nineteenth century. To name but a few, mention is frequently made of the role of the American Peace Society in the first plan for the Permanent Court of Arbitration; the role of the Geneva Public Welfare Society in the adoption of the 1864 Geneva Convention for the Amelioration of the Condition of the Wounded in Armies in the Field; the role of all the peace societies which sent representatives to the First and Second Hague Peace Conferences the role of the Inter-Parliamentary Union and the World Court League in the establishment of the Permanent Court of International Justice; and the occasional role of NGOs in the committees and conferences of the League of Nations. A similar role played by the private sector in the same period in the meetings of the International Telegraph Union, the annual conferences of the International Labour Organization or the Pan American Conferences is also invoked, *see*, generally, S Charnovitz, 'Two Centuries of Participation: NGOs and International Governance' (1997) 18 Michigan Journal of International Law 103. It could also be said that the idea of a Westphalian State-centric order has never really existed and has been a straw man created by inter-war international lawyers, *see* R Collins, 'Classical Positivism in International Law Revisited' in J d'Aspremont and

institutions of international law. In that sense, inclusiveness is simultaneously managerial as it is about subjecting new actors to the rule(s) of international law and evaluating their behaviour according to the very standards set by international law. Indeed, once one includes them in the realm of international law, one can evaluate their behaviour according to the standards of international law and attach to departures from such standards the consequences prescribed by international law.[65] They actually are included in the regulative space of international law and given the necessary existence that allows them to be subjected to international regulatory frameworks and the standards set by the latter.

It will not come as a surprise that, as far as this managerial aspect of the inclusiveness of the notion of non-State actors is concerned, international law, humanitarian law, and the law of armed conflict have constituted a fertile ground. Whilst reflections about the binding-ness of humanitarian law, especially that of provisions like Common Article 3 of the Geneva Conventions upon insurgents, pre-date the post-1990 scholarly frenzy,[66] the pre-1990 debates seemed to have regained momentum. Interestingly, all the stakeholders in this debate ended up agreeing that such non-State actors are bound by some rules of international humanitarian law but kept

J Kammerhofer (eds), *International Legal Positivism in a Post-Modern World* (Cambridge University Press 2012); J d'Aspremont and J Kammerhofer, 'Introduction: The Future of International Legal Positivism' in J Kammerhofer and J d'Aspremont (eds), *International Legal Positivism in a Post-Modern World* (Cambridge University Press 2014) 1; *see* also A Osiander, 'Sovereignty, International Relations, and the Westphalian Myth' (2001) 55 *International Organization* 251; P Piirimäe, 'The Westphalian Myth and the Idea of External Sovereignty' in Q Skinner and T Kalmo (eds), *Sovereignty in Fragments: The Past, Present and Future of a Contested Concept* (Cambridge University Press 2010) 64–80; B Teschke, *The Myth of 1648: Class, Geopolitics, and the Making of Modern International Relations* (Verso 2009).

65 F Megret, 'Where Does the Critique of International Human Rights Stand An Exploration in 18 Vignettes' in JM Beneyto and D Kennedy, *New Approaches to International Law: The European and American Experiences* (TMC Asser Press 2012).

66 On this question in general, *see* M Bothe, KJ Partsch, and WA Solf, *New Rules of Victims of Armed Conflicts: Commentary on the Two 1977 Protocols Additional to the Geneva Conventions of 1949* (Martinus Nijhoff 1982); A Cassese, 'The Status of Rebels under the 1977 Geneva Protocol on Non-International Armed Conflicts' (1981) International and Comparative Law Quarterly 416; C Ryngaert, 'Human Rights Obligations of Armed Groups' (2008) 1–2 Revue Belge de droit international 355; L Zegveld, *Accountability of Armed Opposition Groups in International Law* (Cambridge University Press 2002); C Tomuschat, 'The Applicability of Human Rights to Insurgent Movements' in H. Fischer (ed), *Crisis Management and Humanitarian Protection: Festschrift für Dieter Fleck* (Berliner Wissenschafts-Verlag 2004), 573–91.

disagreeing about what justifies the binding-ness of such rules on non-State actors. Said differently, they all came to claim that non-State actors are bound by (certain rules of) international humanitarian law but stopped inquiring about the foundations thereof. This is why this new post-1990 momentum ended with a consensus on the idea that non-State actors are bound by international law. Yet, this consensus fell short of any common theory of international obligations in relation to non-State actors.[67]

The managerial inclusiveness of the concept of non-State actors did not stop with international humanitarian law. Having agreed on these findings regarding insurgents, international legal scholars turned their attention to other actors. They raised the same question of binding-ness of the rules of international law in relation to NGOs[68] and multinational companies.[69] In this case, however, no consensus was reached and scholars remained deeply divided.[70] Here too, they suffered from the absence of a theory of international obligations. Yet, this did not preclude international legal scholarship to embark on studies over the consequences of the breach of such obligations in terms of responsibility, thereby engaging in ambitious transposition of the Articles on State Responsibility (hereafter ASR) to non-State actors,[71] not always with tangible success.[72] It remains that by subjecting more actors to

67 *See* e.g. L Zegveld, *Accountability of Armed Opposition Groups in International Law* (Cambridge University Press 2002).

68 *See*, generally, PM Dupuy (ed), *NGOs in International Law, Efficiency in Flexibility?* (Edwar Elgar 2008).

69 On the famous *Texaco v Libya* arbitration (1977), *see* A Fatouros, 'International Law and the Internationalized Contract' (1980) 74 American Journal of International Law 134.

70 R Hoffmann (ed), *Non-State Actors as New Subjects of International Law: from the Traditional State Order towards the Law of the Global Community* (Duncker & Humblot 1999).

71 For instance, the *UN Basic Principles and Guidelines on the Right to a Remedy and Reparation for Victims of Gross Violations of International Human Rights Law and Serious Violations of International humanitarian law* (UNBPG) state that where 'a person, a legal person, or other entity is found liable for reparation for a victim, such party should provide reparation to the victim or compensate the State if the State has already provided reparation to the victim' (Principle 15); it is also noteworthy that the ILA Committee on Reparations for Victims of Armed Conflict affirmed that armed opposition groups can be held responsible to provide reparations where they commit violations of international humanitarian law, for an attempt of transposition of the paradigms of the 2001 Articles on State Responsibility to armed groups, *see* J d'Aspremont, A Nollkaemper, I Plakokefalos, and C Ryngaert, 'Sharing Responsibility Between Non-State Actors and States In International Law: Introduction' (2015) 62 Netherlands International Law Review 49.

72 *See* 3rd report prepared by the co-rapporteurs, Cedric Ryngaert and Jean d'Aspremont, available at www.ila-hq.org/index.php/committees?committeeID=41.

international legal rules, this other aspect of the inclusiveness of non-State actors has reinforced the pluralism and cosmopolitanism of international law while also conveying the image that international law subject actors to its rule in order to serve the interest of individuals.

The foregoing shows that, despite the theoretical paucity of scholarly debates, the notion of non-State actors has continued to perform an inclusive function, filling the space open by the 1949 Advisory Opinion and allowing new actors to contribute to international lawmaking processes on the one hand, while also subjecting those actors to the rule(s) of international law. In performing this twofold inclusive function, the concept of non-State actors has allowed international law to be represented as a pluralistic order at the service of a cosmopolitan project.

The attention must now turn to the other managerial aspect of the notion of non-State actors, namely its exclusiveness, or, said differently, its ability to create otherness. It is submitted here that the inclusiveness of the concept of non-State actors, as was described above, has simultaneously been accompanied by exclusive practices.[73] Indeed, the notion of non-State actors is concurrently deployed in an exclusionist way; that is, as a mechanism of 'othering'. As has been observed elsewhere,[74] the notion of non-State actors whether deployed in relation to arguments about legal personality, rights and duties, or lawmaking privileges, has largely been relied on in international legal thought and practice to promote a certain configuration of international law and exclude certain actors from the centre thereof. The notion is about constructing the idea that certain actors are 'the others'.[75] It thus puts in place a fundamental narrative of ostracisation.[76] Whilst the concept of non-State actors is not alone in functioning as an othering mechanism,[77] it certainly is one of the most powerful constructions of this kind in international legal thought and practice.

Recognising the ostracisation – and more generally the mechanism of othering – that accompany the notion of non-State actors is not ground-breaking. For the sake

73 On the idea that inclusiveness of human rights comes at the cost of exclusive practices, *see* Megret (n 65) 7.

74 This is one of the main ideas of the book by Nijman (n 48) 454 onwards.

75 S Jodoin, 'International Law and Alterity: The State and the Other' (2008) 21 Leiden Journal of International Law 1.

76 It is in this sense that Philip Alston claims that 'these negative euphemistic terms … have been intentionally adopted in order to reinforce the assumption that the state is not only the central actor, but also the indispensable and pivotal one around which all other entities revolve', Alston (n 55) 3.

77 This is a process that has been ascribed to human rights in general, *see* Megret (n 65); *see* also M Mutua, 'Savages, Victims, and Saviors: The Metaphor of Human Rights' (2001) 42 Harvard International Law Journal 201.

of the argument made here, it is of greater relevance to highlight that the othering performed by the notion of non-State actors comes with a specific vision of what constitutes order and disorder. By othering, the notion of non-State actors comes to constitute order and disorder.[78] In fact, the realm of the State becomes equated with order as it falls under international law. In contrast, disorder is associated with the realm of the non-State (or the 'others'). By associating chaos and disorders with the others, the notion of non-State actors allegedly pushes chaos, unsettled competition of interests, and disorder outside international law, thereby simultaneously reinforcing the idea that international law replaces chaos and conflict thanks to the rational consensus that allegedly informs its foundations and mode of operation.[79]

It will not come as a surprise that the otherness of the notion of non-State actors, like inclusiveness, bears a managerial dimension. Indeed, just like the inclusiveness of the concept of non-State actors allowed the modulation of the ambit of international law and the imposition of rights and duties on other actors than States and international organisations, relegating non-State actors to the realm of the disorder allows international lawyers to pass a judgment on those fringe entities and unruly creatures with a view to legitimising attempts to regulate their practice. In other words, the disorder constituted by the notion of non-State actors carries an invitation for international lawyers to intervene with a view to ironing out disorders through the subjection of those actors to the rule(s) of international law.[80]

It is argued here that recognising the two managerial dimensions of the notion of non-State actors, and especially its inclusive and exclusive dimensions, can prove instrumental in renewing the categories through which discourses on the contribution of non-State actors to the formation of custom are formulated. It is the

78 On the rage for order of international lawyer, *see* J Crawford, 'International Law as a Profession and Discipline', Manley O Hudson Medal Lecture (2012) 106 Proceedings of the American Society of International Law 471, 472.

79 On the idea that rejecting chaos, plurality of interest and disorder to the periphery of international law and thus ascribing them to the others, is the expression of liberal pattern of thought, *see* S Marks, 'International Judicial Activism and the Commodity-Form Theory of International Law' (2007) 18 European Journal of International Law 199, 202.

80 cf with the justification of the intervention of international law (and international lawyers) by virtue of narratives of crisis, *see*, generally, A Orford, 'The Destiny of International Law' (2004) 17 Leiden Journal of International Law 441; on international lawyers' inclination to seek and find crisis to develop international law, *see*, generally, H Charlesworth, 'International Law: A Discipline of Crisis' (2002) 65 *Modern Law Review* 377; for an illustration of such use of crisis narratives, *see* J d'Aspremont, 'Jenks' Ethic of Responsibility for the Disillusioned International Lawyer' (28 October 2016), Amsterdam Law School Research Paper no 2016-63, available at SSRN: https://ssrn.com/abstract=2860610.

ambition of the next and last section of this chapter to touch on the argumentative space that can potentially be made available by gainsaying the three main constructions discussed in sections 1–3.

4 Non-State actors and customary international law: where do we go from here?

Reinvention is punishing. In fact, as was discussed in this chapter, reinventing the debate on the contribution of non-State actors to custom-forming processes calls for some kind of 'unlearning',[81] in this case the unlearning of the categories of thoughts which international lawyers have been trained to continuously repeat and articulate their thoughts around. In particular, the previous sections have sought to show that international lawyers' reflections on the contribution of non-State actors to customary law are not bound to be conducted under the umbrella of Article 38 and that of the two-element doctrine which they have never applied systematically and rigidly. In the same vein, the previous sections have shown that deploying the notion of non-State actors in relation to international customary law inevitably mobilises some of the managerial dimensions of that notion, and especially its inclusive and exclusive features. It is submitted, at this concluding stage, that the argumentative space opened by the challenging of these three common tropes is significant. This section is, of course, not the place to dictate how the argumentative space created by such an unlearning should be used and the specific direction that the debate on non-State actors and custom should take. Instead, these ultimate paragraphs limit themselves to a few new thoughts that now seem possible by virtue of the emancipatory exercise promoted here.

81 I have further explored the idea of 'unlearning' elsewhere, *see* J d'Aspremont, *International Law as a Belief System* (Cambridge University Press 2017); for some critical remarks on the idea that works of critical theory are designed to demystify, *see* A Rasulov, 'Writing about Empire: Remarks on the Logic of a Discourse' (2010) 23 Leiden Journal of International Law 449, esp. 450; Derrida argued that mysticism – which is how he construes fabricated genealogy – is what gives law a 'deconstructible' structure, thereby allowing the possibility of deconstruction, *see* J Derrida, 'Force of Law: The "Mystical Foundation of Authority"' in G Anidjar (ed), *Acts of Religion: Jacques Derrida* (Routledge 2002) 230–98 – he writes (242–43ff) that the mystical character of law means that 'law is essential deconstructible, whether because it is founded, that is to say constructed, upon interpretable and transformable textual strata … or because its ultimate foundation is by definition unfounded. The fact that law is deconstructible is not bad news. One may even find in this the political chance of all historical progress … it is this deconstructible structure of law … that also ensures the possibility of deconstruction'.

1. The role of non-State actors in the formation of custom is not a matter that is dependent on any interpretation of Article 38 of the Permanent Court of International Justice Statute. In other words, the debate about non-State actors and customary international law does not need to be conducted as a question of hermeneutics.
2. In the same vein, the debate on non-State actors' contribution to customary international law should not be carried out from the perspective of the sources of international law. In fact, the making of the doctrine of customary international law and the determination of those who potentially play a role in the formation of custom cannot be seen as a legalist rule-making process. Instead, it should be seen as the coalescing of a number of State and non-State actors that have imposed certain modes of legal reasoning about custom on all the professionals involved in the business of international legal argumentation.
3. Because the determination of the role of non-State actors in custom-forming processes does not boil down to a hermeneutical question nor a sources-based inquiry, one can realise that the very attribution of a role to non-State actors can possibly be determined by all those intervening in these debates, including a series of non-State actors whose say is held to be authoritative (scholars, codifying bodies, non-governmental organisations, etc.). In that sense, the question of the role of non-State actors in custom-forming processes is partly to be answered by non-State actors themselves.
4. As the debate on non-State actors' contribution in custom-forming processes ought not to be conducted in hermeneutical or source-based terms, it becomes possible to conduct these debates in the very managerial terms of the notion of non-State actors and consciously choose what kind of lawmaking process one wants and which actors should be given a voice without having to hide behind the smokescreen of sources or interpretation. In other words, claims on this matter should not be presented as inductive constructions based on interpretation or sources but, rather, as normative choices about how to design and shape the politics of international lawmaking.

The abovementioned novelties are only a few of the new constructions enabled by the unlearning of the three key tropes gainsaid in this chapter. Whether these constructions actually serve the agendas of international lawyers and all those having a stake in the debate about non-State actors' contribution to customary international law is a question for another day. For now, it is just hoped that international lawyers will not be daunted by the punishing character of the unlearning process promoted here and dare to take advantage thereof in order to renew their thinking.

Part II

Field perspectives and case studies

Chapter 8

International organizations and non-State actors in the International Law Commission's conclusions on identification of customary international law

*Michael Wood**

The present volume is a timely addition to the vast (and still growing) literature on customary international law. In 2018 the United Nations International Law Commission adopted, on second and final reading, a set of sixteen conclusions (with commentaries) on identification of customary international law, thus bringing to completion a six-year study of the topic.[1] Throughout that time, the question whether, and if so how, the practice of international (intergovernmental) organizations may contribute to the formation and identification of customary international law was much debated, both within and outside the Commission. The role that may be played in this regard by actors other than States and international organizations, by contrast, proved largely uncontroversial. Intended to offer practical guidance on these and other matters to those called upon to identify and apply customary international law, the Commission's conclusions seek to capture the present position in international law, as it appears from the approach of States and in the case law of courts and tribunals.

It may be useful to clarify, at the outset, what the Commission did and did not say with regard to the role of international organizations and that of 'non-State actors', since some of the contributions in this volume (like one or two States in the

* The author thanks Mr Omri Sender for his invaluable assistance.

1 *See* A/73/10: *Report of the International Law Commission on the work of its seventieth session (30 April–1 June and 2 July–10 August 2018)*, 119–56. In addition to the conclusions and commentaries, the Commission's output under this topic includes a bibliography prepared by the Special Rapporteur (A/CN.4/717/Add.1) and a study by the Secretariat on 'Ways and means for making the evidence of customary international law more readily available' (A/CN.4/710*).

UN General Assembly's Sixth Committee) seem not to have fully appreciated what was said within the Commission or what the Commission itself actually said in its second reading texts. The Commission's second reading in 2018 involved a detailed review of the earlier draft conclusions and commentaries (adopted on first reading in 2016) in light of comments received from governments and others.[2] The review led to rather few changes in the text of the conclusions; but the commentaries were adjusted in many respects. This was mainly to increase their clarity, but also – and this was particularly the case with the role of international organizations – to take account of suggestions made and concerns expressed about the first reading texts.[3]

The issues covered by the present volume are chiefly dealt with in three of the conclusions: conclusions 4, 10, and 12. Conclusion 4, entitled 'Requirement of practice', stipulates that while it is 'primarily … the practice of States that contributes to the formation, or expression, of rules of customary international law', '[i]n certain cases, the practice of international organizations also contributes' to this end.[4] The conclusion further provides that '[c]onduct of other actors is not practice that contributes to the formation, or expression, of rules of customary international law, but may be relevant when assessing the practice [of States and international organizations]'.[5] The Commission thus makes a clear distinction between States and international organizations on the one hand, and actors that are neither States nor international organizations on the other; it does not lump them together, as a superficial reading of some of the contributions to this book might suggest.

Conclusion 10, which deals with forms of evidence of acceptance as law (*opinio juris*), is drafted so as to apply equally to States and international organizations, with the exception of conclusion 10, paragraph 2; in that case the commentary states that the paragraph 'applies *mutatis mutandis* to the forms of evidence of acceptance of law (*opinio juris*) of international organizations'.[6]

2 *See*, for example, *Identification of customary international law: Comments and observations received from Governments* (A/CN.4/716). Several institutions hosted meetings on the topic, including the 2017 conference hosted by the Manchester International Law Centre at the University of Manchester, which was the origin of the present volume.

3 For some of the questions about the treatment of international organizations in first reading text, *see* N Blokker, 'International Organizations and Customary International Law: Is the International Law Commission taking International Organizations Seriously?' 14 International Organizations Law Review (2017) 1–12; N Blokker, *International Institutional Law* (6th edn, Brill Nijhoff 2018) para 1579.

4 *Supra* note 1, 119, conclusion 4, paras 1 and 2.

5 ibid para 3.

6 ibid 141, para 7 of the commentary to conclusion 10.

Conclusion 12, which deals with the significance of resolutions of international organizations (and intergovernmental conferences), states that '[a] resolution adopted by an international organization or at an intergovernmental conference cannot, of itself, create a rule of customary international law'.[7] It specifies, however, that such a resolution 'may provide evidence for determining the existence and content of a rule of customary international law, or contribute to its development'.[8] The conclusion further provides that '[a] provision in a resolution adopted by an international organization or at an intergovernmental conference may reflect a rule of customary international law if it is established that the provision corresponds to a general practice that is accepted as law (*opinio juris*)'.[9] The Commission thus recognized (as does, for example, Brölmann in chapter 2 of this volume) that international organizations may prove relevant to the formation and identification of customary international law both as actors in their own right and as fora for State practice.[10]

If for some scholars, including some of the contributors to this volume '[i]t seems uncontested that international organisations can contribute [in their own right] to the making of customary international law',[11] this proposition (as enshrined in conclusion 4, paragraph 2) was the subject of a range of strongly held views, both within the Commission and among States, including in the course of the 2018 Sixth Committee debate on the second reading text.[12] As noted above, the text eventually adopted aimed to meet the concerns of all sides, with the relatively detailed commentary to conclusion 4 playing a crucial role in that respect. As stated therein,

> The practice of international organizations in international relations (when accompanied by *opinio juris*) may count as practice that gives rise or attests to rules of customary international law, but only those rules (a) whose subject matter falls within the mandate of the organizations, and/or (b) that are addressed specifically to them (such as those on their international responsibility or relating to treaties to which international organizations may be parties). The words 'in certain cases' in paragraph 2 indeed serve to indicate that the practice of international organizations will not be

7 ibid 121, para 1 of conclusion 12.
8 ibid para 2.
9 ibid para 3.
10 As the commentary puts it, '[w]hile international organizations often serve as arenas or catalysts for the practice of States, [conclusion 4, paragraph 2] deals with practice that is attributed to international organizations themselves, not practice of States acting within or in relation to them (which is attributed to the States concerned)': *supra* note 1, 130, para 4 of the commentary to conclusion 4.
11 *See* Chapter 13 in this volume.
12 For the Sixth Committee debate, *see* A/C.6/SR. 20–24 and (for the USA) A/C.6/SR.29.

> relevant to the identification of all rules of customary international law, and further that it may be the practice of only some, not all, international organizations that is relevant.[13]

The commentary further explains that:

> Within this framework, the practice falling under paragraph 2 arises most clearly where member States have transferred exclusive competences to the international organization, so that the latter exercises some of the public powers of its member States and hence the practice of the organization may be equated with the practice of those States. This is the case, for example, for certain competences of the European Union. Practice within the scope of paragraph 2 may also arise where member States have not transferred exclusive competences, but have conferred competences upon the international organization that are functionally equivalent to powers exercised by States. Thus the practice of international organizations when concluding treaties, serving as treaty depositaries, in deploying military forces (for example, for peacekeeping), in administering territories, or in taking positions on the scope of the privileges and immunities of the organization and its officials, may contribute to the formation, or expression, of rules of customary international law in those areas.[14]

It is also noted that:

> At the same time, caution is required in assessing the weight of the practice of an international organization as part of a general practice. International organizations vary greatly, not just in their powers, but also in their membership and functions. As a general rule, the more directly a practice of an international organization is carried out on behalf of its member States or endorsed by them, and the larger the number of such member States, the greater weight it may have in relation to the formation, or expression, of rules of customary international law. Among other factors that may need to be considered in weighing the practice are: the nature of the organization; the nature of the organ whose conduct is under consideration; whether the conduct is *ultra vires* the organization or organ; and whether the conduct is consonant with that of the member States of the organization.[15]

To suggest that the conclusions assign to international organizations only a 'modest role' in the formation of customary international law, as some scholars seem to do, is misguided for at least three reasons. First, those scholars overlook (if not contest) the fact that it is States that are the primary subjects of international law. International organizations, which are entities established and empowered by States (or by States and/or other international organizations) to carry out certain functions, are not 'reduced' by the conclusions to agents of States:[16] even if they have

13 *Supra* note 1, 131, para 5 of the commentary to conclusion 4 (footnotes omitted).
14 ibid para 6 of the commentary to conclusion 4 (footnotes omitted).
15 ibid para 7 of the commentary to conclusion 4.
16 *See* the Introduction to the present volume.

separate legal personality and a 'juridical will' that may be independent of that of their members, they are in fact agents of States, not having the degree of autonomy enjoyed by the latter. Scholars are, of course, free to suggest changing this state of the world; but this was not what the Commission sought to do.[17]

Second, and closely related, the argument that a uniform basic approach to customary international law necessitates treating States and international organizations in exactly the same way,[18] is unconvincing. As the International Court of Justice put it as long ago as in 1949, '[t]he subjects of law in any legal system are not necessarily identical in their nature or in the extent of their rights'.[19]

Third, the conclusions do recognize the potential role of international organizations in the formation of customary international law and indeed highlight it. To the extent that 'such a role has never been captured by the modern categories of the doctrine of the sources of international law',[20] then the conclusions are to be welcomed for doing just that. One may add in this connection that Article 38 of the Statute of the International Court of Justice, the importance of which is difficult to deny notwithstanding occasional assertions to the contrary,[21] does leave room for recognizing the possible contribution of the practice of international organizations to the formation and identification of customary international law: unlike some earlier proposals for what became Article 38, it refers to '[i]nternational custom, as

17 To suggest that the Special Rapporteur considered the proposition enshrined in conclusion 4(2) to represent a progressive development of the law, as Voulgaris does in this book, is wrong, as is his assertion that the conclusion was 'the product of a gut feeling'.

18 *See* Chapters 1 and 4 in this volume.

19 *Reparation for injuries suffered in the service of the United Nations, Advisory Opinion, ICJ Reports 1949*, 174, 178ff. *See* also the articles on responsibility of international organizations adopted by the Commission in 2011, paragraph 7 of the general commentary: 'International organizations are quite different from States, and in addition present great diversity among themselves. In contrast with States, they do not possess a general competence and have been established in order to exercise specific functions ("principle of speciality"). There are very significant differences among international organizations with regard to their powers and functions, size of membership, relations between the organization and its members, procedures for deliberation, structure and facilities, as well as the primary rules including treaty obligations by which they are bound' (*Yearbook of the International Law Commission 2011*, vol II (Part Two), 47).

20 *See* Chapter 7 in this volume. *See* also Chapter 11 in this volume ('The International Law Commission study has an original feature which has no precedent in either the previous work of the International Law Commission on customary international law or the academic literature: according to the Draft Conclusions, the practice of international organizations as such may, under certain circumstances, be constitutive of custom').

21 *See* Chapters 6 and 7 in this volume.

evidence of a general practice accepted as law' without including the word 'State' or 'nation'.[22]

Nor is it convincing to suggest, as some scholars do, that the Commission limited the possible contribution of international organizations to the objective element of customary international law and set aside any inquiry that pertains to the subjective element (*opinio juris*).[23] The fact that practice of international organizations is referred to explicitly only in conclusion 4 (on the requirement of practice) certainly does not imply that: not only are the conclusions to be read together, but any practice that may be of relevance to the formation of customary international law – including that of international organizations – must inherently be one that is accompanied by *opinio juris*. The commentary states that '[t]he practice of international organizations in international relations (when accompanied by *opinio juris*) may count as practice that gives rise or attests to rules of customary international law'.[24] It provides, moreover, that '[i]n those cases where the practice of international organizations themselves is of relevance … references in the draft conclusions and commentaries to the practice of States should be read as including, *mutatis mutandis*, the practice of international organizations'.[25]

Nor does establishing acceptance as law (*opinio juris*) on the part of international organizations raise any special difficulties. As noted above and as those who have worked for international organizations will surely appreciate, the forms of evidence referred to in the Commission's conclusion 10 may well apply, *mutatis mutandis*, to international organizations.[26] Statements of senior officials of the organization, legal opinions by the legal advisers of the organization,

22 The suggested Root-Phillimore formulation of '[i]nternational custom, as evidence of a common practice in use between nations and accepted by them as law', like Baron Descamps's original reference to international custom as 'being practice between nations accepted by them as law', ended up on the Advisory Committee of Jurists' cutting-room floor. Authors have thus argued that 'custom … [is] not required to be followed or acknowledged "by states" only, as it is actually required [in the Statute] … when referring to conventions. So that, in principle, practices may emanate from state and non-state actors': JP Bohoslavsky, Y Li, and M Sudreau, 'Emerging Customary International Law in Sovereign Debt Governance?', 9 *Capital Markets Law Journal* (2013) 55, 63.

23 *See* Chapter 1 in this volume. *See* also Chapters 2, 4, and 13 in this volume.

24 *Supra* note 1, 131ff, para 5 of the commentary to conclusion 4.

25 ibid 130, para 4 of the commentary to conclusion 4.

26 This is expressly stated in the commentary to conclusion 10: *see* ibid; J Odermatt, 'The Development of Customary International Law by International Organizations', 66 *International and Comparative Law Quarterly* (2017) 491, 493.

correspondence of the organization with its member States (or others), acceptance by the organization of treaty provisions explicitly incorporating rules of customary international law, or official publications of an organization, may indeed attest to the 'juridical will' of the organization concerned. A recent example is the Joint Statement submitted to the United Nations Legal Counsel on 31 January 2017 by some twenty-four international organizations, in which the signatories expressed their view, inter alia, on the legal status of the rules contained in the International Law Commission's articles on the responsibility of international organizations.[27]

Resolutions adopted by organs of international organizations may, of course, in addition serve as important evidence of the *opinio juris* of their members, and that is part of what conclusion 12 seeks to capture. The Commission did not define resolutions as acts of States;[28] the commentary indeed explains that '[a]lthough resolutions of organs of international organizations (unlike resolutions of intergovermental conferences) emanate, strictly speaking, not from the States members but from the organization, in the context of the present draft conclusion what is relevant is that they may reflect the collective expression of the views of such States'.[29] It is equally mistaken to suggest that the conclusion makes no reference to the purpose which the resolution in question is to serve, or that a single resolution (as opposed to several resolutions) cannot serve as evidence.[30] Like the International Court of Justice, the Commission recognizes that a resolution may sometimes offer valuable evidence for establishing the existence of a rule or the emergence of an *opinio juris*, particularly when it purports to be declaratory of an existing rule of customary international law (in which case it may serve as evidence of the acceptance as law of such a rule by those States supporting the resolution).[31]

Turning to those 'other actors' referred to in conclusion 4, paragraph 3, it should first be noted that the term 'non-State actors' is not without ambiguity: as Bílková

27 'Response to the request of the Under-Secretary-General for Legal Affairs and United Nations Legal Counsel of February 8, 2016, for comments and information relating to the draft articles on the responsibility of international organizations pursuant to UN General Assembly resolution 69/126 (2014)', available online at http://opil.ouplaw.com/view/10.1093/law-oxio/e204.013.1/law-oxio-e204-regGroup-1-law-oxio-e204-source.pdf. *See* also the reference, in Chapter 12 in the present volume, to legal opinions published by secretariats of international organizations; as another example, Veber points in Chapter 13 to protests of international organizations against certain acts of States.

28 *See contra* Chapter 11 in this volume.

29 *Supra* note 1, 147ff, para 3 of the commentary to conclusion 12.

30 *See* Chapter 11 in this volume.

31 *See supra* note 1, 147–48ff, para 5 of the commentary to conclusion 12.

recognizes in Chapter 9 of this volume, there is no accepted definition in general use. In the Commission, too, some members understood the term to include international organizations, while others questioned such classification; hence 'other actors' in paragraph 3 of conclusion 4, directly following the reference to States and to international organizations in paragraphs 1 and 2. As the commentary explains, the term refers to such actors as non-governmental organizations and private individuals, as well as transnational corporations and non-State armed groups.[32]

More significantly, the text of paragraph 3, which makes explicit that conduct of entities other than States and international organizations is neither creative nor expressive of customary international law, does not 'suggest that non-States actors and customary international law do not have much in common'.[33] Far from disregarding the potential influence that such actors may have with regard to customary international law, the conclusion explicitly recognizes that their conduct 'may have an indirect role in the identification of customary international law, by stimulating or recording the practice and acceptance as law (*opinio juris*) of States and international organizations'.[34] As mentioned above, this paragraph did not prove controversial within the Commission or among States. Any concern that it might not do justice to the International Committee of the Red Cross were soon allayed since the International Committee of the Red Cross supported the approach taken in the conclusions, and indeed has itself followed a similar approach, as Müller's contribution explains.[35]

The Commission's commentary explains that the conduct of 'other actors' may well contribute to the development and determination of customary international law in various informal and indirect ways, such as those surveyed by Azarova in chapter 19 of this volume. Alleged 'lawmaking' activities described by others in terms of '[putting] pressure on the people working for States' and 'provid[ing] technical information, lobby[ing] for a particular agenda, promot[ing] diplomatic conferences or writ[ing] drafts of treaties or soft law instruments, or simply … [writing] and disseminat[ing] studies and proposals',[36] in fact fall squarely within

32 ibid 132ff, para 8 of the commentary to conclusion 4.

33 *See* Chapter 9 in this volume.

34 *Supra* note 1, 132ff, para 8 of the commentary to conclusion 4. As is noted in a footnote 696, the Commission considered a similar point with respect to practice by 'non-State actors' under its topic 'Subsequent agreements and subsequent practice in relation to interpretation of treaties': *see* conclusion 5, paragraph 2, adopted on second reading under that topic (*see supra* note 1, 14ff, with commentary 39–43ff).

35 The commentary addresses the role of the ICRC: *see* ibid para 9. *See* also Chapter 14 in this volume.

36 *See* Chapter 6 in this volume.

the Commission's conclusion, since such activities are intended precisely to stimulate or record the practice and *opinio juris* of States and international organizations.

Some scholars, including several contributors to this book, also appear to be disappointed that the Commission, which according to one of them 'is expected to produce innovative developments on [international law], leading old traditions into the newest realities and not a room to celebrate academic anachronisms',[37] did not recognize a more central role for actors other than States and international organizations in the creation of customary international law. Yet producing 'innovative solutions' is not what the Commission set out to do in the present context;[38] and there would anyway have been no basis for such a more 'inclusive' approach. The significant participation and impact of 'other actors' in international relations, to which some contributors to this volume appear to attach great weight, does not in itself change the status and competence of such actors in the international legal system. Nor does the fact that some of them may be bound by at least some rules of international law, or subjective arguments as to the legitimacy of international law. What is also clear is that international law – as any law – cannot afford to depend on 'the theoretical standpoint of the observer',[39] however appealing such a standpoint may be. The approach of States, on the other hand, is crucial.[40]

37 *See* Chapter 6 in this volume; the author also asserts that the International Law Commission 'should be a place to make international law useful and practical and not just another place for mere theoretical reflection and repetition'. *See* also Chapter 9 in this volume (while recognizing that the International Law Commission's conclusion 4 reflects 'the lex lata' and that '[a]ll this is certainly true', Bíková nonetheless argues that a different approach should have been taken given an alleged lack of 'a total consensus' on this among 'States, international courts, legal scholars').

38 Suggestions that to some extent it did so, such as those made in the Sixth Committee by the USA (A/C.6/SR.29), are unconvincing.

39 *See* Chapter 6 in this volume.

40 *See* General Assembly resolution 73/265 of 22 December 2018. *See* also the debates in the Sixth Committee of the UN General Assembly in 2013–2016 and in 2018, as well as the comments and observations submitted by States in writing (A/CN.4/716); *see* also, for example, the judgment of the Court of Appeal of England and Wales in *Freedom and Justice Party v Secretary of State for Foreign and Commonwealth Affairs* [2018] EWCA Civ 1719 (19 July 2018).

Chapter 9

The International Law Commission perspective on non-State actors and customary international law

Veronika Bílková

In 2018, the United Nations International Law Commission adopted, on second reading, a set of *Conclusions on Identification of Customary International Law*.[1] The document, now submitted to the United Nations General Assembly, contains sixteen conclusions relating to various aspects of the formation and identification of customary international law. The basic approach that the document embraces is a traditional one. A rule of customary international law emerges when there is 'a general practice that is accepted as law (*opinio juris*)'.[2] The practice is primarily that of States and, to a certain extent, of international organizations. 'Conduct of other actors is not practice that contributes to the formation, or expression, of rules of customary international law but may be relevant when assessing the practice referred to in paragraphs 1 and 2' (i.e. practice of States and international organizations).[3] Conclusion 9, dealing with the requirement of *opinio juris*, does not explicitly indicate which actors have to accept the general practice as law.[4] Yet, the wording of the Conclusion, under which 'the practice in question must be undertaken with a sense of legal right of obligation',[5] implies that the relevant *opinio juris* is that of the actors whose practice counts, that is, again, of States and, sometimes, international organizations.

The place that the International Law Commission reserves to non-State actors in the formation of customary international law is therefore a marginal one. Their conduct does not count as the general practice (*usus longaevus*); their views do not qualify as the acceptance of the binding nature of the practice (*opinio juris*). At most, their conduct can be relevant for the assessment of the practice of States

1 UN Doc A/73/10, Report of the International Law Commission on the Work of the Seventieth Session, 2018, 117–56.
2 ibid 119 (Conclusion 2).
3 ibid 119 (Conclusion 4(3)).
4 *See* Chapters 1, 2, and 5 in this volume.
5 ibid 120 (Conclusion 9(1)).

and international organizations. All that would suggest that non-State actors and customary international law do not have much in common. This chapter casts some doubt on such a view, arguing that the International Law Commission fails to do justice to the complex relationship that nowadays exists between non-State actors and customary international law. Ignoring this relationship or, even, denying it may downplay the value that the Conclusions could have in offering practical guidance to international or national actors tasked to identify, apply, or implement customary international law. Section 1 traces the history of the Conclusions in the International Law Commission work. Section 2 introduces alternative views on the role of non-State actors in the formation of customary international law, expressed by other international bodies and by scholars. Section 3 critically assesses the Conclusions in light of these alternative views, identifying several shortcomings in the International Law Commission approach.

It is important to recall that there is no uniformly accepted definition of non-State actors in international law. In the broadest meaning, the term is used to denote any actors that are not States.[6] In a narrow meaning, it refers to collective organized entities that are neither comprised of, nor governed by, States – thus excluding not only States but also international organizations (which are comprised of and governed by States) and individuals (who are not collective organized entities).[7] The International Law Commission, although it has never provided a definition of non-State actors, seems to opt for a middle-ground approach. The examples of 'other actors', as the International Law Commission has been usually referring to non-State actors since 2015,[8] provided in the commentaries to the 2018 *Conclusions on Identification*

6 P Alston, 'The "Not-a-Cat" Syndrome: Can the International Human Rights Regime Accommodate Non-State Actors?' in P Alston (ed), *Non-State Actors and Human Rights* (Oxford University Press 2005) 3–36.

7 *Non-State Actors in International Law*, Final Report of the ILA Committee on Non-State Actors, Johannesburg, 2016, 4–6.

8 In the first years of its work on the topic, the International Law Commission used the term 'other non-State actors'. The change occurred in 2015 at the initiative of the Drafting Committee, with the aim of distinguishing between non-State actors ('other actors') and international organizations. The International Law Commission is however not fully consistent in its terminology. For instance Conclusion 5(2) of the *Conclusions on subsequent agreements and subsequent practice in relation to the interpretation of treaties*, adopted on second reading in 2018, which also relates to the practice of non-State actors, uses the term 'non-State actors'. *See* UN Doc A/73/10 (n 1) 14. The word non-State actors also appears in the bibliography on the topic of identifcation of customary international law, contained in the addendum to the fifth report by the Special Rapporteur. *See* UN Doc CN.4/717/Add.1, *Fifth report on identification of customary international law, Addendum*, 6 June 2018, 20 (Section B.3. Non-State actors and customary international law).

of Customary International Law, include 'non-governmental organizations (NGOs) and private individuals … transnational corporations and non-State armed groups'.[9] Thus, non-State actors as understood by the International Law Commission encompass any entities other than States and international organizations. States, institutions, and scholars commenting upon the work of the International Law Commission may have their own conception of non-State actors. This chapter therefore adopts a flexible approach, taking note of any position expressed with respect to non-State actors (or 'other actors') in the context of the debate on the formation and identification of customary international law, regardless of how broad the range of actors denoted by this term for those expressing their position is.

1 Formation of customary international law and non-State actors in the work of the International Law Commission

The International Law Commission has been dealing with customary international law since 2012, when it decided to include this topic in its programme of work under the title *Formation and evidence of customary international law*[10] (later on changed to *Identification of customary international law*[11]). Michael Wood was appointed as the Special Rapporteur for the topic. In his initial note, he indicated that the aim was to produce 'a practical guide, with commentaries, for judges, government lawyers and practitioners'.[12] In the syllabus on the topic submitted one year earlier, Wood made it clear that he intended to take a traditional approach to customary international law that would focus on State practice and State *opinio juris*.[13] This was confirmed in the first report submitted in 2013, in which the Special Rapporteur noted, and implicitly criticized, the existence of 'calls for opening the process of customary law creation to non-State actors, namely, international organizations and their agencies, as well as individuals'.[14] He labeled these calls as one of the implications of '"conceptual stretching", celebrated as the "new vitality of custom"'.[15]

9 UN Doc A/73/10 (n 1) 132.
10 UN Doc A/CN.4/SR.3132, Summary record of the 3132nd meeting, 7 June 2012.
11 Despite the change of the title, the Conclusions contain more references to the formation, than to the identification, of customary international law.
12 UN Doc A/CN.4/653, Formation and evidence of customary international law, Note by Michael Wood, Special Rapporteur, 30 May 2012, para 3.
13 UN Doc. A/66/10, Annex A – Formation and evidence of customary international law (Mr. Michael Wood), 2011, 307.
14 UN Doc A/CN.4/663, First report on formation and evidence of customary international law, 17 May 2013, 52 (para 98).
15 ibid.

The second report, submitted in 2014, contains the most detailed, albeit still a rather short comment on the role of non-State actors in the formation of customary international law.[16] This comment is present in the section pertaining to Draft Conclusion 5 on the role of practice, which reads as follows:

> The requirement, as an element of customary international law, of a general practice means that it is primarily the practice of States that contributes to the creation, or expression, of rules of customary international law.[17]

There is, on the contrary, no reflection on non-State actors in the section relating to Draft Conclusion 10 on the role of acceptance of law, which stipulates that 'the requirement … that the general practice be accepted as law means that the practice must be accompanied by a sense of legal obligation'.[18] The relevant *opinio juris* is thus that of actors whose practice counts in the development of *usus longaevus*, which makes an autonomous debate on actors under Conclusion 10 unnecessary. This approach has been maintained in subsequent years as well. The comments on, and revisions of, Conclusion 10 (to become later Conclusion 9) have therefore had virtually no relevance for the topic of this chapter.

Draft Conclusion 5 is accompanied by a commentary which is, in our context, interesting in two respects. First, the report makes a distinction between international (intergovernmental) organizations and 'other non-State actors'.[19] As far as the former are concerned, the report concludes, in somewhat mysterious terms, that 'considerations that apply to the practice of States may also be relevant to the practice of international organizations'.[20] It also declares, less mysteriously, that the practice of international organizations in the areas in which these organizations have exclusive competences 'may be equated with that of States'.[21] Thus, the report does not conceive of customary rules as rules created solely by States but opens the norm-creating process to at least one non-State actor (NSA in the broad sense).

Secondly, the report has a short section on what the Special Rapporteur labels as 'other non-State actors'. The section notes that it has been suggested that these actors, such as non-governmental organizations and individuals, could contribute to the development of customary international law.

16 UN Doc A/CN.4/672, Second report on identification of customary international law, 22 May 2014, 32–34 (para 45–46).
17 ibid 18 (para 36).
18 ibid 56 (para 69).
19 ibid 32 (para 45).
20 ibid 31 (para 43).
21 ibid 31 (para 44).

> The better view, in Wood's opinion, however, is that, while individuals and non-governmental organizations can indeed 'play important roles in the promotion of international law and in its observance' … their actions are not 'practice' for purposes of the formation or evidencing of customary international law.[22]

The view is substantiated by several quotes from scholarly literature, two statements made by States (Iran and Israel) in the Sixth Committee of the United Nations General Assembly and one of the International Law Commission Conclusions on subsequent agreements and subsequent practice in relation to the interpretation of treaties.[23] Somewhat surprisingly, the subsection on 'other non-State actors' ends with a paragraph pertaining to the decisions of international courts and tribunals. The report notes, this time unsurprisingly, that such decisions serve as subsidiary means for the determination of rules of law. It however does not explain whether this is supposed to turn international courts and tribunals into non-State actors endowed with some formal role in customary international law creation or whether their case-law is relevant merely for the purposes of ascertaining the norm-creating status of other non-State actors.[24]

Draft Conclusion 5 became the object of an intense debate in the International Law Commission during its 2014 session.[25] In this debate, the members were divided. Some suggested that the word 'primarily' should be removed from the provision, because it would suggest – wrongly, in the opinion of these members – that the practice of entities other than States could be relevant in the formation of customary international law. Other members were ready to condone that at least the practice of international organizations could matter in this context, though there was no consensus as to when this would be the case. The role of other non-State actors was not discussed at any length but, as the International Law Commission Annual Report notes, some members 'considered that the study of the role, if any, of the practice of non-State actors would be

22 ibid 32–33 (para 45).

23 Conclusion 5(2) which nowadays reads: 'Other conduct, including by non-State actors, does not constitute subsequent practice under articles 31 and 32. Such conduct may, however, be relevant when assessing the subsequent practice of parties to a treaty.' UN Doc A/73/10 (n 1) 14.

24 In the third report, the Special Rapporteur introduced a special conclusion on Judicial decisions and writing (Draft Conclusion 14). The provision was later on divided into two separate Conclusions, one on Decisions of courts and tribunals (Draft Conclusion 13), the other on Teachings (Draft Conclusion 14). No link is any more made between courts and tribunals and non-State actors.

25 UN Doc A/69/10, Report of the International Law Commission on the work of its sixty-sixth session, 2014, 244 (para 159–61).

worthwhile'.[26] The text was passed to the Drafting Committee. The Committee revised Conclusion 5 – newly Conclusion 4 [5] – adding a new paragraph 2 which read '[i]n certain cases, the practice of international organizations also contributes to the formation, or expression, of rules of customary international law'.[27] As the chairman of the Drafting Committee noted, members of the Committee all agreed that the State practice was crucial for the formation of customary international law but there was less concord as to the role of international organizations. 'The question of the role, if any, of other non-state actors was also raised'[28] but apparently without any clear outcomes.

In November 2014, the work of the International Law Commission was discussed in the Sixth Committee. The positions of States with respect to the role of non-State actors in the formation of customary international law, and to Conclusion 4[5], were divided. Some States expressed preference for a narrow approach that would only focus on the practice of States and, possibly, international organizations. Other States favoured a broader approach that would not leave actors other than States and international organizations completely aside. Finally, yet other States – a majority indeed – did not comment on the issue at all or did it in an ambiguous way.

The first group encompassed Belarus, Israel, Romania, the Russia Federation or Slovakia. Belarus noted that:

> with respect to the role of practice in the formation of customary rules, it was necessary to understand the practice of States, including within the framework of international organizations. For that reason, it was not appropriate to include the word 'primarily' in draft conclusion 5.[29]

Israel was very explicit in declaring that 'only State practice should be looked at for the purpose of identifying international customary law'.[30] Israel therefore 'supported an approach that placed emphasis on States as the sole developers of international rules of a customary nature'.[31] Romania noted that it 'shared the view expressed by the Special Rapporteurs … in respect of the practice of non-State actors'.[32] The Russian Federation

26 ibid (para 160).

27 Identification of customary international law. Statement of the Chairman of the Drafting Committee, Mr Gilberto Saboia, 7 August 2014.

28 ibid 8.

29 UN Doc A/C.6/69/SR.26, Sixth Committee, Summary Record of the 26th Meeting, 3 November 2014, 20 November 2014, 4 (para 21).

30 UN Doc A/C.6/69/SR.23, Sixth Committee, Summary Record of the 23rd Meeting, 31 October 2014, 24 November 2014, 17 (para 82).

31 UN Doc A/C.6/69/SR.25, Sixth Committee, Summary Record of the 25th Meeting, 3 November 2014, 28 November 2014, 14 (para 83).

32 UN Doc A/C.6/69/SR.26 (n 29) 15 (para 85).

stressed that 'the practice of international organizations and other entities could only be used as a subsidiary tool for the identification of the practice and opinion juris of States'.[33] Slovakia declared that it 'could agree to the inclusion of the practice of international organizations, but preference should be given to the practice of States'.[34]

Whereas the first group encompassed mostly States of Central and Eastern Europe, the second one was made up primarily by those of Central and Western Europe, such as Austria, France, Poland, and Portugal. Austria noted that:

> Concerning the scope of potential actors in the process of the creation of customary international law, a limitaton to the practice of states, or to states as only potential creators of customary international law would be misguided. The Austrian delegation thinks that this potential norm creating role should be kept open for other subjects of international law. In that regard we would prefer that the Special Rapporteur's approach could be expanded.[35]

France declared that 'the question could be raised whether international organizations were the only other entities to play a role in the formation of customary international law or whether all subjects of international law could potentially do so'.[36] Portugal, in a similar way, noted that while the practice of international organizations was relevant for the identification of customary law, 'the practice of other non-State actors might also be worth exploring'.[37] Poland agreed, stressing that 'the Commission's conception of the scope of practice and *opinio juris* was too narrow. States were, of course, the primary subjects of international law and their practice was the most significant, but consideration of the practice of secondary subjects of international law should not be limited to that of international organizations'.[38]

Finally, some countries commented on Conclusion 4 [5] in a way that allows for several interpretations. This is typically the case of Germany which stated that 'Draft conclusion … confirmed that States were the primary subjects of international law. Although other subjects of international law, such as international organizations

33 UN Doc A/C.6/69/SR.25 (n 31) 16 (para 93).

34 UN Doc A/C.6/69/SR.23 (n 30) 19 (para 88).

35 Statement by Prof August Reinisch, 3 November 2014. *See* also UN Doc A/C.6/69/SR.25 (n 32) 17 (para 107).

36 UN Doc A/C.6/69/SR.22, Sixth Committee, Summary Record of the 22nd Meeting, 29 October 2014, 11 November 2014, 7 (para 30).

37 UN Doc A/C.6/69/SR.26 (n 29) 2 (para 3).

38 UN Doc A/C.6/69/SR.26 (n 29) 11 (para 57). Poland also opined that 'the Commission should … investigate to what extent non-State actors were bound by general customary law' (ibid), though this would go beyond the scope of the International Law Commission topic which is only – rightly or wrongly – concerned with the identification, and the formation, of customary international law, not with its scope of application.

and the International Committee of the Red Cross, might have a role in setting practice and expressing opinio juris, States were the most important source for both purposes'.[39] The statement can be read in a narrow way, as limiting the scope of actors contributing to the formation of customary international law to States, or in a broad way, opening the area to international organizations and other non-State actors, though relegating these actors to the position secondary to that of States. As noted above, most States present in the Sixth Committee did not comment on Conclusion 4[5] and their position in this respect thus remained unclear.

In 2015, the Special Rapporteur published his third report,[40] in which he further elaborated on the role of international organizations. He also proposed two amendments to Conclusion 4 [5], both concerning non-State actors. First, the word 'primarily' was to be deleted from paragraph 1 which would now read: 'The requirement … of a general practice means that it is the practice of States that contributes to the creation, or expression, of rules of customary international law'. Secondly, a new paragraph 3 was to be introduced to the Conclusion stating that: '[c]onduct by other non-State actors is not practice for the purposes of formation or identification of customary international law'.[41] The Special Rapporteur added no commentary, simply noting that the amendments were proposed 'in order to clarify the position in regard to non-State actors, as reflected in the 2014 debate'.[42]

The Drafting Committee adopted a critical stance to the proposed revisions.[43] The word 'primarily' was reintroduced to paragraph 1, to make justice to the role of international organizations. Paragraph 3 was accepted but its wording changed in two respects. First, the expression 'other non-State actors' was replaced by 'other actors', because it was felt that international organizations did not truly qualify as non-State actors. Secondly, the provision was revised to reflect the view that although the practice of 'other actors' could not contribute to the formation of customary international law, it could have a role in the identification of this law. On its leaving the Drafting Committee, paragraph 3 thus read as follows:

> Conduct of other actors is not practice that contributes to the formation, or expression, of rules of customary international law, but may be relevant when assessing the practice referred to in paragraphs 1 and 2.

39 UN Doc A/C.6/69/SR.26 (n 29) 14 (para 79).

40 UN Doc A/CN.4/682, Third report on identification of customary international law, 27 March 2015.

41 ibid 54 (para 79).

42 ibid.

43 UN Doc A/CN.4/L.869, Identification of customary international law. Text of the draft conclusions provisionally adopted by the Drafting Committee, 14 July 2015.

In this wording, the provision made part of eight draft conclusions which were provisionally adopted by the Committee in 2015, completing eight draft conclusions adopted the previous year. When addressing the Sixth Committee, the International Law Commission chairman Singh indicated that

> several Commission members had supported the Special Rapporteur's view … that the conduct of other non-State actors did not constitute practice for the purposes of formation or identification of rules. Some members had considered the proposal too strict, particularly in view of the significance of the practice of certain non-State actors and the importance of activities involving both States and non-State actors.[44]

During the debate in the Sixth Committee held in November 2015, the amendments to Draft Conclusion 4[5] gave rise, again, to mixed reactions. Most countries commenting on the issue expressed their support to the position of the Special Rapporteur. Australia, for instance,

> was of view that the conduct of other non-State actors did not contribute directly to the formation or expression of customary international law, although their work might operate as a catalyst for State action or comment.[45]

Germany 'appreciated the approach taken in draft conclusion 4 [5]'[46] and Turkey 'agreed that conduct by other non-State actors was not practice for the purposes of formation or identification of customary international law'.[47] A minority of States held a different view. Austria noted that 'the wording of draft conclusion 4, paragraph 3 … did not do justice to the important contribution of the International Committee of the Red Cross to international practice'.[48] Greece declared that 'with regard to rules of international law whose addressees included non-State actors … it could not easily be argued that the behaviour of the addressees was irrelevant for the formation of customary international law'.[49]

Already in 2013, the International Law Commission requested States to provide information on their practice relating to the formation of customary international law and the types of evidence suitable for establishing such law, as set out in their

44 UN Doc A/C.6/70/SR.19, Sixth Committee, Summary Record of the 19th Meeting, 4 November 2015, 20 November 2015, 12 (para 59).

45 UN Doc A/C.6/70/SR.22, Sixth Committee, Summary Record of the 22nd Meeting, 6 November 2015, 23 November 2015, 9 (para 51).

46 ibid 3 (para 10).

47 ibid 17 (para 108).

48 UN Doc A/C.6/70/SR.20, Sixth Committee, Summary Record of the 20th Meeting, 4 November 2015, 13 November 2015, 6 (para 28).

49 ibid 8 (para 43).

official statements and judicial decisions. Only a handful of States responded to this request.[50] Two of them expressly addressed the issue of the role of non-State actors in the formation of customary international law. The first one was, in 2015, Austria, which however merely cited the position presented by its representative during the 2014 session of the Sixth Committee.[51] The second one was, in 2016, Switzerland, which included a whole section entitled 'the work of nonstate actors and especially the ICRC'.[52] Despite the title and the word especially, the section comments solely on the practice of the ICRC. It declares that the Swiss authorities have often relied on the practice of the ICRC to confirm the customary nature of a norm of international law, adding however that

> The different analysed extracts seem … to suggest that the acts of the ICRC, to the extent that they make it possible to clarify the content of international customary law, are considered by the Swiss authorities more as sources of the identification rather than as an element of the identification stricto sensu of constitutive elements of international humanitarian law.[53]

In the fourth report, published in 2016, the Special Rapporteur engaged with the comments made by States in the Sixth Committee and in other meetings, including the meeting of the Asian-African Legal Consultative Organization (AALCO) informal expert group on customary international law held in Malaysia in August 2015. As far as paragraph 3 of Conclusion 4[5] was concerned, he noted that:

> a couple of delegations were concerned that the wording … was too strict, in that it does not adequately recognize the important contribution that such actors may make to international practice related to their work and the possible development of customary international law.[54]

In light of these concerns, Wood proposed a minor change in the wording of paragraph 3, where 'formation' would be replaced by 'creation'.[55] This proposal did not gather sufficient support in the International Law Commission and the wording

50 2014 – Belgium, Botswana, Cuba, the Czech Republic, El Salvador, Germany, Ireland, the Russian Federation, the United Kingdom, the US; 2015 – Austria, Belgium, the Czech Republic, Finland, Germany, the Republic of Korea, the United Kingdom; 2016 – the Netherlands, Switzerland; 2017 – El Salvador.

51 Information submitted by Austria, 10 March 2015.

52 La pratique suisse relative à la détermination du droit international coutumier, Information submitted by Switzerland, 2016, 37–38.

53 ibid.

54 UN Doc A/CN.4/695, Fourth report on identification of customary international law, 8 March 2016, 7, para 21.

55 ibid 21.

of paragraph 3, as provisionally adopted by the Drafting Committee, remained unchanged from that approved in 2015.[56]

On 2 July 2016, the International Law Commission adopted, on first reading, a set of sixteen *Draft Conclusions on Identification of Customary International Law*, including Draft Conclusion 4 (Requirement of practice) with its three paragraphs.[57] The commentary to the Draft Conclusions notes that Conclusion 4(3) 'makes explicit … that the conduct of entities other than States and international organizations … is neither creative nor expressive of customary international law'.[58] Thus, this conduct, in the International Law Commission view, does not constitute relevant practice for the formation of customary international law and it cannot serve as direct evidence of the existence and content of customary international law either. Yet, the commentary to Conclusion 4(3) recognizes that

> such conduct may have an important indirect role in the identification of customary international law, by stimulating or recording practice and acceptance as law (*opinio juris*) by States and international organizations.[59]

Two non-State actors, non-State armed groups, and the International Committee of the Red Cross are invoked as examples of the actors which may indirectly contribute to the development or determination of customary international law, for instance by inducing State reactions or by recording the relevant practice. The commentary also notes that 'the acts of private individuals may also sometimes be relevant, but only to the extent that States have endorsed or reacted to it'.[60]

The Draft Conclusions, adopted on first reading, were transmitted, through the United Nations Secretary General, to States for comments and observations that were to be submitted, again through the United Nations Secretary General, by 1 January 2018. By then, thirteen States responded to the request.[61] Some of them,

56 UN Doc A/CN.4/L.872, Identification of customary international law. Text of the draft conclusions provisionally adopted by the Drafting Committee, 30 May 2016.

57 UN Doc A/71/10, Report of the International Law Commission on the work of the sixty-eighth Session, 2016, 74–117. Draft Conclusion 4(3) read as follows: 'Conduct of other actors is not practice that contributes to the formation, or expression, of rules of customary international law, but may be relevant when assessing the practice referred to in paragraphs 1 and 2.'

58 ibid 89 (para 9).

59 ibid 89–90 (para 9).

60 ibid 90 (para 9).

61 2016 – Austria; 2017 – Austria, Belarus, China, the Czech Republic, Denmark (on behalf of the Nordic countries), El Salvador, Israel, the Netherlands, New Zealand, the Republic of Korea, Singapore and the US.

and also several other States, commented on the Draft Conclusions in the meeting of the Sixth Committee held in autumn 2016. This time, virtually all intervening States expressed their support to the position expressed in Draft Conclusion 4(3). New Zealand noted that it 'agree[d] with the conclusion regarding the practice of non-State actors'.[62] Singapore also 'agree[d] that the conduct of non-State actors … is not practice that contributes to the formation, or expression of rules of customary international law'.[63] The view was shared by Chile[64] and China.[65] The latter raised doubts whether 'an ambiguous phrase such as "may be relevant" should be retained in the draft conclusion'.[66] Belarus,[67] Israel,[68] the Russian Federation,[69] and the US[70] went even further and made it clear that for them, the only practice which counted for the formation of customary international law was that by States. Austria,[71] Denmark[72] (on behalf of the Nordic group), and the Netherlands[73] disagreed with this view but the disagreement concerned the practice of international organizations, not that of non-State actors.

In 2017, the topic of *Identification of customary international law* was not considered by the International Law Commission. The role of non-State actors was however briefly discussed within the topic of *Peremptory rules of general international law (jus cogens)*. In the second report on this topic submitted in 2017, the Special Rapporteur Dire Tladi noted that 'for a rule to qualify as a norm of jus cogens it has to be a norm of general international law and it has to be accepted and recognized as a norm from which no derogation is permitted'.[74] He further proposed that

62 UN Doc A/CN.4/716, Identification of customary international law. Comments and observations received from Governments, 14 February 2018, 18.
63 ibid.
64 UN Doc A/C.6/71/SR.21, Sixth Committee, Summary Record of the 21st Meeting, 26 October 2016, 16 November 2016, 13 (para 99).
65 UN Doc A/C.6/71/SR.20, Sixth Committee, Summary Record of the 20th Meeting, 24 October 2016, 11 November 2016, 14 (para 66).
66 ibid.
67 UN Doc A/CN.4/716 (n 62) 14.
68 UN Doc A/CN.4/716 (n 62) 15–16.
69 UN Doc A/C.6/71/SR.21 (n 65) 7 (para 49).
70 UN Doc A/CN.4/716 (n 62) 18–23.
71 UN Doc A/CN.4/716 (n 62) 13.
72 UN Doc A/CN.4/716 (n 62) 14.
73 UN Doc A/CN.4/716 (n 62) 16.
74 UN Doc A/CN.4/706, Second report on *jus cogens* by Dire Tladi, Special Rapporteur, 16 March 2017, 19 (para 39).

> while the attitudes of actors other than States may be relevant in assessing the acceptance and recognition of the international community of States as a whole, these cannot, in and of themselves, constitute acceptance and recognition by the international community of States as a whole. The attitudes of other actors may be relevant in providing context and assessing the attitudes of States. (Draft Conclusion 7(2))[75]

When noting so, the Special Rapporteur explicitly referred to Draft Conclusion 4(3).[76] Unlike this provision, however, Draft Conclusion 7(2) does not relate to the practice of non-State actors but to their attitudes. The parallel that the Special Rapporteur drew between the provisions seems to confirm the close link between the material and mental aspects underpinning the creation of norms (as manifested in the two elements of customary rules). The Drafting Committee accepted this approach, limiting itself to terminological changes, including the replacement of 'actors other than States' by 'other actors' in line with the Draft Conclusion 4(3).[77]

The topic of *Identification of customary international law* got back to the agenda of the International Law Commission in 2018. In March 2018, the Special Rapporteur submitted his fifth and last report.[78] The section dealing with Conclusion 4 is rather lengthy but only two paragraphs effectively deal with non-State actors. Noting that 'paragraph 3 of the draft conclusion, concerning the conduct of other actors, was generally endorsed',[79] the Special Rapporteur suggested only a minor change in the wording of the Draft Conclusion (replacing 'formation' with 'creation') and some further changes in the commentary, which

> would need to address the concerns raised, in particular by clarifying further that 'other actors' have no direct role in the creation or expression of rules of customary international law, and the circumstances in which their conduct could be taken into consideration when assessing relevant practice.[80]

The Drafting Committee accepted some changes in the commentary but not in the Draft Conclusion itself. Moreover, as the chairman of the Committee revealed in his report,

75 ibid 46.

76 ibid 36 (para 71). The Special Rapporteur also referred to Draft Conclusion 5(2) of the Draft Conclusions on subsequent agreements and subsequent practice in relation to the interpretation of treaties.

77 *Peremptory norms of general international law (Jus Cogens)*, Statement of the Chairman of the Drafting Committee Mr Aniruddha Rajput, 26 July 2017, 9.

78 UN Doc A/CN.4/717, Fifth report on identification of customary international law, 14 November 2018.

79 ibid 18 (para 40).

80 ibid 22 (para 49).

> the Drafting Committee discussed the view that, as currently drafted, paragraph 3 may be considered as too restrictive in relation to the conduct of non-State actors, for example in relation to self-determination and non-international armed conflicts. It was decided to retain the language adopted on first reading, not least given the positive consideration thereof by States, on the understanding that the commentary would clarify the possible relevance of the conduct of actors other than States and international organizations.[81]

On 25 May and 2–3 August 2018 respectively, the International Law Commission adopted the *Conclusions on Identification of Customary International Law* and the commentaries thereto. The wording of Conclusion 4(3) remained identical to the one adopted on first reading in 2016.[82] The commentaries were slightly revised, to further emphasize that the conduct of non-State actors 'does not contribute to the formation, or expression, of rules of customary international law, and may not serve as direct (primary) evidence of the existence and content of such rules'.[83] The Conclusions with their commentaries have been submitted to the United Nations General Assembly with the recommendation by the International Law Commission that the Assembly take note of the documents and commend them to the attention of States.

For the sake of completeness, it may be useful to recall that the topic *Identification of customary international law* is not the first one relating to customary international law that the International Law Commission has had on its agenda. As early as in 1949, the Commission began to 'consider ways and means for making the evidence of customary international law more readily available, such as the collection and publication of documents concerning State practice and of the decisions of national and international courts on questions of international law', as Article 24 of its Statute incites it to do. One year later, in 1950, it completed the consideration and submitted a short report to the United Nations General Assembly.[84] The report limited itself to identifying concrete sources (juridical yearbooks, legislative series, etc.) that could help in the process of the identification of customary international law. In line with the wording of Article 24 of the International Law Commission Statute, only sources produced by States and, occasionally, the United Nations, were

81 *Identification of customary international law, Statement of the Chair of the Drafting Committee Mr Charles Chernor Jalloh*, 25 May 2018, 7.

82 Draft Conclusion 4(3) therefore reads: 'Conduct of other actors is not practice that contributes to the formation, or expression, of rules of customary international law, but may be relevant when assessing the practice referred to in paragraphs 1 and 2.' UN Doc A/73/10 (n 1) 130.

83 ibid 132.

84 International Law Commission, Ways and means for making the evidence of customary international law more readily available, Report of the International Law Commission, 1950, 367–74.

enlisted, with no attention paid to 'sources' produced by non-State actors. No objection was raised against this approach which indicates that in the given period, the State origin of customary rules was not questioned. This, as the statements States have made with respect to the current International Law Commission work show, is no longer the case. Despite that, Conclusion 4(3) reveals that the International Law Commission view on the role of non-State actors in the formation of customary international law has not radically changed since the mid-twentieth century.

2 Alternative views on the formation of customary international law and non-State actors

The International Law Commission is not the only entity which has considered the role that non-State actors play in the formation and identification of customary international law. This issue has been, albeit not very thoroughly, discussed by other international bodies as well. It has also featured, again not very prominently, in the scholarly literature. This section gives an overview of the views expressed by the International Law Association, the International Committee of the Red Cross, the International Criminal Tribunal for the Former Yugoslavia, and various scholars.

The International Law Association is a professional non-profit association with more than 4,000 members all over the world, which establishes committees and study groups to analyse specific areas and topics of international law. In 1985, the International Law Association established the *Committee on Formation of Customary (General) International Law*. The Committee completed its work in 2000, with the publication, at the International Law Association bi-annual conference held in London, of the *Statement of Principles Applicable to the Formation of General Customary International Law* (also known as the London Statement).[85] The London Statement does not discuss the role of non-State actors in the formation of customary rules at any length. It notes, however, that:

> a rule of customary international law is one which is created and sustained by the constant and uniform practice of States and *other subjects of international law* in or impinging upon their international legal relations, in circumstances which give rise to a legitimate expectation of similar conduct in the future.[86]

The commentary adds that this definition 'indicates that subjects of international law other than States can contribute to the formation of customary law; for instance,

85 Statement of Principles Applicable to the Formation of General Customary International Law, Final Report of the Committee, ILA London Conference, 2000.

86 ibid 8 (emphasis added).

international organizations'.[87] The fact that international organizations are cited merely as an example of non-State subjects of international law that can contribute to the formation of customary law, suggests that non-State actors, at least those endowed with legal subjectivity under international law (such as the ICRC or insurgent groups), could have some contribution in this area as well. The London Statement, however, fails to give any further specification in this respect. Since, moreover, the section dealing with the objective element of custom is entitled 'State practice' and since even the practice of intergovernmental organizations is qualified as a form of State practice,[88] one may doubt whether the International Law Association Committee truly intended to broaden the scope of actors whose conduct count in the formation of customary international law.

In 2008, the International Law Association established another committee with the interest in, inter alia, the role of non-State actors in the formation and identification of customary international law – the Committee on Non-State Actors. Before completing its work in 2016, the Committee adopted four reports, including the final report. Three of these reports discuss the role that non-State actors play in norm-creation. The discussion is much more extensive than in the London Statement and the conclusions are much less definitive than those reached by the International Law Commission. The Committee makes a distinction between three types of situations in which non-State actors, defined in the reports as 'legally recognized and organised entities that are not comprised of nor governed or controlled by States nor groups of States and that actually perform functions in the international arena that have real or potential effects on international law',[89] could somehow affect the formation of customary rules.

In the first situation, the conduct of non-State actors is carried out on behalf of States or adopted (ratified) by them.[90] The conduct then makes part of State practice. It affects the formation of customary rules, but not as an autonomous form of practice. In the second situation, non-State actors contribute to the formation of customary rules indirectly, by affecting State practice or *opinio juris*. This is so, for instance, when non-governmental organizations, through their advocacy and naming and shaming campaigns, prompt States to change their behaviour. The third situation is that of the conduct of non-State actors serving as an autonomous type of practice. Yet, as the Committee admits, 'it is not entirely clear whether the

87 ibid 9.

88 ibid 19 (Section 11 entitled 'The practice of intergovernmental organizations in their own right is a form of "State practice"').

89 *Non-State Actors*, Final Report, Johannesburg Conference, 2016, 4.

90 This scenario is also described in the London Statement, *see Statement of Principles* (n 85) 16.

contribution of NSAs are taken into account for purposes of ascertaining the existence of customary international law'.[91] While inconclusive on this point, the report expresses some sympathy for the concept of quasi-custom promoted by certain scholars[92] and it does not exclude the possibility of giving the conduct of non-State actors some weight in the formation of norms that govern the behaviour of these very actors. No further details are provided on either of these points.

It might be interesting to know what non-State actors themselves think about their own norm-creating powers and those of their 'peers'. Most non-State actors, however, have failed to articulate any position in this respect. One, and probably the only, exception to this rule is the International Committee of the Red Cross. In 2005, the International Committee of the Red Cross published an impressive two-volume *Study on Customary International Humanitarian Law*.[93] In the Introduction to the Study, the methodology used to ascertain rules of customary international humanitarian law is exposed. The International Committee of the Red Cross takes a double-track approach. On the one hand, it includes the practice of international organizations as well as its own official statements under the relevant practice that can contribute to the formation of customary international humanitarian law. This is justified by the fact that both international organizations and the International Committee of the Red Cross have international legal personality.[94] On the other hand, the conduct of other non-State actors, including armed opposition groups, is listed under 'other practice' with the note that 'its legal significance is not clear'.[95] Provided that the International Committee of the Red Cross at the same time holds that armed opposition groups are bound by international humanitarian law which entails that they also have some international legal personality, it is not clear why the logic applied in the first track does not apply in the second one as well.

91 *Non-State Actors*, Report, Sofia Conference, 2012, 5.

92 ibid 6.

93 J-M Henckaerts and L Doswald-Beck (eds), *Customary International Humanitarian Law, Volume I: Rules, Volume II: Practice* (Cambridge University Press 2005).

94 'International organisations have international legal personality and can participate in international relations in their own capacity, independently of their member States. In this respect, their practice can contribute to the formation of customary international law. […] In addition, official ICRC statements, in particular appeals and memoranda on respect for international humanitarian law, have been included as relevant practice because the ICRC has international legal personality.' ibid volume I, xli.

95 ibid volume I, xlii.

Despite the cautious approach embraced in it, the Study gave rise to sharp criticism, particularly by the United States. In its official reaction, the United States stated, inter alia, that 'the Study gives undue weight to statements by non-governmental organizations and the ICRC itself, when those statements do not reflect whether a particular rule constitutes international law accepted by States'.[96] In his response, one of the editors of the Study, Jean-Marie Henckaerts, repeated that 'official ICRC statements … have been included as relevant practice because the ICRC has international legal personality',[97] adding nonetheless that 'the Study did not … use ICRC statements as primary sources of evidence supporting the customary nature of a rule. They are cited to reinforce conclusions that were reached on the basis of state practice alone'.[98] As regards non-governmental organizations, Henckaerts explained that:

> NGO statements were included … under the category of 'Other Practice', which served as a residual category of materials that were not given any weight in the determination of what is customary. The term 'practice' in this context was not at all used to denote any form of state (or other) practice that contributes to the formation of customary international law.[99]

The International Committee of the Red Cross, despite its readiness to pay some attention to its own statements, thus shares the International Law Commission scepticism as to the norm-creating capacity of non-State actors. Other international institutions have shown more openness in this respect. This is especially the case of the International Criminal Tribunal for the Former Yugoslavia, which, though it belonged to the United Nations system, was sometimes also considered as a specific non-State actor.[100] When establishing the existence of a customary rule of international humanitarian law applicable in non-international armed conflicts, the International Criminal Tribunal for the Former Yugoslavia took into account not only the practice of States but also that of non-State parties to the conflict.

For instance, in the *Tadić* Case, the International Criminal Tribunal for the Former Yugoslavia Appeals Chamber considered the practice of the Chinese

96 J Bellinger III and W Haynes II, *US Initial Reactions to ICRC Study on Customary International Law*, 3 November 2006, 1.

97 J-M Henckaerts, 'Customary International Humanitarian Law: A Response to US Comments' (2007) 89 IRRC 478.

98 ibid.

99 ibid 479.

100 *See* M Hakimi, 'Custom's Method and Process, Lessons from Humanitarian Law', in CA Bradley (ed), *Custom's Future: International Law in a Changing World* (Cambridge University Press 2016) 165.

People's Liberation Party, the Farabundo Martí National Liberation Front,[101] and several other armed opposition groups. It also listed 'the behaviour of belligerent States, Governments and insurgents' among factors that 'have been instrumental in bringing about the formation of the customary rules',[102] without making distinction between States and non-State actors. More specifically, the International Criminal Tribunal for the Former Yugoslavia stressed the contribution made by the ICRC, stating that 'the practical results the ICRC has thus achieved in inducing compliance with international humanitarian law ought … to be regarded as an element of actual international practice; this is an element that has been conspicuously instrumental in the emergence or crystallization of customary rules'.[103] The statement is not completely clear, yet it suggests that the exclusion of non-State actors from the norm-making processes was not considered absolute by the International Criminal Tribunal for the Former Yugoslavia.[104]

Other judicial bodies have either not commented on the issue or have taken more cautious approach. Yet, it is interesting to note that even some of the International Court of Justice judges have not completely discarded the possibility of non-State actors involvement in the formatiom of customary international law. In his dissenting opinion in the *Case Concerning the Arrest Warrant (Belgium v Congo)*, Judge Van den Wyngaert criticized the Court for adopting a formalistic reasoning with respect to the rules on international accountability ignoring 'the opinion of civil society, an opinion that cannot be completely discounted in the formation of customary international law today'.[105]

The legal doctrine is not uniform in its view on the issue either. Most authors adopt the traditional approach, defining customary rules as rules created by States and, to some extent, international organizations. Mendelson, for instance, while

101 International Criminal Tribunal for the Former Yugoslavia, *Prosecutor v Duško Tadić* (IT-94-1-AR72), Appeals Chamber, Decision on the Defence Motion for Interlocutory Appeal on Jurisdiction, 2 October 1995, paras 102, 103, and 107.

102 ibid 108.

103 ibid 109.

104 In other cases, however, the International Criminal Tribunal for the Former Yugoslavia took a more traditional approach. For instance in the *Vasiljević* case, it held that '[a]s useful as the Commentaries to the 1949 Geneva Conventions may be to interpret the Conventions, they do not constitute state practice'. International Criminal Tribunal for the Former Yugoslavia, *Prosecutor v Mitar Vasiljević* (IT-98-32), Trial Chamber, Judgment, 29 November 2002, 78 (footnote 549).

105 Case Concerning the Arrest Warrant (Belgium v Congo) ICJ Reports 2002, Judge Van den Wyngaert (Dissenting Opinion), para 27.

recognizing that non-State actors may have indirect contribution to the formation of customary international law, concludes that 'in the ultimate analysis, it is only the practice of the organs and instrumentalities of States which is taken into account when deciding whether a rule of customary international law has come into being'.[106] Byers is of the same opinion, noting that

> States are the principal, if not the exclusive, direct participants in the process of customary international law ... International organizations do play an increasing role in the customary process ... Other entities, and individuals, are excluded from the customary process to an even greater degree.[107]

Similarly as the International Committee of the Red Cross, Byers links the capacity to take part in the norm-creating process to international legal personality, without elaborating on this point in any detail. Kyriakopoulos also opines that 'so far, only state practice, as opposed to non-state actor practice, appears to be, formally and directly, taken into account for the formation and identification of international customary law'.[108] Geiss and Zimmermann concur that 'it is widely agreed that, in principle, non-State actors such as the ICRC do not have the capacity to contribute directly to the formation of customary international law'.[109] Classical international law textbooks often take the State origin of customary international law as granted and their authors therefore do not feel any need to engage in a debate about the role of other actors.[110]

There are however other views in the doctrine as well. Noortmann draws attention to the fact that Article 38 of the International Court of Justice Statute defines custom as evidence of a general practice accepted as law, not as evidence of a general *state* practice. For him, thus, 'theoretically, or perhaps within a different

106 MH Mendelson, *The Formation of Customary International Law* (Martinus Nijhoff 1999) 203.

107 M Byers, *Custom, Power and the Power of Rules, International Relations and the Customary International Law* (Cambridge University Press 2001) 78.

108 GD Kyriakopoulos, 'Formation of International Custom and the Role of Non-State Actors' in P Pazartzis et al (eds), *Reconceptualising the Rule of Law in Global Governance, Resources, Investment and Trade* (Hart 2016) 58.

109 R Geiss and A Zimmermann, 'The International Committee of the Red Cross: A Unique Actor in the Field of International Humanitarian Law Creation and Progressive Development' in R Geiss, A Zimmermann, and S Haumer (eds), *Humanizing the Laws of War* (Cambridge University Press 2017) 236.

110 *See*, for instance, J Crawford (ed), *Brownlie's Principles of Public International Law* (8th edn, Oxford University Press 2012) 23–27; MN Shaw, *International Law* (7th edn, Cambridge University Press 2014) 51–63.

intersubjectively constructed interpretation, article 38 of the Statute … includes "evidence of a general non-state practice" as well. In that way, non-state entities would not merely be vehicles in a transnational legal process but figures in that process'.[111] Charlesworth and Chinkin refer to 'more radical suggestions made for new methods of international law', including one that would allow 'the activities of NGOs as constitutive of practice for determining rules of customary international law'.[112] Gunning notes that 'customary international law … should look to non-state actors as having the ability to create custom'.[113] Discussing specifically the legal status of individuals, Ochoa opines that 'the proposal that individuals ought to be included in the process of customary international law formation is both theoretically grounded and technically feasible'.[114]

Some authors put forward more concrete proposals as to what the role of non-State actors in the formation of customary international law could or should be. Arend suggests a model with 'multiple levels of customary international law'.[115] Some customary rules would apply to all actors – and they would be formed based on the practice and *opinio juris* of all actors. Other rules would only bind certain actors – and only the practice and *opinio juris* of those actors would be relevant. Roberts and Sivakumaran propose the theory of quasi-customary international law.[116] In this theory, customary rules would emerge based on the practice and *opinio juris* of all relevant actors. The practice and views of non-State actors, such as armed opposition groups, would therefore count. Yet, they would not necessarily be given the same weight as those of States. Furthermore, non-State actors would not be able to establish new customary rules on their own. They would 'contribute to the process of customary law, without being able to control its outcome'.[117] What

111 M Noortmann, 'Understanding Non-State Actors in the Contemporary World Society: Transcending the International, Mainstreaming the Transnational, or Bringing the Participants Back In?' in M Noormann and C Ryngaert (eds), *Non-State Actor Dynamics in International Law: From Law-Takers to Law-Makers* (Ashgate 2010) 160.

112 H Charlesworth and CM Chinkin, *The Boundaries of International Law: A Feminist Analysis* (Manchester University Press 2000) 172.

113 IR Gunning, 'Modernizing Customary International Law: The Challenge of Human Rights' (1991) 31 *Virginia Journal of International Law* 221.

114 C Ochoa, 'Individual and Customary International Law Formation' (2007) 48 Va J Int'l L 169.

115 AC Arend, *Legal Rules and International Society* (Oxford University Press 1999) 177.

116 A Roberts and S Sivakumaran, 'Lawmaking by Nonstate Actors: Engaging Armed Groups in the Creation of International Humanitarian Law' (2012) 37 Va J Int'l L 149–51.

117 ibid 151.

exactly this contribution would consist of and what its proportion in relation to that of States would be, remains unclear.

The two proposals thus introduced are made from the *de lege ferenda* perspective.[118] The authors putting them forward consider how non-State actors *could be made* part of the process leading to the formation of customary international law. Some authors, however, are persuaded that non-State actors already *make part* of this process. Hakimi opines that the traditional view on the formation of custom is outdated, because it ignores the fact that finding custom and making custom are intertwined processes. This, for her, entails that non-State actors charged with finding custom, such as international courts or the International Committee of the Red Cross, also contribute to the creation of this custom.[119] Arajärvi argues that 'non-state actors do shape the international law-making, not only indirectly by influencing states, but by having a direct bearing on the development of customary rules through their own actions and statements'.[120] She however bolsters this argument by few examples, which are moreover largely limited to international organizations. Carrillo-Santarelli draws attention to the fact that although non-State actors lack the general entitlement to participate in the development of international humanitarian law, they can contribute to this development in informal and indirect ways. In addition, 'States have the power to authorize non-state actors to participate in the shaping of customary law'.[121]

The thesis that non-State actors already actively contribute to the formation of customary international law also finds support among certain liberal and critical legal scholars.[122] These scholars do not necessarily share the traditional view on how norms in international law, including customary rules, are generated. McCorquodale, for instance, opines that

> to consider only state practice and state opinions … to determine customary international law as a 'source' of international law is a fiction created by the dominant legal doctrine … In an international legal system where non-state actors are participants, the practice of these actors, their role in the creation, development and enforcement of law and their

118 *See* Chapter 6 in this volume.

119 Hakimi (n 100) 163–64.

120 N Arajärvi, 'From State-Centrism to Where? The Formation of (Customary) International Law and Non-State Actors' (2010) SSRN 23.

121 N Carrillo-Santarelli, 'The Possibilities and Legitimacy of Non-State Participation in the Formation of Customary Law' (2017) 19 International Community Law Review 103.

122 Symposium on Contemporary Conceptions of Customary International Law, ASIL Proceedings (1998) 37–63.

> actions within the international and national communities … can, and should, be considered to form a part of customary international law.[123]

By the same token, Cardenas in chapter 6 of this volume shows that the exclusionist approach to non-State actors adopted by mainstream positivist scholars (labelled as formalists) is not necessarily shared by those studying the topic from a more empirical perspective or those conceptualizing, as the author does, customary international law as the product of successful argumentative campaigns.[124] The overview of the scholarly literature thus reveals that the State origin of customary rules is no longer taken for granted and that some form of contribution by non-State actors to the formation of customary international law is increasingly seen as both possible and desirable.

3 Critical assessment of the International Law Commission views on the formation of customary international law and non-State actors

The *Draft Conclusions on Identification of Customary International Law*, adopted by the International Law Commission on second reading in 2018, take a sceptical view on the role of non-State actors in the formation and identification of customary international law. The conduct of non-State actors does not count as the general practice (*usus longaevus*), their views do not qualify as the acceptance of the binding nature of the practice (*opinio juris*). At most, their conduct can be relevant for the assessment of the practice of States and international organizations. This approach mirrors the one adopted by the International Law Commission in 1950 in the study on *Ways and means for making the evidence of customary international law more readily available.* And although the Conclusions, with their commentaries, are much more elaborated than the 1950 study, the space reserved to the discussion on non-State actors is again quite limited and the conclusions of this discussion are virtually identical to those reached almost seventy years earlier. The statements made by States in the Sixth Committee and the views expressed by other international organs and by scholars reveal however that the International Law Commission view is problematic on at least five accounts.

123 R McCorquodale, 'An Inclusive International Legal System' (2004) 17 LJIL 498. *See* also R McCorquodale, 'Beyond State Sovereignty: The International Legal System and Non-State Participants' (2006) 8 International Law: Revista Colombiana de Derecho Internacional 103–59.

124 *See* Chapter 6 in this volume.

First of all, the conclusions that the International Law Commission has reached with respect to the role that non-State actors have, or rather do not have, in the formation and identification of customary international law are formulated in very categorical terms. This may, indeed, be warranted for Conclusions, whose aim after all is to 'offer practical guidance without being overly prescriptive'.[125] Thus, Conclusions should, and as far as Conclusion 4(3) is concerned, they most likely do, reflect international law as it stands today. It is the current *lex lata*, understood within the mainstream positivist paradigm, that those who are called upon to apply or advice on customary international law need to have the knowledge of. At the same time, being aware that the *lex lata* in a certain area is not, or no longer, the object of a total consensus and that there are actors (States, international courts, legal scholars) advocating for its change or, even, believing that such a change has already occurred, is also important for specialists in international law. Acknowledging this in the commentaries and giving information on the alternative positions and proposals would therefore provide a more complete, and more useful, description of the current normative landscape.

Secondly, while the International Law Commission contests that non-State actors play any role in the formation of customary international law, it accepts that their conduct may be relevant when assessing the practice of States and, potentially, international organizations. It is, however, not clear, whether the International Law Commission embraces the distinction described in the reports of the ILA Committee on Non-State Actors[126] between situations where the conduct of non-State actors makes part of State practice, because it is carried out on behalf of States or adopted by them, and situations, when non-State actors contribute to the formation of customary rules wholly indirectly. The commentaries foresee the case when an act of private individuals can be endorsed by States. They do not however explain what the nature and consequences of such an endorsement would be. It thus remains uncertain whether the conduct of non-State actors could in some cases (e.g. analogical to those that entail attribution of the acts of non-State actors to States under the 2001 International Law Commission *Articles on Responsibility of State for internationally wrongful acts*[127]) qualify as a form of State practice. While the wording of Conclusion 5 ('State practice consists of conduct of the State') suggests a negative answer, having clearer guidance in this respect

125 UN Doc A/73/10 (n 1) 122.

126 *Non-State Actors*, Report, Sofia Conference, 2012, 5.

127 UN Doc A/56/10, *Report of the International Law Commission on the work of its Fifty-third session*, Supplement No 10, November 2001, 59–365.

provided in the commentaries would be helpful for those tasked to identify the rules of customary international law.

Thirdly, the same applies with respect to situations when the conduct of non-State actors contributes to the formation, or expression, of customary international law wholly indirectly. The commentaries note that the conduct may either stimulate practice and *opinio juris* by States and international organizations, or record that practice and *opinio juris*. In the former case, non-State actors indirectly contribute to the formation of customary international law, in the latter case, they help identify customary international law. The commentaries add that in the latter case, the conduct of non-State actors may fall under teachings, which qualify as a subsidiary means for determining the rules of customary international law under Article 38(1)(d) of the International Court of Justice Statute.[128] All this is certainly true. Yet, if the Conclusions with their commentaries are to serve as a practical guidance, they should go beyond general statements, providing users with more concrete instructions on how to weigh the relevance of various forms of conduct as well as the conduct of various non-State actors.

Fourthly, another issue on which the Conclusions and the commentaries could and should be more unequivocal is the relation between the formation and the identification of customary international law. On the one hand, Conclusion 4(3) indicates that the conduct of non-State actors does not contribute to the formation or expression of rules of customary international law but that it 'may be relevant when assessing the practice' of States and, potentially, international organizations. Here, the International Law Commission draws a clear line between the formation (and the expression[129]) of customary international law, where non-State actors has no role, on the one hand, and the identifation of customary international law, where non-State actors can have some role, on the other hand. In the commentaries, however, we read that 'in practice identification cannot always be considered in isolation from formation; the identification of the existence and content of a rule of customary international law may well involve consideration of the processes by which it has developed'.[130] If this is so and if non-State actors, or at least some non-State actors, indeed contribute somehow to the identificion of customary international

128 ibid 132.

129 In Conclusion 4, the International Law Commission distinguishes between the formation and the expression of rules of customary international law. The latter term, not defined in the text, probably refers to the application of rules of customary international law after their formation, though in case of rules of customary international law, which are formed and re-formed continuously, such a distinction may seem contentious.

130 ibid 124.

law, it is not fully clear why they do not, or could not, contribute to the formation of customary international law as well.

Fifthly, and taking a broader perspective this time, one may wonder whether the decision of the International Law Commission to focus solely on the formation and identification of customary international law has been a wise one. It is certainly important for specialists in international law to know 'the way in which the existence and content of customary international law are to be determined' (Conclusion 1). Yet, it is equally important for them to know to whom customary international law applies. This question is not, in fact, left completely unaddressed in Conclusions and the commentaries. Conclusion 15, for instance, deals with the doctrine of persistent objector. Although the commentaries affirm that the doctrine 'not infrequently arises in connection with the identification of rules of customary international law',[131] it is in reality linked to the personal scope of application of customary international law. It can even be argued that determining the scope of application of customary international law is part of the process of its identification. In a similar vein, Conclusion 16, focusing on particular customary international law, indicates that a rule of particular customary international law 'applies only among a limited number of *States*' (emphasis added). The commentaries add that particular customary international law is to be distinguished from general customary international law, which 'in principle applies to all *States*' (emphasis added).[132]

These statements show that the International Law Commission pronounces upon, albeit cursorily and without giving any details, the personal scope of application of customary international law. And it does so in a way which, this time, does not seem to reflect the *lex lata*. There is quite a large consensus both within the international community and among scholars that at least some customary rules bind at least some non-State actors.[133] This is the case, for instance, of armed opposition groups which are bound by the rules of international humanitarian law (both treaty and customary rules) applicable in non-international armed conflicts.[134] As D'Aspremont notes in Chapter 7, it was exactly this recognition of the fact that non-State actors may be bound by norms of customary international law, which

131 ibid 152.

132 ibid 155.

133 *See* C Ryngaert, 'Non-State Actors: Carving Out a Space in a State-Centred International Legal System' (2006) 63 Neth Int Law Rev 183–95.

134 *See* L Zegveld, *Accountability of Armed Opposition Groups in International Law* (Cambridge University Press 2002); S Sivakumaran, 'Binding Armed Opposition Groups' (2006) 55 ICLQ 369–94; JK Kleffner, 'The Applicability of International Humanitarian Law to Organized Armed Groups' (2011) 93 IRRC 443–61.

prompted the debates about whether they may also contribute to its formation.[135] And although the two processes do not necessarily go hand in hand (an actor may be bound by norms without taking part in their formation and vice versa), non-State actors' effective contribution to the formation of customary international law could help answer the intriguing question as to the legal grounds for the binding effect of international law for non-State actors.

The International Law Commission does not explicitly address this question (which is not a problem, as doing so would go beyond the scope of the topic). It however also denies the relevance of the question by simply excluding non-State actors from the area of customary international law almost completely – not only for the formation of customary international law but also for its application (which is a problem, as it does not reflect reality). This is so surprising that one may wonder whether Conclusion 4(3) and, in fact, the Conclusions in general, deal with customary international law as a whole or whether they focus on a special part thereof – customary rules only applicable to States and, hence, only formed by them. That would leave space for other customary rules – those that would apply to States and (some) non-State actors alike and could (but would not need to) be formed by non-State actors as well; and those that would apply solely to (some) non-State actors and could (but, again, would not need to) be formed solely by them. It is not likely that the International Law Commission intended to embrace such an approach or that it even considered it. Yet, by treating custom as almost a purely inter-State phenomenon and by excluding non-State actors from this normative space (or simply ignoring them), the International Law Commission risks decreasing the value of its product not only on the theoretical level but also on the practical one, making practitioners unprepared to deal with non-State actors when they encounter them. Since such encounters become more and more frequent and since, moreover, an increasing number of States, scholars, and other actors consider that customary international law and non-State actors no longer live in two separate worlds, this position does not seem truly convincing.

135 *See* Chapter 7 in this volume.

Chapter 10

The International Law Commission in the eyes of the International Law Commission: mirror or looking-glass?

Luíza Leão Soares Pereira

This chapter addresses one specific aspect of the International Law Commission's work on the identification of customary international law: how it sees *its own* output in relation to custom. While in the latest Conclusions and Commentary on the Identification of Customary International Law (hereafter 'the Conclusions') it dedicates specific sections to 'teachings of publicists' and judgments, the Commission chose not to dedicate a discrete sub-heading to its own work, instead mentioning it in passing in the commentary preceding the 'Significance of certain materials for the identification of customary international law' section. The subject matter of this chapter might seem narrow at first glance, but the International Law Commission's difficulty in classifying its work is symptomatic of the project's deeper problems.

This chapter will first set out the Commission's ambiguous stance on its own work in the Conclusions and Commentary. This will be followed by a reasoned praise of the International Law Commission's choice not to classify its work under Conclusion 14, 'Teachings'. It will be argued subsequently, however, that the Commission did not appropriately grapple with its own role in relation to custom – despite the peripheral participation of states in its work, International Law Commission output has at times fundamentally shaped customary rules, and this is not reflected in the Conclusions and Commentary. It will be concluded that the problematic position of the International Law Commission on this subject is the triumph of pragmatism over accuracy. This isolated stance of inaccuracy is symptomatic of deeper problems with the project as a whole – the artificiality of the two-element approach, the excessive emphasis on state practice, and the impossibility of extricating 'identification' from 'formation' of custom. A closer look at the Commission's purported mirror-image reveals distortions more akin to a looking-glass.

1 Background: the International Law Commission's report and output

In its 64th Session, in 2012, the International Law Commission decided to include the 'Formation and evidence of customary international law' in its programme, having appointed Sir Michael Wood as its Special Rapporteur.[1] Sir Michael's first report was presented in the 65th Session, and, upon suggestion of the Special Rapporteur, the title of the topic was changed from 'Formation' to 'Identification of customary international law'.[2] At the 66th and 67th Sessions, subsequently to the presentation of the Second[3] and Third Reports[4] by the Special Rapporteur, draft Conclusions were submitted to the Drafting Committee, which the International Law Commission then 'took note of'.[5] Upon the submission of the fourth report by the Special Rapporteur,[6] in its 68th Session, the Commission adopted the sixteen Conclusions elaborated by the Drafting Committee alongside its commentary, produced by the Special Rapporteur in conjunction with an open-ended working group chaired by Marcelo Velázquez-Bermúdez.[7] In several stages during their drafting, the Conclusions and Commentary were submitted to States for their comments and observations. In August 2018 at its 70th Session, the Commission adopted the Conclusions and Commentary, submitted the Conclusions to the General Assembly, and recommended that the General Assembly take note thereof.

The Conclusions are divided into seven parts – scope and purpose, three sections on the basic or 'two-element approach' to identification and guidance on the two elements, significance of certain materials for the identification of custom, and

1 International Law Commission, 'Note by Michael Wood, Special Rapporteur, Formation and evidence of customary international law' (2012) UN Doc A/CN.4/653.
2 International Law Commission, 'First report on formation and evidence of customary international law by Michael Wood, Special Rapporteur' (2013) UN Doc A/CN.4/663.
3 International Law Commission, 'Second report on identification of customary international law by Michael Wood, Special Rapporteur' (2014) A/CN.4/672.
4 International Law Commission, 'Third report on the identification of customary international law by Michael Wood, Special Rapporteur' (2015) A/CN.4/682.
5 International Law Commission, 'Identification of customary international law, Text of the Conclusions and commentary provisionally adopted by the Drafting Committee' (2015) A/CN.4/L.869.
6 International Law Commission, 'Fourth report on identification of customary international law by Michael Wood, Special Rapporteur' (2016) A/CN.4/695; International Law Commission 'Fourth report on identification of customary international law by Michael Wood, Special Rapporteur Addendum' (2016) A/CN.4/695/Add.1.
7 International Law Commission, 'Report of the International Law Commission on the Work of it Sixty-Eighth Session' (2 May–10 June and 4 July–12 August 2016) A/71/10, 76–117.

a special part on the persistent objector and particular custom. The Commission chose to adopt the 'two-element' approach to Customary International Law, which enshrines State practice and *opinio juris* as the elements that constitute custom – 'for a persuasive analysis of whether a rule of customary international law exists, "it would be necessary to be satisfied that such a rule meets the conditions required for the birth of an international custom"'. This is also the personal position of Sir Michael, expressed in a lecture: 'what is needed to ascertain a rule of customary international law is, first, a general practice (often referred to as a "State practice") and, second, evidence of the acceptance of that practice as law (often referred to by the Latin term "*opinio juris*")'.[8] Although this two-element approach debate will come up in this chapter, its importance here is only tangential – the focus here is on Part Five of the Conclusions and Commentary, entitled 'Significance of certain materials for the identification of customary international law',[9] more specifically in the treatment it accorded to its own work[10] for the identification of custom.

One must begin with the caveat that 'formation' and 'identification' of custom are intimately intertwined. Although the Commission has attempted to limit the scope of its work by changing the name of the project from 'Formation and evidence' to 'Identification' of customary international law, as mentioned above, that this differentiation is artificial. This might have been an attempt on the part of the Commission to circumvent systemic implications that a statement made by it on the formation of custom would have for international law,[11] which in itself raises interesting issues of the perception of the Commission regarding its own work, but this is outside the scope of this chapter. The Commission has, to an extent, admitted to the problems in this distinction between identification and formation. In an earlier report, one of its footnotes cited Sir Robert Jennings,[12] who rightly stated that 'in international law the questions of whether a rule of customary law exists,

8 Sir M Wood and O Sender, '2014 Jonathan J Charney Distinguished Lecture in Public International Law: International Organisations and Customary International Law' (2015) 48 Vanderbilt Journal of Transnational Law 609, 612.

9 International Law Commission, A/71/10 (n 7), 78, 101–12.

10 ibid 101–12.

11 The change in name from 'Formation' to 'Identification' and the presentation of the Conclusions as a guide for domestic practitioners rather than a way to settle the theoretical debates on custom (*see* International Law Commission, A/71/10 (n 7), 305) are, in the author's view, are part of this attempt to limit the influence of this work in general international law. If it will be successful in doing this, given the key role the International Law Commission plays in international law today, as it is argued below in this chapter, remains to be seen.

12 International Law Commission, A/CN.4/672 (n 3), 2/68, fn 6.

and how customary law is made, tend in practice to coalesce'.[13] It also alluded to this in the latest version of the Conclusions, where it stated that 'in practice identification cannot always be considered in isolation from formation'.[14] Accordingly, this chapter will appropriately deal with the role of International Law Commission output in the *formation* of custom, and, consequently, its identification. The terms 'formation', 'making', and 'creation' of custom will be used interchangeably.

The focus of this chapter will be on the International Law Commission's appreciation of its own output in the formation of customary international law. At the beginning of the fifth part of the Commentary to the Conclusions, it is stated that 'other than primary evidence' of State practice and *opinio juris* cited in the previous section, other materials 'may be consulted' in ascertaining the existence of customary rules. These may 'assist in collecting, synthesizing or interpreting practice relevant to the identification of customary international law', guiding one seeking to determine the two constituent elements.[15] Whilst 'teachings of publicists' received their specific conclusions in Part Five – alongside 'treaties', 'resolutions of international organizations and intergovernmental conferences', 'decisions of courts and tribunals' – the Commission's own materials do not feature therein. Instead, the International Law Commission chose to include its output in the introduction to the Commentary to Part Five, in the following terms:

> (2) The Commission decided not to include at this stage a separate conclusion in the output of the International Law Commission. Such output does, however, merit special consideration in the present context. As has been recognized by the International Court of Justice and other courts and tribunals, a determination by the Commission affirming the existence and content of a customary rule *may have particular value*; as may a conclusion by it that no such rule exists. This flows from the Commission's *unique mandate from States* to promote the progressive development of international law and its codification, the thoroughness of its procedures (including the consideration of extensive surveys of *State practice*), and its *close relationship with States* as a subsidiary organ of the General Assembly (*including receiving oral and written comments* as it proceeds with its work). The weight to be given to the Commission's determinations depends, however, on various factors, including sources relied upon by the Commission, the stage reached in its work *and above all upon States' reception of its output*.[16] (some footnotes omitted, emphasis added)

13 Sir RY Jennings, 'What Is International Law and How Do We Tell When We See It' in Martti Koskenniemi (ed), *The Library of Essays in International Law: Sources of International Law* (Ashgate 1981) 60.
14 International Law Commission, A/71/10 (n 7), 81.
15 ibid 101.
16 Once the General Assembly has taken action in relation to a final draft of the Commission, such as by commending and annexing it to a resolution, the output of

The International Law Commission's approach to its own work is interesting for three reasons: firstly, due to it not having included its work in the 'teachings' category of the Conclusions. This is surprising because the majority of the literature that applies the strict two-element approach to custom adopted by the Commission classifies it as such.[17] Having added a specific draft conclusion on 'teachings' and not including it therein signals that it perceives itself as different, and a more significant contributor to custom, than scholars writing in their private capacity.

Secondly, the Commission's statement that its output '[merits] special consideration', and 'may have particular value' is telling, insofar as it is evidence of its recognition that it has *some* role in the making of customary international law. Nonetheless, the Commission tempers these statements regarding its role in the making of custom with the use of vague language – '*may* have particular value' (emphasis added) – and attribution of said importance to its links to States, as will be explored below, demonstrating difficulty on how to best articulate, and maybe how to come to terms with, its own systemic role.

Finally, the Commission's choice to attach its importance to States is significant. The Commission chose to attribute its importance to 'its unique mandate *from States* to promote progressive development of the law and its codification', 'its close relationship *with States*' though the GA in which it receives 'oral and written comments [*from States*]', and '*above all* upon *States' reception* of its output' (emphasis added).[18] Its (possible) importance in the formation of custom hinges on its relationship with States, and not its functional/organizational/membership particularities. This further highlights the ambiguity of the Commission's relationship with its own work. One can see this passage as evidence of its struggle to come to terms with its

the Commission may also be considered under Draft Conclusion 12 (Resolutions of International Organisations and Intergovernmental Conferences).

17 A Oraison, 'Reflexions Sur La Doctrine Des Publicistes Les Plus Qualifies Des Differentes Nations' (1991) 21 Revue Belge de Droit International 507, 510; M Peil, 'Scholarly Writings as a Source of Law: A Survey of the Use of Doctrine by the International Court of Justice' (2012) 136 Cambridge Journal of International and Comparative Law 1–16, 136; James Crawford, *Brownlie's Principles of Public International Law* (8th edn, Oxford University Press 2012) 43–44; H Thirlway, *The Sources of International Law* (Oxford University Press 2014) 19. Even Sir Michael himself, when writing on 'teachings' as a source of international law in his personal capacity, states that 'The collective product of [the International Law Commission and other] learned bodies should be seen as part of the teachings for the purposes of Article 38(1)(d) International Court of Justice Statute'. Sir Michael Wood, 'Teachings of the Most Highly Qualified Publicists (Art 38(1) ICJ Statute)', *MPEPIL* (2010) para 11.

18 International Law Commission, A/71/10 (n 7), 101.

importance in the international sphere despite its relative detachment from States' interests that permeates United Nations political organs, and its attempt to attach itself to States in order to justify its own importance. This is a display of the difficulty experienced by the Commission in particular and of international lawyers in general to acknowledge members of the profession who act independently from states.

2 Why are International Law Commission documents *not* 'teachings'

2.1 Ordinary meaning and discussions at the Advisory Committee of Jurists

Although much of the literature on teachings includes International Law Commission output and other 'soft' materials under the 'teachings' classification, it is argued here that this is not correct; in this sense, the International Law Commission took the right approach in leaving its own materials outside Conclusion 14, 'Teachings'. This is, first of all, because the 'teachings' category encompasses work of an academic/scholarly nature, and not materials produced with an immediate practical aim such as those drafted by the International Law Commission, which is a body whose mandate is to promote 'codification' and 'progressive development' of the law.

One must look first to the ordinary meaning of 'teachings of publicists'. The International Court of Justice Statute's Article 38(1)(d), which the International Law Commission Conclusion paraphrases, reads as follows:

> 1. The Court, [...], shall apply:
> [...]
> d. [...] *the teachings* of the most highly qualified *publicists* of the various nations, as subsidiary means for the determination of rules of law. (Emphasis added)

Both the words 'teachings' and 'publicists' denote works of a scholarly or academic nature; the terms used in the Statute are not 'secondary materials' or an equivalent, but specifically 'teachings', and what is a 'teaching' if not the product of scholarly, versus practice-type, activities. In turn the term 'publicist', although uncommon in the English language, denotes a jurist that writes about public law,[19] thus also possessing an academic connotation. The scholarly nature of the materials enshrined in this provision is confirmed by the French text ('*la doctrine*' as it is produced by '*[les] publicistes*'). The term '*Doctrine*' comes from the Latin term '*docere*', which is

19 Sir M Wood, 'Remarks on the Importance Of "Teachings" in International Law, with Particular Reference to the Melland Schill Lecture Series', Manchester International Law Centre (2016) 7.

translated as 'to teach', often being defined in opposition to judgments or '*la jurisprudence*'. In the words of Andre Oraison, '*la doctrine*' in its original meaning[20] designates 'the understanding of a sage on a point of law, or the solution that he gives to a question that is the object of controversy',[21] in which one acts individually or collectively but independently from States, about a topic of their own choice.

Even if one could argue that the meaning of 'teachings' is unclear, and could encompass International Law Commission output, the debates before the Committee of Jurists support this chapter's abovementioned conclusions, and only speak of academic works properly so-called. The terminology used by the Commissioners when drafting this provision makes this clear; they use terms such as 'doctrines of jurists',[22] 'opinions of authors',[23] 'opinions of highly recognized authors',[24] 'doctrine of legal writers',[25] 'works of writers',[26] amongst others. The original Phillimore-Root proposal, referring to 'works of writers' rather than 'teachings of publicists', denotes academic work. The concerns raised by some of the members of the Committee regarding the inclusion of a provision on 'teachings' provide further confirmation. When presented with the Phillimore-Root proposal that listed 'opinions of writers' as materials to be taken into account by the Court – albeit only after treaties, custom, and general principles had been considered – the Italian Commissioner Arturo Ricci-Busatti 'denied most emphatically that the opinions of authors could be considered a *source of law* to be applied by the Court, and he was above all astonished that Mr. Root had agreed to a formula containing this idea'.[27] In turn, the French representative Albert De

20 Although he later on argues doctrine evolved as to encompass that which is produced by practitioners as well as academics. 'À cette doctrine classique de theóriciens purs […] dont les membres interviennent quand ils veulent et sur les sujets de leur choix s'est graduellement superpose, dès l'aube du XXe siècle, unne doctrine nouvelle de praticiens […] engagée dans les procédures spécifiques de nature diplomatique, normative ou contentieuse', Oraison (n 7) 509.

21 '[L]a conviction d'un Savant sur un point de droit ou la solution qu'il donne à une question qui fait l'objet d'une controverse', Oraison (n 7) 508.

22 Permanent Court of International Justice Advisory Committee of Jurists, 'Procès-Verbaux of the Proceedings of the Advisory Committee of Jurists June 16th-July 24th 1920' (1920) www.icj-cij.org/pcij/serie_D/D_proceedings_of_committee_annexes_16june_24july_1920.pdf, accessed 6 July 2020 331.

23 ibid 332.

24 ibid 333.

25 ibid 333.

26 ibid 334.

27 ibid 332.

Lapradelle stated that 'jurisprudence was more important than doctrine, since the judges in pronouncing the sentence *had a practical end in view*'[28] (emphasis added), implying that 'writers' were those acting privately to produce academic/scholarly publications without a specific practical end in mind.

The International Law Commission's work, on the other hand, is not of an academic/scholarly nature, and aims at having direct practical consequences. The practical nature of the work of the International Law Commission can be drawn both from its mandate as well as its procedural practices. Its mandate, pursuant to Article 1, paragraph 1, of the Statute of the International Law Commission, provides that the 'Commission shall have for its object the promotion of the *progressive development* of international law and its *codification*' (emphasis added). Article 15 distinguishes the Commission's two functions: progressive development is defined as 'the preparation of draft conventions on subjects which have not yet been regulated by international law or in regard to which the law has not yet been sufficiently developed in the practice of States', whereas codification is defined as 'the more precise formulation and systematization of rules of international law in fields where there already has been extensive State practice, precedent and doctrine'. Both functions are closer to practice than to scholarship – preparing conventions and formulation and systematization of rules of international law – and cannot be classified as academic 'teachings'.

Its procedural practices also highlight that, although its activities are investigative, and thus involve extensive legal research, the International Law Commission's role is to facilitate the application and development of international law, and not produce academic treatises or studies. Aside from the fact that some of its members are diplomats and not scholars, and that even the majority of its academic members are also prolific practitioners, the International Law Commission maintains continuous communication with States and other actors regarding its work. Its proceedings take considerable time to achieve results, allowing for adaptation and refinement of any by-product of discussions; the interaction between the Commission and other United Nations organs when drafting its materials, namely the Sixth Committee and the General Assembly, provide the Commission with feedback and to some extent promote the exchange of views between United Nations bodies. Moreover, although some of the International Law Commission's work may be close to scholarship – a prime example of this being the work on fragmentation led by Special Rapporteur Martti Koskenniemi – these are the exception rather than the rule. The final versions of its output generally comes in a 'legislative format' (draft articles, draft conclusions),

28 ibid 336.

a characteristic which also distinguishes its work from that produced by academics.[29] Furthermore, although there is some degree of flexibility, it cannot be said that Commissioners 'intervene when they want on subjects of their own choice'; their agenda is set conjointly with States and other United Nations organs, and although the timeframe can be set out by the Commission according to the extension of the project concerned, discussions take place at specific times of the year in structured sessions.

Thus, it is argued that (1) 'teachings of [the most qualified] publicists' cannot be construed as including International Law Commission output, because (a) the Commission's work is imminently practical – codification and progressive development – and does not fit the ordinary meaning of 'teachings', and (b) even if the meaning of the term was ambiguous, the debates amongst the drafters of Article 38(1)(d) confirm that they only envisaged academic works, and not those of a practical nature, such as the Commission's, to be encompassed by this provision. It is thus concluded that the Commission was right not to classify its own work as 'Techings' under Draft Conclusion 14.

2.2 More than 'teachings': International Law Commission documents as part of the formation of custom

This chapter argues that International Law Commission output should not be under the 'teachings of publicists' rubric due first to its practical nature, but also because it is part of the process whereby custom is formed. In this sense, this chapter sees custom as not emanating exclusively from States, but arising from a complex, decentralized process. Custom can be seen 'in motion over time, as States and other actors – operating not in isolation, but through collective judgments that build incrementally on existing institutions – engage in dialogue about its development'.[30] The Commission and the individuals that compose it, interacting with other institutions, especially the International Court of Justice, has often modified and created customary international law.

Similar points were made by Sir Robert Jennings, who stated that the work of the International Law Commission is 'not limited to drafting and proposing but is, within its limits, genuinely law-making'.[31] Jennings makes a case for a need of

29 Exceptions to this are the work of the Institut de Droit International and, sometimes, the International Law Association, which also adopt the 'legislative' format.

30 J Crawford, 'Chance, Order, Change: The Course of International Law' (2013) 365 Recueil des Cours para 89.

31 Sir RY Jennings, 'Recent Developments in the International Law Commission: Its Relation to the Sources of International Law' (1964) ICLQ 897. In this sense, *see* also G

international lawyers to detach themselves from domestic legislation analogies, and accept that in the international legal system authority is material, rather than formal. Although the Commission's work is not binding as a formal source of law, law in the material sense might be created from International Law Commission output, especially if that output is combined with an interaction with other international bodies, such as the International Court of Justice.[32]

If this was true when Jennings described the phenomenon in the 1960s, when codification by treaty was still on the rise, this is even more accurate today. The Commission has often submitted its output to the General Assembly, which in turn 'takes note' of the work, instead of organizing a conference to convert it into a treaty. The Conclusions themselves have gone through this process. This point is particularly well articulated by Santiago de Villalpando, who states that 'the codification and progressive development of international law at the United Nations appears to have shifted away from the conventional form'. He argues that 'it is indeed possible to identify the existence of an "autocatalytic process", by which the consolidation of legal regimes is achieved through informal channels, as a result of a dialogue between international lawyers in different roles … in the absence of any for negotiation by government representatives and adoption of an international convention'.[33] Villalpando contends that non-binding instruments become legally binding custom due to external confirmations and re-statements of authoritativeness, such as citations by international courts and tribunals, which in turn profit from the International Law Commission's authority and the availability of its formulations in convenient written form.[34]

Fernando Lusa Bordin makes a similar point, expressing the view that the work of the International Law Commission is neither State practice nor 'teachings', but something more.[35] The process of re-statement of the Commission's work by other bodies and the blurred lines between codification and progressive development

Abi-Saab, 'La Commission Du Droit International, La Codification et Le Processus de Formation de Droit International', *Making Better International Law: The International Law Commission at 50 Proceedings of the United Nations Colloquium on Progressive Development and Codification of International Law* (1998).

32 Jennings (n 31) 893.

33 S Villalpando, 'The "Invisible College of International Lawyers" Forty Years Later', *ESIL Conference Paper Series* (2013) 11.

34 S Villalpando, 'Codification Light: A New Trend in the Codification of International Law at the United Nations' (2013) 8 Brazilian Yearbook of International Law 117, 121 vi.

35 FL Bordin, 'Reflections of Customary International Law: The Authority of Codification Conventions and ILC Draft Articles in International Law' (2014) 63 ICLQ 535–67, 537.

in its work portray an 'image that the resulting texts constitute the most authoritative restatement of the existing law'.[36] Although at first he appears to adopt an ambiguous position – whilst maintaining that they are 'subsidiary means for the determination of the rules of law', and analogizing International Law Commission materials to the work of the International Court of Justice – he also states that 'non-legislative codification may be part of the *process* whereby international custom is formed',[37] and that only addressing them as 'teachings' or State practice 'falls short of properly appraising the pivotal role that these texts have played and continue to play in articulating rules of general international law'.[38]

The best example of the pervasive influence of the International Law Commission on the development of customary international law is its contribution to the law on State Responsibility.[39] The International Law Commission Articles on State Responsibility have been cited widely by international and national courts and tribunals in subject areas that range from investment to international criminal law. Villalpando uses the defence of necessity to illustrate how the work of the International Law Commission can change international law. He argues that prior to the latest Special Rapporteur's work, the existence of such a defence under international law was uncertain. Once it was included in the International Law Commission's work, however, it became part of the international legal vocabulary, having been incorporated in the jurisprudence of the International Court of Justice and, later on, in that of other international courts and tribunals; this 'autocatalytic process', in which the International Law Commission played a key role, elevated necessity from controversial legal doctrine to widely recognized circumstance precluding wrongfulness.[40] Thus, this chapter argues that the final reason the International Law Commission was correct in not classifying its own work as 'teachings' is because they are not merely 'subsidiary means for the determination' of international law, but part of the complex system whereby custom develops.

3 Why the Commission did not go further

As explained above, the Commission did not go far enough in assessing its role in the development of custom. Although it accepted that its output 'may have

36 ibid 535.
37 ibid 564.
38 ibid 567.
39 For instance in the fields of diplomatic protection and responsibility of international organizations.
40 Villalpando (n 33).

particular value', it attached this value to its 'special relationship to states', which is only part of the story. It also only addressed its role in the commentary, not in the conclusions themselves. This is in contrast with 'Teachings' and 'Decisions of courts and tribunals', addressed in their own discrete Conclusions.

The Commission took this approach for at least three reasons. Firstly, from a stylistic standpoint, it did not want to appear self-congratulatory. In a project that places such emphasis on states and their practice, and that takes little notice of other actors' roles in relation to custom, highlighting its own importance in this way could appear crass. The second justification for this conservative approach to its own output is technical – accrediting a central role for a non-State actor such as itself in the formation of customary international law is incompatible with the 'neatness' of the two-element approach framework the Commission adopted. The International Law Commission is not only part of an international organization, which in itself does not sit well with the cautious approach it adopted, but its members are elected in an individual capacity, and not as diplomats representing States' interests. The State practice plus *opinio juris* approach ties custom very strongly to acts and views of States, and cannot be easily reconciled with giving a prominent role to an organ that is moved largely by individuals with strong personal views and autonomy. Sir Michael's second report is evidence of this concern, when it stated that 'practice of organs or other bodies … composed of individuals serving in their personal capacity … cannot be said to represent States', and thus cannot 'contribute or attest to the formation of a general practice'.[41] Not only would this explain the hesitance in taking a firmer stance on its importance, it would also explain the Commission's choice to tie its own importance to its 'special relationship to *States*', its 'unique mandate *from States*', 'the thoroughness of its procedures (including consideration of extensive surveys on *State practice*', and '*its close relationship to States*', and subsidiarity to the *State* composed 'General Assembly'[42]). Special Rapporteur Sir Michael Wood in particular, like the majority of current International Law Commission members, is committed to a strict adoption of the two-element approach when it comes to custom. Not only were Sir Michael's previous reports on the subject even more firm in his adoption of the two-element approach, his personal academic work is revealing of a strong belief in the pivotal role of State practice in the formation of custom.[43] Adopting a different model that is inconsistent with the two-element approach only in relation to its own work somewhat

41 International Law Commission, A/CN.4/672 (n 3), para 43.

42 International Law Commission, A/71/10 (n 7), 101.

43 See this in Sir M Wood and Sender, '2014 Jonathan J. Charney Distinguished Lecture in Public International Law: International Organisations and Customary International Law'; Sir M Wood and O Sender, 'State Practice', *MPEPIL* (2015); Sir M Wood,

compromises the project, and goes against personal positions of the Commissioners involved. Work of bodies such as the International Law Commission, which have a strong individual component, are especially problematic for those advocating a State-centric view of international lawmaking, and further highlight the reluctance international lawyers have in acknowledging any significant role for individual members of the profession. Sources literature struggles to reconcile itself with the profession's role in international lawmaking and its relative independence from states – see the general rejection of any significant role for academic 'teachings'.

Thirdly, and tied to both previous justifications provided above for the position adopted by the International Law Commission, is a more pragmatic reason. The Commission may have been hesitant to take a different stance due to a perception that it was required to remain deferential to States, to avoid backlash and maintain its current influential position. Although the Commission might be part of a *sui generis* process of international lawmaking, the impact of its work is still dependent on either express endorsement by States of International Law Commission positions or their silence. Overtly acknowledging its own importance may lead to rejection by States of the Commission's work, and set back one of the main processes by which international law has managed to develop without the need for cumbersome and excessively politicized treaty-making – in a sense, admitting its own prominence might contribute towards diminishing it. It is thus a political choice to limit its overt importance, and a small price to pay in order to keep its position intact.

As suggested by the contributor during the conference that preceded this volume, a good strategy would have been to include International Law Commission output under a separate category of Part Five, similarly to what was done with 'Decisions of courts and tribunals' which play a comparable role. Although it would not solve systemic problems inherent to the methodology the Commission adopted, including International Law Commission output as its own conclusion would be a pragmatic way to avoid dealing with theoretical debates, and simultaneously draw domestic practitioners to

'Editorial Comment: The Present Position within the ILC on the Topic "Identification of Customary International Law": In Partial Response to S Yee, Report on the ILC Project on "Identification of Customary International Law"' (2016) Chinese Journal of International Law 3–15; Sir M Wood, 'Remarks on the Importance Of "Teachings" in International Law, with Particular Reference to the Melland Schill Lecture Series'; Sir M Wood and O Sender, 'Discussion of Stefan Talmon's "Determining Customary International Law: The ICJ's Methodology between Induction, Deduction and Assertion'; Sir M Wood and O Sender, 'The International Court of Justice and Customary International Law: A Reply to Stefan Talmon'; Sir M Wood and O Sender, 'Identifying the Rules for Identifying Customary International Law: Response from Michael Wood and Omri Sender'.

the importance to the role of the Commission. It seems remiss that a project pitched at aiding domestic practitioners not well-versed in international law[44] to identify custom does not expressly point towards the Commission's valuable materials.

4 Concluding remarks

The first conclusion of the analysis of the International Law Commission's approach to its own output in the Identification of Customary International Law project is that the Commission made a conscious decision to extricate itself from the 'teachings' category, and that it was correct in doing so. Firstly, its work is not 'scholarly' in the traditional sense, but practical, hence its mandate of 'codification and progressive development'. Secondly, and most importantly, the International Law Commission features much more prominently than 'teachings' in how customary international law evolves. Whereas teachings' contribution to custom is much more diffuse, the Commission's influence has, in many instances, been paramount. The International Law Commission and the materials it produces are a fundamental part of a complex system whereby customary international law is formed, at times with little State input.

Following from this, the second conclusion reached here is that the International Law Commission did not go far *enough* in acknowledging its own role in relation to custom. For the reasons expounded above – not wanting to appear self-congratulatory, the strictness of the two-element approach, and its deference to States – it adopted an ambiguous stance. The Comission's output was not included in the conclusions themselves and relegated to the Commentary to the Introduction of Chapter 4. Although accepting its work 'may have particular value' in this context, the International Law Commission did not extrapolate on what this value is, and attributed said value exclusively to its 'special relationship' with States.

In choosing pragmatism over accuracy on this point, the International Law Commission failed to provide much-needed clarification as to how its materials inform custom. The impossibility of simplifying the complexity of customary international law's ebb and flow become evident when the issue of International Law Commission output is scrutinized. In the small gesture of pulling this one thread, this contribution unraveled other aspects of the debate surrounding the project as a whole, adding to other critical voices in this volume. Beyond the narrow confines of the role performed by the International Law Commission in relation to custom, deeper questions about the inadequacy of the two-element approach and the artificiality of the division between formation and identification come to the fore.

44 International Law Commission, A/71/10 (n 7), 305. *See* n 11 for more on this.

Chapter 11

The riddle of custom: General Assembly resolutions

Rossana Deplano

On 30 May 2016 the International Law Commission adopted a set of sixteen Conclusions aimed at explaining how a customary rule is formed and how it is possible to identify either an emerging or a fully formed rule of customary law. However, being the process of custom creation entirely informal and unstructured, the International Law Commission Conclusions do not, and cannot, represent an objective method for ascertaining customary rules. They thus fail to provide authoritative guidance to practitioners in the field of international organizations' practice, which is flagged as the stated aim of the study.

The study of the International Law Commission on the Identification of Customary International Law represents nonetheless an ambitious attempt to clarify how to spot the presence of a customary rule. In particular, in the Conclusions, the process of identification of customary rules runs in parallel with the stages of formation of such rules, which leads the International Law Commission to equate the process of identification of international customary law with a type of legal methodology largely grounded on the traditional, normative analysis of law. However, the International Law Commission study has an original feature which has no precedent in either the previous work of the International Law Commission on international customary law or the academic literature: according to the Conclusions, the practice of international organizations as such may, under certain circumstances, be constitutive of custom. Such a proposition has revived the scholarly debate on the sources of international law in general, and the relevance of international customary law in the modern international legal system in particular. Within this context, scholars and practitioners alike are now engaged in trying to conceptualize the specific role international organizations play in the process of custom creation.

This chapter examines the role of resolutions adopted by intergovernmental organizations in the International Law Commission Conclusions on Identification of Customary International Law with a view to assessing the effectiveness of the proposed methodology. The analysis unfolds along three lines of inquiry. Firstly, it critically analyses the methodology devised by the International Law Commission to ascertain the existence of a customary rule with specific reference to the work of international organizations (1). Secondly, it examines the definition of resolution contained in the Conclusions and compares it with the mainstream literature on the concept of resolution to see whether in the International Law Commission Conclusions there is any significant departure from the dominant conception (2). Thirdly, it evaluates the practical implications of the International Law Commission Conclusions by using the resolutions of the United Nations General Assembly as a case study (3). By focusing on the group of fifty re-stated resolutions on the implementation of the Declaration on the Granting of Independence to Colonial Countries and Peoples by the Specialized Agencies and the other international institutions associated with the UN, this section shows that over time the resolutions of the General Assembly have acquired a systemic character and, therefore, do not exist in isolation from each other. It then relates the findings back to the relevant International Law Commission Conclusions on Identification of Customary International Law with a view to establishing whether they adequately account for the peculiarities of the decisions of international organisations in the process of custom creation. A last section offers concluding observations (4). The argument is made that providing a step-by-step methodology on how to identify a rule of customary international law proves to be an elusive task due to the spontaneous character of custom creation. In particular, the dual nature of resolutions of international organizations as both political and normative acts, like those of the General Assembly, proves that a methodology focusing on the normative character of resolutions cannot explain how a customary rule comes into existence. Hence, the International Law Commission Conclusions can be at best effective in identifying already formed customary rules, eventually adding little to the previous International Law Commission study on identification of international customary law (1950).

1 Methodology

Questions of method are questions about the identity of international law, including international customary law. The stated purpose of the International Law Commission Conclusions is to clarify the legal methodology required to detect the presence of a customary rule.[1] The suggested methodology consists of 'elucidat[ing]

1 International Law Commission, 'Report of the International Law Commission on the work of its sixty-eighth session, 2 May–10 June and 4 July–12 August 2016', UN Doc A/71/10 81 para 1 and 82 para 5.

the process of formation and identification of customary international law through guidance and practice'[2] for those called to apply customary rules, including national and international judges.[3] In practice, the methodology devised by the International Law Commission consists in the application of the two-element approach contained in Article 38(1)(b) of the International Court of Justice Statute[4] according to the interpretation given to each element (general practice and acceptance as law) by the International Court of Justice itself.[5]

The decision of the International Law Commission, which is strongly supported by the Special Rapporteur, to equate the mandate of providing authoritative guidance to practitioners with fully endorsing the International Court of Justice's pronouncements on formation and evidence of international customary law appears like a sensible attempt to bring together what is otherwise a fragmented, and at times incoherent,[6] picture of authoritative statements. However, it is questionable whether the International Law Commission Conclusions, as they stand, are able to achieve their stated goal. Two main objections come to the fore.

The first one refers to the relationship between the aim of the Conclusions and the remit of the International Law Commission mandate. Article 24 of the International Law Commission Statute reads:

> The Commission shall consider ways and means for making the evidence of customary international law more readily available, such as the collection and publication of documents concerning State practice and of the decisions of national and international courts on questions of international law, and shall make a report to the General Assembly on this matter.[7]

Article 24 refers to 'ways and means' for making evidence of international customary law available whereas the International Law Commission Conclusions aim

2 Note by the Special Rapporteur, Sir Michael Wood, UN Doc A/CN.4/653 (30 May 2012) para 24.

3 Recommendation of the Working Group, UN Doc A/66/10 305 para 4.

4 Commentary to Draft Conclusion 2, in International Law Commission, UN Doc A/71/10 (n 1), 82 para 1.

5 International Law Commission, 'Report of the International Law Commission on the work of its sixty-fourth session, 7 May to 1 June and 2 July to 3 August 2012', UN Doc A/67/10, 108 para 161. *See* also UN Doc A/CN.4/SR.3148 4.

6 S Talmon, 'Determining Customary International Law: The ICJ's Methodology between Induction, Deduction and Assertion' 26(2) European Journal of International Law (2015) 417.

7 Statute of the International Law Commission, UNGA res 174, UN Doc 174(II) (21 Nov 1947), as amended by UNGA res 36/39, UN Doc A/RES/36/39 (18 November 1981).

at providing a 'methodology' for detecting the presence of custom. Both expressions, 'ways and means' and 'methodology', are quite broad and open to interpretation. However, unless they are regarded as synonymous to each other, they seem to cover different aspects of the process of identification of customary rules.

On the one hand, 'ways and means' appears to refer to the identification of already formed rules. The 1950 International Law Commission study (whose title – 'Ways and Means for Making the Evidence of Customary International Law More Readily Available' – replicates verbatim the first part of Article 24 of the International Law Commission Statute) considered as evidence of State practice statements contained in treaties, either ratified or signed but not brought into force, and decisions of national and international courts on questions of international law while recognizing that providing a full list of the types of materials which reveal State practice is neither practicable nor useful.[8] Accordingly, the 1950 study limited itself to providing a list of private and public collections of both the text of treaties and decisions of national and international courts.[9] Constitutions and national legislation as well as diplomatic correspondence also feature as sources able to 'supply abundant evidence of [customary international law]'.[10] Much more succinct was the treatment of the practice of international organizations, which is exhausted in one sentence: 'Records of the cumulative practice of international organizations may be regarded as evidence of customary international law with reference to States' relations to the organization.'[11]

On the other hand, the term 'methodology' covers the process of formation of a customary rule. Evidence in this context refers to both the identification of an already formed rule and the realization that a rule is in the process of crystallizing. In relation to this point, several members of the International Law Commission have expressed doubt and concern about the expanded interpretation of the scope of the Conclusions. The lack of unanimity among the International Law Commission members also represents the second objection to the methodological stance taken by the International Law Commission.

Some International Law Commission members have firmly opposed the idea of bringing together the topic of *formation* and *evidence* of international customary

8 Report of the International Law Commission on its Second Session, Yearbook of the International Law Commission, 1950, vol 2, 367–68.

9 Report of the International Law Commission on its Second Session, Yearbook of the International Law Commission, 1950, vol 2, 368–70.

10 Report of the International Law Commission on its Second Session, Yearbook of the International Law Commission, 1950, vol 2, 371.

11 Report of the International Law Commission on its Second Session, Yearbook of the International Law Commission, 1950, vol 2, 372.

law within the scope of the Conclusions. Mr Murase, for instance, has pointed out the impossibility of applying the two-element approach to both the process of formation and evidence, since the former is a dynamic concept whereas the latter is a static one.[12] He argues that the word 'evidence' means stopping the clock and trying to ascertain the applicable law at a given moment in time. This, by logic, makes it impossible to talk simultaneously of formation and evidence 'without causing some methodological confusion'.[13] Mr Wisnumrti,[14] Mr Petrič,[15] and Mr Kamto[16] share his interpretation. In addition, it is noteworthy that the desirability of engaging in this type of inquiry about international customary law had already been denied in an unofficial survey on items that should not be inscribed on the International Law Commission's agenda.[17]

An even more radical position is the one taken by Mr Forteau, who is resolute in proclaiming the scope of the Conclusions as falling outside the remit of the International Law Commission's mandate. He suggests keeping a tight focus on the identification of already formed rules only.[18] More softly, Mr Park points out that it is preferable to focus on evidence rather than formation.[19]

Equally strong is the position taken by other International Law Commission members in favour of including the process of formation of customary rules within the Conclusions. Mr Gevorgian, for example, argues that formation and identification are part of the same process of searching for evidence of the existence of a customary rule.[20] Similarly, Mr Hassouna shares the Special Rapporteur's decision to focus on the formative stage of the process of custom creation[21] while Mr Nolte has referred to it as an essential step of the inquiry.[22]

Overall, the Conclusions appear not to be particularly innovative in terms of the methodology adopted, since it consists of a full endorsement of the International Court of Justice's pronouncements on international customary law. At the same

12 UN Doc A/CN.4/SR.3148, 8.
13 UN Doc A/CN.4/SR.3150, 6.
14 UN Doc A/CN.4/SR.3151, 7.
15 UN Doc A/CN.4/SR.3150, 9.
16 UN Doc A/CN.4/SR.3151, 10.
17 As reported in First report on formation and evidence of customary international law (17 May 2013), 5 para 10.
18 UN Doc A/CN.4/SR.3150, 11.
19 UN Doc A/CN.4/SR.3151, 9.
20 UN Doc A/CN.4/SR.3151, 5.
21 UN Doc A/CN.4/SR.3150, 8.
22 UN Doc A/CN.4/SR.3151, 13.

time, they raise concern, since they require to apply the same requirement – namely, the two-element approach – to the identification of both already formed rules and rules in the process of crystallizing. In this respect, it seems that the International Law Commission position on the role of resolutions in the process of identification of international customary law is contradictory, for two main reasons.

Firstly, Conclusion 4(2) establishes that, in certain cases, the practice of international organizations may be constitutive of custom. However, the Commentary clarifies that this holds true only in relation to decisions of international organizations endowed with exclusive competence.[23] This amounts to considering international organizations as mere agents of States. Secondly, since the Conclusions do not treat international organizations as autonomous subjects of international law for the purpose of creation of international customary law, the practice of international organizations is not seen in its temporal dimension as a series of interconnected acts aimed at developing the politics of the international organization. What instead transpires from the text of the Conclusions is a strict focus on the text of resolutions as possible evidence of international custom.[24] The general word of caution given by the Special Rapporteur that due consideration must be given to the relevant circumstances does not seem to provide any authoritative guidance in context of a methodological question about the identification of customary rules.[25]

The process of ascertaining the evidentiary value of resolutions is further complicated by the application of the two-element approach to the formative stage of custom. As a matter of methodology, the Commentary to Conclusion 2 states that two distinct inquiries are to be carried out about the empirical evidence necessary for the identification of international customary law in relation to each of the two elements.[26] Whereas detecting a general practice requires an inductive

23 Second report on identification of customary international law (22 May 2014), para 43. *See* also M Wood, 'International Organizations and Customary International Law' 48 Vanderbilt Journal of Transnational Law (2015) 617.

24 The Commentary to Draft Conclusion 1 clearly states that the Draft Conclusions do not directly address the process by which international customary law develops over time. Report of the International Law Commission on the work of its sixty-eighth session, 2 May–10 June and 4 July–12 August 2016, UN Doc A/71/10, 81 para 4.

25 'It should not be expected that the outcome of the [ILC] work will be a series of hard-and-fast rules for the identification of rules of [CIL]. Instead, the aim is to shed light *on the general process* of formation and evidence of rules of [CIL]'. First report on formation and evidence of customary international law (17 May 2013), UN Doc A/CN.4/663 (17 May 2013), 7 para 18 (statement by the Special Rapporteur, Sir Michael Wood; emphasis added).

26 Report of the International Law Commission on the work of its sixty-eighth session, 2 May–10 June and 4 July–12 August 2016, UN Doc A/71/10, 86 para 6.

approach,[27] the Conclusions turn out to be fully contradictory in relation to the assessment of the evidentiary value of the acceptance as law, so long as at times they prescribe to follow an inductive analysis[28] and at times to perform a deductive type of inquiry.[29]

The considerations above suggest that trying to explain, and interpret, the 'inherently flexible'[30] process of custom creation by devising a rigid methodology is eventually not very helpful.

2 Defining resolutions

To ask whether resolutions contribute to the creation of international customary law amounts to ask how a decision of an international organization can affect the behaviour of States.[31] In the International Law Commission study, resolutions are defined as 'all decisions and other acts adopted by international organizations or at intergovernmental conferences, whatever their designation and whether or not they are legally binding'.[32] Since evidence of this gradual process does not emerge from the text of individual resolutions, it is not possible to find evidence of either State practice or *opinio juris* by looking at the text of the resolutions alone, as recognized by the Special Rapporteur himself in his third report.[33] However, the International Law Commission study simply states that the resolutions drafted in normative language 'are those that might be of relevance, and the choice (or avoidance) of

27 Report of the International Law Commission on the work of its sixty-eighth session, 2 May–10 June and 4 July–12 August 2016, UN Doc A/71/10, 84 para 5.

28 Report of the International Law Commission on the work of its sixty-eighth session, 2 May–10 June and 4 July–12 August 2016, UN Doc A/71/10, 84 para 5.

29 The Commentary to Conclusion 10 states: 'Draft conclusion 10 concerns the evidence from which acceptance of a given practice as law (*opinio juris*) may be *deduced*'. Report of the International Law Commission on the work of its sixty-eighth session, 2 May–10 June and 4 July–12 August 2016, UN Doc A/71/10, 99 para 1 (emphasis added).

30 Second report on identification of customary international law (22 May 2014), UN Doc A/CN.4/672 (22 May 2014) para 12.

31 This is also referred to as the need to explore the interrelationship between non-binding norms and the formation of rules of international customary law. Topical summary of debate in the Sixth Committee, UN Doc A/CN.4/666, 11, para 44.

32 Commentary to Draft Conclusion 12, Report of the International Law Commission on the work of its sixty-eighth session, 2 May–10 June and 4 July–12 August 2016, UN Doc A/71/10, 107, para 2.

33 Third report on identification of customary international law (27 March 2015), UN Doc A/CN.4/682, para 29.

particular terms may be significant'.[34] No reference is made to the purpose resolutions, as one of the many forms of decisions of international organizations, serve.

The concept of resolution dates back to the international conference model of the early nineteenth century.[35] As the conference model represented a whole new form of diplomacy in which the interests of all States concerned were represented, the object of the deliberations was intended to be a vision for the future based on the existent balance of power. Resolutions were thus adopted to solve practical problems and, although they often involved questions of law, they were not intended to establish general principles governing international politics.[36]

The system of conferences was designed to regulate inter-State relations mostly for the purpose of achieving international peace and security. A peculiarity of the conference system, in this respect, is that the results of any conference required subsequent ratification and enforcement by participants.[37] However, social, economic, and technological advancements in the nineteenth century multiplied the possibility of interaction among people in their private capacity.[38] More transnational integration thus facilitated the emergence of common interests of various nature, including commerce. The institutionalization of transnational relationship between members of civil society brought to the emergence of international unions, private and public alike, which adopted the method of the conference to serve their function.[39]

Subsequently, the League of Nations, the first ever international conference endowed with a permanent character, adopted the conference method for the functioning of its political organs – the Council and the Assembly – while retaining the power to create specialized institutions to deal with technical issues such as those arising in the fast developing area of telecommunications.[40] The technical agencies of the League of Nations were inspired by the public international union model. Apart from the resolutions on administrative and budgetary issues, none of the League of Nations' decisions, including resolutions, were binding. However,

34 Third report on identification of customary international law (27 March 2015), UN Doc A/CN.4/682, para 48.
35 Norman L Hill, *The Public International Conference* (Stanford University Press 1929) 82. *See* also Sir EM Satow, *International Congresses* (HM Stationery Office 1920) 20–23.
36 DW Bowett, *The Law of International Institutions* (2nd edn, Stevens & Sons 1970) 2–3.
37 NL Hill, *The Public International Conference* (Stanford University Press 1929) 131.
38 DW Bowett, *The Law of International Institutions* (2nd ed, Stevens & Sons 1970) 4.
39 NL Hill, *The Public International Conference* (Stanford University Press 1929) 202.
40 MO Hudson, *Progress in International Organization* (Stanford University Press 1932) 41–45.

the Assembly resolutions requiring action from the League of Nations were almost invariably addressed to the Council, the reason being that the Council was a standing body as such able to supervise the execution of the Assembly's wishes.[41] This shows that, bearing in mind the inherent inequality of power among the members of the Council, resolutions were meant to be an expression of the politics of the international organization rather than a manifestation of the will of the States represented in the Assembly.

Conversely, the resolutions of the United Nations are directly addressed to their recipients, be they States, individuals, United Nations, or other institutions. With regard to the resolutions adopted by the General Assembly, they are only recommendatory, with the exception of those regulating administrative and budgetary matters.[42] Despite their non-binding nature, the Assembly's resolutions serve the function of developing the values of the United Nations over time and, as such, should be regarded as acts of the United Nations rather than acts of States.[43] The International Law Commission Conclusions, in this respect, go in the opposite direction, since they define resolutions as acts of States.[44] Such a qualification holds true in relation to the resolutions adopted at international conferences, whether organized under the aegis of the United Nations or not, the reason being that they are unmediated manifestations of State will rather than the practice of an international organisation. Conversely, it does not appear to reflect, and capture, the nature of resolutions of international organizations.

The considerations above suggest that the International Law Commission position seems too restrictive to accurately consider the role resolutions play in contemporary international relations. Instead, the inquiry into the contribution of resolutions to the

41 On the character of the Assembly's decisions, *see* ME Burton, *The Assembly of the League of Nations* (University of Chicago Press 1941) 184–88. On the relations character of the Council as a standing organ as opposed to the limited availability of the Assembly during any regular session of the League of Nations, *see* 'Report Presented by the British Representative, Mr AJ Balfour, and Adopted by the Council of the League of Nations, Meeting at San Sebastian, on 2nd of August, 1920', League of Nations Doc 20/48/16, 3, available at https://archive.org/details/relationsbetweenooleag (accessed 20 November 2018); 'The Execution of the Assembly Resolutions', April 1921, available at https://archive.org/details/executionofassemooleag (accessed 20 November 2018).

42 Charter of the United Nations (adopted 26 June 1945, entered into force 24 October 1945) 1 UNTS XVI (UN Charter), Article 25.

43 N White, *The United Nations System: Toward International Justice* (Lynne Rienner 2002) 12 and 18.

44 Report of the International Law Commission on the work of its sixty-eighth session, 2 May–10 June and 4 July–12 August 2016, UN Doc A/71/10, 107 para 3.

process of custom creation should be broadened as to include how States use international organizations, in addition to the use of relevant resolutions by States and other international actors. It follows that any inquiry into the evidentiary value of General Assembly resolutions as either general practice or *opinio juris* should be complemented by an empirical study of the systemic character groups of resolutions have acquired over time. The following section presents an original database of General Assembly practice with a view to assessing the relevant findings in the light of the methodology devised by the International Law Commission to detect the presence of custom.

3 Case study: United Nations General Assembly resolutions

The United Nations General Assembly is often described as the parliament of the world and the study of the legal effects of its resolutions has fascinated generations of scholars. However, no specific account of how, if at all, resolutions contribute to the creation of customary rules has ever been provided. One of the reasons for such a gap in the literature may be attributed to the difficulties related to quantifying how many resolutions have been adopted by the United Nations General Assembly over time and the subject matters addressed by them. The process of counting is made particularly challenging by both the sheer number of resolutions so far adopted and the changes occurred from time to time in the General Assembly's working methods. The latter affect the counting of resolutions in two ways.

Firstly, groups of closely related resolutions are often assigned the same document number followed by a Latin letter – for example, A/RES/70/249A-C. Such resolutions are at times listed as a group[45] or as individual resolutions,[46] or both.[47] Secondly, the method of adoption of individual resolutions – namely, without voting, by majority, by consensus, by unanimity or by acclamation – is at times provided for the individual resolutions, at times for the group of resolutions[48] while sometimes it is omitted.[49] For the purposes of this study, individual resolutions accompanied

45 For example, UNGA res 63/108A-B, UN Doc A/RES/63/108A-B (5 December 2008).

46 For example, UNGA res 70/238A, UN Doc A/RES/70/238A (23 December 2015); UNGA res 70/238B, UN Doc A/RES/70/238B (1 April 2016); and UNGA res 70/238C, UN Doc A/RES/70/238C (17 June 2016).

47 For example, UNGA res 36/234A-B, UN Doc A/RES/36/234A-B (18 December 1981); UNGA res 36/234A, UN Doc A/RES/36/234A (18 December 1981) and UNGA res 36/234B, UN Doc A/RES/36/234B (18 December 1981).

48 For example, UNGA res 63/108, UN Doc A/RES/63/108A-B (5 December 2008), adopted without voting.

49 For example, UNGA res 36/321A-B, UN Doc A/RES/36/231A-B (18 December 1981).

with an indication of their method of adoption count as one resolution.[50] Likewise, groups of resolutions adopted without a vote[51] and groups of unqualified resolutions[52] count as one resolution.

From 1946 to 2016, the General Assembly has adopted 16,935 resolutions, of which 6,362 with a vote and 10,564 without voting.[53] Of all the resolutions, the overwhelming majority have been adopted by the six main committees rather than in plenary session, subject only to approval in plenary session.[54] The findings also show that the majority of resolutions adopted in plenary session and by the Second, Third, Fifth, and Sixth Committees have been adopted without voting whereas the majority of resolutions adopted by the First and Fourth Committees have been put to vote.

A closer look at the composition by subject matter of the resolutions adopted within individual committees shows that, with a handful of exceptions,[55] resolutions form groups of re-stated resolutions and such groups of re-stated resolutions tend to refer to each other, thus forming broader thematic areas. Table 11.1 illustrates a fraction of the pattern of clustering which has developed over time in the practice of the Fourth Committee.

Albeit partial, the empirical reconstruction of the General Assembly's behavioural patterns demonstrates that resolutions have gradually acquired a systemic character – that is to say, they do not exist in isolation from each other. This in turn suggests that, when it comes to identifying international customary law, there is little or no value in trying to establish how a specific resolution has contributed, or is contributing, to the development of a customary rule. In this respect, looking at the

50 For example, UNGA res 70/248, UN Doc A/RES/70/248A (23 December 2015); UNGA res 70/248B, UN Doc A/RES/70/248B (1 April 2016) and UNGA res 70/248C, UN Doc A/RES/70/248C (17 June 2016).

51 For example, UNGA res 63/108A-B, UN Doc A/RES/63/108A-B (5 December 2008).

52 For example, UNGA res 36/231, UN Doc A/RES/36/231A-B (18 December 1981) (no indication of method of adoption is provided).

53 Among the resolutions adopted with a vote, 360 have been adopted unanimously; however, for nine resolutions, the voting pattern is unknown. The figures refer to the author's calculation based on the data freely available on the United Nations website: www.un.org/en/sections/documents/general-assembly-resolutions/index.html, 9 July 2017. For the purposes of this chapter, only the resolutions adopted during regular sessions are considered. In counting the resolutions, consideration has been given the fact that the working methods of the General Assembly have changed over time.

54 In addition, the Special and Political Committee (1952–1992) and other committees have adopted 762 resolutions.

55 Examples include the resolutions appointing the new Secretary-General or merely celebratory resolutions such as those instituting international days or years.

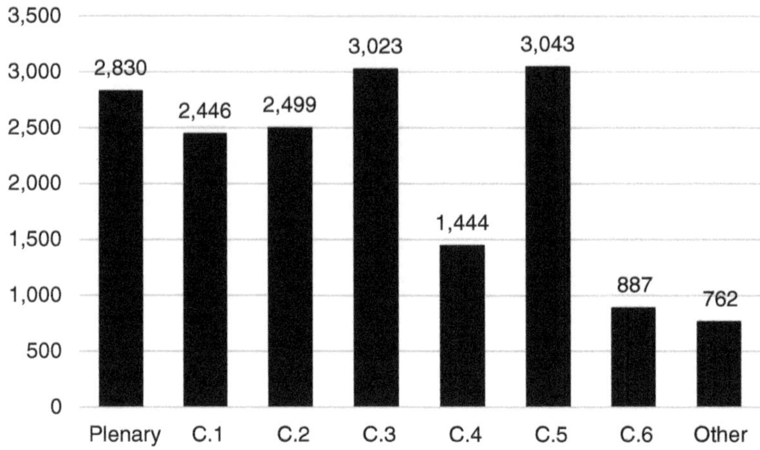

Figure 11.1 Resolutions adopted in plenary sessions and individual committees (1946–2016).
Bar chart providing the breakdown by plenary session and the six main committees of the number of resolutions adopted by each individual body. The category 'other' refers to resolutions adopted by several ad hoc committees.

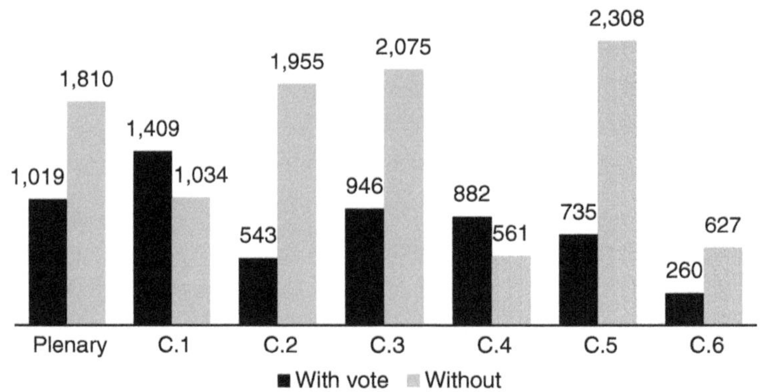

Figure 11.2 Resolutions adopted with or without a vote (1946–2016).
Bar chart providing the breakdown by plenary session and the six main committees of the number of resolutions adopted with or without voting by each individual body.

normative content of individual resolutions does not reveal whether a resolution is per se contributing to the development of a customary rule.

For example, in the field of human rights the Universal Declaration of Human Rights[56] cannot be regarded as evidence of international custom in its own right. On

56 UNGA res 217C, UN Doc 217(III)C (10 December 1948).

Table 11.1 Example of resolutions adopted by the Fourth Committee (1946–2016)

Subject matter of resolutions	No. of resolutions adopted
Implementation of the Declaration on the Granting of Independence to Colonial Countries and Peoples	13
Economic and other activities affecting Non-Self-Governing Territories	20
Activities of foreign economic and other interests which are impeding the implementation of the Declaration on the Granting of Independence to Colonial Countries and Peoples	30
Implementation of the Declaration on the Granting of Independence to Colonial Countries and Peoples by the Specialized Agencies and the International Institutions associated with the United Nations	49

Fraction of the practice of the Fourth Committee illustrating that most of the resolutions adopted is grouped in thematic clusters. The left column indicates the subject matter of resolutions. The right column provides the number of resolutions adopted by the Fourth Committee within thematic cluster.

the one hand, the practice of the General Assembly shows that the recognition of both certain rights of women and the freedom of association precedes the adoption of the Universal Declaration of Human Rights.[57] The continuing relevance of both issues has then been reiterated in groups of thematic resolutions up to today. On the other hand, once adopted, the Universal Declaration of Human Rights has appeared as a stand-alone issue only in General Assembly resolutions celebrating the various anniversaries of the Declaration[58] while the individual rights proclaimed in it have been discussed and refined over time as separate thematic issues.[59] Similar considerations apply to the Declaration on Friendly Relations in the field of international peace and security. Adopted in 1970, the Declaration has been preceded by six resolutions on the same subject-matter.[60] Individual provisions of the Declaration have then been discussed by the General Assembly under the narrower items of non-use of force in international relations and peaceful settlement of international disputes.[61]

57 *See* resolution UNGA res 56, UN Doc 56(I) (11 December 1946) (rights of women) and UNGA res 128, UN Doc 128(II) (17 November 1947) (freedom of association).

58 *See*, for instance, UNGA res 36/169, UN Doc A/RES/36/169 (16 December 1981).

59 *See*, for instance, UNGA res 1780, UN Doc 1780(XVII) (7 December 1962) and following ones (racial discrimination) and UNGA res 1386, UN Doc 1386(XIV) (20 November 1959) (the rights of the child) and following ones.

60 UNGA res 1815, UN Doc 1815(XVII) (18 December 1962) and following ones.

61 UNGA res 2936, UN Doc 2936(XXVII) (29 November 1972) and following ones; UNGA res 3283, UN Doc 3283(XXIX) (12 December 1974) and following ones.

A more recent example of resolutions acquiring a systemic character is Resolution 71/104 (2017), which is the last of a group of 50 re-stated resolutions adopted yearly by the General Assembly since 1967.[62] Aimed at facilitating the implementation of the Declaration on the Granting of Independence to Colonial Countries and Peoples (the Decolonization Declaration), it imposes a duty on both the Specialized Agencies and the international institutions associated with the United Nations to implement relevant resolutions. A passage from the resolution reads:

> [The General Assembly] Reaffirm[s] the mandates of the specialized agencies and other organizations of the United Nations system to take all appropriate measures, within their respective responsibilities, to ensure the full implementation of General Assembly resolution 1514(XV) and relevant ones.[63]

The 'relevant resolutions' referred to in the passage above are those on the issue of decolonization[64] and are not limited to those adopted by the General Assembly.[65] However, taken in isolation from the wider practice of the General Assembly, the text of the resolution does not reveal the imperceptible stages of evolution undergone by the duty imposed on the Specialized Agencies and international institutions associated with the United Nations and their implications for the development of the wider United Nations system. Such incremental changes have occurred through the practice of reiteration of resolutions and provide the evidence of the systemic character of the group of resolutions under scrutiny.

Resolution 71/104 qualifies the duty placed upon the Specialized Agencies and other international institutions associated with the United Nations as a duty of assistance to the remaining Non-Self-Governing Territories, which is aimed at 'accelerat[ing] progress in the economic and social sector of those Territories'.[66] Initially, the Territories beneficiary of the duty of assistance were those territories in Africa where national liberation movements were fighting the colonial rule in general and the apartheid regime in particular.[67] It thus follows that the legal roots of the duty of assistance lie in the inalienable right to self-determination

62 UNGA res 71/104, UN Doc A/RES/71/104 (6 December 2016).

63 UNGA res 71/104, UN Doc A/RES/71/104 (6 December 2016) Preamble para 13. The origins of the duty trace back to UNGA res 3300, UN Doc 3300(XXIX) (13 December 1974) Preamble para 6.

64 UNGA res 71/104, UN Doc A/RES/71/104 (6 December 2016) para 5.

65 UNGA res 71/104, UN Doc A/RES/71/104 (6 December 2016) para 4.

66 UNGA res 71/104, UN Doc A/RES/71/104 (6 December 2016) para 9.

67 *See*, for instance, UNGA res 2311, UN Doc 2311(XXII) (14 December 1967) Preamble para 6; UNGA res 2704, UN Doc 2704(XXV) (14 December 1970) Preamble para 6; UNGA res 41/15, UN Doc A/RES/41/15 (31 October 1986) Preamble para 7.

and independence of colonial countries and peoples. Paragraph 4 of Resolution 71/104 reads:

> [The General Assembly] reaffirms that the recognition by the General Assembly, the Security Council and other United Nations organs of the legitimacy of the aspirations of the peoples of the Non-Self-Governing Territories to exercise their right to self-determination entails, as a corollary, the extension of all appropriate assistance to those peoples.

However, reference to the right to self-determination of Non-Self-Governing Territories in Resolution 71/104 bears a completely different meaning to the reference to the same right in the first resolutions on the implementation of the Decolonization Declaration by the Specialized Agencies and other international institutions associated with the United Nations. Whereas the latter group of re-stated resolutions refers to the recognition of the inalienable right to self-determination and independence from the colonial rule of Namibia and Zimbabwe,[68] Resolution 71/104 refers to the right to self-determination of the remaining Non-Self-Governing Territories, which all happen to be small islands.[69] The different nature of the remaining Non-Self-Governing Territories entails that preserving their right to self-determination of the peoples living in those areas requires a sustained intervention to mitigate their chronic vulnerability to natural disasters.[70] In other words, the duty of assistance to the Non-Self-Governing Territories is now instrumental to achieving goals of sustainable development rather than supporting the fight of national liberation movements against the colonial powers. A passage from Resolution 71/104 reads:

> because the development options of the small island Non-Self-Governing Territories are limited, there are special challenges to planning for and implementing *sustainable development* and that those Territories will be constrained in meeting those challenges without the continuing cooperation and assistance of the specialized agencies and other organizations of the United Nations system.[71]

Nothing of the historical account of the legal basis of the duty of assistance emerges from the text of Resolution 71/104 as such. Yet the historical background of this group of re-stated resolutions is essential to qualify the scope of the obligation

68 UNGA res 37/32, UN Doc A/RES/37/32 (23 November 1982) para 14 and previous ones.
69 UNGA res 71/104, UN Doc A/RES/71/104 (6 December 2016) Preamble para 7.
70 UNGA res 71/104, UN Doc A/RES/71/104 (6 December 2016) para 17 ('Bearing in mind the extremely fragile economies of the small island Non-Self-Governing Territories and their vulnerability to natural disasters, such as hurricanes, cyclones and sea-level rise').
71 UNGA res 71/104, UN Doc A/RES/71/104 (6 December 2016) Preamble para 11 (emphasis added). *See* also UNGA res 48/47, UN Doc A/RES/48/47 (10 December 1993) para 9 and UNGA res 49/41, UN Doc A/RES/49/41 (9 December 1994) para 10.

placed on the Specialized Agencies and the other institutions associated with the United Nations to implement the Decolonization Declaration as well as the related duty of collaboration individual State members of the concerned Specialized Agencies and associated institutions.

On the one hand, by reiterating the inviolability of the right to self-determination of the inhabitants of Non-Self-Governing Territories, Resolution 71/104 can be regarded as directly contributing to the development of United Nations law when read in the light of its historical background. Indeed, Resolution 71/104 does not exist in isolation from the wider practice of the General Assembly: its text as such does not reveal the normative significance of the resolution in terms of its relationship with both other groups of resolutions and the goals of the United Nations system.

With regard to the first point – the relationship of Resolution 71/104 with other groups of resolutions – it must be noted that the group of re-stated resolutions to which Resolution 71/104 belongs is part of the wider programme of decolonization progressively developed by the General Assembly's Fourth Committee. Specifically, it supplements the group of re-stated resolutions monitoring the implementation of the Decolonization Declaration by member states[72] and the group of re-stated resolutions addressing the exploitation of natural resources of Non-Self-Governing Territories by foreign economic actors[73] as well as the effects of foreign investments in those territories.[74] In addition, a conspicuous number of resolutions on the implementation of the Decolonization Declaration has been adopted by the General Assembly in plenary session rather than the Fourth Committee.[75] Like the group of re-stated resolutions adopted by the Fourth Committee, they contribute to the systemic character of resolutions.

With regard to the second point – that is to say, the relationship of Resolution 71/104 with the goals of the United Nations system – Resolution 71/104 aims at facilitating the implementation of the Decolonization Declaration in the remaining small island Non-Self-Governing Territories. To achieve its goal, it posits that taking appropriate measures to fully implement the Decolonization Declaration is part of the mandate of all the Specialized Agencies and the other institutions associated with the United Nations. For example, paragraph 3 of Resolution 71/104 states that, in carrying out their duty of assistance, the Specialized Agencies and the other institutions of the United Nations system must be guided by the relevant resolutions of

72 UNGA res 71/122, UN Doc A/RES/71/122 (28 December 2016) and previous ones.
73 UNGA res 51/140, UN Doc A/RES/51/140 (19 February 1997) and previous ones.
74 UNGA res 71/103, UN Doc A/RES/71/103 (23 December 2016) and previous ones.
75 UNGA res 58/111, UN Doc A/RES/58/111 (9 December 2003) and previous ones.

the UN. As a corollary, the resolution requests the administering powers to facilitate the participation of representatives of Non-Self-Governing Territories in the work of the relevant Specialized Agencies from which those Territories benefit.[76] This is another adaptation of the original request to allow the participation of the leaders of national liberation movements in the colonial Territories of Africa in the work of the Specialized Agencies to the post-colonial scenario.[77] Nowadays, the participation of representatives of Non-Self-Governing Territories in the work of the United Nations mainly constitutes a general requirement of democratic governance.

On the other hand, Resolution 71/104 recommends the United Nations member States to intensify their efforts through the Specialized Agencies and the other organizations of the United Nations system of which they are members to accord priority to the question of providing assistance to Non-Self-Governing Territories, thus contributing to a collective effort to achieve the goals of the United Nations.[78] It is in the light of the role of member States of Specialized Agencies and associated institutions that certain statements contained in Resolution 71/104 – either praising the work of certain Specialized Agencies and associated institutions[79] or lamenting the lack of cooperation by others[80] – must be read.

Overall, by reiterating the need to build on previous United Nations resolutions, Resolution 71/104 and previous ones contribute to the development of the law of the United Nations, both directly and indirectly. Directly, by creating an original duty of assistance not contemplated in the text of either the United Nations Charter or the constitutive treaties of the Specialized Agencies and institutions associated with the United Nations. Indirectly, by reiterating that there exists a 'United Nations system' thus strengthening the identity of a family of institutions working together to achieve the goals of the United Nations Charter.[81] In turn, Resolution 71/104 and previous ones have developed a customary rule formally placed on their addressees: namely, the Specialized Agencies and the institutions associated with the United Nations as well as their member States.

The considerations above show that to fully appreciate the normative significance of Resolution 71/104, and therefore its actual or potential contribution to the

76 UNGA res 71/104, UN Doc A/RES/71/104 (6 December 2016) para 18.

77 UNGA res 2704, UN Doc 2704(XXV) (14 December 1970) para 10.

78 UNGA res 71/104, UN Doc A/RES/71/104 (6 December 2016) para 19.

79 UNGA res 71/104, UN Doc A/RES/71/104 (6 December 2016) para 5 (mentioning the United Nations Development Programme).

80 UNGA res 71/104, UN Doc A/RES/71/104 (6 December 2016) para 10.

81 *See* N White, 'The United Nations System: Conference, Contract or Constitutional Order?' 4 Singapore Journal of International and Comparative Law (2000) 291.

formation of customary rules, the text of the resolution must be read in conjunction with the preceding re-stated resolutions and in the light of the goals of the United Nations. This, in turn, suggests that General Assembly resolutions are better understood as a complex construct comprising both legal and political elements.

On the one hand, the legal element lies in the fact that resolutions can be seen as the formalization of interactions between States and international institutions into a written text. On the other hand, the political element lies in the effects the adoption of resolutions produce on States. If the analysis of resolutions is conducted exclusively from the perspective of law, as suggested in the International Law Commission Conclusions, the political element of resolutions ends up being neglected. This leads to the further conclusion that the methodology for identifying customary rules contained in the Conclusions almost deprives the process of custom creation of its spontaneity and informality.[82] Nor does it explain the role of international organizations in the creation of customary law. A better approach is to consider resolutions as political acts of international organizations capable of producing a range of legal effects, including contributing to the creation or development of customary rules, the assessment of which must be conducted on a case-by-case basis.

4 Concluding remarks

The text of the Conclusions raises a number of questions. The main one refers to the assumption that international organizations are agents of States which generates a lack of clarity about the role of international organizations in the process of formation of customary rules as well as the relevance of resolutions as evidentiary sources of custom. The approach endorsed by the International Law Commission, according to which resolutions adopted by intergovernmental organs reflect the views expressed and the votes cast by States, plainly fails to recognize that the resolutions of international organizations in general, and those of the General Assembly in particular, have now acquired a systemic character. Consequently, focusing on individual resolutions as evidence of custom in a decontextualized way does not, and cannot, account for the role resolutions play in the process of custom creation. The statement that resolutions framed in normative language have a special evidentiary value for the purposes of identification of international customary law is therefore not entirely convincing.[83]

82 cf *Summary record of 3301st meeting* (A/CN.4/SR.3301), 15, statement by Murase ('[CIL] could be created spontaneously and there [is] no way of knowing systematically when and how a rule of [CIL is] created').

83 Third report on identification of customary international law (27 March 2015), UN Doc A/CN.4/682, para 48.

Another problematic aspect is that Conclusions 4 and 12 are rooted on the assumption that, for the purposes of custom creation, resolutions count as acts of states rather than acts of the international organizations. A passage from the Special Rapporteur's third report reads:

> [I]f one were not to equate the practice of such international organizations with that of States, this would mean not only that the organization's practice would not be taken into account, but also that its Member States would themselves be deprived of or reduced in their ability to contribute to state practice.[84]

From this limited perspective, the International Law Commission Conclusions mirror the position of a much criticized strand of scholarship which, moving from the assumption that the General Assembly is a permanent diplomatic conference, qualify resolutions as acts of States participating in the work of the institution while denying that they constitute formal sources of international law. At the same time, the Conclusions recognize that the practice of international organizations as such may contribute to the development of international custom. However, in the plenary debate the Special Rapporteur, faced with criticism by other members of the International Law Commission, clarified that although the adoption of resolutions can be equated to the practice of states, the practice of the international organization is a different issue.[85] By making this remark, the Special Rapporteur has ended up endorsing another, and radically opposed, understanding of the nature of General Assembly resolutions as acts of the international organization rather than of states.

The overall impression one has of Conclusions 4 and 12 is that they do not either reflect a common position of States or provide any authoritative guidance for practitioners. Quite the contrary, they confirm that it is impossible to try to make objective an inherently flexible process such as the one of custom creation. By refusing to engage with the theoretical underpinnings of the nature of international organizations, the International Law Commission has deliberately left open the option for practitioners to pick and choose the conception of resolution as well as the one of custom that best fits their particular needs. In this respect, the International Law Commission study has failed to achieve its goal of providing authoritative guidance.

In conclusion, while it seems unquestionable that resolutions can be *evidence* of custom, especially in the form of acceptance as law (*opinio juris*), the combined interpretation of Conclusions 4(2) and 12(2) is problematic in relation to the

84 Third report on identification of customary international law (27 March 2015), UN Doc A/CN.4/682, para 77.

85 *See*, for instance, Fourth report on identification of customary international law (8 March 2016), UN Doc A/CN.4/695, 20 para 7; and A/CN.4/SR.3250 (8 March 2016) 10–11.

constitutive function of resolution: if resolutions are regarded as a simple form of collective State practice, then they turn out to be a manifestation of State will and the spontaneous character of custom creation is lost. Furthermore, when it comes to General Assembly resolutions, the type of message the Conclusions send out to practitioners is somehow misleading, since they ignore the systemic character the resolutions have acquired over time.

Excessive reliance on the normative propositions contained in the text of resolutions is also misleading. When States frame resolutions in normative language, they do so for the purpose of creating standards of behaviour and not binding rules. It follows that, depending on the support they receive once adopted, the concerned resolutions can lead to the adoption of a treaty or the creation of a customary rule, but only when they are spontaneously followed by States and, perhaps, other international actors. In a sense, the rule of international customary law generated by a resolution lies outside the text of the resolution: it is triggered by the resolution, but it is not the resolution.

If the purpose of the International Law Commission is to provide a methodology on how to identify a customary rule, then the Commission has set out an impossible task for itself, at least in relation to the role of international organizations in the process of custom creation. Possible recommendations on how to ameliorate the Conclusions are, firstly, to restrict the scope of the Conclusions to the practice of States, thus excluding the practice of international organizations; and secondly, to focus on the identification of fully formed rules of international customary law only, even if this does not make the Conclusions particularly original when compared to the 1950 International Law Commission study on evidence of international customary law.

Chapter 12

The United Nations Secretariat and custom

*Jean-Baptiste Merlin**

As other chapters in this volume confirm, the role of international organisations in the formation and expression of rules of customary international law, as well as the extent of such a role, remains controversial in legal doctrine and practice. This chapter explores several aspects of the practice of the Secretariat of the United Nations as a specific example in an attempt to identify significant points that may inform the general debate on the issue. In so doing, it follows a practical approach based on the recent work of the International Law Commission that touches upon this matter.

The draft conclusions with accompanying commentaries adopted by the International Law Commission on second reading in 2018[1] acknowledge the contribution of international organisations to the formation and expression of rules of customary international law.[2] Conclusion 4(2), read together with the commentary thereto, constitutes the central provision on the matter, conclusions 6 and 12 covering specific aspects. After acknowledging the primacy of State practice as creative or expressive of rules of customary international law in the first paragraph, conclusion 4 affirms in its second paragraph that '[i]n certain cases, the practice of international organizations also contributes to the formation, or expression, of rules of customary international law'. The third paragraph excludes the conduct of

* The author is indebted to Sir Michael Wood for his remarks and suggestions. The views expressed remain the author's alone.

1 Report of the International Law Commission on the work of its seventieth session (2018), General Assembly, official records, 73rd session, supplement No. 10, A/73/10, 119–56, paras 65–6; *see* also the statement of the Chair of the Drafting Committee of 25 May 2018 introducing the third report of the Drafting Committee for the session (most documents of the Commission on the topic are available online in the analytical guide to the ILC's work on the Commission's website: http://legal.un.org/ilc/guide/1_13.shtml). For a clarification on what the Commission did and did not do in its work on the topic, *see* Chapter 8 in this volume.

2 In this chapter, reference to 'contribution' without further qualification means contribution to the formation and/or identification of rules of customary international law, depending on the context.

other actors from what may count as practice, although it acknowledges the possible relevance of such actors when assessing the practice of States and international organisations. The discussions within the Commission and the drafting history of conclusion 4(2) with its accompanying commentary highlight the controversy that surrounds the role of international organisations in relation to customary international law.[3] Indeed, the very idea that international organisations may have a self-standing role to play in the customary process in general, an idea that was defended by the Special Rapporteur[4] and reflected the view of a majority of the Commission members and beyond,[5] remained questioned by some of its members[6] as well as several representatives of States in the Sixth Committee.[7] According to the position

3 Discussions in plenary at the 68th session (2016) leading up to the first reading (3301st to 3303rd, 3309th and 3338th to 3340th meetings), and discussions in plenary at the 70th session (2018) leading up to the second reading (3396th to 3402nd, 3412th, 3441st to 3444th meetings). Discussions also took place within the Working Group and Drafting Committee although their proceedings are not published; for a limited account of these, *see* the statements of the Chair of the Drafting Committee of 2 June 2016 and 25 May 2018.

4 A/CN.4/SR.3303 (24 May 2016), 8 (M Wood), also minimising the practical implications of the controversy among Commission members: 'the practical differences between members were not so great'.

5 P Daillier, M Forteau, and A. Pellet, *Droit international public* (8th edn, LGDJ 2009) 355, para 209. A list of recent writings on the issue may be found in the updated bibliography submitted by the Special Rapporteur as Annex II of his Fifth Report on identification of customary international law, A/CN.4/717/Add.1 (6 June 2018), section B2.

6 A/CN.4/SR.3301 (19 May 2016), 16–17 (SD Murphy); A/CN.4/SR.3302 (20 May 2016), 5 (M. D Hmoud). *See* also the Special Rapporteur's Fourth Report on identification of customary international law, A/CN.4/695 (8 March 2016) paras 19–20; and Fifth Report on identification of customary international law, A/CN.4/717 (14 March 2018) paras 41–48. During the plenary debate on second reading in 2018, the idea that generally speaking the practice of international organisations could not as such result in the formation of rules of customary international law was still suggested, sometimes in a qualified manner, by several members: *see* statements of e.g. SD Murphy (A/CN.4/SR.3397, 8 May 2018, 7–8), MD Hmoud (A/CN.4/SR.3398, 9 May 2018, 13), and H Huang (A/CN.4/SR.3400, 11 May 2018, 5). The delicate balance reached by the Commission's output on the issue most likely contributed to resolving the controversy.

7 A/C.6/71/SR.20 (24 October 2016) para 57 (United States of America); A/C.6/71/SR.21 (25 October 2016) para 49 (Russian Federation) and para 86 (United Kingdom); A/C.6/71/SR.22 (26 October 2016) para 22 (Mexico); Doubts or reservations were expressed again at the 73rd session of the Sixth Committee after the second reading: New Zealand, Russian Federation, Turkey (22nd meeting, 24 October 2018), Israel (23rd meeting, 24 October 2018), Iran (24th meeting, 25 October 2018), United States of America (29th meeting, 31 October 2018). On the whole, nevertheless, States were appreciative of the efforts made by the Commission to reach a balanced solution on this issue on second reading.

that sometimes underlies such minority views, although it is not disputed that international organisations enjoy international legal personality, their acts and the decisions they take would eventually rest on the will of their member States and thus in most cases would be deprived of real autonomy. The scope and instances of the international organisation's role as expressive or creative of rules of customary international law would therefore be reduced to exceptional circumstances, and such role could presumably not be considered in general as reflecting existing law.

As this chapter endeavours to show, this view does not fully take into account the current state of international law. In so doing, the reflection follows a practical approach, focusing on just one of the principal organs of the United Nations, namely the Secretariat, with a view to offering leads for reflection as part of the general debate on the topic. The contribution of the Secretariat is examined both from the perspectives of formation and identification (sometimes also referred to as evidence or expression) of rules of customary international law. Although the International Law Commission sought to distinguish clearly between these two dimensions by renaming the topic in 2013 and by limiting the scope of the draft conclusions to issues of identification,[8] it also admitted that both dimensions may be closely intertwined in practice,[9] which is clearly shown in the case of the Secretariat.

The United Nations holds a special place within the international legal order. Indeed it counts as one of the few existing fora of a universal character[10] where States usually articulate, speak out, and coordinate their views (including legal positions) on a very wide range of international matters. This unique position among international organisations unavoidably fosters the role of the Organisation within the machinery of international lawmaking. Therefore, and as this chapter suggests, the role of the United Nations in the formation and identification of customary international law could arguably be described as a

8 Summary record of the 3181st meeting (17 July 2013), *Yearbook of the International Law Commission, 2013*, vol I, 84, para 20 (M Forteau); *Yearbook of the International Law Commission*, 2013, vol II, part 2, 64–5, paras 65, 69, 76–77; A/73/10 (n 1), 124, para 66, para 5 of commentary to conclusion 1.

9 *Yearbook of the International Law Commission, 2013*, vol II, part 2 (n 8), 65, para 77. *See* also the discussion on the dual interpretation of the term 'determination' in M Shahabuddeen, *Precedent in the World Court* (Cambridge University Press 1996) 77–78. Although Shahabuddeen's point is limited to judicial decisions of the International Court of Justice the general distinction made undoubtedly has a wider scope and may also apply to the context of the Secretariat's conduct.

10 Other such universal or nearly universal fora include for instance the Universal Postal Union.

specificity within a specificity. This assertion warrants a few qualifications. First, far from covering all organs, agencies and programs that constitute the United Nations, in this chapter, focus is placed on one of the principal organs of the United Nations, namely the Secretariat. This should be kept in mind, since the contribution of the United Nations to the formation and identification of rules of customary international law is far from uniform, being rather unequally distributed throughout the Organisation. Second, the universal character of the United Nations places it in the best comparative position, relatively to other international organisations, to contribute, at various levels, in various ways and often involving the combined conduct of several organs, to the formation and expression of rules of general customary international law. This is all the more so that the United Nations has been closely associated with the development of international law since its creation in the aftermath of the Second World War. The Secretariat indeed interacts, among others, with the Security Council and the General Assembly as well as the International Law Commission, which typically is vested with the double mandate of promoting the development of international law and its codification.[11]

1 Direct contribution versus indirect contribution

To better grasp the complexity of the role of the Secretariat in the formation and identification of rules of customary international law, it may be useful to say a word about some elements that seem to emerge from the general discussion on international organisations and customary international law. Generally speaking, the contribution of the United Nations to the formation of rules of customary international law may be divided into what may be termed direct and indirect contribution. This distinction may be helpful methodologically in assessing the value of a given conduct with regard to custom.[12]

Direct contribution may be defined, for present purposes, as covering conduct by United Nations organs that contributes as such to the two elements of the customary process. Such conduct may be equated with the conduct of States for the purpose of creating a rule of customary international law. In this context, the conduct of organs of international organisations is practice and/or *opinio juris* that in turn gives rise to a rule of customary international law. However, the criteria for

11 International Law Commission Statute (Resolution 174 (II) of the General Assembly of 21 November 1947) Article 1(1).

12 *See* e.g. A/CN.4/717 (14 March 2018) (n 6), paras 48–9.

the identification of such relevant conduct of international organisations in general, and of the United Nations in particular, has been much debated.[13] The precise criteria have not been definitely fixed, a task that is complicated by the great diversity of international organisations. Several converging points, however, may be identified, including from the compromise attempted by the draft conclusions on identification of customary international law (and especially the commentaries thereto) as adopted on second reading.

First, the international organisation should either be vested with delegated powers by States (e.g. exclusive competences of the European Union, competences of the United Nations Security Council) or be entrusted with powers functionally equivalent to those of States (e.g. practice of secretariats of international organisations, such as the United Nations Secretariat, in certain subject areas),[14] making the organisation act on behalf of its member States in the fulfilment of a specific mandate. Second, the conduct should be attributable to the international organisation per se, as distinct from its individual member States acting within it.[15] This aspect remains quite controversial, as discussions at the Sixth Committee on the first reading text in 2016 showed.[16] To be able to make a direct contribution to the customary process, the organisation should act in its own capacity as opposed to being a mere platform for the conduct of individual member States, although it will of course remain important to assess whether the conduct of the organisation is consonant with that of its member States.[17] This aspect highlights the primary relevance of conduct carried out by the organisation as part of its external relations as well as internal conduct with international relevance or implications. Third, the conduct should relate to an area of competence of the international organisation, pursuant to the principle of

13 Including in this volume; *see* Chapters 1 and 2 in this volume.

14 A/73/10 (n 1), 131, para 66, para 6 of commentary to conclusion 4; Special Rapporteur's Third Report on identification of customary international law, A/CN.4/682 (27 March 2015) paras 76–77. On the specific case of the European Union, *see* in particular J Odermatt, 'The Development of Customary International Law by International Organizations', 66(2) *International & Comparative Law Quarterly* (2017), 503–510.

15 A/73/10 (n 1), 31, para 66, paras 5–6 of commentary to conclusion 4. The requirement that the organisation have at least one organ with a will of its own is also one element of the definition of an international organisation proposed in HG Schermers and NM Blokker, *International Institutional Law: Unity Within Diversity* (5th revised edn, Martinus Nijhoff 2011) 44.

16 Topical summary of the discussion held in the Sixth Committee of the General Assembly during its seventy-first session, A/CN.4/703 (22 February 2017) para 83.

17 A/73/10 (n 1) 131, para 66, para 7 of commentary to conclusion 4, providing also for further elements of caution to be taken into account, including the question of acts *ultra vires*.

specialised competences of international organisations (principle of speciality).[18] In relation to this, it would appear that an international organisation should be able to contribute to the formation of those customary rules of international law by which it will be bound.[19] Fourth, the violation by the international organisation of a rule it has contributed to create could in principle engage its international responsibility. This point raises the question of which organs of the organisation may contribute to the formation or identification of rules of customary international law. Although the draft conclusions on the identification of customary international law acknowledge that States and international organisations are different,[20] the draft articles on the responsibility of international organisations largely echo the articles on State responsibility,[21] which confirms that international organisations could in principle be held responsible for the conduct of their organs in the same way as States. Organs composed of experts acting in their individual capacity are not likely to reflect the position of the organisation although their works may at times influence such position.

Besides direct contribution by the United Nations covering both formation and identification, indirect contribution of the United Nations seems to be limited to the formation of rules of customary international law. This is the case insofar as indirect contribution may not constitute practice or *opinio juris*, but may only influence these elements. In comparison to direct contribution, indirect contribution is a much more diffuse and softer phenomenon, at the margins of legal and formal procedures. It covers the various ways and dynamics by which the activities and functioning of various United Nations organs stimulate the emergence and crystallisation of rules of customary international law. Indirect contribution is not to be apprehended through the status or legal force of a conduct per se but rather through its effect (of an extra-legal nature) on the passage of principles from *lex ferenda* into *lex lata*. By contrast to the forms of direct contribution, which are of a legal character, the forms of indirect contribution are essentially political in nature. This does not mean that a direct contribution such as State conduct might not be politically motivated. Rather, in the perspective of indirect contribution, conduct is not part of the materials on

18 A/73/10 (n 1) 131, para 66, para 5 of commentary to conclusion 4, and footnote 693.
19 ibid.
20 Ibid. Footnote 693 refers to para 7 of the general commentary to the draft articles on the responsibility of international organisations. *See* also Article 57 of the draft articles on the responsibility of States for internationally wrongful acts, in *Yearbook of the International Law Commission, 2001*, vol II, part 2, 141–2.
21 *See* para 3 of the general commentary to the draft articles on the responsibility of international organisations, in *Yearbook of the International Law Commission, 2011*, vol. II, part 2, 46 (limiting the scope of the draft articles to 'secondary rules').

which the existence of the customary rule rests (counting towards each of the two elements). Instead, it forms an external context or stimulating factor, the value of which ultimately relies on the reaction it generates from subjects of international law. The relevant United Nations organs play a role of exhortation and stimulation that helps shape the conduct of States by calling for and eventually provoking their reactions. As indirect contribution is not in itself constitutive of the practice and *opinio juris* of the Organisation, it does not need to be limited to organs acting on behalf of member States or with their active participation. Rather, it may extend to any organs, including technical organs, bodies of experts acting in their individual capacity, bodies tasked with monitoring the application of a General Assembly Declaration, Special Rapporteurs, etc. as long as such entities or persons exert an actual influence on the conduct or positions of States or other organs of the Organisation, or call for States' reaction. Indeed, eventually States' reactions to the conduct of the Organisation are critical in attributing indirect contributing value to the Organisation's conduct for the purpose of formation or identification of rules of customary international law. Treaty bodies may only exert a limited influence because their conduct, findings, and recommendations to States are mainly related to conventional obligations.[22]

The distinction between direct and indirect contribution is not absolute,[23] as the case of the United Nations Secretariat will show. It may nevertheless cast useful light on processes of formation of a rule of customary international law, but its relevance seems more limited when it comes to identifying existing rules of customary international law. The distinction could, however, provide a helpful tool in assessing the various nuances of possible contributions and the role of organs which on their face could seem without real influence on the customary process. Its interest also lies in accounting for the specificity of international organisations, which appear able to bring both kinds of contribution to the customary process, by contrast with States' contribution which seems to be primarily direct, and non-State actors' contribution which is exclusively indirect.[24]

22 On this point in the context of human rights, *see* Chapter 15 in this volume.

23 G Cahin, *La coutume et les organisations internationales – L'incidence de la dimension institutionnelle sur le processus coutumier* (Pedone 2001) 30–44, 79–81. *See* also A/CN.4/682 (27 March 2015) (n 14) paras 74–6, and S. Mathias, 'The Work of the International Law Commission on Identification of Customary International Law: A View from the Perspective of the Office of Legal Affairs', 15(1) Chinese Journal of International Law (2016), 24, para 35, that adopt a three-fold distinction. The present contribution is not concerned with those acts of the organisation that reflect the practice and opinio juris of States per se, except insofar as they are influenced by the institutional context or by the organisation itself.

24 A/73/10 (n 1) 132, para 66, para 8 of commentary to conclusion 4.

2 Contribution of the United Nations Secretariat

The United Nations Secretariat is composed of international civil servants working for and in the name of the Organisation, the Secretary-General being the first among them as the chief administrative officer of the Organisation.[25] International civil servants are statutorily prohibited from seeking and/or receiving instructions from any governments in performing their tasks, while member States retain a possibility to react to the conduct of the Secretariat through their participation in other organs of the Organisation.[26] Thus, the Secretariat, as the central administrative service of the UN, qualifies as an organ the conduct of which may make a contribution to the formation or identification of rules of customary international law.[27]

The Secretary-General stands for the Organisation as a whole and is able to take a stance on issues of international law in front of the main organs and member States. One example of this is the Secretary-General's yearly speech in opening the general debate of the General Assembly's annual session.[28] These speeches at times contain positions and assertions on the state or the desired evolution of rules of international law and provide general orientations for the Organisation's conduct. The Secretariat also facilitates access to the materials to be used when identifying the two elements of the customary process through substantial publication activities that help rationalise and compile the conduct of subjects of international law, although admittedly this is not conduct per se for the purpose of customary international law. Besides International Law Commission documents and Yearbooks, the Secretariat

25 United Nations Charter, 26 June 1945, Article 97.

26 ibid Article 100(1).

27 Para 6 of commentary to conclusion 4 as adopted on first reading, citing as examples the relevant conduct of secretariats of international organisations as treaty depositaries, in deploying military forces (including for peacekeeping purposes), or in taking position on the scope of the privileges and immunity of the organisation and its officials (Report of the International Law Commission on the work of its sixty-eighth session (2016), General Assembly, official records, 71st session, supplement no 10, A/71/10, 89). One may add, under certain circumstances, the conduct of the United Nations Secretariat, in particular through its Department of peacekeeping operations, in territories under international administration. On this last point, *see* Chapter 16 in this volume. The specific reference to secretariats of international organisations in para 6 of the commentary to conclusion 4 was abandoned on second reading, but the remaining, broader terms of 'international organizations' certainly do cover such organ in the case of the UN.

28 *See* e.g. general debate of the 58th session of the General Assembly, A/58/PV.7 (23 September 2003) 2–4.

also compiles the practice of member States in various sectors[29] and the practice of the UN, as with the *Repertory of Practice of United Nations Organs*, the *Repertoire of the Practice of the Security Council*, the *United Nations Juridical Yearbook*, or the *Summary of Practice of the Secretary-General as Depositary of Multilateral Treaties*, among other publications.

3 Complementary conducts of the Secretariat/Secretary-General and other United Nations organs

The influence of the Secretary-General may be substantial in the progressive development of legal standards through the activities of the main United Nations organs. This way the Secretary-General and the Secretariat may promote the adoption of legal positions by other organs. As a form of indirect contribution, such exhortatory conduct of the Secretariat and Secretary-General enjoys a high degree of authority and influences State conduct or call for State reaction. As his reports show,[30] the pervasive authority of the findings and recommendations of the Secretary-General might rest on political and moral grounds, but they often also rely on legal findings (by him or by other organs) and ultimately they form part of the role of the Secretariat to preserve the principles of the Charter. This provides the room necessary to the exhortatory role of the Secretary-General in the formation and identification of rules of customary international law.

The conduct of the Secretariat, and in particular of the Secretary-General, generally unfolds in interaction with other organs of the Organisation. Consequently, it is often the combination of these various forms of conduct that enable customary rules to emerge and be identified. Such interaction should be appreciated in the context of Article 98 of the United Nations Charter which provides that:

> [t]he Secretary-General shall act in that capacity [as chief administrative officer of the Organisation] in all meetings of the General Assembly, of the Security Council, of the Economic and Social Council, and of the Trusteeship Council, and shall perform such other functions as are entrusted to him by these organs.

An instance of these interactions is the Secretary-General's practice to prepare and submit reports to other United Nations main organs, in particular to the General

29 *See* e.g. *Maritime Boundary Agreements 1970–1984*, Office for Ocean Affairs and the Law of the Sea, E.87.5.V.12 (1987); Memorandum on ways and means for making the evidence of customary international law more readily available, A/CN.4/710 (12 January 2018); *United Nations Legislative Series*; *Diplomatic Conferences*, among others.

30 'Oceans and the law of the sea', Report of the Secretary-General, A/68/71 (8 April 2013) paras 111–12 and 114.

Assembly and the Security Council, which may also contribute for their part to the formation and identification of rules of customary international law.[31] Such reports are generally requested by these organs either on an occasional basis or on a regular basis in relation to topics placed on their agenda; they may relate to the Secretariat's activities, such as good offices, or may be aimed at providing thematic update and support to the requesting organ to assist its decision-making. Although such reporting activities form part of the political activities of the Organisation, they leave room for limited legal influence to infuse over time into the conduct of other United Nations organs, and of States eventually. These reports may indeed include legal positions expressed by the Secretary-General and may provide recommendations for further action of the main organ concerned. This is the case for instance of the well-known *Agenda for peace* presented by the Secretary-General in 1992,[32] of the Secretary-General's bulletin 'setting out fundamental principles and rules of international humanitarian law applicable to United Nations forces conducting operations under United Nations command and control',[33] and of the Secretary-General's regular reports on the responsibility to protect.[34]

The progressive development of the principle of responsibility to protect through various United Nations organs highlights the joint influence of several organs, as well as the stimulating role played by the Secretariat, in attempting gradually to confer some (still controversial) legal force to an initially political or moral principle. A few years after the ICISS report was published in 2001 under the auspices of the Canadian Ministry of Foreign Affairs,[35] the Secretary-General relayed the conclusion of the High-level Panel on Threats, Challenges and Change 'endors[ing] the emerging norm that there is a collective international

31 *See* G Fox, K Boon, and I Jenkins, 'The Contributions of United Nations Security Council Resolutions to the Law of Non-International Armed Conflict: New Evidence of Customary International Law', 67(3) *American University Law Review* (2018), 692–724; O Corten, 'La participation du Conseil de sécurité à l'élaboration, à la cristallisation ou à la consolidation de règles coutumières', 2004/2 *Revue belge de droit international* (2004) 560–64.

32 Secretary-General, 'An Agenda for Peace: Preventive Diplomacy, peacemaking and peace-keeping', A/47/277 (17 June 1992).

33 ST/SGB/1999/13 (6 August 1999).

34 In the same vein, *see* Mathias (n 23) 29–30, para 58.

35 'The Responsibility to Protect', Report of the International Commission on Intervention and State Sovereignty, December 2001, annexed to UN Doc A/57/303 (14 August 2002). *See* also Secretary-General's Millenium report 'We the peoples: The role of the United Nations in the twenty-first century', A/54/2000 (27 March 2000) para 217, and more generally the debate on humanitarian intervention during the 1990s.

responsibility to protect' and linking such norm to Chapter VII of the United Nations Charter.[36] Shortly thereafter he repeated his agreement with this view and endorsed the list of criteria proposed by the High-level Panel for the authorisation of the use of force.[37] He also submitted to the General Assembly and Security Council a series of reports dealing with the implementation of the principle.[38] These two organs have in turn adopted a series of resolutions which rely on the principle of responsibility to protect as conceptualised in the Secretary-General's reports and sometimes refer explicitly to his findings.[39] In particular, the Security Council has reaffirmed the principle in Resolution 1674[40] and has later applied it to authorise the deployment of a peacekeeping mission in Darfur,[41] regarding the situation in Libya,[42] and in a number of other occasions.[43] These elements suggest a joint progressive contribution by these United Nations organs to the crystallisation of the principle into a legal norm. Although it remains debatable whether this outcome has been reached as of yet, the institutional interaction between these United Nations organs on this question, the articulation of the concept and the application of it in some concrete cases, as well as the reaction of member States they call for provide a strong indication that such process is indeed ongoing. Of course, none of these resolutions or reports should be held alone as constitutive or expressive of a rule of customary international law. Rather, the process as a whole should be acknowledged as contributing to the progressive crystallisation of the principle of responsibility to protect.

36 Note by the Secretary-General, A/59/565 (2 December 2004) paras 199–203.

37 Report of the Secretary-General, 'In larger freedom: towards development, security and human rights for all', A/59/2005 (21 March 2005) para 135.

38 *See* in particular A/63/677 (12 January 2009) paras 2–3; A/64/864 (14 July 2010) and more recently A/70/999-S/2016/620 (22 July 2016). Annual reports have been issued by the Secretary-General since 2009. Since 2008, the Secretary-General has appointed a Special Adviser on the responsibility to protect.

39 Resolution 60/1 of the General Assembly of 16 September 2005, paras 138–9. This Resolution enjoys greater visibility with member States since it was adopted as part of the 2005 World Summit.

40 Security Council, Resolution 1674 of 28 April 2006, Article 1 (noting with appreciation of the findings of the Secretary-General in the matter and taking note of his conclusions).

41 Security Council, Resolution 1706 of 31 August 2006.

42 Security Council, Resolution 1970 of 26 February 2011 and Resolution 1973 of 17 March 2011.

43 Côte d'Ivoire (Resolution 1975 of 30 March 2011), South Sudan (Resolution 1996 of 8 July 2011), Yemen (Resolution 2014 of 21 October 2011), Central African Republic (Resolution 2121 of 10 October 2013).

Of particular interest is the interaction between the Secretariat and the Sixth Committee and the International Law Commission as a subsidiary organ of the General Assembly. The relation of the Codification Division of the Secretariat with the work of the International Law Commission and the Sixth Committee includes not only organisational support to the annual sessions of these organs as well as ensuring a consistent editing of International Law Commission documents[44] in all United Nations official languages, but also a material contribution to substance, both in its reports and behind the scenes. In particular, some procedures of work of the International Law Commission provide considerable room for input by the Secretariat, thus contributing to the mandate of the General Assembly and Commission to promote the development of international law and its codification.[45] At the Commission's request, the Secretariat prepares memorandums and studies from time to time to assist the work of the Commission in various topics. Such documents usually consist in legal and/or historical analysis of certain concepts and issues, compilations of practice of States or the United Nations, etc. As such they guide the work of Special Rapporteurs and inform the output of the Commission by providing factual and legal support. At the plenary debate on the topic of identification of customary international law during the International Law Commission's 70th session in 2018, at the request of the Special Rapporteur, the Secretariat formally introduced its *Memorandum on ways and means for making the evidence of customary international law more readily available* to the Commission right after the Special Rapporteur had introduced his Fifth Report,[46] and the Commission decided to recommend to the General Assembly to

44 Articles 14, 16(e, g, j), 17(1), 19(2), 21(1), 22, 25(2) of the International Law Commission Statute.

45 The work of the International Law Commission on various topics are referred to and taken note of in a General Assembly resolution when they reach the first reading and second reading stages. On the support provided to the International Law Commission by the Secretariat, and in particular the Codification Division, *see The Work of the International Law Commission* (9th edn, United Nations 2017) vol I, 85–7; R Higgins, P Webb, D Akande, S Sivakumaran, and J Sloan, *Oppenheim's International Law: United Nations* (Oxford University Press 2017) 502 (and footnote 44) and 943; C-A Fleishhauer, 'Les organisations internationales face à la codification du droit international', in Société française pour le droit international, *Colloque d'Aix-en-Provence: La codification du droit international* (Pedone 1999) 295; H Llewellyn and T Bektas, 'United Nations, Sixth Committee', *Max Planck Encyclopedia of Public International Law* (online edition, May 2019) paras 5–6 and 11–12; draft resolution A/C.6/73/L.22 (7 November 2018) negotiated by the Sixth Committee (n 47) para 26.

46 A/CN.4/SR.3396 (7 May 2018), 12 (M Wood) and 13–4 (D Nanopoulos).

note the Memorandum and follow up on its recommendations.[47] Memorandums of the Secretariat submitted to the International Law Commission may also be referred to in the case law of international courts and tribunals to inform their interpretation of a particular point of international law.[48] Coordination between the International Law Commission and the Secretariat is also visible in the traditional visit and statement of the Legal Counsel to the Commission at each of its annual sessions. Moreover, the International Law Commission usually requests States but also at times international organisations to provide comments on its outputs between the first and the second readings, which in the case of the United Nations typically occurs through the Secretariat. The International Law Commission takes these comments into account when finalising its works on second reading.[49] Thus interaction with the International Law Commission points to the Secretariat's role in the identification of rules of customary international law as well as its (admittedly modest and residual) contribution to the formation of such rules.

The Secretariat also contributes to the progressive consolidation of International Law Commission outputs into positive law.[50] For instance, in a 1972 legal opinion the

47 A/73/10 (n 1) 118, para 63(d) and (e). *See* also draft resolutions A/C.6/73/L.22 (Report of the International Law Commission on the work of its seventieth session, 7 November 2018, para 26) and A/C.6/73/L.24 (Identification of customary international law, 7 November 2018, preamble) negotiated at the 73th session of the Sixth Committee and adopted by it on 13 November 2018 (Report of the Sixth Committee, A/73/556). Both draft resolutions were adopted without a vote by the General Assembly in plenary as Resolution 73/203 of 20 December 2018 (Identification of customary international law) and Resolution 73/265 of 22 December 2018 (Report of the International Law Commission on the work of its seventieth session).

48 *See* e.g. *South China Sea Arbitration* (Philippines v People's Republic of China), PCA case no 2013–19, award of 12 July 2016, para. 222, were the Tribunal relied inter alia on a 1962 study prepared by the Secretariat on the juridical regime of historic waters including historic bays (doc. A/CN.4/143, in *Yearbook of the International Law Commission, 1962*, vol II, 1–26) in interpreting the concept of 'historic title'. The International Court of Justice relied on this same document in applying the concept of 'historic bay' to the Gulf of Fonseca (*Land, Island and Maritime Frontier Dispute (El Salvador/Honduras: Nicaragua intervening*), judgment of 11 September 1992, *ICJ Reports 1992* (351), 593–4, para 394.

49 *See* e.g. para 6 of the commentary to Article 7 of the draft articles on the responsibility of international organisations in *Yearbook of the International Law Commission, 2011*, vol II, part 2 (n 21), 57, which took note of the position expressed by the United Nations Legal Counsel in response to the Commission's request for comments and observations.

50 This concerns those areas of the output that correspond to the progressive development part of the ILC's mandate.

Secretariat has relied on the draft articles on succession of States in respect of treaties in assessing the procedure followed by the World Health Organization concerning the succession of newly independent States to World Health Organization regulations.[51] Although in this opinion the practice of the secretariat of an organisation is considered in particular under the perspective of institutional custom the opinion suggests that such practice may also be understood in the light of the general regime defined in the draft articles, which are concerned with questions of general international law outside the institutional context.[52]

The United Nations Secretariat's contribution to the progressive consolidation of International Law Commission outputs into *lex lata* lies generally in a combined conduct together with the General Assembly. The fate of the draft articles on the responsibility of States for internationally wrongful acts, among other topics, provides an illustration of this. Every three years since the adoption of the draft articles on second reading in 2001, the General Assembly has been considering, in adopting a resolution as part of its agenda, the question of possible future action regarding these draft articles, including the opportunity to prepare a Convention.[53] The consideration of the matter and the comments received from States are based among others on a report entitled 'Compilation of decisions of international courts, tribunals and other bodies'[54] on the topic of the draft articles. This report is prepared and regularly updated by the Secretary-General on request of the General Assembly. This reflects the role played by the Secretariat in the consideration by the General Assembly of further actions to be taken regarding International Law Commission completed works. Admittedly in this case however, since the role of the Secretariat is mainly limited to administrative and institutional support, its contribution to the formation and identification of rules of customary international law might appear relatively minor in comparison with other examined situations.

4 Legal opinions of the Secretariat

When it comes to assessing the role of the Secretariat in the formation and expression of rules of customary international law it seems particularly interesting to focus

51 'Draft articles on succession of States in respect of treaties – Procedure followed by the World Health Organization concerning the succession of newly independent States to WHO regulations', *United Nations Juridical Yearbook (UNJY)*, 1972, 195–99.

52 ibid 197–98.

53 As a recent example, *see* Resolution 74/180 of 18 December 2019.

54 *See* e.g. A/62/62 (1 February 2007).

on the conduct of the Office of Legal Affairs, and in particular on the legal opinions that are delivered from time to time by the Under-Secretary-General for Legal Affairs, the Legal Counsel, on request of various Secretariat departments or offices,[55] the Secretary-General or other United Nations organs. Although the Office of Legal Affairs is by no means the only organ of the Secretariat by which legal advice may be delivered to the Secretary-General and other United Nations organs, it nevertheless appears as possibly the most straightforward case study for the purpose of this chapter. Even though the function of the Office of Legal Affairs to provide legal advice to the Secretary-General, Secretariat departments and offices, and other United Nations organs could seem on its face to limit the contribution of its legal opinions to the field of identification or codification of rules of international law, as Schachter highlighted, the legal opinions of the Secretariat may also play a role in the development of international law.[56] This role is relatively specific, however. Legal opinions of the Secretariat fulfil the Organisation's need for formal legal advice in real time in order to guide the Organisation's conduct,[57] and it is all the more so that permanent representatives and delegates of member States taking decisions within main organs such as the General Assembly and the Security Council are generally not very prone to seeking legal advice from the Secretariat.[58] Although the request for and delivery of legal opinions are in principle internal to the Organisation,

55 Secretary-General's bulletin – Organization of the Office of Legal Affairs, ST/SGB/2008/13 (1 August 2008) Section 2.1. These legal opinions are published yearly in Chapter VI of the *UNJY*.

56 O Schachter, 'The Development of International Law through the Legal Opinions of the United Nations Secretariat', 25 *British Yearbook of International Law* (1948), 91–132. The publication of the *UNJY* itself is a measure that was directed to the Secretary-General by the General Assembly in order to help promoting the development of international law (*see* Resolution 1292 (XIII) of 5 December 1958, the Secretary-General's report of 1959 and Resolution 1814 (XVII) of 18 December 1962). *See* also the Statement of the United Nations Legal Counsel, Mr Miguel de Serpa Soares, at the 70th session of the ILC, A/CN.4/SR.3398 (9 May 2018) 7.

57 Schachter (n 56) 93; R Zacklin, *The United Nations Secretariat and the Use of Force in a Unipolar World: Power v. Principle* (Cambridge University Press 2010) 4; J Sloan and GI Hernández, 'The Role of the International Court of Justice in the Development of the Institutional Law of the United Nations' in CJ Tams and J Sloan (eds), *The Development of International Law by the International Court of Justice* (Oxford University Press 2013) 200.

58 M Wood, 'The UN Security Council and International Law', *Lecture Series* (Lauterpacht Centre for International Law 2006); 'The Interpretation of Security Council Resolutions', 2 Max Planck Yearbook of United Nations Law (1998), 80; 'The Interpretation of Security Council Resolutions, Revisited', 20 Max Planck Yearbook of United Nations Law (2016), 12. This does not mean that the Secretariat is not involved in preparing reports that often provide the basis for the adoption of decisions and resolutions by these organs.

these documents may be concerned both with matters internal to the Organisation or other organisations of the United Nations system and with issues between the Organisation and its member States or third States.[59] Only those legal opinions that are concerned (even incidentally) with the external relations of the Organisation are likely to be of concern for the purpose of the formation or identification of rules of customary international law; in the specific case of the United Nations, the relations between the Organisation and its member States arguably may also fall within this scope because the universal character of the United Nations tends to attenuate the distinction between the internal or institutional relation of the Organisation with its member States, on the one hand, and the external relations of the Organisation with States, on the other.

The contribution of legal opinions of the Secretariat to the formation of rules of customary international law lies in part in their influence in shaping and orienting the conduct of the Secretary-General, the Secretariat, and other United Nations organs. The role of the legal opinions that are prepared by the Office of Legal Affairs[60] and generally attributed to the Legal Counsel (and sometimes to the Secretary-General himself) is particularly related to custom as a source of international law. As statements on the state or the evolution of rules of international law delivered by a principal organ of the United Nations within its mandate, legal opinions are neither decisions by a judicial organ nor teachings of the most highly qualified publicists under Article 38.1.d of the Statute of the International Court of Justice. Some opinions may be purely advisory or may have legal effect, depending on the context

59 ST/SGB/2008/13 (n 55) para 3.3. *See* for instance legal opinions relating to organisations' internal matters (although with possible international implications): 'Status of the Global Environment Facility', *UNJY 1994*, 469–73; 'Resolutions under Chapter VII adopted by the Security Council – Practice of the Council', *UNJY 1994*, 502–3. Legal opinions relating to relations between the Organisation and States: 'Question of whether the staff of permanent missions are obliged to reside in Switzerland – Section 11 of the 1946 Agreement with the Swiss Federal Council on Privileges and Immunities of the United Nations – Article 7 of the 1975 Vienna Convention on the Representation of States in Their Relations with International Organizations of a Universal Character', *UNJY 1994*, 444–46; 'Succession in the membership of the International Cocoa Organization – Succession of States in respect of State property – 1983 Vienna Convention on Succession of States in respect of State Property, Archives and Debts', *UNJY 1994*, 491–94.

60 Although the Legal Counsel is the senior legal adviser to the Secretary-General on legal matters generally, legal opinions on issues of public international law are usually prepared by the Office of the Legal Counsel within the OLA whereas legal opinions on issues of the Organisation's internal administrative law as well as private international law are usually prepared by the General Legal Division (ST/SGB/2008/13 (n 55), sections 3.3, 6.2(a), 7.2(a)).

in which they are delivered.[61] Moreover, when they assess the existence of a rule of customary international law legal opinions of the Secretariat rarely proceed to a detailed analysis of the two elements.[62] Legal opinions of the Secretariat that make a determination on a customary process or an emerging rule of customary international law, or repeated opinions making a legal assessment on the desirability of a rule could arguably be considered as reflecting the *opinio juris* of the Organisation as a qualified legal assessment informing the specific conduct of an organ. In this context, when it can be assessed that a legal opinion was actually relied upon by the Secretary-General or any United Nations organs in their later conduct, the finding in this opinion on the existence of a rule of customary international law may reasonably be counted as reflecting the *opinio juris* of the Organisation.

An example of this is the role played by legal opinions of the Secretariat in shaping the Secretariat's positions and conduct towards the end of the war in Bosnia.[63] In this case, legal opinions have helped the Secretariat and the Secretary-General define a position that would eventually lead to influence the international law on the use of force and could arguably be considered as the *opinio juris* of such conduct. In these circumstances, legal opinions may be regarded as contributing to the practice and/or *opinio juris* of the Organisation.

As another illustration, in a legal opinion delivered in 1994 on the 'Question of whether the staff of permanent missions are obliged to reside in Switzerland', the Legal Counsel was asked whether it would be appropriate for the receiving State of the office of an international organisation to categorically request that diplomatic personnel of missions to this office reside within the boundaries of the host State. He came to the conclusion that 'one could argue as to whether a customary rule has not been established in this area of relations'.[64] In reaching this conclusion, the Legal Counsel based his reasoning on State practice but also on a review of relevant United Nations practice, including a memorandum of the Secretariat submitted to the International Law Commission and further International Law Commission works based on it.[65] Since then this rule seems to have been followed by consistent

61 Schachter (n 56) 95.

62 'Water project concerning an international river flowing across Namibia and South Africa…', *UNJY 1984*, 171, para 2; 'The right of self-defense of United Nations peace-keeping forces and the exercise of that right…', *UNJY 1993*, 371, para 2; Mathias (n 23) 30, para 61, and 31, para 63.

63 Zacklin (n 57) 63–64. *See* also 144 in the context of Iraq.

64 'Question of whether the staff of permanent missions are obliged to reside in Switzerland' (n 59), *UNJY 1994*, 446, para 11.

65 ibid para 10.

practice, which illustrates both the indirect contribution of the legal opinion and the direct contribution of the Organisation to the emergence of the rule as a matter of customary international law.

Although legal opinions of the Secretariat are in principle addressed to the Organisation, they are at times also relied upon by States, and thus enjoy a wider impact. For instance, in a legal opinion delivered in 2002 in the context of the Western Sahara conflict, the Legal Counsel both affirmed the customary character of the principle of permanent sovereignty over natural resources and helped define its scope when it comes to activities related to natural resources undertaken by an administering Power, also recognising that such aspect remained controversial.[66] As part of the negotiation process under United Nations auspices, the reactions of Morocco and Algeria to the legal opinion[67] and the subsequent practice of the United Nations, in particular the Secretary-General and the Security Council, seem to have followed the findings of the Legal Counsel,[68] and thus the legal opinion can arguably be counted as contributing to the consolidation and clarification of the principle of permanent sovereignty over natural resources under customary international law.

The contribution of legal opinions may be further found in cases when such opinions purport to identify an existing rule of customary international law, or to qualify a given principle as a legal rule.[69] As a negative example, in a legal opinion delivered in 2007 the Legal Counsel denied the existence of the prohibition

66 Letter dated 29 January 2002 from the Under-Secretary-General for Legal Affairs, the Legal Counsel, addressed to the President of the Security Council, S/2002/161 (12 February 2002) paras 14 and 21.

67 Letter dated 1 February 2002 from the Permanent Representative of Algeria to the United Nations addressed to the Secretary-General, A/56/809 – S/2002/144 (5 February 2002); Letter dated 8 February 2002 from the Permanent Representative of Morocco to the United Nations addressed to the President of the Security Council, S/2002/153 (8 February 2002).

68 Report of the Secretary-General on the situation concerning Western Sahara, S/2002/178 (19 February 2002), para 19.

69 'Privileges and immunities issues related to "Delivery as One" and United Nations Volunteers', *UNJY 2009*, 393–4, para 10 (examining State practice to deny that the privileges and immunities of the United Nations Volunteers have developed into rules of customary international law); 'Certain labour claims filed against the United Nations Logistics Base in [City] in the Court of [City] by five former individual contractors', *UNJY 2012*, 461 (affirming the customary character of the jurisdictional immunities of States and the absence of immunity when a State acts as a private person in a commercial context); 'Note to the Assistant Secretary-General for Political Affairs, regarding the usage of the term "civil war"', *UNJY 2007*, 459, para 4 (affirming the customary character of Additional Protocol II to the 1949 Geneva Conventions).

of death penalty as a rule of customary international law, yet at the same time he underlined a diverging practice of the Secretariat to eventually support the latter's position not to cooperate with judicial bodies that are empowered to apply the death penalty.[70] Although not making this point directly, such reasoning might support an argument in favour of the emergence of a rule of customary international law prohibiting the death penalty, and to the contribution of the Secretariat to such process.

There are also instances in which legal opinions have expressly purported to identify the possible emergence of a rule of customary international law, pointing to the customary process itself.[71] In such cases related to identification, the legal opinions are to be construed as self-standing, external findings on a given conduct or situation as opposed to a constitutive element of it. They constitute a formal manifestation of the legal advisory role entrusted to the Office of Legal Affairs vis-à-vis the Secretary-General. They are instances of interpretation of the Charter and of rules of international law by the very United Nations organ in charge of safeguarding the Charter and its principles. As such, even though the legal opinions of the Secretariat are not legally binding they constitute authoritative statements of the state of international law since they emanate from the competent, central body in charge of providing legal advice to the Secretariat as the central organ in charge of upholding the principles of the Charter,[72] and to the Secretary-General as the chief administrative officer[73] in charge of liaising and coordinating the activities of the United Nations main organs. It is often in this role that the Secretary-General seeks legal advice from the Legal Counsel. As such, legal opinions are to be presumed to have a high legal pervasiveness, which probably explains in part why they tend to be followed by their addressees and why they provide a powerful legal – as opposed to political – guidance to the conduct of the Secretary-General. As external determination on the state of the law, such legal advice arguably entails a contribution by legal opinions to the identification of customary international law.[74]

70 'The death penalty under international law and the position of the United Nations Secretariat', *UNJY 2007*, 476, para 7.

71 'Question of whether the staff of permanent missions are obliged to reside in Switzerland' (n 59), *UNJY 1994*, 446, para 11.

72 Secretary-General's bulletin – Organization of the Secretariat of the United Nations, ST/SGB/2015/3 (22 July 2015), Section 2.

73 United Nations Charter, Article 97; Resolution 13(1) of 13 February 1946 of the General Assembly.

74 Mathias (n 23) 30, para 60.

5 Treaty depositary practice

The conduct of the Secretary-General and the Secretariat in relation to the function of depositary of multilateral treaties stands as a telling illustration of their contribution to the formation and consolidation of rules of customary international law. The practice of the Secretary-General as treaty depositary presumably lies at the same level as State practice for purposes of customary international law, not least because it typically was, and still is, otherwise performed by States,[75] which therefore makes it functionally equivalent to State practice.[76] As the Secretary-General is the principal depositary of multilateral treaties worldwide,[77] he holds a central depositary role since 1945, succeeding to the Secretariat of the League of Nations in this role. Thus, his practice, in fact discharged by the Treaty Section of the Office of Legal Affairs, has been central in shaping the legal rules pertaining to treaty deposit, which have been essentially customary up to their partial codification by the 1969 Vienna Convention on the Law of Treaties.[78] The Secretary-General's depositary practice has developed and evolved in close connection with other United Nations organs and States' reactions and practice, consistently responding to a need for pragmatism in the face of new situations.[79] As an example of this functional approach, the fact that States often only designate the Secretary-General as the depositary when concluding a treaty without specifying all tasks that he is supposed to carry out (as used to be specified in the past) suggests that the practice followed by him has been accepted as law by States and arguably amounts to more than mere habit or convenience.

While it is generally accepted that the depositary practice of the Secretary-General is nowadays guided by treaty provisions, customary international law, and decisions of relevant United Nations organs (including resolutions of the General Assembly),[80] it is interesting to note how such practice contributed to the

75 'Summary of Practice of the Secretary-General as Depositary of Multilateral Treaties', Treaty Section of the Office of Legal Affairs, ST/LEG/7/Rev.1 (1999) para 12.

76 A/73/10 (n 1) 131, para 66, para 6 of the commentary to conclusion 4.

77 ST/LEG/7/Rev.1 (n 75) para 1.

78 ibid paras 101, 161, 204, 252. However, caution should be exercised as all provisions of the Convention did not necessarily codify customary international law at the time the Convention was signed: for instance the ninety-day time limit for objections to proposed corrections of the original text to be raised by States reflects the usual practice of the Secretary-General (ibid para. 55) but it is doubtful whether this practice actually reflects a legal rule.

79 ibid paras 4, 6, 13.

80 ibid paras 14 and 291; 'Practice of the Secretary-General in his capacity as depositary of multilateral treaties regarding (1) reservations and objections to reservations relating to

consolidation of rules of customary international law in this field in the period leading up to the 1969 Vienna Convention. In 1950, long before the Convention was signed and at a time when the International Law Commission's work on the law of treaties was still at an early stage, the General Assembly requested the International Court of Justice to deliver its famous Advisory Opinion on the legality of reservations to the Convention on the Prevention and Punishment of the Crime of Genocide.[81] The Resolution requesting the opinion from the Court also invited the International Law Commission to prepare a study on the question of reservations to multilateral conventions as part of the related topic on the law of treaties that was on its program of work, and to report to it at the following session; it further requested the Secretary-General to keep on with his then depositary practice relating to treaty reservations pending the delivery of the Advisory Opinion.[82] The Resolution adopted by the General Assembly in the aftermath of the Advisory Opinion in turn directed the Secretary-General to adapt his practice to the conclusions of the Court and to the report submitted by the International Law Commission on the topic.[83] The depositary practice of the Secretary-General prior to the signature of the 1969 Vienna Convention also relied on several legal opinions of the Secretariat. These in fact provided legal guidance to the Secretary-General whenever a new situation arose.[84] In this context it does not seem unreasonable to conclude that the Secretary-General's conduct in relation to multilateral treaty deposit matters constitutes practice attributable to the UN, the *opinio juris* of the Organisation being reflected in the International Court of Justice 1951 Advisory Opinion, International Law Commission works, and relevant legal opinions of the Secretariat, as legal statements some of which have been in turn endorsed by the General Assembly.

treaties not containing provisions in that respect (2) correction of errors in the original of a treaty', *UNJY 1976*, 210, para 5; 'Question whether it is possible for a State party to a treaty having formulated reservations at the time of deposing its instrument of ratification to formulate further reservations at a subsequent stage', *UNJY 1984*, 183.

81 ICJ, *Reservations to the Convention on Genocide*, Advisory Opinion of 28 May 1951, *ICJ Reports 1951*, 15. In this Advisory Opinion, the Court took the depositary practice of the Secretary-General into account (25).

82 Resolution 478 (V) of 16 November 1950.

83 Resolution 598 (VI) of 12 January 1952.

84 'Accession of new States to multilateral conventions concluded under the auspices of the League of Nations – Legal implications of a proposal to open those conventions to new parties with the tacit consent of a majority of the States already parties', *UNJY 1962*, 264–5; 'Question whether the instruments of ratification of the amendments to the Charter provided in Articles 108 and 109 thereof should be deposited with the Secretary-General or with the Government of the United States of America as the depositary of the original

6 Concluding remarks

More than any other United Nations organ the Secretariat stands for the Organisation as a subject of international law distinct from its member States. Thus it is in a position to adopt a certain conduct as part of establishing practice and/or *opinio juris* attributable to the Organisation itself, but also to stimulate State practice and *opinio juris*. As the central administrative organ of the United Nations in charge of safeguarding the principles of the United Nations Charter, the Secretariat contributes to the formation and identification of general rules of customary international law, often in combination with other organs at many levels. The Secretariat can fully take part in practice and *opinio juris* of the Organisation by its conduct, which is identified above as direct contribution. Its contribution may also be indirect by stimulating and orienting the crystallisation of a rule, often through political and institutional influence of the conduct of other United Nations organs and of member States. In the latter case, States' reactions to the conduct of the Organisation are critical in attributing contributing value to the Organisation's conduct.[85] Direct and indirect contributions of the Secretariat often coalesce.

Although the United Nations holds a special place in the international legal order that facilitates its role as a central contributor to the development of international law and its codification, it is usual for international organisations to have a secretariat. While the direct contribution of a secretariat (i.e. its capacity to be the source of a practice accepted as law attributable to the organisation) is related to the legal status and competences vested in such organ in the founding treaty or other statutory act of the organisation, the faculty of such organ to bring an indirect contribution to the identification or formation of rules of customary international law typically depends on the room left for initiatives and political leadership to develop with practice over time. When the position of a secretariat within the institutional structure of an international organisation enables it to play a politically emancipated role, it appears more likely to be in a position to stimulate and orient member States in shaping a general practice that is accepted as law.[86]

text of the Charter', *UNJY 1964*, 249; 'Certain aspects of the depositary practice of the Secretary-General in respect of constituent instruments of international organizations', *UNJY 1964*, 249–50.

85 Use of the Terms 'Declaration' and 'Recommendation', Memorandum by the OLA, E/CN.4/L.610 (2 April 1962) para 4.

86 For an insightful analysis of the political role of the Secretariat and the Secretary General in an institutional context, *see* E. Giraud, 'Le secrétariat des institutions internationales', 79 *Collected Courses of the Hague Academy of International Law* (1951-II), 369–509.

The draft conclusions on identification of customary international law as adopted by the International Law Commission on second reading and endorsed by the General Assembly, and the commentaries, fully acknowledge the role of international organisations in the identification of rules of customary international law, although the exact scope of such role has been much debated.[87] As far as the United Nations is concerned, with its special place as an international organisation of a universal character, the reality of its contribution, both direct and indirect, to the formation and identification of rules of customary international law is beyond doubt, as exemplified by the Secretariat.

87 At an earlier point of the consideration of the topic by the Commission, options included, among others, distinguishing the issue of international organisations in a separate conclusion, limit the mention of international organisations to the commentaries, or delete altogether references to the role of international organisations (although this more radical option was quickly dropped). On second reading, the proposal by the Special Rapporteur to delete the term 'primarily' in conclusion 4(1) was much discussed and was eventually not adopted (*see* statements by B Aurescu, P Galvão Teles, MD Hmoud, H Huang, CC Jalloh, G Nolte, N Oral, A Reinisch, and DD Tladi, among others, during the plenary debate in May 2018). *See* also further Comments and observations received from Governments, A/CN.4/716 (14 February 2018), 13–23, and A/CN.4/717 (14 March 2018) (n 6) paras 35–49.

Chapter 13

The making of custom through sanctions of international organisations

Maruša T. Veber

It seems uncontested that international organisations[1] can contribute to the making of customary international law.[2] Interestingly, however, the attention of international legal scholars has mostly been drawn to the role international organisations play as

1 For the purposes of this chapter the term 'international organisations' is used as defined by the International Law Commission (ILC) in its work on the responsibility of international organisations. *See* Article 2 Articles on Responsibility of International Organisations (2011) YILC vol II, Part Two.

2 M Wood, 'International Organizations and Customary International Law' (2015) 48 Vanderbilt Journal of Transnational Law 609; DM DeBartolo, 'Identifying International Organizations' Contribution to Custom' (2014) 108 American Journal of International Law 174; G Cahin, *La Coutume Interantionale et les Organisations Internationales: L'incidence de la Dimension Institutionelle sur le Processus Coutumier* (Pedone 2001); A Pellet, 'Article 38' in Andreas Zimmermann et al (eds), *The Statute of the International Court of Justice: A Commentary* (2nd edn, Oxford University Press 2012); T Treves, 'Customary International Law' *Max Planck Encyclopedia of Public International Law* (MPEPIL), para 50; J d'Aspremont, 'The Decay of Modern Customary International Law in Spite of Scholarly Heroism' (2015) 2015 Global Community: Yearbook of International Law and Jurisprudence; J Klabbers, 'International Organizations in the Formation of Customary International Law' in E Cannizzaro and P Palchetti, *Customary International Law on the Use of Force: A Methodological Approach* (Martinus Nijhoff 2005); A Cassese, *International Law* (2nd edn, Oxford University Press 2005) 165; MH Mendelson, *The Formation of Customary International Law* (Recueil des cours, Collected courses of the Hague Academy of International Law 272, Martinus Nijhoff 1998) 201; Memorandum by the Secretariat, Formation and evidence of customary international law, Elements in the previous work of the International Law Commission that could be particularly relevant to the topic (2013) UN Doc A/CN.4/659, Observation 13; Third report on the identification of customary international law by Michael Wood (2015) UN Doc A/CN.4/682; Fifth report on the identification of customary international law by Michael Wood (2018) UN Doc A/CN.4/717 14–22; Conclusion 4(2), Identification of customary international law, Report of the International Law Commission, Seventieth session (2018) UN Doc A/73/10.

forums for evidence of practice and *opinio juris* of States,[3] rather than their direct involvement as independent international legal persons. This chapter aims to fill the shortfall of international organisations-focused research. It seeks to demonstrate the increasingly important role of international organisations in relation to the formation of customary international law rules by virtue of the sanctions they adopt in response to violations of *erga omnes* obligations.

The main claim advanced by this chapter is that international organisations can be conducive to the emergence or consolidation of the customary status of those primary rules of international law which their sanctions are meant to vindicate. It will show that the contribution of sanctions to the formation of custom varies significantly depending on the concrete situation we are looking at. In cases where international organisations react to breaches of obligations that already have an *erga omnes* status and their standing to adopt sanctions is uncontested under the law of countermeasures, international organisations contribute to consolidation and clarification of custom. Ironically, however, the potential for customary lawmaking is greater when the *erga omnes* status of an obligation towards which an international organisation is reacting to is not yet confirmed. The illegality or legal uncertainty shrouding such sanctions under the law of responsibility does not preclude their potential in customary lawmaking. On the contrary, it seems to maximise their contribution. In discussing these situations, the present chapter makes an important distinction between the act of sanction and the act of protest. This makes it possible to argue that it is protests accompanying the act of sanction that have a role to play in custom making, rather than the act of sanction itself.

Four preliminary caveats must be formulated in order to further delineate the ambit of this chapter. First, this chapter does not attempt to provide a definite answer on the question of the entitlement of international organisations under general international law to adopt sanctions in the general interest, nor answer the entangled question of identification of *erga omnes* rules. Rather, it attempts to assess whether through the adoption of sanctions international organisations can contribute to the consolidation, expression, or formation of customary status of certain

3 *See* e.g. MH Mendelson, *The Formation of Customary International Law* (Recueil des cours, Collected courses of the Hague Academy of International Law 272, Martinus Nijhoff 1998) 201; R Jennings and A Watts (eds), *Oppenheim's International Law* (9th edn, Vol I, Peace, Introduction and part 1, Longman 1992) 46–47; L Hannikainen, 'The Collective Factor as a Promoter of Customary International Law' (2006) 6 Baltic Yearbook of International Law; Conclusions VII and VIII of the Institute de droit international, Session of Cairo, 1987, The Elaboration of General Multilateral Conventions And of Non-contractual Instruments Having a Normative Function or Objective; *Legality of the Threat or Use of Nuclear Weapons, Advisory Opinion* [1996] ICJ Rep 226, 258, para 81.

primary rules of international law.[4] Second, it should be emphasised that the focus is on the adoption of sanctions by international organisations in their external relations as opposed to conducts of organisations relating to the internal operation of the organisation,[5] which is also an approach adopted by the Special Rapporteur of the International Law Commission on the topic of identification of customary international law.[6] Third, it is acknowledged that international organisations play a dual role[7] in customary lawmaking: international organisations as forums of States and international organisations as independent actors. In this sense ascertainment and assessment of practice of international organisations must be dealt with caution since it is sometimes difficult to differentiate between practice of States and intentional organisations as such.[8] This chapter does not aim to assess the importance of the e.g. resolutions adopted by the United Nations organs or positions adopted within the European Union that are mostly considered as collective practice of States and not international organisations as such. Last but not least, this contribution does not address the practice relating to the adoption of countermeasures by international organisations themselves, and more generally the so-called secondary rules of international law pertaining to countermeasures and reaction to wrongfulness.[9]

4 Third report on the identification of customary international law by Michael Wood (2015) UN Doc A/CN.4/682, para 70.
5 A Pellet, 'Article 38' in A Zimmermann et al (eds), *The Statute of the International Court of Justice: A Commentary* (2nd edn, Oxford University Press 2012) 731–870.
6 Third report on the identification of customary international law by Michael Wood (2015) UN Doc A/CN.4/682, para 72.
7 *See* Chapter 4 in this volume.
8 T Treves, 'Customary International Law', MPEPIL, para 50.
9 It is argued by Dawidowicz that practice of States on third-party countermeasures 'appears to be sufficiently widespread, representative and consistent to form the basis of a rule of customary international law'. M Dawidowicz, 'Third-Party Countermeasures: A Progressive Development of International Law?' (2016) QIL www.qil-qdi.org/third-party-countermeasures-progressive-development-international-law/ accessed 11 July 2017. For an opposing view *see* Focarelli, having doubts on the legal meaning of secondary rules contained in Articles on Responsibility of States for Internationally Wrongful Acts this being a doctrinal product, 'hence they are nothing "legal" at all'. C Focarelli, 'International Law and Third-Party Countermeasures in the Age of Global Instant Communication' (2016) QIL www.qil-qdi.org/international-law-third-party-countermeasures-age-global-instant-communication/ accessed 11 July 2017, 19. On the question of the adoption of countermeasures by not-directly injured States *see* also: C Tams, *Enforcing Obligations Erga Omnes in International Law* (Cambridge University Press 2005) 231. On the question of the adoption of countermeasures by international organisations *see*: F Dopagne, *Les contre-mesures des organisations internationals* (Parution 2010).

This chapter is structured as follows. It first explains and defines relevant basic concepts including the notion of sanctions, protest, *erga omnes* obligations, and briefly addresses the question of attribution (1). It then turns to clarify the role that sanctions adopted by international organisations play in consolidation, clarification, and prevention of emergence of customary international law (2). Finally, the contribution of sanctions to the ascertainment of custom, with a specific focus on distinction between the objective (practice) and subjective (*opinio juris*) element (3) is assessed. In closing, the chapter offers some concluding remarks (4).

1 Setting the stage: sanctions adopted by international organisations in response to violations of *erga omnes* obligations

1.1 Sanctions

There is no common understanding of the notion of sanction in positive international law.[10] Against this background the notion of sanctions is a source of significant controversy and is associated with various notions that have different legal connotation (e.g. retorsion, institutional sanctions or collective measures, countermeasures).[11] For the purpose of this chapter defining the criteria for identification of sanction will not be of paramount importance; it suffices to accept that sanctions are coercive reactions to previous wrongful acts.[12] It is acknowledged that in its work on responsibility the International Law Commission reserved the term sanctions for measures adopted on the basis of the constitutive acts of international organisations against their member States, and therefore distinguished them from the notion of

10 *Encyclopaedia of Public International Law* (Max Planck Institute for Comparative Public Law and International Law 2000) vol 4, 313.

11 Third report on State responsibility by Mr Gaetano Arangio-Ruiz and Add.1 (1991) UN Doc A/CN.4/440 YILC vol II part one, para 8; A Pellet and A Miron, 'Sanctions' The Max Planck Encyclopedia of Public International Law 6 (2012).

12 Regardless of different uses of the notion of sanctions, most authors agree that sanctions are reactions to a prior breach of international law. H Morgenthau, 'Théorie des sanctions internationales' (1935) 16 Rev Droit Int'l & Legis Comp 809–36; H Kelsen, 'Sanctions in International Law under the Charter of the United Nations' (1945) 31 IOwa l rEv 499; K Zemanek, 'The Unilateral Enforcement of International Obligations' (1987) 47 ZaöRV 32; M Doxey, 'International Sanctions in Theory and Practice' (1983) 15 Case W Res J Int'l L 273; JL Kunz, 'Sanctions in International Law' (1960) 54.2 AJIL 324–47; M Noortmann, *Enforcing International Law: From Self-Help to Self-Contained Regimes* (Ashgate 2005) 53; J d'Aspremont, 'The Collective Security System and the Enforcement of International Law' in M Weller, *The Oxford Handbook of the Use of Force in International Law* (Oxford University Press 2015) 131.

countermeasures.[13] However, this narrow understanding of sanctions as proposed by the International Law Commission is not accepted in this chapter, which uses sanction as a general term for measures which mean reaction to wrongfulness. Excluded from the analysis of this chapter are sanctions adopted by international organisations against their member States on the basis of provisions in their constitutive acts, including sanctions adopted under Chapter VII of the United Nations Charter.[14] The focus rather is on sanctions adopted against third States or against their member States on the basis of general international law. In respect of the latter cases the following discussion is without prejudice to the Article 22/2(b) of the Articles on the Responsibility of International Organizations[15] prescribing that measures adopted against member States remain consistent with the rules of the concerned international organisation.

Sanctions are unilateral acts opposite to those of recognition and their essence is to make it obvious that the international organisation perceives certain acts as inadmissible or wrongful under general international law. Protest is therefore an inherent part of every sanction.[16] The unilateral character of sanctions goes hand in hand with their self-assessed character,[17] which is important for the formation of customary international law, since it may disclose perception of an imposing authority of the status of acts to which they are reacting.

A wide range of types of sanctions are being adopted by international organisations. These include but are not limited to complete or partial interruption of economic relations, import and export restrictions, freezing of foreign assets, embargoes, travel restrictions, expulsion from or suspension of membership, suspension of aviation agreements, and severance of diplomatic relations.[18]

1.2 Distinguishing between the act of sanction and the act of protest

As has been stated above, sanctions are reactions to wrongful acts and protest is an inherent part of every sanction.[19] However, further delimitation of these two notions is necessary in order to discern and determine the role they play in the making of custom.

13 Articles on Responsibility of States for Internationally Wrongful Acts (2001) YILC, 2001, vol II Part Two 75.
14 Article 41 of the United Nations Charter 1945, 1 UNTS XVI.
15 Articles on the Responsibility of International Organizations (2011) YILC vol II, Part Two.
16 C Eick, 'Protest' MPEPIL, para 2.
17 D Alland, 'The Definition of Countermeasures' in J Crawford, A Pellet, S Olleson, and K Parlett, *The Law of International Responsibility* (Oxford University Press 2010) 1129.
18 *See* e.g. EU restrictive measures, Factsheet (2014) www.consilium.europa.eu/uedocs/cms_data/docs/pressdata/EN/foraff/135804.pdf accessed 11 July 2017.
19 C Eick, 'Protest' MPEPIL, para 2.

The act of sanction can be described as the adoption of a measure which is usually not reciprocal to the previous breach of international legal rule. International organisations, for example, commonly adopt measures in the form of e.g. suspension of landing rights, travel restrictions, and economic measures to react to breaches of e.g. genocide, human rights violations, and humanitarian law. It follows from this that the nature of a breach to which international organisations are reacting is in no way related to the nature of the act of sanction itself. In fact, the effects of the act of sanction are limited to the law in the field of which sanctions are adopted: e.g. suspension of landing rights or adoption of economic measures. In terms of material behaviours relevant for the formation of modern customary international law, sanctions in the form of e.g. countermeasures are often stated as being particularly strong evidence of practice.[20] However, on the basis of the above stated, it would be very difficult to argue that the act of sanction as such could be seen as practice relevant for the ascertainment of the customary nature of primary rules that are being breached and are the reason for the adoption of sanctions. While the very act of the adoption of sanction could fulfil the criteria of practice relevant for the ascertainment of custom in general, it cannot be seen as instrumental for the confirmation of customary status of primary rule as a reaction to which the sanction was adopted.

On the other hand, protest is understood here as a 'formal objection by subject of international law … against a conduct or claim purported to be contrary to or unfounded in international law'.[21] Even though protest is inherent to the notion of sanction, it is generally treated as a distinct legal institution.[22] Protests can be expressed in numerous ways: through diplomatic notes, orally, or in official documents and legislative acts. The purpose and legal effect of protest is to show that the protesting entity 'does not recognize, accept or acquiesce in the act or action, or preserves the right to challenge that act or action'.[23] It therefore relates to the statement made by international organisations on the wrongfulness of certain conduct that prompted the adoption of sanctions. Through protests, international organisations either express dissatisfaction with certain activities of States towards which they are reacting or provide legal justification for the adoption of sanctions under international law. They relate to the supposedly wrongful acts and occasionally include express referral to primary rules, the violation of which was a

20 T Treves, 'Customary International Law' MPEPIL, para 27.
21 C Eick, 'Protest' MPEPIL, para 2.
22 ibid. Occasionally protest can also be considered as being implied in the act of sanction, provided that the intention to protest is clear, ibid para 7.
23 A Cassese, *International Law* (2nd edn, Oxford University Press 2005) 184.

reason for the adoption of sanctions in the first place. It seems therefore that as opposed to the acts of sanctioning protests are of the greatest relevance for the customary status of primary rules, which is the focus of this chapter. In Section 4 I will assess their importance in terms of the two-element doctrine: practice and *opinio juris*.

1.3 Erga omnes *obligations*

In practice sanctions are increasingly being adopted by international organisations in cases where they cannot be considered as being individually affected by a certain breach of international law. Instead of protecting their individual interest, they shield and act in protection of a general interest. In particular, we have been witnessing a growing practice whereby international organisations adopt sanctions - occasionally referred to as 'solidarity measures',[24] 'collective countermeasures',[25] 'community measures',[26] or 'third-party countermeasures'[27] - against other subjects of international law (mostly States) on the occasion of what they consider as a breach of *erga omnes* obligations. These obligations are derived from general international law[28] and they exist between all subjects of international law, therefore, their application is in the interest of the international community as a whole.[29] Accordingly, they have to be distinguished from their treaty-based counterpart, *erga omnes*

24 JR Crawford, 'The Relationship Between Sanctions and Countermeasures' in V Gowlland-Debbas, MG Rubio, and H Hadj-Sahraoui, *United Nations Sanctions and International Law* (vol 1, Martinus Nijhoff 2001) 57–68; J Petman, 'Resort to Economic Sanctions by Not Directly Affected States' in LP Forlati and L-A Sicilianos (eds), *Les sanctions économiques en droit international/Economic sanctions in International Law* (Hague Academy of International Law, Martinus Njihoff 2004).

25 L-A Sicilianos, 'Countermeasures in Response to Grave Violations of Obligations Owed to the International Community' in J Crawford, A Pellet, S Olleson, and K Parlett, *The Law of International Responsibility* (Oxford University Press 2010) 1137.

26 J Petman, 'Resort to Economic Sanctions by Not Directly Affected States' in LP Forlati and L-A Sicilianos (eds), *Les sanctions économiques en droit international/Economic sanctions in International Law* (Hague Academy of International Law, Martinus Njihoff 2004) 315.

27 M Dawidowicz, *Third-Party Countermeasures in International Law* (Cambridge University Press 2017).

28 C Tams, *Enforcing Obligations Erga Omnes in International Law* (Cambridge University Press 2005)123.

29 *Barcelona Traction, Light and Power Company, Limited (Belgium v Spain)* (Judgment) ICJ Rep 3 [1970] para 33. *See* also M Ragazzi, *The Concept of International Obligations Erga Omnes* (Clarendon Press 1997).

partes.[30] When an obligation is classified as having *erga omnes* status this has certain effects under international law, due to the importance of rights involved in these obligations.[31] In particular, it transcends the traditional bilateral nature of obligations by affecting the rules of standing[32] to enforce such rights and the invocation of responsibility.[33] This manifests itself in the right of not-directly affected international organisations or States[34] to institute judicial proceedings or adopt countermeasures to enforce such rights.[35] It is on the latter consequence that this chapter focuses.

1.4 Attribution

Scholars nurture caution when it comes to assessing the practice of international organisations as autonomous subjects of international law, since it is sometimes difficult to differentiate between the practice of States and intentional organisations as such.[36] For international organisations to be able to contribute to customary law-making independently, the conduct must namely be attributable to international

30 *Erga omnes partes* is not perceived as conventional equivalent of obligations *erga omnes.* Christian Tams, *Enforcing Obligations Erga Omnes in International Law* (Cambridge University Press 2005) 125.

31 ibid 97.

32 *Barcelona Traction, Light and Power Company, Limited (Belgium v Spain)* (Judgment) ICJ Rep 3 [1970] para 33.

33 C Tams, *Enforcing Obligations Erga Omnes in International Law* (Cambridge University Press 2005) 99. For other effects *see* ibid 106–16. *See* also, Article 48 Articles on Responsibility of States for Internationally Wrongful Acts and corresponding commentary, Articles on Responsibility of States for Internationally Wrongful Acts (2001) YILC, 2001, vol II Part Two 126–27.

34 G Gaja, *The Protection of General Interests in the International Community* (Recueil des cours 364, Martinus Nijhoff 2011) 21; L-A Sicilianos, 'Countermeasures in Response to Grave Violations of Obligations Owed to the International Community' in J Crawford, A Pellet, S Olleson, and K Parlett, *The Law of International Responsibility* (Oxford University Press 2010) 1137.

35 Articles 48, 54 Articles on Responsibility of States for Internationally Wrongful Acts; Articles 49, 57 Articles on the Responsibility of International Organizations. *See* below, Chapter 3.

36 Second report on the identification of customary international law by Michael Wood (2014) UN Doc A/CN.4/672, para. 43; Third report on the identification of customary international law by Michael Wood (2015) UN Doc A/CN.4/682, para. 71; T Treves, 'Customary International Law' MPEPIL, para 50. It is acknowledged that certain acts of international organisations may reflect (collective) practice of its member States or that international organisations often act as a catalyser of State practice in terms of prompting reactions of member States, which counts as practice of States relevant for customary

organisations as such and not to their member States. A common argument undermining the importance of international organisations in customary lawmaking pertains to the relationship between organisations and their members stating that States create and control international organisations and therefore continue to be the leading actors,[37] while organisations are only vehicles for their member States.[38]

This chapter does not aim to answer the entangled question of attribution. It submits that occasions whereby international organisations as such and not their members adopt sanctions in reaction to the breach of *erga omnes* obligation and subsequently contribute to consolidation or emergence of custom exist. It suffices to mention only one case where this question seems to be fairly straightforward. That is in relation to adoption of sanctions by the EU. It is accepted today that the EU, as a supranational organisation, clearly has a place in customary international lawmaking and its practice is to be equated with that of States.[39] This is especially the case when sanctions are adopted in the form of economic measures which fall into the common commercial policy and are therefore under the exclusive competence of the EU.[40] Such measures are adopted by a regulation which is an act of legislation binding on all member States and has specific features of EU law. This was acknowledged by the EU itself[41] and the Special Rapporteur:

international lawmaking, e.g. through the adoption of resolutions. MH Mendelson, *The Formation of Customary International Law* (Recueil des cours 272, Martinus Nijhoff 1998) 201; R Jennings and A Watts (eds), *Oppenheim's International Law* (9th edn, vol I, Peace, Introduction and part 1, Longman 1992) 46–47; *Legality of the Threat or Use of Nuclear Weapons* (Advisory Opinion) ICJ Rep 226 [1996] 258, para 81.

37 Third report on the identification of customary international law by Michael Wood (2015) UN Doc A/CN.4/682, para 70. *See* also L Hannikainen, 'The Collective Factor as a Promoter of Customary International Law' (2006) 6 Baltic Yearbook of International Law 125, 130.

38 J Klabbers, 'International Organizations in the Formation of Customary International Law' in E Cannizzaro and P Palchetti, *Customary International Law on the Use of Force: A Methodological Approach* (Martinus Nijhoff 2005) 179, 183.

39 Third report on the identification of customary international law by Michael Wood (2015) UN Doc A/CN.4/682, para 77.

40 In certain cases, practice may count as that of member States as well as that of international organisations. Such would be the case for example in cases of the adoption of measures by the EU which fall under shared competences of the EU. MH Mendelson, *The Formation of Customary International Law* (Recueil des cours 272, Martinus Nijhoff 1998) 201, 202, ft 94.

41 'The Union acted on the international plane on the basis of competences conferred upon it by its founding treaties. It was a contracting party to a significant number of international agreements, alongside States. Moreover, in several areas covered by international law it had exclusive competences. Those special characteristics gave it a

> the practice of those international organizations (such as the European Union) to which member States sometimes have transferred exclusive competences, may be equated with that of States, since in particular fields such organizations act in place of the member States. This applies to the actions of such organizations, whatever forms they take, whether executive, legislative or judicial. If one were not to equate the practice of such international organizations with that of States, it would in fact mean that, not only would the organization's practice not count for State practice, but its Member States would be deprived or reduced of their ability to contribute to State practice in cases where the Member States have conferred some of their public powers to the organization.[42]

2 Consolidation and clarification of existing custom and prevention of the emergence of new customary international law

In the following two sections this chapter distinguishes between two situations in the course of which sanctions adopted by international organisations will play a different role in relation to customary international law.

The first situation refers to instances where an international organisation is reacting to breaches of obligations that already have an *erga omnes* status and therefore legal basis for the adoption of such sanctions can be found in the secondary rules on the responsibility of States and international organisations, in particular the law of countermeasures. Countermeasures are governed by the Articles on Responsibility of States for Internationally Wrongful Acts,[43] the Articles on the Responsibility of International Organizations,[44] and customary international law[45] and are one of the circumstances precluding wrongfulness, giving a State or an international organisation injured by a wrongful act of the responsible State a right to take measures that would otherwise be contrary to international law.

particular role in the formation of customary international law, to which it could contribute directly through its actions and practices.' Statement on behalf of the European Union (2013) A/C.6/68/SR.23, para 37. *See* also Jan Vanhamme, 'Formation and Enforcement of Customary International Law: the European Union's Contribution' (2008) 39 Netherlands Yearbook of International Law 127–54.

42 Footnotes omitted. UN Doc. A/CN.4/672, para 44. *See* also T Treves, 'Customary International Law' MPEPIL, para 52.

43 Articles on Responsibility of States for Internationally Wrongful Acts (2001) YILC, 2001, vol II Part Two.

44 Articles on the Responsibility of International Organizations (2011) YILC vol II, Part Two.

45 *Naulilaa Incident Arbitration (Portugal v Germany)* 2 RIAA [1928] 1012; *Gabčíkovo-Nagymaros Project (Hungary v Slovakia)* (Judgment) ICJ Rep 7 [1997]; *Air Services Agreement of 27 March 1946 between the United States of America and France*, RIAA [1978] vol XVIII.

Apart from these 'classical' countermeasures, the law of responsibility also presupposes countermeasures by not-directly affected States or international organisations[46] in cases of breaches of *erga omnes* obligations,[47] which are relevant for the present chapter. Even though the International Law Commission left the legality of the adoption of such measures to be determined by further development of international law,[48] the view that they can legally be taken in the contemporary international community due to increased practice in this respect is becoming firmly established amongst international lawyers[49] and other important international institutions, such as the Institut de droit international.[50]

When it comes to the entitlement of international organisations to adopt countermeasures in response to breaches of *erga omnes* obligations, it also remains questionable to what extent such entitlement depends upon their competences. While international organisations are deemed to have 'those powers which, though not expressly provided in the Charter, are conferred upon it by necessary implication as being essential to the performance of its duties',[51] it is less clear to what extent the application of such powers in the form of the adoption of countermeasures is

46 Article 54 Articles on Responsibility of States for Internationally Wrongful Acts; Article 57 Articles on the Responsibility of International Organizations.

47 *Barcelona Traction, Light and Power Company, Limited (Belgium v Spain)* (Judgment) ICJ Rep 3 [1970] para 33. *See* also *The case of East Timor (Portugal v Australia)*, 90 ICJ Rep [1995] 102; Report of the International Law Commission (2001) UN Doc A/56/10, 208.

48 UN Doc A/56/10, Commentary to Chapter II, 139.

49 M Dawidowicz, *Third-Party Countermeasures in International Law* (Cambridge University Press 2017); Martin Dawidowicz, 'Third-Party Countermeasures: A Progressive Development of International Law?' (2016) QIL www.qil-qdi.org/third-party-countermeasures-progressive-development-international-law/ accessed 11 July 2017; Christian Tams, *Enforcing Obligations Erga Omnes in International Law* (Cambridge University Press 2005); F Dopagne, *Les contre-mesures des organisations internationals* (Parution 2010); F Dopagne, 'Sanctions and Countermeasures by International Organisations' in R Collins and ND White (eds), *International Organizations and the Idea of Autonomy: Institutional Independence in the International Legal Order* (Routledge 2011); J d'Aspremont, 'The Multifaceted Concept of the Autonomy of International Organizations and International Legal Discourse' in R Collins and ND White (eds), *International Organizations and the Idea of Autonomy: Institutional Independence in the International Legal Order* (Routledge 2011) 63–86; EK Proukaki, *The Problem of Enforcement in International Law: Countermeasures, the Non-Injured State and the Idea of International Community* (Routledge 2010). For the contrary view *see* J Crawford, *State Responsibility: The General Part* (Cambridge University Press 2013) 706, 709.

50 Institut de droit international, Krakow resolution 2005.

51 *Reparation for injuries suffered in the service of the United Nations* (Advisory Opinion) ICJ Rep [1949] 182. Seyersted concludes in this respect that '[intergovernmental

limited to breaches of rules, the observation of which falls in the functions of a particular organisation. As regards the adoption of countermeasures in response to violations of *erga omnes* obligations, the International Law Commission in its work on the responsibility of international organisations resorted to a conservative view. It adopted a position that a not-directly injured international organisation is entitled to invoke responsibility for breaches of *erga omnes* obligations only insofar as safeguarding these obligation falls within the functions of the international organisation invoking responsibility.[52] According to this view, the adoption of countermeasures by international organisations in response to *erga omnes* violations is therefore limited with the functions of the international organisation. Some authors, however, are of the opinion that such limitations are not warranted, and are probably based on a confusion between the notion of the standing of the international organisation to resort to countermeasures (as a question of general international law) and competence of an international organisation to take a particular countermeasure (a question subject to rules of the organisation). Entitlement under general international law namely cannot be conditioned upon the rules of a particular organisation.[53] The question of the entitlement of international organisations and States is, however, not the object of the present research and will therefore not be further considered.

In cases of the adoption of sanctions in response to violations of *erga omnes* obligations, an international organisation will found legal basis in the Articles on Responsibility of States for Internationally Wrongful Acts,[54] whereas in cases of sanctions against other international organisations, provisions of the Articles on the Responsibility of International Organizations will come into play.[55] The examples

organizations have also presented international claims and made representations and protests to States, despite the fact that hardly any constitution of an intergovernmental organization (or State) authorizes them to do so'. F Seyersted, 'Objective International Personality of Intergovernmental Organizations: Do Their Capacities Really Depend upon the Conventions Establishing Them' (1964) Nordisk Tidsskrift Int'l Ret 26.

52 This is due to the fact that international organisations do not possess a general competence under international law, but have been established to exercise specific functions (the so-called 'principle of speciality'). Articles on the Responsibility of International Organizations (2011) YILC vol II, Part Two 3. *See* also: C Eick, 'Protest' MPEPIL, para 3; UN Doc A/CN.4/672, para 43.

53 J d'Aspremont, 'The Multifaceted Concept of the Autonomy of International Organizations and International Legal Discourse' in R Collins and ND White (eds), *International Organizations and the Idea of Autonomy: Institutional Independence in the International Legal Order* (Routledge 2011) 72.

54 Articles 48 and 54 Articles on Responsibility of States for Internationally Wrongful Acts.

55 Articles 49 and 57 Articles on the Responsibility of International Organizations.

of existing obligations that have *erga omnes* status include prohibition of the act of aggression and genocide, principles and rules concerning the basic rights of the human person, including protection from slavery, racial discrimination,[56] self-determination of peoples,[57] some obligations of international humanitarian law,[58] and prohibition of the use of force.[59] On the occasions when an international organisation is reacting to breaches of such already established *erga omnes* obligations which subsequently also have a status of custom, their sanctions will contribute not to the making of new custom, but to consolidation and clarification of existing custom and prevention of the emergence of new customary international law. By definition, *erga omnes* obligations namely derive from general international law.[60]

In terms of consolidation of customary status of these *erga omnes* obligations, sanctions help to strengthen the existing rule of customary international law.[61] The process of the creation of custom is namely a continuing one, 'and every act which conforms to an established practice helps to strengthen it, and every act which violates it helps to undermine it'.[62] Therefore, objections in the form of sanctions to violations of customary international law rules help to neutralise violations and in cases where they are successful even help to strengthen the existing rule of customary international law.[63]

In a similar vein, such sanctions and their legal justifications can provide clarification as to the content of a particular existing customary rule. In what is sometimes called the 'mature stage of customary rule', the adoption of sanctions by international organisations and their subsequent interpretative practice can contribute to the clarification of certain customary international law rule.[64]

56 *Barcelona Traction, Light and Power Company, Limited (Belgium v Spain)* (Judgment) [1970] ICJ Rep 3, 32, para 34; M Ragazzi, *The Concept of International Obligations Erga Omnes* (Clarendon Press 1997) 74–117.
57 *Case Concerning East Timor (Portugal v Australia)* (Judgement) ICJ Rep 90 [1995] 102, para 29.
58 Legal Consequences of the Construction of a Wall in the Occupied Palestinian Territory (Advisory Opinion) [2004] ICJ Rep 136, paras 155–57.
59 *See* e.g. Commentary by the International Law Commission to Article 53 of the subsequent Vienna Convention on the Law of Treaties (1966) YILC Vol II, 248, para 3.
60 T Treves, 'Customary International Law' MPEPIL, para 82.
61 MH Mendelson, *The Formation of Customary International Law* (Recueil des cours 272, Martinus Nijhoff 1998) 283, ft 352.
62 ibid.
63 ibid.
64 ibid 283–84. Some scholars warn that such practice has to be carefully distinguished from behavioural practice supporting this very same legal rule. J d'Aspremont,

In addition, acts of international organisations in the form of the adoption of sanctions with the aim of opposing certain behaviour of States can also prevent certain customary international rule from coming into being. For a rule to become part of custom, one of the preconditions namely is that practice is sufficiently representative.[65] If there exist protests of international organisation against certain behaviour of another international legal subject, this may contribute to prevention of such behaviour from becoming part of customary international law. The value of protests in the prevention of customary law from coming into being was confirmed by the Permanent Court of International Justice in the *Lotus* case.[66]

It is acknowledged that contribution of sanctions to custom in accordance to this first scenario remains rather modest and it is in the framework of the second situation that sanctions have greater potential to custom making.

3 Ascertainment of new customary international law

It is on the occasions when international organisations react to breaches that do not yet have a status of an *erga omnes* obligation that their contribution to customary lawmaking is the most prominent. This chapter approaches the question of sanctions' contribution to custom from the perspective of the traditional two-element doctrine for the ascertainment of customary international law[67] as it has

'Customary International Law as a Dance Floor: Part II' (2014) EJIL: *Talk!* www.ejiltalk.org/customary-international-law-as-a-dance-floor-part-ii/ accessed 11 July 2017.

65 MH Mendelson, *The Formation of Customary International Law* (Recueil des cours 272, Martinus Nijhoff 1998) 227.

66 *SS 'Lotus' (France v Turkey)* [1927] PCIJ Series A, no 10, 29. *See* also IC MacGibbon, 'Customary International Law and Acquiescence' (1957) 33 Brit YB Int'l L 124.

67 Article 38/1(b) of the Statute of ICJ; UN Doc A/CN.4/672, para 21; R Jennings and A Watts (eds), *Oppenheim's International Law* (9th edn, vol I, Peace, Introduction and part 1, Longman 1992) 25–31; A Cassese, *International Law* (2nd edn, Oxford University Press 2005) 156. This approach was also confirmed by the ICJ in *Continental Shelf (Libyan Arab Jamahiriya v Malta)* (Judgment) [1985] ICJ Rep 13, 29; *Jurisdictional Immunities of the State (Germany v Italy: Greece intervening)* (Judgment) [2012] ICJ Rep 99, 122, para 55; *North Sea Continental Shelf (Federal Republic of Germany v Denmark; Federal Republic of Germany v Netherlands)* (Judgment) [1969] ICJ Rep 3, 44, para 77; *Case Concerning Military and Paramilitary Activities in and against Nicaragua (Nicaragua v United States of America)* (Merits) [1986] ICJ Rep 14, 97. For deficiencies of this approach *see*: J d'Aspremont, 'The Decay of Modern Customary International Law in Spite of Scholarly Heroism' (2015) 2015 Global Community: Yearbook of International Law and Jurisprudence 2016.

been confirmed by the International Law Commission in its recent work on customary international law.[68]

3.1 Protests as a form of practice

One of the mysteries permeating debates about custom relates to finding of relevant practice necessary for the ascertainment of custom. This element is based on the series of instances of conducts in which a pattern may be observed.[69] When assessing practice relevant for custom, we have to distinguish between two separate issues: 'the selection of practice that contributes to the creation of customary international law and the assessment of whether this practice establishes a rule of customary international law'.[70] It is the former that is addressed in this chapter.

The question whether and to what extent international organisations can contribute to practice relevant for custom has been subject to debates in the International Law Commission. Conclusion 4(2) confirms that 'in certain cases, the practice of international organizations also contributes to the formation, or expression, of rules of customary international law'.[71] However, the final version of the commentaries limited practice of international organisations relevant for the formation of custom to those rules '(a) whose subject matter falls within the mandate of the organizations, and/or (b) that are addressed specifically to them (such as those on their international responsibility or relating to treaties to which international organizations may be parties)'.[72] This position implies that international organisations will only be able to contribute to customary status of those (*in statu nascendi*) *erga omnes* obligations falling within their functions or codified in treaties to which an international organisation adopting sanctions is a party. The International Law

68 *See* Conclusion 2, Identification of customary international law, Report of the International Law Commission, Seventieth session (2018) UN Doc A/73/10: 'To determine the existence and content of a rule of customary international law, it is necessary to ascertain whether there is a general practice that is accepted as law (*opinio juris*).' *See* also UN Doc A/CN.4/672, Chapter IV.

69 ibid para 32.

70 International Committee of the Red Cross (ICRC), Customary Humanitarian International Law, Assessment of customary international law https://ihl-databases.icrc.org/customary-ihl/eng/docs/v1_rul_in_asofcuin accessed 11 July 2017.

71 Conclusion 4(2), Identification of customary international law, Report of the International Law Commission, Seventieth session (2018) UN Doc A/73/10.

72 Commentary to Conclusion 4(2), Identification of customary international law, Report of the International Law Commission, Seventieth session (2018) UN Doc A/73/10.

Commission again resorted to a restrictive approach[73] which preposterously limits the role of international organisations in custom making even in relation to those general international legal rules which by definition exist between all subjects of international law.[74] All States and international organisations are considered to have an interest in respect of *erga omnes* obligations[75]and are subsequently deemed capable to contribute to their customary status.

It is important to distinguish between internal, purely institutional practice 'giving rise to a customary rule within the "proper law" of the organisation concerned',[76] also referred to as 'the practice of the organization',[77] and practice of international

73 *See* above analysis on the adoption of countermeasures by international organisations in response to *erga omnes* violations.

74 When talking about practice of international organisations in relation to *erga omnes* obligations and their customary status, we have to distinguish between practice relevant for the ascertainment of custom from practice relevant for the identification of *erga omnes* obligations. As opposed to the ascertainment of custom, there is no prescribed way of identification of *erga omnes* obligations. Sanctions could be perceived as one of the 'ways and means of identifying obligations' with the *erga omnes* character, since status of concepts is often inferred from responses against misconduct. The very act of the adoption of sanction by not-directly injured international organisation that manifests itself in breach of a certain (non-reciprocal) international legal rule owed to the perpetrating State, can have a bearing on the *erga omnes* status of primary rule the breach of which prompted such reaction. When the not-directly injured international organisation reacts to a breach of primary rule with the adoption of non-reciprocal measures that are contrary to its international legal obligations, this may demonstrate its belief that it is reacting to the breach of *erga omnes* obligation owed to the international community as a whole. This is the so called 'indirect evidence' for the determination of the *erga omnes* status of certain obligations and must be differentiated from practice relevant for the secondary rules of international law pertaining to countermeasures and reaction to wrongfulness as well as practice relevant for the ascertainment of custom. *See* also C Tams, *Enforcing Obligations Erga Omnes in International Law* (Cambridge University Press 2005) Chapter 4, 154.

75 Article 48/1(b) Articles on Responsibility of States for Internationally Wrongful Acts, Article 49 Articles on the Responsibility of International Organizations.

76 A Pellet, 'Article 38' in A Zimmermann et al (eds), *The Statute of the International Court of Justice: A Commentary* (2nd edn, Oxford University Press 2012) 817; C Peters, 'Subsequent Practice and Established Practice of International Organizations: Two Sides of the Same Coin?' (2011) 3 Goettingen Journal of International Law; D Vignes, 'The Impact of International Organizations on the Development and Application of Public International Law' in RStJ Macdonald and DM Johnston (eds) *The Structure and Process of International Law: Essays in Legal Philosophy, Doctrine and Theory* (vol 6, Martinus Nijhoff 1986) 828.

77 *See* definition of 'rules of organisation' in the Vienna Convention on the Law of Treaties between States and International Organizations or between International Organizations

organisations in their external relations, which this chapter focuses on. In 1950 the International Law Commission stated that 'records of the cumulating practice of international organisations may be regarded as evidence of customary international law with reference to States' relations to the organisations',[78] however, it is clear today that the practice of international organisations has broader implications for customary lawmaking and is especially important in their external relations.[79]

Scholarly views on the nature of protests and their relevance for customary lawmaking are divided. Traditionally, protests are considered as an evidence of practice[80] and were historically particularly important for the creation of customary law when manifested in the form of diplomatic protest.[81] According to this view protests can be, as any other written statements,[82] considered as practice relevant for

(1986) Article 2/1(i) and Article 2(a) Articles on the Responsibility of International Organizations.

78 Report of the International Law Commission, Ways and means for making the evidence of customary international law more readily available (1950) YILC, vol II, 372.

79 Third report on the identification of customary international law by Michael Wood (2015) UN Doc A/CN.4/682; A Pellet, 'Article 38' in A Zimmermann et al (eds), *The Statute of the International Court of Justice: A Commentary* (2nd edn, Oxford University Press 2012) 817; MH Mendelson, *The Formation of Customary International Law* (Recueil des cours 272, Martinus Nijhoff 1998) 201.

80 MH Mendelson, *The Formation of Customary International Law* (Recueil des cours 272, Martinus Nijhoff 1998) 204, 291; T Treves, 'Customary International Law' MPEPIL, para. 50; International Committee of the Red Cross (ICRC), Customary Humanitarian International Law, Assessment of customary international law https://ihl-databases.icrc.org/customary-ihl/eng/docs/v1_rul_in_asofcuin accessed 11 July 2017. Unilateral acts such as protests are sometimes also considered as possible additional sources or lawmaking processes, however, for the purpose of this contribution we will not evaluate the nature of protests as a separate independent source, but rather their role in customary lawmaking. *See* e.g. A Cassese, *International Law* (2nd edn, Oxford University Press 2005) 184; H Thirlway, 'The Sources of International Law' in MD Evans, *International Law* (3rd edn, Oxford University Press 2010).

81 MH Mendelson, *The Formation of Customary International Law* (Recueil des cours 272, Martinus Nijhoff 1998) 205, 206. *See* case *De Meeüs v Forzano* [1939] Italian Court of Cassation.

82 Verbal acts are considered as practice that contributes to the creation of customary international law by the International Court of Justice, the International Law Commission, the International Law Association, and the International Committee of the Red Cross. *See* respectively *Case Concerning Military and Paramilitary Activities in and against Nicaragua (Nicaragua v United States of America)* (Merits) [1986] ICJ Rep 14, 100, para 190; YILC (1950) vol II, 368–372; ILA, Final Report of the Committee on the Formation of Customary (General) International Law, Statement of Principles Applicable to the

customary international lawmaking.[83] The Special Rapporteur's non-exhaustive list of types of practice and its manifestation contains 'diplomatic acts and correspondence' which include protests against the practice of other subjects.[84] On the other hand, however, some scholars warn over deficiencies related to this reasoning and pinpoint confusion and complexity relating to the separation of two elements of custom.[85] According to this view it remains questionable whether we could understand practice to include written documents whereby intentional organisations state their opinion on the existing rule of international law and provide qualification of certain situations.[86] Rather, practice should be seen as something subjects actually do (physical acts) and not what they say about certain rules (verbal acts).

It is acknowledged that differentiating between the two elements of custom, practice and *opinio juris*, is sometimes difficult, which makes it hard to consider them separately.[87] However, since protests can disclose a perception of an international organisation about what is possibly prohibited under general international law, it seems more reasonable to conclude that protests have a more significant role to play in the determination of *opinio juris* than they do in terms of practice. The International Law Commission seems to have adopted a middle ground solution in

Formation of General Customary International Law (2000), Report of the Sixty-Ninth Conference, Principle 4 and commentary (a), 725–26; International Committee of the Red Cross (ICRC), Customary Humanitarian International Law, Assessment of customary international law https://ihl-databases.icrc.org/customary-ihl/eng/docs/v1_rul_in_asofcuin accessed 11 July 2017.

83 MH Mendelson, *The Formation of Customary International Law* (Recueil des cours 272, Martinus Nijhoff 1998) 204, 291; T Treves, 'Customary International Law' MPEPIL, para 50.

84 UN Doc A/CN.4/672, 22. *See* also Report of the International Law Commission, Sixty-Sixth session (2014) UN Doc A/69/10, 245; Report of the International Law Commission, Sixty-Eighth session (2016) UN Doc A/71/10, 99.

85 *See* J d'Aspremont, 'Customary International Law as a Dance Floor: Part II' (2014) EJIL: *Talk!* www.ejiltalk.org/customary-international-law-as-a-dance-floor-part-ii/ accessed 11 July 2017; J d'Aspremont, 'The Decay of Modern Customary International Law in Spite of Scholarly Heroism' (2015) 2015 Global Community: Yearbook of International Law and Jurisprudence 2016.

86 On the importance of distinction between declarative and constitutive processes of customary lawmaking *see* J d'Aspremont, 'Customary International Law as a Dance Floor: Part II' (2014) EJIL: *Talk!* www.ejiltalk.org/customary-international-law-as-a-dance-floor-part-ii/ accessed 11 July 2017.

87 UN Doc A/CN.4/672, para 28; MH Mendelson, *The Formation of Customary International Law* (Recueil des cours 272, Martinus Nijhoff 1998) 290–93.

this respect by arguing that protests are relevant for the ascertainment of practice as well as for the ascertainment of *opinio juris*.[88]

3.2 *Protests as a form of* opinio juris

In its earlier work the International Law Commission adopted a State-centric approach to the second element of custom;[89] however, in the final version of the commentaries to conclusions it rightfully recognised that forms of evidence of *opinio juris* as specified in Conclusion 10(2) *mutatis mutandis* apply to the forms of evidence of *opinio juris* of international organisations.[90]

To fulfil the criteria of *opinio juris*,[91] sanctions of international organisations must be carried out in such a way as to be evidence of a belief that they are based on the existence of a breach of a primary international rule which is legally binding under customary law.[92] In other words, there needs to exist legal conviction that conduct of international organisations is justified in legal terms, they have to believe that they are applying 'a mandatory rule of customary international law'.[93] This psychological element distinguishes mere practice or usage from custom.[94]

88 For protests amounting to practice *see*: UN Doc A/CN.4/672, 22. *See* also UN Doc A/69/10, 245. For protests being understood as *opinio juris see* the explanation given by the chairman of the drafting committee on the notion of 'public statements made on behalf of States' which 'comprises all kind of declarations made publicly by States or State officials in domestic or international *fora*, such as official statements by a Government official, official statements before legislatures or courts, or public protests'. Identification of customary international law, Statement of the Chairman of the Drafting Committee, Mr Mathias Forteau (2015).

89 *See* Draft conclusions 9 and 10 with commentaries, Report of the International Law Commission Sixty-eighth session (2016) UN Doc A/71/10.

90 Commentaries to Conclusion 10, Identification of customary international law, Report of the International Law Commission, Seventieth session (2018) UN Doc A/73/10. *See* also Fifth report on the identification of customary international law by Michael Wood (2018) UN Doc A/CN.4/717, para 83; Statement of the Chair of the Drafting Committee, Mr Charles Chernor Jalloh, Identification of customary international law (2018) 12.

91 *See* also Chapters 2 and 5 in this volume.

92 Article 38 of the Statute of the ICJ; *North Sea Continental Shelf (Federal Republic of Germany v Denmark; Federal Republic of Germany v Netherlands)* (Judgment) [1969] ICJ Rep 3, para 77.

93 ibid para 76.

94 UN Doc A/CN.4/672, para 61.

Indeed, protests often indicate such belief and may 'afford evidence of the acceptance of practice as law'.[95] They disclose a certain legal view of the protesting party on the matter in question. Examples relevant for this chapter include cases where an international organisation reacts to a certain breach of obligation with which it cannot be seen as directly affected and that does not have a clear *erga omnes* status yet. Reaction to such breaches may indicate that an international organisation believes that these norms have a status of custom (or should become part of it) and subsequently consider themselves as deemed to enforce them. Even though the legality of the act of sanction itself under the law of countermeasures may be questioned in these situations, this does not undermine the contribution of a protest inherent in the sanction to the formation of customary international law. Legal uncertainty instead has the potential to reinforce the *opinio juris* inherent in protest against certain breaches of international law that they perceive as being customary. International organisations namely risk breaching the law themselves in order to protest against breaches of other subjects.

This being said, there however exists a hindrance to the contribution of international organisations to *opinio juris* as described above. In practice, international organisations, like States,[96] avoid clearly stipulating the legal framework of their coercive conducts. Most of the time they do not refer to the precise breach of international law they are reacting to. When adopting sanctions against Russia, the EU for example adopted them inter alia on the basis of 'Russia's actions destabilising the situation in Ukraine'.[97] In cases like this, it is not clear in what way the EU perceives the actions of Russia to be contrary to international law. Similarly, when adopting sanctions against Libya[98] the EU argued that sanctions are necessary due to the 'threat that continues to be posed to the peace, stability or security of Libya' and the 'seriousness of the situation in Libya'.[99] Another

95 IC MacGibbon, 'Customary International Law and Acquiescence' (1957) 33 Brit YB Int'l L 124. *See* also UN Doc A/CN.4/672, para 75.

96 EK Proukaki, *The Problem of Enforcement in International Law: Countermeasures, the Non-Injured State and the Idea of International Community* (Routledge 2010) 93.

97 Council Decision 2014/512/CFSP of 31 July 2014 concerning restrictive measures in view of Russia's actions destabilising the situation in Ukraine, OJEU L 229/13; Council Regulation (EU) no 833/2014 of 31 July 2014 concerning restrictive measures in view of Russia's actions destabilising the situation in Ukraine OJEU L 229/1.

98 On this occasion the EU adopted sanctions that were additional to the ones imposed by the United Nations.

99 Council decision 2011/137/CFSP of 28 February 2011 concerning restrictive measures in view of the situation in Libya.

example is the adoption of Arab League sanctions against Syria, in the form of suspension of membership and economic sanctions, without having legal basis in the constitutive act.[100] The main reason for the adoption of sanctions was continued violence and non-adherence of Syria to the Plan of Action which it has agreed upon.[101]

These examples confirm that legal reasoning for the adoption of sanctions is often rather scant and can hardly be seen as sufficient for the ascertainment of customary status of particular international rule. As was stressed by the Special Rapporteur, 'mere adherence to an alleged rule does not generally suffice as evidence of opinion juris'.[102] Indeed, the adoption of sanctions manifests the evidence that international organisations perceive certain activities to be inadmissible or contrary to international law, however, it is sometimes less clear which exact international legal rule is being breached. This necessarily limits the value of such practice for subjective element in customary international lawmaking. Often these are politically motivated measures adopted without proper legal assessment[103] and clarification of legal positions of international organisations. It is therefore hard to distinguish between voluntary participation in practice and practice accompanied by the sense of a legal obligation aimed at recognising the legal character of an emerging rule.[104] Another difficulty relates to the fact that often sanctions themselves amount to breaches of intentional law.[105] Without substantial legal justification for the adoption of sanction it will therefore be hard to distinguish between measures not compatible with existing international law from those that are the beginning of an evolution of the law.[106]

4 Concluding remarks

Through the adoption of sanctions in response to violations of *erga omnes* obligations and in particular protests inherent to them, international organisations can

100 *See* also M Dawidowicz, *Third-Party Countermeasures in International Law* (Cambridge University Press 2017) 224–25.

101 Arab League Council Resolution 7438, adopted at a resumed extraordinary Session on 12 November 2011.

102 UN Doc A/CN.4/672, para 72.

103 *Asylum Case (Colombia v Peru)* (Merits) [1950] ICJ Rep 266, 277.

104 GM Danilenko, 'The Theory of International Customary Law' (1988) 31 German YB Int'l L 32, 33.

105 For example, measures in the form of asset freezes and economic sanctions may amount to violation of bilateral or multilateral agreements (e.g. World Trade Organization agreements).

106 T Treves, 'Customary International Law' MPEPIL, para 28.

contribute to the making of customary international law. In assessing this contribution, we have to differentiate between two different situations. The first situation refers to instances whereby international organisations react to breaches of obligations that already have an *erga omnes* status and their standing to adopt sanctions is uncontested. In such instances, international organisations contribute to consolidation and clarification of custom and may prevent the custom from coming into being. Ironically, however, the potential for customary lawmaking is greater in the second situation, when the *erga omnes* status of an obligation towards which an international organisation is reacting to is not confirmed yet. In fact, the illegality or legal uncertainty shrouding such sanctions does not preclude their potential in customary lawmaking. On the contrary, it seems to maximise their contribution, which is not entirely surprising, since the emergence of customary law has always included behaviour that has departed from existing legal standards.

However, the assessment of the contribution of sanctions adopted by international organisations to the customary lawmaking process must be approached with caution. Even though this chapter acknowledges the potential of the international organisations as separate legal subjects for the making of custom, this potential should not be overblown because sanctions in some cases are not adopted with the sense of illegality which limits their relevance for the subjective element (*opinio juris*).

Chapter 14

The International Committee of the Red Cross and custom

*Iris Müller**

International humanitarian law[1] is a branch of international law whose core treaties enjoy wide support: in particular, the 1949 Geneva Conventions have been universally acceded to or ratified.[2] Significant numbers of States have also become parties to other international humanitarian law treaties, such as the 1977 Protocols Additional to the Geneva Conventions: Additional Protocol I,[3] relating to international armed conflicts,[4] and Additional Protocol

* Legal Adviser, Legal Division, International Committee of the Red Cross. The views expressed in this chapter are those of the author alone and do not necessarily reflect those of the International Committee of the Red Cross. The chapter is based on a presentation given by the author at the workshop 'The Role of International Organizations and Non-State Actors in the Formation of Customary International Law' in Manchester, United Kingdom, on 27 January 2017.

1 International humanitarian law is sometimes also referred to as the 'law of armed conflict', the 'law of war' or 'jus in bello'.

2 Convention (I) for the Amelioration of the Condition of the Wounded and Sick in Armed Forces in the Field, Geneva, 12 August 1949; Convention (II) for the Amelioration of the Condition of Wounded, Sick and Shipwrecked Members of Armed Forces at Sea, Geneva, 12 August 1949; Convention (III) relative to the Treatment of Prisoners of War, Geneva, 12 August 1949; Convention (IV) relative to the Protection of Civilian Persons in Time of War, Geneva, 12 August 1949. For a regularly updated overview of parties to the main international humanitarian law treaties, including the Geneva Conventions, *see* 'Treaties, States Parties and Commentaries' (*ICRC*) https://ihl-databases.icrc.org/ihl accessed 16 November 2018.

3 Protocol Additional to the Geneva Conventions of 12 August 1949, and relating to the Protection of Victims of International Armed Conflicts (Protocol I), Geneva, 8 June 1977. At the time of writing, there were 174 States parties to Additional Protocol I; *see* ibid.

4 International armed conflicts are generally understood as armed conflicts between States. For details, *see* e.g. International Committee of the Red Cross, 'Commentary on the First Geneva Convention: Convention (I) for the Amelioration of the Condition of the Wounded and Sick in Armed Forces in the Field' (2nd edition, 2016), commentary to common Article 2, https://ihl-databases.icrc.org/ihl/full/GCI-commentary accessed 16 November 2018.

II,[5] relating to non-international armed conflicts.[6] The continuing relevance of customary international humanitarian law may therefore not be immediately evident.

However, the non-universal adherence to Additional Protocol I means that in international armed conflicts the applicable international humanitarian law treaty provisions can vary considerably, as the Protocol only applies between States that are parties to the Protocol.[7] In a non-international armed conflict, the applicability of Additional Protocol II – in addition to Article 3 common to the Geneva Conventions, which is the fundamental treaty provision governing non-international armed conflicts – depends on whether the State party to the conflict is a party to that Protocol and, furthermore, depends on additional conditions.[8] Moreover, even in a non-international armed conflict in which both common Article 3 and Additional Protocol II apply, their provisions are far from being as numerous and detailed as those laid down for international armed conflict in the Geneva Conventions and Additional Protocol I. Customary international humanitarian law is therefore often still of decisive importance in the regulation of today's armed conflicts, complementing treaty law as an equally relevant source of international law.

Questions related to customary international law – and especially customary international humanitarian law – have therefore long been of importance to the International Committee of the Red Cross (ICRC). The publication of the

5 Protocol Additional to the Geneva Conventions of 12 August 1949, and relating to the Protection of Victims of Non-International Armed Conflicts (Protocol II), Geneva, 8 June 1977. At the time of writing, there were 168 States parties to Additional Protocol II; *see* 'Treaties, States Parties and Commentaries' (*ICRC*) https://ihl-databases.icrc.org/ihl accessed 16 November 2018.

6 Non-international armed conflicts are generally understood as armed conflicts with at least one non-State party. For details, *see* e.g. International Committee of the Red Cross, 'Commentary on the First Geneva Convention: Convention (I) for the Amelioration of the Condition of the Wounded and Sick in Armed Forces in the Field' (2nd edition, 2016), commentary to common Article 3, https://ihl-databases.icrc.org/ihl/full/GCI-commentary accessed 16 November 2018.

7 In international armed conflicts to which more than two States are parties, of which some but not all are parties to Additional Protocol I, this can also mean that the Protocol is, for example, applicable between opposing States A and B, if both are party to the Protocol, but not between opposing States A and C, if State C is not a party to the Protocol.

8 *See* Article 1(1) of Additional Protocol II: 'which take place in the territory of a High Contracting Party between its armed forces and dissident armed forces or other organized armed groups which, under responsible command, exercise such control over a part of its territory as to enable them to carry out sustained and concerted military operations and to implement this Protocol' (emphasis added). These conditions do not govern the applicability of common Article 3.

International Committee of the Red Cross's study on 'Customary International Humanitarian Law' (the Study) in 2005 is a testament to that.[9] Since 2010, the Study has also been available on the International Committee of the Red Cross's online database on customary international humanitarian law (the Database), complemented by regular updates of the Study's practice part.[10] The International Committee of the Red Cross therefore also followed the work of the International Law Commission on the topic of the 'Identification of customary international law' with great interest.

This chapter is intended to address two main points: first, it gives an overview of the International Committee of the Red Cross's experience in the identification of customary international humanitarian law, related to its work on the Study (1). Second, it addresses specific questions concerning the role of non-State actors in the formation of customary international humanitarian law (2). It ends with a few concluding remarks (3).

1 The International Committee of the Red Cross's experience in the identification of customary international humanitarian law

In 1993, the International Conference for the Protection of War Victims, held in Geneva, reaffirmed in its final declaration 'the necessity to make the implementation of international humanitarian law more effective' and called upon 'the Swiss Government to convene an open[-]ended intergovernmental group of experts to study practical means of promoting full respect for and compliance with that law'.[11]

The Intergovernmental Group of Experts for the Protection of War Victims, thus convened in Geneva in January 1995, adopted a number of recommendations, among them that:

> the International Committee of the Red Cross be invited to prepare, with the assistance of experts on international humanitarian law representing various geographical regions and different legal systems, and in consultation with experts from governments and international organisations, a report on customary rules of international humanitarian law

9 Jean-Marie Henckaerts and Louise Doswald-Beck, *Customary International Humanitarian Law*, vol I (Rules), vol II (Practice) (Cambridge University Press and ICRC 2005, 2009 reprint).

10 'IHL Database, Customary IHL' (*ICRC*) https://ihl-databases.icrc.org/customary-ihl/eng/docs/home accessed 16 November 2018.

11 *See* 'Final declaration of the International Conference for the Protection of War Victims' (*ICRC* 1993) www.icrc.org/eng/resources/documents/misc/57jms8.htm accessed 16 November 2018.

applicable in international and non-international armed conflicts, and to circulate the report to States and competent international bodies.[12]

In December 1995, the 26th International Conference of the Red Cross and Red Crescent (International Conference)[13] endorsed the final declaration of the International Conference for the Protection of War Victims and the recommendations of the Intergovernmental Group of Experts for the Protection of War Victims, and, among other points, '*urge[d]* the International Committee of the Red Cross (ICRC) … to carry out the tasks entrusted to [it] by the Recommendations'.[14] Among those tasks was, as noted, the preparation of a 'report on customary rules of international humanitarian law applicable in international and non-international armed conflicts'.

The International Committee of the Red Cross 'accepted this mandate with gratitude and humility – gratitude because it appreciate[d] the international community's confidence in it as symbolised by this assignment, and humility since it was fully aware of the difficulty involved'.[15]

After worldwide research and consultation, the Study was published in 2005, almost ten years after the mandate given by the 26th International Conference. This interval alone indicates that the identification of customary international law

12 *See* 'Meeting of the intergovernmental group of experts for the Protection of War Victims, Geneva, 23–27 January 1995: Recommendations' (*ICRC* 1995) www.icrc.org/eng/resources/documents/article/other/57jmbm.htm accessed 16 November 2018.

13 According to Article 8 of the Statutes of the International Red Cross and Red Crescent Movement, the International Conference is the 'supreme deliberative body for the Movement'. It brings together the components of the Movement (National Red Cross and Red Crescent Societies, International Committee of the Red Cross, International Federation of Red Cross and Red Crescent Societies) and, notably, the States parties to the Geneva Conventions; *see* 'Statutes of the International Red Cross and Red Crescent Movement', adopted by the 25th International Conference of the Red Cross at Geneva in October 1986 and amended by the 26th International Conference of the Red Cross and Red Crescent at Geneva in December 1995 and by the 29th International Conference of the Red Cross and Red Crescent at Geneva in June 2006 (*ICRC* 2007) www.icrc.org/eng/resources/documents/misc/statutes-movement-220506.htm accessed 16 November 2018.

14 *See* operative paragraphs 3, 4, and 8 of Resolution 1 of the 26th International Conference, 'Resolutions of the 26th International Conference of the Red Cross and Red Crescent: Resolution 1' (*ICRC* 1996) www.icrc.org/eng/resources/documents/article/other/57jmvh.htm accessed 16 November 2018, emphasis in original.

15 *See* the foreword to the 2005 Study by then International Committee of the Red Cross President Jakob Kellenberger, in Jean-Marie Henckaerts and Louise Doswald-Beck, *Customary International Humanitarian Law*, vol I (Rules), vol II (Practice) (Cambridge University Press and ICRC 2005, 2009 reprint) xvi.

is not an easy undertaking, raising challenges ranging from methodological questions over the collection of relevant material, to, ultimately, the careful assessment of that material.[16] The fact that, to the author's knowledge, no similar study has been undertaken, either in the field of international humanitarian law or other areas of international law, may be another indication of the challenges involved.

Volume I of the Study identified 161 rules of customary international humanitarian law. Many – but not all – of them were found to be equally applicable in international and non-international armed conflict.[17] Volume II of the Study made accessible the material collected in the preparation of the Study. Since its publication, the Study has been referred to by a range of actors, such as national and international courts, United Nations bodies, and academia. It is also a regular reference in the International Committee of the Red Cross's own work. The same has been the case for the online Database since its creation in 2010.[18]

The Study's publication has also given rise to intense debate.[19] This was not a surprise, though; rather, it was one of the Study's objectives. As Yves Sandoz, then member of the International Committee of the Red Cross and former director of its department of international law and policy, noted in his foreword to the Study:

16 For a detailed overview of the Study's organisation and its approach in the assessment of customary international law, *see* ibid xxxvii–lviiff.

17 Examples of customary international humanitarian law rules that were found to be applicable only in international armed conflict include those related to occupation and to prisoner-of-war status (*see* e.g. rule 51 and rule 106, available at 'IHL Database, Customary IHL, Rules by Rule' (*ICRC*) https://ihl-databases.icrc.org/customary-ihl/eng/docs/v1_rul accessed 16 November 2018). Treaty international humanitarian law on non-international armed conflict does not contain provisions on these matters either.

18 For a detailed recent overview of the Study's and Database's use, *see* J-M Henckaerts and E Debuf, 'The ICRC and the Clarification of Customary International Humanitarian Law' in BD Lepard (ed), *Reexamining Customary International Law* (Cambridge University Press 2017) 161–88, 168–78ff.

19 *See*, for example, the critical comments by JB Bellinger III and WJ Haynes, 'A US Government Response to the International Committee of the Red Cross Study Customary International Humanitarian Law' 89 International Review of the Red Cross 443, www.icrc.org/en/international-review/article/us-government-response-international-committee-red-cross-study accessed 16 November 2018. *See* further Jean-Marie Henckaerts, 'Customary International Humanitarian Law: A Response to US Comments' 89 International Review of the Red Cross 473 www.icrc.org/en/international-review/article/customary-international-humanitarian-law-response-us-comments accessed 16 November 2018. As an example of further comments, *see* Elizabeth Wilmshurst and Susan Breau (eds) *Perspectives on the ICRC Study on Customary International Humanitarian Law* (Cambridge University Press 2007).

> The study is a still photograph of reality, taken with great concern for absolute honesty, that is, without trying to make the law say what one wishes it would say. I am convinced that this is what lends the study international credibility. But though it represents the truest possible reflection of reality, the study makes no claim to be the final word. It is not all-encompassing – choices had to be made – and no one is infallible … May it be read, discussed and commented on. May it prompt renewed examination of international humanitarian law and of the means of bringing about greater compliance and of developing the law … The study on customary international humanitarian law is more than the record of a worthy project – it is above all a challenge for the future.[20]

During the work on the Study, the International Committee of the Red Cross had to address many of the methodological questions that the International Law Commission faced in its work on the identification of customary international law. As its fundamental starting point, the Study decided to proceed on the understanding that the existence of a rule of customary international law – i.e. including customary international humanitarian law – requires the presence of two elements. Its introduction noted:

> The Statute of the International Court of Justice describes customary international law as 'a general practice accepted as law'. It is generally agreed that the existence of a rule of customary international law requires the presence of two elements, namely State practice (*usus*) and a belief that such practice is required, prohibited or allowed, depending on the nature of the rule, as a matter of law (*opinio juris sive necessitatis*).[21]

This fundamental understanding has been reaffirmed by the International Law Commission's Conclusions on the identification of customary international law and commentaries thereto adopted on second reading in 2018.[22]

As noted in the Study's introduction, though, the 'exact meaning and content of these two elements has been the subject of much academic writing'. As the introduction further explains, the 'approach taken in this study to determine whether

20 Jean-Marie Henckaerts and Louise Doswald-Beck, *Customary International Humanitarian Law*, vol I (Rules), vol II (Practice) (Cambridge University Press and ICRC 2005, 2009 reprint) xxiii–xxiv.

21 ibid xxxvii–xxxviiiff, footnote omitted, emphasis in original.

22 Report of the International Law Commission, Seventieth session (30 April–1 June and 2 July–10 August 2018), General Assembly, Official Records, Seventy-third session, Supplement no 10 (A/73/10), United Nations, New York, 2018, Chapter V. Identification of customary international law, 117–156, Conclusion 2 ('Two constituent elements') and commentary thereto, 124–26ff http://legal.un.org/docs/?symbol=A/73/10 accessed 16 November 2018.

a rule of general customary international law exists is a classic one, set out by the International Court of Justice in a number of cases'.[23]

Among the issues the Study faced in this respect, to name but one well-known example, was the question what forms of practice to take into account: only physical ('battlefield') practice or also verbal practice? The method adopted by the Study was to consider both physical and verbal acts of States as contributing to the formation of customary international law.[24] The appropriateness of this approach has now been clearly confirmed by the International Law Commission's Conclusions and commentaries.[25]

2 Non-State actors and the formation of customary international humanitarian law

Another question the Study needed to address when applying the fundamental two-elements approach was whose acts to take into account as 'general practice'? Turning from the International Committee of the Red Cross's experience in the identification

23 Jean-Marie Henckaerts and Louise Doswald-Beck, *Customary International Humanitarian Law*, vol I (Rules), vol II (Practice) (Cambridge University Press and ICRC 2005, 2009 reprint) xxxviii.

24 ibid xxxviii–xxxixff.

25 Report of the International Law Commission, Seventieth session (30 April–1 June and 2 July–10 August 2018), General Assembly, Official Records, Seventy-third session, Supplement no 10 (A/73/10), United Nations, New York, 2018, Chapter V. Identification of customary international law, 117–56, Conclusion 6 ('Forms of practice') and commentary thereto, 133–34ff. Conclusion 6 notes:

1. Practice may take a wide range of forms. It includes both physical and verbal acts. …
2. Forms of State practice include, but are not limited to: diplomatic acts and correspondence; conduct in connection with resolutions adopted by an international organization or at an intergovernmental conference; conduct in connection with treaties; executive conduct, including operational conduct 'on the ground'; legislative and administrative acts; and decisions of national courts.
3. There is no predetermined hierarchy among the various forms of practice.

The commentary to Conclusion 6 states:

(2) … While some have argued that it is only what States 'do' rather than what they 'say' that may count as practice for purposes of identifying customary international law, it is now generally accepted that verbal conduct (whether written or oral) may also count as practice.

For a discussion *see* also J-M Henckaerts and E Debuf, 'The ICRC and the Clarification of Customary International Humanitarian Law' in BD Lepard (ed), *Reexamining Customary International Law* (Cambridge University Press 2017) 161–88, 179–81ff.

of customary international humanitarian law in general to the particular question of 'Non-State Actors and the Formation of Customary International Law', the following aims to share some thoughts on non-State actors and the formation of customary international law in the specific area of international humanitarian law.

In its introduction, the Study is clear on the pre-eminence of States in the formation of customary international humanitarian law, pointing out that it is 'generally agreed that the existence of a rule of customary law requires the presence of two elements, namely *State* practice'[26] and *opinio juris*.

Concerning actors other than States, the introduction notes with respect to international organisations:

> International organisations have international legal personality and can participate in international relations in their own capacity, independently of their member States. In this respect, their practice can contribute to the formation of customary international law. Therefore, this study has included, for example, the United Nations Secretary-General's Bulletin on observance by United Nations forces of international humanitarian law as relevant practice.[27]

The International Law Commission's Conclusions appear to be based on a similar understanding of a clearly hierarchical relevance of the acts of States, on the one hand, and international organisations, on the other hand, as 'practice' that contributes to the formation of customary international law. Paragraphs 1 and 2 of the International Law Commission's Conclusion 4 state:

1. The requirement of a general practice, as a constituent element of customary international law, refers primarily to the practice of States that contributes to the formation, or expression, of rules of customary international law.
2. In certain cases, the practice of international organizations also contributes to the formation, or expression, of rules of customary international law.[28]

The commentary to paragraph 2 of Conclusion 4 explains:

> (5) International organizations are not States. They are entities established and empowered by States (or by States and/or other international organizations) to carry out

26 J-M Henckaerts and L Doswald-Beck, *Customary International Humanitarian Law*, vol I (Rules), vol II (Practice) (Cambridge University Press and ICRC 2005, 2009 reprint) xxxvii–xxxviii.

27 ibid xliff, emphasis added, footnote omitted.

28 Report of the International Law Commission, Seventieth session (30 April–1 June and 2 July–10 August 2018), General Assembly, Official Records, Seventy-third session, Supplement no 10 (A/73/10), United Nations, New York, 2018, Chapter V. Identification of customary international law, 117–56, Conclusion 4 ('Requirement of practice') and commentary thereto, 130–32ff.

> certain functions, and to that end have international legal personality, that is, they have their own rights and obligations under international law. The practice of international organizations in international relations (when accompanied by *opinio juris*) may count as practice that gives rise or attests to rules of customary international law, but only those rules (*a*) whose subject matter falls within the mandate of the organizations, and/or (*b*) that are addressed specifically to them (such as those on their international responsibility or relating to treaties to which international organizations may be parties). The words 'in certain cases' in paragraph 2 indeed serve to indicate that the practice of international organizations will not be relevant to the identification of all rules of customary international law, and further that it may be the practice of only some, not all, international organizations that is relevant.
>
> (6) … Practice within the scope of paragraph 2 may also arise where member States have not transferred exclusive competences, but have conferred competences upon the international organization that are functionally equivalent to powers exercised by States. Thus the practice of international organizations when concluding treaties, serving as treaty depositaries, in deploying military forces (for example, for peacekeeping), in administering territories, or in taking positions on the scope of the privileges and immunities of the organization and its officials, may contribute to the formation, or expression, of rules of customary international law in those areas.[29]

While the International Law Commission's Conclusions thus consider the possibility that acts of international organisations may, in 'certain cases', count as 'practice', they do not extend this understanding to the acts of other actors. Paragraph 3 of the International Law Commission's Conclusion 4 states:

> 3. Conduct of other actors is not practice that contributes to the formation, or expression, of rules of customary international law, but may be relevant when assessing the practice referred to in paragraphs 1 and 2.[30]

In the field of international humanitarian law, such 'other actors' are, in particular, non-State parties to armed conflicts. It is widely accepted that such parties to armed conflict are bound by international humanitarian law applicable in non-international armed conflict.[31] A challenge sometimes encountered when engaging with such actors, though, is that they might 'deny the applicability of humanitarian law by refusing to recognize a body of law created by States' or 'by claiming that

29 ibid 131ff, footnotes omitted, emphasis in original.

30 ibid 130ff.

31 For an overview of views, with further references, *see* e.g. ICRC, 'Commentary on the First Geneva Convention: Convention (I) for the Amelioration of the Condition of the Wounded and Sick in Armed Forces in the Field' (2nd edn, 2016), commentary to common Article 3, at paras 505–508 https://ihl-databases.icrc.org/ihl/full/GCI-commentary accessed 16 November 2018.

they cannot be bound by obligations ratified by the government against whom they are fighting'.[32] The question has therefore been raised whether the acceptance by non-State parties to armed conflict of at least customary international humanitarian law could not be increased by taking into account their acts as 'practice' that contributes to the formation of customary international humanitarian law.[33] However, while the International Committee of the Red Cross is, of course, highly aware of the challenges involved in encouraging non-State parties to armed conflict to comply with their obligations under treaty and customary international humanitarian law, the approach chosen for the Study was as follows:

> The practice of armed opposition groups, such as codes of conduct, commitments made to observe certain rules of international humanitarian law and other statements, does not constitute State practice as such. While such practice may contain evidence of the acceptance of certain rules in non-international armed conflicts, its legal significance is unclear and it has therefore been listed under 'Other Practice' in Volume II.[34]

As further explained, the category of 'Other Practice'

> served as a residual category of materials that were not given any weight in the determination of what is customary. The term 'practice' in this context was not at all used to denote any form of state (or other) practice that contributes to the formation of customary international law.[35]

It would appear that the cautious approach chosen by the Study with respect to acts of non-State parties to armed conflicts is in line with the International Law Commission's understanding as expressed in paragraph 3 of Conclusion 4.

32 'Increasing respect for international humanitarian law in non-international armed conflicts' (*ICRC* 2008) 11 www.icrc.org/en/publication/0923-increasing-respect-international-humanitarian-law-non-international-armed-conflicts accessed 16 November 2018.

33 *See* e.g. Marco Sassòli, 'Taking Armed Groups Seriously: Ways to Improve their Compliance with International Humanitarian Law' (2010) 1.1 Journal of International Humanitarian Legal Studies 5, 20–21ff; *see* also 13ff for the question why 'armed groups are … bound by certain international humanitarian law rules'.

34 J-MHenckaerts and L Doswald-Beck, *Customary International Humanitarian Law*, vol I (Rules), vol II (Practice) (Cambridge University Press and ICRC 2005, 2009 reprint) xlii.

35 *See* J-M Henckaerts, 'Customary International Humanitarian Law: A Response to US Comments' (2007) 89 International Review of the Red Cross 473, 479–80ff, in the context of non-governmental organisations, noting further: 'Hence, only part of the practice collected in Volume II was actually taken into account in Volume I. In that respect, Volume II may give the wrong impression that everything included in it was somehow considered relevant for the establishment of customary law.' For added clarity, the online customary IHL Database refers to the category discussed merely as 'XII. Other'.

Another question that is raised by the International Law Commission's Conclusion 4 is where the International Committee of the Red Cross itself fits in the system of States, international organisations, and 'other actors', and, as a consequence, what the role of the International Committee of the Red Cross's own acts is in the formation of customary international law.[36]

Consisting of five personalities appointed by the 'Geneva Public Welfare Society', a local charitable organisation, the committee that would eventually become known as the International Committee of the Red Cross was established in Geneva in 1863.[37] In the following year, the original Geneva Convention for the 'Amelioration of the Condition of the Wounded in Armies in the Field' was adopted by a Diplomatic Conference convened in Geneva in August 1864, using a draft convention prepared by the committee as the basis of discussion.[38]

Today, the International Committee of the Red Cross is explicitly referred to in, especially, the 1949 Geneva Conventions and their Additional Protocols,[39] which, for example, recognise its specific right to visit prisoners of war and civilian persons

36 For a recent consideration, *see* e.g. Robin Geiß and Andreas Zimmermann, 'The International Committee of the Red Cross: A Unique Actor in the Field of International Humanitarian Law Creation and Progressive Development' in Robin Geiß, Andreas Zimmermann, and Stefanie Haumer (eds), *Humanizing the Laws of War: The Red Cross and the Development of International Humanitarian Law* (Cambridge University Press 2017), 215–55, 236–37ff, noting that 'there is no evidence that [the International Committee of the Red Cross's] practice – however, important, relevant and persuasive it might be – (currently) directly contributes to the formation of customary international law'.

37 *See* e.g. François Bugnion, 'Birth of an Idea: The Founding of the International Committee of the Red Cross and of the International Red Cross and Red Crescent Movement: From Solferino to the Original Geneva Convention (1859–1864)' (2012) 94 International Review of the Red Cross 1299, 1308–21ff, www.icrc.org/eng/assets/files/review/2013/irrc-888-bugnion.pdf accessed 16 November 2018.

38 ibid 1321–27ff.

39 *See* Article 3 common to the four Geneva Conventions; Articles 9, 10, 11, and 23 Geneva Convention (I); Articles 9, 10, and 11 Geneva Convention (II); Articles 9, 10, 11, 56, 72, 73, 75, 79, 81, 123, 125, and 126 Geneva Convention (III); Articles 10, 11, 12, 14, 30, 59, 61, 76, 96, 102, 104, 108, 109, 111, 140, 142, and 143 Geneva Convention (IV); Articles 5, 6, 33, 78, 81, 97, and 98 Additional Protocol I; Article 24 Additional Protocol II; as well as Articles 3, 4, and 13 of the Protocol Additional to the Geneva Conventions of 12 August 1949, and Relating to the Adoption of an Additional Distinctive Emblem (Protocol III), 8 December 2005. For an overview of the International Committee of the Red Cross's role, *see* also Article 5 of the 'Statutes of the International Red Cross and Red Crescent Movement', adopted by the 25th International Conference of the Red Cross at Geneva in October 1986 and amended by the 26th International Conference of the Red Cross and

protected under the Fourth Geneva Convention who are deprived of their liberty, and, for instance, to interview them without witnesses.[40]

Concerning its legal status, from the national law perspective, the International Committee of the Red Cross is an association governed by the Swiss Civil Code.[41] Regarding the international law perspective, the International Committee of the Red Cross's Statutes state:

> In order to fulfil its humanitarian mandate and mission, the International Committee of the Red Cross enjoys a status equivalent to that of an international organization and has international legal personality in carrying out its work.[42]

However, the International Committee of the Red Cross is not an international organisation as understood by the International Law Commission's Conclusions. According to the commentary to Conclusion 4, the

> term 'international organizations' refers, in these draft conclusions, to organizations that are established by instruments governed by international law (usually treaties), and possess their own international legal personality. The term does not include non-governmental organizations.[43]

The International Committee of the Red Cross is recognised in 'instruments governed by international law', especially in the Geneva Conventions and their Additional Protocols, but it was not 'established' by them, as demanded by the International Law Commission's first criterion above. Indeed, the International

Red Crescent at Geneva in December 1995 and by the 29th International Conference of the Red Cross and Red Crescent at Geneva in June 2006 (*ICRC* 2007) www.icrc.org/eng/resources/documents/misc/statutes-movement-220506.htm accessed 16 November 2018.

40 *See* Article 126 of Geneva Convention (III) and Articles 76 and 143 of Geneva Convention (IV).

41 *See* paragraph 1 of Article 2 ('Legal status') of the 'Statutes of the International Committee of the Red Cross', most recently adopted on 21 December 2017 and entered into force on 1 January 2018, www.icrc.org/en/document/statutes-international-committee-red-cross-0 accessed 16 November 2018.

42 ibid para 2 of Article 2. For a discussion, *see* Els Debuf, 'Tools to Do the Job: The ICRC's Legal Status, Privileges and Immunities' (2015) 97 International Review of the Red Cross 319, www.icrc.org/en/international-review/article/tools-do-job-icrcs-legal-status-privileges-and-immunities accessed 16 November 2018.

43 *See* Report of the International Law Commission, Seventieth session (30 April–1 June and 2 July–10 August 2018), General Assembly, Official Records, Seventy-third session, Supplement no 10 (A/73/10), United Nations, New York, 2018, Chapter V. Identification of customary international law, 117–56, Conclusion 4 ('Requirement of practice') and commentary thereto, 130ff, footnote 691.

Committee of the Red Cross's origins pre-date the instruments that recognise it, and it exists independently of them.

However, the International Committee of the Red Cross's 'own international legal personality' – the International Law Commission's second criterion for an international organisation in the sense of the Conclusions – has found wide support. For example, the International Criminal Tribunal for the Former Yugoslavia (ICTY) noted in the *Simić* case in 1999 that '[i]t is generally acknowledged that the International Committee of the Red Cross, although a private organization under Swiss law, has an international legal personality'.[44] This is, of course, not the full international legal personality of States, but rather a personality linked to the International Committee of the Red Cross's functions.[45]

Against this background, as noted in the introduction to the Study, '[o]fficial International Committee of the Red Cross statements, in particular appeals and memoranda on respect for international humanitarian law, have been included as relevant practice because the International Committee of the Red Cross has international legal personality'.[46] As further explained, the

> Study did not, however, use International Committee of the Red Cross statements as primary sources of evidence supporting the customary nature of a rule. They are cited to reinforce conclusions that were reached on the basis of state practice alone. Hence, International Committee of the Red Cross practice likewise never tipped the balance in favour of a rule being customary.

44 International Criminal Tribunal for the Former Yugoslavia, The Prosecutor v Blagoje Simić et al, Case no IT-95-9-PT, Decision on the prosecution motion under Rule 73 for a ruling concerning the testimony of a witness, 27 July 1999, § 46, footnote 9. For a discussion and further references, *see* Els Debuf, 'Tools to Do the Job: The ICRC's Legal Status, Privileges and Immunities' (2015) 97 International Review of the Red Cross 319, especially 324ff. For a different view *see* e.g. Tarcisio Gazzini, 'A Unique Non-State Actor: The International Committee of the Red Cross' (2010) 4 Human Rights and International Legal Discourse 32.

45 *See*, with further references, also to a different view, e.g. Alfred Verdross and Bruno Simma, *Universelles Völkerrecht, Theorie und Praxis* (Unchanged reprint of 3rd completely revised edition of 1984, Duncker und Humblot 2010) at §§ 375–77 and 418–21, concerning the International Committee of the Red Cross as a non-State subject of international law linked to its functions, based on the understanding of subjects of international law as those who are bearers of international legal rights and/or obligations, ie whose behaviour is directly governed by international law.

46 J-M Henckaerts and L Doswald-Beck, *Customary International Humanitarian Law*, vol I (Rules), vol II (Practice) (Cambridge University Press and ICRC 2005, 2009 reprint) xli.

State reactions to International Committee of the Red Cross memoranda or appeals would clearly be a more important source of evidence.[47]

Since the International Committee of the Red Cross is thus not an international organisation as described by the International Law Commission's criteria for the Conclusions, its acts can only fall under paragraph 3 of the International Law Commission's Conclusion 4. And indeed, the commentary specifically addresses the International Committee of the Red Cross, noting that:

> (9) Official statements of the International Committee of the Red Cross (ICRC), such as appeals for and memorandums on respect for international humanitarian law, may likewise play an important role in shaping the practice of States reacting to such statements; and publications of the International Committee of the Red Cross may assist in identifying relevant practice. Such activities may thus contribute to the development and determination of customary international law, but they are not practice as such.[48]

In view of the broad scope of paragraph 3 – understanding as 'other actors' entities as diverse as 'for example, non-governmental organizations and private individuals, but also transnational corporations and non-State armed groups'[49] – the particular consideration given to the International Committee of the Red Cross is a helpful recognition of its specific characteristics.

In particular, the express affirmation that 'official statements' of the International Committee of the Red Cross, 'such as appeals for and memorandums on respect for' international humanitarian law 'may … play an important role in shaping the practice of States reacting to such statements', that 'publications of the International Committee of the Red Cross may assist in identifying relevant practice', and that '[s]uch activities may thus contribute to the development and determination of customary international law' is a useful acknowledgement of the International Committee of the Red Cross's special role.

Insofar as the commentary ends by noting that such activities of the International Committee of the Red Cross 'are not practice as such', this conclusion follows logically from the system underlying Conclusion 4. Notably, this ultimate conclusion is complemented by a footnote, which clarifies that '[t]his is without prejudice to the

47 *See* J-M Henckaerts, 'Customary International Humanitarian Law: A Response to US Comments' (2007) 89 International Review of the Red Cross 473, 478ff.

48 *See* Report of the International Law Commission, Seventieth session (30 April–1 June and 2 July–10 August 2018), General Assembly, Official Records, Seventy-third session, Supplement no 10 (A/73/10), United Nations, New York, 2018, Chapter V. Identification of customary international law, 117–56, Conclusion 4 ('Requirement of practice') and commentary thereto, 132ff.

49 ibid.

significance of acts of the International Committee of the Red Cross in exercise of specific functions conferred upon it, in particular by the Geneva Conventions for the protection of war victims of 12 August 1949'.[50] In view of the distinctive character of the International Committee of the Red Cross described above – not an international organisation established by instruments governed by international law, but exercising specific functions recognised in such instruments, and in this respect widely acknowledged as having an international legal personality – this footnote recognises, in the context of the identification of customary international law, that acts of the International Committee of the Red Cross in carrying out its unique functions do have a special significance.

3 Concluding remarks

More than twenty years have passed since the International Committee of the Red Cross embarked on the endeavour to identify rules of customary international humanitarian law applicable in international and non-international armed conflicts, based on the mandate of the 26th International Conference in 1995. The Study's publication in 2005 sparked significant discussions not only on the substance of customary international humanitarian law as such, but also on the identification of customary international law more widely. Many of the challenging questions that needed to be addressed in the preparation of the Study are today reflected in the International Law Commission's Conclusions on the identification of customary international law and the commentaries thereto. This notably includes the question of the role of non-State actors in the formation of customary international law.

50 ibid.

Chapter 15

Treaty bodies and States: shaping custom

Kasey McCall-Smith

With the proliferation of international legal actors, each of whom has the potential to contribute to the creation of international law, it is timely to consider the influence of the United Nations human rights treaty bodies on the development of customary international law. These supervisory mechanisms warrant special attention as several of them enjoy an easily recognised status as the longest continual treaty supervisory mechanisms in the international legal system.[1] The significance of treaty bodies has, in fact, made such an impact on the international community's understanding of 'law' that multiple International Law Commission studies have acknowledged the relevance of the human rights treaty bodies, including the ongoing work on subsequent agreement and subsequent practice in relation to interpretation of treaties,[2] the 2011 Guide to Practice on Reservations to Treaties[3] and its current examination of customary international law.

This chapter proceeds from the accepted notion that international organisations contribute to international lawmaking in a number of ways.[4] Tracking the possibility

1 E.g. the Human Rights Committee commenced its supervisory role in 1976, with the entry into force of the International Covenant on Civil and Political Rights, 16 December 1966, 999 UNTS 171, entered into force 23 March 1976. This excludes the European Court of Human Rights, as its function is solely adjudicatory rather than supervisory with the same competences as the United Nations human rights treaty bodies.

2 International Law Commission, Fourth report of the Special Rapporteur on Subsequent agreements and subsequent practice in relation to the interpretation of treaties, UN Doc A/CN.4/694 (2016), paras 17 *et seq*, looking at the pronouncements of expert bodies and the decisions of domestic courts.

3 International Law Commission, Guide to Practice on Reservations to Treaties, UN Doc A/66/10 (2011), para 75, guidelines 3.2–3.2.5. Although not expressly referring to the human rights treaty bodies in the guidelines, the commentary to the guidelines makes clear that human rights treaty bodies are a consideration.

4 *See* e.g. J Alvarez, *International Organizations as Law-Makers* (Oxford University Press 2005).

acknowledged in the International Law Commission conclusions on the identification of customary law,[5] the chapter argues that the responses by States to human rights treaty body interpretations support a conclusion that treaty bodies can, and do, contribute to the development of customary international law, albeit in often subtle ways and through their relationships with States parties. Conclusion 4(2) speaks specifically on the practice of international organizations and Conclusion 6(1) admits a 'wide range of forms'. Yet, the more telling measure of the contribution of the treaty bodies is the way in which the broad range of States parties to the various human rights treaties have engaged with the practice and jurisprudence of the treaty bodies. Thus, the following looks not only at the practice of the treaty bodies, but at State responses to, and reliance on, rules as interpreted by treaty bodies and how the responses ultimately do and could support the development of customary international law.

Responses to treaty body practice are often marked by inaction, a point recognised in Conclusion 6(1). However, conduct in connection with treaties (Conclusion 6(2)) can be charted across States in their engagement with the treaty bodies and must be considered as a whole, as outlined in Conclusion 7(1). For this reason, State practice in response to the supervisory dialogues with the treaty bodies, whether marked by inaction or further responsive measures, warrants attention in the determination of customary international law. Treaty body jurisprudence is almost entirely in the public domain and includes the decisions taken in regard to the review of States' periodic reports and individual communications, their observations in General Comments on States parties' conduct across all parties, and on their procedural practices. Collectively, treaty body outputs are viewed as soft law, though arguably should be assumed as further means of interpreting the treaty texts in line with the rules on interpretation in Article 31(3)(b) the Vienna Convention on the Law of Treaties.[6] Furthermore, there is demonstrable evidence that this body of soft law is influencing domestic human rights accounts.[7] In light of the readily

5 International Law Commission, Conclusions on identification of customary international law, with commentaries, UN Doc A/73/10 (2018), para 66 (Identification of customary international law).

6 Vienna Convention on the Law of Treaties, 23 May 1969, 1155 UNTS 331, art 31(3)(b): 'any subsequent practice in the application of the treaty which establishes the agreement of the parties regarding its interpretation'.

7 K McCall-Smith, 'Interpreting International Human Rights Standards – Treaty Body General Comments as a Chisel or a Hammer' in S Lagoutte, T Gammeltoft-Hansen, and J Cerone (eds), *Tracing the Roles of Soft Law in Human Rights* (Oxford University Press 2016); R Van Alebeek and A Nollkaemper, 'The Legal Status of Decisions by Human Rights

available exchanges between treaty bodies and States, this chapter will examine how, within the regimented parameters of the various treaty body competences, an effective account of the existence of customary law is delivered in a way that ably presents evidence both of State practice and *opinio juris*.

As a starting point, this chapter delivers an account of the treaty bodies as primary interpreters of human rights treaties and contributors to the development of human rights law (1). The next section follows with consideration of the prohibition against torture as a human right that is also recognised as a customary rule of international law (2). In line with the International Law Commission's decision to keep the consideration of customary international law and peremptory norms separate, the prohibition as a peremptory norm (*jus cogens*) will not be addressed.[8] The chapter will then present the interplay between States and the treaty bodies in terms of developing rules of customary international law (3). Section 4 will offer final comments on how the engagement between States and treaty bodies plays a clear, but often overlooked, role in the identification and development of customary international law.

1 Human rights treaty bodies as interpreters

Because the value of utilising the treaty bodies as the ultimate interpreters has been addressed by the author and others elsewhere, this section simply will recap the important role played by the treaty bodies in interpreting human rights.[9] United Nations human rights treaty bodies have been accepted as expert interpreters of human rights treaty obligations across many international fora, though this idea is

Treaty Bodies in National Law' in H Keller and G Ulfstein (eds), *UN Human Rights Treaty Bodies: Law and Legitimacy* (Cambridge University Press 2012) 356, 357; International Law Association, *Committee on International Human Rights Law and Practice, Final Report on the Impact of Findings of the United Nations Human Rights Treaty Bodies* (ILA 2004).

8 International Law Commission, 'First report on formation and evidence of customary international law', UN Doc A/CN.4/663 (17 May 2013) (First report on customary international law) paras 24–27. *See* also A Bianchi, 'Human Rights and the Magic of *Jus Cogens*' (2008) 19 EJIL 491.

9 McCall-Smith (n 7); K McCall-Smith, 'Reservations and the Determinative Function of Human Rights Treaty Bodies' (2012) 54 German YbIL 521. *See*, generally, G Ulfstein, 'Law-Making by Human Rights Treaty Bodies' in R Liivoja and J Petman (eds), *International Law-Making: Essays in Honour of Jan Klabbers* (Taylor & Francis 2013); H Keller and G Ulfstein (eds), *UN Human Rights Treaty Bodies: Law and Legitimacy* (Cambridge University Press 2012); Y Tyagi, *The UN Human Rights Committee: Practice and Procedure* (Cambridge University Press 2011) esp 56–58.

equally contested. The International Court of Justice has clarified that even though under no obligation to do so, it 'ascribe[s] great weight to the interpretation adopted by [the Human Rights Committee]' as the body 'established specifically to supervise the application of [the International Covenant on Civil and Political Rights]'.[10] The International Court of Justice further opined on clarity and the consistent interpretation of the rights of aliens lawfully in a foreign state to review of an expulsion order by a competent authority and how the Human Rights Committee's interpretation of this right echoed across regional human rights systems.[11] This 'echo' and the way in which States respond to it feeds into a determination of a rule of customary international law.

In the national context, States often underscore the non-binding nature of treaty body opinions.[12] This overt eschewing of treaty body interpretations tends to feed into the State-centric, sovereigntist arguments necessary to massage isolationist approaches to international law that bubble underneath the skin of even the most human rights-forward States. Even with resistance to treaty body interpretations, there are clear instances of States' uptake of treaty body jurisprudence, which speak directly to the development of consensus on the content of a normative rule.[13] In line with International Law Commission Conclusion 7(1), implementation of treaty body decisions and recommendations is part of the holistic practice that contributes to the development of customary law as repeated implementation of a rule helps crystallise State practice. Even where a government asserts that compliance with a treaty body decision is 'voluntary', the way in which the State implements that decision can ultimately generate customary law.[14]

10 *Ahmadou Sadio Diallo (Republic of Guinea v Democratic Republic of the Congo)*, 2010 ICJ Reports 639, para 66. *See* also, Legal Consequences of the Construction of a Wall in the Occupied Palestinian Territory, Advisory Opinion, 2004 ICJ Reports 136, para 109, recounting the Human Rights Committee interpretation of the applicability of the International Covenant on Civil and Political Rights outwith the territory of the State.

11 *Diallo* (n 10) para 66.

12 E.g. *Perterer v Land Salzburg and Austria*, 1Ob8/08w [ORIL, ILDC 1592 (AT 2008)], 6 May 2008, Supreme Court of Justice [OGH], paras 9–10 (noting the need for direct implementation of the International Covenant on Civil and Political Rights); *Hauchemaille v France*, Judicial Review, Case no. 238849 [ORIL, ILDC 767 (FR 2001)] 11 October 2001, Council of State, para 22; *PM v Criminal Chamber of the Supreme Court*, Constitutional appeal (*recurso de amparo*) [ORIL, ILDC 1794 (ES 2002)] 3 April 2002, Constitutional Court, para 7.

13 McCall-Smith, 'Interpreting International Human Rights' (n 7). Although the chapter discusses general comments primarily, final views have been of similar interest to national courts.

14 E.g. Senate (Australia) *Select Committee on Ministerial Discretion in Migration Matters*, Report, March 2004, Recommendation 18, para 2.24: 'However, the views of these committees are not legally binding or enforceable, and the efficacy of these committees relies on

Pursuant to rule 71(5) of the Human Rights Committee's rules of procedure, a State should provide follow-up information as to how it is implementing the Committee's concluding observations. This practice has been in place since 2001 and offers a realistic, albeit limited, overview of how States respond to the interpretations of the Human Rights Committee. Even with the substantial amount of legal analysis produced by the Human Rights Committee and other treaty bodies, it is clear that many States continue to fail to implement the decisions made by the treaty bodies.[15] This failure to respond to treaty body opinion is reflected in the International Law Commission's conclusions on customary international law noting that inaction may also aid in a determination of customary international law (Conclusion 6(1)). This is particularly true when it is necessary to refine the further reaches of a human rights rule in terms of both positive and negative duties of the State. Whether interpreted as inaction or as a partial response to treaty body jurisprudence, the key is that a State's aggregate engagement with treaty obligations may be considered when evaluating evidence of a rule of customary international law (Conclusion 7(1)).

2 The interplay between treaties and customary international law

The Universal Declaration of Human Rights[16] is often asserted as the basis for several customary international rules for human rights.[17] Although there is not universal agreement to what extent each of the rights set out in the Universal Declaration of Human Rights has transformed into a customary rule, a survey of State actions across national and international practice suggests that a number of the rules are definitively accepted as customary whilst others are slowly gathering support in a transition towards customary rules. Support for this proposition can be found in the strength of the ratifications across the core human rights treaties, particularly where there is cross-manifestation of the same right, such as the right to life or the prohibition against torture. The International Court of Justice has acknowledged that there is interplay between treaties and the identification or development of customary law.[18] Due to the brevity of this chapter, the following only examines the prohibition against torture as a treaty obligation and a rule of customary international law.

parties voluntarily agreeing to implement their views.' www.aph.gov.au/~/media/wopapub/senate/committee/minmig_ctte/report/report_pdf.ashx accessed 4 November 2018.

15 *See* Report of the Human Rights Committee, vol. I, UN Doc A/69/40 (vol. I) iii.

16 Universal Declaration of Human Rights, UNGA Res. 217A, UN Doc A/810 (1948).

17 H Hannum, 'The Status of the Universal Declaration of Human Rights in National and International Law' (1995–96) 25 Ga J Int'l & Comp L 287, 317 *et seq.*

18 *Continental Shelf case* (*Libya v Malta*) 1985 ICJ Reports 13, para 27.

2.1 The prohibition against torture as a treaty obligation and State practice

The prohibition against torture is a bedrock norm in the international human rights paradigm. It is usually expressed as a negative obligation on the State – the State and its representatives are prohibited from engaging in action that amounts to torture. Subsequent to the adoption of the Universal Declaration of Human Rights in 1948, which recognised the right to be free from torture in Article 5, the United Nations General Assembly affirmed the prohibition on a number of occasions through the adoption of several resolutions, including: Resolution on the Protection of All Person from Being Subjected to Torture and Other Cruel, Inhuman or Degrading Treatment or Punishment (1975);[19] Resolution on the adoption of the United Nations Convention against Torture and Other Cruel, Inhuman or Degrading Treatment or Punishment (1985);[20] Resolution adopting the Optional Protocol to the Convention against Torture and Other Cruel, Inhuman or Degrading Treatment or Punishment (2002);[21] and, more recently, in the Revised Standard Minimum Rules for the Treatment of Prisoners[22] (Mandela Rules) (2015). Ultimately, it was also codified in the Geneva Conventions,[23] the International Covenant on Civil and Political Rights[24] Article 7, the Convention against Torture and Other Cruel, Inhuman or Degrading Treatment or Punishment,[25] and the Convention on the Rights of the Child[26] Article 37(a), as well as in three regional human rights conventions.[27] Despite high levels of ratification – the International

19 UNGA Resolution 3452 (XXX), UN Doc A/RES/30/3452, 9 December 1975.

20 UNGA Resolution 39/46, UN Doc A/RES/39/46, 26 June 1987.

21 UNGA Resolution 57/199, UN Doc A/RES/57/199, 18 December 2002.

22 Revised Standard Minimum Rules for the Treatment of Prisoners, UNGA Resolution 70/175, UN Doc A/RES/70/175 (17 December 2015), Rule Nos 1, 8d, 32d, 34, 43, 71, 76b.

23 Common Article 3 of the following: Geneva Convention for the Amelioration of the Condition of the Wounded and Sick in Armed Forces in the Field, 12 August 1949, 75 UNTS 31; Geneva Convention for the Amelioration of the Condition of Wounded, Sick and Shipwrecked Members of Armed Forces at Sea, 12 August 1949, 75 UNTS 85; Geneva Convention Relative to the Treatment of Prisoners of War, 12 August 1949, 75 UNTS 135; Geneva Convention Relative to the Protection of Civilian Persons in Time of War, 12 August 1949, 75 UNTS 287.

24 International Covenant on Civil and Political Rights (n 1).

25 10 December 1984, 1465 UNTS 85 (UNCAT).

26 20 November 1989, 1577 UNTS 3 (UNCRC).

27 European Convention on Human Rights and Fundamental Freedoms, 4 November 1950, 213 UNTS 221; American Convention on Human Rights, 22 November 1969, 1144 UNTS 144; African Charter on Human and People's Rights, 27 June 1981, 21 ILM 58 (1982).

Covenant on Civil and Political Rights has been ratified by 172 States, the Convention against Torture by 164 States, the Convention on the Rights of the Child by 196 States[28] it is clear that ratification of treaties expressly outlining a rule does not automatically confer the status of customary law upon the rule,[29] though today the prohibition against torture is generally recognised as one of custom.[30] In fact, the high levels of reservations to these treaties make the determination of a clear baseline of protection inherently difficult.[31]

The identification of customary international law is an imprecise legal inquiry. A number of International Court of Justice decisions have examined the two elements that together form a rule of customary law, State practice and *opino juris*;[32] yet, across the decisions there are unspoken variables that are understood to influence the weight ascribed to each of these elements and it is acknowledged that the distinction between the two is, at best, a *non sequitur* oft repeated by international lawyers to validate their craft.[33] Nonetheless, the following discussion attempts to distinguish State responses to treaty body jurisprudence in line with the

28 Ratifications numbers at the time of writing. All available on https://treaties.un.org accessed 4 November 2018.

29 *North Sea Continental Shelf* (*Germany v Denmark/Netherlands*) 1969 ICJ Reports 3, paras 75–78; *Military and Paramilitary Activities in and against Nicaragua* (*Nicaragua v United States*) 1986 ICJ Reports 14, paras 183–84.

30 E.g. *Questions Relating to the Obligation to Prosecute or Extradite* (*Belgium v Senegal*), 2012 ICJ Reports 422, para 97; *Filartiga v Pena-Irala*, 630 F.2d 876, 884 (2nd Cir 1980) ('torture is prohibited by the law of nations'). S Greer, 'Is the Prohibition against Torture, Cruel, Inhuman and Degrading Treatment Really "Absolute" in International Human Rights Law' (2015) 15 Human Rights Law Review 101, 108; D Weissbrodt and C Heilman, 'Defining Torture and Cruel, Inhuman, and Degrading Treatment' (2011) 29 Law & Inequity 343, 348; TP Crocker, 'Overcoming Necessity: Torture and the State of Constitutional Culture' (2008) 61 SMU Law Review 221, 222–23 (torture as a norm of *jus cogens*).

31 UNCHR, Chairpersons of the human rights treaty bodies Report on Reservations, UN Doc HRI/MC/2009/5 (2009) 4. *See* also K McCall-Smith, 'Mind the Gaps: The ILC Guide to Practice and Reservations to Human Rights Treaties' (2014) 16 International Community Law Review 263.

32 E.g. *North Sea Continental Shelf* case (n 29) paras 75–79; *Military and Paramilitary Activities in and against Nicaragua* (n 29) paras 183–85; *Jurisdictional Immunities of the State* (Germany v Italy, Greece Intervening) 2012 ICJ Reports 99, para 55.

33 As Kammerhofer sagely notes that 'the range of uncertainty in international law' is often the result of basing our arguments 'on what other lawyers before us have said, not an any objective "proof"'. J Kammerhofer, 'Uncertainty in the Formal Sources of International Law: Customary International Law and Some of Its Problems' (2004) 15 EJIL 523, 524.

traditionally accepted distinct elements. However, this examination cannot help but conclude that the distinction between *opinio juris* and State practice is often blurred in terms of responses to the treaty bodies and, therefore, this chapter ultimately aligns with other recent literature to demonstrate that the finite distinction between the two is untenable in practice and, ultimately, an unwarranted distraction in the articulation of customary international law.[34]

In terms of United Nations human rights treaties, membership is a two-fold contribution to the development of customary law. Initially, it is the affirmation of the obligation as a rule of law that could potentially be recognised as a customary rule. Implementation of the obligation is demanded under the terms of each of the treaties[35] and this delivers the initial element of a customary rule – State practice. The majority of States have criminalised torture or recognise the prohibition through a constitutional or legislative provision, such as those found in the United Kingdom,[36] the United States,[37] and Spain,[38] to name but a few. To deliver more comprehensive protection, States may choose to incorporate the treaties explicitly. Australia's most recent legislation on torture, the Crimes Legislation Amendment (Torture Prohibition and Death Penalty Abolition) Act 2010, specifically amended the Australian Criminal Code in order to directly incorporate provisions of the United Nations Convention against Torture and make specific reference to the International Covenant on Civil and Political Rights.[39] These instances of legislative and constitutional action amount to tangible physical evidence of State practice.[40]

Akehurst offered a similar introduction to the subject of custom: '[international lawyers] invoke rules of customary international law every day, but they have great difficulty in agreeing on a definition of customary international law'. M Akehurst, 'Custom as a Source of International Law' (1977) 47 BYBIL 1, 1.

34 *See* e.g. Chapters 5 and 7 in this volume; Kammerhofer (n 33).

35 E.g. International Covenant on Civil and Political Rights (n 1) art 2. Similar obligations are reflected in United Nations Convention against Torture (n 25) art 2 and Convention on the Rights of the Child (n 26) art 4.

36 UK Criminal Justice Act 1988, §134.

37 Torture Victims Protection Act, 28 USC § 1350; War Crimes Act, 18 USC § 2240–41.

38 Constitution of Spain, 1978, art 15; Organic Law 10/1995 (23 November 1995) of the Penal Code, art 173.

39 Crimes Legislation Amendment (Torture Prohibition and Death Penalty Abolition) Act 2010, No 37, 2010 (replacing the Crimes (Torture) Act, 1988 and amending the Criminal Code Act 1995), Division 274.1 – Torture (in total) and para 274.2(4), respectively. Torture is otherwise criminalised on a state-by-state basis within Australia.

40 *See* e.g. M Meguro, 'Distinguishing the Legal Bindingness and Normative Content of Customary International Law' (2017) 6:11 ESIL Reflection.

While the general core of the right – not to engage in or support behaviour that amounts to torture – is broadly accepted (though notably not always observed), the Human Rights Committee and the Committee against Torture spend a great amount of effort addressing the nuances of what observance of the rule specifically requires. Much of this effort is invested in the bilateral relationship between States allegedly in breach of the obligation under the International Covenant on Civil and Political Rights or the United Nations Convention against Torture, but also in the delivery of general comments on aspects of the prohibition. The Human Rights Committee's General Comment No. 20 is illuminating for the present analysis as it specifically acknowledges the value of maintaining a vague core concept of the prohibition:

> The Covenant does not contain any definition of the concepts covered by article 7, nor does the Committee consider it necessary to draw up a list of prohibited acts or to establish sharp distinctions between the different kinds of punishment or treatment; the distinctions depend on the nature, purpose and severity of the treatment applied.[41]

Maintaining a vague definition of the core right leaves space for dynamic interpretation and ensures that the treaty bodies, courts, and States can respond to the evolving problems across societies. Though it is difficult to discern identical or even consistent State practice in implementation, State engagement with and response to treaty body interpretations of human rights over the past few decades have delivered a more coherent understanding of the core human rights obligation. Ensuring a consistent interpretation of core rights is essential for clarity in the international rule of law.[42]

In addition to being obliged to implement the rules outlined in human rights treaties upon ratification, in the United Nations system States parties also become objects of supervision by the treaty bodies. With this objectification, the State becomes the recipient of the interpretations put forward by the treaty body as it carries out its multi-functional exercises in supervision. States' implementation of the core rights set out by a human rights treaty is ultimately a demonstration of State practice but also may be indicative of *opinio juris*.

2.2 Implementation and recognition of a treaty obligation as opinio juris

One reason that makes consensus among States on various human rights rules difficult to ascertain is the very nature of the rules. Unlike more exacting rules of

41 Human Rights Committee, General Comment No 20 (replacing General Comment No 7) on Article 7, UN Doc CCPR/C/GC/20 (1992) para 4.

42 *Diallo* (n 10) para 66.

customary international law, the core of a human rights obligation can be more fluid. Establishing the minimum core right is further complicated due to the broad scope for limiting those rights that are not absolute by definition, which is often manifested through the use of reservations to the various treaties. This section considers the way in which responses to a treaty body interpretation might generate *opinio juris* in order to further entrench emerging contours of the prohibition against torture into customary international law. The specific ways in which States implement the core obligations as well as emerging aspects of the rule will be examined below in section 4 in an effort to demonstrate how treaty bodies contribute to customary international law.

The prohibition against torture is one of the most highly publicised and politically charged human rights due the range of associated issues, such as *non-refoulement* (United Nations Convention against Torture Article 3), that are inherent in the complete observance of the prohibition. While the core of the right is widely accepted across States, the tangential aspects mandated by the complete prohibition are often controversial, as was demonstrated repeatedly in the *Abu Qatada* case in the UK.[43] However, it is the implementation of these incremental expansions of the right that offer a view into a State's understanding of the breadth of the rule. As acknowledged in the *Continental Shelf* case, the application of a norm of customary international law can be debated because though a particular standard might be defined by the norm, States determine how to achieve the standard.[44] Both the Human Rights Committee and the Committee against Torture have been instrumental in articulating the outer and evolving dimensions of the prohibition against torture as the primary supervisory mechanisms of the International Covenant on Civil and Political Rights and United Nations Convention against Torture, respectively. International Covenant on Civil and Political Rights Article 7, the entirety of the United Nations Convention against Torture and Convention on the Rights of the Child Article 37(a) are directed at ensuring the prohibition and articulating emerging actions that breach the prohibition. The nuances between the treaty bodies and the recognition of their opinions by States are addressed below.

It is in negotiating the emerging interpretations of the prohibition by the treaty bodies that States offer what might establish *opinio juris* and therefore shape customary international law. Although the International Court of Justice has rejected the idea that implementation of a treaty obligation equates to *opinio juris*, notably in the application of the equidistance principle in the *North Sea Continental Shelf*

43 *Othman (Abu Qatada) v United Kingdom* (2012) 55 EHRR 1.

44 *Continental Shelf* case (n 18) para 28.

case,[45] the interplay between States and treaty bodies suggests that State responses to new, evolutive interpretations may support identification of customary international law when taken as a whole along with other manifestations of their obligations, in line with International Law Commission Conclusions 6(2) and 7(1) and the increasing literature recognising the obfuscation in identifying distinctions between State practice and *opinio juris*.[46] This phenomenon will now be examined.

3 States' responses to treaty bodies

This section examines how responses to treaty body jurisprudence in the national setting can be drawn upon to identify either or both elements of customary international law – State practice and *opinio juris*. As acknowledged by the International Law Commission in the course of its study of customary international law, States operate in their own domestic legal order.[47] In most systems there is a distinct separation between the executive, legislative, and judicial branches of the State. Each contributes to State practice and *opinio juris* in varying ways. Legislative acts can be drawn upon to demonstrate State practice in the determination of a customary rule of international law. Judicial decisions are highly suggestive of *opinio juris* while policies and practice of the executive can lend support to both elements of customary law. Admittedly, none of these assignments of a particular branch of the State to an element of customary law is definitive.

The following analysis draws upon domestic law, policy decisions, and judicial opinions responding to treaty body jurisprudence. It relies heavily upon the follow-up procedures of the treaty bodies, especially those of the Human Rights Committee and the Committee against Torture in the context of reviewing the implementation of final views on individual communications under the Optional Protocol to the International Covenant on Civil and Political Rights[48] or United Nations Convention

45 *North Sea Continental Shelf* case (n 29) para 76.

46 *See* n 34.

47 International Law Commission, First report on customary international law (n 8) paras 83–84.

48 Optional Protocol to the International Covenant on Civil and Political Rights, 16 December 1966, 999 UNTS 171, art 5(4). As of March 2016, the Human Rights Committee had delivered final views in 1155 of the 2756 individual communications received. The Human Rights Committee maintains a Special Rapporteur for the express purpose of pursuing follow-up to individual communications and has since 1990. The Human Rights Committee has repeatedly reminded States parties of their obligation to comply with the views of the body, *see* General Comment No 33 on the Obligations of

against Torture Article 22.[49] The treaty body–State party dialogues produced in the furtherance of the periodic reporting process or the review of individual complaints for convention breaches deliver a prime opportunity for the development and dissemination of progressive rights interpretation and can influence the law, policy, and practice of States. These processes also allow States to moderate conflicting interpretations of the treaty bodies. For example, the Committee against Torture has repeatedly interpreted the prohibition against torture as limited to actions by a State or its agents. The Human Rights Committee, however, has gone a step further to imply a further positive obligation on the State to prevent torture by non-State actors, in line with other international opinions on the obligations of the State to prevent human rights breaches by third parties or private actors.[50] This suggests that at least in terms of the treaty regime, the observance of the prohibition is limited by the nature of the specific terms of the treaty. However, in terms of the development of a rule of customary international law, these subtle differences can influence the uptake of a potential new rule. The way in which States have responded to treaty bodies on various aspects of the prohibition against torture is highly relevant for assessing the development of customary international law. The following analysis provides a glimpse into the ways in which treaty bodies may shape the development of law through their engagement with, and influence on, States.

3.1 Why States respond to issues of core implementation

Core to the right to be free from torture is the negative obligation on the State not to engage in acts amounting to torture in any situation and this is frequently reiterated

States Parties under the Optional Protocol to the International Covenant on Civil and Political Rights, UN Doc CCPR/C/GC/33 (5 November 2008).

49 As of 13 May 2016, the Committee against Torture had reviewed a total of 376 of the 400 State reports received pursuant to art 19 and as of 15 August 2015 had delivered final views in 272 of the 697 cases submitted to it under art 22(1). The Committee against Torture adopted similar follow-up procedures as a way of assessing State compliance with its final observations on United Nations Convention against Torture implementation. *See* Committee against Torture, Guidelines for follow-up to concluding observations, UN Doc CAT/C/55/3 (17 December 2015).

50 *X and Y v the Netherlands*, Ser A No 91 [1985] 8 EHRR 235; *Velásquez-Rodríguez v Honduras* (Merits), Ser C, No 4 (1988), paras 172–175, the Inter-American Court of Human Rights opined that the failure to prevent harm by a third party triggered the international responsibility of the State; reaffirmed in *Ximenes-Lopes v Brazil*, Ser C, No 149 (2006); 55/96, *SERAC and CESR v Nigeria*, 15th Annual Report of the ACHPR [2002] 10 IHRR 282 (2003).

by the treaty bodies.[51] Where torture is determined to have been committed, a concomitant obligation is one of compensation to the victim. In response to determinations of breaches of the prohibition against torture, Argentina, for example, has increasingly implemented the decisions of the Human Rights Committee recognising that compensation is necessary for victims of torture and that impunity must be eliminated by adopting a range of initiatives, as required by the United Nations Convention against Torture.[52] Compensation for victims of torture is not explicitly mentioned in International Covenant on Civil and Political Rights Article 7 but has been 'read in' to its interpretation by the Human Rights Committee. Therefore, fulfilment of compensation awards amounts to compliance with treaty obligations under the United Nations Convention against Torture (Article 14); however, in terms of the International Covenant on Civil and Political Rights the same behaviour could be viewed as State practice in support of this dimension of the prohibition while changes to the law to ensure compensation or prevent impunity may be regarded as *opinio juris*. For Argentina, which is party to both treaties, implementation continues to be the subject of review by both by the Human Rights Committee and the Committee against Torture. On this issue, therefore, it appears that giving effect to the core obligation is far from straightforward in practice and the State's difficulties are borne out by its responses to both committees and its collective responses aid in the identification of customary international law.

National courts have increasingly recognised the interpretative value of treaty body jurisprudence and some have relied upon findings of the treaty bodies to sustain redress compensation in civil claims even where domestic criminal proceedings failed to deliver a guilty verdict against a State actor for engaging in torture.[53] These cases are particularly interesting where the government of the State has explicitly denied the lack of status for treaty bodies in domestic law in direct opposition to the ultimate findings of the highest national court.[54] In these instances where the branches of a government

51 E.g. Committee against Torture, Conclusions and Recommendations of the Committee: Argentina, UN Doc CAT/C/CR/33/1 (10 November 2004) para 5.

52 Human Rights Committee, Follow up on *LNP v Argentina*, UN Doc A/69/40 (Vol. I) (2014) 182, *see* original case Communication No 1610/2007, UN Doc CCPR/C/102/1610/2007 (18 July 2011); Committee against Torture, Conclusions and Recommendations of the Committee: Argentina, UN Doc CAT/C/CR/33/1 (10 November 2004) para 7.

53 E.g. Committee against Torture, Follow-up on *Gerasimov v Kazakhstan*, Communication No 433/2010, UN Doc CAT/C/53/2 (11 December 2014) para 26. *See* generally Machiko Kanetake, 'UN Human Rights Treaty Monitoring Bodies Before Domestic Courts' (2018) 67 ICLQ 201.

54 ibid para 27.

compete, support for custom is difficult to identify. However, how these competing views are ultimately reconciled within the State will either lend or detract from the determination of a customary rule.

Also fundamental to the prohibition is the impartial and full investigation into claims of torture. Many States reported as running afoul of the torture prohibition do so expressly due to a failure to investigate claims of torture or ill-treatment.[55] In these instances, the treaty body will generally request that the State amend its procedures or take action to ensure an effective investigation. When the executive or judicial branches respond directly to a treaty body decision in an individual complaint or review of a periodic report, or both, the influence of the treaty body on national practice is clear.[56] Engaging with the treaty body decisions on core issues of implementation highlights the State's commitment to its treaty obligations and reform at the national level and often assuages pressure from civil society organisations.

The potential for judicial activism in terms of utilising treaty body jurisprudence is important in the development of human rights norms, particularly in States where no regional human rights system currently operates or where entrenchment of human rights has been arduous. Article 2 of the Lebanese Code of Civil Procedure outlines that courts must consider any relevant ratified treaties. A similar provision is found in Article 9 of the Iranian Constitution. These provisions, along with provisions such as Article 2(6) of the 2010 Kenyan Constitution, suggest that these are monist States in terms of the relationship between international and national law. From a strictly legal view, this ensures a fairly simple access point to treaty body jurisprudence in terms of applicability in the national legal system as the obligation to take the treaty body decisions into account is

55 Human Rights Committee, Follow-up on *Baustista de Arellana v Colombia*, Communication No 563/1993, UN Doc A/69/40 (Vol I) (2014) 191; Human Rights Committee, Follow-up on *Zhumabaeva v Kyrgyzstan*, Communication No 1756/2008, UN Doc A/69/40 (Vol I) (2014) 195; Human Rights Committee, Follow-up on *El Hagog v Libya*, Communication No 1755/2008, UN Doc A/69/40 (Vol I) (2014) 199; Committee against Torture, Follow-up on *Aarrass v Morocco*, Communication 477/2011, UN Doc CAT/C/53/2 (11 December 2014) paras 32–33; Committee against Torture, Follow-up on *Sanko v Spain*, Communication 368/2008, UN Doc CAT/C/56/2 (22 December 2015) 2; Committee against Torture, Follow-up on *Ntikarahera v Burundi*, Communication 503/2012, UN Doc CAT/C/56/2 (22 December 2015) 8–9.

56 E.g. elements of both the Spanish executive (Fiscalía General del Estado) and the judiciary adopted measures and took action to implement the Committee against Torture decision in *Sanko v Spain*, Committee against Torture, Follow-up on *Sanko v Spain* (n 55) 2.

inherent in the treaty. National human rights institutions also offer a strong voice in this context when reminding States about their international obligations.[57]

Further impetus for a State to respond to a treaty body decision is that it may be engaged in a multi-party, multi-level dialogue or campaign to address institutional torture. For example, in the follow-up dialogue to a 2011 complaint against Morocco for breaches of the United Nations Convention against Torture, the State party reported that it had reopened the complainant's case even prior to the Committee against Torture's decision and highlighted that it was committed to working with the United Nations human rights mechanisms, including the Special Rapporteur on torture, and was also considering Amnesty International's torture eradication campaign.[58] This type of report by a State suggests that changes in both State practice and *opinio juris* are influenced by a multitude of actors, including the treaty bodies. The remainder of section 4 will review further dimensions of the prohibition against torture in order to demonstrate how treaty body–State engagements might expand the outer reaches of the rule in terms of development of the customary rule of international law.

*3.2 Non-*refoulement

The principle of non-*refoulement*, also known as non-return, has been at the heart of many political controversies during the war on terror years.[59] This aspect of the prohibition is expressly outlined in United Nations Convention against Torture Article 3 and the Human Rights Committee has interpreted International Covenant on Civil and Political Rights Article 7 to include the principle of non-return when there is a strong possibility that the individual might be subjected to torture by the receiving State.[60] An examination of the bilateral dialogues between States and treaty bodies on non-*refoulement* highlights how the principle is not yet cemented as part of the customary rule on the prohibition of torture despite the tendency of scholars to refer to it as such.[61]

57 E.g. Kenya National Commission on Human Rights, National Values & Principles of Governance: An Alternative Report of State Compliance on Obligations Under Article 132(c)(I), Constitution of Kenya 2010 on Realization of Article 10, 20 www.knchr.org/Portals/0/CivilAndPoliticalReports/National%20Values%20and%20Principles%20of%20Governance.pdf?ver=2016-08-01-154241-273 accessed 4 November 2018.

58 Committee against Torture, Follow-up on *Aarrass v Morocco* (n 55) paras 32–33.

59 E.g. *Othman* (n 43).

60 Human Rights Committee, General Comment 21, UN Doc HRI\GEN\1\Rev.1, 33 (1994).

61 *See* C Costell and M Foster, 'Non-refoulement as Custom and Jus Cogens? Putting the Prohibition to the Test' (2015) 46 Netherlands Yearbook of International Law 273, 282 *et seq.*

Australia's engagement with the Committee against Torture highlights the slow progress in the entrenchment of this aspect of the prohibition. In 2000, the Committee against Torture recommended that it consider 'providing a mechanism for independent review of ministerial decisions in respect of cases coming under article 3 of [UNCAT]'.[62] Failure to comply with the obligation of non-*refoulement* was determined in a previous complaint against Australia before the Committee against Torture.[63] Following the determination of a breach of United Nations Convention against Torture Article 3 in that complaint, the responsible government minister allowed a subsequent protection visa application, which was also rejected and the applicant was expelled. Ultimately, following the fourth finding of a breach of non-*refoulement* within the treaty body complaints system, the Senate Select Committee on Ministerial Discretion recommended to the Australian government that a new system be put in place to record immigration cases and establish the compliance of the ministerial decisions with the United Nations Convention against Torture, the Convention on the Rights of the Child, and the International Covenant on Civil and Political Rights, reflecting the recommendations made by the relevant treaty bodies.[64] Subsequent to the suggested changes to domestic procedures, Australia has been the subject of additional complaints on the issue of non-*refoulement* and has further indicated that it will take heed of the Committee against Torture's decisions in complaints where it determined a breach of Article 3.[65] How this dimension of the obligation will eventually be entrenched remains to be seen, though movement can be tracked across various State organs and ultimately each movement feeds into a developing State practice and Australia's understanding of the obligation of non-*refoulement*. As the progress continues, the discussions surrounding new policies and procedures will undoubtedly reflect the view of Australia in terms of non-*refoulement* therefore contributing to *opinio juris* in the evolution of the prohibition against torture.

Despite slow movement in Australia, the Committee against Torture has experienced some success in its complaints procedures in terms of pushing States

62 *Concluding Observations of the Committee against Torture: Australia*, 25th session, 13–24 November 2000, UN Doc CAT A/56/44/2001 (2001).

63 E.g. Committee against Torture, *Elmi v Australia*, Communication No 120/1998, UN Doc CAT/C/22/D/120/1998 (1998).

64 Senate (Australia) *Select Committee on Ministerial Discretion in Migration Matters*, Report (n 14) Recommendation 18, para 8.29.

65 Committee against Torture, Follow-up on *Dewage v Australia*, Communication No. 387/2009, UN Doc CAT/C/53/2 (11 December 2014) para 19 (stay of deportation to Sri Lanka or any other country that might return him to Sri Lanka on humanitarian grounds); Follow-up on *Ke Chun Rong v Australia*, Communication No 46/2010, UN Doc CAT/C/53/2 (11 December 2014) para 21 (stay of deportation to China).

to reconsider expulsion cases in order to enforce the right of non-*refoulement*, as observed in the follow-up procedures with Norway,[66] Sweden,[67] Kazakhstan,[68] Switzerland,[69] and other States.[70] In some cases, States have noted that the national law has changed to better reflect their international obligations.[71] In other cases, well-crafted opinions deliver interpretative value in subsequent cases. A Finnish case demonstrates the strength of conviction with which counsel for complainants place upon decisions of the treaty bodies. In the follow-up procedure on the case of *Mr X and Mr Z v Finland* (non-return to Iran) it was found that Finland had complied with the Committee against Torture's suggested redress following the Committee's decision that the State breached the obligation of non-return, thereby negating the need for follow-up.[72] Finland complained that the Committee should remove the decision from its list due to the compliance. The complainant's counsel, however, argued that the decision should not be struck from the list because 'the Committee's decision is important in order to improve national jurisprudence and procedures in similar cases'.[73] It is this incremental improvement that aids in developing customary international law. While improvements do not follow the same pace across all States, the marked increase in 'chatter' surrounding treaty body jurisprudence cannot be

66 Committee against Torture, Follow-up on *Eftekhary v Norway*, Communication No 312/2006, UN Doc CAT/C/53/2 (11 December 2014) paras 8–9 (stay of deportation to Iran on humanitarian grounds).

67 Committee against Torture, Follow-up on *Njamba and Balikosa v Sweden*, Communication 322/2007, UN Doc CAT/C/53/2 (11 December 2014) para 10 (stay of deportation to Democratic Republic of the Congo on humanitarian grounds).

68 Committee against Torture, Follow-up on *Nasirov v Kazakhszan*, Communication 475/2011, UN Doc CAT/C/53/2 (11 December 2014) para 30 (stay of extradition to Uzbekistan).

69 Committee against Torture, Follow-up on *KN, FW and SN v Switzerland*, Communication No 481/2011, UN Doc CAT/C/53/2 (11 December 2014) para 30 (stay of deportation to Iran)

70 Committee against Torture, Follow-up on *EKW v Finland*, Communication No 490/2012, UN Doc CAT/C/56/2 (22 December 2015) 1 (removal to the Democratic Republic of the Congo).

71 Committee against Torture, Follow-up on *Mopongo et al v Morocco*, Communication No 321/2007, UN Doc CAT/C/56/2 (22 December 2015) 3. 'The State party had provided information on the introduction of a new migration policy in September 2013 that is more humane and in conformity with its international obligations.'

72 Committee against Torture, Follow-up on *Mr X and Mr Z v Finland*, Communication No 483/2011, UN Doc CAT/C/53/2 (11 December 2014) para 38 (obligation to refrain from forcibly returning the complainants to Iran). Finland granted the complainant refugee status shortly after the decision.

73 ibid para 39.

ignored. Once the chatter cements into policy, *opinio juris* may be extracted to support this dimension of the prohibition.

Similarly, in *Thuraisamy v Canada*, the Human Rights Committee determined that the applicant's claim of torture in violation of International Covenant on Civil and Political Rights Article 7 if returned to Sri Lanka mandated reconsideration of his claim for asylum based on humanitarian and compassionate grounds.[74] In consideration of the Committee's views, Canada reconsidered the application and ultimately granted leave to remain.[75] This pattern is tangible across a range of States and suggests that the right of non-return is increasingly recognised. Even where the State and treaty body views diverge, the various intricacies of the protection are being explored in terms of how best to adhere to the protection.[76] Once a tipping point has been reached, it will be only a matter of time until this aspect of the prohibition against torture is viewed as customary international law and this will be due in many ways to the treaty bodies' elaboration of non-*refoulement*.

3.3 Rehabilitation for victims of torture

The obligation to provide medical treatment to victims of torture is a further dimension of the prohibition against torture that could gain traction as a customary rule of international law. Unlike the *prima facie* prohibition, this feature of the protection acknowledges the breach and requires that States deliver relief in the form of both physical and mental rehabilitation. While the text of International Covenant on Civil and Political Rights is silent on the issue, the right to medical treatment is protected by United Nations Convention against Torture Article 14. Failure to provide victims of torture with rehabilitative medical treatment is repeatedly recognised as a breach of the prohibition by the European Court of Human Rights.[77] Both the Committee against Torture and the Human Rights Committee have confirmed that rehabilitation to the extent possible is a necessary part of the protection against torture.[78]

74 Human Rights Committee, *Thuraisamy v Canada*, Communication No 1912/2009, UN Doc CCPR/C/106/D/1912/2009 (31 October 2012).

75 Human Rights Committee, Follow-up on *Thuraisamy v Canada*, Communication No 1912/2009, UN Doc A/69/40 (Vol. I) (2014) 190.

76 Committee against Torture, Follow-up on *Khan v Canada*, Communication No 015/1994, UN Doc CAT/C/56/2 (22 December 2015) 7–8.

77 *Kudla v Poland* (Application No 3021/96) ECtHR Judgment of 26 October 2000, at para 94; *McGlinchey v the United Kingdom*, ECtHR Judgment of 29 April 2003, at paras 57–58; *Sarban v Moldova*, ECtHR Judgment of 4 October 2005, at paras 83 and 89–91; *Hummatov v Azerbaijan*, ECtHR Judgment of 29 November 2007, at para 121 (mental suffering).

78 Committee against Torture, *Gerasimov v Kazakhstan*, Communication No 433/2010, CAT/C/48/D/433/2010 (24 May 2012); Committee against Torture, Follow-up on

For torture victims with a multitude of physical and psychological symptoms, rehabilitation cannot easily be quantified, nor is there a one-size-fits-all approach to be applied. Whether the victim is incarcerated or living freely, there are many variables that will influence rehabilitation options. In the event that provision of healthcare is offered, either practically or by subsidisation, States vary considerably as to how they approach the issue. When torture is directly attributable to a State actor, such as a police officer or prison guard, the duty to ensure appropriate medical care often requires that victims, especially those who are incarcerated, balance their safety and their health, thus adding a further level of issues to consider.[79] Therefore, the way in which rehabilitation is provided is highly variable but as previously noted, it is for the State to determine how to comply with a customary norm, thus precise levels of rehabilitation need not be identified across State practice in order to support an expansion of this dimension of the prohibition.[80]

The variables at stake extend to how the State ensures accessible treatment. Cameroon, for example, responded positively to a decision calling for compensation to facilitate rehabilitation of a victim of ill-treatment following the determination of a breach of the International Covenant on Civil and Political Rights. The complainant suffered severe physical symptoms of ill-treatment and was diagnosed with post-traumatic stress disorder.[81] Though Cameroon acknowledged the need to cover medical care for the victim and offered an amount substantially lower than that sought by the victim, the State noted that a specific amount was not required by the Committee.[82] The victim sought cover for private services while the State seems to have relied in part on its own public services. This speaks to the fluidity of the developing rule in that it is for States to determine how medical treatment is to be

Keremedchiev v Bulgaria, Communication No 257/2004, UN Doc CAT/C/56/2 (22 December 2015) 3; Committee against Torture, *Ntikarahera v Burundi*, Communication 503/2012, UN Doc CAT/C/52/D/503/2012 (12 June 2014) para 6.5; Committee against Torture, General Comment No 3 Implementation of article 14 by States parties, UN Doc CAT/C/GC/3 (13 December 2012) paras 11–14; Human Rights Committee, General Comment No 20 (30 September 1992) para 15.

79 Committee against Torture, Follow-up on *Aarross v Morocco* (n 55) 4–6. This case repeatedly has been the subject of follow-up procedures due to the tension between the complainant's health needs and the risk to his personal security following complaints of ill-treatment by prison guards in prison.

80 *Continental Shelf* case (n 18) para 28.

81 Human Rights Committee, *Afuson Njaru v Cameroon*, Communication No 1353/2005, UN Doc CCPR/C/89/D/1353/2005 (19 March 2007).

82 Human Rights Committee, Follow-up on *Afuson Njaru v Cameroon*, Communication No 1353/2005, UN Doc A/69/40 (Vol. I) (2014) 188.

delivered, whether by compensation for private services or by State services. This also is contingent on the service provision available as it will not be the same among States. At this moment, provision of medical rehabilitation remains a demand of the treaty prohibition against torture as there is no bright line test for determining what amounts to adequate rehabilitation that equates to 'the extent possible' demanded by the Committee against Torture and the Human Rights Committee. The coming years will reveal how States come to approach this developing dimension of the prohibition.

3.4 Corporal punishment as a form of cruel, inhuman, or degrading treatment

A slightly different angle on the prohibition includes actions that do not amount to torture but do breach human rights in the form of actions amounting to cruel, inhuman, or degrading treatment. United Nations Convention against Torture Article 16 prohibits other acts of cruel, inhuman, or degrading treatment while lesser forms of prohibited treatment are also included in International Covenant on Civil and Political Rights Article 7 and Convention on the Rights of the Child Article 37. Of the further dimensions of the prohibition against torture introduced above, the ban on corporal punishment of children is steadily gaining the requisite support to evidence a documented evolution in the prohibition as a rule of customary international law.

It is commonly recognised that the judiciary generally cannot impose corporal punishment on adults or children and the number of states with laws permitting corporal punishment for certain crimes are few.[83] The expansion of the protection outside the judicial or penal system to include a prohibition against corporal punishment against children as a form of cruel, inhuman, or degrading treatment gained great momentum in the early 2000s. Both the Human Rights Committee and the Committee against Torture had previously issued opinions citing that corporal punishment violated the prohibition.[84] When the opinions were further reinforced by the Committee on the Rights of the Child, which oversees the Convention on the Rights of the Child, the international interpretation of the treaty prohibition and its extension to corporal punishment was sealed. The Committee on the Rights of the Child issued General Comment No. 8 on the right of children to be free

83 *See* generally Nigel Rodley and Matt Pollard, *The Treatment of Prisoners under International Law* (Oxford University Press 2011) chapter 10 'Corporal Punishment'.

84 Human Rights Committee, General Comment No 20 (n 41) para 5; Committee against Torture, Report of the Committee, UN Doc A/50/44 (1995) para 169.

from corporal punishment in 2006.[85] The comment noted that over 100 States had banned corporal punishment in schools and penal systems and many had also forbidden it in the home, which was the agreed interpretation of the prohibition in this context.[86]

While the prohibition of corporal punishment in schools and detention facilities is widely enforced, a complete ban in the home is less congealed across States outside Europe. For example, between consideration of the first and second periodic reports of South Africa on compliance with the Convention on the Rights of the Child, the State adopted a law prohibiting corporal punishment of children in detention and alternative care settings though it is still permits the practice in the home.[87] Notably, the Human Rights Committee also addressed the issue of corporal punishment in South Africa in its 2016 concluding observations calling for an absolute prohibition.[88] The dialogue with South Africa suggests that the State's views on corporal punishment in schools was shaped by the treaty bodies and both *opinio juris* and State practice can be derived from its adoption of new laws and the enforcement of the law in line with the rule outlined by the treaty bodies.

Referring to the Human Rights Committee in 2004, among other foreign judicial systems, the Canadian Supreme Court noted that corporal punishment in schools triggered a breach of the prohibition against cruel, inhuman, or degrading treatment found in International Covenant on Civil and Political Rights Article 7.[89] The Court recognised that both international law and other national jurisdictions had acknowledged that corporal punishment as a form of corrective force was prohibited in schools.[90] The examination by the Court in identifying common practice across other jurisdictions and international mechanisms was not unlike that undertaken by the International Court of Justice in its determination of customary international law. These examples provide support for the idea that treaty bodies can influence the development of customary international law from the earliest stages, even if

85 UN Doc CRC/C/GC/8 (2 March 2007).

86 ibid paras 4 *et seq*. provide general background information of the CRC and its role in the promotion of this prohibition as well as some statistics.

87 Concluding observations on the second periodic report of South Africa, UN Doc CRC/C/ZAF/CO/2 (27 October 2016) para 35, welcoming the adoption of the South African Children's Act of 2005.

88 Human Rights Committee, Concluding observations on the initial report of South Africa, UN Doc CCPR/C/ZAF/CO/1 (14 April 2016) paras 24–25.

89 Canadian Foundation for Children, Youth and the Law v Canada, 2004 SCC 4, [2004] 1 SCR 76, 30 January 2004, para 33.

90 ibid para 34.

only nominally or in conjunction with other actors. Ultimately, conduct in connection with treaties, including responses to treaty body jurisprudence, contribute to the identification of customary international law, as outlined by International Law Commission Conclusion 6(2).

The Committee on the Rights of the Child continues to raise the issue of banning corporal punishment in the home and repealing laws that permit 'reasonable chastisement' during its bilateral dialogues with States parties.[91] Picking up issues raised by the Committee on the Rights of the Child, national human rights institutions are actively promoting State compliance with a full ban and continue to note that even where there are limited bans there has been a failure to promote alternative forms of discipline in line with the suggestions of the Committee on the Rights of the Child.[92] Thus whether directly through a dialogue with the State or through promotion of its jurisprudence by a national human rights institution or civil society, treaty bodies are impacting the way in which human rights rules are expanding rules of customary international law.

4 Concluding remarks

The overarching aim of this chapter was to deliver an account of the way in which the engagement between States and treaty bodies plays a clear, but often overlooked, role in shaping customary international law. Engagement with the treaty bodies varies wildly among States. This chapter presented a mere glimpse of the influence of the treaty bodies on the development of customary international law through the incidental behaviour of States in response to treaty body jurisprudence. While it is clear that the core prohibition against torture is undoubtedly recognised in customary international law, the analysis demonstrates that further dimensions of the prohibition reflecting treaty body interpretations are on the horizon.

91 E.g. Committee on the Rights of the Child, Concluding observation on the fifth periodic report of the United Kingdom, UN Doc CRC/C/GBR/CO/5 (12 July 2016) para 41; Concluding observations on the first periodic report of South Africa, UN Doc CRC/C/15/Add.122 (2000) para 28; Concluding observations on the second periodic report of South Africa (n 87) paras 33, 35, and esp 36.

92 E.g. Scottish Human Rights Commission, 'Submission to the UN Committee on the Rights of the Child' April 2016, 7–8 www.scottishhumanrights.com/international/international-treaty-monitoring/the-convention-on-the-rights-of-the-child-crc/ accessed 4 November 2018.

Chapter 16

The contribution to customary international law by territories under international administration

William Thomas Worster

Although it is often argued that international organizations do not contribute to customary international law in the same manner as States, this position ignores situations where an international organization assumes the governance of a State or territory. In these cases, the usual paradigm distinguishing states from international organizations fails and the organization takes on the function of a State. A survey of citations shows that International Territorial Administrations, where an organization functions as a State government, do contribute to customary international law. This result means that this situation would be an example of an international organization contributing to customary international law in the same or similar manner as a State. However, although they do contribute to customary international law, authorities do appear to be reluctant to cite to International Territorial Administrations generally for proof of norms.

The first section of this chapter will use citations to the practice of International Territorial Administrations when discussing norms of customary international law as evidence that the International Territorial Administration is indeed contributing to the custom at issue. Admittedly, the reason for authorities to cite to International Territorial Administration practice is not always explicitly stated.[1] It may have been that the authority was citing the practice because the administration was contributing to the formation of customary international law (formal source) or was citing the

1 Further, this concern overlaps in many cases with larger theoretical questions of how to assess the value of practice for secondary rules on law formation, *see* International Law Association, Committee on Formation of Customary (General) International Law, Maurice Mendelson, et al., Statement of Principles Applicable to the Formation of General Customary International Law, Final Report of the Committee (International Law Association, Mendelson Statement of Principles), principle 6, n.6 (2000); and the fundamental problem of the State-centric or participatory nature of the international legal system, *see* J d'Aspremont, 'International Law-Making by Non-State Actors: Changing the Model or Putting the Phenomenon into Perspective?' in M Noortmann and C Ryngaert (eds), *Non-State Actor Dynamics in International Law – From Law-Takers to the Lawmakers* 171 (Routledge 2010).

practice because the actor had correctly identified the existence of a rule of customary international law (material/evidentiary source).[2] For example, the International Committee of the Red Cross cited as State practice for customary international humanitarian law that a Belgian military court relied on the practice of UNOSOM II for determining customary international law.[3] So is the International Committee of the Red Cross relying on the UNOSOM II practice to directly contribute to customary international law? Or the Belgian practice of relying on the UNOSOM II practice? Or is the Belgian practice of citing to UNOSOM II evidence of the rule? The approach taken in this chapter is to rely only on citations to actors that manifest a positive act, not citations to actors in turn citing the practice of other actors, so as to eliminate this aspect of the problem. Further, this chapter will consider citation to practice as evidence of a formal contribution to customary international law by the cited actor. Generally citations to the practice of International Territorial Administrations were made alongside citations to the practice of States without comment. Because authors did not distinguish between International Territorial Administration and State practice in their citations, and States are comfortably understood to contribute to customary international law, we can infer that International Territorial Administration practice was viewed in the same light as that of States.

This section will survey citations to several forms of International Territorial Administration in major studies on customary international law for comparative purposes. There are a variety of International Territorial Administration forms ranging from governance assistance to full governance. There is no precise definition of practices that qualify as International Territorial Administrations and those that do not.[4] This chapter is focused on whether governance of a territory by the United Nations produces effects in customary international law, so it will consider examples

2 Also in this regard *see* International Law Commission, Michael Wood, Special Rapporteur, First report on formation and evidence of customary international law, UN Doc A/CN.4/663, paras 13–15 (17 May 2013); International Law Association, Mendelson Statement of Principles, prins. 28–32 (2000).

3 *See* International Committee of the Red Cross, Customary International Humanitarian Law Database (ICRC Database), Rule 33. Personnel and Objects Involved in a Peacekeeping Mission, available at https://ihl-databases.icrc.org/customary-ihl/eng/docs/v2_rul_rule33 (citing a 1997 Belgian military court's decision in the Violations of IHL in Somalia and Rwanda case making reference to practice of UNOSOM II).

4 *See* R Wilde, 'From Danzig to East Timor and Beyond: The Role of International Territorial Administration', *American Journal of International Law*, 95(3), 583 (2001); R Wilde, 'Quis Custodiet Ipsos Custodes? Why and How UNHCR Governance of Development Refugee Camps Should Be Subject to International Human Rights Law', *Yale Human Rights and Development Law Journal*, 1, 5 (1998).

of that practice regardless of whether the particular nuances of the administration might fall under a strict definition of International Territorial Administration. Specifically, this chapter will survey citations to the practice of UNTAES (United Nations Transitional Authority in Eastern Slavonia, Baranja, Western Sirmium), UNMIK (United Nations Mission in Kosovo), and UNTAET (United Nations Transitional Administration in East Timor) as the best examples of full administration of a State's governance mechanisms by the United Nations. UNOSOM II (Somalia) and the Office of the High-Representative for Bosnia-Herzegovina will also be examined as they are good examples of a less intrusive, co-administration approach. Other International Territorial Administrations will also be included. In searching for instances of citation to these International Territorial Administrations, the author examined the records of the International Law Commission, International Law Association, as well as the International Committee of the Red Cross study on customary international humanitarian law, and other scholarly writing on the subject. In addition to studying these expected forms of International Territorial Administrations, this study will also briefly examine by way of analogy comparable cases of territorial governance by foreign entities, such as colonialism, and whether that practice also contributed to customary international law.

1 References to International Territorial Administration practice

In order to determine the trends in practice, we will examine a survey of the various ways in which International Territorial Administrations are cited by authorities to determine customary international law.

UNTAES was the governance organ for Eastern Slavonia in Croatia based on United Nations Security Council Resolution 1037 (1996).[5] It was created to transition from Republika Srpska Krajina governance back to Croatian control. While the region remained formally part of Croatia, the United Nations took over full authority and complete control as administering authority during those two years including all executive and administrative authority.[6]

5 *See* Basic Agreement on the Region of Eastern Slavonia, Baranja and Western Sirmium, UN Doc S/1995/951, Ann.; United Nations Security Council (UNSC) Resolution 1037 (15 Jan 1996), para 2; A Zimmermann and C Stahn, 'Yugoslav Territory, United Nations Trusteeship or Sovereign State? Reflections on the Current and Future Legal Status of Kosovo', *Nordic Journal of International Law* 70, 423, 433 (2001).

6 *See* J-P Klein, 'The United Nations and Administration of Territory: Lessons from the Front Line, The United Nations Transitional Administration in Eastern Slavonia (UNTAES)', *Proceedings of the American Society of International Law* 97, 205 (2003).

There is very little reference to UNTAES practice for customary international law with one significant exception. The International Committee of the Red Cross, in preparing its Customary International Humanitarian Law Database, included the practice of UNTAES on the issue of the return of displaced persons.[7] It was indexed as the practice of an international organization. This author could not find any citation to UNTAES practice in scholarly opinion.

UNTAET was created in 1999 by United Nations Security Council Resolution 1272[8] in order to govern East Timor while it was in transition from disputed Indonesia occupation to independence. The Special Representative of UNTAET was empowered to adopt, amend or repeal legislation and regulations.[9] East Timor had been listed on the United Nations list of non-self-governing entities and its status was maintained there during UNTAET's existence, although the administering power was changed from Indonesia to UNTAET.[10] Upon independence, in 2002 UNTAET was dissolved and replaced with UNMISET which had less power, and served effectively as a co-administration.[11]

There are several instances where UNTAET practice has been cited for customary international law. The International Committee of the Red Cross cited extensively to UNTAET regulations for a number of norms of customary international humanitarian law pertaining to prosecution for crimes.[12] It has also included UNTAET practice on both individual and State responsivity in the Customary International Humanitarian Law Database.[13] The International Law Commission Special

7 *See* International Committee of the Red Cross, Database, Rule 132. Return of Displaced Persons, available at https://ihl-databases.icrc.org/customary-ihl/eng/docsLight/src_ITr; Rule 132. Return of Displaced Persons: Sec. B. Measures to facilitate return and reintegration, available at https://ihl-databases.icrc.org/customary-ihl/eng/docs/v2_rul_rule132.

8 *See* United Nations Security Council Resolution 1272 (1999). Also *see* United Nations Security Council Resolutions 1338 (21 January 2001) para 2; 1392 (31 January 2002) para 2; 1410 (17 May 2002) para 1; 1480 (19 May 2003) para 1.

9 *See* UNTAET Regs 1999/2 (2 December 1999); 1999/3 (3 December 1999); 2000/1 (14 January 2000); 2001/1 (31 January 2001).

10 *See* www.un.org/Depts/dpi/decolonization.

11 *See* United Nations Security Council Resolution 1410 (17 May 2002) paras 1, 2 (a).

12 *See* International Committee of the Red Cross, J-M Henckaerts and L Doswald-Beck (eds), *Customary International Humanitarian Law* (ICRC, Henckaerts & Doswald-Beck, *Customary IHL*), Vol I: Rules pp 346, 554, 556, 558, 566, 567, 568, 616 (2005) (respectively citing UNTAET Regulation 2000/15, §§ 6(1)(a)(vii), 14, 49(2), 14(3), 14(3) and 16, 21, 21, 6(1), and 17(1)).

13 *See* International Committee of the Red Cross, Database, Rule 88. Non-Discrimination, available at https://ihl-databases.icrc.org/customary-ihl/eng/docs/v1_rul_rule88 (citing

Rapporteur on Crimes against Humanity, Sean Murphy, has cited to UNTAET practice for the customary international law substance of those crimes,[14] as has the Special Rapporteur on immunity of State officials, Concepción Escobar Hernández, on the topic of immunity.[15] Scholarly opinion has largely avoided citation to UNTAET practice, with a single exception on the responsibility to protect.[16]

UNMIK is similar to the two administrations above but is in many ways more well-known due to the notoriety of the Kosovo controversy and continuing existence of the administration. UNMIK was created by United Nations Security Council Resolution 1244[17] and holds all legislative, judicial, and executive

UNTAET Reg. 2000/15, §6(1)(j)); Rule 113. Treatment of the Dead: Section A. Respect for the dead, available at https://ihl-databases.icrc.org/customary-ihl/eng/docs/v2_rul_rule113_SectionA (citing UNTAET Reg. No. 2000/15); Rule 151. Individual Responsibility, available at https://ihl-databases.icrc.org/customary-ihl/eng/docs/v1_cha_chapter43_rule151 (citing UNTAET Reg No 2000/15, §14); Rule 152. Command Responsibility for Orders to Commit War Crimes, available at https://ihl-databases.icrc.org/customary-ihl/eng/docs/v1_cha_chapter43_rule152 (citing UNTAET Regulation No. 2000/15, § 14(3)).

14 *See* International Law Commission, Sean D Murphy, Special Rapporteur, First report on crimes against humanity, UN Doc A/CN.4/680 (17 February 2015) (citing practice of the Special Panels for Serious Crimes in East Timor although unlike the ICTY and ICC, the Panels were created solely by UNTAET, *see* UNTAET Reg. 2000/15, § 5); International Law Commission, Sean D Murphy, Special Rapporteur, Second report on crimes against humanity, UN Doc A/CN.4/690 (21 January 2016) (citing UNTAET Reg. 2000/15, §§5, 10, 12–14, 16, 21, 17.1).

15 *See* International Law Commission, Concepción Escobar Hernández, Special Rapporteur, Fifth report on immunity of State officials from foreign criminal jurisdiction, UN Doc A/CN.4/701 (14 June 2016) (citing practice of the Special Panels, *see* UNTAET Reg No 2000/15, § 15.2).

16 Some scholars have also cited to UNTAET practice, *see* e.g. P Stockburger, 'The Responsibility to Protect Doctrine: Customary International Law, an Emerging Legal Norm, or Just Wishful Thinking', *Intercultural Human Rights Law Review* 5, 365 (2010) (citing UNTAET Reg No 200/15).

17 *See* United Nations Security Council Resolution 1244 (1999) (authorizing the UNSG to create the United Nations Mission in Kosovo); C Tomuschat (ed), *Kosovo and the International Community: A Legal Assessment* (Brill 2002); B Knoll, 'From Benchmarking to Final Status? Kosovo and the Problem of an International Administration's Open-Ended Mandate', *European Journal of International Law* 16, 637 (2005); A Yannis, 'The UN as Government in Kosovo', *Global Governance* 10, 67 (2004); M Ruffert, 'The Administration of Kosovo and East Timor by the International Community', *International and Comparative Law Quarterly* 50, 613 (2001); ICTY, *Prosecutor v Haradinaj*, Case No IT-04-84-AR65.1, Decision on R. Haradinaj's Modified Provisional Release (10 March 2006).

power.[18] Over time, the objective is to phase out UNMIK and transition to local governance. Formally under Resolution 1244, Kosovo remains a part of the Federal Republic of Yugoslavia (now Serbia). However, the resolution also excludes all authority of Yugoslavia/Serbia in the region.

A preliminary observation is that UNMIK's governance, while not formally the government of Kosovo, is sometimes assimilated to a State government from a functional perspective. In the *Kosovo* advisory opinion, the International Court of Justice found that UNMIK regulations are not to be considered domestic acts of Kosovo, but legislation imposed by the United Nations on the basis of the United Nations Charter, i.e. from international law obligations.[19] However, this view was not unanimous. Cançado Trindade took a different approach, concluding that Kosovo under UNMIK was a trusteeship.[20] Yusuf went further and concluded that UNMIK regulations were the domestic law of Kosovo.[21] In his view, we can distinguish between the authority to govern Kosovo, which does indeed come from international law, from the domestic legal order of Kosovo, which is prescribed by UNMIK. The split between the Court majority and Yusuf in particular falls on the conception of UNMIK governance being that of an international organization or effectively a national government.

Turning to the European Court of Human Rights, the Court takes an approach more like that of the International Court of Justice majority in regards to UNMIK practice. In the *Behrami and Saramati* case, the Court held that, for purposes of attribution, UNMIK is a subsidiary organ of the United Nations created under

18 *See* United Nations Security Council Resolution 1244 (1999); UNMIK Reg 2001/9 on a Constitutional Framework for Provisional Self-Government (15 May 2001); European Court of Human Rights, *Azemi v Serbia*, Appl. 11209/09, Decision on the admissibility; ICTY, *Prosecutor v Haradinaj*, Case No IT-04-84-AR65.1, Decision on R Haradinaj's Modified Provisional Release (10 March 2006); ICTY, *Prosecutor v Limaj, et al*, Case No IT-03-66-AR65, Decision on F. Limaj's Request for Provisional Release, para 25 (31 October 2003).

19 *See* International Court of Justice, Accordance with International Law of the Unilateral Declaration of Independence in Respect of Kosovo, Advisory Opinion, 2010 ICJ Reps 403 (22 July 2010).

20 *See id* at C Trindade, sep op, para 64, in International Court of Justice (n 19).

21 *See id* at Yusuf, sep op, para 18, in International Court of Justice (n 19). Also *see* J Cerone, 'The Human Rights Framework Applicable to Trafficking in Persons and its Incorporation into UNMIK Regulation 2001/4', *International Peacekeeping* 7, 43 (2001) (arguing that there is an international obligation on Kosovo to combat trafficking in persons and, on that basis, UNMIK could promulgate UNMIK Regulation 2001/4 address the problem).

Chapter VII[22] so when the European Roma Rights Centre brought an action against UNMIK as government of Kosovo responsible for lead poisoning, the European Court of Human Rights rejected the case.[23] However, both of these decisions could have been different if UNMIK (and/or Kosovo) was (or could have been) party to the European Court of Human Rights. In *Azemi v Serbia*, the Court concluded that '[t]here is no international mechanism of review with respect to acts of UNMIK',[24] which is not completely true for a subsidiary organ of the United Nations. The view of the European Court of Human Rights appears to be that UNMIK is, first and foremost, an international organization.

But other bodies have taken the opposite view. ECOSOC determined that UNMIK could act as if it was the government of Kosovo regarding reporting on compliance with human rights obligations.[25] Similarly, the United Kingdom High Court of Justice and Immigration Appeals Tribunal have held that UNMIK is not formally the government of Kosovo, but that its practice might rise to quasi-governmental nature in providing protection in a way that the applicant does not have a fear of persecution.[26] The International Criminal Tribunal for the former Yugoslavia has concluded that UNMIK (and KFOR) have the role and

22 *See* European Court of Human Rights, *Behrami & Behrami v France; Saramati v France, Germany & Norway*, Applications No. 71412/01 & 78166/01, Decision as to the admissibility (2 May 2007) paras 29–33, 133, 139–43.

23 *See* European Roma Rights Centre, 'European Court of Human Rights Has No Jurisdiction in Kosovo Lead Poisoning Case' (3 April 2006) available at www.errc.org/cikk.php?cikk=2568; European Court of Human Rights, *Azemi v Serbia*, Application 11209/09, Decision on the admissibility.

24 *See* European Court of Human Rights, *Azemi v Serbia*, Application 11209/09, Decision on the admissibility, para 75.

25 *See* United Nations Committee on Economic, Social and Cultural Rights, 'Concluding observations of the Committee on Economic, Social and Cultural Rights, Consideration of reports submitted by States parties under articles 16 and 17 of the Covenant – Concluding Observations', Document submitted by the United Nations Interim Administration Mission in Kosovo, 41st sess, [2008] UNCESCRCO 19, UN Doc E/C.12/UNK/CO/1, para 2 (1 December 2008) (finding that UNMIK could submit information on Kosovo compliance with the ICESCR).

26 *See* United Kingdom High Court of Justice, Queen's Bench, *R on the application of Vallaj v Special Adjudicator*, Case No CO/2738/2000, [2000] EWHC Admin 438 (21 December 2000); United Kingdom Immigration Appeals Tribunal, STARRED FD (Protection – UNMIK – Arif – IFA – Art1D) (Kosovo) CG [2000] UKIAT 00001, para 12 (30 August 2000) ('UNMIK and KFOR are not in any real sense "the authorities of the Federal Republic of Yugoslavia"').

are capable of protecting the public in Kosovo[27] and it has concluding that an order for monitoring terms of releases are properly addressed to UNMIK as the effective authority in Kosovo.[28] These decisions perhaps imply that Kosovo could be assimilated to a State, and UNMIK could be assimilated to a government, for certain purposes.[29]

UNMIK practice has been cited far more than either UNTAES or UNTAET to support findings on customary international law. The International Committee of the Red Cross has included its practice in the Customary International Humanitarian Law Database[30] and in the study on customary international humanitarian law regarding restitution of property[31] and compensation for displaced persons.[32] Significantly, the International Committee of the Red Cross indexed the practice of UNMIK on the application of the precautionary principle in armed conflict as *both* the practice of an international organization and the practice of the Federal Republic of Yugoslavia.[33] In addition, the International Law Commission Special

27 *See* International Criminal Tribunal for the former Yugoslavia, *Prosecutor v Haradinaj*, Case No IT-04–84-AR65.1, Decision on R Haradinaj's Modified Provisional Release (10 March 2006).

28 *See* ibid; International Criminal Tribunal for the former Yugoslavia, *Prosecutor v Limaj, et al*, Case No IT-03–66-AR65, Decision on F Limaj's Request for Provisional Release, para 25 (31 October 2003) para 25; ICTY, *Prosecutor v Seselj*, Case No IT-03–67-PT, Decision on the Defence Motion for Provisional Release para 7 (23 July 2004).

29 *See* International Criminal Tribunal for the former Yugoslavia, *Prosecutor v Limaj, et al*, Case No IT-03–66-AR65, Decision on F Limaj's Request for Provisional Release, para 25 (31 October 2003) para 25; International Criminal Tribunal for the former Yugoslavia, *Prosecutor v Seselj*, Case No IT-03–67-PT, Decision on the Defence Motion for Provisional Release para 7 (23 July 2004).

30 *See* International Committee of the Red Cross, Database, Rule 44. Due Regard for the Natural Environment in Military Operations: Section B. The precautionary principle, available at https://ihl-databases.icrc.org/customary-ihl/eng/docs/v2_cha_chapter14_rule44_sectionb.

31 *See* International Committee of the Red Cross, Henckaerts and Doswald-Beck, *Customary IHL*, Vol I: Rules 547 (2005) (regarding restitution of property) (citing UNMIK Reg No 2000/60, §§2(2) (5) (6)).

32 *See* ibid at Vol I: Rules 548 (2005) (regarding compensation for displaced persons) (citing Agreement on Refugees and Displaced Persons annexed to the Dayton Accords, Article XI; UNMIK Reg No 2000/60, § 2(2)).

33 International Committee of the Red Cross, Database, Rule 44. Due Regard for the Natural Environment in Military Operations: Section B. The precautionary principle, available at https://ihl-databases.icrc.org/customary-ihl/eng/docs/v2_cha_chapter14_rule44_sectionb.

Rapporteur on immunity of State officials has cited UNMIK alongside UNTAET in the fifth report on that topic.[34]

Moving away from the complete governmental control, the United Nations has also exercised joint administration of territories. The two most relevant examples of this practice are UNOSOM II in Somalia and the High-Representative for Bosnia-Herzegovina.

UNOSOM II was formed in 1993 to administer Somalia[35] alongside the Somali Transitional National Council. It held administrative and legislative authority,[36] and used that authority to create a viable, independent judiciary.[37] Perhaps significantly, UNSOM II was not created with the consent of Somalia; instead the United Nations Security Council adopted a Chapter VII resolution,[38] like the approach followed for UNTAES, UNTAET, and UNMIK. Unfortunately, UNOSOM II was not successful and the United Nations abandoned Somalia in 1995.

There is little evidence that the actions of UNOSOM II have ever been cited as forming customary international law, with the exception of the International Committee of the Red Cross. The International Committee of the Red Cross cited the administration for three different practices: treatment of medical units,[39] peacekeeping personnel,[40] and the deceased[41] in armed conflict. Giorgio Gaja,

34 *See* International Law Commission, Concepción Escobar Hernández, Special Rapporteur, Fifth report on immunity of State officials from foreign criminal jurisdiction, UN Doc A/CN.4/701 (14 June 2016) (citing UNMIK Regulation 2003/25, art 10).

35 *See* United Nations Security Council Resolution 814 (26 March 1993). Also *see* J Chopra, *Peace-Maintenance: The Evolution of International Political Authority* 123–60 (Lynne Rienner 1998); D Sarooshi, *The United Nations and the Development of Collective Security: The Delegation by the UN Security Council of its Chapter VII Powers* 63 (Clarendon Press 1999).

36 *See* United Nations Security Council Resolution 814 (26 March 1993), paras 4 (c) and (g), 14.

37 *See* UN Doc S/26317 (1993) Ann 1, paras 29 *et seq.*

38 *See* United Nations Security Council Resolution 814 (26 March 1993). Also *see* United Nations Security Council Resolutions 878 (29 October 1993) para 1; 886 (18 November 1993) para 3; 923 (31 May 1994).

39 *See* International Committee of the Red Cross, Database, Rule 28. Medical Units, available at https://ihl-databases.icrc.org/customary-ihl/eng/docs/v2_rul_rule28.

40 *See* International Committee of the Red Cross, Database, Rule 33. Personnel and Objects Involved in a Peacekeeping Mission, available at https://ihl-databases.icrc.org/customary-ihl/eng/docs/v2_rul_rule33.

41 *See* International Committee of the Red Cross, Database, Rule 113. Treatment of the Dead: Section A. Respect for the dead, available at https://ihl-databases.icrc.org/customary-ihl/eng/docs/v2_rul_rule113_SectionA.

as International Law Commission Special Rapporteur on the Responsibility of International Organizations, cited to the attacks on UNOSOM II personnel for purposes of customary international law.[42] However, this citation was not for the value of UNOSOM II actions in themselves, but rather for UNOSOM II peacekeepers as objects of the practice, so this citation is unlikely to prove the point.

Another relevant co-administration effort was the High-Representative for Bosnia-Herzegovina. The High-Representative for Bosnia-Herzegovina was created in 1995 by United Nations Security Council resolution pursuant to the Dayton Agreements establishing peace in the region.[43] The structure was a co-administration alongside the Bosnian federal system that monitored and guaranteed the implementation of the Dayton Agreement.[44] Its powers included the authority to remove an elected or appointed official from office and even promulgate legislation where the Bosnia authority had not acted.[45] While the institution was the result of the consensual Dayton Agreement, the actual adoption of the Bosnia constitution and legal order was based on United Nations Security Council resolution.[46]

42 *See* International Law Commission, Giorgio Gaja, Special Rapporteur, Second report on responsibility of international organizations, UN Doc. A/CN.4/541, *Yearbook of the International Law Commission*, Vol. II (2004) para 29 (regarding conduct of organs placed at the disposal of an international organization by a State or another international organization, observing practice pertaining to attribution for armed attacks on UNOSOM II personnel, citing Note by the Secretary-General, UN Doc S/1994/653, 45, paras 243–44; Report of the Secretary-General, UN Doc A/51/389, 6, paras 17–18, 11, para 44.

43 *See* General Framework Agreement for Peace in Bosnia and Herzegovina ('Dayton Agreement'), 14 December 1995, 35 ILM 89, Ann. 10; United Nations Security Council Resolution 1031 (15 December 1995) para 27. Also *see* High-Representative for Bosnia-Herzegovina decisions at www.ohr.intidecisions/archive.asp, and extensions of the High-Representative for Bosnia-Herzegovina mandate, *see* United Nations Security Council Resolutions 1088 (12 December 1996) para 18; 1174 (15 June 1998) para 10; 1247 (18 June 1999) para 10; 1305 (21 June 2000) para 10; 1357 (21 June 2001) para 10; 1423 (12 July 2002) para 10; 1491 (11 July 2003) para 10.

44 *See* United Nations Security Council Resolution 1031 (15 December 1995) para 27.

45 *See* Conclusions of the Peace Implementation Conference in Bonn of 10 December 1997, paras XI(2)(a)–(c). Also *see* United Nations Security Council Resolution 1144 (19 December 1997) para 2; T Banning, 'The "Bonn Powers" of the High Representative in Bosnia Herzegovina: Tracing a Legal Figment', *Goettingen Journal of International Law* 6, 259–302 (2014).

46 *See* D Agreement, 35 ILM 89, Ann 4, Constitution of Bosnia-Herzegovina. Also *see* TD Grant, 'Internationally Guaranteed Constitute Order: Cyprus and Bosnia as Predicates for a New Non-Traditional Actor in the Society of States', *Transnational Law and Contemporary Problems* 20–21, 37–38 (1998).

In some respects, the High-Representative for Bosnia-Herzegovina has been treated as the government of Bosnia, for example when the Office filed the report on Bosnia's implementation of the International Covenant on Economic, Social and Cultural Rights,[47] and cited measures adopted by the High Representative as evidence of compliance with the ICESCR.[48] The International Committee of the Red Cross has cited to the practice of the High-Representative for Bosnia-Herzegovina especially in regard the treatment of missing or displaced persons.[49]

Prior to the modern territorial administrations, there have been a variety of experiments with differing forms of similar administrations.[50] There are models for this practice going back to the League of Nations,[51] and, if we can stretch the analogy, perhaps even to colonial or protectorate/trust territory administrations.

47 *See* Bosnia and Herzegovina – Initial reports submitted by States parties under articles 16 and 17 of the Covenant [2005] UNCESCRSPR 2; UN Doc E/1990/5/Add.65 (3 February 2005) (OHR submitting reporting on the implementation of the International Covenant on Economic, Social and Cultural Rights by Bosnia).

48 *See* Bosnia and Herzegovina – Initial reports submitted by States parties under articles 16 and 17 of the Covenant [2005] UNCESCRSPR 2; UN Doc E/1990/5/Add.65, paras 13, 42, 87 (3 February 2005) (presenting measures adopted by the High Representative for Bosnia and Herzegovina as compliance measures by Bosnia).

49 *See* International Committee of the Red Cross, Henckaerts and Doswald-Beck, *Customary IHL*, Vol I: Rules 426 (2005) (citing High-Representative for Bosnia-Herzegovina for the Implementation of the Peace Agreement on Bosnia and Herzegovina); International Committee of the Red Cross, Database, Rules 117. Accounting for Missing Persons, available at https://ihl-databases.icrc.org/customary-ihl/eng/docs/v1_cha_chapter36_rule117, Rule 132. Return of Displaced Persons, available at https://ihl-databases.icrc.org/customary-ihl/eng/docs/v2_rul_rule132, Rule 133. Property Rights of Displaced Persons, available at https://ihl-databases.icrc.org/customary-ihl/eng/docs/v2_cha_chapter38_rule133_sectiona.

50 Also *see* ONUC (United Nations Operation in the Congo) which performed a variety of governmental functions and technical assistance from 1960–64; UNTEA (United Nations Temporary Executive Authority) to briefly exercise executive power in West Irian (West New Guinea) from 1962–63; UNDOF (United Nations Disengagement Observer Force) in Syria in 1974; UNFOCYP (United Nations Peacekeeping Force in Cyprus) since 1964. Even before the creation of the United Nations, there were a few cases of international territorial administration that are potentially relevant. For example, following the Second World War, the victorious Allies assumed the governance of Germany although this author could not find reliable evidence that the practice of the Allies in right of Germany was regarded as constitutive of customary international law.

51 *See* R Wilde, 'From Danzig to East Timor and Beyond: The Role of International Territorial Administration', *American Journal of International Law* 95(3), 583 (2001).

From 1920 to 1935, the Saar was administered by the League of Nations.[52] While treaties between France and Germany pertaining to the subject of the Saar have been cited by the International Law Commission for customary international law,[53] the International Law Commission has also cited legislation on Saar nationality and practice in terms of attribution to the Saar as State practice for purposes of the formation of custom, alongside the practice of other States.[54]

Danzig was also placed under international administration as a 'free city' following the First World War.[55] While it was primarily self-governing, the League of Nations retained certain powers to ensure its status and free governance.[56] A similar arrangement was created for Trieste, though never implemented.[57] For some purposes, Danzig has been treated as a State.[58] The International Law Commission has cited practice by Danzig as State practice for

52 *See* Treaty of Peace between the Principal Allied and Associated Powers and Germany ('Treaty of Versailles'), 28 June 1919, Pt III, § IV, Ann, art 19.

53 *See* International Law Commission, Humphrey Waldock, Special Rapporteur, Second report on the law of treaties, UN Doc A/CN.4/156 & Add.1–3, *Yearbook of the International Law Commission*, Vol II, 54 (1963), UN Doc A/CN.4/Ser.A/1963/ADD.1.

54 *See* International Law Commission, Roberto Cordova, Special Rapporteur, Report on the elimination or reduction of statelessness, UN Doc A/CN.4/64, *Yearbook of the International Law Commission*, Vol II, 170 (1953), UN Doc A/CN. 4/8ER. A/1953/Add. 1 (citing 1949 legislation of the Saar); International Law Commission, Roberto Ago, Special Rapporteur, Fourth report on State responsibility, UN Doc A/CN.4/264 & ADD.l, *Yearbook of the International Law Commission*, Vol II, 111 (1972), UN Doc A/CN.4/SER.A/1972 /Add. 1 para 108 (citing practice of the Governing Commission of the Saar on attribution); International Law Commission, Ivan S Kerno, Expert, Nationality, including Statelessness – Analysis of Changes in Nationality Legislation of States since 1930, UN Doc A/CN.4/67, 2, 4, 5 (Apr. 6, 1953) (including the Saar in several of its lists of State legislation).

55 *See* Treaty of Versailles, 28 June 1919, arts 100–108. Also *see* JK Bleimaier, 'The Legal Status of the Free City of Danzig 1920–1939: Lessons to Be Derived from the Experience of a Non-State Entity in the International Community', *Hague Yearbook of International Law* 69, 70–78 (1989).

56 *See* e.g. PCIJ, Jurisdiction of the Courts of Danzig, Advisory Opinion, 1928 PCIJ, Series B, No 15 (3 March 1928); PCIJ, Treatment of Polish Nationals and Other Persons of Polish Origin or Speech in the Danzig Territory, Advisory Opinion, 1932 PCIJ Series A/B, No 44 (4 February 1932).

57 *See* Peace Treaty with Italy, Feb 10, 1947, pt II, § 111, arts 21–22, & Anns VI-VIII, 49 UNTS 126.

58 *See* Statute of the Permanent Court of International Justice, art 71(2) (treating the City of Danzig as a State); Crawford, *Creation of States*, at 21–22.

purposes of customary international law on State succession[59] as well as for State responsibility.[60]

In addition to these cases above, a few other International Territorial Administrations are relevant. The Coalition Provisional Authority in Iraq[61] appears to have only been cited once for contributing to customary international law.[62] Also, the UNTAC (United Nations Transitional Authority in Cambodia),[63] where the United Nations assumed governmental functions for an entire State for the first time,[64] was considered as the government of the State of Cambodia for purposes of refugee status,[65] though not cited as contributing to customary international law. The United Nations Council for Namibia (Namibia Council) was not an International Territorial Administration per se although it effectively operated as a governance mechanism by an international organization for a territory.[66] It was also not cited

59 *See* UN Secretariat, Digest of Decisions of National Courts Relating to Succession of States and Governments, UN Doc A/CN.4/157, *Yearbook of the International Law Commission* Vol II, 97 (1963), UN Doc A/CN.4/Ser.A/1963/ADD.1; International Law Commission, Ivan S. Kerno, Expert, Nationality, including Statelessness – Analysis of Changes in Nationality Legislation of States since 1930, UN Doc A/CN.4/67, 2 (Apr 6, 1953) (noting that the Hague Protocol relating to a Certain Case of Statelessness was signed 'but not ratified' by the Free City of Danzig).

60 *See* International Law Commission, Report of the International Law Commission on the work of its twenty-fifth session, 7 May–13 July 1973, UNGAOR 28th sess, Suppl No 10, UN Doc A/9010/Rev.1, *Yearbook of the International Law Commission*, Vol II (1973).

61 *See* United Nations Security Council Resolution 1483 (22 May 2003) para 4.

62 *See* R Bejesky, 'CPA Dictates on Iraq: Not an Update to the Customary International Law of Occupation but the Nucleus of Blowack with the Emergence of ISIS', *Syracuse Journal of International Law and Commerce* 42, 273 (2014–15).

63 *See* Agreement on a Comprehensive Political Settlement of the Cambodian Conflict, 30 October 1990 (Paris Agreements) (Doc S/23177 of 30 October 1991) (Paris Agreement), 31 ILM 183, esp Annex 1, Section A, para 1; United Nations Security Council Resolution 745 (1992).

64 *See* B Kondoch, 'Human Rights Law and UN Peace Operations in Post-Conflict Situations' in ND White and D Klaasen (eds), *The United Nations, Human Rights and Post-Conflict Situations* 19, 86 (Manchester University Press 2005); SR Ratner, 'The Cambodia Settlements Agreements', *American Journal of International Law* 87, 10, 12–25 (1993).

65 *See* Australian Refugee Review Tribunal, *Case No N95/08421*, Decision and Reasons for Decision, [1997] RRTA 729 (4 Mar 1997) (appearing to view UNTAC as the government of Cambodia for purposes of a refugee status determination).

66 The United Nations revoked the South African mandate over Namibia in 1966, *see* United Nations General Assembly Resolutions 2145 (XXI) (27 October 1966); 2248 (19 May 1967); 2372 (12 June 1968); United Nations Security Council Resolution 435 (1978), and in 1967 established the Namibia Council to administer the territory, *see* United Nations

for customary international law, but its other practice suggests that it could be. It was clearly intended to fill the legal 'vacuum' and held the lawful authority to govern the territory.[67] The International Law Commission did briefly consider whether agreements with the Namibia Council would be effective in binding Namibia under international law, but eventually excluded this question from the study on the law of treaties,[68] and practice shows that agreements with the Council were considered binding.[69]

We might also draw a comparison with foreign administration of colonial and trust territories. Both the International Court of Justice[70] and the International

Security Council Resolution 264 (1969); 276 (1970); International Court of Justice, Legal Consequences for States of the Continued Presence of South Africa in Namibia (South West Africa) notwithstanding Security Council Resolution 276 (1970), Advisory Opinion, 1971 ICJ Reps. 58.

67 *See* John Dugard, *The Southwest Africa / Namibia Dispute: Documents and Scholarly Writings on the Controversy Between South Africa and the United Nations* (University of California Press 1973) 409–13, 436–46; Lawrence L. Herman, 'The Legal Status of Namibia and of the United Nations Council for Namibia', *Canadian Yearbook of International Law* 306 (1975); M Sinjela, 'The Role of the United Nations Transition Assistance Group (UNTAG) in the Independence Process of Namibia', *African Yearbook of International Law* 1, 13 (1993). The Council accordingly exercised wide governmental powers, *see* United Nations Council for Namibia, Decree No. 1 on Natural Resources of Namibia, UN Doc A/C.131/33, in Report of the Council for Namibia, Add., UN GAOR, 29th Sess, Supp No 24A, at 27, UN Doc A/9624/Add.1 (1974); United Nations Council for Namibia, UNGAOR 28th sess, Suppl No 24, UN Doc A/9024, para 336(17), and had the authority to act on behalf of Namibia internationally 'in international organizations, at conferences and on any other occasion as may be required', *see* United Nations General Assembly Resolution 2871 (XXVI); 3031 (XXVII) (18 December 1972). Also *see* United Nations General Assembly Resolution 2248 (S-V) (19 May 1967).

68 *See* International Law Commission, 1429th mtg, Friday, 27 May 1977, at 11.05 am, para 7, *Yearbook of the International Law Commission*, Vol I (1977), UN Doc A/CN.4/Ser.A/1977.

69 *See* International Law Commission, United Nations Secretariat, Possibilities of participation by the United Nations in international agreements on behalf of a territory, Study prepared by the Secretariat, UN Doc A/CN.4/281, para 23 (10 June 1974), *Yearbook of the International Law Commission*, Vol II(2) (1974), UN Doc A/CN.4/Ser.A/1974/Add.l (Part 2).

70 *See* International Court of Justice, Land & Maritime Boundary (Cameroon v Nigeria: Equatorial Guinea, intervening) Judgment, 2002 ICJ Reps 303, para 33 (10 Oct 2002) (citing colonial treaty making of Germany, France and Great Britain for territories in Africa as binding); International Court of Justice, Temple of Preah Vihear (Cambodia v Thailand), Merits, Judgment, 1962 ICJ Reps. 6 (15 June 1962) (relying on the practice of the French colonial government); International Court of Justice, Right

Law Commission[71] have referred to the practice of colonial powers over territories as evidence of customary international law. The International Court of Justice jurisprudence on *uti possidetis juris* also comes to mind,[72] although it is not entirely clear from the Court's judgments whether it was finding the rule to be a general principle of law, customary international law, or simply 'logical'.[73] In its replies to inquiries from the International Law Commission, Austria cited to one case before its Supreme Court where the court looked to, inter alia, the practice of the Imperial Economic Conference of the British Empire of 1923 as evidence of customary international law.[74] In addition, some domestic courts have been willing to view State acts of the prior, colonial administration as State acts of the succeeding State.[75] Turning to trust territories, practice also seems to accept

of Passage Over Indian Territory (Portugal v India), Merits, Judgment, 1960 ICJ Reps 6 (12 Apr 1960) (relying on the colonial practice of the British and Portuguese in India).

71 *See* International Law Commission, Mohammed Bedjaoui, Special Rapporteur, Third report on succession in respect of matters other than treaties, Draft articles with commentaries on succession to public property, UN Doc A/CN.4/226 (24 March 1970) (citing extensive practice during colonial administrations of territories regarding customary international law on cessation and succession); International Law Commission, Humphrey Waldock, Special Rapporteur, Third report on succession in respect of treaties, UN Doc A/CN.4/224 & ADD.l, *Yearbook of the International Law Commission*, Vol II (1970), UN Doc A/CN.4/Ser.A/1970/Add.l; United Nations Secretariat, Succession of States to multilateral treaties: seventh study prepared by the Secretariat, UN Doc A/CN.4/225 (24 April 1970); United Nations Secretariat, Succession of States to bilateral treaties: study prepared by the Secretariat, UN Doc A/CN.4/229 (28 May 1970).

72 *See* e.g. International Court of Justice, Western Sahara, Advisory Opinion, 1975 ICJ Reps 12; International Court of Justice, Frontier Dispute (Burkina Faso/Mali), Judgment, 1986 ICJ Reps 554.

73 *See* e.g. International Court of Justice, Frontier Dispute (Burkina Faso/Mali), Judgment, 1986 ICJ Reps 554, para 20.

74 *See* International Law Commission, 67th sess, Reply by Austria, UN Doc A/69/10 (10 March 2015), Statement by Ambassador Helmut Tichy, Legal Adviser, Austrian Ministry for European and International Affairs, New York, 29 October 2012 available at http://legal.un.org/docs/?path=../ilc/sessions/67/pdfs/english/icil_austria.pdf&lang=E (citing *Dralle v Czechoslovakia*, Judgment, OGH 1 Ob 171/50, SZ 1950 No 23/143, 304–332, 17 ILR 155, 157–61 (Sup Ct, Aust, 10 May 1950). *Dralle* was in turn positively cited by the Special Rapporteur on Customary International Law, *see* International Law Commission, Michael Wood, Special Rapporteur, Second report on identification of customary international law, UN Doc A/CN.4/672 (22 May 2014) para 41.

75 *See* Nazar Mohammad & others v The Crown, Pakistan L Reps, Vol I, 19 (1948) (High Ct Lahore, Pakistan, 1948), *Annual Digest*, 1948, Case 28 (recognizing a judgment under British rule as a domestic judgment).

foreign governance acts as contributing to international law in the territory's name. The United Nations Secretariat, in a memo prepared for the International Law Commission's study on customary international law, pointed to significant practice of the UN, as administering authority, adhering to treaties in the name of the administered territory.[76]

2 Analysis of the practice

All of the citations above to the practice of International Territorial Administrations lead to several conclusions. To sum up the patchy practice outlined above, we see a general aversion to relying on the practice of an International Territorial Administration, though not an absolute prohibition. Firstly, this practice confirms that indeed International Territorial Administrations do contribute to customary international law. However, secondly, the reliance on the practice of International Territorial Administrations is not widespread and examples are infrequent. We can resolve these two points by concluding that while International Territorial Administrations do contribute formally to the creation of customary international law, their practice is not strong evidence of the content of the rules.

Whether it is possible for an International Territorial Administration to contribute to customary international law is a binary question. Certainly some actors can influence or create factual social conditions that promote certain norms, but whether an actor in a legal system has the competence to create a legal act by force of its own will, is not a spectral question. The survey of practice shows that International Territorial Administrations of various forms and natures have been viewed to hold the competence to create a legal act. In considering this question, whether the governed territory is a State is not relevant. Where the territory that is under International Territorial Administration is a State (e.g. UNOSOM or UNMIK), then that State has the potential to contribute to customary international law just as any other State would, even though it may be under an unusual (or non-democratic) governance system. In cases of co-administration, the practice could more easily be considered State practice anyway because of the presence of State organs accountable to and representative of the local population. Where the territory is not a State (e.g. UNTAES or UNTAET, at the time of is operation), the territory is still a part of some State. As

76 *See* generally United Nations Secretariat, Possibilities of participation by the United Nations in international agreements on behalf of a territory, Study prepared by the Secretariat, UN Doc A/CN.4/281 (10 June 1974), *Yearbook of the International Law Commission*, Vol II(2) (1974), UN Doc A/CN.4/Ser.A/1974/Add.l (Part 2).

such, following the logic of attribution,[77] it is a sub-State region and can contribute to customary international law within the scope of its competences.

However, the government of the territory is still an international organization. One question is whether the practice above is being cited because it is the practice of the State being governed or the practice of the international organization. Significantly, usually the practice is cited as being that of the organization, not the organization as proxy for the governed State or territory. For example, as mentioned above, the practice of UNMIK is indexed as organization practice by the International Committee of the Red Cross,[78] and both the International Court of Justice[79] and European Court of Human Rights[80] consider the practice of UNMIK as organization practice, at least for purposes of attribution. That being said, international organizations can contribute to customary international law in their own name to the degree that their activities fall within the scope of 'internal' activities or to the degree to which they have been delegated State-like competences (e.g. the European Union). Even though the administration can fully contribute to customary international law due to its governance of a qualifying territory, its ability to do so is constrained by its nature as an international organization. In the case of International Territorial Administrations, the organization has been granted

77 *See* International Law Commission, Draft conclusions on identification of customary international law, with commentaries, UN Doc A/73/10 (2018) 130, Conclusion 4, commentary (4) ('While international organizations often serve as arenas or catalysts for the practice of States, the paragraph deals with practice that is attributed to international organizations themselves, not practice of States acting within or in relation to them (which is attributed to the States concerned)'); International Law Commission, Michael Wood, Special Rapporteur, Second report on identification of customary international law, UN Doc A/CN.4/672 (22 May 2014) para 33 ('It is the conduct of States which is of primary importance for the formation and identification of customary international law, and the material element of customary international law is thus commonly referred to as "State practice", that is, conduct which is attributable to States').

78 International Committee of the Red Cross, Database, Rule 44. Due Regard for the Natural Environment in Military Operations: Section B. The precautionary principle, available at https://ihl-databases.icrc.org/customary-ihl/eng/docs/v2_cha_chapter14_rule44_sectionb.

79 *See* International Court of Justice, Accordance with International Law of the Unilateral Declaration of Independence in Respect of Kosovo, Advisory Opinion, 2010 ICJ Reps 403 (22 July 2010).

80 *See* European Court of Human Rights, *Behrami & Behrami v France; Saramati v France, Germany & Norway*, Applications No 71412/01 & 78166/01, Decision as to the admissibility (2 May 2007) paras 29–33, 133, 139–43; European Court of Human Rights, *Azemi v Serbia*, Application 11209/09, Decision on the admissibility, para 75.

considerable State-like competences, in fact going beyond the types of competences held by the European Union. Thus, it is not important whether the International Territorial Administration is a State, a territory, or an organization with State-like competences for purposes of customary international law.

One aspect of citation to this practice is notable: there are no recorded objections by States, scholars, members of the International Court of Justice or International Law Commission or other relevant actors to reliance on the acts of International Territorial Administrations, or colonial practice for that matter, for establishing customary international law. For example, while the US criticized the International Committee of the Red Cross customary international humanitarian law study in a letter to the organization stating that the 'the Study frequently fails to apply this approach [assessment of State practice] in a rigorous way' and identified several alleged State practice methodological flaws in the study, it did not identify any reliance on International Territorial Administration practice as one of those flaws.[81] Sean Murphy, among other members of the International Law Commission has been especially critical of citing practice of international organizations generally for establishing customary international law, yet his reports as Special Rapporteur on Crimes against Humanity have cited to UNTAET practice. We can understand this apparently inconsistency and failure to object by concluding that when the practice is undertaken by an international organization acting as an International Territorial Administration, the practice must be assimilated to State practice for purposes of customary international law.

Thus it appears that it is, in principle, acceptable to consider an International Territorial Administration as capable of contributing to customary international law whether it is considered practice of the territory or practice of the organization. At the end of the day, there is practice of a territorial governance unit with State-like character that can contribute to customary international law.

81 *See* e.g. US Department of State, John B Bellinger III, and US Department of Defense, William J Haybes II, Letter to the International Committee of the Red Cross, Dr Jakob Kellenberger, President, US Initial Reactions to International Committee of the Red Cross Study on Customary International Law (3 November 2006) available at https://2001–2009.state.gov/s/l/rls/82630.htm. Similarly, scholars that have criticized the International Committee of the Red Cross study also did not specifically mention reliance on international territorial administration practice as problematic. *See* e.g. I Scobbie, 'The Approach to Customary International Law in the Study' in E Wilmshurst and S Breau (eds), *Perspectives on the ICRC Study on Customary International Humanitarian Law* 15 (Cambridge University Press 2007).

However, we need to account for the thin degree of practice. While International Territorial Administrations are cited, it is infrequent and sparse. Also, while all forms of International Territorial Administrations are cited, there is inconsistency in reliance on various forms of International Territorial Administrations to establish norms of customary international law. Where practice is cited, the administration is usually exercising total authority, not partial authority, and has the ability to bind the State internationally (UNTAES, UNTAET, UNMIK, Saar, etc.). While this authority might be on the basis of a United Nations Security Council resolution under Chapter VII, it does not appear to be a requirement (see e.g. the Saar).

In addition, differing legal authorities have slightly different views on when it is appropriate to rely on the practice of International Territorial Administrations. The International Committee of the Red Cross appears to be the most open to referencing practice of International Territorial Administrations (UNTAES, UNTAET, UNMIK, UNOSOM II, High-Representative for Bosnia-Herzegovina), looking beyond situations of complete authority, although it avoids reference to colonial practices. The International Law Commission is somewhat more conservative (UNTAET, UNMIK, Saar, Danzig), although conversely it has been more open to citing practice of colonial entities. The United Nations Secretariat and International Court of Justice, as well as scholarly opinion and States themselves, are the most conservative, generally not citing to such practice as contributing to customary international law, although not excluding it either.

These considerations of existing, yet sparse practice, and reliance, though fluctuating appreciation, do not mean that International Territorial Administrations do not contribute. After all, as discussed above, these authorities do rely on International Territorial Administration practice at one time or another. Instead, this citation to practice appears to show an uncertainty, and perhaps hesitation, in using this kind of practice to prove customary international law. But if it is permissible to rely on the practice of International Territorial Administrations, then we might expect it to be far more frequent on a wide range of issues. One explanation is that there are so few International Territorial Administrations that there is less practice to cite compared to the practice of States. However, International Territorial Administrations are generally very well managed in practice, or at least well documented with freely available material, perhaps better than some States. And since they are administered by international civil servants under international organization oversight, we might expect them to be far better representatives of global State practice than the practice of a few eccentric States. Yet, citation to International Territorial Administration practice is still infrequent. This conclusion might seem paradoxical, but we can separate the two questions of contribution and evidence of contribution.

We can reconcile the binary problem of eligibility to contribute with the problem of proof, by understanding that this uncertainty is a spectral problem of the degree to which the practice is probative of the norm at issue. This analysis links back to the initial methodological difficulty of this chapter which was separating the formal from the material, since by using a citation survey it studies the question of contribution from both perspectives. Thus, the sparse practice can be explained as a statement that the practice of International Territorial Administrations is seen as less probative of norms than the practice of States. After all, organizations, in principle, hold a limited range of competences, each being slightly different from the next, and this limitation might impact the degree to which the International Territorial Administration can function. It is when it comes to proving the content of the practice, that we would place little evidentiary weight in International Territorial Administrations.

Practice shows that citation to an administration that has fully displaced the local governance is more prevalent than cases of co-administration. In order to be considered persuasive, the administration needs complete authority (UNMIK, UNTAET, etc.); a co-administration (UNOSOM II, High-Representative for Bosnia-Herzegovina, etc.) is apparently not very persuasive of the norm being formed.

3 Concluding remarks

At this point, we can draw some conclusions. First, there is, in principle, no *a priori* exclusion of International Territorial Administrations from contributing to customary international law. By administering the sovereignty of a State, the International Territorial Administration exercises in trust the State's capacity to create legal acts. Where it is only a territory of a State that is being administered, the same principle applies, though the International Territorial Administration is more akin to an organ of the State, than a State government. And though an International Territorial Administration is limited in its own competences and ability to contribute to customary international law, it may contribute when it exercises State-like competences. Thus, it has the capacity to contribute and does not have any inherent limitations on the exercise of that capacity.

However, authorities are reluctant to rely on International Territorial Administration practice as evidence for customary international law. While there are a number of explanations for why this approach might be followed, the best explanation is that International Territorial Administration practice is not as probative of customary international law as that of States with more typical governance arrangements.

Chapter 17

The formation of customary international law by *de facto* regimes

Antal Berkes

The International Law Commission's work on the identification of customary international law raised the question whether actors other than States may play a role in the formation or expression of customary international law. Beyond international organisations whose contribution to the formation of customary international law is covered in detail in the Special Rapporteur's third report, the role of 'other non-State actors' such as non-governmental organisations and even individuals was only briefly invoked by the Special Rapporteur. Indeed, scholar works referring to the role of non-State actors in the formation of customary international law mainly refer to non-governmental organisations, transnational corporations, or individuals.[1] However, there has been no discussion about the role of *de facto* regimes, whose State-like characters such as their territorial control, the exercise of governmental functions, and especially their limited, but existing participation in some international negotiations might lead to some speculation about their eventual role in the formation of customary norms.

The notion of *de facto* regime is the product of mainly German doctrine which defines it as an entity 'that exercises at least some effective political authority over a territory within a State', 'without being recognised as independent State or government of an already existing State'.[2] This definition depends neither on the existence of an armed conflict or a period of peace, nor on the question of attribution of a legal personality to the *de facto* regime, nor on its political ambitions, nor again on its

1 *See* the references in Second report on identification of customary international law, by Michael Wood, Special Rapporteur, UN Doc A/CN.4/672 (22 May 2014) para 45, fn 136.

2 Jochen Abr Frowein, '*De facto* Regime', *Max Planck Encyclopedia of Public International Law* (Oxford University Press 2014); Michael Schoiswohl, '*De facto* Regimes and Human Rights Obligations – The Twilight Zone of Public International Law' (2001) 6 Austrian Review of International and European Law 45, 50–51; Hans-Joachim Heintze, 'Sind De-Facto-Regime an Die Menschenrechte Gebunden?', *OSZE-Jahrbuch 2009: Jahrbuch zur Organisation für Sicherheit und Zusammenarbeit in Europa (OSZE).*

political independence. However, it uses objective elements and especially the main criterion, the exercise of effective control over a part of the territory of a State – which is the minimum condition of the State appearance of an armed insurgent group. The effectiveness of the territorial control necessarily implies a certain stability of the given entity – an element distinguishing it from a high number of armed groups.

Another important element that distinguishes *de facto* regimes from the community of States is their non-recognition as a State. However, the group of past and existing *de facto* regimes includes a variety of territorial entities recognised by no State or one or more, or even a group of States, but certainly not the majority of States. As a working definition, a *de facto* regime is recognised by no State (e.g. the 'Moldovan Republic of Transnistria', 'Nagorno-Karabakh Republic') or only a small number of States such as Abkhazia, South-Ossetia (both recognised by four States[3]) or Taiwan (recognised by twenty-one States[4]). Entities recognised by at least half of, but not the overwhelming majority of, United Nations member States such as currently Kosovo (recognised by 113 States[5]) or the State of Palestine (recognised by 137 States[6]) are not covered by this definition, but are considered as States *in statu nascendi*. However, their practice is taken into account in the chapter as far as their current status was preceded by a state of *de facto* regime and all references to Kosovo and Palestine will be expressly justified. Needless to say, the working definition of *de facto* regimes is based on the predominant doctrinal view under which statehood is a question of fact whose criteria are determined by law.[7] Without taking position

3 Russia, Venezuela, Nicaragua, and Nauru; two other States, Tuvalu and Vanuatu having granted, but subsequently withdrawn recognition. Angelika Nußberger, 'South Ossetia', *Max Planck Encyclopedia of Public International Law* (Oxford University Press 2013) para 1 http://opil.ouplaw.com/view/10.1093/law:epil/9780199231690/law-9780199231690-e2068 accessed 29 December 2017.

4 *See* the Ministry of Foreign Affairs of the Republic of China (Taiwan), www.mofa.gov.tw/en/AlliesIndex.aspx?n=DF6F8F246049F8D6&sms=A76B7230ADF29736 accessed 15 December 2016.

5 *See* the website of the Ministry of Foreign Affairs, Republik of Kosovo, www.mfa-ks.net/?page=2,224 accessed 5 January 2017.

6 *See* the website of the Permanent Observer Mission of the State of Palestine to the United Nations, New York, http://palestineun.org/about-palestine/diplomatic-relations/ accessed 5 January 2017; The resolution adopted by the General Assembly on the observer State status of Palestine was voted by 138 in favour to 9 against (Canada, Czech Republic, Israel, Marshall Islands, Micronesia (Federated States of), Nauru, Panama, Palau, United States), with 41 abstentions. *See* UN Doc GA/11317 (29 November 2012) and Res. 67/19. Status of Palestine in the United Nations, UN Doc A/RES/67/19 (4 December 2012).

7 *See* the definition of the 'State' by the International Criminal Tribunal for the former Yugoslavia: 'A State Member or non-Member of the United Nations or a self-proclaimed

in the debate on the question whether the *de facto* regimes analysed in the present chapter fulfil the factual criteria of statehood, it suffices to note that the final decision is incumbent upon the community of States through the act of recognition.

The lawmaking capacity of *de facto* regimes is a complex issue, depending on their concrete rights and obligations, understood as their legal capacity. Among subjects of international law, only States, original subjects of international law have the full legal personality, whereas all other subjects may have only partial legal personality, derived from the rights and obligations of States.[8] *De facto* regimes, however, possess rights and obligations as far as States allow them at the international level, for example in multilateral status settlement negotiations, in territorial or maritime boundary delimitation, and commercial law matters, etc.

Some doctrinal works have already observed, without examining the question in details, that it is still obscure in international law whether the conduct of a *de facto* regime that engages in a potentially custom-creating practice can be considered as relevant practice.[9] One can also ask whether such a *de facto* regime must, if the practice is regarded as relevant, similarly be inspired by *opinio juris* as States are, and if

entity *de facto* exercising governmental functions, whether recognized as a State or not'. *See* International Criminal Tribunal for the former Yugoslavia, Rules of procedure and evidence, Version 3, IT/32/Rev.3, 30 January 1995, Article 2 and its version in force, Rules of procedure and evidence of the International Criminal Tribunal for the former Yugoslavia, Version 49, IT/32/Rev. 49, 22 May 2013, Article 2; OAS Charter, Article 13 ('The political existence of the State is independent of recognition by other States'); Document Regarding the Situation in the Former Yugoslavia (September 25, 1991–November 16, 1992): Conference on Yugoslavia Arbitration Commission: Opinions on Questions Arising from the Dissolution of Yugoslavia, Opinion no. 1, *ILM*, 1992, vol 31, 1495; Théodore Christakis, 'The State as a "Primary Fact": Some Thoughts on the Principle of Effectiveness' in Marcelo G Kohen (ed), *Secession: International Law Perspectives* (Cambridge University Press 2012); Anthony Cullen and Steven Wheatley, 'The Human Rights of Individuals in *de facto* Regimes under the European Convention on Human Rights' (2013) 13 Human Rights Law Review 691, 696.

8 Only the State possesses the original legal personality and enjoys general competences in all domains of international law whereas other subjects derived from the legal personality of the State which can be called 'non-state actors' dispose of rights and obligations of international law only in certain matters, according to their specific status. *Legality of the Use by a State of Nuclear Weapons in Armed Conflict*, Advisory Opinion, *ICJ Reports* 1996, 78, para 25 (in respect of international organisations); Christian Walter, 'Subjects of International Law', *Max Planck Encyclopedia of Public International Law* (2007) para 23 http://opil.ouplaw.com/view/10.1093/law:epil/9780199231690/law-9780199231690-e1476?rskey=SUFjJt&result=1&prd=EPIL accessed 29 December 2017.

9 Hugh Thirlway, *The Sources of International Law* (1st edn, Oxford University Press 2014) 56, n 14.

so, what form this might take. While numerous doctrinal works have analysed the lawmaking activities of armed opposition groups[10] and even of *de facto* regimes,[11] no study has considered the impact of *de facto* regimes specifically on customary international law.

The chapter does not examine whether *de facto* regimes can participate in the formation of sources of international law other than customary international law (international conventions, acts of international organisations and especially of international tribunals). Those sources form State practice, one of the constitutive elements of customary international law,[12] to which *de facto* regimes might *indirectly* contribute, together with States. Instead of this *indirect* role, the chapter focuses on the question whether *de facto* regimes may *directly* contribute to the formation of customary international law through their conduct, which is not necessarily, but might be, considered as State practice.

The International Law Commission held that as a non-State actor, the conduct of *de facto* regimes 'is not practice that contributes to the formation, or expression, of rules of customary international law' for the sake of the identification of customary international law.[13] However, the present chapter argues that the activities of *de facto* regimes can be considered as properly speaking 'practice' that contributes to the formation, or expression, of rules of customary international law under two scenarios. Firstly, the custom-creating or custom-strengthening conduct of the *de facto* regime might be attributed to a State, usually to an occupying power or a State supporting in various means the *de facto* regime by exercising effective control or at least decisive influence over it. As Section 1 explains, this is the first scenario where the conduct of *de facto* regimes can be regarded as 'practice' for the identification of customary international law (1). Secondly, *de lege ferenda*, Section 2 argues that even without attributing the *de facto* regime's conduct to a State, its conduct should be

10 Anthea Roberts and Sandesh Sivakumaran, 'Lawmaking by Nonstate Actors: Engaging Armed Groups in the Creation of International Humanitarian Law' (2012) 37 Yale Journal of International Law 4; Sophie Rondeau, 'Participation of Armed Groups in the Development of the Law Applicable to Armed Conflicts' (2011) 93 International Review of the Red Cross 649.

11 Sandesh Sivakumaran, 'Lessons for the Law of Armed Conflict from Commitments of Armed Groups: Identification of Legitimate Targets and Prisoners of War' (2011) 93 International Review of the Red Cross 1, 5–6.

12 *North Sea Continental Shelf*, Judgment, *ICJ Reports* 1969, 44, para 77.

13 International Law Commission, Identification of customary international law, Text of the draft conclusions provisionally adopted by the Drafting Committee, UN Doc A/CN.4/L.872 (30 May 2016), Draft conclusion 4[5](3).

taken into account as strengthening the practice forming customary international law at least in subject matters governing the rights and obligations of the *de facto* regime itself (2). Although both scenarios may raise various theoretical and practical objections, it will be explained that in areas under-regulated by international law, the conduct of *de facto* regimes may be relevant as 'practice' revealing a State's practice. The chapter ends with a few concluding remarks (3).

1 Attribution of the *de facto* regime's conduct to a State

The unlawful conduct of *de facto* regimes may be attributed to an outside State – defined as a State other than the territorial State in which the *de facto* regime operates – under one of the International Law Commission's Articles on the Responsibility of States for Internationally Wrongful Act,[14] for example if the outside State exercises 'effective control' over the entity.[15] There is a growing international case law on such attribution of the conduct of *de facto* regimes – it suffices to think to the case law of the European Court of Human Rights with regard to the conduct of the Turkish Republic of Northern Cyprus/Turkey,[16] the 'Moldovan Republic of Transnistria'/ Russia,[17] the 'Nagorno-Karabak Republic'/Armenia.[18] One can presume that under the same logic, if a *de facto* regime has a lawful, custom-relevant conduct, the latter can similarly be attributed to the same State and consequently, the conduct becomes State practice, considered as practice by the International Law Commission for the sake of the formation of customary international law. However, this hypothesis raises various theoretical and practical difficulties.

The theoretical difficulty is that attribution of conduct has been constructed with regard to unlawful and not lawful conduct. The International Law Commission has

14 Draft articles on responsibility of States for internationally wrongful acts and commentary thereof, *YbILC*, 2001, vol II (Part Two), Articles 4–11.

15 ibid Article 8.

16 European Court of Human Rights, *Loizidou v Turkey (Merits)* [GC], Appl no 15318/89, judgment of 18 December 1996, paras 49–57, esp para 56; *Cyprus v Turkey* [GC], Appl no 25781/94, Judgment of 10 May 2001, para 77.

17 European Court of Human Rights, *Ilaşcu and Others v Moldova and Russia* [GC], Appl. no. 48787/99, judgment of 8 July 2004, para 392; *Catan and Others v Moldova and Russia* [GC], Appl nos 43370/04, 8252/05 and 18454/06, judgment of 19 October 2012, para 150; *Mozer v the Republic of Moldova and Russia*, Appl. no 11138/10, judgment of 23 February 2016, para 110.

18 European Court of Human Rights, *Chiragov and Others v Armenia (Merits)* [GC], Appl no 13216/05, Judgment of 16 June 2015, para 186; *Muradyan v Armenia*, Appl no 11275/07, judgment of 24 November 2017, para 126.

theorised attribution in its works on the responsibility of States for internationally wrongful acts and the responsibility of international organisations for internationally wrongful acts. However, if one closely examines the notion of attribution, one finds that it has an independent character, unrelated to the unlawfulness of the act. Since States can only act through the person of their agents and representatives,[19] attribution determines the persons who should be considered as acting on behalf of the State, constituting an 'act of the State' for the purposes of the law of State responsibility.[20] Attribution is only the first constitutive element of the internationally wrongful act of a State, whereas the second element is the breach of an international obligation of the State.[21] Thus, one can suppose that attribution can be applied even outside the context of international responsibility for unlawful conduct, whenever it has to be decided whether a conduct can be considered as an act of the State or of an international organisation. Indeed, the International Law Commission did use the concept of attribution in its reports on the identification of customary international law.[22] Therefore, there is no valid theoretical objection against such an attribution.

Another classical counter-argument against this hypothesis is the unrecognised nature of *de facto* regimes and the eventual duty of States not to recognise any acts of *de facto* regimes as valid. While several binding Security Council resolutions imposed such a duty of non-recognition on States, it was doubtful whether States had to consider all conducts of *de facto* regimes as null and void. In the *Legal consequences for States of the continued presence of South Africa in Namibia (South West Africa) notwithstanding Security Council resolution 276 (1970)* advisory opinion, the International Court of Justice clarified those obligations. Whereas the Court

19 *Certain questions relating to settlers of German origin in the territory ceded by Germany to Poland*, advisory opinion, 10 September 1923, Series B, no 6, 22.

20 Articles on responsibility of States for internationally wrongful acts and commentary thereof, *YbILC*, 2001, vol II (Part Two), 35, para 4 (Commentary to Article 2).

21 Articles on the Responsibility of States for Internationally Wrongful Act (n 14), 26–30, Article 2.

22 Report of the International Law Commission, Sixty-eighth session (2 May-10 June and 4 July-12 August 2016), UN Doc A/71/10 (2016), 88, para 3 (Commentary of para 2, Conclusion 4: 'The paragraph deals with practice attributed to international organizations themselves, not that of their member States acting within them (which is attributed to the States in question)'); Third report on identification of customary international law, by Michael Wood, Special Rapporteur, UN Doc A/CN.4/682 (27 March 2015), para 71 ('The present report, like the second report, proceeds on the basis of the determination that, where appropriate, the practice of States within international organizations is to be attributed to States themselves').

confirmed that 'official acts' performed by South Africa concerning Namibia are 'illegal and invalid', it identified one exception of the absolute invalidity rule:

> In general, the non-recognition of South Africa's administration of the Territory should not result in depriving the people of Namibia of any advantages derived from international Co-operation. In particular, while official acts performed by the Government of South Africa on behalf of or concerning Namibia after the termination of the Mandate are illegal and invalid, this invalidity cannot be extended to those acts, such as, for instance, the registration of births, deaths and marriages, the effects of which can be ignored only to the detriment of the inhabitants of the Territory.[23]

Although the scope of these acts is not clearly defined,[24] at least one can conclude that the so-called Namibia-exception, i.e. the non-application of the absolute nullity rule to certain acts concerning the inhabitants of the territory, has humanitarian considerations. Domestic[25] and international case law[26] has latter confirmed the Namibia-exception and allowed the validity of non-political acts, i.e. acts of ordinary administration of *de facto* regimes as lawful. Consequently, the lawfulness of certain conducts of *de facto* regimes would not raise any difficulty, within the limits of the *Namibia*-exception.

23 *Legal consequences for States of the continued presence of South Africa in Namibia (South West Africa) notwithstanding Security Council resolution 276 (1970)*, Advisory Opinion, *ICJ Reports* 1971, 55–56, para 125.

24 Verhoeven qualified this paragraph as 'perplexed'. Joe Verhoeven, 'Relations Internationales de Droit Privé En l'absence de Reconnaissance d'un État, d'un Gouvernement Ou d'une Situation' (1985) 192 Recueil des Cours 9, 92.

25 E.g. English Court of Appeals, *Hesperides Hotels Ltd v Aegean Turkish Holidays Ltd*, 1978 QB 205, [1978] 1 All ER 277 (CA), 218.

26 E.g. European Court of Human Rights, *Loizidou v Turkey* [GC], Application no 15318/89, judgment of 18 December 1996, para 45; *Cyprus v Turkey* [IV] [GC], Application no 25781/94, judgment of 10 May 2001 [*Cyprus v Turkey* [IV]], para 96; *Takis Demopoulos and Others* [GC], Application nos 46113/99, 3843/02, 13751/02, 13466/03, 10200/04, 14163/04, 19993/04, 21819/04, decision of 1 March 2010 on the admissibility [*Demopoulos and Others*], para 94; European Commission for Democracy through law (Venice Commission), Comments on the Law on occupied territories of Georgia, Ms Angelika Nussberger (Substitute Member, Germany), Opinion no 516/2009, CDL(2009)045, Strasbourg, 4 March 2009; Interim opinion on the Draft amendments and annexes to the Law on occupied territories of Georgia, Adopted by the Venice Commission at its 80th Plenary Session (Venice, 9–10 October 2009), Opinion no 552 / 2009, CDL-AD (2009)046, Strasbourg, 13 October 2009, para 22; Special Follow-Up Mission to the Areas Affected by the South Ossetia Conflict: Implementation of the Commissioner's six principles for urgent human rights and humanitarian protection, by Thomas Hammarberg, Commissioner for Human Rights of the Council of Europe,

The practical difficulties are more significant: to be able to attribute lawful conduct of *de facto* regimes to a State, the conduct must be known and available for judges or the International Law Commission. However, judges or the International Law Commission are rarely aware of the conduct and especially legal acts of unrecognised *de facto* regimes and it is even more exceptional that they are aware of lawful conducts. Some International Law Commission members complained, while discussing the relevance of the conduct of non-State armed opposition groups in the identification of customary norms, that they had insufficient information on the practice of non-State armed groups.[27] The situation is not much better in the case of *de facto* regimes that, although they have effectively operational governmental, legal and judicial systems, rarely publish their practice and case law in a transparent, available manner. Most *de facto* regimes, because of their lack of international relations, resources, and competences, are unable to make available and transparent their legal sources. Moreover, the above-mentioned international case law about attribution of the conduct of *de facto* regimes to States has usually arisen in cases involving violations of international humanitarian or international human rights law, thus unlawful conduct. Lawful acts and omissions simply do not reach the level of international disputes since they are rarely relevant. Nevertheless, there are some cases where courts considered some conducts of *de facto* regimes as lawful.

The first example where courts found the conduct of a *de facto* regime as lawful concerns the law of the Turkish Republic of Northern Cyprus on compensation of lost property of internally displaced persons. The antecedents of the law go back to the decade-long case law of the European Court of Human Rights on northern Cyprus. In those cases, the Court systematically found that Greek Cypriot

Doc CommDH(2008)33, Strasbourg, 21 October 2008, 25 to 27 September 2008, para 81; Human Rights Council, Report of the Representative of the Secretary-General on the human rights of internally displaced persons, Walter Kälin, Addendum, UN Doc A/HRC/10/13/Add.2 (13 February 2009) para 56; International Law Commission, *Yearbook of the International Law Commission*, 1982, vol II(1), UN Doc A/CN.4/SER.A/1982/Add.1 (Part 1) (1982) 49, para 8.

27 E.g. International Law Commission, Provisional summary record of the 3266th meeting, UN Doc A/CN.4/SR.3266 (30 May 2016) 7–8 (Mr Park); Second report on the protection of the environment in relation to armed conflicts, Submitted by Marie G Jacobsson, Special Rapporteur, UN Doc A/CN.4/685 (28 May 2015) para 9; Third report on the protection of the environment in relation to armed conflicts, submitted by Marie G Jacobsson, Special Rapporteur, UN Doc A/CN.4/700 (3 June 2016) para 15; International Law Commission, Provisional summary record of the 3265th meeting, UN Doc A/CN.4/SR.3265 (7 August 2015) 9 (Mr Forteau).

applicants, displaced from northern Cyprus to the south because of the Turkish occupation, were denied access to the control, use, and enjoyment of their property and any compensation for the interference with their property rights in the Turkish Republic of Northern Cyprus.[28] As a consequence of the systematic condemnation of Turkey and the unsatisfactory legislation of the Turkish Republic of Northern Cyprus, the Turkish Cypriot authorities decided to adopt a law for the compensation, exchange, and restitution of immovable properties, which provided that all natural and legal persons claiming rights to immovable or movable property might bring a claim before the Immovable Property Commission.[29] The Immovable Property Commission shall examine and reach decisions on applications, determine the amount and method of payment of compensation to be paid for the applicants. Based on the structure and the operation of the mechanism, the European Court of Human Rights held in subsequent northern Cyprus property cases that the Turkish Republic of Northern Cyprus law 'provides an accessible and effective framework of redress in respect of complaints about interference with the property owned by Greek Cypriots'.[30]

Similarly, the friendly settlements concluded between a *de facto* regime and an individual are conform to international law and the European Court of Human Rights recognised their validity as a friendly settlement concluded between the applicant and the respondent State. For example in the *Tymvios* case, the applicant, a Cypriot national, complained before the European Court of Human Rights that he had been unable to access or enjoy his property in the northern part of Cyprus. After the decision of the Immovable Property Commission to receive compensation for his lost property and an exchange of property, he accepted the decision and signed a friendly settlement agreement formally with the Turkish government, executed by the Turkish Republic of Northern Cyprus.[31] Before the European Court of Human Rights, Turkey confirmed the agreement, the payment of compensation, and 'the exchange of property insofar as the exchange decision can be executed within the control and power of the authorities of the Turkish

28 E.g. *Cyprus v Turkey* [IV] (n 26) paras 187, 189; *Xenides-Arestis v Turkey (merits)*, Application 46347/99, Judgment of 22 December 2005, para 32.

29 *Demopoulos and Others* (n 26) para 35.

30 ibid para 127; *Anastasia Ioannou Iacovou and Others v Turkey*, Applications nos 24506/08, 24730/08, 60758/08, partial decision of 5 October 2010 on the admissibility.

31 *See* in this sense: Note verbale dated 28 March 2008 from the Permanent Mission of Turkey addressed to the Office of the United Nations High Commissioner for Human Rights, Annex ('Turkish Republic of northern Cyprus Deputy Minister and Ministry of Foreign Affairs'), UN Doc A/HRC/7/G/16 (1 April 2008) 7–8.

Republic of Northern Cyprus'.[32] Recognizing the friendly settlement as lawful, the Court

> welcomes the agreement reached between the parties (Article 39 of the Convention) and takes note of the explanation given by the Government concerning the conditional nature of the agreement insofar as it concerned a possible exchange of property. It is satisfied that the settlement is based on respect for human rights as defined in the Convention or its Protocols (Article 37 § 1 *in fine* of the Convention and Rule 62 § 3 of the Rules of Court) and that it is equitable within the meaning of Rule 75 § 4 of the Rules.[33]

The practice of the Turkish Republic of Northern Cyprus in the matter of the right to property of internally displaced persons and compensation claims is likely to confirm the existing customary norms in international humanitarian and human rights law[34] or to give rise to new customary rules (e.g. as regards the procedure, friendly settlement, compensation). However, one may object to this hypothesis by claiming that the authorities of the Turkish Republic of Northern Cyprus, and thus Turkey acted not under an *opinio juris*, but under a treaty obligation, namely the provisions of the European Convention on Human Rights and its protocols protecting the right to property and the right to fair trial and the subsequent condemning judgment of the European Court of Human Rights. It is possible that the isolated act of adopting the Turkish Republic of Northern Cyprus law on property compensation reflected a compliance with a treaty, but in a repeated and systematic way, its application by the Turkish Republic of Northern Cyprus authorities and its eventual adaptation by other *de facto* regimes certainly reflect an acceptation by a sense of legal right or obligation.

It is less disputed that *de facto* regimes are bound by customary international law – such a principle was reiterated in international humanitarian law, as far as *de facto* regimes are parties to armed conflicts,[35] and in international human rights law,[36] as far as *de facto* regimes govern persons under their control. Some of the *de facto* regimes have vaguely recognised their commitment to respect customary

32 European Court of Human Rights, *Eugenia Michaelidou Developments Ltd and Michael Tymvios v Turkey (Just satisfaction, friendly settlement)*, Application no 16163/90, judgment of 22 April 2008, para 14.

33 ibid para 15.

34 Jean-Marie Henckaerts and others, *Customary International Humanitarian Law*, vol 1 (Rules) (Comité international de la Croix-Rouge ed, Cambridge University Press 2009) 472–74 (Rule 133. Property Rights of Displaced Persons).

35 ibid 299.

36 Report of the independent international commission of inquiry on the Syrian Arab Republic, UN Doc A/HRC/21/50 (15 August 2012), Annex II: Applicable law, 47, para 10.

international law in unilateral acts[37] or bilateral agreements concluded with States.[38] They are sometimes aware of their obligations under customary international law and try to comply with it. Thus, at least one can say that that the detailed elaboration of the Turkish Republic of Northern Cyprus law and its domestic mechanism may contribute to a growing customary norm. Beyond attribution of conduct to a State, there have been some instances where certain International Law Commission members or other international bodies examined the conduct of *de facto* regimes to identify or clarify the state of customary international law.

2 Consideration the conduct of *de facto* regimes as such

There were some isolated cases where International Law Commission members seemed to take into account the conduct of certain *de facto* regimes not as an act

37 Constitution of the 'Pridnestrovskaia Moldavskaia Respublika' adopted on 24 December 1995 at the national referendum and signed by the President of the 'Pridnestrovskaia Moldavskaia Respublika' on 17 January 1996, accessible in English at the website of the 'PMR Constitutional Court', www.kspmr.idknet.com/eng/k_I.htm accessed 23 August 2016, preamble and Article 10(2) ('Universally recognised principles and norms of international law [...] shall be the basis for relations with other states and the constituent part of the legal system.'); *Конституция Республики Южная Осетия* [Constitution of South-Ossetia], adopted by referendum on 8 April 2001, available in Russian at http://south-ossetia.info/respublika-yuzhnaya-osetiya-segodnya/konstituciya-osnovnoj-zakon-respubliki-yuzhnaya-osetiya/ accessed 4 October 2016, Articles 2(5), 11(2), 18 ('universally recognised principles and norms of international law'); Abkhazia, 'People's Assembly – the Parliament of the Republic of Abkhazia', To the Secretary General of the United Nations, president of the Security Council of the United Nations, Parliaments of the countries of the world, 7 March 2008, available at www.kapba.de/AppealByUN.html accessed 21 November 2016, paras 15, 17 ('compliance with the recognised norms of international law'); *Конституция Донецкой Народной Республики* [Constitution of the People's Republic of Donetsk], 14 May 2014, available at the website of the self-proclaimed entity, https://dnrsovet.su/konstitutsiya/ accessed 10 February 2018, Article 12(1) ('guarantees the rights and freedoms of man and citizen according to the universally recognised principles and norms of international law'); *Конституция Луганской народной республики* [Constitution of the People's Republic of Lugansk], 18 March 2014, available at the website of the self-proclaimed entity, http://lug-info.com/documents/one/12 accessed 16 December 2016, Article 12(1) ('guarantees the rights and freedoms of man and citizen according to the universally recognised principles and norms of international law').

38 E.g. the commitment of the FARC in the signed peace agreement: *Acuerdo final para la terminación del conflicto y la construcción de una paz estable y duradera* [Final Peace Accord for the Conclusion of the Conflict and the Construction of Stable and Lasting Peace], Bogotá, 24 November 2016 (ratified by the Colombian Congress on 30 November 2016), preamble, para 25.

attributed to an outside State, but as a relevant conduct, similar or assimilated to 'practice'. The first is the conduct of *de facto* regimes as parties to armed conflicts, as far as they are bound by customary international humanitarian law (2.1). The second case is a rather *de lege ferenda* proposition to assimilate the conduct of the *de facto* regime either to the territorial State (2.2) or to a new State (2.3) and consider it as State practice for the formation of customary international law. These three categories show that there is certainly more space to consider the conduct of *de facto* regimes for the sake of customary international law than only in cases where it is attributed to an outside State.

2.1 De facto *regimes as parties to armed conflicts*

First of all, international humanitarian law binds 'parties' to the armed conflict, i.e. both States and non-State armed groups in a non-international armed conflict, and not only States.[39] Since most *de facto* regimes gained their effective control over a territory in armed hostilities with the governmental forces of the territorial State, they had and, if hostilities are ongoing, still have the status of non-State armed opposition group under international humanitarian law. Thus, *de facto* regimes as armed opposition groups were or are bound by the rules of international humanitarian law applicable to non-State parties to non-international armed conflicts. Without examining in details the complicated questions whether, how, and how far non-State armed groups could contribute to the formation of customary international humanitarian law, it suffices to indicate a growing number of authors and international bodies who take into account in international humanitarian law the conduct of non-State armed groups in the analysis of 'practice'.

The International Criminal Tribunal for the former Yugoslavia held in the *Tadić* Decision on Defence Motion for Interlocutory Appeal on Jurisdiction, that beyond the practice of States, the behaviour of insurgents has been 'instrumental in bringing about the formation of the customary rules' protecting civilians from hostilities in the course of internal armed conflicts.[40] However, the decision proved

39 Convention (IV) relative to the Protection of Civilian Persons in Time of War. Geneva, 12 August 1949, 75 *UNTS* 31, Article 3; Protocol Additional to the Geneva Conventions of 12 August 1949, and relating to the Protection of Victims of Non-International Armed Conflicts (Protocol II), 8 June 1977, 1125 *UNTS* 609; Convention for the Protection of Cultural Property in the Event of Armed Conflict, 14 May 1954, 249 *UNTS* 240, Article 19, etc. For a detailed list of conventions binding non-State armed groups, *see* Roberts and Sivakumaran (n 10) 108, n 1–2.

40 International Criminal Tribunal for the former Yugoslavia, *The Prosecutor v Dusko Tadić aka 'Dule'*, Decision on Defence Motion for Interlocutory Appeal on Jurisdiction,

to remain a rather isolated case that did not make any echo in the later case law. The International Committee of the Red Cross, in its Study on Customary International Humanitarian Law, excluded the conduct of non-State armed groups from 'State practice' as such, but accepted that 'such practice may contain evidence of the acceptance of certain rules in non-international armed conflicts', while 'its legal significance is unclear and it has therefore been listed under "Other Practice" '.[41] Indeed, if one cautiously examines the International Committee of the Red Cross's Study on Customary International Humanitarian Law, one finds that certain unilateral commitments of non-State armed groups are indeed cited to confirm State practice.[42]

The International Law Association, in its second report on non-State actors, accepted that non-State actors' practice 'can be taken into account to ascertain norms that govern their own behavior'.[43] Furthermore, it was favourable to the doctrinal opinion that proposes to give non-State armed groups a role in the formation of 'quasi-custom', to 'allow armed groups to play some role in the creation of customary norms without ceding all, or even equal, control to armed groups'.[44] This suggestion forms a middle ground between excluding any role for armed groups in the formation of customary international law on the one hand, and treating such groups on par with States on the other.

Finally, the International Law Commission, although refusing to consider the conduct of non-State armed groups as 'practice' relevant to the formation of customary international law, adopted a somewhat different view in its ongoing work on the 'Protection of the environment in relation to armed conflicts'. During the codification work, several members of the International Law Commission recommended the Special Rapporteur that she should examine the practice of non-State actors further and 'that she should not let the Commission's tendency not to include practice by non-State actors as part of the concept of customary international law deter her from doing so'.[45] The Special Rapporteur herself expressed her some sympathy for

Appeals Chamber, 2 Oct 1995, Case No IT-94-1-AR72 [*Tadić*, Decision on Defence Motion for Interlocutory Appeal on Jurisdiction] para 108.

41 Henckaerts and others (n 34) xlii, para vii.

42 SPLM/A Penal and Disciplinary Laws, cited ibid 423, 424 (Commentary of Rule 117).; statement of FARC-EP and the reported practice of the SPLM/A, cited ibid 454 (Commentary to Rule 128).

43 International Law Association, Sofia Conference (2012), Non-State Actors, Second Report of the Committee, Non-State Actors in International Law: Lawmaking and Participation Rights, 6.

44 ibid referring to Roberts and Sivakumaran (n 10) 143–44, 151.

45 International Law Commission, Provisional summary record of the 3269th meeting, UN Doc A/CN.4/SR.3269 (22 September 2015) 11 (Ms Jacobsson, Special Rapporteur);

the proposal.[46] The most often cited arguments for this proposal were the grave consequences of the armed groups' activities for the environment and their obligations under international humanitarian law;[47] therefore 'their practice should be taken into consideration and analysed from a legal perspective, even if it was to condemn them for violations'.[48]

It is not by accident that the International Law Commission members expressed much more sympathy towards the consideration of the conduct of non-State armed groups in matter of the protection of the environment in armed conflicts rather than in the discussions about the formation of customary international law in general. Non-State actors with a territorial control, and, at a stabilised phase, with governmental functions as *de facto* regimes can more effectively undertake and comply with international norms, and thus contribute to the formation of customary international law. It is also telling that the only international judicial decision citing acts of non-State armed groups as constituting practice for customary international law, the above-mentioned *Tadić* decision, cited the rules of conduct of two more or less stabilised non-State armed groups with a considerable territorial control. The first was the Chinese People's Liberation Army, the second the FMLN of El Salvador – both insurgent movements becoming victorious, acquiring governmental functions.[49] It is submitted that the more stabilised the *de facto* regime is and the more governmental functions is exercises, the more it can participate in lawmaking activities in international relations and contribute to the formation of customary international law. Furthermore, because the *de facto* governmental functions of *de facto* regimes may extend to more subject matters than the conduct of mere armed groups with remote or no territorial control, their contribution to the formation of customary international law is not necessarily limited to international

International Law Commission, Provisional summary record of the 3268th meeting, UN Doc A/CN.4/SR.3268 (11 May 2016) 14 (Ms Escobar Hernández). *a contrario*: International Law Commission, Provisional summary record of the 3266th meeting, UN Doc A/CN.4/SR.3266 (30 May 2016) 13 (Mr Kittichaisaree).

46 International Law Commission, Provisional summary record of the 3266th meeting, UN Doc A/CN.4/SR.3266 (30 May 2016) 5 (Mr Hassouna); International Law Commission, Provisional summary record of the 3254th meeting, UN Doc A/CN.4/SR.3254 (10 May 2016) 3 (Ms Jacobsson).

47 International Law Commission, Provisional summary record of the 3254th meeting, UN Doc A/CN.4/SR.3254 (10 May 2016) 3 (Ms Jacobsson).

48 International Law Commission, Provisional summary record of the 3264th meeting, UN Doc A/CN.4/SR.3264 (6 May 2016) 16–17 (Mr Saboia).

49 *Tadić*, Decision on Defence Motion for Interlocutory Appeal on Jurisdiction (n 40) paras 102, 107.

humanitarian law, but may extend to related fields. Such fields might include human rights law, the law of cultural heritage, the law of the sea, or – as the recent statements of the International Law Commission members in the codification work on natural resources in armed conflicts suggest – environmental law.

2.2 Acts of de facto *regimes assimilated to those of the territorial State*

As it is recognised, the actions of all branches of government (whether exercising executive, legislative, judicial, or other functions) and all levels (whatever its character as an organ of the central government or of a territorial unit of the) of the State administration may count as State practice for the purposes of customary international law.[50] By a legal fiction, the practice of *de facto* regimes can eventually be taken into account as the practice of a territorial unit of the territorial State, without specifying the status of the *de facto* regime and while 'disregarding any controversial aspects of the status of that entity'.[51] Some members of the International Law Commission seemed to be in favour of a solution that treats the domestic law or acts of a *de facto* regime, for the sake of international law, as law and acts of the territorial State. This was the case of the 'nationality' of the residents in the Bantustan home-states for the sake of the nationality, considered by International Law Commission members as South African while analysing the State practice.[52] The assimilation of acts of the *de facto* regime to acts of the territorial State is not an attribution of conduct, defined above as the determination of the 'act of the State' for the purposes of the responsibility of States, but the classification of a *sui generis* entity's act according to the recognised nationalities. Such a solution would be pertinent in the case of identifying customary international law where the State practice would be strengthened by the conduct of a *de facto* regime.

This is also confirmed by the United Nations' practice with regard to certain unrecognised *de facto* regimes. In the case of Taiwan, since the adoption of resolution 2758 (XXVI) of 25 October 1971 on the 'Restoration of the lawful rights of the People's Republic of China in the United Nations', the established practice of the United Nations has been to use the term 'Taiwan, Province of China' when a reference to 'Taiwan' in United Nations Secretariat documents.[53] However, even

50 Second report on identification of customary international law, by Michael Wood, Special Rapporteur, UN Doc A/CN.4/672 (22 May 2014) para 34.

51 Seventh report on unilateral acts of States, by Mr Víctor Rodríguez Cedeño, Special Rapporteur, UN Doc. A/CN.4/542 (22 April 2004) paras 31, 131.

52 2486th meeting, 30 May 1997, in: *YbILC*, 1997, vol I, 86, para 68 (Mr Crawford); 2499th meeting, 25 June 1997, in: *YbILC*, 1997, vol I, 173, para 50 (Mr Crawford).

53 *UNJYB*, 2010, Part II, 516, para 3.

the neutral denominations 'Taiwan' or 'Kosovo' are used in United Nations documents, with a usual footnote to the United Nations' official position about the *de facto* regime's non-recognition ('In accordance with United Nations terminology, reference to Taiwan in the present document should read Taiwan, Province of China';[54] 'All references to Kosovo in the present document should be understood to be in compliance with Security Council resolution 1244 (1999)'[55]). The status-neutral denominations led certain International Law Commission members to consider the conduct of those entities as relevant State practice. For example the Special Rapporteur on unilateral acts of States referred to the protest, promise, and other acts of Taiwan as forming the customary norms in the matter of unilateral acts of States.[56] These references provoked harsh debates within the International Law Commission: some members considered the references to Taiwan as a 'wandering into a political minefield',[57] while others explained that the issue is 'an internal matter of China', a question of recognition of governments rather than recognition of States since 'Taiwan was part of China'.[58] Notwithstanding the Special Rapporteur's references, the International Law Commission followed the majority view of States when it decided that the references 'in the report in relation to Taiwan as a subject of international law were not in keeping with general Assembly resolution 2758 (XXVI) of 25 October 1971 and should therefore not have been included'.[59] Thus, in case of recorded objections, the International Law Commission prefers to follow the opinion of States and not to include the conduct of *de facto* regimes as relevant practice in its reports as it did in the final outcome on unilateral declarations of States.[60]

It is not without importance that the International Law Association, in its first report on 'Non-State Actors', while reiterating its former conclusion that acts of non-State actors 'do not count as State practice, unless carried out on behalf of

54 ibid 517, para 6.
55 E.g. Report of the Working Group on Enforced or Involuntary Disappearances, Mission to Serbia, including Kosovo, UN Doc A/HRC/30/38/Add.1 (17 August 2015); Report of the Special Rapporteur on adequate housing as a component of the right to an adequate standard of living, and on the right to non-discrimination in this context on her mission to Serbia and Kosovo, UN Doc A/HRC/31/54/Add.2 (26 February 2016).
56 ibid para 131; 2811th meeting, 5 July 2004, in: *YbILC*, 2004, vol I, 144, para 13.
57 2816th meeting, 13 July 2004, in: *YbILC*, 2004, vol I, 169, para 6 (Mr Kateka).
58 ibid 171–72, para 25–27 (Ms Xue).
59 Report of the International Law Commission, Fifty-sixth session (3 May–4 June and 5 July–6 August 2004), UN Doc A/59/10 (2004), in: *YbILC*, 2004, vol II (Part Two) 95, para 233.
60 Guiding Principles applicable to unilateral declarations of States capable of creating legal obligations, with commentaries thereto, in: *YbILC*, 2006, vol II (Part Two) 159–66.

the State or adopted ("ratified") by it',[61] excluded from its examination 'territorial entities such as Kosovo and Palestine'.[62] Somewhat ambiguously, the ILA justified this exclusion by stating that '[s]uch entities present the rather different question of whether it is a State or a component of a State than that of whether it is a non-State actor'.[63] The report was prepared at a moment where both Kosovo and Palestine did not reach a considerable number of State recognitions and were not States parties to any international organisations. However, at least the later statement indicates that the International Law Association considered it possible to treat such *de facto* regimes as 'a component of a State'. Consequently, where the *de facto* regime seeks independence from a State that the international community accepts as the territorial State, one might regard the conduct of the *de facto* regime as that of a territorial unit within the later State. This would not raise any problem if the territorial State followed the same practice and accepted the conduct of the *de facto* regime. However, such an analogy would be problematic if the territorial State followed a contrary practice and would even oppose the *de facto* regime's conduct.

2.3 Acts of de facto *regimes assimilated to a new State*

Even if *de facto* regimes remain unrecognised by the majority of States, the State-like conduct of a *de facto* regime recognised by a small number of States might be considered as State practice if it strengthens the practice of other States. It is not recommended that the International Law Commission or the International Court of Justice resort to this assimilation, because their views necessarily reflect the current state of international law as perceived by the majority of States. As the above-mentioned example of the Taiwanese practice shows, the International Law Commission is likely to follow the majority view of the international community on the statehood of an entity. Nothing excludes, however, that other expert bodies or scholars consider the relevant acts of partially recognised *de facto* regimes as 'practice' for the sake of the identification of customary international law.

61 International Law Association, The Hague Conference (2010), Non-State Actors, First Report of the Committee. Non-State Actors in International Law: Aims, Approach and Scope of Project and Legal Issues [International Law Association, Non-State Actors, First Report], 11; International Law Association, London Conference (2000), Committee on Formation of Customary International Law, Final Report of the Committee: Statement of principles applicable to the formation of general customary international law, 16 (Principle no. 7).

62 International Law Association, Non-State Actors, First Report (n 61) 6.

63 ibid.

The International Law Association, for example, in its report on the rights of indigenous peoples, while identifying the relevant State practice for the establishment of customary international law, referred to the legislation of Taiwan without any discussion about its contested status.[64] There are no available data about debates on this inclusion, similar to those at the International Law Commission. This is not without importance and shows that even without universal recognition, an entity recognised by at least some States could be considered as an actor whose conduct amounts to 'practice' of States. The boundary to draw between unrecognised and partially recognised State is however difficult, but it shows that *de facto* regimes might not be entirely excluded from the identification of customary international law.

All the above-mentioned scenarios (2.1–2.3) are especially relevant when considering the conduct of *de facto* regimes as proper 'practice' for the identification of customary international law strengthens the practice of States in subject matters governing the rights and obligations of the *de facto* regime itself. Possible matters might be certain legal domains not yet examined by the International Law Commission such as the privileges and immunities of international organisations binding *de facto* regimes or the legal regime applicable to internal ceasefire lines.

3 Concluding remarks

This chapter argued that several instances of the *de facto* regimes' lawmaking capacity and conduct should be taken into account either as relevant sources for identifying the 'practice' of States or the conduct of international organisations, or as relevant 'practice' as such. As to the counterarguments invoked above, the main reason for considering the conduct of *de facto* regimes in certain circumstances as relevant practice for the formation of customary international law is their State-like nature. If one accepts that armed opposition groups do have a custom-creating capacity in international humanitarian law, one could argue that armed opposition groups with stable control over a territory, considered as *de facto* regimes in a period of armed conflict, *a fortiori* have such a custom-creating capacity in international law and not only in the domain of international humanitarian law. Some States held that '[c]olonies and similar entities given some measure of authority in foreign relations, especially when approaching statehood', should dispose of lawmaking

64 ILA, The Hague Conference (2010), Rights of Indigenous Peoples, Interim Report, 27, fn 163 and 50, fn 366.

capacity[65] – arguably this might equally apply to a *de facto* regime as far as it has been granted the authority to act in foreign relations.

The International Law Commission may be inspired by the acts of *de facto* regimes and agreements to which *de facto* regimes are parties in various domains of international law. Such domains are typically not regulated by treaty law such as the access and privileges of international organisations in the territory controlled by *de facto* regimes, the procedural rights and obligations of *de facto* regimes in multilateral status negotiations, etc. Thus, the International Law Commission may be inspired by the practice of States, international organisations, and *de facto* regimes in such domains, especially as the Commission is also tasked with 'the preparation of draft conventions on subjects which have not yet been regulated by international law or in regard to which the law has not yet been sufficiently developed in the practice of States'.[66]

The conclusions also confirm, however, that even if international organisations and States might recognise the rule-making practice of certain *de facto* regimes, the general practice as a constituent element of customary international law refers primarily to the practice of States. Thus, even if the activities of *de facto* regimes might have some relevance in assessing the practice of States and international organisations, the fact remains that States have 'the last word and the legal authority to recognise a certain practice by a non-State actor as legally relevant'.[67]

65 Submission of the United States of America, Law of Treaties: Comments by Governments on the draft articles on the law of treaties drawn up by the Commission at its fourteenth, fifteenth and sixteenth session, UN Doc A/CN.4/182 and Corr.1&2 and Add.1, 2/Rev.1 & 3 (1966), in: *YbILC*, 1966, vol II, 346 (Comment to draft Article 3).

66 Statute of the International Law Commission, Article 20(a)–(b).

67 Sixtieth session (Second part), provisional summary record of the 2980th meeting, 17 July 2008, UN Doc A/CN.4/SR.2980 (5 August 2008), in: *YbILC*, 2008, vol I, 145–57, para 19 (Mr Nolte).

Chapter 18

Investors in the formation of customary international law

*Tomoko Yamashita**

International lawmaking is no longer a privilege exclusively reserved for States. As mentioned by the International Law Commission in its Conclusion 13(1) on the Identification of Customary International Law in 2018, decisions of international tribunals serve as a subsidiary means for the ascertainment of rules of customary international law.[1] That said, in light of the principle *non ultra petita*, the real contributors appear to be the claimants who raise discussions for customary international law determination before a tribunal, which then decides only upon the pleadings and observations submitted by both parties. From the moment when international tribunals opened the door for direct access by non-State actors, private persons acting as claimants actively began to affect the formation of international law through the tribunals. Such international tribunals are commonly created under a special treaty regime; however, their decisions may be extended to the interpretation and identification of a specific rule of customary international law as long as such an argument is raised by the claimant and it falls within their jurisdiction.

Nowadays, investors have emerged as the most powerful claimants who certainly influence the clarification of customary international law rules through investor–State dispute settlement on the international sphere, which is created by international investment agreements (hereafter IIAs) or by bilateral investment treaties (hereafter BITs).[2] Because of the procedural bias built in the system,

* Chapter 18 is a part of the author's research project supported by JSPS KAKENHI Grant Numbers JP14J03085 and JP17K13617.

1 International Law Commission Conclusions on Identification of Customary International Law with commentaries, in UN Doc A/73/10 (2018). International Law Commission considers 'international courts and tribunals' in this context as including any type of 'arbitral tribunals applying international law' ibid, Commentary to Conclusion 13, para 4.

2 Almost all the investment arbitrations based on IIAs are between investors and the host State, although inter-State disputes could arise under IIAs. A few inter-State cases have

investor–State dispute settlement arbitrations sustain a pro-investor nature[3] to the extent that some States withdraw or refuse their consent to investor–State dispute settlement,[4] and others have reinforced a mandatory requirement to exhaust local remedies before investor–State dispute settlement.[5] These phenomena eloquently show how loud the investors' voices are in investor–State dispute settlement to the extent that they may control the tribunals' rulings.[6] Here arises questions: how and to what extent are these references to customary international law justified and may they influence the formation of customary international law?

In the present chapter, I propose to answer these questions through the combination of two concepts – namely, 'framing' and 'spilling-over effect'. Briefly, I argue that investors who raise questions of customary international law have a significant ability to frame the debates that lead to a final award. Furthermore, I argue that the arguments investors put forward have a spill-over effect, i.e. their impact can be felt beyond the immediate realities of the case at hand. The present chapter unpacks both arguments through the study of one case, namely, the exceptions to the local remedies rule by examining the *lex lata* customary international

been observed until the time of writing, including *Mexico v United States* [2000], *Italy v Cuba* [2003], *Peru v Chile* [2003], *Ecuador v United States* [2011]. *See* N Bernasconi-Osterwalder, 'State-State Dispute settlement in Investment Treaties: Best Practices Series-October 2014' (2014) *International Institute for Sustainable Development* www.iisd.org/sites/default/files/publications/best-practices-state-state-dispute-settlement-investment-treaties.pdf accessed on 30 November 2018; UNCTAD Series on Issues in International Investment Agreements, 'Dispute Settlement: State-State' (2003) UNCTAD/ITE/IIT/2003/1, 6–8.

3 M Toral and T Schultz, 'The State, a Perpetual Respondent in Investment Arbitration? Some Unorthodox Considerations' in M Waibel et al (eds), *The Backlash against Investment Arbitration: Perceptions and Reality* (Kluwer 2010) 578–80; D Tamada, 'Host States as Claimants: Corruption Allegations' in S Lalani and RP Lazo (eds), *The Role of the State in Investor-State Arbitration* (Brill-Nijhoff 2015) 103.

4 Although Latin American States have traditionally been sceptical about international resolution of investor–State disputes (e.g. discussion concerning Calovo clause), they once joined the ICSID Convention, the most famous ground of investor–State dispute settlement, in the 1990s. However, after being largely targeted in the increasing arbitrations, Bolivia, Ecuador, Venezuela, and Argentina have successively withdrawn from ICSID.

5 MD Brauch, 'Exhaustion of Local Remedies in International Investment Law', *International Institute for Sustainable Development Best Practices Series* (January 2017) 1.

6 This constitute an example of 'successful argumentative campaigns' as is put forward by Fabian Cardenas in Chapter 6 in this volume.

law of diplomatic protection and emerging interpretations in investor–State dispute settlement, with a special focus on the 'futility exception' to the exhaustion of local remedies.

This case provides good material for the ascertaining of the full impact of the arguments investors put forward before investor–State dispute settlement tribunals. This occurs because, as it is the most elusive exception enumerated in the International Law Commission's Articles on Diplomatic Protection completed in 2006 (hereafter the '2006 International Law Commission Articles'),[7] the futility of local remedies is widely argued in various forms. Indeed, the practice of international litigation only discusses the exceptions rather than the principle because the claimants argue exceptional circumstances precluding the application of the principle in order to circumvent local remedies. This tendency is aggravated in investor–State dispute settlement, even when the investment treaty establishing the jurisdiction of such arbitrations explicitly requires the investor to exhaust all local remedies before submitting international claims. For that purpose, the investors argue customary international law exceptions developed through diplomatic protection, which is somehow antiquated, and ascertain them in order to interpret implicit exceptions that may be included in the provisions of IIAs/BITs. For the sake of investors, such customary international law exceptions are frequently required to be identified in this regard.

The chapter is organised as follows. As a prerequisite to this discussion, section 1 is devoted to identifying exceptions to the local remedies rule under customary international law in the traditional discussion of diplomatic protection. Section 2 explores specific features of the investor–State dispute settlement procedure and the tribunals' understandings of the local remedies rule and its exceptions. This section scrutinises how the futility exception are integrated into investor–State dispute settlement practice and vice versa. Section 3 ascertains the spill-over effect of the arguments that investors make in the context of investor–State dispute settlement proceedings. Although it places focus on the case subject of the present study, many of its findings are generalisable. Finally, section 4 wraps up the argument and concludes.

1 Historical origin of the futility exception under customary international law

The local remedies rule has its origin in the concept of 'denial of justice (*denegatio justitiae*)', which was generated through the private reprisals of the medieval

7 International Law Commission Articles on Diplomatic Protection with commentaries, in UN Doc A/61/10 (2006) Article 15.

age.[8] Since private reprisals came to be prohibited in the modern age because of the emergence of the law of nations between 'States' who claimed full control of legal processes in their territory, the exercise of diplomatic protection replaced this ancient practice.[9] The practice of diplomatic protection itself and the relevant rules had been largely developed throughout international arbitrations during the eighteenth and nineteenth centuries.[10] In the beginning of the twentieth century, the arbitral tribunals started to discuss the applicability of the local remedies rule as one of the main issues.[11]

The exhaustion of local remedies is one of the procedural prerequisites for exercising diplomatic protection, which is nowadays considered to be 'a well-established rule of customary international law'.[12] This rule has been repeatedly recognised and confirmed by judicial decisions, as well as State practice and writings of jurists.[13] Indeed, from the very beginning, it was not the rule itself but its exceptions that were argued in international proceedings. This is because, unlike the exceptions for external reasons such as the immunity of diplomats, the exceptions for an intrinsic cause of the rule cannot be easily identified. Even so, some

8 HW Spiegel, 'Origin and Development of Denial of Justice' (1938) 32 AJIL 63, 63–64; Jan Paulsson, *Denial of Justice in International Law* (Cambridge University Press 2005) 23; JR Crawford and TD Grant, 'Local Remedies, Exhaustion of' [2007] *MPEPIL* http://opil.ouplaw.com/home/EPIL accessed on 30 November 2018, paras 1–2; GG Fitzmaurice, 'The Meaning of the Term "Denial of Justice"' (1932) 13 BYBIL 93, 95–96. *See also* Article IV of American Institute of International Law, Projects on 'Responsibility of Governments' and 'Diplomatic Protection' (1925): Project no 15 Responsibility of Governments; Paragraph 7 of League of Nations Committee of Experts for the Progressive Codification of International Law, Conclusion amended by Rapporteur Gustavo Guerro of Questionnaire No 4 on 'Responsibility of States for Damage Done in Their Territories to the Person or Property of Foreigners' (Geneva 1926); and Article V of Institute of International Law, Draft on 'International Responsibility of States for Injuries on Their Territory to the Person or Property of Foreigners' (Lausanne 1927), all reproduced in UN Doc A/CN.4/SER.A/1956/Add.1, 222, 227–28.

9 Paulsson (n 8) 14.

10 D Müller, 'The Work of García Amador on State Responsibility for Injury caused to Aliens' in James Crawford, A Pellet, and S Olleson (eds), *Oxford Commentaries on International Law: The Law of International Responsibility* (Oxford University Press 2010) 70; Phillip Jessup, *A Modern Law of Nations* (Macmillan 1958) 96.

11 *Robert E Brown* (USA v UK) [1923] 6 UNRIAA 120; *Rhodope central (fond)* (Greece v Bulgaria) [1933] 3 UNRIAA 1405, 1420; *Panevezys-Saldutiskis Railway* (Estonia v Lithuania) [1939] PCIJ Series A/B, No 76, 19; *Ambatielos* (Greece v UK) [1956] 12 UNRIAA 83, 120.

12 *Interhandel* (Switzerland v USA) [1959] ICJ Reports 6, 27. *See also Elettronica Sicula SpA* (USA v Italy) [1989] ICJ Reports 15, 42, para 50.

13 International Law Commission Articles on Diplomatic Protection with commentaries (n 7), Article 14 and its commentary para (1).

academics, including those at the Harvard Law School in 1929[14] and l'Institute de Droit International in 1956,[15] attempted to codify some exceptional situations precluding the applicability of the local remedies, by featuring the availability of the remedies as a key to understanding the exceptions to the local remedies rule.[16] Combined with some arbitral practices, these academic arguments proved that a loose international consensus was made in the beginning of the twentieth century for exceptions to the rule, especially when the local remedies were not 'available' for the injured persons; however, such situations were not yet fully consolidated at that time.[17] Moreover, these arguments consider an admissible exception not as a logical conclusion from the historical concept of denial of justice but as a practical consideration for the actual international dispute settlement proceedings.

In 2006, Article 15 of the International Law Commission Articles on Diplomatic Protection identified exceptional situations where the local remedies do not need to be exhausted:

(a) There are no reasonably available local remedies to provide effective redress, or the local remedies provide no reasonable possibility of such redress;
(b) There is undue delay in the remedial process which is attributable to the State alleged to be responsible;
(c) There was no relevant connection between the injured person and the State alleged to be responsible at the date of injury;
(d) The injured person is manifestly precluded from pursuing local remedies; or
(e) The State alleged to be responsible has waived the requirement that local remedies be exhausted.[18]

Besides paragraph (e) concerning waivers, the other exceptions (a)–(d) basically stem from the idea of the 'availability' of the local remedies for the injured persons. However, among them, only the futility exception as codified in paragraph

14 Art 9 of Draft Convention on the Responsibility of States for Damage Done in Their Territory to the Person or Property of Foreigners prepared by Harvard Law School, reproduced in UN Doc A/CN.4/SER.A/1956/Add.1 (1956),229.
15 Résolution concernant la règle de l'épuisement des recours internes, Session de Grenade, 1956 [1956] 46 *Ann. de l'Institut de D. Int'l*, 364. Translation and emphasis by the author.
16 EM Borchard, *Diplomatic Protection of Citizens Abroad* (Banks Law 1915) 822; FS Dunn, *The Protection of Nationals* (Johns Hopkins Press 1932) 156–57; R Jennings and A Watts (eds), *Oppenheim's International Law* (vol 1 Peace, 9th ed, Longman, 1992) 362; AV Freeman, *The International Responsibility of States for Denial of Justice* (Longmans 1938) 215–63.
17 J Dugard, 'Second Report on Diplomatic Protection', UN Doc A/CN.4/514 (2001), para 17; 'Third Report on Diplomatic Protection', UN Doc A/CN.4/523 and Add.1 (2002) para 26.
18 International Law Commission Articles on Diplomatic Protection (n 7).

(a), because of its conceptual broadness, needs clarification and embodiment in practice. In this vein, the commentary to the 2006 International Law Commission Articles introduces criteria for the futility of local remedies by examining judicial decisions of State-to-State disputes or of human rights court:[19] the local court has no jurisdiction over the dispute in question;[20] the national legislation justifying the acts of which the alien complains will not be reviewed by local courts;[21] the local courts are notoriously lacking in independence;[22] there is a consistent and well-established line of precedents unfavorable to the alien;[23] the local courts do not have the competence to grant as appropriate and adequate remedy to the alien;[24] or the respondent State does not have an adequate system of judicial protection.[25]

2 Procedural feature of investor–State dispute settlement in relation to the local remedies

The most distinct aspect of the investor–State dispute settlement from other international procedures is, without any doubt, the involvement of investors. Since

19 International Law Commission Articles on Diplomatic Protection with commentaries (n 7), Commentary to Article 15, para (3).

20 *Panevezys-Saldutiskis Railway* (n 11), 18, Arbitration under Article 181 of the Treaty of Neuilly, in [1934] 28 AJIL 760, 789; *R Gelbtrunk and 'Salvador Commercial Co' et al,* 15 [1902] UNRIAA 467, 476–477; *'The Lottie May' Incident* (Honduras v UK), [1899] 15 UNRIAA 29, 31; Judge Lauterpacht's separate opinion in the *Norwegian Loans case* (France v Norway), [1957] ICJ Reports 9, 39–40; *Finnish Ships* (Greece v UK) [1934] 3 UNRIAA 1479, 1535.

21 *Arbitration under Article 181 of the Treaty of Neuilly*, [1934] 28 AJIL 789. *See* also *Forêts du Rhodope Central (Fond)* [1933] 3 UNRIAA 1405; *Ambatielos* (n 11), 119; *Interhandel* (n 12), 28.

22 *Robert E Brown* (n 11), 120; *Vélasquez Rodríguez* (1988) IACHR, Series C, no 4, paras 56–78.

23 *Panevezys-Saldutiskis Railway* (n 11), 18; *SS 'Lisman'* (USA v UK), [1937] 3 UNRIAA 1767, 1773; *SS 'Seguranca'* (USA v UK), [1939] 3 UNRIAA 1861, 1868; *Finnish Ships* (n 20), 1495; *X v FRG*, [1956] 1 YB ECHR 138; *X v FRG*, 2 YB ECHR 342, 344; *X v Austria*, 3 YB ECHR 196, 202.

24 *Finnish Ships* (n 20), 1496–1497; *Vélasquez Rodríguez* (n 22), para 64; *Yağci and Sargin v Turkey*, Judgment of 8 June 1995, ECHR, Reports and Decisions, no 319, 3 at 17 ff, para 42; *Hornsby v Greece*, Judgment of 19 March 1997, ECHR, Reports and Decisions, 1997–11, no 33, 495 at 509 ff, para 37.

25 *Mushikiwabo and others v Barayagwiza*, 9 April 1996, ILR, vol 107, p 457 at 460. During the military dictatorship in Chile the Inter-American Commission on Human Rights resolved that the irregularities inherent in legal proceedings under military justice obviated the need to exhaust local remedies; resolution 1a/88, case 9755, [1987/88] Ann Rep Int Am Com HR.

investor–State dispute settlement has rapidly developed from the 1990s, there remains a certain amount of technical defaults in IIAs and BITs which establish the jurisdiction of international arbitration. The uncertainty concerning the futility exception is one such example, and the terminology within IIAs and BITs are not always clear enough in this regard, or they sometimes explicitly refer to customary international law as a formal source to be applied by the arbitral tribunal to resolve the disputes arising from the interpretation of these treaties.

In such cases, the tribunal needs to review the customary international law that has emerged out of the practice of diplomatic protection as a traditional form of international legal investment protection,[26] explicitly or implicitly, to fulfil the legal lacuna existing in the IIAs. This is in principle the question of treaty interpretation, however, at the same time, that of identification of customary international law. As Paparinskis points out, there exists an incomplete overlap between the legal regimes of customary international law concerning State responsibility and of investment arbitration for the issues of lawmaking and the nature of disputing parties, as well as the decentralised structure of dispute settlement, which raises questions about the place of non-State actors in international law for its sources and interpretation.[27] In addition to this point, an overview of the special feature of investor–State dispute settlement in relation to the local remedies rule is needed, because the futility exception cannot go out of this framework set forth by each IIA/BIT.

2.1 A hybrid of public and private international law

Although IIAs are creatures of public international law, they are distinct from most public international law not only for permitting investors to bring direct claims against host States but also for grafting private international law dispute resolution mechanisms at the procedural level.[28] Regardless of clear differences between classical commercial arbitration and investment arbitration, investor–State dispute settlement can be dealt by institutions for commercial arbitration. In addition to the International Centre for Settlement of Investment Disputes (hereafter ICSID) and the Permanent Court of Arbitration, there is, for instance, the International

26 Even when IIAs exclude the possibility of inter-State arbitration, States can exercise diplomatic protection in favour of their nationals abroad as foreign investors as a final resort. *See* Article 27 of ICSID Convention, [1966] 575 UNTS 159.

27 M Paparinskis, 'Investment Treaty Arbitration and the (New) Law of State Responsibility' [2013] 24 EJIL 617, 617–21.

28 A Roberts, 'Clash of Paradigms: Actors and Analogies Shaping the Investment Treaty System' (2013) 107 AJIL 45.

Chamber of Commerce, the London Court of International Arbitration, and the Regional Arbitration Centres in the world.[29] Since arbitrators are always those who enjoy the confidence of the disputing parties and have the necessary expertise in the field, arbitration is usually more efficient than judicial settlement for disputes of such kind.[30] In addition, the third party has no right to intervene in nor attend to the arbitral proceedings thus the sole audience consists of the disputing parties,[31] except for some rare cases where the treaties creating jurisdiction of the tribunals so stipulate.[32] This private nature of arbitration assuring the confidentiality of proceedings is often valued by parties to major economic development projects, although the transparency of proceedings such as access to information and third party participation has been called for in recent investment arbitrations in light of the public nature of the disputes involving judicial review of administrative acts of the host States.[33]

At the same time, these private aspects of investor–State dispute settlement mechanisms strengthen the voices of investors to the level that their claims equate to those of States. Indeed, it is the procedural rules of these fora, rather than a substantive mixture of public and private international law, which affect the applicability of the local remedies rule.[34] Article 26 of the ICSID Convention mentions 'any other remedies' that do not have to be exhausted unless the State explicitly opts in. The Report of the Executive Directors explains this provision to be a rule of interpretation at the ICSID, but this provision is not intended to modify customary international law rules concerning the exhaustion of local remedies.[35] The non-ICSID tribunals do not mention exhaustion, so that the tribunals tend to consider consent to arbitration as a waiver of the local remedies rule based on the understanding that the arbitration clause operates as fork-in-the-road, by which

29 R Dolzer and C Schreuer, *Principles of International Investment Law* (2nd edn, Oxford University Press 2012) 241.

30 ibid 236.

31 CH Brower II, 'Arbitration' (2007) *MPEPIL* http://opil.ouplaw.com/home/EPIL accessed on 30 November 2018, para 5.

32 Art 56 of 1899 Hague Convention for the Pacific Settlement of International Disputes, Art 84 of 1907 Hague Convention for the Pacific Settlement of International Disputes, and Art 1128 of North American Free Trade Agreement (1992).

33 Dolzer and Schreuer (n 29) 237, 286–88.

34 Paparinskis (n 27) 642.

35 Report of the Executive Directors on the Convention and the Settlement of Investment Disputes between States and Nationals of other States I (Resolution No 214, adopted by the Board of Governors of the IBRD on 10 Sep 1964), reprinted in AR Parra, *The History of ICSID* (Oxford University Press 2012) 415–16, at para 32.

the investor can choose either between the investor–State dispute settlement or the local remedies.[36] Considering the fact that in diplomatic protection the investors' intentions have been disregarded as it is within a State's discretion, the arbitral tribunals of investor–State dispute settlement certainly consider them as important factors for final outcome including ascertainment of customary international law.[37]

2.2 Types of IIAs concerning the local remedies rule

The local remedies rule is integrated into treaty regimes, commonly with specific characterisations depending on the treaty. In human rights treaties, local remedies are an important factor for facilitating the domestic implementation of human rights protection and therefore their exhaustion is positively supervised by the treaty bodies which are, in principle, subsidiaries to the national courts. On the other hand, IIAs are basically oriented to skip the local remedies by inserting investor–State dispute settlement clauses which allows investors' direct access to international arbitrations against the host State of the investment.

In IIAs, there exist five types of approaches towards the local remedies rule: (i) no reference; (ii) fork-in-the-road; (iii) no U-turn; (iv) parallel proceedings; and (v) the investor–State dispute settlement is available only after the exhaustion of local remedies.[38] Although exceptions to the rule are quite rarely stipulated in IIAs, and this is the reason for controversy, these different contexts wherein the 'principle' operates certainly have an impact on exceptions and their various modalities.

The first type (No-Reference type), no reference to the local remedies rule can be found in several model BITs as well as in actual BITs. An example is Article 8 of Netherland-Czech BIT.[39] Because of this provision, the tribunal in *CME v Czech* exercised its jurisdiction over the dispute before the conclusion of domestic

36 *RosInvest Co UK Ltd v Russia*, [2008] SCC V 79/2005, Award on Jurisdiction, para 153; *Mytilineos v Serbia*, [2006] UNCITRAL Case, Partial Award on Jurisdiction, paras 220–21.

37 International Law Commission Articles on Responsibility for Internationally Wrongful Acts, Commentary to Art 20, UN Doc A/56/10 (2001) para 10.

38 K Abe, '*Nikokucan Toushi Jyoyaku/Keizai Renkei Kyotei ni okeru Toshityuusai to Konunaikyusai Tetsuduki tono Kankei* (Arbitration Clauses in BITs/EPAs and the Local Remedies Rule)', RIETI Discussion Paper Series 07-J-40 (2007), 6–18 (in Japanese) www.rieti.go.jp/jp/publications/summary/07100002.html accessed on 30 November 2018.

39 signed on 29 April 1991. All the IIAs mentioned here are available at the UNCTAD Investment Policy Hub http://investmentpolicyhub.unctad.org/IIA accessed on 30 November 2018.

proceedings before Czech national court.[40] The same type of provisions can be found in numerous BITs, for instance, in Egypt-Denmark BIT (Article 9),[41] Germany-Bolivia BIT (Article 11, BIT terminated),[42] Hungary-Mongolia BIT (Article 8),[43] Turkey-South Africa BIT (Article 7),[44] Lebanon-Sweden BIT (Article 7),[45] Swiss-Pakistan BIT (Article 9),[46] and UK-Kazakhstan BIT (Article 8).[47] This type of provision is also quite common for model BITs, including that of Sweden 2002 (Article 8), Denmark 2000 (Article 9), Germany 2008 (Article 10), Mongolia 1998 (Article 8), Netherlands 2004 (Article 9), South Africa 1991 (Article 7), Switzerland (Article 8), Turkey 2009 (Article 9), and UK 2008 (Article 8).

In relation to the second type (Fork-in-the-Road type) of approach, the investor can choose either investor–State dispute settlement or the local remedies, but once such a decision is made, the treaty normally prescribes that it is to be final and irrevocable.[48] There numerous BITs which have such provisions, including US-Argentina BIT (Article 7),[49] US-Czech/Slovakia BIT (Article 6),[50] France-Argentina BIT (Article 8),[51] Swiss-Philippines BIT (Article 8(2)),[52] South Korea-Japan BIT (Article 15),[53] Turkey-Australia BIT(Article 13),[54] Japan-Viet Nam BIT (Article 14),[55] Japan-Kenya BIT(Article 15)[56] etc. For model BITs, Chile 1994 (Article 8), Croatia 1998 (Article 10), Iran (Article 12), Thailand 2002 (Article 11), Peru 2000 (Article 8), US 1994/1998 (Article 9), and Southern African Development Community (SADC) 2012 (Article 29.4) have such a provision. In this type, the nature of an investors'

40 *CME Czech Republic BV v Czech Republic*, [2001] UNCITRAL, Partial Award of 13 September 2001, para 410.
41 Signed on 24 June 1999.
42 Signed on 23 March 1987.
43 Signed on 13 September 1994.
44 Signed on 23 June 2000.
45 Signed on 15 June 2001.
46 Signed on 11 July 1995.
47 Signed on 23 November 1995.
48 Z Douglas, 'The Hybrid Foundations of Investment Treaty Arbitration' (2004) 74 BYBIL 151, 274.
49 Signed on 14 November 1991.
50 Signed on 22 October 1991. After the break-up of Czechoslovakia in 1993, this treaty continued in effect for the successor States, the Czech Republic and Slovakia.
51 Signed on 3 July 1991.
52 Signed on 31 March 1997.
53 Signed on 22 March 2002.
54 Signed on 16 June 2005.
55 Signed on 14 November 2003.
56 Signed on 28 August 2016.

claims can be a subject of dispute at domestic courts, i.e. whether their contractual claims are identical to the disputes within the meaning of the BIT, which needs to be waived before investor–State dispute settlement.[57]

In the third type (No U-Turn type), the investor–State dispute settlement is available only when the investor waives the local remedies, even when the local proceedings are ongoing. In other words, once investors bring their case before investor–State dispute settlement arbitration, they need to abandon all possibilities at the local level. The most famous provision is Article 1121 of NAFTA.[58] The purpose of this provision, as explained in *Waste Management*, is to avoid situations where investors obtain the double benefit in its claim for damages both at domestic court and at international arbitration.[59] In general, this type is different from Fork-in-the-Road type on the point that No U-Turn type allows investors to change the forum even if they firstly proceed before domestic courts; in Fork-in-the-Road type, they need to choose either an international arbitration or a domestic proceeding at the beginning. In other words, type (iii) does not permit a party to go back to the local remedies once an international arbitration has started (in this sense, it is 'No U-Turn' type). The number of BITs having such a provision is increasing: Chile-US FTA (Article 10.17),[60] Canada-Ecuador BIT (Article 13),[61] Japan-Mexico EPA (Article 81),[62] Oman-US FTA (Article 10.17),[63] Peru-US FTA (Article 10.18),[64] Uruguay-US BIT (Article 26),[65] Japan-Kuwait BIT (Article 16),[66] and Japan-Ukraine BIT (Article 18).[67] Relevant model BITs include the Canada 2004 (Article 26), Finland 2001 (Article 9), US 2004/2012 (Article 26), DR-CAFTA (Article 10.18),[68] and US-Peru Trade Promotion Agreement (Article 10.18(2)).[69]

57 For instance, there is a sharp contrast of opinions between Award 21 November 2000 (para 55) and Decision on Annulment 3 July 2002 (paras 38, 55) even in the same case concerning *Compañía de Aguas del Aconquija SA & Compagnie Générale des Eaux v Argentina*, ICSID No ARB/97/3.

58 32 ILM 289, 605 (1993).

59 *Waste Management Inc v United Mexican States*, [2000] ICSID No ARB(AF)/98/2, Award, 235–236.

60 Signed on 6 June 2003.

61 Signed on 29 April 1996.

62 Signed on 17 September 2004.

63 Signed on 19 January 2006.

64 Signed on 12 April 2006.

65 Signed on 4 November 2005.

66 Signed on 22 March 2012.

67 Signed on 5 February 2015.

68 Signed on 24 September 2001.

69 Signed on 1 February 2009.

Under the fourth type (Parallel Proceedings type), few IIAs/BITs allow investors to proceed both in investor–State dispute settlement and in the domestic court of the host State at the same time. Article 11 of Australia-Czech BIT is such an example.[70] Other examples are Australia-Hungary BIT (Article 12)[71] and Australia-Poland BIT (Article 13).[72]

Finally, there are few BITs that adopt the fifth type (Prior Exhaustion of the Local Remedies type). Nonetheless, these BITs are important as most of these BITs were concluded by Argentina, the State that has received the highest amount of ICSID claims. For instance, Argentina-UK BIT interestingly provides in its Paragraph (2) (a) (i), which sets the time-limit for eighteen months after the initiation of the judicial proceeding at the local court, along with Paragraph (2) (a) (ii) just confirming the customary international law rule on the local remedies.[73] Nearly identical provisions are included in Argentine-Netherlands BIT (Article 10),[74] Argentine-Canada BIT (Article 10),[75] Argentine-Spain BIT (Article 10),[76] Argentina-Italy BIT (Article 8),[77] Argentina-Germany BIT (Article 10),[78] and all of them are with the eighteen-month limitation. Another example is Article 7 of Turkey-Turkmenistan BIT,[79] whose deadline is 'within one year'. BITs of this type are particularly important to understand customary international law in investor–State dispute settlement, since the clause for prior-exhaustion of the local remedies induces the tribunal to explicitly mention whether there is an exceptional situation for the rule, and whether the criteria developed in customary international law are applicable to the case.

Therefore, among the aforementioned types of BITs, the futility exception is mostly discussed in relation to Prior Exhaustion of the Local Remedies type. In disputes that fall within the fifth type, Prior Exhaustion of the Local Remedies type, the situation is quite similar to the application of customary international law for diplomatic protection since they both discuss the application of unwritten procedural exceptions to the case, so long as the deadline prescribed in BITs has not been exceeded. A comparison with customary international law and investor–State dispute

70 Signed on 30 September 1993.
71 Signed on 15 August 1991.
72 Signed on 7 May 1991.
73 Signed on 11 December 1990.
74 Signed on 20 October 1992.
75 Signed on 5 November 1991.
76 Signed on October 1991.
77 Signed on 22 May 1990.
78 Signed on 9 April 1991.
79 Signed on 2 May 1992.

settlement on this point is useful for examining the impact that investors have on the development of law in investor–State dispute settlement.

3 Investors' impact on customary international law through the futility exception claim in investor–State dispute settlement

Except for some manifest cases, the futility of the local remedies is indeed difficult for international tribunals to declare because there is a lack of absolute criteria for the evaluation of the situation and the host State bears the burden of proof for the availability of the local remedies.[80] Traditionally, the futility exception is seen in very exceptional situations such as, inter alia, when the local courts are notoriously lacking in independence, or when local courts are unable to review, or refuse to review, the domestic acts that underpin the complaints of foreign investors.

However, such manifest defaults can be the object of severe contestation before the host State invites foreign direct investment. In most investor–State dispute settlement cases, the futility is hidden in a normal but intricate procedure of the local remedies which appear to lack deficiencies *prima facie*. In order to establish the futility of local remedies, there is no need to show that the system as a whole is paralysed as it is required under the customary international law for diplomatic protection, though this threshold is sufficient for the purpose of investor–State dispute settlement.[81] In addition, the aforementioned different types of investor–State dispute settlement clauses require different interpretations of the futility of local remedies. Thus, the argument of futility needs updating in the relevant context of investor–State dispute settlement. In this regard, any arbitral determinations of futility cannot be made without claims of investors indicating negligence of local remedies, which are invisible at the national standard but arguable at international standard set forth in IIAs/BITs. The impact of investors is therefore shown firstly in the ascertainment of customary international law, then the embodiment of the futility through their claims, and finally such investor–State dispute settlement practices have the potential to be ploughed back into customary international law as will be elaborated below.

80 *Chevron Corporation (USA) and Texaco Petroleum Company (USA) v Ecuador,* [2010] UNCITRAL, Permanent Court of Arbitration Case No 34877, Partial Award on the Merits, paras 328–29.

81 *Apotex v USA*, [2013] ICSID Case No UNCT/10/2 [hereafter, *Apotex UNCITRAL*], Award, paras 280, 282.

3.1 Theoretical basis for the futility exception of the original customary international law rule

In the first place, there has been a long academic customary international law debate for the reason to require exhaustion of local remedies before resorting to international litigation. As mentioned above, the futility of local remedies has been discussed in the context of denial of justice. According to Borchard, the responsible State has the primary obligation to make municipal remedies available to foreigners, and the failure to comply with this duty involves an international responsibility owed to the national State of the victim. The individual's claim is transformed into 'the correlative right of the injured state' whose infringement allows that State to demand reparation on behalf of its national.[82] In his view, the fact that a higher authority did not correct the wrongful act is deemed as a deliberate act between States.[83] This idea has been coined by Ago as the hypothesis of '*délits internationaux complexes* (complex international tort)'. Even if wrongful treatment against a foreigner is originally a mere violation of domestic law, once it is composed with a denial of justice, the first tort is to be transformed into an international wrongful act, comprising of the sum effect of conduct by differing organs.[84]

In other words, there are two international obligations by which the territorial State is bound: (1) local remedies must be open for foreigners who suffer from wrongful acts domestically, and (2) if they cannot obtain reparation in exhausting local remedies, another international wrongful act results from this failure. This distinction is formulated in the first reading of the International Law Commission's Articles on State Responsibility as obligations of conduct and result.[85] The violation of the latter obligation is considered as a denial of justice, an international obligation owed to the victim's State of nationality by the territorial State.[86] This amounts to a failure in the administration of justice,

82 E Borchard, 'Responsibility of States for Damage Done in Their Territory to the Person or Property of Foreigners' (1929) 23 AJIL Special Supplement 133, 150.

83 E Borchard, 'Theoretical Aspects of the International Responsibility of States' (1929) 1 ZaöRV 223, 241.

84 R Ago, '*Le délit international*' (1939-II) 68 RCADI, 512–17.

85 Article 20 and 21, UN Doc A/CN.4/L.263/Add.1 (1997) 278; This distinction has vanished in the Second Reading (2001) since, according to Crawford, it derives from civil law systems and is not known to the common law and should be treated as a problem of primary rule. J Crawford, 'Second Report on State Responsibility', UN Doc A/CN.4/498(1999) paras 53–80.

86 *See* e.g. J Combacau, 'Obligations de résultat et obligations de comportement: quelques questions et pas de réponse', *Mélanges offerts à Paul Reuter: le droit international, unité*

comprising of an improper act or omission on the part of the judiciary or of some other organ of the State.[87] In the context of diplomatic protection, at least, the obligation to make available local remedies for foreigners composes a part of the meta-obligation in customary international law of fair and equitable treatment, while the original violations to individuals alone are not regarded as violations of international law. Brierly points out that 'the injurious results of a denial of justice are not, or at any rate are not necessarily, confined to the individual sufferer or his family, but include such consequences as the "mistrust and lack of safety" felt by other foreigners similarly situated'.[88] In this sense, the original local remedies rule has developed upon customary international law in order to link the suffering of individual nationals to their national State, when these individuals were a mere 'object' of international law and a convenient scale for the calculation of the reparation due to the State.[89] This is in fact a very important point of departure from investor–State dispute settlement where treaties (IIAs/BITs) directly protect the rights of investors to the extent that they can claim remedies against the host State at international level.

In the framework of investor–State dispute settlement, Article 27 of the ICSID Convention, for instance, preserves the possible invocation of diplomatic protection by the national State of investors when the host State of investment has failed to abide by and comply with the award rendered by ICSID in investor–State arbitration. This provision suggests that such arbitrations consist of 'the remedies to be exhausted' before resorting to diplomatic protection. Therefore, the rule of the (local) remedies and its exceptions are not identical under the customary international law on diplomatic protection and investor–State dispute settlement, and there would not be any mutual direct influences between these two dimensions of law.

et diversité (A Pedone 1981) 181–204; P Daillier and A Pellet, *Droit international public* (6th edn, LGDJ 1999) paras 139, 473; P-M Dupuy, 'Le fait générateur de la responsabilité internationale des Etats' (1984) 188 RCADI, 43–54; I Brownlie, *State Responsibility – Part I* (Clarendon Press 1983), 241; C Tomuschat, 'What is a "Breach" of the European Convention on Human Rights", *Essays in Honour of Henry G. Schermers* (vol 3, M. Nijhoff 1994) 315; Eric Wyler, *L'illicité et la condition des personnes privées: La responsabilité internationale en droit cotumier et dans la convention européenne des droit de l'homme* (A Pedone 1995) 17–43.

87 Fitzmaurice (n 8) 102–104; Freeman (n 16) 50–51.

88 JL Brierly, 'The Theory of Implied State Complicity in International Claims' (1928) 9 BYBIL 42, 48.

89 *Factory at Chorzów* (Germay v Poland) [1928] PCIJ Series A, No 17, Judgment, 28; *Mavrommatis Palestine Concessions* (Greece v UK) [1924] PCIJ Series A, No 2, Judgment, 12.

3.2 *Ascertainment of the futility exception of customary international law through investor–State dispute settlement*

From a practical point of view, the investors wish to circumvent the local remedies even when the applicable BITs are of Prior Exhaustion of the Local Remedies type. As investor–State dispute settlement is a mechanism designed principally to pursue the liability of States,[90] their first achievement was made in 2000 by the tribunal in *Maffezini v Spain* which allowed, because of a most favoured nation (hereafter MFN) clause within the Spain-Argentina BIT, the investor to avail himself of the more favorable treatment contained in the Chile-Spain BIT.[91] According to Douglas, it was the first case where a party has been permitted to rely upon an MFN clause to modify the jurisdictional mandate of an international tribunal.[92] Although this approach was followed by a certain number of cases,[93] it was harshly criticised by academics and is far from being generally accepted since MFN cannot be used to modify the treaty's threshold requirements.[94]

In this vein, the futility exception under customary international law has emerged into investor–State dispute settlement as another strategy for litigation.[95] The first case which explicitly utilised this new approach was the tribunal in *Ambiente Ufficio v Argentina*, which found 'the strong structural parallels' between Article 15(a) of

90 Tamada (n 3) 103.

91 *Maffezini v Spain*, [2000] ICSID Case No ARB/97/7, Decision on Jurisdiction.

92 Z Douglas, 'The MFN Clause in Investment Treaty Arbitration: Treaty Interpretation off the Rails' (2011) 2 J of Int'l Dispute Settlement 97, 101.

93 *Impregilo SpA v Argentine*, [2011] ICSID Case No ARB/07/17, Award; *Hochtief v Argentine*, [2011] ICSID Case No ARB/07/31, Decision on Jurisdiction; *Gas Natural SDG, SA v Argentine*, [2005] ICSID Case No ARB/03/10, Decision of the Tribunal on Preliminary Questions on Jurisdiction; *Suez, Sociedad General de Aguas de Barcelona, SA and Interagua Servicios Integrales de Agua SA v Argentine*, [2006] ICSID Case No ARB/03/17, Decision on Jurisdiction; *Telefónica SA v Argentine*, [2006] ICSID Case No ARB/03/20, Decision of the Tribunal on Objections to Jurisdiction; *Teinver SA, Transportes de Cercanías SA and Autobuses Urbanos del Sur SA v Argentine*, [2012] ICSID Case No ARB/09/1, Decision on Jurisdiction; *Siemens AG v Argentine*, [2004] ICSID Case No ARB/02/8, Decision on Jurisdiction.

94 G D'Agnone, 'Recourse to the "Futility Exception" within the ICSID System: Reflections on Recent Developments of the Local Remedies Rule', [2013] 12 The Law and Practice of Int'l Courts and Tribunals 343, 345–51.

95 ibid 345.

the 2006 International Law Commission Articles and Article 8 of Argentina-Italy BIT.[96] The tribunal states as follows:

> Accordingly, in view of the strong structural parallels between these two types of clauses, the Tribunal does not consider it a far-fetched conclusion to assume that the futility exception to the exhaustion of local remedies rule in the field of diplomatic protection is, *in the light of Art. 31(3)(c) of the VCLT*, also applicable to clauses requiring recourse to domestic courts in international investment law. The conclusion that the futility of local remedies constitutes an exception to the duty of having recourse to local courts is also affirmed in the case-law and in legal academia.
>
> [...]
>
> What is more, since the futility exception is even capable of disposing of a duty to exhaust local remedies – i.e. the use of (virtually) all means offered by the domestic dispute settlement system for a (virtually) unlimited amount of time –, this must hold true a fortiori for a duty to have recourse to local remedies for a limited amount of time. Accordingly, the only aspect where there exists a major difference between the two types of clauses, i.e. the time aspect, does not prevent the drawing of a parallel between them regarding the futility exception; it rather militates in favour of drawing this parallel.[97]

A reference to Article 31(3)(c) of the Vienna Convention on the Law of Treaties is convincing enough if one understands the dispute as a problem involving the interpretation of the given BIT. Indeed, several other tribunals are following the approach of *Ambiente Ufficio*.[98] Some authors and the tribunal in *İçkale İnşaat v Turkmenistan*, based on literal interpretations, deny this approach because the concerned BITs do not mention the existence of exceptions explicitly.[99] However,

96 *Ambiente Ufficio v Argentina*, [2013] ICSID Case No ARB/08/9, Decision on Jurisdiction and Admissibility, paras 599–603. *See* also *Abaclat and Others (Case formerly known as Giovanna Beccara and Others) v Argentine Republic* [2011] ICSID Case No ARB/07/5, Decision on Jurisdiction and Admissibility, paras 582–84, 588.

97 ibid, paras 603 and 606.

98 *Wintershall Aktiengesellschaft v Argentina*, [2008] ICSID Case No ARB/04/14, Award; *Apotex v USA*, [2014] ICSID Case No ARB(AF)/12/1 [hereafter, *Apotex AF*], Award; *Loewen v USA*, [2001] ICSID Case No ARB(AF)/98/3, Decision on Hearing of Respondent's Objection to Competence and Jurisdiction; *Chevron Corporation (USA) and Texaco Petroleum Company (USA) v Ecuador*, [2010] UNCITRAL, Permanent Court of Arbitration Case No. 34877, Partial Award on the Merits; *Apotex UNCITRAL* (n 81); *Corona v Dominica*, [2016] ICSID Case No ARB(AF)/14/3, Award, paras 261–65; *Flughafen v Venezuela*, [2014] ICSID Case No ARB/10/19, Award; *Yukos v Russia*, [2014] UNCITRAL, Permanent Court of Arbitration Case No AA 227; *Loewen v USA*, [2003] ICSID Case No ARB(AF)/98/3, Award.

99 D'Agnone (n 94) 357–61; *İçkale İnşaat Limited Şirketi v Turkmenistan*, [2016] ICSID Case No ARB/10/24, Award, paras 260–61.

I submit that this criticism is not fair since the principle accompanies the exceptions as an analogy of law, and I argue that it neglects why the tribunal relies on customary international law for interpreting BITs – such a reference is made when the stipulations of BITs are not clear enough for application to the case.

Nevertheless, a profound doubt may arise if one considers diplomatic protection as a rule under customary international law. In other words, the rule is applicable only between States, since Article 31(3)(c) referrers to 'any relevant rules of international law applicable in the relations between *the parties*', but the dispute here is not that of the contracting States of the BIT but of the investor-to-State relationship. This point can be an important milestone for evaluating the investor's impact in making the rule of exceptions in the local remedies rule.

On the other hand, this debate over the futility exception made clear that the local remedies and its futility is a pure procedural rule pertaining to the admissibility of claims in investor–State dispute settlement. In the traditional discussion of customary international law, the doctrine of denial of justice and the local remedies rule are two sides of the same coin; they are commonly conflated, despite the local remedies being a rule relating to admissibility of claims and denial of justice is itself an international wrongful act.[100] Considering the genesis of the rule, customary international law could not clearly distinguish between them, however, investor–State dispute settlement perceives the local remedies rule and its futility exception as a genuine procedural question.

3.3 Embodiment of the futility exception in investor–State dispute settlement

As mentioned above, a problem arises when the foreign investors are barred from effective access to the local remedies because of hidden default, which cannot be observed in the text of domestic law and regulations. It is on this point that investor–State dispute settlement and the investors' claims may have a creative impact on the customary international law rules of admissibility, by identifying certain deficiencies of the host State as examples of futile local remedies in the sense of international law. Broadly speaking, three types of investors' claims are observed in relation to the futility of local remedies.

The first one relates to IIAs/BITs of Fork-in-the-Road type or No U-Turn type. The futility exception is claimed in investor–State dispute settlement when

100 AO Adede, 'A Fresh Look at the Meaning of the Doctrine of the Denial of Justice', Canadian YB of Int'l L, 14 (1976), 76–77; C de Visshher, 'Le déni de jusitice en droit international', RCADI 52 (1935-II) 371.

investors did not manifestly choose the forum for dispute settlement in bringing cases before investor–State dispute settlement arbitral tribunals but have not suspended the procedures at national courts of the host State. In such situations, investors insist that they have tacitly waived their claims before national courts since the local remedies are futile. However, the arbitral tribunals consistently deny such allegations.[101] Furthermore, as the Tribunal of *Commerce Group* points out, 'a waiver must be more than just words; it must accomplish its intended effect'.[102] As stated in *Renco*, the purpose of these types of IIAs/BITs are to avoid the burden and risk of a multiplicity of proceedings commenced in parallel or sequentially.[103]

The second type relates to the waiting period or cooling-off period set forth in IIAs/BITs of Prior Exhaustion of the Local Remedies type. The investors argue that they can initiate investor–State dispute settlement before the period is up since the local remedies are futile. In this regard, their claim is much more convincing than the first one since the wording of IIAs/BITs do not clearly require certain actions taken by the disputing parties. The conclusions of the arbitral tribunals are largely divided into two groups: the first sustains the procedural requirement of IIAs/BITs in any case;[104] and the second accepts the investors' claims in admitting that the procedural default of the waiting period can be cured by the futility of the local remedies.[105] In *Abacrat*, in which 60,000 Italian bondholders brought their claims against Argentina on the basis of Argentina-Italy BIT, the majority of the Tribunal affirmed its jurisdiction and admissibility to entertain such a 'mass claim' before the ICSID arbitration for practical considerations.[106] Thus, the tribunals principally

101 For example, *Waste Management v Mexico (I)*, ICSID Case No ARB (AF)/98/2, Award, 2 June 2000, paras 18, 24; *Ethyl Corporation v Canada*, UNCITRAL, Award on Jurisdiction, 24 June 1998, paras 90–91; *Mondev International Ltd v US*, Award, ICSID Case No ARB(AF)/99/2, 11 October 2002, para 86; *International Thunderbird Gaming v Mexico*, Award, UNCITRAL Ad hoc, 26 January 2006, paras 117–18.

102 *Commerce Group Corp v El Salvador*, ICSID Case No ARB/09/17, Award, 14 March 2011, para 80.

103 *Renco v Peru*, ICSID Case No. ARB(AF)04/6, Partial Award, 5 July 2016, paras 86–88.

104 *ICS Inspection v Argentina*, UNCITRAL, Permanent Court of Arbitration Case No 2010–9, 10 February 2012, para 269; *Wintershall Aktiengesellschaft v Argentina*, ICSID Case No ARB/04/14, Award, 8 December 2008, paras 126–27; *Teinver SA and others v Argentina*, ICSID Case No ARB/09/1, Decision on Jurisdiction, 21 December 2012, paras 135–36.

105 *Abaclat v Argentina*, ICSID Case No ARB/07/5, Decision on Jurisdiction and Admissibility, 4 August 2011, paras 582–89.

106 *Abaclat v Argentina*, ibid, para 537. Admissibility of 'mass claim' is a separate but intrinsically related question. *See* K Nakajima, 'Beyond Abaclat: Mass Claims before

observe the waiting period, but this can be ignored in certain cases such as a mass claim considering the adverse impact that may be brought against investors if the tribunal denies the admissibility of their claims.

The third category concerns procedural defaults hidden in the local remedies. This category corresponds to the futility exception in a narrow and traditional sense; therefore, it is on this point that investor–State dispute settlement and the investors' claims may have an impact on the creation of pure procedural customary international law rules of admissibility, which are, at least, applicable in investor–State dispute settlement. The tribunal in *Apotex Holdings, ICSID(AF) 2014* clarified that 'exceptional circumstances' of a particular case may also indicate futility,[107] and this is an innovative point for understanding futility in investor–State dispute settlement. Therefore, some particular measures targeted to the particular investor are also taken into account when considering the futility rule in recent cases. In *Loewen v USA*, the tribunal clarified that futility does not consist of the award of punitive damages in ordering the investor an exorbitant amount,[108] nor of the extreme bonding requirements for the appeal to the extent that its execution on the investors' assets bankrupts them.[109] If the investors prepare for the settlement agreement because of these financial restrains, they are not considered to have exhausted the local remedies.[110] If recusals directed at resolving delays are available besides normal judicial procedure, the investors cannot claim the futility of the local remedies, even when the litigation continues over fifteen years, according to the tribunal of *Chevron I*.[111] In this sense, importance appears to be attached to the formal availability of the local remedies rather than the effective remedies for the investors in investor–State dispute settlement.

Nevertheless, there are some observations which narrow the application of the futility rule compared with the customary international law on diplomatic protection. Although the 2006 International Law Commission Articles considers that administrative remedies in general must also be exhausted,[112] investor–State dispute

Investment Treaty Arbitration and Regulatory Governance for Sovereign Debt Restructuring' (2018) Journal of World Investment & Trade 1–40.

107 *Apotex AF* (n 98) para 9.58.

108 *Loewen v USA*, ICSID Case No ARB(AF)/98/3, Decision on Hearing of Respondent's Objection to Competence and Jurisdiction, 5 January 2001, paras 53–60.

109 *Loewen v USA*, ICSID Case No ARB(AF)/98/3, Award, 5 June 2003, para 207–17.

110 *ibid*, paras 167, 215–17.

111 *Chevron Corporation (USA) and Texaco Petroleum Company (USA) v Ecuador*, UNCITRAL, Permanent Court of Arbitration Case No 34877, Partial Award on the Merits, 30 March 2010, para 331.

112 International Law Commission Articles on Diplomatic Protection with commentaries (n 7), Commentary to Article 14, para (5).

settlement goes a different path. The tribunal of *Yukos v Russia* clarifies that the local remedies include administrative remedies only when the concerned IIAs or BITs so stipulate.[113] The unanswered Motion for Reconsideration addressed to the administrative body does not show the futility of the local remedies.[114] However, in any case, there would be no doubt that the futility exception is embodied in these discussions. In this sense, such embodiment may be also an indicator for identifying futile local remedies in future customary international law discussion of diplomatic protection cases.[115]

4 Concluding remarks

International lawmaking is nowadays also opened to investors, though their impact is rather indirect through the claims they bring before investor–State dispute settlement arbitral tribunals. By employing the example of exceptions to the local remedies rule, this chapter considered whether investors, through the arbitral tribunal, are eligible for creating new customary international law in investor–State dispute settlement[116] or modifying old customary international law which emerged out of State-to-State practices.

In formulating the basis for the tribunal's arguments, investors are indirectly taking part in the formation of customary international law in this regard, since the arbitrations are basically bilateral and legally independent but are nonetheless influential in practice. This is so even between arbitrations based on different BITs. As each award of investor–State dispute settlement arbitration does not have the effect of *res judicata* on other tribunals, it would be reasonable to consider, at least, that these interactions are subsidiary means for the ascertainment of customary international law in investor–State dispute settlement. However, discussions in investor–State dispute settlement may also have an impact for identifying futile local remedies in future customary international law discussions of diplomatic protection cases. Such a spill-over effect can be justified because, as mentioned by the tribunal of *Ambiente Ufficio*, 'strong structural parallels' exist between the customary international law on diplomatic protection and regulations concerning investor–State dispute settlement, at least for this subject.

113 *Yukos v Russia* (n 98) paras 1426–28.

114 *Corona v Dominica*, ICSID Case No ARB(AF)/14/3, Award, 31 May 2016, paras 262–64.

115 In the other context, investor–State dispute settlement cases already cited by International Law Commission Articles on Diplomatic Protection with commentaries (n 7), Commentary to Article 5, para 5.

116 A 'particular customary international law' in the sense that this customary international law is not applicable to the States not taking part in investor-State dispute settlement arbitration system. *See* Conclusion 16 of the International Law Commission's Conclusions (n 1).

From a practical point of view, as I have discussed above, investors' contributions are, at least in the context of the futility exception, firstly ascertaining customary international law in the context which has been long discussed for diplomatic protection and secondly embodying the situations where the exception applies in the context of the present legal system of the host State inviting foreign direct investment. Although the situation does not fall within any of the traditional extreme criteria, certain types of democratic legal instruments, inter alia, punitive damages, may be examples of the futility of local remedies in a specific context. This is because investor–State dispute settlement takes some particular measures targeted at the particular investor into account when considering the futility of local remedies. In light of the principle of *non ultra petita*, it is the claimant investors' arguments rather than the tribunals' final finding that frame the futility exception in investor–State dispute settlement. Indeed, this tendency appears to be strengthened by the fact that arbitral awards do not have the effect of *res judicata* on other tribunals, since the arbitral tribunals can much more focus on the dispute settlement by hearing the claims of the disputing parties rather than paying attention to the consistency of jurisprudences.

Investor–State dispute settlement is definitely one of the most employed methods of international dispute settlement. Accordingly, the power of investors is growing in the international fora, and in some instances, it has become much stronger than the power of States.[117] This is one of the results of the treaty-based mechanism of investor–State dispute settlement in which resolutions are achieved within the interpretation of IIAs or BITs, but there is still a margin of appreciation within the customary international law of investor–State dispute settlement, especially in relation to the unwritten exceptions accompanying the principles. Since there is currently a new trend in avoiding investor–State dispute settlement and shifting to a hybrid type of dispute settlement,[118] the accumulation of such permeation would be useful to resolve investment dispute in whatever form.

117 In *'ARA Libertad'* case (Argentina v Ghana), International Tribunal for the Law of the Sea Case No 20 (a US investor sought to obtain satisfaction of a New Yourk judgment debt from Argentina in Ghana, where an Argentinean military vessel was docked, and succeeded in obtaining the seizure of the vessel. The International Tribunal for the Law of the Sea has ordered release of the vessel).

118 Brazil has never joined in investor–State dispute settlement, and concludes IIAs which do not allow investors to directly bring arbitration; rather, they foresee the establishment of a joint committee made up of governmental representatives of the signatory State to steer investment cooperation, and the private sector and the civil society are allowed to participate in the meetings. Art 15.6 of the Brazil-Mozambique, Brazil-Angola ACFIs; Art 13.6 of the Brazil-Malawi ACFI; Art 19.1 of the Brazil–Mexico ACFI.

Chapter 19

Adjudicators, guardians, and enforcers: taking the role of non-governmental organisations in customary international lawmaking seriously

Valentina Azarova

As States and intergovernmental organisations (IGO) face a range of new challenges, non-governmental organisations are playing an increasingly important role in global governance.[1] Non-governmental organisations have led the development of a range of international treaties, triggered the domestication of international norms in a host of states, and documented abusive State and non-State actor practices in the most perilous environments. Non-governmental organisations are commonly referred to as norm entrepreneurs, but a substantial number of actors consider them as informal arbiters of the international legality of State and other actors' actions.[2] It is no overstatement that non-governmental organisations have acted as *de facto* adjudicators and enforcers of international norms in the international and domestic arenas, both instigating respect for the law and progressing its development. The role of non-governmental organisations in the making of customary international law is, according to the International Law Commission, limited to their ability to 'stimulate and record' the acceptance by States and intergovernmental organisations of certain rules as customary; their practice is not directly adducible in the identification of a customary international law norm.[3]

Within this dynamic and rich domain of activity, this chapter focuses on the work of non-governmental organisations that aim to promote and protect the rule of international law – under different branches of public international law, including international human rights law, international humanitarian law, weapons law, criminal law, and environmental law – and engage in its progressive

1 *See* e.g. S Charnovitz, 'Nongovernmental Organizations and International Law' (2006) 100 AJIL 348, 349.

2 M Finnemore and K Sikkink, 'International Norm Dynamics and Political Change' (1998) 52 International Organization 887.

3 Draft conclusions on identification of customary international law, with commentaries 2018, 132, paras 8–9.

development. In order to assess how non-governmental organisations contribute to and influence the identification, formation, and application of customary international law norms, the chapter surveys relevant non-governmental organisation activities and how they interface with customary international lawmaking, by defending, solidifying, and crystallising customary international law norms; as well as the growing reliance of States, as well as other international actors and institutions, on non-governmental organisations for information gathering, reviewing foreign policy, and triggering the enforcement of domestic law.

The chapter endeavours to demonstrate the significance of the role of non-governmental organisations in customary international lawmaking. It explores their defensive role, holding ground against State practice and positions that could threaten the customary international law status of certain IL norms, as well as their offensive role – in both senses of the term, some States would say – in developing the content of customary international law norms and settling their interpretation. The chapter's basic claim is that non-governmental organisations have made a substantive contribution to customary international lawmaking and their activities should be accounted for as part of the genealogy of customary international law norms.[4] Such processes of customary international law-formation are distinct from the identification of a customary international law norm – an account of customary international lawmaking should include the backstage role of non-governmental organisations, and an account of the application of customary international law norms should similarly include non-governmental organisation activity, alongside that of experts and scholars. The chapter argues that non-governmental organisations perform an increasingly sophisticated and influential role in customary international lawmaking that is not limited to the classical, constructivist view of non-governmental organisations as norm entrepreneurs in international relations literature[5] – i.e. promoters of norms who aim to change the behaviour of social actors.[6] Non-governmental organisations act as norm identifiers, defenders, and progressors as well as solidifiers of State practice.

4 On the decay of the modern way of organising the behavioural generation of legal normativity in international law, J d'Aspremont, 'The Decay of Modern Customary International Law in Spite of Scholarly Heroism' (2016) Global Community: Yearbook of International Law and Jurisprudence 9.

5 J Brunnée and S Toope, 'Constructivism and International Law' in J Dunoff, M Pollack (eds), *Interdisciplinary Perspectives on International Law and International Relations* (Cambridge University Press 2013) 119.

6 On norm entrepreneurship, C Ingebritsen, 'Norm Entrepreneurs Scandinavia's Role' (2002) 37 Journal of the Nordic International Studies Association 12. Finnemore and Sikkink (n 2) 897.

This discussion cannot encompass the enormous diversity and breadth of non-governmental organisation activity. Nor does it attempt to assess the ways that differences between non-governmental organisations – be they national, regional, or international; focused on different themes or issues; and with different institutional structures, mandates, methods, and standing – might well affect the nature and quality of their influence on the formation and identification of customary international law norms. This survey of the different roles played by non-governmental organisations in international lawmaking seeks to account for activities that affect the norms and the perceptions of the norms' subjects and objects, and that address international law issues to an appropriate audience in international or domestic fora with the aim of enhancing the normative force and 'behavioural relevance of international law'.[7] The chapter's sample of non-governmental organisations comprises civil society actors that seek the protection and promotion of international law,[8] but excludes non-State actors in the broader category of global civil society such as trade unions and businesses, who may contribute to the promotion and development of customary international law norms implicitly in coalition with non-governmental organisations.[9] The discussion also assumes that the non-governmental organisations whose activities it samples genuinely consider international law as their normative frame of analysis;[10] it excludes the oxymoronic GONGOs ('government non-governmental organisations') and non-governmental organisations that merely mobilise international law claims in open pursuit of political agendas.

To evaluate the role of non-governmental organisations in customary international lawmaking, the chapter proceeds in three steps. Section 1 provides an empirical typology of non-governmental organisations' various methods and means in furthering the application and determination of international norms, based on

7 J Dill, *Legitimate Targets? Social Construction, International Law and US Bombing* (Cambridge University Press 2014) 349.

8 While the International Committee of the Red Cross is not a non-governmental organisation in the proper sense, the effects of its activities are arguably mutadis mutandis equivalent to those of non-governmental organisation for the purpose of this analysis. A-K Lindblom, *Non-Governmental Organisations in International Law* (Cambridge University Press 2005) 495–96. G Rona, The ICRC's Status: In a Class of Its Own, ICRC, 17 February 2004 www.icrc.org/eng/resources/documents/misc/5w9fjy.htm accessed 16 July 2017.

9 *See* e.g. on the involvement of business in the promotion and development of international law standards in the field of business and human rights; N Bernaz and I Pietropaoli, 'The Role of Non-Governmental Organizations in the Business and Human Rights Treaty Negotiations' (2017) 9 Journal of Human Rights Practice 2, 287.

10 *See* generally, A Vedder (ed), *NGO Involvement in International Governance and Policy: Sources of Legitimacy* (Martinus Nijhoff 2007).

what they do to and with international norms. By claiming rights on behalf of victims, adjudicating wrongs, and potentiating accountability processes, it maps out the means non-governmental organisations deploy in global governance (1). Section 2 suggests an effects-based analysis of the quality of the different non-governmental organisation activities observed in Section 1 in terms of the way that non-governmental organisations engage with and influence the identification, formation, and application of customary international law norms (hereinafter: customary international lawmaking). The chapter argues that by acting as defenders and solidifiers of customary international law norms, and not merely as their entrepreneurs, non-governmental organisations play both a formal-indirect and an informal-indirect role in such processes (2). Section 3 offers a preliminary assessment of what the preceding analysis means for the role of non-governmental organisations in customary international lawmaking and international lawyers' understanding of these processes and their effects (3). We conclude with reflections on the responsibilities that these under-appreciated roles of non-governmental organisations attract (4).

1 A typology of non-governmental organisation activity in global governance

In general, non-governmental organisations seek to 'use the power of their information, ideas, and strategies to alter the information and value contexts within which states make policies' by re-constructing their cognitive frames.[11] Keck and Sikkink summarise the activities of transnational non-governmental organisation advocacy networks as consisting of four modes of *interception* in international politics: information politics; symbolic politics; leverage politics; and accountability politics.[12] Wouters and Rossi describe the roles of non-governmental organisations as including agenda-setting; standard-setting; enforcement; and aid and education.[13] While advocacy to influence action by others may not be the explicit or main focus of many non-governmental organisations, their activities on the domestic, regional, and international planes are such that non-governmental organisations play an unequivocal and decisive role in global governance.

11 M Keck and K Sikkink, *Activists Beyond Borders: Transnational Advocacy Networks in International Politics* (Cornell University Press 1998) 16–17.

12 ibid, 18–25. *See* also J Ron, H Ramos, and K Rodgers, 'Transnational Information Politics: NGO Human Rights Reporting, 1986–2000' (2005) 49 International Studies Quarterly 557–87.

13 J Wouters and I Rossi, 'Human Rights NGOs: Role, Structure and Legal Status' (2001) Institute for International Law Working Paper No 14.

A European convention has codified the international legal personality of associations, foundations, and other private institutions with a non-profit aim of international utility.[14] Domestic and international non-governmental organisations are interdependent, often work together in coalitions, and coordinate and complement each other's efforts.[15] Domestic non-governmental organisations are usually more familiar with victims' situations, developments on the ground, and domestic politics, including attitudes towards international law and institutions, and can relay this information to international non-governmental organisations with access to international fora and the potential to draw on transnational pressure groups,[16] and which may wield more hard power than smaller domestic non-governmental organisations. Both contribute to global civil society's ability to affect State, intergovernmental organisation, and other actors' behaviour and commitment to respect international law.

Non-governmental organisations mobilise international law with the hope of raising global standards of human security and offering greater protection to marginal and vulnerable populations.[17] To achieve these goals, non-governmental organisations propagate legal norms that are intended to bring about change in the behaviour of specific actors as well as in the very forms of behaviour that may represent socially accepted norms in a given situation.[18] Non-governmental organisations straddle the divide between legal enforcement, often conceived of as a form of coercion by its recipients, and social processes of persuasion, discourse, and capacity-building.[19]

This chapter begins by proposing a typology of non-governmental organisation activity in global governance related capacities that is based on non-governmental organisations' principal means and methods of mobilising and propagating international law norms. This typology has an eye for the influence of non-governmental organisations on international law itself as well as its subjects' declarative and

14 Article 1, European Convention on the Recognition of the Legal Personality of International non-governmental organisations, 24 April 1986, Eur TS 124.

15 Finnemore and Sikkink (n 2) 902ff.

16 On the significance of non-governmental organisation relationships with states and the informal channels they create, P Willetts, *Non-Governmental Organizations in World Politics: The Construction of Global Governance* (Routledge 2011) 62.

17 B Simmons, *Mobilizing for Human Rights: International Law in Domestic Politics* (Cambridge University Press 2009) 6–8.

18 S Calnan, *The Effectiveness of Domestic Human Rights NGOs: A Comparative Study* (Martinus Nijhoff 2008) 20–25. P Burstein, 'Legal Mobilisation as a Social Movement Tactic: The Struggle for Equal Opportunity' (1991) 96 American Journal of Sociology 1201, 1209.

19 T Risse, S Ropp, and K Sikkink, *The Persistent Power of Human Rights: From Commitment to Compliance* (Cambridge University Press 2013) 12–16.

operative practice (both what they actually do and what they think and say about the practice of others), and includes four categories of activity, differentiated according to their purpose and effects on the conduct of those whose practice can substantiate the customary status of norms. The first category is the documentation and reporting activity by non-governmental organisations, and their analysis of State, intergovernmental organisations, and other actors' policies and activities. The second includes mobilisation activities with the goal of awareness raising, including campaigning, media rallying, and coalition building. The third category consists of political and legal lobbying activity that often targets specific decision-makers on policy or legislative questions, and can engage the development of new international legal standards.[20] Non-governmental organisations hire and work with international legal experts, scholars, and practitioners to engage in legal argumentation to defend or further social justice agendas with the support of international law claims and mechanisms. The fourth category is thus domestic and transnational litigation, often with a strategy to change State conduct or the law, including expert-witness and amicus interventions by non-governmental organisations.[21] The rest of this section considers the contours and potential effects of each.

First, a classical role of international non-governmental organizations as prominent members of international civil society and frontline defenders of international law is to independently establish facts in controversial incidents through investigation and expert analysis. For example, non-governmental organisations are developing increasing expertise in forensic investigations, which they know key policy and decision makers rely on.[22] Such information and analysis often establishes the record of pertinent facts, as well as setting out the state of the law and its specific normative thresholds.[23] The information gathered, analysed, and disseminated

20 On legislative and 'counteractive' lobbying, D Austen-Smith and J Wright 'Competitive Lobbying for a Legislator's Vote' (1992) 9 Social Choice and Welfare 229–57. D Austen-Smith, 'Counteractive Lobbying' (1994) 38 American Journal of Political Science 25.

21 On the impact of such activity, CC Barber, 'Tackling the Evaluation Challenge in Human Rights: Assessing the Impact of Strategic Litigation Organisations' (2012) 16 The International Journal of Human Rights 411.

22 P Alston and C Gillespie, 'Global Human Rights Monitoring, New Technologies and the Politics of Information' 23 (2012) European Journal of International Law 1089–1123. *See* e.g. Forensic Architecture, About, www.forensic-architecture.org/project/ accessed 16 July 2017. *See* also E Weizman, 'Forensic Architecture: Only the Criminal Can Solve the Crime' (2010) 164 Radical Philosophy 9.

23 Guidelines on International Human Rights Fact-Finding Visits and Reports: The Lund-London Guidelines, 1 June 2009 www.factfindingguidelines.org/guidelines.html accessed 17 July 2017.

by non-governmental organisations may be targeted at or percolate into State and intergovernmental organisation documentation, media reports, scholarly works and teaching, businesses' decision-making processes, and indeed other non-governmental organisation reports.[24] The cumulative effect of the dissemination of information, particularly by leading non-governmental organisations, can and has influenced the prevailing objective narrative on certain situations (e.g. the public record on the legality of a military attack), and contributed to the push-back against States' attempts to deny and cover-up for violations through justificatory argumentation.[25]

Dissemination and campaigning form a second category.[26] Non-governmental organisations often plan their research and fact-finding with a view to disseminating and leveraging the information in tailored advocacy campaigns, but the two remain distinct activities; larger domestic and international non-governmental organisations typically have specific staff or even departments devoted to 'communications', 'advocacy', 'press', or 'campaigning', as distinct from research. Non-governmental organisations seek to influence public opinion and mobilise constituencies through the press, social media, and other outlets.[27] International non-governmental organisations increasingly use social media channels, in addition to targeting traditional newspapers and television outlets, to reach publics and a broad range of officials, including in other countries. Some campaigns by a group of non-governmental organisations may form a transnational advocacy network with often domestic and regional non-governmental organisations based in another State with the aim of pressuring the government of the other State into compliance.[28] What is most important for the present discussion is that the information disseminated by non-governmental organisations often includes their analysis

24 L Mallinder, 'Review: Law, Politics and Fact-finding: Assessing the Impact of Human Rights Reports' (2010) 2(1) Journal of Human Rights Practice 166–76. DR Davis, A Murdie, and CG Steinmetz, '"Makers and Shapers": Human Rights, INGOs and Public Opinion' (2012) 34 Human Rights Quarterly 199–224.

25 S Cohen, 'Government Responses to Human Rights Reports: Claims, Denials and Counterclaims' (1996) 18 Human Rights Quarterly 517–43. *See* e.g. S Dubberley, Embarking on the Path of Verification, Digital Verification Corps, Amnesty International citizenevidence.org/2016/10/06/embarking-on-the-path-of-verification/ accessed 17 July 2017.

26 *See* e.g. LN Kingston and KR Stam, 'Online Advocacy: Analysis of Human Rights NGO Websites' (2003) 5 Journal of Human Rights Practice 46–74.

27 *See* e.g. on Greenpeace's mass mobilisation techniques, RC Mitchell, AG Mertig, and RE Dunlap, 'Twenty Years of Environmental Mobilization: Trends among National Environmental Organizations' (1991) Society & Natural Resources 219–34.

28 On the 'boomerang effect', Keck and Sikkink (n 2) 13.

of State practice, its codification, and in some cases a concerted legal analysis of domestic laws and public policy that assesses the State's level of commitment to the international law norms in question. In this way, non-governmental organisation activity may have the effect of propagating and raising the profile of certain norms amongst both specialist and general publics, as well as the law's subjects. Similarly, non-governmental organisations have made concerted efforts to regulate the activities of non-State actors under international law by signing non-State armed groups up to informal international humanitarian law instruments[29] and persuading businesses in the extractive sector to subscribe to anti-corruption standards.[30]

The third category of relevant non-governmental organisation activity is lobbying, which includes demarches and interventions intended to raise the awareness of both specific decision-makers and their constituencies traditionally at the State level but also in international organisations.[31] Lobbying is made somewhat easier by the formal incorporation of non-governmental organisation participation in the work of intergovernmental organisations, at least since the League of Nations, and has increasingly diversified through their participation in the sessions of different UN bodies,[32] review of and input to specific processes of monitoring compliance with the law, as well as development of specific rules in the course of drafting and legislative processes.[33] This is what might be called 'legal lobbying': engagement in drafting legislation and legislative review of the content of specific provisions

29 P Bongard and J Somer, 'Monitoring Armed Non-State Actor Compliance with Humanitarian Norms: A Look at International Mechanisms and the Geneva Call Deed of Commitment' (2011) 93 IRRC 673. *See* e.g. Deed of Commitment under Geneva Call for the Protection of Children from the Effects of Armed Conflict www.genevacall.org/wp-content/uploads/dlm_uploads/2013/12/DoC-Protecting-children-in-armed-conflict.pdf accessed 16 July 2017.

30 J Nelson, 'The Operation of Non-Governmental Organisations in a World of Corporate and Other Codes of Conduct' (2007) Corporate Social Responsibility Initiative, Working Paper No 34. SA Aaronson, 'Limited Partnership: Business, Government, Civil Society, and the Public in the Extractive Industries Transparency Initiative (EITI)' (2011) 31 Public Administration and Development 50–63.

31 *See* e.g. DC Esty, 'Non-Governmental Organisations at the World Trade Organisation: Cooperation, Competition or Exclusion' (1998) 1 Journal of International Economic Law 123–47.

32 C Stahn, 'NGOs and International Peacekeeping: Issues, Prospects and Lessons Learned' (2001) 61 ZaöRV 323–55.

33 On non-governmental organisations in lawmaking and the relationship between international organisations and non-governmental organisations, A Boyle and C Chinkin, *The Making of International Law* (Oxford University Press 2007) 282ff.

at the international or domestic levels, including the adoption of laws following treaty ratification,[34] by consulting domestic executives and legislatures on the alignment of existing laws and practices with international law.[35] Domestic jurisdictions may require non-governmental organisation staff who advocate with government officials to 'register' as lobbyists, and international and regional organisations use formal and informal processes to vet the standing and access they grant non-governmental organisations.[36]

Associated with lobbying activity are non-governmental organisations' involvement at different stages and with different degrees of ownership in international law-making processes. For instance, non-governmental organisations were instrumental to the evolution of some of the most seminal instruments of international law dating back to the 1840 World Anti-Slavery Convention; the 1997 Ottawa Anti-Personnel Mines Convention,[37] the 1998 International Criminal Court Rome Statute;[38] the 2002 Optional Protocol to the Convention on the Rights of the Child on the Involvement of Children in Armed Conflict; and the 2014 Arms Trade Treaty. Non-governmental organisations are currently leading campaigns such as an international treaty on business and human rights[39] and for a ban on autonomous weapons.[40] In addition to a range of soft lawmaking at the UN and other intergovernmental organisations, non-governmental organisations have engaged in informal codification and adjudication projects to advance the law, which are commonly referenced as part of the law

34 On ratification as a form of promotion of compliance with human rights, Simmons (n 17). *See* also, HH Koh, 'The 1998 Franckel Lecture: Bringing International Law Home' (1998) 35 Houston Law Review 623.

35 PH Verdier and M Versteeg, 'Modes of Domestic Incorporation of International Law' in W Sandholtz and CA Whytock (eds), *Research Handbook on the Politics of International Law* (Elgar 2017) chapter 6.

36 D Coen and Jeremy Richardson (eds), *Lobbying the European Union: Institutions, Actors and Issues* (Oxford University Press 2009); H Klüver, *Lobbying in the European Union Interest Groups, Lobbying Coalitions, and Policy Change* (Oxford University Press 2013). *See* also Overview of Lobbyists at the US Senate www.senate.gov/reference/reference_index_subjects/Lobbying_vrd.htm accessed 16 July 2017.

37 K Anderson, 'The Ottawa Convention Banning Landmines, the Role of International Non-Governmental Organisations and the Ideal of International Civil Society' in A Bianchi (ed), *Non-State Actors and International Law* (Routledge 2009).

38 On the participation of non-governmental organisation in the Rome Statute conference, Lindblom (n 8) 463ff. Z Pearson, 'Non-Governmental Organisations and the International Criminal Court' (2006) 39 Cornell Journal of International Law 243.

39 *See* generally: Bernaz and Pietropaoli (n 9).

40 Non-governmental organisations' 'Campaign to Stop Killer Robots', Official Website www.stopkillerrobots.org/ accessed 16 July 2017.

and defended by other non-governmental organisations as an emerging custom.[41] These include: the Maastricht Principles on Extraterritorial Obligations of States in the area of Economic, Social and Cultural Rights; the Siracusa Principles on the Limitation and Derogation Provisions in the International Covenant on Civil and Political Rights; the Montréal Principles on Women's Economic, Social and Cultural Rights; and the Princeton Principles on Universal Jurisdiction.

The involvement of non-State actors in European Union based lobbying has been categorised by Voltolini in terms of their effects on European Union foreign policy-making: as dialogue-builders, voice-articulators, and opponents,[42] moving from private to public lobbying and thus also from the most consensual to the most adversarial. The use of 'technical frames' by non-governmental organisation lobbyists to mobilize law put forward legal arguments may, in the case of a 'mixed frame', include political claims.[43] Non-governmental organisation lobbying often mobilises international law claims alongside domestic legislative and policy arguments, counterbalances diagnoses and criticisms of the deficient implementation of obligations and commitments under both bodies of law and policy, and proposes prospective resolutions.[44] Other hybrid processes at the domestic level include what is known as 'regulatory lobbying': when non-governmental organisations address decision-makers with a specific mandate and competence to apply domestic law on matters within their competence, and solicit them on technical grounds to apply or review the application of domestic law in line with international law. Such non-adversarial domestic law-based approach to the enforcement of international law norms can be highly effective in pacifying the political discretion commonly associated with international law-based decisions.

The fourth category that should be considered in canvassing the global governance role of non-governmental organisations is that of litigation both at the domestic court level, invoking either international law alone or a mix of international and

41 On the work of the Extraterritorial Obligations Consortium www.etoconsortium.org accessed 16 July 2017. For a critical enquiry into their work and its effects on legal practice and the development of the law: R Wilde, 'Dilemmas in Promoting Global Economic Justice through Human Rights Law' in N Bhuta (ed), *The Frontiers of Human Rights: Extraterritoriality and its Challenges, Collected Courses of the Academy of European Law* (Oxford University Press 2016) 127–75.

42 B Voltolini, *Lobbying in EU Foreign Policy-Making: The Case of the Israeli-Palestinian Conflict* (Routledge 2015) 19–20.

43 *See* on the juridical approach of non-governmental organisation as distinct from others, K Martens, 'Mission Impossible? Defining Nongovernmental Organizations' (2002) 13 Voluntas: International Journal of Voluntary and Nonprofit Organizations 271–85.

44 Voltolini (n 42) 22–23.

domestic legal arguments, and at the international level, in both regional and international courts and tribunals.[45] Non-governmental organisations have contributed hugely to the case docket and evidence files of the International Criminal Court; what is more, they have also strengthened the role of this Court in the international legal system after having contributed the Court's establishment.[46] The normative pull of regional courts' decisions may be under threat given the bleak record of their implementation at the domestic level and the limitations created by the Court's inability to contend with its overwhelming workload. But non-governmental organisations which have effectively contributed to the development of international human rights law norms through litigation before the European Court of Human Rights, the Inter-American Court of Human Rights, and the African Commission on Human and People's Rights, including as applicants, are now also beginning to attend to the challenge of furthering these judgments' implementation.[47] In addition to regional courts, UN treaty bodies act as quasi-judicial bodies with more universal representation.[48] By contrast to lobbying, the mobilisation of law through litigation is limited by a given court's temporal, territorial, and material jurisdiction. Moreover, although judicial processes can offer remedies to some victims and exert a deterrence effect for broader categories of future perpetrators of international crimes and serious human rights violations, such court suits are at risk of political interference and selectivity, widely criticised by non-governmental organisations.[49] Domestic judges remain generally averse to international law-based

45 D Shelton, 'The Participation of Nongovernmantal Organisations in International Judicial Proceedings' (1994) 88 American Journal of International Law 611–42.

46 On the lawmaking roles of non-governmental organisations in the case of the Rome Statute, Boyle and Chinkin (n 33) chapter 4.2.3.

47 Recognising and denoting the role of civil society in the implementation of ECtHR judgments, 10th Annual Report of the Committee of Ministers of the Council of Europe, Supervision of the Execution of Judgements of the European Court of Human Rights 2016, 66ff. *See* the European Implementation Network, Vision, Mission & Goals http://einnetwork.org/misson-aims/. JL Cavallaro and SE Brewer, 'The Virtue of Following: The Role of Inter-American Litigation in Campaigns for Social Justice' (2008) 5 Sur International Journal on Human Rights 85–96.

48 FD Gaer, 'Implementing International Human Rights Norms: UN Human Rights Treaty Bodies and NGOs' (2003) 2 Journal of Human Rights 339. On the involvement of non-governmental organisations in the UN Treaty Body 2020 Reform, HRW, UN Treaty Bodies Reform: NGOs respond, 2 December 2010 www.hrw.org/news/2010/12/02/un-treaty-bodies-reform-ngos-respond accessed 10 December 2017.

49 Amnesty International, Universal Jurisdiction: A Preliminary Survey of Legislation Around the World – 2012 Update, 9 October 2012 www.amnesty.org/en/documents/ior53/019/2012/en/ accessed 10 December 2017. *See* e.g. HRW, UN Security

claims, and require executive approval, particularly in cases of transnational litigation against partner and politically powerful countries.[50] Where judicial processes remain remiss, non-governmental organisations have used such initiatives as the Bertrand Russell tribunal and the Permanent Peoples' Tribunal in Mexico to invigorate international and transnational justice processes.[51]

In addition to their roles as norm entrepreneurs, non-governmental organisations are also subjects of international law obligations to which they must conform their activity. International law governs aspects of the operations of humanitarian and development non-governmental organisations in conflict zones or post-conflict environments to provide services, support peacekeeping efforts, and implement transitional justice processes.[52] As service-providers, non-governmental organisations incur obligations under international humanitarian law to ensure that their humanitarian operations are undertaken in a neutral and impartial manner, and in line with the principle of non-discrimination.[53] The practical challenge in such cases is often to reconcile the need for access with the non-governmental organisation's responsibility to maintain its neutrality and ensure that it 'does no harm', including by abstaining from giving effect to and treating as lawful the unlawful practices of an authority that controls the group's access to a certain area or population or that regulates the activity the group is looking to engage in.[54] The need to balance these imperatives is particularly acute for non-governmental organisations that

Council: Refer Burma to the International Criminal Court, 3 November 2017 www.hrw.org/news/2017/11/03/un-security-council-refer-burma-icc 10 December 2017. *See* also HRW, Pressure Point: The ICC's Impact on National Justice, 3 May 2018.

50 DL Sloss and MP Van Alstine, 'International Law in Domestic Courts', in W Sandholtz and CA Whytock (eds), *Research Handbook on the Politics of International Law* (Elgar 2017) chapter 4.

51 D Otto, 'Impunity in a Different Register: People's Tribunals and Questions of Judgement, Law and Responsibility' in K Engle et al (eds), *Anti-Impunity and the Human Rights Agenda* (Cambridge University Press 2016) 291. R Falk, 'People's Tribunals, and the Roots of Civil Society Justice', Open Democracy, 12 May 2015.

52 *See* e.g. Stahn (n 32).

53 B Demeyere, 'Turning the Stranger into a Partner: The Role of Responsibilities of Civil Society in IHL Formulation and Application', Thematic Brief, Program on Humanitarian Policy and Conflict Research, Harvard University.

54 *See* on the relevance of the CRPD to humanitarian assistance work; M Kett, Emergency & Humanitarian Assistance and the UN Convention on the Protection and Promotion of the Rights and Dignity of Persons with Disabilities IDDC Task Group on Conflict & Emergencies www.ucl.ac.uk/lc-ccr/lccstaff/maria-kett/iddc_conflict_and_emergencies_taskgroup accessed 10 December 2017. *See* generally on the tensions between law and practice, Liesbet Heyse, *Choosing the Lesser Evil: Understanding Decision Making*

fulfil life-saving functions in conflict and post-conflict situations where intergovernmental organisation and State agencies incur access restrictions.[55] Such non-governmental organisations are increasingly invoking international law to place demands on responsible authorities, and guarantee their non-acquiescence in its violations. The experiences of non-governmental organisations have furthered States and international organisations' appreciation for and compliance with their obligations to accept and facilitate humanitarian assistance.[56]

2 Non-governmental organisation activity and customary international law: an effects-based analysis

Given the range of activities through which non-governmental organisations seek to propagate international norms, what is the scope and quality of their influence on the identification, formation, and application of customary international law norms?[57] Research suggests that the influence of non-governmental organisations on the construction and diffusion of norms can be profound: Finnemore and Sikkink find that non-governmental organisations have contributed to the full span of a norm's life-cycle, by influencing the 'emergence' of norms, driving 'norm cascades', and furthering the 'internalisation' of norms.[58] An effects-based analysis of non-governmental organisation activity on customary international lawmaking may approach the scope and extent to which non-governmental organisations that mobilise international legal argument to address a range of international actors (e.g. State officials, intergovernmental organisations, business, academia, as well as social

in Humanitarian Aid NGOs (Ashgate 2006) Part II. *See* on the requirement to obtain a permit for the construction of schools, clinics etc in the so-called 'Area C' of the West Bank: Diakonia IHL Resource Centre, Planning to Fail: The planning regime in Area C of the West Bank (September 2013) 33–35 www.diakonia.se/globalassets/documents/ihl/ihl-in-opt/planning-to-fail.pdf accessed 1 December 2018.

55 On non-governmental organisation contribution to treaty-making efforts in which non-governmental organisation have played a critical part: J Becker, *Campaigning for Justice: Human Rights Advocacy in Practice* (Stanford University Press 2012) 2.

56 R Barber, 'Facilitating Humanitarian Assistance in International Humanitarian and Human Rights Law' (2009) 91 International Review of the Red Cross 874, 371.

57 The phenomenon of groups of individuals working to influence intergovernmental policymaking is hardly new. SE Baldwin, 'The International Congresses of the Last Century as Forces Working Toward the Solidarity of the World' (1907) 1 AJIL 565, 576; cited in Charnovitz (n 1) 349.

58 On the life cycle of norms, Finnemore and Sikkink (n 2) 895–96.

movements and other civil society actors) influence customary international law-making in at least three ways.[59]

First, non-governmental organisations generate evidence relevant to the identification of the customary status of certain norms of international law by bringing about the actual practice commensurate with the application of a particular rule of international law by a State or intergovernmental organisation,[60] and furthering the articulation of the belief of a State or intergovernmental organisation that their practice is legally required or binding (generating *opinio juris*).[61] Second, non-governmental organisations invoke existing norms of customary international law to adjudicate the conduct of other subjects of international law. They do so in order, thirdly, to influence the application and implementation of existing customary international law norms by and to other subjects of international law. Non-governmental organisations affect the manner in which international law's subjects perceive the content, weight, and compliance pull and bindingness of certain rules (or the 'intellectual effect of international law' norms, as a compromise between utility and appropriateness[62]).

The effects of non-governmental organisation activity may thus progress the substantive scope of specific customary international law norms, the significance of customary international law as a whole, as well as the acceptance of a particular normative content of a given customary international law norm by its subjects, enforcers (e.g. international courts and institutions), and audiences (e.g. scholars and practitioners).[63] We consider these effects along three categories of activities: those that defend the customary status and interpretative content of certain international law norms; those that solidify the content of specific customary international law norms; and those that progress the substantive content of existing customary

59 *See* e.g. J d'Aspremont, 'The Professionalisation of International Law' in J d'Aspremont et al (eds), *International Law as a Profession* (Cambridge University Press 2017) 19. *See* also J d'Aspremont, *Epistemic Forces in International Law* (Elgar 2015).

60 M Wood, 'International Organizations and Customary International Law' (2015) 48 Vanderbilt Journal of Transnational Law 609.

61 J Crawford, *Brownlie's Principles of Public International Law* (Oxford University Press 2012) 23–25.

62 Dill (n 7) 349.

63 For an analysis of the effects of non-governmental organisation on states, intergovernmental organisations, firms, other non-governmental organisations, P Spiro, 'Nongovernmental Organisations in International Relations (Theory)' in J Dunoff and M Pollack (eds), *Interdisciplinary Perspectives on International Law and International Relations* (Cambridge University Press 2013) 228ff.

international law norms and the customary status of emerging customary international law norms.

Non-governmental organisations defend customary international law norms through the dissemination of information and analyses that document State practice (often, wrongful practice) in a manner that upholds the status and content of customary international law norms, such as the prohibition of torture, the freedom of expression, or the right to life.[64] Non-governmental organisations engage in activity intended to police the enforcement of customary international law norms through domestic litigation and regulatory interventions, and submissions to international bodies and third party interventions before international and regional courts.[65] By holding State and intergovernmental organisation practice to existing customary international law rules, non-governmental organisations have arguably contributed to countering attempts to erode those rules or to hamper the emergence of treaty-based rules as customary international law norms. Through, inter alia, educational campaigns and expert reports, non-governmental organisations have defended from disruption norms that were in the process of crystallisation as customary, such as the emerging customary international law status of the prohibition on the death penalty,[66] and furthered the application of the customary international law doctrine of sovereign (non)immunities by aligning State practice therewith with the standards of the Rome Statute of the International Criminal Court.[67]

64 *See* e.g. on non-governmental organisations' work on the development of the definition of psychological torture, PP Sales, *Psychological Torture: Definition, Evaluation and Measurement* (Routledge 2017). *See* e.g. on the protection of the right to life in time of hostilities, Amnesty International, Families Under the Rubble: Attacks on Homes in Gaza (November 2014). *See* also D Murray et al, *Practitioner's Guide to Human Rights in Armed Conflict* (Oxford University Press 2017). The Camden Principles on Freedom of Expression and Equality (April 2009).

65 L McGregor, 'The Role of Supranational Human Rights Litigation in Strengthening Remedies for Torture Nationally' (2012) 16 International Journal of Human Rights 737–54. JA Goldston, 'The Struggle for Roma Rights: Arguments that Have Worked' (2010) 32 Human Rights Quarterly 311–25.

66 *See* e.g. Campaign to End the Death Penalty www.nodeathpenalty.org/ accessed 16 July 2017. R Linde, *The Globalisation of Childhood: The International Diffusion of Norms and Law Against the Child Death Penalty* (Oxford University Press 2016); J Pitzpatrick, 'Relevance of Customary International Norms to the Death Penalty in the United States' (1995) 25 Georgia Journal of International and Comparative Law 165.

67 *See* e.g. FIDH France in Violation of Law Grants Donald Rumsfeld Immunity, Dismisses Torture Complaint 21 November 2007 www.fidh.org/en/region/americas/usa/USA-Guantanamo-Abu-Ghraib/FRANCE-IN-VIOLATION-OF-LAW-GRANTS,4932

Non-governmental organisation networks undertook the pursuit of accountability for the abuses perpetrated by the United States and its allies in the so-called 'global war on terror' by recording violations, demanding transparency from States, and addressing a range of international and domestic mechanisms.[68] Non-governmental organisations have responded and sought to thwart some State-led efforts to mobilise divisive interpretations of international law and engage in campaigns to revise the content of certain norms.[69] They have affirmed the applicability of international law to non-State actors[70] in response to the exclusion of whole groups from the basic protections of international humanitarian and human rights law, such as fair trial and due process rights;[71] challenged States that have sought to expand the permissible scope of the extraterritorial use of lethal force under the pretext of the existence of an armed conflict against a global network of loosely organised non-State groups; and challenged States who became complicit in the use of drone warfare in a global campaign of 'targeted assassinations'.[72] For instance, Human Rights Watch recalled that 'the United States has long considered article 75 to be part of

accessed 10 December 2017. Human Rights Watch, Memorandum for the Twelfth Session of the International Criminal Court Assembly of States Parties, 12 November 2013. *See* also D Akande and S Shah, 'Immunities of State Officials, International Crimes, and Foreign Domestic Courts' (2010) 21 EJIL 815–52.

68 *See* e.g. on bringing Charles Taylor to justice and on accountability for war crimes in Sri Lanka, Becker (n 55) chapters 6 and 8. Trial International, Criminal Complaint in Geneva against George W Bush: What Has Trial Done?, 17 July 2017 trialinternational.org/latest-post/criminal-complaint-in-geneva-against-george-w-bush-what-has-trial-done/ accessed 18 July 2017.

69 *See* generally, J Ohlin, *The Assault on International Law* (Oxford University Press 2013).

70 *See* e.g. upholding the international human rights law obligations of states towards members of such groups: HRW, US: Prolonged Indefinite Detention Violates International Law, 24 January 2011.

71 *See* e.g. 25 Non-Governmental Organisations Urge Obama to Close Guantanamo, 11 April 2013 www.cejil.org/en/25-ngos-urge-obama-close-guantanamo accessed 17 July 2017. DJ Kochan, 'The Political Economy of the Production of Customary International Law: The Role of Non-Governmental Organizations in U.S. Courts' (2004) 22 Berkeley Journal of International Law 240.

72 *See* e.g. framing the effects of the use of drones as a set of issues beyond international humanitarian law and international human rights law: International Human Rights and Conflict Resolution Clinic, Stanford Law School; NYU School of Law, Global Justice Clinic, Living Under Drones: Death, Injury and Trauma to Civilians from US Drone Practices in Pakistan (September 2012) law.stanford.edu/publications/living-under-drones-death-injury-and-trauma-to-civilians-from-us-drone-practices-in-pakistan/ accessed 10 December 2017. *See* for an overview of these practices: C Powell, 'The Role of

customary international law';[73] and Amnesty International that 'Torture and other cruel, inhuman or degrading treatment or punishment is prohibited under international law and is a rule of customary international law' that is 'absolute and can never be subject to any limitation'.[74] Whereas, for instance, Human Rights Watch has observed that 'Some experts contend that Article 36 [obligating states to review modified weapons for their compliance with international law] is customary international law binding on all states, while others see it as a best practice'.[75]

Non-governmental organisation activity has also had a norm-solidifying effect on customary international law. Non-governmental organisations collate and frame evidence of State and intergovernmental organisation practice and *opinio juris* to substantiate the emergence or existence of customary international law norms in a given field of international law. A non-governmental organisation may investigate and document a State's or intergovernmental organisation's practices, policies, or obligations under its internal regulatory order in order to substantiate that political actor's acknowledgement that it has a legal obligation to undertake a particular course of action. Examples include non-governmental organisation work on domestic laws to criminalise war crimes, and to ensure respect for international human rights and environmental law norms.[76] Some non-governmental organisation reporting and analysis has aimed to directly refute misperceptions and claims that certain wrongful State and intergovernmental organisation actions were lawful or driven by a sense of legal obligation, by pointing out internal contradictions in a State's law or public policy, or by mounting challenges against such actions based on legal expertise that demonstrates the customary international law status of a given norm or seeks to progress its interpretative

Transnational Norm Entrepreneurs in the US "War on Terrorism"' (2004) 5 Theoretical Inquiries in Law 47. *See* the work of the International Commission of Jurists (ICJ), through legal lobbying and analysis including of abusive developments in domestic counter-terrorism laws; ICJ Eminent Jurists Panel, Terrorism, Counterterrorism and Human Rights 2009.

73 *See* e.g. HRW, Summary of International and US Law Prohibiting Torture and Other Ill-Treatment of Persons in Custody, 24 May 2004, pantheon.hrw.org/legacy/english/docs/2004/05/24/usint8614.htm accessed 10 December 2017.

74 Amnesty International and Omega Research Foundation, The Human Rights Impact of Less Lethal Weapons and Other Law Enforcement Equipment (2015) 6.

75 HRW, Losing Humanity: The Case Against Killer Robots, 19 November 2012 www.hrw.org/report/2012/11/19/losing-humanity/case-against-killer-robots accessed 10 December 2017.

76 On respect to weapons law, L Doswald-Beck, 'Participation of Non-Governmental Entities in Treaty Making: The Case of Conventional Weapons' in V Gowland-Debbas (ed), *Multilateral Treaty Making* (Springer 2000) 41–44. *See* on the enduring role of non-State

content.[77] Non-governmental organisations have furthered the customary status of the prohibition of the trial of civilians by military courts;[78] the content of the State's duty to investigate international humanitarian law violations;[79] the human rights obligations of corporate actors;[80] and the obligations of States to share the burden and responsibility towards refugees, inter alia.[81] Human Rights Watch has held that '[a]s an international organization the World Bank derives human rights obligations from customary international law and general principles of law',[82] and Amnesty International that 'the prohibition of apartheid forms part of customary international law' and indirectly furthered its normative scope by applying it to Myanmar's 'state-sponsored discrimination and persecution which has targeted the Rohingya population'.[83]

actors in progressive political development, R Pierik and G Gordon, 'Liberal Political Philosophy: The Role of Non-State Actors and Considerations of Global Justice' in B Reinalda (ed), *The Ashgate Research Companion to Non-State Actors* (Ashgate 2011) 133–46.

77 Voltolini (n 42) chapter 4.

78 International Federation for Human Rights, UN demands release of lèse-majesté detainee, raises specter of crimes against humanity, 27 January 2017 www.fidh.org/en/region/asia/thailand/un-demands-release-of-lese-majeste-detainee-raises-specter-of-crimes accessed 10 December 2017.

79 On the customary status of the doctrine of universal jurisdiction: HRW, Syria: Criminal Justice for Serious Crimes under International Law, 17 December 2013. International Federation for Human Rights (FIDH), A Step by Step Approach to the Use of Universal (Criminal) Jurisdiction in Western European States (2009) www.fidh.org/IMG/pdf/ComUniv522a2009.pdf accessed 10 December 2017. Amnesty International, International Law Commission: Second Report on Crimes Against Humanity: Positive Aspects and Concerns (2016).

80 *See* e.g. International Federation for Human Rights, Corporate Accountability for Human Rights Abuses A Guide for Victims and NGOs on Recourse Mechanisms (May 2016) www.fidh.org/IMG/pdf/corporate_accountability_guide_version_web.pdf accessed 10 December 2017.

81 *See* e.g. Joint NGOs Statement ahead of the New York summit on refuges and migrants: Amnesty International et al, Rising to the challenge: world leaders need to urgently adopt solutions for refugees and migrants beyond the UN Summit (September 2016) refugees-migrants-civilsociety.org/wp-content/uploads/2016/09/Civil-society-statement-scorecard-in-response-to-2016-New-York-Declaration-as-of-14-Sept_16.00-hrs.pdf accessed 10 December 2017.

82 *See* e.g. HRW, Submission re International Financial Institutions and Human Rights to the UN Independent Expert on the promotion of a democratic and equitable international order, 25 April 2017 www.hrw.org/news/2017/04/25/human-rights-watch-submission-re-international-financial-institutions-and-human accessed 10 December 2017.

83 *See* e.g. Amnesty International, Myanmar: 'Caged Without a Roof': Apartheid in Myanmar's Rakhine State (2017) 90.

Many non-governmental organisation activities have incidental effects on the formation or identification of State practice and *opinio juris*. In addition, some non-governmental organisations' explicit goals to expand or restrict rights or obligations could also affect the customary status of certain norms.[84] Cases filed with the support of non-governmental organisations or third-party non-governmental organisation interventions in the Inter-American Court of Human Rights and the European Court of Human Rights have both successfully progressed the law and shown its remedial limits.[85] Non-governmental organisation-led soft law initiatives have foregrounded the extraterritorial orientation of human rights law through the 2011 Maastricht Principles on the Extraterritorial Obligations of States in the area of Economic, Social and Cultural Rights.[86] The enforcement of soft instruments,[87] particularly in the field of international environmental law, relies on the work of non-governmental organisations.[88]

As noted, non-governmental organisations mobilise arguments based on customary international law norms thereby contributing to their application by and to others. One way in which this happens is when States apply international law to review the practice of a non-State actor whose international law based obligations hinge on the customary status of the specific norm. Non-governmental organisation activity has thus contributed to the substantiation of non-State armed groups and businesses obligations under international law.[89] They have trained and signed

84 *See* e.g. HRW, The Legal Prohibition on Torture, 11 March 2003. NGO Shipbreaking Platform, Make the Polluter Pay! Why We Need the Ship Recycling License (2016) www.shipbreakingplatform.org/platform-news-ngo-shipbreaking-platform-demands-european-ship-reycling-licence/ accessed 17 July 2017.

85 LMI Sundstrom, 'Russian NGOs and the European Court of Human Rights: A Spectrum of Approaches to Litigation' (2014) 36 Human Rights Quarterly 844; LH Mayer, 'NGO Standing and Influence in Regional Human Rights Courts and Commissions' (2010–11) 36 Brooklyn Journal of International Law 911.

86 *See* e.g. T van Boven, 'Role of NGOs in International Human Rights Standard Setting: A Prerequisite of Democracy' (1990) 90 California Western International Law Journal. *See* on the mixed prospects of extraterritoriality: Wilde (n 41) 127–75.

87 *See* on the relationship between soft law and customary international law: A Pellet, The Normative Dilemma: Will and Consent in International Law-Making (1989) 12 Australian Year Book of International Law 30.

88 *See* on non-governmental organisation involvement in the Aarhus Convention procedure for individual communications; Lindblom (n 8) 285–88. *See* also D Tarlock, 'The Role of Non-Governmental Organisations in the Development of International Environmental Law' (1992) 68 Chicago-Kent Law Review 61.

89 Business and Human Rights Resource Center, International business and human rights organizations business-humanrights.org/en/international-business-and-human-rights-organizations accessed 17 July 2017.

armed groups up to political declarations and 'deeds of commitment' in furtherance of their respect for international law;[90] and in particular the rules of international humanitarian law and international human rights law applicable in armed conflict.[91] Similarly, non-governmental organisations have led the application of international law to businesses,[92] by activating the practice of domestic courts in prosecuting businesses under domestic laws that incorporate international law, and the International Criminal Court's capacity for such prosecutions.[93] Concerted non-governmental organisation efforts have trickled down into States' and international organisations' public policy-making, furthering the application of customary international law norms to non-State actors as subjects of international law,[94] for instance, by calling for reforms in the mandate and practice of international bodies such as the Security Council and the International Criminal Court.[95]

90 J Somer, 'Engaging Armed Non-State Actors to Protect Children from the Effects of Armed Conflict: When the Stick Doesn't Cut the Mustard' (2013) 5 Journal of Human Rights Practice. C Hofmann, Reasoning with Rebels: International NGOs' Approaches to Engaging Armed Groups, SWP Research Paper 2012, www.swp-berlin.org/fileadmin/contents/products/research_papers/2012_RP11_hof.pdf accessed 17 July 2017.

91 R Geiss et al (eds), *Humanising the Laws of War: The Red Cross and the Development of International Humanitarian Law* (Cambridge University Press 2017).

92 HRW, Amnesty International and FIDH investigate activities of businesses and international financial institutions. *See* e.g. FIDH, Corporate Accountability for Human Rights Abuses. A Guide for Victims and NGOs on Recourse Mechanisms 3rd edition May 2016. International Commission of Jurists, Report of the Expert Legal Panel on Corporate Complicity in International Crimes (2008).

93 *See* e.g. on the International Criminal Court's widening its remit to investigate business, Human Rights Coalition Calls on International Criminal Court to Investigate Role of Chiquita Executives in Contributing to Crimes against Humanity, May 2017 www.fidh.org/en/region/americas/colombia/human-rights-coalition-calls-on-icc-to-investigate-role-of-chiquita accessed 17 July 2017. *See* also S Khoury and D Whyte (eds), *Corporate Human Rights Violations: Global Prospects for Legal Action* (Routledge 2017).

94 S Herr, 'Binding Non-State Armed Groups to International Humanitarian Law Geneva Call and the Ban of Anti-personnel mines: Lessons from Sudan' (2010) Peace Research Institute Frankfurt, PRIF-Report No 95. *See* also, on the practice of the Human Rights Council in applying international law to armed groups, to which non-governmental organisations contribute, A Bellal, 'Human Rights Obligations of Armed Non-State Actors: An Exploration of the Practice of the UN Human Rights Council' (2016) Geneva Academy In-Brief No 7.

95 *See* e.g. criticism of the failures of the Security Council to respond to global crisis: Amnesty International, Annual Report 2014/5 www.amnesty.org/en/latest/research/2015/02/annual-report-201415/ accessed 10 December 2017. On challenges to the International Criminal Court: Human Rights Watch, Human Rights Watch Briefing Note for the Sixteenth Session of the International Criminal Court Assembly of States

In the formation of customary international law norms, non-governmental organisations have triggered international lawmaking initiatives with the effect of solidifying the customary status and progressing the content of specific norms. Non-governmental organisations lobby for State participation in international legislative processes that codify customary international law norms – including processes that were initiated and led by non-governmental organisations.[96] Such efforts are often matched by lobbying and campaigning activities at the domestic level to further the domestication of international law norms, including through legislation, which can contribute to the consolidation of *opinio juris* with respect to a State's practice of a norm,[97] for instance, by substantiating its internalisation of the obligation to do so in its public policy and institutional practice.

As Table 19.1 summarises, non-governmental organisation activity can influence any one of the three domains of customary international lawmaking – the identification, application, and formation of customary international law norms – in a range of overlapping and interrelated ways. Almost all the non-governmental organisation activities listed above can contribute to the identification of customary international law norms by unearthing relevant State practice and *opinio juris* and analysing their adequacy, and as such defending and solidifying customary international law norms. The fact that most non-governmental organisation contributions to domestic and international lawmaking remain under-documented has invariably lead to an under-valuing of the effects non-governmental organisations have on international law and its subjects, also making the aggregate effects of a cacophony of non-governmental organisation activities on a particular issue and set of norms difficult to capture.

Critically, the likelihood that non-governmental organisation activity will defend, solidify, or progress a given customary international law norm, and hence customary international law as a whole, depend on the intensity of such effects, as well as their issue-focus, target audience, and methodological orientation.[98] The consequentiality

Parties, November 2017 www.hrw.org/news/2017/11/20/human-rights-watch-briefing-note-sixteenth-session-international-criminal-court accessed 10 December 2017.

96 *See* e.g. International binding instrument for BHR; Ottawa anti-personnel mines convention; and ongoing work on the use of schools for military purposes protocol. *See* the case-studies in Boyle and Chinkin (n 33) chapter 4.

97 *See* e.g. HRW's role in analysis the flaws, lobbying, and legislative review of the 2014 Tunisian Constitution to 'include a clause directly incorporating human rights, as defined under customary international law'; HRW, Tunisia: Events of 2012, World Report 2014 www.hrw.org/world-report/2014/country-chapters/tunisia accessed 10 December 2017.

98 Finnemore and Sikkink (n 2) 896ff.

Table 19.1 Effects of non-governmental organisation activity on customary international lawmaking

CIL-making element	Examples of relevant non-governmental organisation activity	Potential effects on State and intergovernmental organisation practice	Effects on customary international law norms
Identification (of customary international law through State and intergovernmental organisation practice, and *opinio juris*)	- Documentation of State practice of customary international law - Legal review of State practice and law - Lobbying to induce decision-making based on customary international law - Domestication of customary international law norms, and substantiation of their content	- Acceptance of customary international law status of norms by states and intergovernmental organisation - Application of customary international law norms	- Defending existing customary international law norms - Solidifying incipient custom
Application (of customary international law norms)	- Reporting and analysis of customary international law-based violations including by non-State actors - Litigation under customary international law - Lobbying UN to condemn actors' violations of customary international law-based obligations	- State and intergovernmental organisation assuming customary international law obligations (through policy, statements) - State and intergovernmental organisation applying customary international law to non-State actors	- Solidifying (and justifying) existing customary international law status of a norm - Defending (protecting) customary international law norms
Formation (of scope and content of customary international law norms)	- Arguing for the customary status of certain IL norms - Potentiating customary international law based decisions by States through lobbying, public pressure - Elaboration of customary international law norms through domestic practice, law - Initiating and contributing to treaty-making processes	- Triggering State and intergovernmental organisation practice - Instigating legislative, policy development (*opinio juris*) - Develop interpretative content of treaty-based rules	- Progressing the interpretation of customary international law norms - Solidifying the substantive scope of customary international law norms

Source: Author's own compilation.

of non-governmental organisation activity may also vary according to the way the non-governmental organisation relates to and is perceived by the political actor whose behaviour it is looking to affect. The non-governmental organisation's relationship with the State or international organisation determines the entry points it has for influencing that actor's decisions and positions, which in turn affects the quality of the non-governmental organisation's influence: from concrete and certain, to diffused and uncertain. It may be possible for a non-governmental organisation to engage a political actor directly, through its own internal regulatory order (direct influence), or indirectly, by affecting its interests through its peers and constituencies (indirect influence). The 'naming and shaming' based theory of change remains prevalent particularly among international non-governmental organisations who have more capacity to influence States and international organisations and has more diffused effects on the practice of wrongdoing or bystander States, and as such also, with diluted effect, on the solidification, defence, and progression of specific customary international law norms.

Even with privileged access to decision-makers, the influence a non-governmental organisation can exert depends on the form and nature of the non-governmental organisation's interactions with the normative actor:[99] prescriptive demands to respect international law are likely to go unheeded, absent other factors, particularly as compared to a process that engages the normative actor's own regulatory framework. The customary international law impact of non-governmental organisation activity may also depend on whether the information it puts forward and the demands it addresses to a normative actor can effectively trigger the latter's re-understanding of its own need to align its conduct with international law – including by abstaining from giving effect to the wrongful conduct of others.[100] Non-governmental organisations have instigated regulatory processes that not only compelled normative actors to align their conduct with international law,[101] but resulted in the reiteration and codification in domestic law and public policy of latent policy preferences and recognised

99 On norm development and interaction, J Brunnee and S Toope, *Legitimacy and Legality in International Law: An Interactional Account* (Cambridge University Press 2008).

100 On the risks entailed for home-state legal orders by their corporate nationals' involvement in extraterritorial international law violations: V Azarova, 'The Bounds of (Il) legality: Rethinking the Regulation of Transnational Corporate Wrongs' in E Yahyaoui (ed), *Human Rights and Power in Times of Globalisation* (Brill 2017).

101 *See* on these processes, P Mueller and P Slominski, 'The Role of Law in EU Foreign Policy-making: Legal Integrity, Legal Spillover, and the EU Policy of Differentiation towards Israel' (2016) Journal of Common Market Studies 1–18. Hugh Lovatt and Matia Toaldo, EU Differentiation and Israeli Settlements (European Council on Foreign Relations 2015). Valentina Azarova, Israel's Unlawfully Prolonged Occupation: Consequences Under An Integrated Legal Framework (European Council on Foreign Relations 2017).

legal imperatives that align with international law norms.[102] Non-governmental organisations' increasing indispensability and embeddedness in the enforcement and development of international law give rise to a responsibility to judge the appropriateness of a particular course of action on a per case basis.

3 The varied, informal roles of non-governmental organisations in customary international lawmaking

The above typology of non-governmental organisation activities and effects-based analysis of their contribution to customary international lawmaking offers only a glimpse into the universe through which non-governmental organisations integrally sustain the veracity and determine the direction of the development of international law by furthering its enforcement, challenging its stagnancy, and stimulating its interpretation.[103] Non-governmental organisations shape not only the way States and intergovernmental organisations actually act and are likely to act, but also how other international actors and institutions perceive and respond to certain State actions, as well as the political orientation that such actors take towards international law. The customary international lawmaking lens enables a more granular and concrete account of the effects of non-governmental organisations' norm entrepreneurship and propagation, one that analyses the wide variety of roles played by non-governmental organisations in terms of what Spiro calls their 'cumulative influence' on international law-based decisions and processes, as well as 'highlight[s] particular junctures at which such influence is probable',[104] and also where the potential for influence perhaps remains latent.

This perspective reminds us that the 'indirect' role non-governmental organisations play in customary international lawmaking has both formal and informal dimensions. Most accounts of non-governmental organisations and customary international lawmaking focus on what may be called their formal-indirect contribution to relatively well-oiled formal institutional processes, which include a range of non-governmental organisation consultations in legislative and other intergovernmental organisations

102 *See* e.g. the interventions made by the expert partnership The MATTIN Group to expose the effects of the European Union's interstate relations with Israel on the full implementation of European Union law, which resulted in the European Union's own correction of its relations and in this context also measures of an enforcing effect on Israeli authorities: Mueller and Slominski (n 98) and Voltolini (n 42) 37–39.

103 *See* generally, I Venzke, *How Interpretation Makes International Law* (Oxford University Press 2012).

104 Spiro (n 63) 226.

and State processes, interventions before courts and quasi-judicial processes.[105] The formalistic view focuses on non-governmental organisations' mobilisation of legal arguments acting as pressure groups in a manner that has a relatively diffused effect on State or intergovernmental organisation actions.[106] In the classic framing of non-governmental organisations as norm entrepreneurs that offer guidance and critique to states,[107] States may wish to utilise non-governmental organisations to plug a democratic deficit of public participation.[108] Non-governmental organisations' influence on customary international lawmaking emanates not only from their ability to mobilise powerful agents (using hard power), but also, in lesser-known cases, from the resources and expertise that permits them to instigate and pursue informal lawmaking processes.[109] Using the lens of Koh's transnational legal process, non-governmental organisations instigate positive State practice and acceptance of legal obligations[110] by potentiating the interpretation of international law in the context of interactions between the authorities of two or more States, and thereby also the internalisation of international norms by States and non-State actors.[111]

The most significant informal way that non-governmental organisations contribute to the solidification and defence of customary international law norms is by instigating State and intergovernmental organisation decision-making processes,

105 K Abbott and D Snidal, 'The Governance Triangle: Regulatory Standards Institutions and the Shadow of the State' in *The Politics of Global Regulation* (Princeton University Press 2009) 44–88.

106 Wendt 1999, 193; cited in Spiro (n 63) 227.

107 K Raustiala, 'States, NGOs, and International Environmental Institutions' (1997) 41.4 International Studies Quarterly, 719–40; K Raustiala, 'Institutional Proliferation and the International Legal Order' (2012) Interdisciplinary Perspectives on International Law and International Relations: The State of the Art, 12–21. Keck and Sikkink evaluate the success of non-State networks by isolating 'stages' in issue politics to include 'defining an issue area, convinc[ing] policymakers and publics that the problems thus defined are soluble, prescrib[ing] solutions, and monitor[ing] their implementation'; Keck and Sikkink (n 2) 201. *See* also Spiro (n 63) 225–26.

108 D Otto, 'Nongovernmental Organisations in the UN System: The Emerging Role of International Civil Society' (1996) 18 Human Rights Quarterly 107. M Edwards, *NGO Rights and Responsibilities: A New Deal for Global Governance* (Foreign Policy Centre 2000) 11.

109 J Pauwelyn et al, 'Informal International Law as Presumptive Law: Exploring New Modes of Law-Making' in R Liivoja and J Petman (eds) *International Law-Making: Essays in Honour of Jan Klabbers* (Routledge 2014) 75ff.

110 Spiro (n 63) 229.

111 On transnational legal process, HH Koh, 'Transnational Legal Process' (1996) 75 Neb L Rev 181.

presenting them with the opportunity to take a position and adopt measures domestically and internationally on previously unheeded situations and issues.[112] Such interventions may not result in compliant behaviour, but they can cause States to admit fault and qualify their actions to protect the erosion of customary international law norms. Much of this activity is based, Spiro notes, on 'agency relationships and causal chains' and as such remains ad hoc and opportunistic. The capability of a non-governmental organisation in this regard depends on the circumstances it finds itself in vis-à-vis the political actor it is looking to influence as a function of its ability to build relationships and pursue longer-term processes for change. A non-governmental organisation that engages a normative actor's internal regulatory order can both elucidate its latent understandings of how it is legally obligated to act in a given situation, and bring it to elaborate its sense of commitment and understanding of the significance of certain international norms, as well as align its actions and engagements with others with these commitments.[113] The limited resources, expertise, and bandwidth of most States means that they are often unable to attend to the growing number of issues regulated by international law.[114] Issues beyond the State's reach in terms of capacity can greatly benefit from intervention and instigation by non-governmental organisations. Such mutually beneficial instigation processes are predicated on a logic that differs from the common perception that the role of non-governmental organisations is simply to confront States and intergovernmental organisations for violations of international law.

NGOs also informally help create a public record of international law violations and violators through concerted documentation, reporting, and analysis of a broad range of facts.[115] Whether this information enters the general court of public opinion, or finds its way to the corridors of power, such discourse-generating activity (the *raison d'être* of leading international non-governmental organizations) raises the significance of certain norms as standards of State conduct, and increases their compliance pull as well as their opposability to the State's or international

112 *See* on the blurring of the distinction between the domestic and the international, Inger Osterdahl, '(International) Law!', in Liivoja and Petman (n 97) chapter 7.

113 On the significance of non-governmental organisation influence in domestic processes, A Chayes and AH Chayes, *The New Sovereignty: Compliance with International Regulatory Agreements* (Harvard 1998) Chapter 11.

114 *See*, on the 'bandwidth hypothesis' and the 'echo hypothesis', S Dotan, 'Social Networks and the Enforcement of International Law' in A Lang and M Hirsch (eds), *Edward Elgar Research Handbook on the Sociology of International Law* (Elgar 2017).

115 J Wouters and I Rossi, 'Human Rights NGOs: Role, Structure and Legal Status' (2001) Institute for International Law, Working Paper No 14. MW Toffel et al, 'Reinforcing

organisation's other interests. Non-governmental organisations are also on guard against abusive norm entrepreneurship by some States and international actors.[116] Although the views of non-governmental organisations are not sufficient to evidence the existence of a customary international law norm, non-governmental organisations can generate both State practice and evidence that a given rule is recognised as a legal obligation by stimulating States and international organisations' actions. To understand non-governmental organisations' ability to influence State and intergovernmental organisation practice, as its enforcer, moral compass, or stimulator,[117] we need to conceptualise the range of non-governmental organisation activities peripheral to formal processes of international lawmaking.

These informal processes of non-governmental organisation engagement with States and international organisations are not new, though they remain curiously absent from accounts of the consequentiality of non-governmental organisations. Yet a growing number of actions and decisions by judicial, executive, and legislative authorities and by intergovernmental organisations were triggered by non-governmental organisations. External instigation is a sine qua non for the activation of certain judicial and administrative processes, such as triggering politically sensitive domestic legislation on international crimes, collecting special-purpose evidence, and raising institutions' awareness of the significance of their action or inaction in a particular case.[118] State or intergovernmental organisation inaction and silence may correlate with the silence or omission of a non-governmental organisation on a given issue, or deficiencies in the manner that such involvement occurs.

Indeed, States and intergovernmental organisations have come to integrally rely on and informally delegate such monitoring and instigation roles to non-governmental

Regulatory Regimes: How States, Civil Society, and Codes of Conduct Promote Adherence to Global Labour Standards' (2013) Corporate Social Responsibility Initiative Working Paper No 65.

116 A Di Lellio and E Castano, 'The Danger of "New Norms" and the Continuing Relevance of IHL in the Post-9/11 Era' (2015) 900 IRRC 1277.

117 Much of non-governmental organisation activity is framed in terms of how it bears on State decision-making; Spiro (n 63) 227–28.

118 It was not until the litigation launched by the Frente Polisario's and Sahrawi civil society e.g. the Western Sahara Campaign in the United Kingdom, at the Court of Justice of the European Union that European Union institutions recognised the harmful effects of Morocco's practice on European Union law and policy: Leigh Day, www.leighday.co.uk/News/News-2018/February-2018/European-judgment-recognises-the-rights-of-Saharwi February 2018 www.leighday.co.uk/News/News-2018/February-2018/European-judgment-recognises-the-rights-of-Saharwi accessed 17 July 2018.

organisations.[119] Non-governmental organisations may offer 'off budget' expertise, resources, and access to certain communities and locations, to support State and intergovernmental organisation compliance with their own obligations. These assets are indispensable to address growing challenges to international law, and to act on urgent cases.[120] The cooperation between States and intergovernmental organisations has presumably also contributed to the growing embeddedness of non-governmental organisations in intergovernmental organisations and State legislative and administrative processes, which has in turn enhanced the intensity of their influence on the internalisation of international law by states and international organisations.[121] The participation of non-governmental organisations in intergovernmental organisation activities, including norm-setting and processes for the review of the actions of States and non-State actors, have palpably affected the quality of their outcomes.[122] Non-governmental organisations maintain a range of agreements with States and intergovernmental organisations to guarantee their right of participation in the instigation and review of their decisions and actions.[123] Most States have ombudsmen and other portals to facilitate and sometimes even ensure non-governmental organisations' participation. States are increasingly factoring in the monitoring role of non-governmental organisations in domestic law and practice, such as the UK Modern Slavery Act.[124] The role of non-governmental organisations in global and domestic governance has, however, also meant that States have become accustomed to these 'parallel and supplementary functions',[125] with potentially worrisome effects on their willingness to ensure their respect for such norms independently of such external interventions.

119 *See* e.g. M Kaldor, 'The Idea of Global Civil Society' (2003) 79 International Affairs, 583–93.

120 Spiro (n 63) 231.

121 *See* on the formal obligations of non-governmental organisations in the context of their cooperation with intergovernmental organisation: Lindblom (n 8) 193ff.

122 R Wedgwood, 'Legal Personality and the Role of Non-Governmental Organizations and Non-State Political Entities in the United Nations System' in R Hofmann (ed), *Non-State Actors as New Subjects of International Law* (Dunker and Humboldt 1999) 21–36.

123 *See* also Report of the Panel of Eminent Persons on Civil Society and UN Relationships, recommending a fortification of these links, including with UN fora such as the UN Security Council and General Assembly: General Assembly, We the peoples: civil society, the United Nations and global governance Report of the Panel of Eminent Persons on United Nations–Civil Society Relations, UN Doc A/58/817, 11 June 2004.

124 CORE Coalition, Beyond Compliance: Effective Reporting Under the Modern Slavery Act: A civil society guide for commercial organisations on the transparency in supply chains clause, February 2016 corporate-responsibility.org/wp-content/uploads/2016/03/CSO_TISC_guidance_final_digitalversion_16.03.16.pdf accessed 17 July 2017.

125 Chayes and Chayes (n 113) 251.

4 Concluding remarks: taking non-governmental organisations seriously

The contribution to and influence of non-governmental organisations on the social construction of customary international law norms is neither stable nor completely ad hoc.[126] This constructivist account of the multiplicity of roles, formal and informal, non-governmental organisations play as instigators or enforces of the practice and *opinio juris* of States and intergovernmental organisations attests to the indirect ways in which non-governmental organisations shape the content of customary international law norms through their influence on States and international organisations' behaviour. Non-governmental organisations further the codification of international law and naturalise its application and enforcement through a wealth of informal processes, outputs, and actors.[127] While the record of the particularities, causes and effects of these influences on customary international law remains incomplete, and the informal roles of different non-governmental organisations multifarious, it is fair to say that non-governmental organisations have become part of the fabric of international law not only from the perspective of the interest groups that their activities seek to serve, but from that of States and international organisations as the 'makers' of customary international law. The International Law Commission cautiously framed non-governmental organisations as having an 'indirect' role in the identification and formation of customary international law norms[128] – an approach that might be viewed as an attempt to deter unprepared enthusiasts from rushing onto customary international law's eclectic 'dance floor'.[129] Notwithstanding this cautionary view, the epistemic force and determinative influence of the activities of non-governmental organisations; the constitutive and generative contribution of these activities to international legal practice, strengthen non-governmental organizations' contribution to customary international lawmaking.

Non-governmental organisations remain subject to access and other restrictions, but their increasing status and rights within States and in international law is such that the merit of their contribution to the much-needed re-orientation of

126 K Martens, 'Examining the (Non-)Status of NGOs in International Law' (2003) 10 Indiana Journal of Global Legal Studies 1.

127 J Pauwelyn et al, 'When Structures Become Shackles: Stagnation and Dynamics in International Lawmaking' (2004) 24 European Journal of International Law 734, fn 3.

128 International Law Commission (n 3).

129 J d'Aspremont, Customary International Law As a Dancefloor: Parts I and II (EJIL: Talk!, 14 and 15 April 2014) www.ejiltalk.org/customary-international-law-as-a-dance-floor-part-i/ and www.ejiltalk.org/customary-international-law-as-a-dance-floor-part-ii/ accessed 17 July 2018.

international law to increase the range of its 'users and beneficiaries',[130] also deserves scrutiny. On the one hand, non-governmental organisations have a unique ability to further the 'behavioural relevance of international law' as residual enforcers, who have often assumed roles that States and intergovernmental organisations claim to be unable to undertake for political or other reasons.[131] They have shaped not only the content and processes of international law, but also perceptions of its remedial nature by the publics it is intended to serve.[132] The professionalisation and proceduralisation of the roles performed by non-governmental organisations and the nature of the interventions they made have sought to make international law more responsive to the needs of its publics,[133] and give 'target state actors a focal point for conforming their practice to a standard', determined by predictable 'legal metrics'.[134]

A downside of this role of non-governmental organisations is that States and other international actors have become increasingly reliant on non-governmental organisations for the instigation of certain decision-making that should not require such prompting and should be performed by the State in compliance with its existing obligations. Leading international non-govenrmental organizations which contribute to and endorse an international legal practice that 'enables particular policies to be furthered',[135] due to a narrow mandate or a tactical focus, have attracted criticism for being agitators of convenience that lose track of the structural biases and protection gaps in the law.[136] In some cases, 'compliance might be part of the problem'[137] necessitating the reconstitution of international law.[138] In Thomas Frank's view, non-governmental organisations 'do not in any sense legitimate the decision-making process' in international law; indeed '[t]hey

130 R Higgins, 'The Reformation in Richard Rawlings (ed) International Law', in R Rawlings (ed) *Law, Society and Economy* (Oxford University Press 1997) 207, 211–15; cited by Charnovitz (n 1), 360.
131 Dill (n 7).
132 Edwards (n 108) 16–27.
133 Charnovitz (n 1) 360.
134 Spiro (n 63) 234.
135 Wilde (n 41) 172.
136 Wilde, for instance, shows how the law's 'narrow conceptions of direct or foreseeable harm, direct territorial control, or vague notions of cooperation, map onto a liberal economic model of laissez faire'. ibid 173.
137 ibid 174. *See* also D Kennedy, 'The International Human Rights Movement: Part of the Problem?' (2002) 15 Harvard Human Rights Journal 99–125.
138 R Dudai, 'Human Rights in the Populist Era: Mourn then (Re)Organise' (2017) 9 Journal of Human Rights Practice 16, 18.

may make it better, sometimes they make it worse, but the legitimacy deficit is not addressed by them'.[139]

Non-governmental organisations claim to serve the interests of their own constituencies, but their influence on customary international law is shaped by how non-governmental organisations may come to serve States' interest in the status quo. Do non-governmental organisations' approaches seek to capture international law's emancipatory potential, and as such a departure from its State-centrist view? What is the shift needed in the strategic and political orientation of non-governmental organisations work? Of course, non-governmental organisations should not engage in boundless activism that irresponsibly dreams up a new international law; doing so risks them rendering their organisations and global civil society more broadly into disrepute.[140] That being said, non-governmental organisations that have become the 'face of international law', and as such also indirect engineers of customary international law, should at a minimum assume a critical orientation towards the strictures of international law so as to offer real answers to well-thought-out questions and reconstruct the predicament Kratochwil aptly describes as follows:

> [S]omething is amiss in thinking that the real problem lies in clarifying principles or codifying best practices while leaving their application to the 'practitioners' on the ground. […] Instead of beginning with a problem and trying to formulate the 'right' question, we begin with a solution, which is looking for problems to be applied to. Here 'the law of the hammer' exerts a powerful pull, since if you have a hammer, the whole world looks suspiciously like a nail, even if we all know that if the task is fetching water, a hammer is of no avail.[141]

But it is not always easy to find a bucket. Non-governmental organisations face the difficult task of synthesising complex patterns of fact, identifying responsibilities and remedies, throughout their efforts to challenge the abusive actions and policies of states and intergovernmental organisations. As actors that engage the law, non-governmental organisations are expected to expose the epistemic forces intended to dilute the normative content of certain international norms. Faced with the limits of the remedial nature of international law in domains like the regulation

139 TM Frank, 'Remarks', in Hofmann (n 124) 151, 152. *See* also TM Franck, *The Empowered Self: Law and Society in the Age of Individualism* (Oxford University Press 2000) 36.

140 On the over-printing and counterfeits of the human rights currency, Dudai (n 138) 18. *See* also DA Bell and JH Carens, 'The Ethical Dilemmas of International Human Rights and Humanitarian NGOs: Reflections on A Dialogue Between Practitioners and Theorists' (2004) 26 Human Rights Quarterly 300–29.

141 F Kratochwil, 'Legalism and the "Dark" Side of Global Governance' in Liivoja and Petman (n 97) 46.

of the conduct of hostilities, the elimination of war, and the migration 'crisis'; however, non-governmental organisations often 'shy away from the idea that [they] too are in charge, that [they] too participate in those decisions'.[142] It is the quality of their political orientation, mandate, methodological posture, and strategy on a given issue[143] that produces the kinds of dynamics in which, as Kratochwil remarks, 'the historical struggles get inscribed and become afterwards through habituation and hindsight, the "way in which things are handled" and taken for granted'.[144]

Non-governmental organisations' aspirations for credibility with decision-makers and relevance to international processes have too often limited their ability to rethink outdated frames and categories of analysis, address root causes of human rights abuses.[145] Paradoxically, non-governmental organisations whose mandates refrain from the application of the legality of the use (*jus ad bellum*)[146] or on the right to self-determination of people[147] do so to maintain a form of 'neutrality' vis-à-vis law-abusing actors so as to be able to leverage their other, considerably more symptomatic actions. These 'awkward silences' by non-governmental organisations may well have contributed to the fading relevance and regulatory potential of certain international norms.[148] It remains to be hoped that a more veridical understanding of the roles non-governmental organisations

142 D Kennedy, 'One, Two, Three, Many Legal Orders: Legal Pluralism and the Cosmopolitan Dream' (2007) 3 New York University Reviews of Law and Change 646; cited by Andrea Bianchi, *International Legal Theories* (Oxford University Press 2017) 243.

143 On the need for explicitness in the example of the Maastricht principles, Wilde (n 41) 141–42. P van Bossche, 'Regulation the Legitimacy of NGO' in A Vedder (ed), *NGO Involvement in International Governance and Policy* (Martinus Nijhoff 2007) chapter 5; M Kaldor, 'Civil Society and Accountability' (2003) 4 Journal of Human Development 5.

144 Kratochwil (n 141) 44.

145 Not unlike the healthy doubts in the appropriateness of the European and US models in understanding the problems for the developing world; A Hirschman, *Essays in Trespassing* (Cambridge University Press 1981) and 'The Search for Paradigms as Hindrance to Understanding' (1970) 21 World Politics 329–43; cited in Kratochwil (n 141) 47.

146 On this shift: S Moyn, 'From Antiwar Politics to Antitorture Politics' in A Sarat et al (eds) *Law and War* (Stanford University Press 2014) 154–97; SR Ratner, 'Jus ad Bellum and Jus in Bello After September 11' (2002) 96 AJIL 905.

147 cf on the efforts to make economic rights justiciable: V Gauri and DM Brinks (eds), *Courting Social Justice: Judicial Enforcement of Social and Economic Rights in the Developing World* (Cambridge University Press 2008); J Gilbert, 'The Right to Freely Dispose of Natural Resources: Utopia or Forgotten Rights?' (2013) 31 Netherlands Quarterly of Human Rights 314.

148 *See* generally on the constraining and legitimising effects of the *jus ad bellum*: M Hakimi, 'The Jus Ad Bellum's Regulatory Form' (2018) 112 AJIL 2 151–90.

have had in customary international lawmaking would in turn enable international lawyers, including those who work with non-governmental organisations, to understand the trajectory and life of customary international law norms and to take a judicious approach to their identification and influence; particularly insofar as such efforts may contribute to the resistance to the erosion of the international rule of law amid mounting populist challenges.

Index

EU authorised representative for GPSR:
Easy Access System Europe, Mustamäe tee 50,
10621 Tallinn, Estonia
gpsr.requests@easproject.com

www.ingramcontent.com/pod-product-compliance
Ingram Content Group UK Ltd.
Pitfield, Milton Keynes, MK11 3LW, UK
UKHW011915150926
8656IPUK00002B/8

* 9 7 8 1 5 2 6 1 3 4 1 5 8 *

List of Contributors

Editors:

Wang Gungwu, Professor, Director, East Asian Institute, National University of Singapore

John Wong, Professor, Research Director, East Asian Institute, National University of Singapore

Harry Harding, Professor, Dean, Elloit School of International Affairs, George Washington University

Kuan Khun Eng, Lecturer, Department of Sociology, University of Hong Kong

Philip A. Kuhn, Francis Lee Higginson Professor of History, Department of History, Harvard University

Lawrence J. Lau, Kwoh-Ting Li Professor of Economic Development, Department of Economics, Stanford University

Luo Qi, Research Fellow, East Asian Institute, National University of Singapore

Dwight H. Perkins, H. H. Burbank Professor of Political Economy, formerly Director of Harvard Institute for International Development, Harvard University

Qiu Zeqi, Associate Professor, Institute of Sociology and Anthropology, Beijing University

Shee Poon Kim, Visiting Senior Fellow, East Asian Institute, National University of Singapore

Friedrich Wu, Vice President, Economic Research Department, DBS Bank, Singapore

Zhao Quansheng, Associate Professor, Department of International Service, American University

Zheng Yongnian, Research Fellow, East Asian Institute, National University of Singapore

Introduction

I

1997 has been truly an eventful year for China with many momentous happenings. In February the paramount leader Deng Xiaopng passed away, thus marking the end of an era. Shortly after, the post-Deng Chinese leadership under Jiang Zemin had to mobilise great efforts to ensure the smooth resumption of sovereignty over Hong Kong on June 30. This was then followed by intensive preparation for the holding of the crucial 15th National Congress of the Chinese Communist Party in September, which set national priorities for China's medium- and long-term development as well as decided on the core team of younger leaders responsible for leading China into the 21st century.

In coping with all these events Jiang Zemin has undoubtedly stood the tests well and further entrenched his power and prestige as to clearly become the unchallenged leader in the post-Deng era. Jiang crowned his achievements in 1997 by making a state visit in late October to the United

States, where he held a successful summit with President Clinton in the White House to mend China's diplomatic fences with the United States as well as to register China as a rising power.

China's success on the economic front is even more remarkable. The Chinese economy has been growing at about 10 percent since the start of economic reform in 1978. Growth has been particularly spectacular for the past five years 1991–96, which averaged at 12.1 percent. In 1996 the economy achieved a successful soft landing with a 9.7 percent real growth on the basis of a much reduced inflation rate of 6.1 percent. In the first half of 1997, China's economy had once again confounded foreign observers by continuing its robust growth at 9.5 percent with inflation further falling to 1.8 percent. More significantly, the Chinese economy apparently stood immune and unscathed as the currency turmoil was hitting one Southeast Asian economy after another. China's strong economic performance has contributed to the strengthening of Jiang's leadership both at home and abroad.

At the same time, Jiang is facing a number of challenges. How to sustain China's high economic growth into the next century? How to come to grips with a myriad of social problems from growing income disparity to rising unemployment (disguised in China under the term *Xia-gang*) that have cropped up in the process of rapid economic growth? China has been eminently successful in the first round of economic reform. Can it be equally successful in the next round by effectively tackling its numerous ailing state-owned enterprises? The reform of state-owned enterprises has promised to be economically complicated and politically and socially difficult to implement. Jiang at the 15th Party Congress has bravely committed its leadership to this task. Furthermore, following closely on the heels of successful economic growth are the much needed institutional changes such as legal and administrative reforms while rising per-capita income will in turn create greater demand for more political participation and openness, though not exactly towards the kind of contentious Western-style democracy as advocated by some Western liberals.

In short, China is in the midst of great political, economic and social changes, which will further compound each other on account of their speed and scale. History has never witnessed before such a huge country as China industrialising and transforming itself so rapidly and so extensively.

Accordingly, China's success or failure in its domestic development carries serious regional and international implications. There is still a great deal of uncertainty as to how soon in the next century China will become the world's most powerful economy. But what is happening in China today has already impinged on many aspects of lives for people in the Asia-Pacific region, either in terms of growing trade and investment opportunities from China or in terms of regional security.

II

The key mission of the East Asian Institute (EAI) is to promote both academic and policy-oriented research on East Asian development, particularly the political, economic and social development of contemporary China (including Hong Kong and Taiwan). Towards this end, EAI started a series of public lectures given by internationally well-known China scholars, and a weekly seminar on East Asian development given by both local and visiting scholars of various disciplines.

This volume is essentially based on a collection of public lectures and seminar papers by our academic visitors and EAI scholars during the past few months. Each was written as a self-contained piece by a China expert, but presented primarily with non-specialist readers in mind. We thought it would serve a useful academic purpose to put them together as a general text on China's recent political economy provided we could bring it out with minimum delay. China, as pointed out earlier, is changing so fast that a general book of this kind covering a wide variety of topics should be useful to both scholars and the informed members of the public by keeping them quickly updated on recent developments in China as well as bringing to the fore some of the dominant problems and issues that is currently engaging China's leadership.

III

CHINA'S ECONOMY

The Chinese economy has experienced phenomenal growth since it started economic growth and the open-door policy some 19 years ago. Such high growth performance owes a great deal to China's success in economic reform.

Chapter One by Dwight Perkins was originally his inaugural Goh Keng Swee Lecture for EAI given in May 1997. Perkins explains China's celebrated economic reform strategy based on a sector by sector approach, to be implemented gradually. The early reform efforts had been a great success and then laid the foundation for further reform, in part because they proved relatively easy to carry out. All this would be mainly of historical interest if it weren't for the fact that gradualism in the mid-1990s in China had become an official excuse for procrastination for tackling the critical problem of reforming the state-owned enterprise sector. The longer China waits to reform the state-owned enterprises, however, the worse the problems connected with this state sector would become. The Chinese leadership essentially knows what needs to be done to reform these enterprises, but, until the recent 15th Party Congress, they lacked the political will to attack this problem head-on.

Chapter Two by Lawrence Lau was originally also a public lecture delivered at the National University of Singapore in July 1997. Lau provides a technical, in-depth explanation of China's economic reform process. Why has China's economic reform not aroused significant political opposition but instead enjoyed widespread popular support? This is because, according to Lau, the Chinese economic reform has adhered to the implicit principle that on one should be made worse off as a result, i.e. only winners but no losers, even though the distribution the gains of the economic reform has been uneven. In fact, China's "dual-track" pricing in the transitional phase has been both Pareto-improving (for having no losers) and fully efficient (with resources being put to their fullest and best use). Hence the maximal "gain without pain".

In Chapter Three, John Wong expounds his thinking on China's medium and longer-term economic growth prospects. If the historical processes of other East Asian economies can be of a general guide, China's economy, from both supply and demand side analyses, should be able to sustain its present momentum of high growth well into the 21st century. However, whether or not China can realise its future growth potential depends critically on how it will come to grips with problems like population and human resources, and immediate constraints like failure to accomplish the remaining economic reform efforts centring on the reform of state-owned enterprises. Long-term constraints like energy shortages and the environment can also trade off for lower growth.

Politics: Rebuilding the Nation-State

When Deng Xiaoping initiated China's reform in the late 1970s, his aim was not much different from his predecessors Sun Yat-sen, Chiang Kai-shek and Mao Zedong, that is, to seek wealth and power for China and to revive China as a nation-state. Due to different domestic and international environments, however, they chose very different strategies of modernisation. China's nation-building has been largely a trial-and-error process. From Sun to Mao, China was constantly in turmoil caused by wars and revolutions. It was only in the late 1970s did China under Deng Xiaoping establish conditions of peace and stability for development into a modern nation-state.

In Chapter Four, Wang Gungwu explores a new concept of Chinese nation building from a historical point of view. Underlying Deng Xiaoping's modernisation programme is the idea that China needs to develop in its own way towards a strong nation-state. Therefore, although Deng Xiaoping opened China's door to foreign capital and foreign technology to facilitate China's economic modernisation, he never stopped his searching for a Chinese way of development (or "modernisation with Chinese characteristics"). Foreign inputs are important, but they have to serve China's own goals. Chinese leaders consciously want to combine China's socialist legacies with foreign development experiences so as to create something like a "Chinese way of socialist economic development" for the rest of the world.

The Chinese way is also reflected in China's political development in the post-Mao era. While in other countries, especially in former European communist states, political reform often means democratisation; but Chinese leaders have their own priority in mind when they come to political reforms. Politics is used to increase the nation's power and wealth and to transform China from a historical empire to a modern nation-state. For Chinese leaders, national re-emergence not just means rapid economic development. More importantly, it also embraces, first, the unification of different parts of China, including Hong Kong, Macao and Taiwan, and secondly, the integration of China's peripheral areas. While fast economic growth has generated very favourable elements for both national reunification and integration, it has also resulted in enormous undesirable consequences. Only by finding a Chinese way can the leadership be able to cope with these consequences and to achieve their goal of political development.

Somewhat similarly, in Chapter Five, Philip Kuhn also argues that one of the most important issues in China's national building is the local-central relationship. When Deng Xiaoping promoted economic reform by decentralisation, it was aimed at promoting growth through fostering local initiatives and incentives, as well as winning provincial and municipal support for his reform programmes by giving them a greater share of power. Yet, while decentralisation had brought about fruitful economic results to China, it also had a negative impact on the central government's relations with the localities. The central government had lost much of its economic power to local governments at different levels. Many Western scholars and Chinese scholars have argued that continued decentralisation, in creating "dukedoms", has significantly weakened the state capacity with potential national disintegration. Based on his rich knowledge of modern Chinese history, Kuhn examines different schools of thoughts regarding changing relations between the centre and the provinces. More importantly, Kuhn finds that while decentralisation has created enormous troubles for

China such as the close linkage between government and business, regionalism, and regional disparities, new elements in favour of institutionalising local-central relations and strengthening central power have also come into being. Implicit in China's economic decentralisation as symbolised by the contract system are elements that carry some form of federalism, a "hopeful sign that central-local relations are entering a more sustainable balance: a balance in which the vast problems of governing China will be shared between central and local units to the ultimate benefit of the nation".

One major problem that Chinese leaders encounter in their efforts of nation building is rising nationalism. Without doubt, nationalism has been an important driving force behind China's modernisation throughout its modern history. The collapse of communist ideology has prompted the Chinese leadership to return to nationalism for a stronger mandate of their rule. Nationalism, however, is a double-edged sword. It inspires political consciousness, democratic participation and a fervent dedication to common goals. But it could also arouse open hostility and fear among those who feel they do not quite belong to the country. Given the fact that China is a multi-national state, the Chinese government has been very cautious in dealing with the newly rising nationalism.

Another important issue facing China's nation building is democratisation. Throughout modern Chinese history, the Chinese have regarded democratisation as an essential part of building strong China. Now, with China's rapid economic development, many Western scholars become optimistic in their belief that economic development is leading the country to democratisation and China has started its "Short March" to democracy.

In Chapter Six, Zheng Yongnian explains how such optimism may be unwarranted. He provides a more realistic picture of Chinese democracy by examining the enormous difficulties that China encounters in its democratic. Economic development has produced an impact on various aspects of China's democratisation, but it has also generated various elements unfavourable for democracy to take place. According to Zheng, Western experience of nation-state building are unlikely to repeat themselves in China, which is clearly not about to develop the kind of democracy that many Western scholars have expected. Hence the need for a new paradigm of China's democratisation.

In Chapter Seven, Zheng Yongnian shows how the Chinese leadership has developed a new concept of "comprehensive national power" as the guiding strategy for national development. "Comprehensive national power" refers to the totality of China's economic, military and political power and signals China's comprehensive development level and its position in the international system. This strategy puts highest priority on China's domestic development, including sustained economic growth, high technological development, military modernisation, and the improvement of population quality, which taken together is also significant for China's foreign policy-making. Even with the rise of nationalistic sentiments among different social groups, the leadership still needs to focus on domestic priority if the strategy of comprehensive national power is to be effectively implemented.

SOCIAL DEVELOPMENT AND STABILITY

Economic development for any country (or "modernisation" in the case of China) is actually a multi-dimensional process of both economic and social changes. Thus, beyond the narrow concept of GNP growth, economic development is also defined in terms of elimination or reduction of poverty, income inequality, and unemployment. China has been eminently successful in terms of chalking up high GNP growth. But has its economic development been accompanied by concomitant social progress?

In Chapter Eight, John Wong discusses the impact of economic growth on people's daily life in terms of the traditional Chinese concept of Xiao-*kang* ("modestly comfortable life"). When Deng Xiaoping initiated China's economic reform in 1978, he aimed at lifting the living standard of the Chinese people to the *Xiao-Kang* (XK) or the satisfaction of their basic needs by 2000. XK has since become a codeword for China's socio-economic development. Wong examines the various technical implications of the official XK index. Thanks to its rapid economic growth, China had achieved its overall XK target by 1994. But, as pointed out by Wong, XK is essentially a normative concept, fuzzy and grossly imprecise, especially when applied to a transitional economy like China. By 2000 a whole new generation will have grown up under market reform who may perceive XK very differently, and are likely to demand a different basket of goods and services for the satisfaction of their own XK.

Economic reform can be socially destabilising. China's economic reform was characterised by the rapid development of the non-state sectors such as private, collective and joint ventures. At the early stages of reform, the expansion of the non-state sector created enormous job opportunities. However, the government has recently targeted the state-owned enterprises (SOEs) for reform and restructuring, which will generate massive unemployment and can possibly pose a threat to social stability in China. How does the Chinese government try to cope with this problem?

In Chapter Nine, Qiu Zeqi and Zheng Yongnian examine what may be called a "Chinese way" of dealing with the problem of employment. Since the early 1990s, the Chinese government has initiated a programme called *Xia-Gang* (literally, off-post) to cope with massive labour redundancy in the state sector . This is done by letting workers be laid off in disguised manner from their original enterprises with partial compensation while allowing the laid-off workers to take on a second, even a third, job in other enterprises. In this way, the *Xia-Gang* has played an important role in alleviating the unemployment problem caused by the SOE reform. However not all workers in SOEs are unwilling to take up these new opportunities. Why? Qiu and Zheng show that the main problem lies in the workers' traditional perception of job. Thus, China's SOE reform still critically depends on the development of the labour market and social security reform rather than on the *Xia-Gang*.

China's social change during the reform period can be externally generated. It is well known that overseas Chinese investment has played an important role in promoting the economic development of China's coastal region. But less known is how the overseas Chinese connection has affected people's daily life, especially in the *Qiaoxiang* (home of overseas Chinese).

In Chapter Ten, Kuah Khun Eng illustrates the social impact of the overseas Chinese money in their native villages. Based on her survey and interviews in China and Singapore, Kuah finds that in recent years among the Singaporean Chinese, there has been a revival of the awareness of their ancestral villages. Many have visited their ancestral villages in China and contributed substantially to the rebuilding of their native villages, especially on social infrastructure development. This includes the development of roads, bridges, education and welfare and rebuilding of old house, ancestral houses and temples. With such financial assistance, these ancestral villages have become prosperous and modern in contrast with those villages that do not have overseas Chinese connections.

EXTERNAL RELATIONS: PRAGMATISM AND CONTINUOUS ADJUSTMENT

One major issue facing China itself and the international community is the rise of China. China is destined to be a major global power with its continuous rapid economic growth. But how China and the world can accommodate each other is still an open question. Many Western scholars and journalists have expressed their concern over the sudden rise of China. Since the early 1990s, various arguments against China such as "China threat" and "containing China" have been developed in the West. The concerns over China's rise are not without any reasons. As Wang Gungwu have argued earlier, since China was once an empire and its influence extended to its neighbouring countries by a tribute system, the rise of China would naturally lead to such concerns. Would a modernised China behave much like the past imperial Britain and France in their quest for maritime empires, or like Russia in its overland drive toward the east? Or would China model itself after the intensely aggressive latecomers like Germany and Japan, or aspire to some version of the American Manifest Destiny?

How China will behave internationally not only depends on domestic conditions in China, but also international factors. In short, Sino-US relationship is the single most important part in China's foreign policy formulation. During the cold war, China and US once formed an alliance against their common enemy, the Soviet Union. But with the collapse of the Soviet Union and the end of the Cold War, such foundation of Sino-US alliance no longer has shifted. The two great powers have to find a new strategic base for their relationship, which is not an easy task, however. Without a common enemy, the two countries often find themselves caught in conflict over various issues such as human rights, trade, and nuclear proliferation. How these issues are handled becomes crucial in developing a new tie between the two countries.

In Chapter Eleven, Harry Harding discusses different approaches to China on the part of the US over different periods since China's reform and open-door policy. Initially, the US expected that China's reform and open-door policy would lead to the development of not just a market economy but also political democracy. But the 1989 Tiananmen Incident shattered this optimistic view of China. Since then, the US began to adjust its China policy. The four policy options identified by Harding comprise enlargement, engagement, integration and containment. Naturally, China has had different responses to these approaches. The Chinese leadership strongly opposed the enlargement and containment policies, while responded positively to the integration and engagement options. China does not want the US to "export" its democracy to China. It also resists the containment policy. Instead, Chinese leaders prefer China to be integrated gradually into the international community. Harding highlights the importance of Sino-US co-operation and the danger of the conflict between the two. Indeed, the recent summit between Presidents Jiang Zemin and Bill Clinton confirms that the two countries are willing to cooperate on a wide range of issues.

In Chapter Twelve, Zhao Quansheng's explores China's changing relations with the two Koreas and shows how China has been flexible enough to change its foreign policy approach to South Korea along with the changing international and domestic environment. Seeking close and beneficial economic ties has been one of China's primary objectives for normalising relations with South Korea. Yet, at the same time, China cannot afford to ignore North Korea altogether and has to balance its actions between the two Koreas so as to meet their conflicting demands from both external and internal fronts. It has taken China more than a decade to complete the smooth transition, which has avoided unnecessary conflicts between China and the two Koreas.

China's gradual and cautious policy adjustment is also reflected in its changing relations with Southeast Asia. While some argue that China is a threat and will be a future hegemon in the Asia-Pacific region, others refute that view as an exaggeration. What does the rise of China mean for the international community, especially its neighbouring countries?

In Chapter Thirteen, Shee Poon Kim examines in detail the meaning and nature of the "China Threat" and assesses the bases of the arguments by both "threat" and "non-threat" proponents. Shee then presents a "middle-of-the-road" picture of the impact of China's rise to the Asia-Pacific region. Some Southeast Asian countries are still apprehensive of the emerging China; but they all have accepted it with a combination of resignation and optimism.

Earlier in Chapter Seven, Zheng Yongnian has emphasised that since the late 1970s, China's international strategy has been based on seeking a peaceful international environment to foster its domestic economic development. Hence the economic imperative in China's foreign policy-making. How the Chinese government has made its foreign economic policy to attract outside investment is already well known. Less known is how local governments in China deal with foreign investment and how foreign investment affects local economies.

In Chapter Fourteen, Luo Qi, in his case study of Xiamen, examines how the Xiamen municipal government has used foreign investment to restructure its local industry. To accelerate local industrial transformation, the Xiamen authorities have decided to use foreign direct investment (FDI) to facilitate the restructuring of local enterprises. However, this is not an easy task for the local government. In using foreign investment to promote local economic development, the local government encounters enormous difficulties, which are not only from the domestic side, but also from the foreign side. This case study thus brings out the interplay between China and the outside world in shaping China's domestic development.

As discussed earlier, the highest priority of China's nation-building efforts has been on the unification of different parts of China, including Taiwan, Hong Kong and Macao. Thus the return of Hong Kong to China need to be smooth and successful. If China were to fail over Hong Kong, it would not succeed over Taiwan. Furthermore, Hong Kong's continuous prosperity will help build international confidence toward China.

In Chapter Fifteen, Friedrich Wu formulates some new scenarios for Hong Kong after 1997. He argues that the autonomy of the Hong Kong Special Administrative Region (HKSAR) government is likely to be more circumscribed by the continuous presence of, and the rise of new, influential players which have close link with powerful institutions in China. According to Wu's observations, a high-profile presence of the Xinhua News Agency Hong Kong Branch could be perceived as a rival political base vis-a-vis the HKSAR government. Likewise, the Ministry of Foreign Affairs (MFA) might become another political heavyweight in the territory's power equation. The People's Liberation Army (PLA) could also come into the limelight, which would bring about a new influx of PLA-based companies to Hong Kong. And finally, Chinese "red chip" companies might emerge as the new "movers and shakers" of Hong Kong stock market, capable of tipping the territory's business playing field in their favour.

It seems quite clear that the imperative of seeking a peaceful international environment to facilitate China's domestic economic development is constantly reflected in China's foreign policy making and its international behaviour. When China runs into conflict with other countries, its pragmatism will emerge to guide its actual behaviour.

November 1997

Wang Gungwu
John Wong

Have China's Economic Reforms Stalled?

Inaugural Goh Keng Swee Lecture
East Asian Institute, National University of Singapore
May 26, 1997

Dwight Heald PERKINS
Harvard Institute for International Development

The strength of China's economic reform process, it has often been argued, is that it was implemented gradually. But, if one looks at these reforms on a sector by sector basis many of these reforms, those in agriculture in the early 1980's for example, were anything but gradual. Other sectors where reforms were carried out within a period of a few years include foreign trade and investment and the Township and Village Enterprise program. The latter was more an accident than a planned effort, but the change in incentives that set off the TVE boom occurred within a time span of a year or two. The real lesson of these early reforms is that they proved relatively easy to carry out. Success in these early efforts then laid the foundation for further reform. All of this would be mainly of historical interest if it weren't for the fact that gradualism in the mid-1990's in China has become an excuse for procrastination particularly in the critical state owned enterprise sector. The longer China waits to reform the state owned enterprises, however, the worse the problems connected with these enterprises are likely to become. Many in China know what needs to be done to reform these enterprises and the key features of what is required can be easily listed. The central issue facing the state owned enterprises, therefore, is not what needs to be done, but when are they going to do it?

(This lecture was given in May 1997 before the meeting of the 15th Congress of the Chinese Communist Party in the fall of 1997. At this Congress, the Chinese leadership for the first time made state-owned enterprise reform the centerpiece of the next stage of reform. If the goals set down at the 15th Congress are implemented in a determined way, many of the issues raised in this essay will be gradually resolved.)

China's economic reforms have been rightfully praised for simultaneously moving China toward becoming a market economy while maintaining an East Asian style economic growth rate of over 9 percent per year for nearly 18 years. The contrast is with the nations of Eastern Europe and the former Soviet Union where similar transitions to the market were accompanied by prolonged economic recessions. Given this contrast in performance, what is there to be concerned about? China has a very high rate of investment, a labour force that is easily trained and is rapidly becoming better educated, and a demonstrated ability to produce manufactures that can be sold around the world. These favourable growth fundamentals ensure that Chinese gross domestic product (GDP) should grow by at least 6 percent per year and possibly at over 9 percent per year for another two decades or longer.

The primary issue that I want to address in this lecture is whether China's current approach to the transition to a market economy is going to work as well in the future as it has in the past. This approach is frequently described as the "gradual" approach to reform in contrast to the "shock therapy" approach that was advocated for Eastern Europe and the states of the former Soviet Union.[1] Leaving aside the question of whether or not the European socialist states ever really tried shock therapy; the question addressed here is whether gradualism is really the most useful way to describe the Chinese approach.

[1]A recent paper exploring the debate over the approach to transition economy reform describes those espousing the gradualist side of the debate as the "experimentalists", as contrasted to the "convergence" school that argues that the faster the convergence to market norms, the better will be the outcome. Jeffrey Sachs and Wing Thye Woo, "Understanding China's Economic Performance", unpublished paper, December 1996.

China's reform effort can be described as gradual if all that is meant by the term is that China did not try to reform the whole economy all at once. China went through the transition to a market economy on a sector by sector basis, completing the transition in one sector before moving on to the next. Within individual sectors, however, the transition to a market economy was not necessarily slow at all. Within agriculture and later within the township and village enterprise sector the major institutional changes were carried out over a period of only a few years, roughly three years in the case of agriculture.

This argument over the pace of economic reform would be largely of interest only to historians if it were not for one contemporary fact. The reputed success of gradualism is being used as a justification in China and elsewhere for procrastination in completing the transition to a market economy in at least one major sector, modern large-scale state owned industrial enterprises. Some in China's leadership support the maintenance of a large state-owned industrial sector much like what exists at present because they see that sector as synonymous with socialism and hence with the underlying justification for a continued monopoly of politics by the Communist Party. But most in China are reluctant to move decisively to transform state-owned enterprises. There is fear of the political consequences of the large lay-offs of enterprise workers that would result. For these politically influential workers any radical change in the way state-owned enterprises are managed and controlled threatens their role in the government and their source of power and income.

None of this would matter if the procrastinating approach to the reform of state owned enterprises would produce the desired market economy in this sector over time. But there is reason to doubt whether state enterprise reform can be completed in this way. In some respects the problems of the state-owned enterprises are getting worse over time not better. Conceivably China can continue to "grow out of the plan"[2] regardless of what is done

[2]The phrase was used in this context by Barry Naughton, *Growing Out of the Plan: Chinese Economic Reform, 1978–1993* (Cambridge: Cambridge University Press, 1995).

by the central leadership, but there are grounds for thinking that this will not happen automatically and that decisive action from the top will be required. I have little doubt that, if decisive action is required, then eventually decisive action will be taken, but that may not happen until after an economic crisis generated by the state owned sector has forced the leadership to act.

The sector by sector approach to the economic transition to a market economy worked well in the first decade of Chinese reform because China had the good sense or the good fortune to begin the transition with sectors that could be converted to the market relatively easily. Reform in these sectors could proceed quickly because the steps involved were simple to carry out at least in a technical sense and, to a lesser degree, in a political sense as well. There was and is nothing simple about how to make large-scale state owned enterprises in industry fit into a market framework. Shock therapy in this sector was never a realistic option in China or in most other socialist economies. Shock therapy may be preferable in this sector where there is a broad national consensus over the desire to be like Western Europe as soon as possible as there may have been in Poland. In that political context, the population may be willing to tolerate the years of lay-offs and lowered incomes as this sector either learns how to operate in the new circumstances or simply goes out of business and is replaced by new firms that start small and then grow. But there was nothing remotely like the Polish political consensus of 1989 in China either in 1978 when the reforms started or in 1997.

The remainder of this lecture is devoted to two broad themes. In the section that follows I shall outline why the introduction of market forces into several Chinese economic sectors was relatively easy to accomplish and why the economic results were so favourable almost immediately. The latter part of the lecture will then return to the issue of what it will take to reform the large scale state owned industrial sector and will speculate about whether the political leadership required to complete this process is likely to be there when needed.

Starting Reform with the Easier to Reform Sectors

China's transition to a market economy, as is well known, began in 1978 and 1979 with the decisions to reform agriculture and to open up to more foreign trade. The foreign trade opening decision was in some respects made as early as 1977, but the export drive does not really start until later.

The initial decision to reform agriculture really only involved a desire to help the poorer rural areas raise themselves up to an above subsistence level, but what started as a limited effort quickly spread across the country. By 1983 if not earlier, rural markets, for the most part, had been freed up and the collectives or production teams had been replaced by household agriculture. Real agricultural output per capita rose by over 50 percent by 1984 and rural incomes rose even more, thanks to an improvement in the rural urban terms of trade. To achieve this result, decisive action by the top leadership, mainly by Deng Xiaoping personally, was required, but the top leadership actions required were very limited in nature. Basically Deng had to step in from time to time to prevent lower level cadres from blocking the reform process. The farmers needed little persuasion to go back to household farming and moved quickly to take advantage of the opportunity. It took political courage on Deng's part to let it happen — he had been purged and sent to the countryside for doing the same thing in the early 1960s — but it did not require much else. When ordered to leave the process alone, the cadres, for the most part, went along.

Why was the agricultural transition to the market so easy to achieve? There are two principal reasons: first, it was comparatively easy to put the requirements of a market system in place in agriculture, and second, few changes in the technology of farming or in the way that crops were raised was required in the Chinese case.

There are essentially five elements required if a market is to function efficiently:

(1) There must be macroeconomic stability in the sense that inflation and balance of payments disequilibria are kept to levels that are both

politically acceptable and economically sustainable so that the government does not feel under pressure to reintroduce direct controls over prices and the flow of imports. China in the first phase of the reform period had little inflation, no foreign debt, and a foreign trade sector that was roughly in balance. Unlike in Russia, Eastern Europe or Vietnam, there was no need for a major stabilisation programme in China until the late 1980s.

(2) Goods must be made available for purchase and sale on the market rather than allocated through administrative channels. In the agriculture sector China had never completely abandoned the use of markets in the distribution of farm products so that all that was required was to expand the scope of those markets. Because of its political sensitivity, a large share of grain output was still allocated through non-market channels, but most other rural products became freely available.

(3) Prices must reflect relative scarcities in the economy. Prices had never been totally abandoned as guides to the allocation of agricultural products and so the degree of distortion from true market prices was probably considerably less than in the urban and industrial sectors. Freeing up prices did not lead to wild movements in prices that could have had a major impact on the distribution of income in rural (and urban) areas and hence could have become a major political headache.

(4) Markets must be competitive in order to avoid monopoly rents and to promote the growth of productivity. Farm households are the textbook example of producing and consuming units in a perfectly competitive market. Monopoly control of rural markets by anyone other than the state is impossible.

(5) Producers in a market system must behave in accordance with the rules of the market. That is they must maximise profits by cutting their costs or raising sales. Increasing income by pleading for more subsidies from the government is not behaving according to the rules. Farm households, however, do not need to be told this or to be retrained to behave in the approved way. Farm households are natural profit or net income maximisers.

Introducing a market system into the agricultural sector, therefore, was a comparatively simple exercise. All the government had to do was to get out of the way and the farmers themselves could do most of the rest. Within a matter of months the market system was up and running. Decollectivisation took longer but even that was not as difficult as it might have been elsewhere. Agricultural production techniques did not change when farmers abandoned the collective and went back to household farming. Labour was allocated in a somewhat different (and more efficient) way but no one had to be retrained. The planting and harvesting of crops was not done in some new way. Even the redistribution of land was not particularly complicated in the Chinese case. Households got a certain share of the team or former collective land based on the size of the household. One did not even have to worry about whether the land should be allocated to the original owners or to those who had supported the revolution, as was the case in Vietnam. In China individual ownership had been abolished a quarter century earlier and few if any were bold or foolish enough to try to assert claims that were that old.

Reforms in the foreign trade area, at least initially, proved to be straightforward as well. Or, to put the issue differently, China did not have to take radical action in order to promote the rapid growth of exports of manufactures. To begin with, China, unlike Vietnam, Russia and Eastern Europe, did not have to deal with the consequences of being a member of a trading bloc, Comecon, that had disappeared. China had broken with the Soviet trading bloc back in 1960 and the break at the time had serious consequences for the Chinese economy. But by 1979 China had long since adjusted its trading relationships to the hard currency markets of the West, Japan, and Southeast Asia. Furthermore, China was an exporter of manufactures, notably textiles, to these markets.

The most obvious problem with China's foreign trade was that it was still monopolised by a handful of foreign trade corporations attached to the Ministry of Foreign Trade. These corporations were not particularly skillful at marketing Chinese manufactures. In fact the very concept of marketing was alien to most Chinese planners and manufacturers. Fortunately these corporations did not have to become skilled at marketing over night. The main trade reform of the early 1980's was the one that broke up the central foreign trade monopolies and created a whole new set of state trading companies at the provincial and lower levels. In principle these new trading companies had full control over their local suppliers, but in practice there was considerably more flexibility than this implies.[3]

The key to China's export success was that these trading companies quickly hooked up with firms in Hong Kong and it was the firms in Hong Kong, some of the ablest traders in the world, that took over the task of selling Chinese manufactures to the world markets.[4] China's exports boomed. By 1984 they had risen to US$26.14 billion, nearly three times the US$9.75 billion level of 1978.

There were other reforms in the trade and foreign investment sphere, but most of these took much longer to have much impact. The government set up export processing zones or Special Economic Zones as the Chinese called them. But these zones got off to a slow start and their full impact was not felt until the late 1980s or early 1990s. Foreign direct investment was also allowed for the first time and a new foreign investment law was passed. But it takes more than a quickly drafted law to stimulate much foreign direct investment, particularly in a society where the rule of law in previous decades had played almost no role at all. FDI in the first four years of reform averaged only US$400 million per year, a tiny sum compared to the tens of billions of dollars of FDI that China was to receive in the 1990's each year. Foreigners wanted to know what taxes they would have to pay and how they were going to repatriate their profits given all of the foreign exchange controls then in place. Small investors from Hong Kong were able to operate profitably in this uncertain environment, but the larger investors stayed away until the rules of the game had become clearer and the foreign exchange market had been progressively liberalised. Perhaps the supporting institutions for FDI could have been put in place faster, but

[3]These and other foreign trade reforms are discussed at length in Nicholas Lardy, *Foreign Trade and Economic Reform in China, 1978–1990* (Cambridge: Cambridge University Press, 1992).

[4]For an in-depth discussion of Hong Kong's role in China's foreign trade, see Yun-Wing Sung, *The China-Hong Kong Connection: The Key to China's Open-Door Policy* (Cambridge: Cambridge University Press, 1991).

there are grounds for skepticism. It takes governments time to figure out what is needed even when they are clear as to their objectives and it takes even longer to get the new institutions up and running. There was nothing particularly slow about China's efforts to promote FDI and the objectives were reasonably clear from the outset, but it was ten years before FDI into China passed the US$3 billion mark and fourteen years (1992) before it passed the US$10 billion annual level.[5]

The successes with agriculture and foreign trade provided the political support needed to carry the reform process in China further. In 1984 the Chinese government under the leadership of then Premier Zhao Ziyang began the process of trying to reform the urban and industrial sectors of the economy. The primary changes were carried out with considerable speed even though there was no consensus among the top leadership of China that moving to a market economy was even the ultimate goal. The phrase that soon came into use was to establish a "planned commodity" economy where the market's role was still seen as subordinate to the machinery of central planning.

The steps taken in the mid 1980s were to make a much larger share of intermediate industrial inputs available on the market, to have those goods sold at market prices, and to abolish the regional monopolies enjoyed by almost all manufacturers large and small. Making only some of the intermediate inputs available on the market at market prices was not as radical as making all inputs available in that way, but the latter step was resisted strongly by the powerful state industrial interests and was simply not politically feasible. The compromise produced the dual price system that was to be a source of more than a little corruption which in turn was to cause major political problems for the reformers, but that was to come in 1988 and 1989.[6] What the dual price and market system allowed China's

[5]Chinese foreign direct investment figures need to be used with a certain amount of caution. Some FDI in China's case was really Chinese funds recycled through Hong Kong to take advantage of tax and other concessions given only to foreigners.

[6]For a discussion of how the dual price system evolved, see Sheng Hua, Xuejun Zhang, and Xiaopeng Luo, *China: From Revolution to Reform* (London: MacMillan, 1993), pp. 119–131.

reformers to do at the outset was to introduce a market system for almost all key inputs except for a few such as electric power and railroad transport. The impact of the abolition of monopolies also had a large and immediate affect. Enterprises throughout the country found themselves facing vigorous competitive pressures particularly in areas where domestic production capacity exceeded domestic demand for the product.[7]

By most standards these mid-1980 urban industrial reforms would be considered radical even if there were a few trial runs before the changes were introduced across the country. Certainly most Chinese by the late 1980s had come to see them as radical and risky. And yet, despite the magnitude and scope of these reforms, the critical state-owned industrial sector responded only slowly. There is a considerable debate among economists about whether the reforms of the mid-1980's had some positive impact on the productivity of state-owned industrial enterprises or none. No one, however, argues that these reforms fundamentally changed the behaviour of the state industrial sector in ways that turned that sector into an efficient, dynamic market oriented set of industries.[8]

The real impact of these radical industrial reforms came from a completely unexpected quarter, what is now known as the township and village enterprise sector or TVEs. The TVEs were in a position to respond rapidly to the new market incentives put in place without much further help from the government and it is instructive to ask why this was the case? The basic answer is that for these industries, all of the key ingredients

[7]One well researched case study of how competition forced change is the case of the challenge faced by the clock and watch makers of Chongqing when they suddenly had to meet the competition of high quality clocks and watches from Shanghai. William A. Byrd and Gene Tidrick, "The Chongqing Clock and Watch Company," in William A. Byrd, editor, *Chinese Industrial Firms under Reform* (Oxford: Oxford University Press, 1992), pp. 58–119.

[8]There is an active ongoing debate on whether or not there was total factor productivity growth in China's state enterprises. See Gary Jefferson, Thomas Rawski, and Yuxin Zheng, "Growth, Efficiency, and Convergence in China's State and Collective Industry", *Economic Development and Cultural Change*, Vol. 40, No. 2, January 1992, pp. 239–266, for one side of the debate. For the other side, see Wing Thye Woo, Wen Hai, Yibiao Jin, and Gang Fan, "How Successful Have Chinese Enterprise Reforms Been? Pitfalls in Opposite Biases and Focus", *Journal of Comparative Economics*, June 1994, pp. 410–437.

of a full market system could be quickly put in place. The TVEs bought and sold their products and inputs on the market at market prices because they lacked the political strength to get large allocations through the central planning process. The TVEs also had little trouble responding to the new rules that allowed them to expand beyond their local, township, or county market. The old rules that forced them to retool and produce a new product once the local market was saturated made little sense except to planners and were easy to jettison.

Most importantly, the TVEs behaved according to the rules of the market. They maximised profits by cutting costs or increasing sales, and, if they failed to make profits, they went out of business. The local governments who supported the TVEs could not afford to keep loss makers afloat. On the contrary, they depended on their share of TVE profits to finance local infrastructure and other necessities. Neither the TVEs nor the local governments had easy access to the banking system for loans at below market interest rates or credits that did not really have to be paid back at all. These local enterprises thus faced hard budget constraints and vigorous competitive pressures. The precise nature of TVE ownership does not appear to have mattered that much. Most were formally collectives, but some were registered as private firms and others were even owned by the local government. Whatever the ownership, however, ties to the local government were close. Local governments helped these enterprises obtain the required higher level authorisations and access to such critical inputs as electric power and the governments in turn received a significant share of the profits. The governments were, in effect, in partnership with the TVEs and like good partners, they tried to be as helpful as possible.

How is it that China acquired local government that saw their role vis-a-vis business in this way? The more typical role for government is to tax and regulate business, not promote it. In socialist systems in particular, governments have elaborate licensing procedures and other controls designed to make sure that enterprises do not deviate from the plan or participate in other activities that are deemed to be harmful to the public or the government. Under the command system, the state-owned enterprises had to turn over all or almost all of their profits to the government so that the enterprises would not use these funds in some creative way not approved by the state.

The only answer to this question that I have found convincing is that the TVEs and the local governments that supported them grew out of the rural communes. The communes were not very successful at efficiently planting and harvesting food and cash crops, but they were a vehicle for the promotion of local industry and related service enterprises. The localities learned during the early 1970s and to some degree earlier how to manage a small industrial firm. Under what was then called the rural small scale industry programme, technicians were sent out from the city enterprises to help the local people to master the technology and to set up a business organisation and train the managers and workers. Local people also went into the city to gain relevant experience. And it was not just the managers and workers that learned how to operate these firms. The cadres in the commune and brigade administration also learned about what it took to make a rural industry successful. When the commune system was abolished in the early 1980s, these cadres did not simply disappear back into farming. They became the cadres of the local township and village governments. As government officials, however, they did not revert to being taxers and regulators. When the opportunity to push local industry presented itself, particularly after the industrial reforms of late 1984, they continued to play the role of promoters.[9]

The close relationship between the earlier rural small industry programme and the TVEs of the late 1980s and 1990s could probably be established statistically but this lecture is not the place to make the attempt.[10] Two kinds of anecdotal "evidence" will be presented instead.

[9]The close mutually supportive ties between local governments and local enterprises is one of the main themes in the works of Jean Oi, including "Fiscal reform and the economic foundations of local state corporation in China", *World Politics*, Vol. 45, No. 1, October 1992, pp. 99–126; and "The role of local state in China's transitional economy", *The China Quarterly*, No. 144, December 1995, pp. 1132–1149.

[10]The main task would be to collect county or lower level data on the size of the TVE sector and its growth rate over some recent period such as 1984–1996 and then to see how those data correlate with the size of rural industry when the commune system was still intact, in 1979, for example, or better still 1975 if the data can be found.

The first is based on a visit I made to China in 1975 as part of a delegation to study rural small scale industry. Two of the counties we visited, that were presented as models of rural industrialisation, were Wuxi County in Jiangsu Province and Nanhai County in Guangdong Province. A dozen years later, when the World Bank and the Chinese Academy of Social Sciences teamed up to do an in depth study of the TVEs, the two counties they studied as models of successful TVE development were Wuxi and Nanhai.[11]

The second kind of evidence in support of this proposition is more in the nature of an indirect argument than it is true evidence. Over the past eight years I have frequently lectured in Vietnam on industrialisation in Asia in general and in China in particular. A standard question from the Vietnamese audiences is how could Vietnam go about creating a dynamic TVE sector of its own. It is a fact that once one leaves the two or three large cities of Vietnam, there is little in the way of local industry of collective, private or even state ownership. The principal explanation appears to be that local governments in Vietnam have usually defined their role to be that of taxers and regulators. Few have seen their role as one of promoting local industry. Local government in Vietnam is an obstacle to be overcome if one wants to set up a business. Local government in China made an effort to be helpful at least in those regions of the country where the TVE sector boomed. Help of this kind may only have been available to local people, not foreigners or even distant Chinese firms, but it was still help. In areas where the TVE sector did not prosper, the World Bank and Chinese Academy of Social Sciences Study found, the explanation was in large part because local governments were more predatory than supportive of the TVE sector.

Thus China's TVE boom that continues to this day was easily achieved once the appropriate external incentives were in place. There were already

[11]The findings of the earlier study can be found in American Rural Small Scale Industry Delegation, *Rural Small Scale Industry in the People's Republic of China* (Berkeley: University of California Press, 1976). The later study was published as William Byrd and Lin Qingsong, editors, *China's Rural Industry* (Oxford: Oxford University Press, 1990).

in place a large number of small enterprises scattered across the nation that were in a position to respond to the new incentives. The incentive reforms required were in a sense radical and were carried out quickly, but like the agricultural reforms earlier; their impact was limited to the one sector that was in a position to take advantage of them. If there had not been a rural small-scale industry programme earlier, it is unlikely that the response to these incentives would have been anywhere near as rapid. There was no such response to similar reforms in Vietnam, for example, even though the freeing up of markets was carried out more rapidly and more completely than was the case in China.

REFORMING LARGE STATE-OWNED ENTERPRISES

If, in the sense explained earlier, the initial reforms carried out by China were easy, the same cannot be said about the task of reforming China's state-owned enterprises. In the case of agriculture, foreign trade, and the TVEs, moving to a market system was mostly a matter of removing barriers to individual and small enterprise initiative. The households and small enterprises to take advantage of the new opportunities presented by the market were already in place or, in the case of farm households, could quickly be put in place. The same cannot be said about the large state-owned enterprises. These SOEs did not respond rapidly and dynamically to the new incentives and their performance has been lagging behind that of the TVEs ever since. The remainder of this lecture is devoted to exploring what China would have to do to change this situation so that the larger SOEs could perform in an internationally competitive and efficient way and thus play a leading role in continued transformation of the Chinese economy. The final part of this lecture will speculate about whether China will in fact take the necessary SOE reform steps.

Before turning to what it would take to reform the SOEs, however, it is necessary to deal with those who argue that reform of SOEs is impossible and that privatisation, the more rapid the better, is the only answer. In many countries and perhaps in most, privatisation may be the best answer and in some, the only answer. Those who start from this ideological position and refuse to consider any alternatives, however, take themselves out of the debate over SOEs at least as that debate is conducted in much of Asia. Well-informed Asians do not automatically buy the "privatisation is the only answer" argument because they can readily point to examples of large SOEs that work and work well.

Any discussion of successful state enterprises in Asia should begin with Singapore.[12] Dr. Goh Keng Swee, in whose honour this lecture is named, was not only one of the principal architects of Singapore's development strategy, he also established a great many SOEs as part of this development effort. In 1990 these SOEs had sales of S$9.2 billion and profits of S$2.1 billion.[13] Perhaps best known among the dozens of Singapore state enterprises is Singapore Airlines, arguably the best airline in the world and one of the most profitable. Singapore Airlines, of course, has no domestic routes and thus must compete with other airlines on every single one of its routes. The Republic of Korea also has a substantial number of state enterprises. At one time these enterprises commanded a share of industrial output comparable to that of India which is often thought of as a country dominated by SOEs.[14] Some of the SOEs in Korea have since been privatised; Korean Airlines for example, but others have not. The latter include POSCO, one of the two or three largest and most profitable manufacturers of steel in the world. POSCO from early on had to export a part of its output and so it too had to learn from the start how to compete in markets it could not control. In Taiwan, virtually all of the early efforts to develop a heavy industry sector were carried out by such state enterprises

[12]For a more comprehensive and up to date discussion of the Singapore experience and the limits of its applicability to China, see John Wong, "Government Participation in Economic Development: Singapore Experiences", Paper presented at the International Symposium on the Government's Role in the Market Economy, China Institute for Reform and Development, Hainan, January 1997.

[13]Dr. Goh Keng Swee, "*Xinjiapo jingji fazhande jingyan ji qianying: zhanlueh bushu ji shishi qingkuang*", East Asian Institute offprint, July 27, 1992.

[14]Leroy Jones, *Public Enterprise and Economic Development: The Korean Case* (Seoul: Korea Development Institute Press, 1976).

as the China Petroleum Corporation. Not all of these state efforts were successful and most of Taiwan's SOEs are oriented mainly toward the domestic market, but they do supply critical industrial inputs and do so, for the most part, at world prices. Taiwan has had plans on the boards to privatise many of these companies, but few as of 1996 had actually been privatised. There are, of course, many other SOEs in East and Southeast Asia that have not been successful in the sense of being able to survive on their own without government subsidies. The largest numbers of examples in the region can be found in Malaysia and Indonesia. Some of these SOEs have now been privatised, the Proton automobile for example, but the firms continue to depend on state support mainly in the form of trade restrictions on competitors.

This brief review of the experience with SOEs elsewhere in East and Southeast Asia was undertaken to make a simple point. Privatisation is neither an absolute prerequisite for the efficient and internationally competitive operation of an industrial enterprise nor is it by itself a sufficient condition for effective performance in all circumstances. Furthermore, most of the economic leadership of China is at least somewhat familiar with the experiences in this area of Singapore, Korea and Taiwan and they very much hope that experience can be duplicated in China. A different ideology, however eloquently presented, is not going to convince them otherwise.

There is no secret about what will have to be done in China if Chinese SOEs are to be made internationally competitive and efficient. There is a large international literature on the subject and there are at least some in China in positions of influence that know what needs to be done. It is certainly possible, of course, that China could do everything right and the SOEs would still fail to become competitive. But then the options facing China would be straightforward — either make the SOEs disappear either through privatisation or failure, or be prepared to waste large resources propping them up indefinitely into the future. The more interesting question, however, is whether the current leadership in China is capable of or willing to do what is necessary to make the SOEs competitive.

There are three broad areas where changes must be made if state enterprises are to be given a chance to become competitive:

(1) The SOEs that don't perform must be allowed to fail in some form or another. In the jargon of the socialist planning and reform literature, they must face a hard budget constraint, not a soft one.
(2) The connection between the top management of SOEs and the Ministries and government offices that oversee them must be broken. As long as the SOEs are tied by an umbilical cord to the government bureaucracy, they will never be able to behave in accordance with the rules of the market except in very unusual circumstances where the government itself is run like a profit maximising enterprise.
(3) The political costs of restructuring the SOEs must be reduced to a politically acceptable level. In China in particular the social and hence political costs of simply letting the state sector go under are especially high because China structured the SOE's to be the principal provider of urban social services including housing.

How can these three broad principles be translated into concrete reform actions? Again, nothing that follows will come as a surprise to those who have wrestled with these problems:

(1) Those SOEs that show little prospect of becoming viable need to be declared bankrupt and their operations closed down. China passed a bankruptcy law a decade ago, but only in the last year or two has a significant number of SOEs been allowed to fail. SOEs, of course, need to have some time to adjust to the new market environment. No large enterprise can restructure itself in a few short years when it starts with a management that will take some time to even begin to understand the nature of the problem. But China's large SOEs have now had over twelve years to become familiar with the requirements of a market system. How much longer do they need?

    Part of the problem facing reformers is that it is often not easy to tell whether an SOE is profitable or not, and that difficulty may be getting worse rather than better as time passes. The failure in the past to close down the chronic losers among the SOEs is that that leaves these losers with two options for covering their deficits. One is to keep on borrowing from the banking system with the clear intent never to repay the loans. The net result of this approach is that the banking system gets loaded up with bad debt and is itself a candidate for bankruptcy and restructuring.

The second option is to give one's suppliers IOUs that one also has no intention of ever honouring. Because the suppliers receive IOUs rather than cash, they too must issue further IOUs to their suppliers and inter-enterprise or triangular debt gets larger and larger. Ultimately this whole mess will have to be refinanced and the books cleared of all of this bad debt. It does not make sense to refinance, however, unless one is also prepared to close down those firms most responsible for the pile up of bad debt, the chronic losers among the SOEs. Once the chronic losers are closed down, it then becomes possible to tell whether the accounts receivable on the books of the remaining enterprises are really future income or ought to be written off. When that is done, it will be a relatively simple matter to tell whether a firm is profitable or not. Until it is done, many firms will be in a position to claim that they would be profitable if others would just pay their bills. If refinancing is done before the chronic losers are closed down, however, the cycle of expanding inter-enterprise debt is likely to simply repeat itself possibly at an even faster pace. The chronic losers, having been bailed out once, will be more confident that they will be bailed out again in the future.

Hardening the soft budget constraint, therefore, is a bit more complicated that just saying that firms should be allowed to go bankrupt. National leadership will be required to straighten out the mess that the failure to deal with the problem earlier has created. Further procrastination on finding a way out of this morass will in all likelihood mean that the process of refinancing will become ever more difficult and politically as well as economically painful. In fact, one possible scenario is that the situation will eventually produce some kind of financial crash followed by a severe recession that would finally force the political leadership to do what is necessary to reform the situation. If this were the 1920s, the financial crash would have already occurred, but fortunately central banks since then have learned a lot about how to rescue failed banks and keep the financial system afloat. The methods can be expensive for the tax-paying public, but they do work.

(2) Breaking the connection between the enterprises and their supervising government bureaucracies is not complicated in a technical sense, but is anything but easy to accomplish politically. The critical step in this process is the one that takes the power to appoint top management away from the central and provincial government ministries and supervising agencies. As long as that power of appointment remains with these government agencies, the principal objective of the appointed managers will be to do what gains them praise from these supervising agencies. In theory the supervising agencies could have the single objective of profit maximisation, but in practice most will have a plethora of objectives both political and personal. They will want to see their political supporters and friends hired and kept on regardless of performance, they will want the enterprise to invest in particular areas of the country rather than others for political or poverty fighting reasons, and much else.

If one is to take the power of appointment of management away from the central ministries and supervising agencies, however, one must have a substitute body of some kind that will play this role. One option is to have the workers given the power to elect their own managers, but this raises numerous other problems because workers as a group are interested in goals other than profit maximisation as well. The enterprise can simply be turned over to the existing managers with no supervising agency above them, but this is, in effect, privatising the enterprise by giving it to the managers. If the privatisation is not done formally, the manager's tenure in office will be insecure and many managers will move quickly to transfer firm assets to some entity over which they have a firmer control. This process of spontaneous "privatisation" or theft of state assets could be seen in most of the transition economies and was particularly prevalent in Russia. In Russia it was one of the major motives behind the decision to formally privatise the economy as fast as possible.

Does the experience of the successful Asian SOEs in Singapore and elsewhere give us any useful guides as to how to get SOEs focused on profit maximisation? The answer, unfortunately, is not very much. POSCO, for example was able to keep the ministry bureaucrats in Korea from interfering with its operations because the head of POSCO was more powerful than most ministers and could report directly to a President (Park Chung Hee). The President in turn was himself primarily interested in making sure that the enterprises the state promoted were commercially successful without having to rely on subsidies. But it is not feasible, when one has several thousand SOEs, to appoint managers who report only to the President unless the President's staff confine their interest in the enterprise to ensuring its profitability and appoints supervisors with that sole purpose in mind. In a sense this is what Singapore has done. In fact the government of Singapore itself is run in many ways like a modern corporation with a heavy emphasis on ensuring that city-state Singapore as a whole and its SOEs in particular remain focused on long run profit maximisation. But few governments are in a position to run themselves in this way however good an idea it might or might not be. Politics and politicians have a plethora of goals other than profit maximisation because the societies they lead and represent have a plethora of other goals and staying in power means being responsive to those other goals.

In the absence of a Singapore-type solution, if one wants to cut the umbilical cord between the enterprises and the state and still retain some kind of public or state ownership, the one practical step available to most countries is to corporatise these enterprises. Corporatisation involves selling shares in the enterprise to others and then letting those others select a board of directors that has the authority to appoint top management. If the shares are sold to individuals or to foreign corporations, this is simply one kind of privatisation. If the shares are sold to other state enterprises or such bodies as state owned pension funds, however, one can still state that in important respects the enterprise is still owned by the state. Distinctions of this sort matter in countries that still consider themselves to be socialist. As long as the shareholding bodies are primarily interested in owning these shares so that they can increase their own income or profits, then corporatisation has succeeded in creating an ownership that is mainly interested in profits, not a whole range of other goals. For public or state organisations such as the Employee Provident Fund of Singapore or the unit trusts under PNB in Malaysia, this assumption that profits will be given primacy over other goals is a plausible one. It may also be a plausible assumption when one state enterprise buys shares in another if the enterprise doing the purchasing is governed by people primarily concerned with profits.

There are, of course, a myriad of issues connected with how the public owners or principals get management or their agents to do their bidding, but this problem exists with fully privatised corporations as well. In a transition economy, it is at least plausible to believe that a large state-owned pension fund will be as effective in keeping management focused on raising the rate of return to the enterprise as would be a few hundred thousand individual shareholders each owning a very tiny fraction of the whole company.

The above analysis is at least a plausible defense of the view that corporatisation could be the solution to making SOEs efficient and internationally competitive and thus avoiding outright privatisation. The problem in the Chinese case is that the country has the form of corporatisation without the substance. A great many SOEs in China now sell shares in themselves to their workers, to other state enterprises, and even to foreigners, but those shares do not give the shareholders the power to appoint management. That power still rests with the central and provincial governments not to mention the Chinese Communist Party. This method of corporatisation makes it possible for some SOEs to raise more capital than otherwise but that is about all. Corporatisation in Vietnam, in contrast, does give shareholders the power to appoint management, but the result is that management resistance has allowed only a handful (less than one dozen) SOEs to be corporatised.

In a situation where formal privatisation is not allowed and coporatisation has taken a form that does not really address the principal problem of supervision over SOE management, it should not come as a surprise that managers are carving out their own solutions. The managers know that many of their enterprises are in deep financial trouble and that they could sink with the enterprise and so they are devising vehicles that will allow them to avoid this fate. They even have a name for it, creating "lifeboats" for themselves. Lifeboats take a number of forms, but they have one central feature in common. The enterprise is restructured in such a way that most of the large liabilities such as the generous pensions given to retired state workers are placed in some kind of holding company. The profitable core parts of the business are separated out and stripped of most of these liabilities. The core business or a part thereof ends up as a joint venture partner with a foreign corporation or is listed directly on the Hong Kong stock exchange. Variations on this theme involve alliances with TVEs and the sale of state assets at very favourable prices to private bodies in which management has a stake.

Conceivably the ownership problem will eventually solve itself through back door approaches of this sort. Over time the TVEs and joint ventures with foreigners could simply replace most of the SOEs. The holding companies set up to take ownership of such things as unfunded pensions and the loss making subsidiaries of the original SOE would eventually collapse in bankruptcy with the state picking up whatever share of the unfunded pensions that it chose to. The main advantage of this approach is that it would allow China's top leadership to avoid making hard decisions that will have political costs at least for a time. In the end, however, this very messy approach to reform could exact a considerable political price of its own for whomever was still around when the loss making holding companies finally collapsed.

(3) Even if China's leadership were all powerful and could carry through the reform of the SOEs without concern for the social consequences, a strong case can certainly be made in social terms that institutions should first be put in place that would cushion the shock of a large

number of SOE bankruptcies. In any case, the Chinese leadership is not all-powerful and thus must be quite careful how it handles the social impact of SOE reform. Certainly that is the case if it wants to avoid a major political backlash from the many powerful people who have not really been supporters of SOE reform from the start. The situation in China is made more difficult by the fact that so many social services in the urban areas are provided, not by national programmes, but by the individual SOEs. This did not have to be the case, it is not the case in Vietnam for example, but it is the case and it greatly complicates the SOE reform issue.

In China there is widespread support for the view that closing down loss making SOEs must be preceded by the introduction of some kind of social safety net. Concretely this means that there should be an unemployment insurance system in place and that worker pensions should become the responsibility of a national system. Health insurance must also be taken away from the enterprises and turned over to a national system. Finally, and in some ways the biggest headache of all, housing, needs to be taken away from the SOEs and distributed through some kind of market mechanism. This latter step sounds simple but it involves major equity issues about how the current occupants of a given apartment should be treated. Should they have to buy the apartment and, if so, at what price and where are they to get the money to do this? Should they be asked to pay the full market value rent in order to stay in the apartment or should they be given a period to adjust and so on.

Given the complications, not to mention the cost, of getting these social reforms in place, it would seem that a good case could be made for delaying SOE reform for some time until this social reform process is well underway. That would be a plausible argument except for the fact that nationwide experiments on all of these fronts have been going on for quite a few years. Housing has been privatised in some areas. An unemployment insurance system has been in place on a limited but substantial scale for several years. Is it really necessary to keep on running trials or are these trials becoming excuses for postponing the hard decisions that will have to be made?

Alternative Paths to the Future

The central issue facing the SOEs , therefore, is not what needs to be done, but when is the government going to do it? I do not know the answer to this question, but it is possible to outline the limited choices available to the Chinese leadership.

The first choice would be to do very little. Inertia and the opposition of those with a vested interest in the status quo would basically win the day at least for a time. This approach will have a number of predictable consequences. Inflation will continue to be a serious problem because loss-making enterprises will continue to try to cover their losses with bank loans that are not going to be repaid and hence will accelerate the growth rate of the money supply. Anti inflationary efforts from time to time will stop the growth of much of this credit, but that will exacerbate the inter-enterprise debt problem.

If this were the 1920s, one could anticipate that China would eventually go through a major financial crisis that would lead to a financial panic and the collapse of the whole system. But this is not the 1920's and central banks, among others, have learned a lot about how to prevent collapses of this sort. The central bank can prop up the commercial banking system more or less indefinitely, but at a price. The most obvious price is the cost to the public of having to continually pay these subsidies to the SOE's, but that is not the only cost. As Japan, Korea, and Thailand have all demonstrated in recent years, continual propping up of the banking system encourages banks and politicians, among others, to make increasingly risky investments in the belief that they will be bailed out when necessary. Eventually the public and political leaders representing the views of that public are likely to arise and try to put an end to these practices with the result that the oft postponed financial crisis is postponed no longer.

This crisis can be avoided if the loss making SOEs somehow managed to disappear on their own. Some kinds of reforms do occur because of local initiative and without much help from the centre. The gradual demise of the dual price system in China is a case in point. The central government did not really make a decision to eliminate the dual price system. In fact during the inflationary pressure of 1989–1990 the government in some cases moved to reinstitute price controls over some goods, but these efforts were rarely successful. Suppliers of these goods had a powerful incentive to sell at the much higher market prices and so took action to avoid the controls. As one acquaintance of mine said, every time the government tried to set low state prices on a good, the enterprise simply changed the name of the good and raised the price anyway.

The SOEs, however, are not likely to disappear as easily as the dual price system. There will be many back door privatisations of the kind described above, but these will only allow some of the more profitable units to escape the downdraft generated by the many failures. But managers, TVEs and foreign direct investors are not rushing to take over the loss-making SOEs.

If the gradual approach to SOE reform means that decisive action is avoided in the hope that the situation will somehow correct itself, then the condition of the SOEs could continue to worsen until a crisis forces action. In a sense this would be somewhat like what happened in Eastern Europe in the 1980's before the collapse of Soviet and Communist Party control in 1989. In Eastern Europe, central planning was dismantled but state enterprises beholden to government ministries remained very much in place. Growth occurred for a time despite the continued weak performance of the SOEs, but taking on more and more foreign debt financed much of this growth. Eventually the system ground to a halt leaving the countries with both stagnant economies and an unsustainable foreign debt. No informed observer of China thinks anything this drastic is likely to happen there among other reasons because China's rising foreign debt is clearly sustainable as long as exports continue to grow so rapidly. In addition, the state sector is no where near as large as it was in Eastern Europe and China's unfunded pension problem is miniscule when compared to the problem of funding the lavish social welfare and pension system that the current Eastern Europeans inherited from the pre-1989 period.[15] The fact

[15]Jeffrey Sachs and Wing Thye Woo, "Structural Factors in the Economic Reforms of China, Eastern Europe, and the Former Soviet Union", *Economic Policy*, April 1994, pp. 102–145.

that China has a more modest form of the same disease, however, does not mean that China's economy is completely healthy or that it is bound to get well without further decisive action.

The second choice facing the Chinese leadership is to take decisive action to solve the state enterprise problem. There is no need to repeat what decisive action would entail. The steps required were outlined above. China's current leadership might prefer to emphasise some of the steps outlined over others, but, to date at least, they have not devised a viable third way. Even the steps outlined above may not complete the job of making the SOEs efficient, profitable, and internationally competitive, but no one will know until they are tried.

What is the probability that China's current leadership will take the necessary steps? A year or more ago I would have been quite pessimistic about the prospects. The last decisive action of this sort taken by the senior leadership was Deng Xiaoping's trip to southern China in early 1992 that reopened the debate over how to make the transition to the market. Since then, China's leaders have often seemed to be avoiding tough decisions while they jockeyed for position in the succession. But in recent months there appears to have been some real movement although only time will tell whether this is more than a mirage.

Two statements by the recent Chinese leadership offer hope that they will take the actions required. One was the apparent decision to concentrate state effort on reforming the largest one or two thousand or so state enterprises while leaving the others to survive or fail on their own. One or two thousand is still a large number, but there were in 1995 some 68,500 SOEs. Even if many of the 66,500 to be cut loose are small, this is still a major change in the role of the state in the economy if it is actually implemented.

The second statement or policy change is more difficult to interpret and may be just wishful thinking on my part. The Chinese have recently tabled a new set of positions on what they are willing to do to get into the World Trade Organisation. Instead of trying to rely on their political clout and sticking to the position that they are a developing country, they have listed a series of steps which, if implemented, would take them a long way toward a true market economy. Most of these steps, in the Chinese view, can only be implemented over a considerable number of years, but no sensible outside observer thinks that China can meet most WTO requirements within a year or two. The potential significance of this changing attitude about how to get into the WTO is that at least some of China's leaders may be coming to the view that meeting these WTO criteria is not only necessary for WTO membership, these criteria would be in China's interests even if there were no WTO.

There are other straws in the wind that provide some evidence that China is now really trying to solve the SOE problem. The number of bankruptcies during the past two or three years has risen substantially and redundant workers are being laid off in considerable numbers. The real proof of Chinese leadership intentions, however, will come several years from now when the SOE's that remain are profitable and internationally competitive and the remainder have been closed down.

Optimists are generally looked down upon in the academic world. It often seems that it is better to be a pessimist if you want the respect of your peers even if being a pessimist leads you to make forecasts that turn out to be untrue. For these past eighteen years, it has been my experience that, when there are steps to be taken that must be taken if economic progress is to continue, the Chinese leadership has eventually gone ahead and made them. In recent years they have often procrastinated for some time before doing what was required, but eventually they moved. Over the long run, I believe, China's leaders will also make the changes required to either make the state-owned enterprises successful or they will curtail their role in the economy sharply. If they do not do so, they could jeopardise China's long-term growth prospects and no Chinese leaders want that as their legacy.

Gain Without Pain

Why Economic Reform in China Worked

Lawrence J. LAU*
Department of Economics
Stanford University

INTRODUCTION

Over the past two decades, East Asia has been the fastest-growing region in the world, and China has been the fastest-growing country in East Asia, with an average annual growth rate of approximately 10 percent since its economic reforms began in 1979. Between 1979 and 1996, Chinese real GDP has quintupled from US$150 billion to US$750 billion (all in 1990 prices). During the same period, real GDP per capita has increased more than fourfold, from US$150 to US$610 (again, all in 1990 prices).[1] China is one of the very few socialist countries that have made a successful transition from a centrally planned economy to a market economy.

*The author is Kwoh-Ting Li Professor of Economic Development, Department of Economics, Stanford University. The author is grateful for discussions with Masahiko Aoki, K. C. Fung, Hyung-Ki Kim, Masahiro Okuno-Fujiwara, Ying-Yi Qian, Dani Rodrik and Gerard Roland. Responsibility for any errors remains with the author.

[1]To put these statistics in perspective, it is useful to remember that real GDP and real GDP per capita in the United States are approximately US$7 trillion and US$25,000 respectively. Thus despite its rapid growth, it will probably take another four decades to half a century before Chinese real GDP and real GDP per capita approach U.S. levels.

Why has China been successful in its economic reforms while others, such as the former Soviet Union, appeared to have failed? Two principal reasons may be identified. First, China has implemented economic reforms in such a way that there are no losers. In other words, no Chinese citizen is made worse off as a result of the Chinese economic reforms. Second, through its high saving rate — approaching 40 percent in some years — China has had an abundant supply of new resources, most of which it has invested efficiently. The resulting rapid economic growth also makes it much easier to assure that there are no losers.[2] The abundance of new resources also makes it far less urgent a matter to try to redeploy the old assets efficiently, which requires the more likely to be painful reform and restructuring of the state-owned enterprises. Our estimates show that almost 80 percent of the fixed capital stock in 1996 is due to gross fixed investments made since 1979. A "gain without pain" strategy might not have been possible if the saving rates were not as high as they were.

THE PROBLEM OF COMPENSATING THE LOSERS

When an economy starts from a state of inefficiency, any efficiency-enhancing economic reform will result in a *net gain* in real output in the aggregate. Thus, in principle, it should be possible to make everyone better off, or at least make nobody worse off, as a result of the reform, by suitably taxing or otherwise redistributing from the winners to compensate the losers. If this can in fact be done, then "gain without pain" is achieved. "Gain without pain" is the dream of all economic reformers (and politicians) because it minimises political opposition to and maximises political support for, reforms *ex ante* as well as maximises political opposition to reversal of reforms *ex post* (because of the new vested interests created).

In practice, potential losers are seldom compensated, and even if they are, they are seldom fully compensated, for several reasons. First, there is imperfect information — it is difficult to identify the potential winners and losers as well as to ascertain the magnitudes of their individual potential

[2]With an economy growing at 10 percent per annum, there is no reason why anyone has to be worse off in absolute terms.

gains and losses. Second, it is difficult to devise implementable general taxation and subsidy schemes that target the potential winners and losers specifically, that is, to tax only the winners and to compensate only the losers. Third, the only way to tax the winners and compensate the losers without introducing distortions in the economy is to use a system of fixed lump sum taxes and subsides, that is, taxes and subsidies whose values do not depend on and hence do not affect the actions of the economic agents. Unfortunately, explicit lump sum taxes and subsidies require such detailed information on the individual economic agents that they are virtually impossible and most general taxation schemes, based on either earnings, income, consumption or retail purchases, are distortionary, that is, they will affect the actions of the economic agents and thereby prevent full economic efficiency from being achieved. Fourth, there are costs of information and implementation, that is, in order to effect transfers from winners to losers, a system of taxation and subsidies with its necessary institutions, e.g. the Internal Revenue Service, may have to be devised and implemented. That is why in many reforming economies, there is frequently no attempt to compensate the losers, and state promises of compensation, when made, generally lack credibility because of the perceived difficulty of implementation. The type of economic reforms implemented in the former Soviet Union and Eastern Europe, sometimes described as "Big Bang" reforms, generally suffers from this inability to compensate the potential losers. Potential losers are therefore likely to oppose the economic reform, often causing the reform to fail before it is even begun, or at least drastically reducing its chance of success.

Unlike economic reforms elsewhere, the Chinese economic reforms have not aroused significant political opposition and enjoyed widespread popular support.[3] This is because the Chinese economic reforms have implicitly adhered to the principle that no one should be made worse off as a result. Thus, there are no losers from the economic reforms, only winners, even though the distribution of the gains from the economic reforms may be highly uneven.

[3]There is, of course, dissatisfaction with the relative distribution of the gains from economic reform. Some have benefited much more than others. But no one will deny that everyone has gained.

But can economic reforms without losers bring about an efficient economy? The answer is an unequivocal yes.[4] It can be shown that, by using a "dual-track" approach, Chinese economic reforms, in addition to being Pareto-improving, that is, having no losers, also simultanously enable the economy to be fully efficient, in the sense that all resources have been put to their fullest and best use. Thus, Chinese economic reforms have not only achieved "gain without pain", but also actually *maximal* "gain without pain."

In Section 2 we briefly review the Chinese economic reforms and the resulting outcomes. In Section 3, we show how the "dual track" approach can simultaneously permit the protection of the pre-reform rights and obligations and yet also enable full economic efficiency, thus achieving "gain without pain". In Section 4, we give examples of the "dual-track" approach from the Chinese experience. In Section 5 we present evidence of how marketisation proceeded under the "dual track" approach in the agricultural, industrial and retail sectors, and how the central plan has been gradually phased out. We conclude with some brief remarks in Section 6.

THE CHINESE ECONOMIC REFORMS (1979–THE PRESENT)

Four essential elements of Chinese economic reforms since 1979 may be identified. They are:

(1) The "open door" — meaning opening the Chinese economy to international trade and foreign investment.
(2) Marketisation — the introduction of markets in goods, factors, and foreign exchange to initially supplement and eventually supplant the plan.
(3) The devolution of decision-making power on the basis of the "contract responsibility system" — the de-communisation of agriculture, empowering provincial and local governments, professionalisation of

[4]See Lau, Qian and Roland (1997).

the management of enterprises, and the granting of autonomy and incentives to enterprises on the margin.

(4) The creation of new, non-state-owned modes of organisation for production. This includes, in agriculture, the return to a system of individual cultivators with fixed rents and taxes in 1979 and in industry, the emergence of "Township and Village" enterprises (TVEs), (foreign) joint-venture, wholly foreign, and private enterprises since 1984. Some state-owned enterprises and/or their subsidiaries have become publicly traded joint stock companies since 1990, with many private citizens becoming shareholders and hence partial owners. The trend corporatisation of state-owned enterprises (SOEs) is poised to accelerate this year.

The results of the Chinese economic reforms may be characterised overall as very successful, with two exceptions. First, the average annual rate of inflation over the post-reform period is approximately 7 percent, much higher than the pre-reform average of less than half a percent per annum. Second, the "contract responsibility" system, so successful in agriculture, failed by and large to elicit the improvement in efficiency in the state-owned enterprises in the industrial sector. We discuss each element of the economic reforms in turn.

The Open Door

The open door policy has been extremely successful. Chinese international trade has increased by leaps and bounds. With the inclusion of Hong Kong, the People's Republic of China is now the world's fourth largest trading nation. It is also by far the largest recipient of foreign direct investment among developing countries.[5] The official foreign reserves of China now

[5]However, the inflow of foreign direct investment only began to be quantitatively significant after 1990s. Even then, at its peak, it accounted for less than 15 percent of gross fixed investment in China.

exceeds US$100 billion, far more than is necessary to support the requirements of her current account transactions.

Marketisation

Marketisation has also been extremely successful. The prices of all consumer goods and more than 95 percent of the producer goods are determined in the market. The price of low-grade grain is controlled (subsidised), only for social welfare purposes. The price of energy is at world market levels. The dual exchange rates were unified in January, 1994. Current account convertibility was achieved in December, 1996. The labour markets have also been liberalised. The state no longer has the responsibility of placing college and university graduates. In return, college and university graduates can work wherever they wish. Stock and bond markets were also established in the 1990s.

The Devolution of Economic Decision Power

A great deal of power has been devolved to the provincial and local government levels. For example, foreign direct investment projects of below US$30 million can be directly approved by the provincial authorities. The managers of enterprises have more autonomy and power than before.

The Growth of the Non-State Sector

The state-owned sector has continuously shrunk *relative* to the aggregate economy; it currently accounts for no more than 30 percent of the aggregate output. The proportion of aggregate economy-wide gross fixed investments accounted for by state-owned enterprises was 72 percent in 1979. It stood at just over 50 percent in 1996. Because of the de-communisation of the agricultural sector, the state-owned sector accounts for only a very insignificant proportion of aggregate agricultural output. In industry,. the state-owned sector's share of gross value of production fell from almost 80 percent in 1979 to just above 30 percent in 1995 (See Figure 1). This decline was caused primarily because of the considerably faster growth of the non-state sector. The growth of the non-state sector has far outstripped the growth of the state sector which has been largely propelled by the growth of the output of the township and village enterprises (TVEs). As of 1994, TVEs accounted for almost half of the aggregate industrial output and almost two-thirds of the aggregate industrial employment of China.

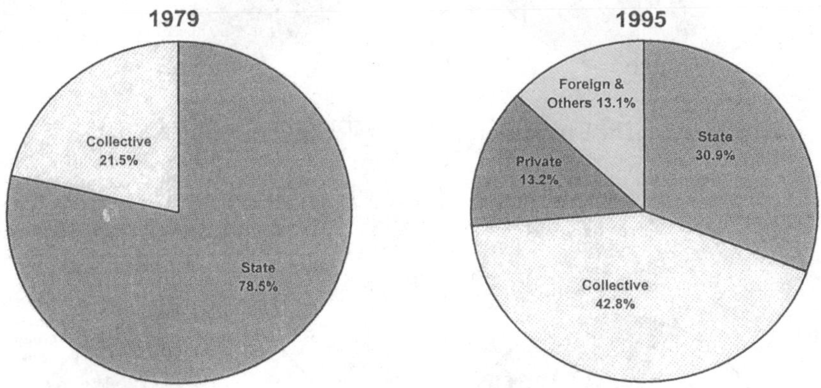

Figure 1 The Distribution of Gross Value of Industrial Production by Ownership (China).

The distribution of retail sales by ownership shows a similar picture (Figure 2). Here the rapid rise in prominence of the private sector in retail sales is clearly evident. From almost nothing in 1979, the private sector is now the largest sector in terms of retail sales.

These trends in the transformation of ownership are not confined to the coastal or the more prosperous provinces. They are indeed nationwide. Even in Guizhou, the poorest province in China in terms of gross provincial product per capita, the distribution of retail sales by ownership is broadly similar to the national pattern (see Figure 3).

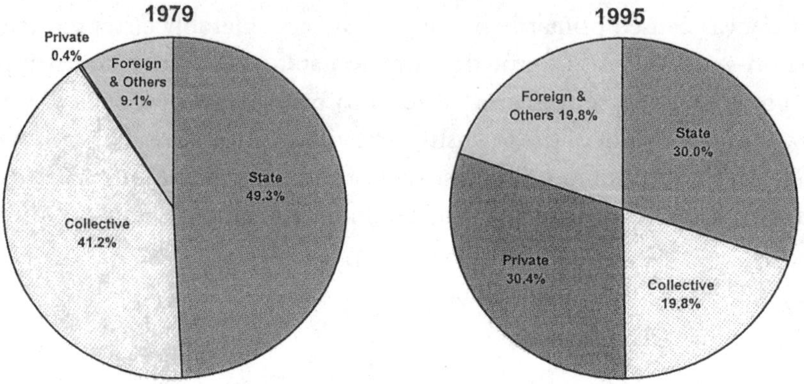

Figure 2 The Distribution of Retail Sales by Ownership (China).

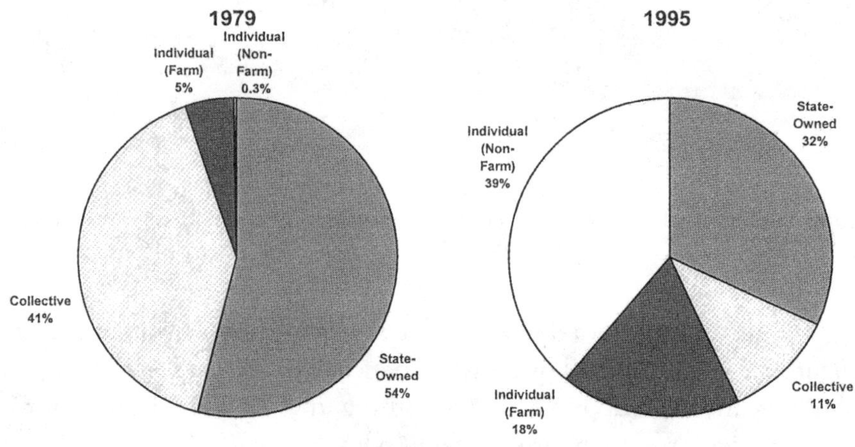

Figure 3 The Distribution of Retail Sales by Ownership (Guizhou Province).

In Table 1, we present selected indicators of the economic performance of China before and after the commencement of economic reforms in 1979. Table 1 shows that in every dimension except one — the rate of inflation, the economic performance in the post-reform period is far superior to that before reform. Of particular interest is the rate of growth of real personal consumption per capita — it went from 2 percent per annum to over 7 percent per annum — indicating a genuine and significant improvement in the standard of living. That is one of the fundamental reasons why a reversal of the economic reforms is most unlikely — everyone in China benefited significantly from the economic reforms.

Table 1 Comparison of the Average Annual Rates of Growth of Selected Economic Indicators.

	1954–1979 Pre-Reform	1979–1995 Reform
Real GDP	5.9	10.0
Real GDP/Capita	3.8	8.5
Real Gross Value of:		
Agricultural Production*	2.9	6.1
Light Industry*	8.7	16.5
Heavy Industry*	12.8	14.4
Real Personal Consumption*	4.0	8.6
Real Consumption/Capita*	2.0	7.1
Real Gross Fixed Investment	7.7	11.9
Capital Stock	5.3	9.1
Employment	2.5	2.6
GDP Deflator	0.4	7.4
Retail Price Index	0.7	8.1
Exports (in current US Dollars)	10.5	15.2
Imports (in current US Dollars)	9.9	13.7

ECONOMIC REFORM WITHOUT LOSERS

The principle of Chinese economic reform is that no one loses as a result. This implies the "grandfathering" of the *status quo ante*, protection of "vested interests" and "discriminating" between the old and the new. For this reason, the availability of new resources and its efficient utilisation takes on additional importance, because they determine how fast a transition economic reforms without losers can be. We have already seen that new enterprises and the new activities have been primarily responsible for the phenomenal economic growth of China since 1979. The new resources come mostly from the high saving rates of between 35 percent and 40 percent. There has been little or no privatisation of existing enterprises as well as little or no successful restructuring of existing enterprises until recently.

Economic Reforms Without Losers: China's "Dual-Track" Approach

A dual-track strategy may be defined as follows:

(1) in one track, the "plan track", the existing (often inefficient) central economic plan, and the distribution of rents under it, are left intact; and

(2) in the other track, the "market track", liberalisation is carried out at the margin, that is, economic agents have both the right and the incentive to participate in the free market provided that the obligations under the original plan are fulfilled. In particular, market resales of plan-allocated inputs and consumption goods, and market purchases of outputs for redelivery are allowed.

The dual-track approach combines the pre-existing plan and at the same time introduces the market; it grandfathers the "vested interests" through the enforcement of the rights and obligations under the pre-existing plan; it uses the "contract responsibility" system to stimulate participation in the market on the margin; it creates new, reform-oriented "vested interests"; it is easy to implement because it relies solely on existing information and institutions, including enforcement. There is no doubt that because it is Pareto-improving, it must be efficiency-enhancing. The question is: can the dual-track approach achieve full efficiency for the economy?

An Economist's Definition of Efficiency

An economy is said to be "efficient" if and only if no one output can be increased without decreasing another output. In other words, all resources in the economy have been put to their fullest and best use.

Comparison of the Big-Bang Strategy and the Dual-Track Strategy to Market Liberalisation

Under the big-bang strategy of market liberalisation, the central plan is completely abolished. All markets are instantaneously open. Producers are completely free to plan their production. Consumers are completely free to plan their consumption. The quantities and prices of all goods are determined through the equilibration between supply and demand in the market. Under the dual-track strategy, the central plan remains (and is frozen except for new increments of state-financed production capacity) but the rights and obligations under the central plan continue to be enforced. All markets are instantaneously open. Producers are completely free to plan their production and sales, provided output delivery obligations under the plan are fulfilled. Consumers are completely free to plan their consumption, given allocated consumption goods. Aggregate quantities and *market* prices of all goods are determined through the equilibration between supply and demand in the market with planned prices remaining fixed.

Making Economic Reforms Painless

The distinction between the big-bang and dual-track strategies lies in the role played by the pre-existing central plan. The sale and purchase obligations of the economic agents remain even after the economic reforms, but they are fixed at the pre-existing levels. In addition, all planned transactions take place at the pre-existing, fixed plan prices. Thus, planned profits and losses (taxes and subsidies) of economic agents remain precisely the same. If economic agents do not do anything outside the plan, they are precisely just as well off as before. If they choose to do anything outside the plan, after fulfilling their obligations under the plan, they must, by definition, expect that they will be better off. Moreover, since the economic agents are free to resell their plan-allocated goods and to purchase from the market goods for re-delivery under the plan, they face, at the margin, the market prices. Any differences between planned and market prices therefore represent implicit feasible lump-sum transfers. The values of these transfers depend on the market prices and are thus not fixed. However, they cannot be affected by the actions of the individual economic agents and hence their existence also does not affect the actions of the economic agents. Planned consumer goods deliveries to the government enable the maintenance of the pre-reform standard of living as a floor (e.g. in the urban areas).

Feasibility of the Pre-Existing Plan

It is reasonable to assume that the pre-existing central plan is feasible, that is, it can in fact be carried out. Otherwise, it may not be possible for all the obligations specified in the pre-existing central plan to be fulfilled and the central plan itself will fail to be a credible arrangement for the lump-sum transfers discussed above. Feasibility of the central plan implies the following conditions:

(1) The production plan for each producer is feasible;
(2) The consumption plan for each consumer is feasible;

(3) Material balance holds in the aggregate; and
(4) The consumption plan for each consumer is affordable at the plan prices.

The Openness of All Markets

Both the big-bang and the dual-track strategies require that all markets are open for economic efficiency. In particular, market resales of plan-allocated inputs and consumption goods, market purchases of outputs for redelivery under the plan, as well as subcontracting, are allowed. Under the dual-track approach, there are two prices for each good — q, the plan price and p, the market price.

The Role of State Power

Under the dual-track approach, the state is required, even after market liberalisation, to enforce the rights and obligations under the pre-existing central plan (as well as any new contracts entered into through the market)[6]. However, as soon as economic agents are allowed to participate in the market, the enforcement of the plan by necessity must shift to the enforcement of specific sales to and purchases from other economic agents as mandated in the pre-existing plan. Simple enforcement of the planned aggregate production no longer suffices because an enterprise, for example, can fulfill its planned aggregate production target and yet at the same time fail to make any planned deliveries to other enterprises at the plan prices. Thus, even if the planned aggregate production target is fulfilled, the plan itself may not be fulfilled because the mandated sales and purchases are not made. But if enforcement is shifted to plan-mandated purchases and

[6]It is important to point out that the enforcement required here is no different from the enforcement of contracts in a market economy.

sales, it is most likely that enforcement actions are taken in response to complaints by other economic agents whose rights have not been honored by specific enterprises. The potential recipients of the planned output deliveries must complain before the state planning commission will begin enforcement actions. The enforcement is not on total production, but on the actual delivery of goods as provided for in the plan. This also makes it likely that absent specific complaints, no enforcement actions are likely to be taken.

Whether the dual-track approach works depends on the credibility of state enforcement, and expectations thereof. If the state is not credible, then the economic agents will have no incentive to fulfill their obligations under the pre-existing plan. And if anyone thinks that the plan-mandated deliveries at planned prices are not going to be received by him or her, he or she will not make the plan-mandated sales at the fixed plan prices either. Thus, if the overall belief or expectation is that there will not be effective enforcement, no one will comply, and the dual-track approach reduces to the big-bang approach. Perceived credibility therefore affects enterprise (and household) behaviour, and hence compliance with the pre-existing plan (post reform). If economic agents do not comply with the pre-existing plan, it is no longer possible to assure that there are no losers.

In general, multiple equilibria (outcomes) are possible under a dual-track approach, depending on expectations of the credibility of state enforcement. If everyone thinks that the state will be able to enforce effectively, everyone will comply, then "gain without pain" can be achieved. If everyone does not expect that there will be credible state enforcement, the dual-track approach will degenerate into the big-bang approach. Thus, in technical terms, there are multiple "rational expectations" (or self-fulfilling) equilibria (a typical example is a bank run).

We have already shown that a dual-track approach assures that there are no losers. In other words, there is Pareto-improvement. In addition, under the above assumptions, a dual-track competitive equilibrium is efficient, that is, all resources are put to their fullest and best use. We note that the assumption allowing resales and purchases for redelivery is essential. Otherwise, the resulting outcome is not necessarily efficient.

Is Chinese Economic Reform Gradualist?

The dual-track approach of the Chinese economic reform is not gradualist because efficiency is instantaneously achieved as if under a big-bang reform. Efficiency is achieved because both the prices and quantities of goods allocated within the plan are *fixed*, and on the margin all economic agents face the market prices. Chinese economic reform *appears* gradualist because the population is protected from shock (pain). However, the pre-existing central plan is "phased out" gradually.

Examples from the Chinese Experience

We provide below nine examples of economic reforms implemented in China that utilise the dual-track approach since Chinese economic reforms began in 1979. Although different in each case, the economic reforms all share the common features described above. The examples are:

(1) The agricultural reform (the introduction of the "contract responsibility system" in agriculture);
(2) The industrial reform;
(3) The "dual-track" price system in urban consumer goods and services;
(4) The foreign exchange reform;
(5) Growth of economic activities outside the "Plan";
(6) Special economic zones and foreign direct investment;
(7) The tax reforms;
(8) The rate of interest on household bank deposits; and
(9) The furloughing of the surplus labour of state-owned enterprises.

(1) The Agricultural Reform

The agricultural reform undertaken in China in 1979 may be regarded as the first successful application of the dual-track approach. Under this reform, the contract responsibility system was introduced in agriculture. The commune is assigned the responsibility to (1) sell a fixed quantity of grain (or other) output to the state procurement agency as previously mandated under the plan at predetermined (plan) prices and (2) to pay a fixed amount of taxes to the state as well as the right to (3) receive a fixed quantity of inputs, principally chemical fertilisers, from state-owned suppliers, again at predetermined (plan) prices. Subject to fulfilling these conditions, the commune is free to do whatever it wishes, e.g., it can produce whatever it considers more profitable, and sell any excess output on the free market, and retain any profit. In fact, under this system, the commune as well as its members are permitted to purchase grain or other output in the market to fulfill the delivery quota (an example of a "wash sale") — it is not required to actually produce the grain or other output itself.

In the implementation of the contract responsibility system, both the mandatory delivery quota and the taxes for the commune are fixed at their original planned levels. The commune in turn reassigns the collective responsibilities (and rights) to the individual farm households, allocating to them their shares of the commune's land and capital (and chemical fertilisers), and making them individually and directly responsible for the fulfilment of their shares of the delivery quota and taxes.

Thus, there is both a plan track and a free market track, each with different prices; however, the quantities of outputs and inputs under the plan track are fixed. It is therefore clear that under this system, only the market prices, and not the plan prices, are relevant for the allocation of resources. Note that both the commune (and its individual members) and the state cannot be worse off than before under this new arrangement. Moreover, as long as the state is not worse off in terms of the quantities of grain and other outputs and taxes delivered to the state, it will continue to be able to supply the urban consumers with food grains and industries with agricultural raw materials (such as cotton) at plan prices, with the consequence that even the urban consumers and industrial enterprises are no worse off as a result of the agricultural reform. Thus, the impact of the liberalisation at the margin must be Pareto-improving for all parties.

Since the agricultural reform is only partial, one cannot assert that the full efficiency of the entire economy is attained. However, since the agricultural reform is Pareto-improving for all parties, overall efficiency of the economy is unambiguously enhanced by the agricultural reform.

The dual-track price system has some historical antecedent. Even prior to the introduction of the contract responsibility system, there were two prices for grain — the plan price paid for mandated grain deliveries to the state and the negotiated (market) price for above-quota transactions.

(2) The Industrial Reform

There have been many studies on the Chinese industrial reform and its associated dual-track price system which was introduced in 1984 (see, e.g., Byrd 1987, Wu and Zhao 1987, and Naughton 1995). The industrial reform represents, in part, an attempt to extend the contract responsibility system to the industrial sector, based on the successful experience of the agricultural reform. Under the reform, the mandatory delivery quotas as well as the quantities of plan-allocated inputs for each enterprise were frozen at their then-existing levels, and the enterprises are free to produce whatever they deem profitable and sell their output on the free market and retain any profit as long as they fulfill their delivery quota. At the same time, parallel free markets for the above-quota outputs of enterprises were introduced, while the within-quota outputs continued to be sold at the generally lower plan prices to authorised purchasers.

This example highlights the crucial elements in a dual-track approach. First, the "market track" must provide for full liberalisation (that is, no intervention of any kind), albeit only at the margin (but as we know, liberalisation at the margin is sufficient for efficiency); second, the enterprises must be allowed to reap the full marginal reward;[7] and third, input and output quotas on the plan track must be enforced as outputs of some enterprises are needed as inputs of other enterprises. The ability of enterprises to meet their planned output quota may depend crucially on their timely receipt of the planned input delivery quotas.

[7]This is for reasons of both incentive and the avoidance of distortions.

(3) The Dual-Track Price System in Urban Consumer Goods and Services

Prior to the economic reforms of 1979, many essential consumer goods and services, such as grain, cooking oil, meat, electricity, housing, and monthly pass for mass transit, are rationed in the urban areas at lower than what would have been free market prices. With the introduction of the free markets and the dual-track price system, urban residents continued to be able to purchase grain, meat, electricity (lifeline rates), and housing (for those who had it) at the same pre-reform prices within the limits of the pre-reform rationed quantities, at the same time that they were able to purchase freely any quantity of any good at free market prices. They were thus no worse off than before. The state was also no worse off because the quantities of goods that it would be obligated to supply at the plan prices remained the same.

(4) The Foreign Exchange Reform

Dual markets were permitted to exist for foreign exchange in China from the mid-1980s to the end of 1993. Between 1985 and 1994, there was an official exchange rate, available only for certain limited approved transactions, as well as an officially sanctioned swap rate, that was determined in Foreign Exchange Adjustment Centres (more commonly referred to as "swap markets") in major cities around the country, among exporters and importers qualified to trade in those markets. The supply of foreign exchange in the swap markets was provided by the exporters through the foreign exchange they were allowed to retain from *net increases* in their export earnings relative to the base period.[8] The government did not control the transactions in the swap market, and the swap market exchange rate was mostly determined by supply and demand (see Khor 1994 for a detailed description). The swap rate was, not surprisingly, significantly higher than the official rate during this period.

[8]At the beginning, the enterprises were permitted to re-purchase part of their foreign exchange earnings at the official exchange rate.

At the same time, foreign visitors to China were required to use "foreign exchange certificates" (FECs), which were available at the official exchange rate, rather than the "renminbi", the Chinese domestic currency, for their transactions.

The dual exchange rate system functioned until January 1, 1994, when the two exchange rates — the official rate and the swap rate — were merged into a single rate, with its level determined in a market consisting of exporters and importers, and the foreign exchange certificates were finally withdrawn from circulation. Under the new system, domestic exporters are required to sell all of their foreign exchange to the interbank market (thus, rights of retentions were abolished); in return, they are allowed to purchase foreign exchange as needed for legitimate business purposes.

At the time of this reform, the share of centrally allocated foreign exchange already fell to only 20 percent of the total. In this last step of the foreign exchange reform, central allocation of foreign exchange was completely abolished, but for those organisations which used to receive cheap foreign exchange, annual lump-sum subsidies in the domestic currency sufficient to enable the purchase of the pre-reform allocation of foreign exchange were offered for five years to assure a smooth transition (in other words, the state tried to maintain the same level of hithertofore implicit subsidies received by these organisations).

The exchange rate reform turned out to be a complete success: the exchange rate has remained stable and even appreciated slightly from 8.7 yuan per US$ to 8.3 yuan per US$ today. Since July 1 of this year, foreign and joint-venture enterprises, which hithertofore must use technically separate foreign exchange swap markets, have been permitted to use the same foreign exchange markets maintained by the banks for the domestic enterprises. The best way to characterise the current exchange rate system is that it is "current-accounts convertible", but not "capital-accounts convertible".

(5) Growth of Economic Activities Outside the "Plan"

A distinctive feature of Chinese economic reform is the growth of economic activities outside the state plan even before state-owned enterprises have begun to be privatised or shut down. These new economic activities are entirely market-oriented and are driven by new investments outside of the state plan (Qian and Xu 1993, and Naughton 1995).[9] Two cases may be distinguished here. The first case is the entry and expansion of new unregulated enterprises, known collectively as "non-state enterprises" in China, such as township and village enterprises, foreign-owned enterprises, joint-venture enterprises, and private enterprises, which face "hard budget constraints". The second is the parallel development of new unregulated and market-oriented activities of state-owned enterprises, commonly described as "one-factory-two-system." For example, state-owned enterprises may set up subsidiaries as collective enterprises, universities may establish high-tech firms, and military hospitals may use slack resources to provide medical services to the public to augment their revenues.

The first case has worked extremely well. A crucial condition for the second case to work is that the regulated activities of the state-owned enterprises must be left to function at its previous level without disruption.[10] Under this condition, new activities can only increase welfare. Sufficient enforcement power of government is an essential condition here to prevent disruptive diversion of resources from the regulated to the unregulated activities of the state sector.

[9]The experience in Taiwan and South Korea showed a similar pattern (Lau and Song 1992).
[10]If entry of new firms reduces profits of SOEs through competition, why does the dual-track approach not hurt SOEs? As SOEs have plan-allocated inputs, they generally benefit from the lower plan prices, competition thus does not seem to be an important factor. The dual-track system also protects producers of intermediate goods from competition because of the planned output deliveries. However, this may not be the case for the producers of final goods. Households are also not always protected by "input quotas," i.e. by rationing at lower than market prices. Thus enterprises in the final goods sector may be hurt by competition from non-state enterprises. They may in the longer run lose their rents, if not fully compensated by the state. One has here an example in which reform does not necessarily leave every one at least as well off as before. However, only a minority of firms can be hurt through this type of competition.

(6) *Special Economic Zones and Foreign Direct Investment*

This is not unlike the entry of new enterprises but takes place at the level of a country. The institution of special economic zones was chosen early as a reform measure in part to minimise its impact on and interaction with the rest of the economic system, which still operated under the state plan. Initially, special economic zones allowed only firms engaged in "material reprocessing", that imported all of their inputs, except labor, and export all of their outputs — thus creating no disruption to the domestic aggregate supply and demand, labour being in surplus. The same rule applied to foreign and joint-venture firms operating in China but outside the special economic zones. The principal purpose of this approach is to minimise the impact of the new economic activities on the old-style domestic state-owned enterprises. Thus, once again, there were two tracks and the reform was Pareto-improving.

The initial success of the special economic zones and foreign direct investment was made possible through (1) the existence of overseas Chinese entrepreneurs willing to invest in China despite the uncertain economic, legal, political and social environment; and (2) the existence of slack and cheap labour in China. After a few years of experimentation, enterprises in the special economic zones as well as foreign and joint-venture enterprises were allowed to buy and sell on the domestic market at market prices.

(7) *The Tax Reforms*

We first discuss the fiscal contracting system introduced in the 1980s (see Bahl and Wallich 1992 for details). The experiment of the fiscal contracting system between the central and provincial governments started in 1980 and the system eventually covered all provinces by the mid-1980s. Under the fiscal contracting system, the province/municipality assumed the responsibility of collecting the taxes for the central government and were committed to deliver to the central government a fixed amount of revenue per year, and allowed to retain any excess. (Thus, this is similar to a tax-farming system.) Since the committed amount to be delivered to the central government would be based on the historical experience, neither the central government, nor the provinces/municipalities, would be worse off under this arrangement.

Of course, it is possible that the provinces/municipalities may fail, or claim to fail, to collect even the fixed amount due the central government. In practice, this applied mostly to the poorer provinces — 19 out of the 35 provinces/municipalities were able to retain 100 percent of the revenues they collected at the margin.

The 1994 tax reform introduced a nationwide value-added tax, abolished the fiscal contracting system and replaced it by a fiscal federalism providing for revenue-sharing as well as a separation of the national and local tax bases. Again, the reform ensured that all provinces were not made worse off. The provincial governments were guaranteed revenue no less than that of their 1993 actual expenditures for the three years between 1994 and 1996. As might be expected, the provinces/municipalities had a major spending spree in the last quarter of 1993, which also attested to their confidence that the central government would in fact be able to carry out their part of the commitment.

(8) The Rate of Interest on Household Bank Deposits

The dual-track approach also applies to the setting of the rate of interest for household bank deposits. During the two high-inflation periods (1988–1989 and 1993–1995), the Chinese government promptly indexed the household bank savings deposit rates for new long-term time deposits to the consumer price index in order to protect depositors from inflation (Qian 1994). Indexation of rate of interest on the savings deposit to the rate of inflation is part of the strategy of "grandfathering" or "not making people worse off". This is in contrast to the rates for short-term deposits which remained negative in real terms until very recently. Indexation of savings deposits was, however, once again abolished as of April 1, 1996, on the grounds that inflationary fears had abated.

A *de facto* dual-track credit market already exists in China although it is not officially sanctioned. The market rate of interest for loans has remained significantly above the official bank lending rate. The practice of "re-lending" by state-owned enterprises with preferential access to credit is widespread.[11] As China moves to develop its money and capital markets, it is inevitable that a dual-track price system for money will eventually develop as a transitional device. Already, an interbank call money market has been introduced in January, 1996. There is a reasonably active secondary market for government bonds. More recently, an auction of ten-year government bonds in the style of the U.S. Treasury Bond aution was successfully carried out in China. All of these developments suggest that in the not too distant future, on the margin, the rate of interest will be set in the market.

(9) *The Furloughing of the Surplus Labour of State-Owned Enterprises*

More recently, workers of state-owned enterprises have been furloughed at a percentage of their pre-existing wages and have been allowed to keep their enterprise-allocated housing. They are given the autonomy to seek alternative employment or to become self-employed. This has worked out quite well in Shanghai, where almost 900,000 of the 1 million workers furloughed have found alternative, gainful employment, possibly at lower marginal wages. The workers, who have been overpaid relative to the market, are no worse than before, taking into account the subsidies received. The enterprises and the state are also better off. In fact, efficiency in the labour market can actually be attained with this type of partial subsidies.

[11] But China has not officially adopted a dual-track approach to its lending activities in the banking sector. This would have guaranteed roll-over to cheap old loans to SOEs while applying the free market rate to new loans. However, in reality, many credits were leaked from state banks to non-state enterprises at market rates.

MARKETISATION UNDER THE DUAL-TRACK APPROACH

Under the dual-track approach, the central plan and the market coexisted at the commencement of economic reform. However, since the central plan has been essentially frozen at the original levels,[12] the output produced outside the plan has grown rapidly and the proportion of output that are sold and purchased at plan prices have declined continuously. In Tables 2, 3 and 4, we present the values of the transactions in each of the sectors of agriculture, industry and retail, that are conducted at plan, guide and market prices respectively. It is clear that by the early 1990s, most of the transactions are conducted at market prices. The plan has been phased out for many goods. These tables demonstrate the effectiveness of the dual-track approach as a strategy of transition from a centrally planned economy to a market economy. They also confirm the unmistakable importance of demand expansion due to the rapid economic growth which takes place outside of the plan. The growth of the market (non-planned) portion of the output is largely due to the rise of new, non-state-owned enterprises established since

Table 2 Phasing Out the Plan-Track: Agricultural Products (% of output value).

	1978	1985	1986	1987	1988	1989	1990	1991	1992	1993
plan price	94.4	37.0	35.0	29.4	24.0	35.5	31.0	22.2	12.5	10.4
guide price	0.0	23.0	21.0	16.8	19.0	24.3	27.0	20.0	5.7	2.1
market price	5.6	40.0	43.7	53.8	57.0	40.4	42.0	57.8	81.8	87.5

[12]This is not true of all industries, however. The planned output was increased in certain limited industries in which the state-owned enterprises had undergone state-financed expansion, e.g., coal mining.

Table 3 Phasing Out the Plan-Track: Industrial Goods (% of output value).

	1978	1985	1986	1987	1988	1989	1990	1991	1992	1993
plan price	100.0	64.0				60.0	44.6	36.0	18.7	13.8
guide price	0.0	23.0					19.0	18.3	7.5	5.1
market price	0.0	13.0				40.0	36.5	45.7	73.8	81.1

Table 4 Phasing Out the Plan-Track: Total Retail Sales (% of sales).

	1978	1985	1986	1987	1988	1989	1990	1991	1992	1993
plan price	97.0	47.0	35.0	33.7	28.9	31.3	30.0	20.9	5.9	4.8
guide price	0.0	19.0	25.0	28.0	21.8	23.2	25.0	10.3	1.1	1.4
market price	3.0	34.0	40.0	38.3	49.3	45.5	45.0	68.8	93.0	93.8

1984 whose sales and purchases are not included in the plan even though a part of it may also be attributed to the participation of the state-owned enterprises in the market.

Concluding Remarks

The Chinese experience shows that by using a dual-track approach to economic reforms, one can achieve gain without pain. Economic reforms without losers are possible. Equity does not necessarily have to be sacrificed in order to achieve efficiency. The necessary conditions for the success of the dual-track approach to the transition from a centrally planned economy to a market economy are: (1) Feasibility of the original plan; (2) Autonomy and incentive for the economic agents to participate in the market on the margin, including, in particular, the freedom of resale of plan-allocated goods, purchase of goods for redelivery under the plan, and subcontracting; and (3) Credibility of state enforcement of the plan-mandated sales and purchases of goods.

Looking ahead, it is most likely that China will still consider the maintenance of political and social stability a goal of the highest priority and will seek to achieve that by adopting economic policies with no or very few losers. For this reason, the creation of new jobs for the new entrants into the labour force (estimated to be approximately 16 million each year) and the preservation/replacement of existing jobs are of paramount importance. The control of inflation may also be viewed in part as an attempt to prevent the emergence of a large group of potential losers (after all, the *status quo ante* has shifted, the reference standard is no longer 1979 or 1984). Moreover, the political economy is such that it may be important to consider the question of "relative" rather than "absolute" losers. Even when no one loses absolutely, large segments of the population may lose relatively. Consistent relative losers can also become discontented. That is one reason why the Chinese Government has recently begun to focus on the development of the interior, to prevent the population in the inland provinces from falling further behind, that is, continuing to be "relative losers", when compared to the coastal population.

References

Arrow, Kenneth J., "Toward a Theory of Price Adjustment", in Moses Abramovitz, *et al.*, 1958.

Arrow, Kenneth J., and Frank H. Hahn, *General Competitive Analysis*, San Francisco: Holden-Day, 1971.

Bahl, Richard, and Christine Wallich, "Intergovernmental Fiscal Relations in China", Working Papers, Country Economics Department, WPS 863, World Bank, 1992.

Boycko, Maxim, Andrei Shleifer and Robert Vishny, *Privatising Russia*, Cambridge, MA: MIT Press, 1995.

Byrd, William A., "The Impact of the Two-Tier Plan/Market System in Chinese Industry", *Journal of Comparative Economics* 11, 295–308, 1987.

Byrd, William A., "Plan and Market in the Chinese Economy: A Simple General Equilibrium Model", *Journal of Comparative Economics* 13, 177–204, 1989.

Diamond, Douglas, and Philip Dybvig, "Bank Runs, Deposit Insurance and Liquidity," *Journal of Political Economy* 93, 401–419, 1983.

Farmer, Roger, *The Macroeconomics of Self-Fulfilling Prophecies*, Cambridge, MA: MIT Press, 1993.

Hammond, Peter J., and Jaime Sempere, "Limits to the Potential Gains from Economic Integration and Other Supply Side Policies", *The Economic Journal* 105, 1180–1204, 1995.

Khor, Hoe Ee, "China's Foreign Currency Swap Market", IMF Paper on Policy Analysis and Assessment, 94/1, International Monetary Fund, 1994.

Lau, Lawrence J., and Dae-Hee Song, "Growth versus Privatisation — An Alternative Strategy to Reduce the Public Enterprise Sector: The Experience of Taiwan and South Korea", Working Paper, Stanford, CA: Department of Economics, Stanford University, 1992.

Lau, Lawrence J., Yingyi Qian and Gerard Roland, "Pareto-Improving Economic Reforms through Dual-Track Liberalisation", *Economics Letters*, 1997, forthcoming.

McMillan, John, and Barry Naughton, "How to Reform a Planned Economy: Lessons from China", *Oxford Review of Economic Policy*, 8, Spring, 1992.

Murphy, Kevin, Andrei Shleifer and Robert W. Vishny, "The Transition to a Market Economy: Pitfalls of Partial Reform", *Quarterly Journal of Economics*, August, 1992.

Naughton, Barry, *Growing Out of Plan*, Cambridge University Press, 1995.

Qian, Yingyi, "Financial System Reform in China: Lessons from Japan's Main Bank System", in M. Aoki and H. Patrick (eds.), *The Japanese Main-Bank System: Its Relevancy for Developing and Transforming Economies*, Oxford University Press, pp. 552–591, 1994.

Qian, Yingyi, and Chenggang Xu, "Why China's Economic Reforms Differ: The M-form Hierarchy and Entry and Expansion of the Non-State Sector", *Economics of Transition* 1(2), 135–170, 1993.

Roland, Gerard, "The Role of Political Constraints in Transition Strategies", *Economics of Transition*, 1994.

Sachs, Jeffery, and Wing Thye Woo, "Structural Factors in the Economic Reforms of China, Eastern Europe, and the Former Soviet Union", *Economic Policy*, Spring 1994.

Wu, Jinglian, and Renwei Zhao, "The Dual Pricing System in China's Industry", *Journal of Comparative Economics* 11, 309–318, 1987.

Some Thoughts on China's Post-Deng Economy

John WONG
East Asian Institute
National University of Singapore

CHINA'S DYNAMIC GROWTH

The Chinese economy has experienced spectacular growth since it started economic reform and the open-door policy some 19 years ago. It chalked up an average annual growth rate of 9.7 percent during 1978–95, and double-digit rates for four consecutive years from 1992 to 1995. Growth for 1996 was still 9.7 percent, with inflation falling to 6.1 percent.

When an economy grows at 7 percent, it will double its GDP in about 10 years, so it is not simple for a gigantic economy like China to achieve such high growth for a sustained period. Japan did so in the 1950s and 1960s, followed by the four newly industrialised economies (NIEs) of South Korea, Taiwan, Hong Kong and Singapore during the 1970s and much of the 1980s (Table 1). Now as these economies have grown mature, they find it more difficult to repeat such phenomenal growth.

Beyond the rise in GNP, China's high economic growth is also reflected in other statistics. Thus, in 1996, China produced 1.4 billion tons of coal,

Table 1 China and Other Asia Pacific Economies

	Area (Thousand of sq. km)	Population Mid 1995 (Million)	GNP per-capita 1995 (US$)	PPP estimates of GNP per-capita, 1995 (US$)	Real GDP Growth (%)						Annual Export Growth (%)		Mfg export as % of total exports, 1993	Export-GDP Ratio, 1995 (%)	Total External Debt 1996 (US$ billion)
					1960–70	1970–80	1980–90	1994	1995	1996	1980–90	1990–95			
China	9,561	1,200.2	620	2,900	5.2	5.8	10.2	11.8	10.2	9.7	11.4	14.3	89	21.3	126.1
Japan	378	125.2	39,640	22,110	10.9	5.0	4.0	0.7	0.8	3.3	5.0	0.4	97	8.7	—
NIEs															
S. Korea	99	44.9	9,700	11,450	8.6	9.5	9.4	8.3	8.2	6.7	13.7	7.4	93	27.5	44.5
Taiwan	36	21.3	12,400	13,200	9.2	9.7	7.1	6.5	6.4	5.5	—	—	93	38.5	—
Hong Kong	1	6.2	22,990	22,950	10.0	9.3	6.9	5.5	5.0	5.1	15.4	15.3	93	120.9	—
Singapore	1	3.0	26,730	22,770	8.8	8.5	6.4	10.1	8.2	7.0	11.0	12.2	80	141.3	—
ASEAN															
Brunei	6	0.3	(21,000)	NA	NA	NA	NA	NA	NA	NA	NA	NA	NA	NA	—
Indonesia	1,905	193.3	980	3,800	3.9	7.6	6.1	7.4	7.5	7.5	5.3	21.3	53	22.9	108.0
Malaysia	330	20.1	3,890	9,020	6.5	7.8	5.2	8.5	9.2	8.5	10.9	12.9	65	86.8	29.0
Philippines	300	68.6	1,050	2,800	5.1	6.3	1.0	4.3	5.5	5.9	2.9	10.2	76	23.6	43.5
Thailand	513	58.2	2,740	7,540	8.4	7.2	7.6	8.5	8.8	6.5	14.3	21.6	72	33.8	75.0
Vietnam	332	73.5	240	—	—	—	—	—	8.5	9.0	—	—	—	—	30.8

Sources: *World Development Report* 1997 and earlier years; for Taiwan, *The Statistical Yearbook of the Republic of China* 1996; and ADB, *Asian Development Outlook 1996 and 1997*.

490 million tons of grain and 101 million tons of steel, ranking as the world's largest producer of all three items. It also manufactured 21 million colour TV sets, 9.3 million refrigerators and 1.5 million automobiles in the same year.[1] Of course, one needs to bear in mind that China is such a huge country with a population of over 1.2 billion so all its statistical aggregates are inevitably in jumbo numbers. China is the world's largest food producer simply because China has the world's largest number of mouths to feed!

If one takes a look at China's external economic activities (which involve foreign partners and, hence, more reliable economic data), one would find equally impressive results. Thus, China's exports in 1996 amounted to US$151 billion (over 80 percent being manufactured products), or to about six times higher than that of India. This ranks China as the world's eleventh largest exporter. On the import side, in 1996, China was a market for US$140 billion worth of goods. China's domestic market today is actually more open than Japan's and South Korea's at their comparable stages of economic development.

During the past few years, China has been the world's most highly favoured destination for foreign investors, with the actual amount of total foreign investment rising from US$11 billion in 1992 to US$28 billion in 1993, US$34 billion in 1994, US$38 billion in 1995 and a further US$42 billion in 1996, even though part of China's foreign direct investment is its own capital "round tripped" back to China via Hong Kong. Furthermore, China's foreign reserves in early 1997 stood at a hefty US$120 billion, the second largest in the world.

In October 1995, the Fifth Plenary Session of the 14th Central Committee of the Chinese Communist Party (CCP) adopted the Ninth Five-Year Plan (1996–2000) and the Long-term Vision of China's Economic and Social Development for 2010. It is envisaged that China's real per-capita GNP by the year 2000 will have quadrupled from the 1980 level, despite the addition of over 300 million more population. China

[1]See "Statistical Communique on the Economic and Social Development of China in 1996", *Jingji Cankou Bao* (Economic Reference News, Beijing, 4 April 1997).

will then have reached the *xiao-kang* (moderately affluent) level of development for having basically eliminated poverty and satisfied the basic needs of its people.[2] From 2000 to 2010, China expects to double its per-capita income so that, 15 years from now it will have developed into a middle-income economy.

IS HIGH GROWTH SUSTAINABLE?

It is clear that China has become the world's most successful "transitional economy" in terms of both dynamic growth and transforming its economic system. Indeed, China's economic reform has gone so far that the process cannot be reversed regardless of the outcome of the post-Deng power struggle. The next question can then be posed: Is China's dynamic economic growth sustainable?

To begin with, it is not possible for any economy to repeat a double-digit rate of growth year after year without getting overheated or running into physical and economic bottlenecks. But considering the historical pattern of China's past economic growth and the existing structural conditions of China's economy, one can be reasonably optimistic about China's future growth potential.

China's dynamic economic growth can indeed be easily analyzed from both demand and supply sides. In terms of technical explanations, China's high economic growth on the demand side stems from its high levels of domestic investment, being matched by equally high levels of domestic savings. According to the Asian Development Bank, China's average gross domestic investment during 1981–90 was 30.5 percent of its GDP while its average gross domestic savings was 30.8 percent. In 1993, for instance, when China had 13.4 percent record growth, its gross domestic investment was 43.5 percent while its gross domestic savings was 41.5 percent, being

[2]For a more detailed discussion of the concept of *Xiaokang*, see John Wong, *Xiao-kang: China's Concepts of Socio-Economic Development*, IEAPE Background Brief No.101 (Singapore, 14 September 1996), 22 pages.

among the highest in the world. In the East Asian NIEs, their past high growth has been similarly due to their high levels of savings and investment.

China's enormous needs for infrastructural investment like transportation and communications, and ports and airports are well known. For instance, China is planning to build 60 new airports and upgrade 25 existing ones. Guangdong province alone has 8 or 9 new airports, either newly completed or are still under construction.

Apart from investment, China's future economic growth can also be boosted by rising consumption. With a moderately affluent middle class of 20–30 million, mainly in urban areas including numerous small towns, China's appetite for consumption goods is similarly enormous. In the rural areas, millions of peasants are still craving for basic household consumer durables like TVs.

Viewed from the supply side, China's economic growth can also be sustained on its own by rising labour force and increasing productivity. As it has happened to Japan and South Korea before, growth of productivity is associated with the shift of labour from low-productivity agriculture to high-productivity manufacturing. In China, the rural sector is a huge reservoir of millions of underemployed labour (i.e. "rural disguised unemployment").

One can, therefore, be justifiably optimistic about the overall growth prospects of the Chinese economy over the medium and long term. In short, if the historical high growth processes of East Asian economies can be of a general guide, the medium-term rate of growth for China's economy should be at 7–8 percent per year.

The development of the Chinese economy is in many ways quite similar to the past growth pattern of the East Asian NIEs. But unlike the NIEs, China is a vast country with a huge resource base and a huge domestic market. China virtually has the whole continent to itself to develop. At present, most of China's economic growth has stemmed from its special economic zones and the coastal provinces, and has yet to spread out to the vast interior. Therefore, it will take a long time for China to exhaust its total development potential.

It stands to reason to argue that in the long run, the Chinese economy has got to grow mainly on domestic demand, quite unlike the smaller NIEs whose economic growth has to be mainly propelled by export growth or external demand. Since the start of economic reform in 1978, China's exports have been growing at the average annual rate of 17 percent. The world market simply cannot continue to absorb such a growing onslaught of labour-intensive manufactured exports. But it is fortunate for China that its sheer size and diversity would provide sufficient internal dynamics to generate its own growth in the long run.

OVERCOMING PROBLEMS AND CONSTRAINTS

Whether or not China can realise its huge growth potential depends critically on how it will come to grips with a number of problems and constraints.

Population and Human Resource Problems

China's population growth has been slowing down considerably from the average annual rate of 1.5 percent during 1980–90 to 1.2 percent during 1990–94 as a result of the successful implementation of its "one-child policy". Accordingly, China's total fertility rate came down from 2.5 in 1980 to 1.8 in 1995, which is slightly below the replacement level of fertility, indicating that China's population growth momentum is slowing down.[3] But it also means that the population has started its ageing process, the effect of which will increasingly be felt at the turn of this century. This will bring changes to China's labour force structure and pose an ultimate constraint on the continuing development of labour-intensive industry in the longer run.

[3]World Bank, *World Development Report 1996*.

On the quality aspects of population, as can be seen from Table 2, China's human resource development is among the weakest in East Asia. Only 2 percent of the relevant age-group in China are receiving tertiary education compared to 42 percent in Korea and 45 percent in Taiwan. About two-thirds of the 220,000 or so Chinese students sent abroad for studies have not returned to China. This will in time pose a problem to China's efforts to restructure and upgrade its economy into more skill-intensive and higher value-added activities. In short, China's human resource gaps can well operate to moderate its long-term growth potential.

Unfinished Reform Constraints

In 1994 China carried out a comprehensive package of economic reforms. In the areas of taxation and foreign exchange, the reform has been quite successful. However, progress in respect of state-owned enterprise (SOE) reform and the financial sector reform is still falling short of their targets.[4]

To realise the objectives of its Ninth Five-Year Plan (1996–2000), China will have to complete the reform of its SOE sector. But this will be an enormously difficult undertaking. In 1978, SOEs accounted for 78 percent of China's total industrial output. By 1995, the figure declined sharply to only 33 percent. But the relative decline of the SOE sector over the years merely reflects the dynamic expansion of the non-sector, which includes township and village enterprises (TVEs) and various forms of individual enterprises and foreign ventures, rather than the government having successfully tackled the SOE problem.

Indeed, despite its relative shrinkage, the SOE sector remains large in size and in terms of employment. In 1995, there were 117,000 or so industrial SOEs, of which 14,000 were considered "large and medium"; together they provided 55 percent of all urban employment. Most SOEs are engaged in

[4]For a further discussion of China's overall economic reform progress, see John Wong, "Assessing China's Economic Reform Progress in 1994", *JETRO China Newsletter* (Tokyo, No. 114, January–February 1995).

Table 2 China and Other Asia Pacific Economies: Social Indicators

	GNP per capita, 1995 US$	Total fertility rate, 1995 (%)	Life expectancy at birth (years) 1995	Infant mortality rate, 1995 (per 1000 births)	Population per doctor, 1993	Adult illiteracy 1995 (%)	Percentage of age group enrolled in education 1993			Human Development Index (1994)	
							Primary (Male)	Secondary (Male)	Tertiary (All)	HDI*	World Ranking
China	620	1.9	69	34	645	19	120	60	4	0.626	108
Japan	39,640	1.5	80	4	609	5	102	95	30	0.940	7
NIEs											
South Korea	9,700	1.8	72	10	855	5	100	93	48	0.890	32
Taiwan	12,400	1.5	74	5	802	8	102	95	45	—	—
Hong Kong	22,990	1.2	79	5	845	8	—	—	21	0.914	22
Singapore	26,730	1.7	76	4	722	9	—	—	30	0.900	26
ASEAN											
Brunei	(21,000)	—	—	—	—	—	—	—	—	—	—
Indonesia	980	2.7	64	51	7,028	16	116	48	10	0.668	99
Malaysia	3,890	3.4	71	12	2,302	17	93	56	—	0.832	98
Philippines	1,050	3.7	66	39	9,689	5	—	—	26	0.672	60
Thailand	2,740	1.8	69	35	4,425	6	98	38	19	0.833	59
Vietnam	240	3.1	68	41	2,491	6	—	—	2	0.557	121
Average of low-income countries	430	3.2	63	69	—	34	112	—	—	—	—
Average of middle-income countries	2,390	3.0	68	39	—	18	105	64	—	—	—

*Human Development Index combines life expectancy, educational attainment and income indicators to give a composite measure of human development.

Sources: *World Development Report 1997*; Asian Development Bank, *Key Indicators of Developing Asian and Pacific Countries 1996*; *Human Development Report 1994*; and *Taiwan Statistical Data Book 1997*; and national sources.

raw materials production and heavy industry, including a wide range of capital-intensive industries which have to operate on the economies of scale and are shunned by TVEs or foreign ventures. Furthermore, the bulk of China's basic industrial raw materials and intermediate products are produced by the SOEs.

China has started to compile its own equivalent to the "Fortune's 500 largest enterprises", and most of them are essentially SOEs, including the annual "best performers". So are those enterprises which have been listed as "H" shares (or "Red Chips") on the Hong Kong Stock Exchange. Therefore, in the words of Secretary-General Jiang Zemin, the SOE sector still "controls the lifeline of the national economy".[5]

Notwithstanding some successful individual SOEs, the overall performance of the SOE sector has remained consistently weak, fundamentally because they still operate under a kind of "soft budget constraints". In the first half of 1996, for instance, 49 percent of China's industrial SOEs were reported to be in the red.[6] According to the State Planning Commission chief, Chen Jinhua, the problem was even more serious as he actually put the figure of loss-making SOEs in 1996 as 75 percent.[7] For China's SOEs operating under the existing half-reformed economy, with their input and output not fully subjected to the free market, it could be quite meaningless to speak of their "profit and loss".

Regardless of the real extent of the SOE losses and their real causes, China's SOE sector without doubt has continued to cause serious problems for the Chinese economy. First, an ailing SOE sector controlling a disproportionately large share of resources badly distorts the whole economy and is a classic case of misallocation of resources. Second, this sector has actually become an obstacle for the reform efforts of the other sectors, particularly the financial sector. When the SOEs were making losses, the state banks had to bail them out, leading to an accumulation of too many bad loans for the state banks. And the problem of bad debt, in turn, hinders banking reform.

[5]"Jiang analyses troubles faced by State firms", *China Daily* (Beijing, 4 March 1997).
[6]"China's economy was stable in first half", *Asian Wall Street Journal* (22 July 1996).
[7]"A guiding hand for China's market", *Asia Times* (Bangkok, 17 January 1997).

In recent years, there has been no lack of open debate among Chinese scholars and officials on how best to reform the SOE sector. The Chinese government has also been quite flexible in experimenting with various reform strategies. Prior to 1993, the focus was placed on improving enterprise governance such as greater managerial autonomy and greater accountability of enterprises. More recently, especially after the enactment of the new Company Law, greater emphasis has been placed on "corporatisation" by converting SOEs (especially the larger ones) into "shareholding companies", the Chinese version of gradual privatisation.

The World Bank has recently recommended additional policy initiatives, which include promoting greater enterprise competition, phasing out easy access to government finance and subsidies to SOEs, cutting off the enterprises' direct links with government bureaus, and transferring enterprise-based welfare and social services to municipal governments.[8] These policy measures are no doubt more effective, albeit also more radical. But the present post-Deng leadership, with their penchant for stability, is clearly in no political mood for a "big bang" approach which requires implementing all the reform measures in full.

Beijing's current policy of reforming the SOEs is to concentrate on 1,000 large SOEs, based on the so-called *Zhua-da fang-xiao* or "managing the larger SOEs and letting go the smaller ones." Admittedly, it is a very cautious strategy, calling for a gradual approach. The Chinese leadership is well aware of the larger political and social risks involved in reforming the SOEs. Prior to the provision of a new social safety net or social security reform, any radical attempt to transform the SOEs by subjecting them to the necessary "hard budget constraints" ran the risk of throwing out millions of redundant workers on the street and create social unrest.

As the crucial banking and SOE reforms (which are actually interdependent), have yet to achieve important breakthroughs, the government's prime objective of establishing a market-based macroeconomic management system remains unfulfilled. This means that the Chinese economy, without the usual built-in macroeconomic stabilisers,

[8]World Bank, *China: Reform of State-Owned Enterprises* (21 June 1996).

will continue to experience instability. But until the transition to a full market economy is completed, China will have to pay for the inefficiency of a partially-reformed economy.

Institutional Constraints

The major challenge faced by China today is not just to "transform" its economic system, but also to "modernise" its institutional structure. China's existing institutional setup and political system were developed primarily to serve the socialist economy based on central planning and dominated by the CCP. They are clearly inappropriate for the market economy.

Liberal distracters would hastily jump to the conclusion that for political reform China must necessarily go for a Western style of democracy. This is quite unwarranted in the East Asian tradition, which has followed instead the sequence of "development first, democratisation later". South Korea's industrial take-off took place under a military dictatorship, Taiwan's under martial law, and Hong Kong's under colonial rule.

Not surprisingly, the Chinese leadership takes the view that any drastic political transformation like a full democratisation is plainly unrealistic for China at its present stage of development: it will simply bring about more chaos (*luan*), particularly if the democratic experiments in several Asian countries can serve as a guide. Nor will political democracy necessarily facilitate China's present economic growth and social progress.

At the same time, however, a Marxist-Leninist state is fundamentally incompatible with a functioning market system. Market forces, operating on their own, only recognise economic signals, not the so-called "Four Cardinal Principles" of the CCP. Either the free market process of economic development would eventually undermine the Marxist-Leninist state or the rigid Marxist-Leninist system would resist crucial changes, the ultimate result of which would be a half-reformed market system, with all its well-known inefficiencies, as mentioned earlier. Hence the CCP must adapt and change.

Assuming that no ruling party is willing to share power on its own volition, the most formidable challenge for the CCP is how to master the political skill to manage institutional changes without losing its total political legitimacy. On the one hand, the CCP has to step up institutional and political reform to facilitate the development of the "socialist market economy"; but on the other, it has to ensure that those changes would not undermine its own rule. Admittedly, this is a highly delicate business, which will test the statecraft of the future CCP leadership.

First of all, for the CCP to retain power, it obviously has to renew itself by attracting more younger and better educated members. To achieve this, it will have to de-emphasise the importance of the class background for its membership and to aim at transforming itself into a modern, development-oriented political organisation based on meritocracy rather than ideological dogma. An authoritarian regime dominated by a ruling party with a modern and pragmatic outlook can still foster economic development; but one with a rigid ideology cannot.

It has now become clear that rapid economic and social changes in China have already led to a serious decay in the CCP's local organisations, especially in the rural areas. This is inevitable once the CCP loses its original revolutionary ideological fervour amidst the spread of prosperity and materialism. One possible scenario in the post-Jiang Zemin period is that the CCP may split into factions. With China getting more developed and the population better educated, it may be possible that some factions break away from the CCP to assume a new label such as social democrats.

In the meantime, China experts are closely watching if the forthcoming 15th Party Congress in the second part of 1997 will reveal any signs of significant changes. For the more likely shape of China's future political system, some China scholars foresee the gradual weakening of the CCP's authority along with the erosion of the state's direct control over the economy and society. In future, even if the CCP continues to remain an important institution, it may not be possible for it to retain its dominance over the overall political system. Rather, the Party, the military, the provincial and municipal bureaucracies, the people's assemblies, and the central economic bureaucracies will all compete in a largely peaceful manner for supremacy. "None of these institutions is likely to emerge as a clear victor, resulting in a complex system of several overlapping yet competing centres of power, with the relative power of each institution varying over time and from place to place."[9]

Whatever is the more likely scenario, successful economic development will eventually bring about significant political pluralisation. In the short run, however, the CCP cannot renounce its Marxist doctrines without immediately losing its own legitimacy, as happened in East Europe. Therefore, the present post-Deng leadership has to be extremely cautious in managing its political reform, perhaps initially more in the nature of improving the "system of government" like separating the Party from the government.

This will in turn pave the way for the reform of the existing "cadre system", with professional civil servants and technocrats gradually replacing the old type "socialist bureaucrats", who are appointed by the Party's organisation department and not by open recruitment based on competition. The role played by technocrats in managing successful economic development in the East Asian NIEs is well known to the Chinese leadership, and hence their recent stress on the importance of civil service reform.

All these political changes may ultimately weaken the CCP's monopoly of power. But at the same time, the CCP is also buying time as the resultant improvement in administrative efficiency and government performance will also help the CCP to stay in power. The potential gain in popularity as a successful moderniser may well offset the loss of its old legitimacy. In the process, a lot still depends on whether or not the top leadership possesses the political skills in managing those changes.

In the meantime, the other aspects of institutional changes involving legal reforms are being stepped up with strong official blessings. All modern states have clear rules and regulations to set out the limits of authority and to define the general behaviour of market participants. It is well known

[9]Michael Okensberg, "China's Political Picture", *JETRO China Newsletter* (No. 120, January–February 1996), p. 2.

that the absence of the rule of law is the weakest link of the Chinese political system due to the Chinese tradition of the "rule of man". Needless to say, a stronger and more transparent legal framework, which reduces transaction costs as well as rent-seeking and corruption activities, for instance, is infinitely more conducive to business and foreign investment.

Since 1976, China has enacted 310 laws and decisions concerning legal matters; promulgated over 700 regulations; and issued over 4,000 administrative rules.[10] Initially, most of the new laws and regulations were related to foreign trade and foreign investment. But recently, efforts were directed at strengthening the legal system, e.g. the recent introduction of the revised Criminal Law. Whereas Mao's China was marked by the absence of lawyers, China today boasts 100,300 full-time lawyers.[11]

Legal reform, however, goes beyond the simple process of law making or setting up law courts. It has to build up an effective legal infrastructure with an independent judiciary (i.e. one that is free from the Party control). Furthermore, China, as primarily a Confucian state with no Greco-Roman legal traditions, needs to undertake greater efforts to foster the necessary "legal culture".

Again, legal reform is not without its political risk to the CCP. The end result of the legal reform could also lead to the weakening of the communist rule, as it means that the Party can no longer remain above the law. The climax of the legal reform will be reached when the CCP agrees to rewrite a new constitution for China, which will remove all its special privileges. All in all, political and institutional changes will hasten the emergence of some kind of democracy in China.

Social Constraints

As China shares the mainstream East Asian cultural tradition of Confucianism, it obviously has similar inherent social capability to sustain

[10] "New Achievements in our Legal System", *Renmin Ribao* (People's Daily) (Beijing, 1 April 1997).

[11] "Legal System Develops Apace", *Beijing Review* (10–16 March 1987).

economic development as the other East Asian NIEs. For the Chinese people in general, there is no lack of such growth-inducing social traits as "savings ethics", "learning ethics" and other similar behaviour patterns that can foster economic growth.[12]

On the other hand, China's rapid economic growth in recent years has given rise to a lot of "negative social externalities", from rising social expectations and widespread social envy to rising crime, which have begun to worry the Chinese leadership. A sense of a general "moral crisis" seems to be sweeping China. To be sure, such a moral crisis is also prevalent (or actually worse) in other transitional economies like Russia and several East European countries. How far does it represent a temporary phenomenon? Will it go away by itself once these socialist countries have completed their economic and social transition?

Most China experts take the view that many of those negative social developments may create frictions in the economic growth process, but they will not, on their own, be serious enough to disrupt the economic development process. The Chinese authorities understandably place a high priority on maintaining social order, on which crucially hinge economic growth and economic reform. It is often the case that the best way to deal with the by-products of rapid economic growth is to continue with rapid economic growth, which can generate more resources to deal with social problems.

Take the case of employment. Between 1978 and 1995, China's labour force increased by 287 million, 73 percent of whom were employed in manufacturing and services. This means that as a result of high economic growth since the reform, a majority of all new entrants into the labour force found productive employment outside of agriculture. If the Chinese economy were to grow at 8 percent or 9 percent a year, a lot of problems like unemployment could be taken care of.

[12]For a more detailed discussion of the role of Confucian values in economic growth in East Asia, see John Wong, "Promoting Confucianism for Socioeconomic Development: The Singapore Experience", in Tu Wei-ming (ed.), *Confucian Traditions in East Asian Modernity* (Cambridge, Harvard University Press, 1996).

However, there are other critical problems which will create strains in Chinese society even with continuing high economic growth. First, the leadership must mobilise all its institutional resources to combat corruption, which is rampant in China today. Economic reform in all transitional economies generates opportunity for excessive rent seeking, profiteering and open graft and corruption. The problem is getting so serious that it threatens to undermine the social fabric of the country as well as the moral authority of the CCP.

So far there has been a lot of official rhetoric from the Chinese leaders on how to combat corruption, however; they have yet to demonstrate a determined political will to tackle this issue. The Chen Xitong affair is manifestly more of an outcome of high-level power struggle than a deliberate attempt by the leadership to crack down on widespread corrupt practices of its high officials.[13]

More than a mere social evil, corruption is actually an anathema to economic growth as it increases transaction costs and reduces efficiency. Rampant corruption also slows down trade and investment. All the four NIEs have made serious attempts to tackle the problem of corruption. China too must manage this problem properly before it can develop into another NIE in future.

Secondly, another macro social issue with serious economic and political consequences is the growing income disparity between the fast-growing coastal zones and the less developed interior provinces, between urban and rural areas, or between industrial and agricultural sectors. The recent Ninth Five-Year Plan, 1996–2000, has emphasised the need for a new development strategy to narrow the various development gaps in China, indicating that Beijing can no longer shrug off this problem.

Underlying the regional development gaps is the deep-rooted inter-regional political rivalry on the one hand, and the political tension between the centre and provinces on the other. Both can pose a threat to China's national unity. Some provinces have from time to time undertaken

[13]Chen Xitong is Party Secretary of Beijing and a member of the Politburo. Chen is so far the highest official to be disgraced for corruption.

unilateral measures to protect their vested economic interests by obstructing the interflow of resources (e.g. inter-provincial "trade wars"), and this affects the efficient operation of the Chinese economy as a single market.[14] Suffice it to say that China needs greater political and economic integration to boost its economic growth, and this in turn depends on closing the regional development gaps.[15]

Thirdly, China has to step up the social security reform, which was actually one of the unfulfilled key areas in China's 1994 reform package. As pointed out earlier, the crucial SOE reform could not take off basically due to the lack of a new social safety net. China's old social security system is based on the *danwei* (work unit), which was developed for the highly regulated society under Mao's time. But economic reform has since eroded the *danwei* system and needs to be replaced by a new social security system to suit the operation of a market economy. A new social security system is needed to deal with such critical problems as labour mobility and the ageing population.

Resource Constraints

China is admittedly a huge country with a vast and diverse natural resource base. But China also has a huge population of 1.2 billion to support.

[14]According to a recent World Bank study, China's economic fragmentation is very serious, as manifested in its lower degree of industrial specialisation and market integration as compared to the EC and USA (The World Bank, *China: Internal Market Development and Regulation*, Washington, DC, 1994).

[15]According to a recent study, China's recent economic reform and economic growth have not actually seriously undermined the political power of the centre, as Beijing, through its highly developed political and bureaucratic controls systems (e.g. reshuffling and rotating top provincial officials), has continued to exert effective compliance from these provinces. So long as China remains politically integrated, regional development disparity may be a source of further economic growth. See Yasheng Huang, *Inflation and Investment Controls in China: The Political Economy of Central-Local Relations during the Reforming Era* (New York, Cambridge University Press, 1996).

Continuing economic growth in future will certainly stretch China's natural resources to the limits, giving rise to acute supply and demand imbalances.

Agriculture has been a constant worry to the Chinese leadership, especially after a 2.6 percent drop in grain production in 1994. Is China "starting to lose the capacity to feed itself", as recently warned by the American environmentalist Lester Brown?[16] There are at present no concrete signs that China is heading for a full-blown food crisis, particularly following two consecutive years of bump harvests.

However, following Brown's recent sensational statement, Chinese specialists have recently re-assessed China's agricultural resource base and its technological foundation, and they have concluded that China by and large will be able to feed itself.[17] China is no longer a "basket case", where the demand for food is calculated in terms of straight per-capita calorie intake from whatever source. Much of the grain demand projection is complicated by the estimates of income elasticity of demand for food (the expected shift from cereals to meat and dairy products as per-capita income rises) and the use of grain as animal feed. However, even if China could feed its people in the crude sense of the term, the government still has

[16]Brown argues that with China's population growing by 14 million a year and increasing meat consumption amidst the rapidly shrinking croplands, by 2030 China could face a serious grain shortfall of 384 million tons or at least 263 million tons, which would exceed the world's entire grain exports of about 200 million tons in 1993. Lester R. Brown, "Question for 2030: Who will be able to feed China?", *International Herald Tribune* (28 September 1994) and "When China's scarcities become the world's problem", *ibid.* (29 September 1994).

[17]China's agricultural economists have since made more realistic demand projections, which show that China's import demand will rise steadily. By 2000, imports are expected to reach 40 million tons, which will impact the world grain market by ending the historical decline in grain prices but will not disrupt the world grain market itself. After 2000, China's grain imports are expected to stabilise on account of China's declining population growth and increases in grain supply from higher productivity. See Justin Yifu Lin, Jikun Huang and Scott Rozelle, "China's Food Economy: Past Performance and Future Trends", paper for the OECD Conference on "China in the 21st Century: Long-Term Global Implications" (Paris, 8–9 January 1996).

cause for real concern over the current state of Chinese agriculture, not least because of frequent outbursts of peasant discontent.[18]

As China is the world's largest producer of grain, it can also be said that China's food problem can also become a world food problem. At present, Chinese grain prices have already exceeded international levels — Chinese rice price is about 50 percent and wheat price 10 percent higher. China has continued to make use of the comparative advantage principle of international trade to import relatively cheaper food like wheat (6 million tons in 1996) to ease domestic distribution. China certainly has sufficient foreign exchange to import a greater amount of food. However, China's sheer population size militates against a higher food import dependency.

If China were to import 5 percent of its present consumption needs, this would be about the level of the total grain trade of the EU; and if China were to import 10 percent, it would seriously disrupt the world grain market! The total world grain trade is about half of China's total grain production.[19] In other words, China must maintain its high level (not necessarily 100 percent) of food self-sufficiency, as it is simply too big to specialise in manufactured exports and import food, as in the case of Japan or the NIEs.

Chinese agriculture is facing a number of daunting challenges. China's 1.2 billion population will increase a further 200 million by 2010, and some 300 million by 2025. With continuing urbanisation and rising per-capita income and hence changes in food consumption patterns, China will have to increase its grain production from its present level of 490 million tons to well over 600 million tons by 2010. And the increased production has to be done with no substantial increase but more likely a decline in arable land.[20]

[18]John Wong, "Why is the Chinese Government so Concerned about Agriculture?", IEAPE Background Brief (Singapore, No. 87, 18 May 1995).

[19]For the relevant grain trade data, see US Department of Agriculture, *Grain: World Markets and Trade* (Washington, D.C., January 1997).

[20]See Justin Yifu Lin, Jikun Huang and Scott Rozelle, "China's Food Economy: Past Performance and Future Trends", paper presented at the OECD Forum "China in the 21st Century: Long-Term Global Implications", (Paris, 8–9 January 1996).

For an effective long-term solution of the agricultural problem, however, the government has to properly manage agricultural development amidst rapid industrial growth — the agricultural sector is set to decline once industrialisation gets under way, e.g. the agricultural labour force has declined from 71 percent in 1978 to 53 percent in 1995. There should be a balanced agricultural development strategy which will not squeeze farmers too hard while promoting agricultural productivity by stepping up technological progress.

In comparison, China's energy sector is giving out an early warning signal, even though energy is less important than agriculture in socio-economic terms.

China's present consumption of energy on per-capita basis is still very low, e.g. its per-capita energy use for 1994 was only 647 kg (oil equivalent), compared to 3,825 kg for Japan and 3,000 kg for South Korea. Also, China's total energy demand grew at the annual rate of only 5.5 percent during 1980–90, which is significantly below its GDP growth.[21] However, further economic growth in future will certainly raise China's overall energy consumption level, with serious implications for the world energy market because of China's huge demand potential. China's share in world primary energy demand will increase from 8.9 percent in 1993 to 10.9 percent for the year 2000.[22]

Despite being the world's sixth largest oil producer (155 million tons in 1996 or about 5 percent of the world's oil output), China has become a net importer of oil since 1993, and its crude oil import in 1996 amounted to 22 million tons. China may have to import 50 million tons of crude oil a year by 2000. Beyond 2000, the situation will depend on China's investment in oil and gas exploitation.[23]

[21]World Bank, *World Development Report 1996*.

[22]See Robert Priddle, "China's Long-Term Energy Outlook", in OECD Forum: "China in the 21st Century: Long-Term Global Implications" (Paris, 8–9 January 1996).

[23]China is likely to be a major player on the world oil market. Recently, China signed a US$4 billion deal with Kazakstan and another US$1.2 billion deal with Iraq, in order to secure China's oil supplies in the 21st century. "Giant oil deals move China onto world stage", *Asia Times* (Bangkok, 6 June 1997).

Similarly, China's dynamic economic growth is already exerting a lot of pressure on China's existing water and land resources as well as on its environment. The Chinese themselves will bear the main costs of pollution: only about 20 percent of industrial waste and 15 percent of sewage flowing into China's rivers are treated. But there is also considerable cross-border pollution due to China's heavy reliance on coal for most of its energy needs. In many parts of China, airborne levels of sulphur dioxide in winter have exceeded World Health Organisation guidelines.

Accordingly, the Chinese government has started to pay serious attention to the environmental issue. But its investment in pollution control is only a small fraction of government expenditure; and enforcement is lax, especially in the rural areas. In the long run, China's economic development is much like a race, whereby new resources have to be quickly created so that the government can use them to cope with such by-products of development as pollution.

Muddling Through?

Each of the above constraints presents a formidable challenge to the Chinese leadership, and they all can, in varying degrees, operate to moderate China's long-term growth capability. It is not certain as to how the Chinese leadership will respond exactly to the above problems and constraints, or how long it will take them to overcome those problems. Many China experts take the view that China will somehow "muddle through".

The point is that China's dynamic economic growth can slow down but it cannot be stifled. Given continuing peace and stability, China will ultimately get there and realise its major economic development objectives, certainly by the first quarter of the 21st century if not by 2015. The following scenario may be instructive:[24]

[24]This simple projection is based on the author's paper "Medium and Long-Term Prospects of PRC's Economic and Social Development", submitted for the "PRC 2020 Project", which was sponsored by China's State Planning Commission and the Asian Development Bank. A workshop for all the experts was held in Beihai, Guangxi, March 1997.

Post-Deng Development to 2000

China is undergoing the post-Deng political and economic transition in the next few years. Politically, the Jiang-centred leadership will consolidate itself, with continuing economic growth to boost its legitimacy. Economically, the leadership will put in place the institutional framework for the next phase of economic reform (which will be technically and politically more difficult) centring on the SOE problem. Legal reform will also be stepped up. Socially, China by 2000 will have reached the *xiao-kang* level of development for having basically eliminated poverty and satisfied the basic needs of its people. Internationally, China will get admitted into the World Trade Organisation (WTO), rendering the Chinese economy even more integrated with the world trade system.

A Full Market Economy by 2010

Major political, economic and social transformation will take place during this period, with all reform measures and institutional changes gearing towards the realisation of a full market economy. By 2010, China will have achieved modest affluence as a lower middle-income economy with per-capita income lying between that of today's Thailand (US$2,410) and Malaysia (US$3,800). Major reform obstacles like the SOEs' reform will have been overcome; and externally, China's economy will be fully integrated with the global economy. Politically, China will be governed by leaders with no previous socialist/revolutionary ideological background — all the former "red guards" of the Cultural Revolution will have retired.

An Economic Superpower by 2020

By 2020 China will become an upper middle-income economy with per-capita income very close to South Korea's level of today (US$8,260). In total GDP terms, however, China will be an economic superpower, with commensurate geopolitical influence regionally and globally. Sustainable development will be a major issue during this period, with China coming to grips with such critical problems as food, energy, natural resources and the environment, and it will carry an inevitable trade-off for lower growth. But how successfully China will come to grips with those problems carry tremendous regional and global implications.

China will also have to adjust to the economic and social requirements of an ageing population. Family structure, and value and belief systems will experience drastic changes.

It is therefore important for all international organisations to start engaging China now on all important global and regional issues. That is why Singapore and many other Asian countries support China's bid to join the WTO, so that China can learn to play by global rules.

China's New Paths for National Reemergence

WANG Gungwu
East Asian Institute
National University of Singapore

It is a great honour for me to be invited to address the Nobel Institute. The Peace Prize and your research done on behalf of nations to ensure peace have made Norway particularly sensitive to important world issues, especially in the years of increasing uncertainty since the end of the Cold War. Recent events have made it difficult to interpret the significance of what is happening around the world. My approach to the subject of China has been guided, and limited, by these wider concerns. On the other hand, China has had an amazing record of economic success for one and a half decades, while most of the world has struggled to show signs of growth. On the other hand, an apparent power vacuum among China's neighbours has encouraged the Chinese to turn their new wealth into a show of strength. Therefore, although I shall be talking about the unique example of an ancient civilisation that has become a potential power, I expect much of what I have to say to resonate elsewhere.

When talking about China, one tends to think only of the People's Republic of China (PRC). This is certainly understandable in the language of international relations, through which the PRC insists, and most members of the United Nations agree, that there is only one China; officially, that means the PRC. At the same time, it is accepted that this "one China" recognises the historical position of Taiwan as part of a divided China. In short, China has always been more than simply the PRC. In the near future, China will incorporate Hong Kong and Macau, and in one way or another, juristically or physically, may well include Taiwan sometime in the 21st century. Thus, the difference between China and the PRC lies largely in current usage. In Chinese eyes, China (Zhongguo or Zhonghua) can refer to a civilisation, a society, or a political entity. For Chinese people, it is both accurate and natural to include all of the People's Republic (or mainland China), the Republic of China on Taiwan, and Hong Kong-Macau (which I shall generally refer to as Hong Kong) as China. This has been confirmed by the fact that Hong Kong and Macau will very soon be part of China, and that the government of Taiwan always has considered and still considers the island to be part of China, albeit a temporarily separate part. Nevertheless, when the term "China" is used, the focus is on the PRC, especially in the context of its position in international relations.

It is also important to note that the Chinese have many words to describe themselves; these vary depending on who the different groups of people are, and on the different historical and geographical contexts in which they need to be identified. But in other languages, a single word suffices: "Chinese" in English and its equivalents in all the others. Thus, this one word is used loosely and widely. It is used as a translation of the many words in the Chinese language for the people, as well as various adjectival words and phrases describing everything that pertains to China. "Chinese" can refer to the written language. As the name of the people, the word describes one-fifth of the world's population. The word also includes millions of people of Chinese origin who do not reside in any part of China but have settled abroad, are foreign nationals, and may not speak the Chinese language at all. Thus, the word itself almost invariably needs a qualifying adjective, as in mainland Chinese, Taiwan Chinese, Hong Kong Chinese, overseas Chinese, and ethnic Chinese, or is itself used adjectivally, as in Chinese diaspora and Chinese American, for example. There is little doubt that the word "Chinese" is overworked.

In short, "Chinese" may merely refer to a national name, like Belgian or Norwegian; it could be construed in the same way as a word like "European" or "Westerner"; and, of course, it can refer to the many varieties of Chinese mentioned above. Obviously, this variable usage could be relevant with regard to China's position in international relations, especially when it is ambiguous or not clearly defined. Thus, it is important to account for the terms "China" and "Chinese", with due regard to each of their respective elements.

My other starting-point is that, despite the differences in geography and modern history that have divided China, there is a great depth and breadth in China's continuous cultural heritage. This China has also claimed that, in its undivided manifestation, it could be a country like other countries. It suggests that whenever it can speak and act as one such country, it expects to behave and be treated like other countries. During the 20th century, all three parts of China have been sharply separated, and at times the people of Taiwan and Hong Kong have been encouraged to behave as if they came from independent countries. In recent years, some of them, together with foreigners, have deliberately and habitually used the name "China" to apply only to the PRC. Sometimes, of course, this use of "China" is convenient shorthand, but it would be misleading if it were employed to suggest that Taiwan and Hong Kong are no longer parts of China.

During the past decade, however, relations between the three parts have become increasingly open and interdependent, and mainland China has joined both Taiwan and Hong Kong in seeking to be open to the rest of the world. Of course, the specific experiences of each part, whether in terms of its internal experiments or its external environment, have had clearly unique features. These experiences determine to a large extent the degree to which the three are open, and if any one of them is more willing than the others to resist global inter-dependence. However, there is no question that the PRC, Taiwan, and Hong Kong also have much in common. For example, during the 20th century, the following have been striking: the speed with which they have changed and seized opportunities; the spirit of defiance they each show when challenged by outsiders; and the propensity of their people to migrate, something that their respective governments have alternately forbidden and encouraged.

Thus, I use the term "China" here to include the PRC, Taiwan, and Hong Kong. However, we now increasingly encounter the term "Greater China" (*The China Quarterly*, Special Issue, no. 136, 1993). What does this mean? When we speak of Greater London or Greater Tokyo, no one is alarmed. The word "Great" in Great Britain does not conjure up images of expansion beyond the British Isles, although some of my Irish friends might object to the inclusion of any part of the island of Ireland. But when "Greater" is attached to large countries like India and China, questions are asked about their imperialist ambitions. In the 1930s, scholars referred to "Greater India", or ancient Hindu colonies in Southeast Asia, when they described Hindu-Buddhist influences in the region. There were objections to this usage, even among Indian scholars themselves, and the term was eventually dropped. Why, then, did a similar term, "Greater China", emerge during the late 1980s? The main reason, of course, is that people have narrowed the term "China" to mean the PRC. Also, developments since 1978 in all three parts of China have shown how readily they can achieve economic integration. With that possibility, it is natural to look at the three areas as a virtual economic entity again. But then, why not simply "China"? Why add the adjective "Greater"?

I have been skeptical of the term from the start and surprised by its persistent use. It seems important, therefore, to try to understand why it has attracted so much attention. This is, of course, a useful way for me to lead into the subject of these lectures — an examination of China's international position and future "great power" role through perceptions of China's historic empire, of a China-based civilisation, of China's ultimate nationhood, and of its divergent market economies.

The origins of "Greater China" may be found in the success of Deng Xiaoping's economic reforms in mainland China, coupled with the powerful economic performances of the Chinese entrepreneurs of Taiwan, Hong Kong, and Singapore. Tentative efforts were made to find terms that would highlight the remarkable developments in South China during the 1980s and connect them directly with, first, Hong Kong and then Taiwan. This is because the capital, business expertise, and skills came mainly from these two territories. The initial concept was largely Hong Kong-centered. Some notable earlier examples describing the increasing economic integration were the "China Economic Circle" (or "China Economic Zone"), the "China Economic Community", and even the "China Economic Sphere". Yet others introduced terms like "Entity" and "Commonwealth", and many began to add "Greater China" (*Da Zhonghua*) as an adjective before the various nouns. Unconsciously, these terms extended the concept to encompass all of China, or even all Chinese. But some terms were more modest, carefully restricting the idea to the three specific areas of Hong Kong, Taiwan, and South China, referring to a "potential Free Trade Area" and to the three as forming the "China Economic Triangle", the "South China Economic Zone", or even "Greater Hong Kong". And "Greater China" somehow became shorthand for some or all of these.

As "Greater China" became more widely used, first by business people and journalists and then by scholars at several major international conferences, various definitions were offered. The most practical and least alarming definition included only the original areas of Hong Kong, Taiwan, and South China. But in the excitement of creating such a striking image of China, other usages expanded the term to include all of the PRC, thereby unconsciously returning to the broader concept of China. Some went even further to include *all* ethnic Chinese settled around the world on the grounds that many of them have invested, and are investing, in all three areas of China and are therefore contributing to the enrichment of the PRC.

The main justification for "Greater China" has been the supposed economic integration of Hong Kong, Taiwan, and the coastal PRC. This is, of course, more apparent than real. The networks of relationships that have been built up in this region are both subtle and complex, and involve processes carried out through informal interactions between industrialists, financiers, and traders in all three areas. These interactions are a part of, and can hardly be separated from, the international interests of the entrepreneurs of Hong Kong, Taiwan, and, increasingly, the Mainland.

They are all dependent on the world's open markets and none of the links have to be specifically Chinese at all. Indeed, the success of both Hong Kong and Taiwan clearly depends on their access to the markets of North America and Western Europe.

But if the concept is extended to include the rest of mainland China, and especially if it includes the ethnic Chinese residing in foreign countries, it does become alarming and needs to be closely scrutinised. In the economic context of how "Greater China" evolved to include all of the PRC, it is different from the historic idea of China, and totally different from the original concept that was centered on Hong Kong. Far from looking only to Hong Kong and Taiwan, most areas of mainland China really look elsewhere for their external relationships. For example, East and North-central China look more readily toward South Korea and Japan; similarly, Northeast China looks toward the Russian Far East, Mongolia, and North Korea; and Northwest China toward the Muslim states of central Asia as well as Russia and Afghanistan. As for Western China (including Tibet), it leans toward Nepal, India, and Pakistan. And then there are the trading routes out of Southwest China, through Yunnan and Guangxi, which have already been linked closely to the economies of Burma, Laos, Thailand, and Vietnam. Surely, "Greater China" was never meant to cover all this.

Furthermore, extending Greater China to include all ethnic Chinese living in foreign countries raises even more problems. Eighty percent of all ethnic Chinese abroad, the Chinese diaspora, live in Southeast Asia. Since the majority of them are nationals of their respective countries, including them would certainly give the term "Greater China" imperialistic overtones in the region. The remaining 20 percent are spread widely throughout the world, but at least 2 million may be found in the Americas, the majority being Chinese-Americans and Chinese-Canadians. To have all these ethnic Chinese linked to a Greater China makes little economic or political sense. It would also create considerable difficulties for the economic freedom and viability of these people in their home countries, especially for those in Southeast Asia, and would undermine their need to identify with their adopted countries, to which they owe ultimate loyalty.

It is clear that some of the uses of "Greater China" are more emotive than others. In particular, if politicians and the media in Southeast Asia use the term to warn and frighten their own peoples about how Chinese economic power could lead to ultimate political dominance and control, there will be repercussions that could destabilise the region and have considerable impact on China's international relations. All the efforts of the overseas Chinese to show loyalty to their adopted countries would be suspect. Any suggestion of a vigorous and aggressive revival of Chinese power and wealth, and any use of "Greater China" to symbolise that rejuvenation, would disturb China's relations with its neighbours. The term could also be used by these neighbours as a warning of future Chinese imperialism and of the possible restoration of former imperial borders, and even as a reminder of the tributary system that China used to control its external relations for over two thousand years.

All these reminders of the past deserve attention when we look at China's international position today. But let me begin with the present economic dimensions on which the term "Greater China" was based, that is, with perceptions of what most Chinese seem prepared to recognise as the socialist market economy of the PRC. The relations that such an economy will have with more conventional economic developments elsewhere, and the possibility of its being any kind of model for others in the region, deserve our special attention.

Much has been written about China's position in international relations following the Chinese revolutions earlier this century and the transformations of the past decades. My lectures cannot hope to cover all of these controversial issues, which so many studies have raised. Instead I will focus mainly on two questions. For reasons of size, influence, and potential power, the PRC deserves much more attention than the other two parts of China. And because of the way I have framed my argument, my lectures will begin with the present before returning to the past to help us look at the future. This lecture deals with the impact of divergent economies. I ask whether the different experiences of the three parts of China can lead to a new model for the region and beyond. The next lecture will deal with the emergence of new frameworks for political and cultural change. To understand how these frameworks have promoted as well as inhibited change, it is necessary to look more closely at the past, from which we can explore some of the possibilities for a future Chinese way. By looking back as well as forward, we may derive some clearer perspectives that could link China's past with its future as a global power.

Both Chinese and foreigners have often asked why China is not a "normal" country; that is, why is China not a nation-state that behaves like most other countries? It seems clumsy in its dealings with other countries, inviting impatience with its seeming intransigence regarding various international issues, for example, its nuclear testing or trade disputes. It is seen alternatively as a civilisation, an empire, or a potential superpower. At times, the PRC is condemned as the last communist giant. At others, there are predictions of disaster and mainland China is seen as a precarious polity on the verge of crumbling into a group of fragmented and warring states. Or, China is considered an unstable hybrid, a strange creature with a socialist body, but parts of it dressed in capitalist clothes. There are numerous paradoxes and contradictions, all giving the impression of instability and the capacity to destabilise the region if not the whole world.

These different images, and the questions they beg, are found not only among those outside China, but also among those within it. We can usefully explore these images through descriptions of China that reflect the different ways the country is perceived by the Chinese themselves. The reactions of the Chinese to pressures from outside are then more readily understood. Views vary from those about the present to those about the past, and also include hopes for the future. Currently there are several layers of such perceptions. "Layers" suggests a chronological sequence, with the present on top and the past arranged in order below, but, just as historical events surface in our minds, each layer of the past can be conjured up whenever appropriate to any discourse. This is how Chinese people habitually make use of their past and how I intend to treat these layers. This does not imply, however, that any of these perceptions are shared by all Chinese. Not all layers may be found among every group of Chinese, nor do they all coexist in people's consciousness at any one time. Also, as is natural for a large and diverse people, each layer, regardless of its overall importance, could be dominant from some Chinese some of the time.

Socialist Market Economy

By divergent economies, I refer to two current terms: "socialist market economy" and "developing economies". The former arouses puzzlement and even scorn among Western and other economists and all those interested in economics or politics. It seems self-contradictory, and many have interpreted its use by the Chinese as a means of hiding their embarrassment that capitalism is now rampant in the country. It is also thought that the Chinese leaders do not understand modern economics and therefore use the term "market economy" incorrectly. But from all accounts, the leaders are perfectly serious about the concept of a socialist market economy that they have developed over the past 15 years, and they have tried to adhere to their interpretation of the term in the face of the many doubts expressed. For whatever reason the term may have been used, and however odd we may consider it to be, we should not underestimate the determination of the present leaders to develop this economic conoction successfully.

I have explained earlier why I begin with the present, with the most immediate issues of wealth and power that concern all Chinese. First, the Chinese face the challenge of socialism in the PRC, that is, the way its communist leaders want to maintain the ideals of socialism as an ideology for the state while developing the economy; they therefore have to deal with a market economy in transition. Second, they see the various parts of China competing with other developing economies, some more successfully than others, but none conforming to the expected norms. And, third, they wonder if a powerful and united China might formulate a universal model from the integration of socialist and capitalist ideals and means. By considering divergent economic solutions to basic problems of livelihood, could Chinese leaders develop a way to position China to play its rightful role in global affairs and thus establish a new basis for its future position in the world?

In less than a decade, the economic reforms of the PRC have transformed the country from a highly centralised planned economy to one that is learning from capitalist practices. There was nothing automatic or inevitable about the decision to carry out economic reforms without political reforms. There were other routes to radical change, and there were examples from central and Eastern Europe that Chinese economists did study closely. But in the late 1970s, partly in reaction to the consequences of the Cultural Revolution and partly because those consequences included the loosening of many of the instruments of central control, Deng Xiaoping decided to promote market reforms as the path to follow.

The Chinese Communist Party and the Beijing government had little choice but to seek reform. Without it, the country would have faced further economic disasters, threatening everything the party leaders had fought for. Even the collapse of the regime might have resulted. But the evidence is clear that the driving forces behind Deng Xiaoping's efforts were more positive than that. His zeal to bring modernity to China had not been diminished by his years in the wilderness. His dedication to a revolution to restore wealth and power to China remained strong. He declared, "We regard reform as a revolution" (from a conversation with Chancellor Helmut Kohl of West Germany, October 10, 1984). The lessons he learned from the mistakes of Mao Tse-tung had heightened his natural pragmatism. In addition, he was correct in believing that the people were deeply disappointed by the poverty in the PRC after 30 years of communism.

The idea that socialism brought betterment not only through a more equitable distribution of wealth, but also through its efficiency in creating more wealth, had been a promise that the people still expected the party to keep. I remember the stirring call by one party leader (An Gang, a former editor of *People's Daily*) at an international conference in 1979 that "socialism should make money", and how that was soon echoed as "get rich first" throughout the country, with the additional exhortation that socialism should be more successful than capitalism! This was when it was obvious that capitalist Hong Kong and Taiwan, the "little Chinas", were each producing greater wealth than their big brother.

The leaders who fought in the battlefields still believe that socialism is superior. But after the bitter and uncertain 30 years of experimentation following 1949, they now agree that learning from capitalism conforms to historical necessity. Capitalism is a stage that cannot be skipped on the way to socialism. It is hard, however, to know how many of the younger leaders still believe in this superiority. Insofar as the picture of capitalism remains that of 19th-century satanic mills and exploited workers, there certainly remains the belief that socialism is superior. But younger party members and intellectuals can now read about what capitalist countries have achieved during the past five decades — not only the obvious examples of Japan and the United States, but also the territories where millions of other Chinese live, Hong Kong and Taiwan. They can see how all of them have been able to raise the standard of living of the vast majority of their peoples. Many PRC leaders can also travel and see for themselves how competitive developments in industrial practices and innovations in financial institutions and managerial methods have made it possible for wealth creation to coexist with the principles of equitable distribution. They can see for themselves that elaborate welfare safety nets for the disadvantaged and disabled have ironically been most developed and successful in these capitalist societies. There is no contradiction in places like Hong Kong and Taiwan; on the contrary, there is actually a direct correlation between newly generated wealth and higher incomes for the working classes.

Nevertheless, despite many vigorous debates, most writings emanating from the PRC today reflect a loyalty to key Marxist principles. The Chinese Communist Party still dictates all analysis of social and political phenomena, even when the economics of the market have been accepted in key aspects of reform policies. Capitalism in its modern and mature form is now recognised as more pluralistic and flexible. It is also seen as more benign and a necessary means to an end. All the same, the official judgment still regards it as a force that will, in the long run, stand in the way of progress toward the socialist ideals that the revolutionaries lived and died for. But crude anti-capitalist rhetoric and righteous pronouncements are now rare. Instead, there is widespread acknowledgment of the strengths of capitalist organisations and the relevance of their skills and experiences for the revival and development of the Chinese economy. The examples of Japan, South Korea, and Taiwan (and cities such as Singapore and Hong Kong) have inspired a younger generation of economists as well as newly emerging private and semi-private sectors on the mainland, and provided lessons from which officials at all levels can learn. In every way possible under a rapidly changing economic system, the most enterprising people are responding to the extraordinary stimulus that Deng Xiaoping has released among them.

Indeed, it is this very speed of change, the bypassing of party and government structures, and the excitement generated by ongoing battles against ingrained bureaucratic habits, especially among the more enterprising officials in the provinces, that have alarmed the leaders in Beijing. It is not capitalism in the abstract that is threatening; it is the perception of a market economy, however modified, that will inevitably unleash social forces that have hitherto been under tight control. Every day, there is evidence that some of the worst features of the pre-1949 world have returned: unemployment, corruption, greed, selfishness, immorality, inequality, even dangers of runaway inflation. The textbooks say the revolution had put an end to these once and for all.

Thus, the perception of a successful market economy becoming less and less socialist hangs like a cloud over the recent triumphs. Ultimately, if mainland Chinese behave like the Chinese of Taiwan and Hong Kong, their economy could head toward a capitalism that would appeal to the young and ambitious, the newly rich and successful, the natural malcontents and rebels, the exploiters, and the potential traitors. How could the party then maintain its tight control? Parts of the outside world, especially the Western world, anticipate the inevitability of a radical change in the capacity to control everything centrally. Some are already portraying the political reforms of Taiwan as the necessary next step for the mainland to follow. In supporting the laws and freedoms of Hong Kong, they point to similar democratic reforms as essential to continued progress on the mainland. The Chinese experiences in the two smaller areas are expected to have a profound impact on the mainland.

The achievements of Deng Xiaoping's reforms have created a new volatile environment in which the hopes for ever better economic performance are matched by fears of social turmoil. The next generation of leaders urgently need to reinspire their people to believe that the socialist way to a market economy is the best road to socialism. For the past 15 years, they have enjoined their economists and policy advisers to define that road more clearly and convincingly. These loyal supporters have been asked to map out how to sustain such a socialist market economy without becoming capitalistic like Chinese Taiwan and Hong Kong. They must demonstrate, in addition, why such an economy is different from what social democrats in the West have been content to accept, that is, the various forms of mixed economies in so-called welfare states. The time has come for the leaders to stop, if I may use their words, "taking one step forward and looking around before taking another" and advancing as if they were, using their words again, "wading across a river by feeling for the rocks under the water" (Zhao Ziyang in January 1985). They still seem to be some way from convincing their people that they have found the right formula with which to enhance, and renew faith in, Marxism. But the perception remains that retaining the ideal of the socialist political order is essential to their particular variety of market economy.

Despite the examples of Taiwan and Hong Kong, for most Chinese people, the key to this primary self-perception of the PRC today is the word "superiority", that is, the superiority of socialism over other systems. The PRC leaders have to believe that the revolution as they see it has not failed. Mistakes have been made, and these are now being rectified through radical reforms. Capitalist methods, where usable, are but the means to an end. To paraphrase an old Chinese saying, "socialism (now with Chinese characteristics) is the base, and capitalism (without its liberal excesses) is only for application." Therefore, greater efforts are needed to show that capitalism may be enough for a city like Hong Kong, or a small "province" like Taiwan, but has no place in a vast country of 1.2 billion people. If the PRC can sustain its successes for another decade or so, it could enshrine the concept of a socialist market economy as the Chinese way for all Chinese, and perhaps for the entire region as well.

In short, what counts is whether market socialism will take root and produce the wealth that the country needs without political reforms. So far, the results have been extraordinary, but now convincing have they been for other countries in similar positions? The dramatic successes seem to have had surprisingly little influence on the former Communist bloc countries. The Soviet Union under Gorbachev chose a different solution by putting political reform ahead of economic reform, a solution that the PRC leaders see as having led to the collapse of the Soviet Union and the end of communism in Europe.

But none of the 20 or so countries that emerged from that debacle have followed the Chinese way. They are trying to harmonise their economies with those of the capitalist West, but are seeking to do so at their own speed. Their various kinds of socialism have, on the whole, accepted new approaches to representative democracy, or at least paid lip service to its principles. Of course, with the exception of Russia and its outreaches in northern Asia, they are all much smaller than, and have nothing in common with, the PRC. Those in Europe have, in any case, economies that are much more like those in neighbouring European nation-states; in addition, there is a greater cultural affinity.

Only the five Muslim states of central Asia, which have remained more loyal to their communist past, might have looked to China. But they all have good reasons to stay close to Russia in the face of a very volatile Muslim world nearby. For similar reasons, in view of their own Muslim minorities in the neighbouring border province of Xinjiang, the Chinese are themselves cautious of intimate relations. Of the remainder, Mongolia and Vietnam seem to have found parts of the Chinese experience instructive, notably the Taiwan and Hong Kong parts. They are certainly studying all three parts with care, and, despite their reservations about the proximity of Chinese power, have not hesitated to follow similar market economy methods when they have found them appropriate. But they might also look more to Japan and South Korea in the long run. Only North Korea has chosen not to change, still being enmeshed in its rhetoric of self-sufficiency. Elsewhere, communist countries like Cuba really have no reason to look to China. When Cuba decides to change, it will most likely have learned from Mexico and make its peace with the United States.

In short, the Chinese version of the market economy has won no converts among former communist countries. What, then, has made the Deng Xiaoping experiment important to the rest of the world, especially the capitalist world?

From one point of view, it is obvious. The size of the labour force and market and the bold decision to open the country to outside investment have attracted foreign capital from all over the world, and from both large and small trading companies. No less important is China's location in East Asia, close to Japan, to the "Little Dragons" of South Korea, Taiwan, Hong Kong, and Singapore, and to the newly emerging economies of the Association of Southeast Asian Nations (ASEAN). Among developing countries, those in this region have responded most successfully to development aid and international trade over the past two decades. China's interactions with the region, and with the West, constitute one of the most important economic phenomena in recent world history. Thus, the importance of the China experiment may be due more to its size and location than to its intrinsic qualities.

I shall return to the perception of what might be called the China model and its future. What needs to be said here is that the PRC's faith in the superiority of socialism, together with the China-U.S. relationship, which is being treated by the American government as the endgame of the historic capitalist-communist struggle, provides a dynamic backdrop for the economic and political transformation of the region.

From the outside, two facts stand out. The first is that communist China has chosen its own way, even though it is yet without followers and allies from the former communist camp. The second is that China has been drawn into a larger Asian region of rapid economic growth. It is one that is likely to expand and, more important, one that offers an interdependence that all three parts of China will increasingly need. These two facts have encouraged the capitalist world to have great hopes for China's further transformation by the eventual integration of its three economies, indeed by the very evolutionary changes that the Chinese leaders believe will prove the superiority of achieving "socialism by capitalist means".

In the PRC's own perception of itself, however, the emphasis is likely to be on the impact its success will have on other developing economies of the world. It could give others hope if they remember that China stood with them during the Cold War period and, despite its limited resources and many tragic mistakes, challenged both the United States and the Soviet Union.

Developing Economies

This brings me to the second layer of self-perception, that China has many of the features of the developing Third World and is not greatly different from most of those countries still considered part of the so-called South. By developing economies, I refer to most of the former colonies of the West that did not come under communist influence, and those countries that had been under Western dominance or some kind of tutelage, in Asia, the Middle East, Africa, and Latin America. The exceptions are the oil-rich countries, which do not quite fit the description.

The obvious examples of countries successfully modernising their economies are found in East and Southeast Asia, notably South Korea, the ASEAN states, and the Chinese territories Taiwan and Hong Kong. They have done this by learning from, depending on, and trading with the capitalist West. Those attracting the most attention in the PRC have been, of course, Taiwan and Hong Kong, where Chinese business and professional leaders have demonstrated their capacity to modernise rapidly by adopting an export expansion strategy. Earlier, in the 1950s, Taiwan had implemented a successful land reform program and a systematic upgrading of education, which both led to considerable upward mobility. Similar successes in South Korea, Hong Kong, and Singapore led to their being grouped together with Taiwan as "Newly Industrialising Countries" (or "NICs"), the "Four Dragons", or the "Little Tigers" and being seen as models of effective development strategies.

However, the PRC leaders have not compared their country directly with any of the developing economies or any of the NICs. They would claim that the PRC has both Chinese and socialist characteristics, and would point to the unique features of their revolutionary experiences that have made the country stronger and more independent. They would insist that their recent reform programs were both original and exceptional. But they would not deny that the similarities are striking. While the PRC is no longer desperately poor, it is still poor by most standards. It needs outside help in the form of both capital and technology, it needs to strengthen its education and training institutions, and it needs all of the trading and financial concessions that have been granted to other developing countries. For these reasons, it is in fact to the PRC's advantage to be treated like a developing economy.

The barrier to equating the Chinese variant of development with that of most developing countries is that it has long been grouped with the alternative model of the Second World, that is, the Soviet Union and all its communist allies. This world was thought to have the solidarity and, therefore, the strength to challenge the First World, the capitalist West. Now that the Communist bloc has been wound up, this picture of the PRC's place in a Second World is clearly no longer applicable. Habits of historical classification are not easy to discard, however. By insisting that it is still dedicated to communist goals and is successfully reforming its way to a more sustainable form of socialism, the PRC seems to be in a state of limbo between the West and the Third World. There are indeed many factors that do not fit the country within the mold of a developing economy: China is a nuclear power; it is an economic giant; its size and location in the North, with Japan and Russia as neighbours, as well as its proven capacity to replicate the latest science and technology to keep pace with the West and Japan, tend to put it in a different category of development.

The concept of "Third World" was, of course, not exactly the same as that of "developing economies". There was always a strong political element in the way Third World countries were the targets of competition and rivalry between the capitalist West and the Communist bloc. Thus, strictly speaking, the PRC was never part of the Third World. However, the intense Sino-Soviet rivalry that started in the 1960s gave the PRC an opening to redefine its role. It distanced itself from the Cold War rivalry between the United States and the Soviet Union and offered leadership to the Third World. It reached out to the Afro-Asian and Latin American countries as a "fellow-sufferer" of superpower ambitions, and wanted to join them to resist being pawns in that "Great Game". Much was written at the time to justify placing this China among the post-colonial developing countries, but one that was separated sharply from Hong Kong, the British colony. It was also quite distinct from Taiwan, the instrument of U.S. intervention in Chinese affairs and therefore a U.S. satellite.

The PRC leaders chose this course for a variety of reasons. Despite the aid missions in the 1970s to help industrialise Africa (many Chinese were sent there to manage these missions), the country never had the resources to offer more than friendly gestures to the developing countries. The Cultural Revolution of 1966–76 destroyed most of what credibility and capability its aid and diplomacy might have had. Therefore, there was no question of setting up as a third superpower offering choices to Third World countries. Also, as an agrarian society still struggling to advance, it was easy for the PRC to portrary itself as undergoing the same development experience as all the others.

By the 1970s, with closer relations growing between China and the West (including the United States), the West had the unexpected opportunity to see China as a powerful counterweight to the Soviet Union. Deng Xiaoping's open-door policies further broke down barriers to trade and investment. The PRC then joined those parts of the Third World that eschewed import substitution policies, including those that have always looked to the West. They adopted instead export-oriented solutions to development, learning directly from Taiwan and the other "Little Tigers". It became an advantage thereafter for the PRC to continue to be seen as a developing country by institutions such as the United Nations, the World Bank, and many others. This image was also helped by policies that encouraged joint ventures with, and investments by, foreign multinationals. Ironically, Chinese entrepreneurs from Hong Kong, Taiwan, and abroad were specially invited to invest in the PRC. Their investments were regularly treated as patriotic contributions by fellow Chinese.

All at once, measured by economic indicators alone, the country could be seen as a supremely successful developing nation. Its performance in social and economic transformation over the past 15 years has been breathtaking. It can now present itself as a "Newly Industrialising Country". Only China's size makes it ridiculous to call itself another "Little Tiger". In fact, there is considerable ambiguity here. In terms of both size and population, China could be compared with developing countries such as India and Brazil. Yet the comparison lacks the one dimension that has aroused controversy within China and among the leaders of the United

States, Japan, and China's closest neighbours. India and Brazil are non-communist and practise versions of democracy that are acceptable to the West. Neither toyed with radical social experiments, as the PRC did for decades. Theirs had never been the "brave new world" of socialist man that Mao Tse-tung tried to lead his people toward. Their minor successes and failures have been mainly incremental. They developed on the margins of capitalism, and, in the case of Brazil, by being dependent on foreign governments as well. Neither had tried the bold leaps into economic revolution that the PRC did. Neither experienced the dramatic ups and downs that brought, alternately, exhilaration and tragedy to hundreds of millions of people and ultimately destroyed a whole ruling class, as happened in China. These bold experiments in social and economic engineering really have no equals among the other developing economies.

Although the PRC does not readily fit the image of a developing country, it has identified itself as one, partly for strategic reasons and partly for short-term economic and diplomatic advantages. And today it is more like a developing economy than it has ever been. By opening its doors to foreign investment on such a large scale, it may seem even more like a developing economy that India. Indeed, if the Chinese leaders were to lose their nerve now and pull back from a greater liberation of the economy, and from going ahead with more thorough legal and administrative reforms, their economy could end up being like that of India. China could share India's fate of having a developing economy with great potential but that, for reasons of inertia, conservatism, and lack of courage and imagination, has become struck in a deep rut. If Chinese leaders see China as a developing economy, they would do well to examine the Indian experience carefully. As in the former Soviet Union, there are lessons there that the Chinese believe they have already learned, lessons from mistakes they are unlikely to repeat, or at least hope not to repeat.

One lesson stands out. India had its variety of socialism, but rejected the revolutionary communist road in favour of a representative democracy. The Soviet Union under Gorbachev also chose political reform, starting with more democracy in order to support economic change. The PRC claims to have avoided both of these approaches in order to concentrate on using strong central control to reform the economy. The fact that the four NICs in the region, from the 1950s to the 1980s, did not need democracy to be economically successful has given the Chinese much encouragement. The NICs' success supports the Chinese position that radical economic reform must precede political change.

Any study of the modernisation process would show that it is a very recent idea to couple democracy with economic growth as part of that process. The imperial powers in Asia and Africa never thought democracy was necessary when they were administering their colonies. Britain and France experimented with democracy only at the final stages of involuntary decolonisation. During the late 19th and the early 20th century, neither Germany nor Japan needed democratic institutions to achieve its own rapid rate of growth. Nor did the new post-colonial nations in the Third World produce any evidence the democracy was necessary for economic development. In many former colonies, democratic institutions did not survive and were never given the chance to prove whether they would have helped or hindered economic development.

In short, one may well conclude that the Western model of liberal democracy can come about in one of only three ways. First, it can evolve organically after several centuries under certain favourable conditions, as it did in Western Europe. This process may or may not include an industrial revolution. Second, it can be part of a colonial heritage, something the British, French, and Americans, each in their distinctive way, tried to leave behind when departing from, for example, India, Malaysia, and Singapore; parts of Africa; and the Philippines. Even Japan could be said to have had democracy imposed on it by an occupying power, the United States, after a disastrous war. Third, it can emerge after decades of economic growth and the rise of a sizable middle class, as in Taiwan, South Korea, and perhaps Thailand. Some point to a fourth example, one following de-Sovietisation in the late 1980s, as in Russia and some Eastern and central European countries. I would rule this out where China is concerned. The Chinese firmly believe that all attempts at democratisation preceding economic reform in communist states were disasters. Of the three main roads to democracy, the first is too slow and depends on unique historical and cultural conditions that cannot be repeated. The second does not apply to China because China was never a British, French, or American colony. If the third were valid, democracy would have to await further economic growth. This would support the PRC's contention that it would take much more time before some kind of democracy could appear in China.

The new kinds of developing economy, like those of South Korea and Taiwan, could be said to have produced models that challenge the idea that democracy is essential for development and should therefore precede it. Instead, their examples show that the people's energies could be channelled toward growth and the production of wealth from the top down, through firm leadership, clear goals, and administrative controls. It is possible for development to succeed through capitalistic methods without the precondition of liberal democracy. And, if either South Korea or Taiwan is any guide, democracy would *follow* successful development. Why could not Taiwan's form of capitalism and the PRC's form of socialism be brought together? Could the two not combine the free and outward-looking structures of Taiwan and Hong Kong with the strength and size of the PRC to promote China's international position and help to find the Chinese way?

China as a Universal Model

I suggest that China's recent economic successes cannot be separated from the way the Chinese see the integration of socialist ideals with capitalist means as a model for the region. This is the third layer of self-perception. Let me start with some earlier Chinese ideas of being an advanced universal model.

Indeed, China is used to the idea of being a model for its neighbours. Many institutions introduced in Korea, Japan, and Vietnam, as well as those adopted in the kingdoms established by the tribal federations of the Turks, the Khitans, the Jurchens, the Tanguts, and — even before they ruled over all of China — the Mongols and the Manchus, were directly modelled on those of China under the Tang (7th–10th centuries), Song

(10th–13th centuries), and Ming (14th–17th centuries) dynasties. So accustomed are the Chinese to being the model for others that their ruling elites have been, for centuries, particularly resistant to learning from others. Similarly, they have never lost the urge to make China a model for others. Thus, the zeal to be a revolutionary model for the developing world after the communist victory in 1949 was almost inevitable. Although this model was inspired by the Russian Revolution, it was seen as having been advanced by the vision and character of Mao Tse-tung. It was therefore natural for the Chinese to expect their country to become a model for other countries again. For a couple of decades, the fact that it could be such a model was also a source of national pride for most Chinese, including many who joined missions to bring the Chinese model to Africa in the 1970s.

Deng Xiaoping's economic reforms were launched with the purpose of saving what had survived the anarchic decade of the Cultural Revolution. Reform was essential to protect what he and his government still believed had been a great, historic revolution. It is in this context that we note it is too early to say that the model for export to the world is free from the shadow of Marxism-Leninism. I mentioned above that the PRC appears to be in limbo between the West and the Third World. From this point of view, more comparisons might be made with the new Russia. But the Chinese perception here seems to be different. The Russians have failed the revolution; the Chinese have not. China is being rescued from the mistakes of some of its leaders, and its success in doing so proves that the revolution is alive and well. Therefore, the earlier Soviet model is seen as irrelevant today only because it was imperfectly implemented, or inadequately adapted to Chinese and Asian conditions. But in its socialist essence, and after due reform, it could still be viable as a model and may still have universal features for others who seek the revolutionary way. If this perception is valid, what kind of model can China present to the world? And how universal can that model be?

The literature describing and extolling the original model in China is vast and erudite. The whole country was saturated with the Thought of Mao Tse-tung. Every word he ever wrote or uttered was near-sacred, so the most careful editing of his works was done at the highest levels to ensure there would be no inconsistency between current policies and what the Great Helmsman had said. Then came the massive effort to popularise his thought and enable every man, woman, and child to understand the profundity of his vision for China. The Little Red Book served as a catechism, and every party member and cadre was expected to act as a priest in this secular faith. Although this is well known, it is important to remind ourselves of how long and deeply the people on the mainland were subjected to this ideological bombardment and how many Chinese rejected it and voted with their feet by moving to Hong Kong, Taiwan, and elsewhere.

We should also remember that the classics of revolutionary theory originated in the West and were the works of Marx and Engels. Great efforts were also made to translate everything they wrote and annotate their most important texts for the whole population. Not far behind were the writings of Lenin and Stalin, and similar complete editions of their works have been made available. Scholarly analyses by generations of young Chinese ideologues of all the antecedents and contemporaries of these four men in Europe have also been made. In addition, all other revolutionary thinkers in the same mode have been given close attention, if not for their originality, at least to demonstrate the universality of the Marxist-Leninist canon. Of course, thousands of scholars and commentators outside China, in the West, in Japan and elsewhere in Asia, in Africa and Latin America, have also contributed to this vast corpus of writings, either critically or in admiration. It is also necessary to remind ourselves of the vitriolic debates between certain Russian and Chinese leaders over the interpretations of the classic texts of revolution. They formed a shared experience that few would care to remember today, but did expose many minds to what the Chinese traditionally call "the end-point of a bull's horn", that is, the epitome of futility.

I have recalled all this to make a point about the great paradox of this layer of self-perception in China. The paradox is that Marxism-Leninism brought an international dimension into the lives of mainland Chinese that they had never experienced before, but this dimension was given a narrow focus through Mao Tse-tung's appeal to the traditions of a peasant rebellion. This narrowness was the very opposite of the universal features of the socialist ideal, but Mao was really a provincial patriot, and this incompatibility was aggravated by the intense rivalry between Chinese and Russian leaders and their respective national interests. In particular, Mao Tse-tung's ambition to be the leader of the socialist world after the death of Stalin, and his conviction that Stalin's successors had perverted the cause of internationalism, led him to excesses of liturgical exposition and in the end to the Cultural Revolution that finally, and ironically, weakened the Chinese people's commitment to socialism and revolution.

If that is the case, is a commitment to an old faith still valid? So far, it still seems to be so among the leaders of the Communist Party. It provides much of the rhetoric in all pronouncements about the ultimate goal of Deng Xiaoping's reform programs. Here I am not referring to the statements simply affirming the authority and existence of the party. I am referring to the justifications for gigantic state projects like the Three Gorges Dam, and massive industrial enterprises to make steel, refine oil, build nuclear weapons, airplanes, and automobiles, and, more recently, create a massive central bank. Despite the reforms and the frequent calls to respect market mechanisms, we observe the survival of Marxist and Maoist ideas in large-scale management, in the practice of law, and in the administration of public order. Of particular importance is the survival of all the control mechanisms that ensure central policies are being implemented. This is because the reforms are limited to economic affairs; political structures, in particular, are not included.

The reforms clearly do not in any way constitute a rejection of the revolution. They presuppose that the revolution of 1949 and its achievements and failures remain the starting-point. Therefore, the injunctions are to learn from the failures and build on the successes. Clearly, the centrally planned policies failed. The isolationist closed economy, out of touch with the developments in the capitalist world outside, also failed. Its structures must be dismantled whenever necessary, but not to the point of endangering the achievements and thus the regime and its leadership.

What achievements of the revolution could strengthen the model for others to follow? It is difficult to be certain about how many of these most

Chinese people could now agree on. The main works of history on the communist period have been written under party supervision. But more and more writings are based on data not previously available to scholars in universities and research institutes. There has also been revisionism in the writings about some aspects of revolutionary mistakes. Foreign scholarship about the revolution is now accessible; many foreign books and articles have even been translated into Chinese and widely read. Despite the constraints, independent thinking has surfaced. At this stage, this is neither wholesale rejection of the post-1949 years nor uncritical praise of the successes during that tumultuous period. Nor is there much regret about what might have been had the revolution been better led, or led by others who might have been more nationalist or more practical. Instead, we see sober preparation for reappraisals that I believe will soon produce more authoritative writings. As for more recent events, like the corruption, inflation, and lack of channels for redress and political dialogue that led to the tragedy at Tiananmen Square in 1989, these are new failures that have yet to be fully addressed. Unless this is done, any model that the PRC has to offer will be tarnished.

In the meantime, there have been some widely accepted claims about the successes. For example, the destruction of the old landed classes that had supported an inefficient and corrupt system of government is seen as a permanent achievement. Also, some of the advances in agriculture, science, and engineering have been widely regarded as outstanding. By and large, enough food was produced in the countryside, and the famines that had occurred regularly during the previous century were brought to an end. There is even some nostalgia for the relatively egalitarian policies that used to prevail but have now been superseded by the universal drive to make money at all costs. But, of all the achievements that are mentioned from time to time, it is probably the unification of China after decades of division under a variety of warlords that is seen by most Chinese as the revolution's greatest achievement. This is what saved China from further imperialist advances by Japan and the West. It protected China from bullying by the Soviet Union at its height. It raised the status of China in international affairs, made it a major player in the Cold War, and, in particular, earned it the respect of the one country for which most Chinese shared a deep but ambivalent respect, the United States.

All this occurred despite the fact that the unification had not been complete. Hong Kong was deliberately left alone after 1949 as a window to the Western capitalist world. By default, arising from China's lack of air and naval power, and because of U.S. support for Taiwan as well as other distractions on the long frontiers to the north and west, the Beijing government could not cross the Taiwan straits. This unfinished business has probably been as important to the Chinese leaders as their visions of communism throughout the past half century. It has always been on their political and military agendas.

What is unfolding today is an intriguing picture of how recent economic developments may alter Chinese perspectives on the issue of integration and eventual unification. The prospect of a coming together of socialist and capitalist ways of achieving progress could determine the shape and nature of a new universal model. In addition, the possibility of new wealth-making partnerships and ventures coming out of all three parts of China even before its unification is a riveting subject for China's neighbours. And it is breathtaking to imagine the potential for some degree of globalisation of trading and financial organisations centered in the East-Southeast Asian region. If this were to become a reality, it would transform the international relations of the world for the next century.

POLITICS AND CULTURE: FROM HISTORIC EMPIRE TO GLOBAL POWER?

Most Chinese believe that the PRC leaders of today got it right by starting with economic reforms and leaving political reforms till later. The Russian experience of the past decade has confirmed the wisdom of their practical approach. With wealth, there will be strength; with wealth and strength, China's power and influence will grow. My second lecture will concentrate on the political and cultural aspects of China's relations with the world. It will examine China as, in turn, a modern nation, a historic empire, a civilisational challenge, and a potential global power.

A Modern Nation

Let me begin with China's perception of itself as a modern nation, or nation-state. China's desire to be a nation predates the launching of the socialist revolution, but not by much. It was really only during the early years of the 20th century that the ideas of nationhood and nationality began to take shape in the minds of Chinese leaders. The emphasis was never on the question of citizenship, nor on political participation by all those who shared a common identity, nor on acquiring an international persona and seeking the protection of international law. What the Chinese leaders saw as nations were clearly the powerful ones like Britain, France, Germany, Russia, and the United States — the great powers with which China compared unfavourably. The importance of national unity was therefore seen from the start as a source of wealth and power, something China badly needed before it could take its rightful place in the world of nations. This picture remained the dominant one during the first half of the century, while China struggled for survival against foreign intervention, especially the Japanese invasions.

But how strong is this self-perception today? It is remarkable how much attention has been given to Sun Yat-sen on the mainland since the early 1980s. What Sun Yat-sen, the father of Chinese nationalism, stood for had never been given much attention in the PRC before. He began as a Han Chinese rebel leader against foreign Manchu rule, but when the Manchus were overthrown in 1911 and the republic inherited the imperial borders, he was forced to change his concerns to those of a multicultural, if not multinational, state in defense of its national borders against foreign enemies. In terms of China's needs today, his original concerns are hardly relevant. Clearly, some of the attention paid to Sun Yat-sen is due to the use of united-front tactics by the Beijing government to win over those who still support the Guomindang, and the ideals of Sun's "Three Principles of the People", in Taiwan and overseas. Thus, in the name of unification and the ideal of One China, Sun Yat-sen the nationalist would certainly have more appeal than Mao Tse-tung or Deng Xiaoping.

But this specific aspect of nationalism is misleading. China as a nation encompasses much more than the question of reunification with Taiwan.

The idea of national identity was a powerful discovery at the turn of the century for the intelligentsia who saw the imperial system collapse. For a people who had lived under an empire for two thousand years, it was remarkable how quickly they accepted the idea of a republic, and they have not seemed to want to return to any sort of imperial or monarchical system since 1911. Indeed, these nationalists started with radical political change. Dynastic overthrow was followed by the complete reform of the system of government, including elected national constituent assemblies. When that failed and the country was dominated for a decade by warlords, both the nationalists and the communists who were allied to fight the warlords agreed that political restructuring was essential.

The first priority was national reunification, seen as political reform or revolution from above. The leaders looked for an alternative to the mainstream Western model, which was seen as an exploitative system that was impoverishing China. Ironically, they looked to the West for an ideology that was more powerful than orthodox capitalism and liberal democracy, something that would help China stand up against the West itself. Some found it in Mussolini's fascism, others in national socialism, and yet others in anarchism, socialism, and communism. In all of these, economic development was subordinated to the political goal of unification and centralised power. And this remained so under both nationalist and communist leaders on the mainland until Deng Xiaoping's reforms after 1978. Only then, for the first time in modern history, was economic reform given the highest priority, an understandable reaction against the Maoist slogan "Put politics in command." This emphasis on putting prosperity before further political reform has brought a totally new dimension to China's nation-building process.

The idea of nationalism itself was an inspiration for all Chinese who felt humiliated by the successive military defeats that led to unequal status for Chinese everywhere, to extraterritorial privileges for foreign residents within China, and to the increasing dominance of foreign enterprises on Chinese soil. Nationalism was tied to anti-imperialism and anti-colonialism as the key to almost all of the political struggles of the 20th century. Both Chiang Kai-shek and Mao Tse-tung were propelled into politics by their nationalistic urges. And, despite the romantic internationalist slogans after the communist victory in 1949, national pride and interests remained in the forefront of the goals of the People's Republic. With the collapse of communist ideology, little now stands in the way of the current leaders' returning to nationalism to seek a stronger mandate for their rule. Simply put, this would mean a return to the quest for wealth and power by the nation-state.

This is obvious. But nationalism could either be a very blunt weapon or be supported by a sophisticated body of ideals for a loyal citizenry, ideals that would inspire political consciousness, democratic participation, and a fervent dedication to common goals. As a blunt instrument, however, it could still be very powerful. It could inspire zealous support or arouse open hostility and fear among those within the country who feel they do not quite belong. If nation-building is not done with the greatest of care, problems of identity could become the cause of much more serious divisions among the ethnic minorities who live within artificial boundaries, or who are forced to accept historical boundaries defined by other than national criteria. Examples abound of what happens when nationalism becomes narrowly defined and fierce passions are aroused both among, and against, those who do not feel that they really belong.

China is more fortunate than most former empires in having a majority — the Han — that numbers more than 90 percent of its population. In 1912 the Republic of China inherited the boundaries that the Manchu Qing armies had extended into northern and central Asia. Some territories acquired in the 17th and 18th centuries, for example Outer Mongolia, had their boundaries redrawn in this century to acknowledge political changes following Russian intervention and support. Most notable was the independence of the modern Mongolian state, although its government is now not entirely secure. Territories such as Manchuria, Xinjiang, and Greater Tibet had also undergone changes when China renegotiated new international borders, but they too had their internal provincial boundaries modified, and not always with the consent of the minorities living within them. Also, many other autonomous provinces, counties, and districts were created to accommodate recognised minority peoples who remain culturally and linguistically distinct from the Han majority. In drawing up criteria for these autonomous areas, the Chinese followed Soviet practice based on Stalin's ideas of nationality. Now that the consequences of those practices have ended in the dissolution of the Soviet Union, the Chinese are concerned about how they might affect ethnic loyalties in China itself.

Indeed, at various layers of self-perception, China cannot help but be conscious of the Soviet model that led China to its present position. The failure of communist ideology is matched by the principles of national differentiation that came from the same source. However, turning to the West for nation-building principles does not make the problem any easier for China. According to those principles, even the smallest ethnic group may, under certain conditions of history, location, language, and culture, seek independent nationhood. The numerous small nations of Western and central Europe attest to the complexities that these national principles can bring. Most notably, the Chinese leaders must view the developments in Europe in recent years with concern, if not alarm. For example, consider the separation of Slovakia; the independence of Slovenia, Croatia, and other former parts of Yugoslavia; and the three Baltic, three Caucasian, and five Muslim republics that, along with Ukraine and Belorussia, pulled out of the Soviet Union. Now as in the past, the end of empires rapidly brings about the addition of new members to the United Nations. There is pressure everywhere for smaller entities to seek their national identities and, should they remain insecure, to find means such as bilateral alliances, commonwealth associations, regional groupings, communities or "unions", and what I have called anti-empires to strengthen their capacity to defend themselves against larger powers.

In this context, the idea of China being a new nation or nation-state is still a very crude one. The government in Beijing seems to be sensitive enough about the dangers of wielding such a double-edged weapon not to make too much of the act of nation-building right now. Official documents today do not attempt any clear exposition of what a Chinese *nation* could mean in the future, and there is no sense of urgency that the country needs such an exposition. Given the unusual fact that the major ethnic minorities have their homes on the extensive borders of China, it appears to be wise for China to leave the concept broadly and inclusively defined. Thus, despite the obvious power of nationalism as a unifying force, the Chinese are not really at liberty to beat the nationalist drum. China remains in the ambivalent position of encouraging national pride in becoming a great power while dampening the national dimensions of minority peoples on its borders. Instead, the focus will, in the long run, have to be on the development of a larger national culture for an "imagined community" that could attract the loyalty of all peoples who live in China.

Here the example of India in a divided Indian subcontinent provides an interesting comparison. India is almost as large and as populous as China, and in many respects, equally poor and backward. It too espoused socialism, but implemented it through representative democracy and in what is effectively a confederated form of state government. India's form of socialism has been no more successful than China's communism. And India's greatest fear is of secession and division into various linguistic or religious states, which would bring about the end of its national identity. As an example of a multinational state, of course, India is very different from China. But as vast countries carefully guarding their national unification goals, China and India have similar concerns. Both central governments have expended immense energy and resources to keep their states and provinces together. But the respective leaders have shown equal determination to succeed in strengthening national unity and in preserving their new nation-states. There is little doubt that this matter will be of central importance to the Chinese leaders in the country's international relations until it is finally resolved to their satisfaction. If other powers actively seek to prevent China's national unification or, worse, encourage parts of China to secede, such action would become a permanent source of instability in the region. Thus, the Chinese believe they must maintain a strong central government, something their history inclines them to do in any case.

A Historic Empire

This leads me to another layer of self-perception in China, namely, that of China as a historic empire. This is quite distinct from the idea of a modern nation discussed above and the pride in China's ancient and continuous civilisation, which I shall come to later. This self-perception is a deep-rooted one that has always been linked to the question of power.

The importance of a glorious imperial past is well attested in thousands of books written by both nationalist and communist historians about China during this century. But let me not suggest that the Chinese are more obsessed with their history than other peoples. All countries that have full records of a long and distinguished past are just as fascinated with their own history. When there exists such a vivid, continuous, and concrete record of the activities of various people living in an extensive territory, which the people themselves recognise as always having had a unified core, it is inevitable that stories of specific successes and failures are regularly invoked. What is unusual is the Chinese attitude toward the uses of history, one that has particular relevance to the idea of a historic empire. The attitude has always been a didactic one — it is believed that history is valuable for the moral and political lessons it might teach future leaders of that empire.

It is this oneness of the historical experience and the didactic quality of historical judgments that make this self-perception of a historic empire especially interesting. Let me address the question of oneness first. Inapplicable to Europe, Africa, and other parts of Asia, where kingdoms and empires rose and fell to form different nations, this sustained picture of historical oneness is unique to a continental territory like China. Most of the core lands of North, Central, and South China, where the Han Chinese have always been the majority, have an unbroken history of two to three thousand years. Others farther north and west have been alternately inside and outside the borders of Chinese empires, but have been regarded as integral parts of the ebb and flow of Chinese history. For example, the fact that many of the more powerful tribal federations, such as the Turks, Mongols, Tibetans, and Jurchen-Manchus, have actually ruled over all or parts of the core lands has established the tradition that they all share a common heritage with the Han Chinese. That many of these people have also been assimilated into the dominant Han culture over time has confirmed this common heritage. Thus, although China has been divided in the past because of the fall of dynasties or foreign conquest, the driving force behind all governments has always been to reunify the empire. The inclusive rhetoric used in historical writings to represent such a theme of unity in diversity is seen to have sanctified the idea that it is the land that is China, and that all those who rule it, whatever their origins, and all those who live there, become Chinese.

The problem with this self-perception is that long stretches of the northern and western borders have never been clearly defined. Understandably, in past centuries, there was no concept of boundary demarcation. Nor was there a concept of sovereignty or jurisdiction. The most important factor was the reach of the central government. However, there are two exceptions in Chinese history, both products of special circumstances — the manipulation of the tributary system by non-Han peoples to secure a large measure of independence. The northern example was that of Korea, which kept itself out of China through a combination of geographical location, self-restraint, and diplomatic skills. The southern example was that of Vietnam. The Vietnamese had to fight their way out of China, then struggled for centuries to define their own nationhood and finally used both military and diplomatic skills to preserve their lands from Chinese invaders. Both Korea and Vietnam were further helped by the crucial fact that neither was ever a threat to China. For all other kingdoms, principalities, and tribal groups that accepted the Chinese tributary system, however, boundaries were either unclear or not contiguous with China, and their tributary missions arrived by sea.

It is clear from the above that China's concept of its historic empire was unlike that of the Persians, Greeks, or Romans, that of Asoka, Tamerlane, or Babur, or, in more modern times, that of the Ottomans, the British, the French, or tsarist Russia. These were empires by conquest; in recent times, they were by conquest over long distances and even across oceans. They lasted only as long as their military forces were victorious. For most of its two thousand years of "imperial" history, this was not the case with China. With the exception of the short Mongol period of 90 years, when China was itself part of the world empire of the Mongols, no armies marched out of traditional Middle Kingdom (*Zhongguo*) lands. The Mongol expeditionary bursts far into Eurasia, and across the seas to Japan and Java, were strictly un-Chinese. On the contrary, the successor dynasty of the Ming, which was led by Han Chinese, strongly resisted the Mongol worldview. After three decades of exceptional voyages by Admiral Zheng He early in the 15th century into the South China Sea and across the Indian Ocean to the shores of East Africa, the Ming emperors insisted on returning to the control of traditional lands and forbade foreign adventures. They saw these voyages as aberrations and turned inward toward their land frontiers. The Ming reaffirmed what had distinguished the Chinese historic empire for more than a thousand years: its self-centredness and its belief in its invulnerability and self-sufficiency. This was reflected in the history of growing complacency and arrogance, and in the empire's adherence to the tributary system that the Chinese rulers had developed internally and then applied in varying degrees beyond China.

I shall return to the tributary system and its relationship with the Chinese concept of empire. Let me now turn to the didactic quality of the Chinese historiographical tradition, in which history was to be studied so that lessons could be learned from the past. This didactic quality has persisted to this day. In all the histories written before the 20th century, the lessons to be learned from the imperial past were that China was a land power, that adventures outside China were to be avoided, and that Chinese rulers who had been ambitious on the borders usually exhausted the empire's resources and failed to profit from their efforts. Also, there are records of a long list of negative and positive role models for future rulers, from examples of those who had impoverished the empire in pursuit of foreign adventures, to those who defended the sacred lands successfully with minimum effort and cost, to those who used the tributary system skilfully to keep the imperial peace and foreigners in their place. Thus, the lessons of political and institutional history were as important as the celebrations of past imperial glories.

But since the turn of the century, modern historians in China have been greatly influenced by their studies of modern Western history. There has been a sharp divergence in historical interpretation since the new historiography of Liang Qichao (1873–1929). Liang had read European history in Japanese translation. He was influenced by the same books that had inspired the Japanese to break from their traditions and embark on modern empire-building along Western lines. Liang had also travelled among the overseas Chinese in British territories and admired the empire that the British had established around the world. With that background, and with the weakness of Qing China in mind, he was the first to record his regret that the Ming navies under Admiral Zheng He did not expand Chinese power into the Indian Ocean and thereby preempt the Portuguese by building a chain of Chinese trading ports all the way to East Africa. He, also for the first time, acknowledged the courageous Chinese pioneers in Southeast Asia and expressed admiration for those who gained fame and wealth outside China without any help from Chinese governments. These Chinese were considered criminals for having left China without official permission.

Since then, a new breed of historians have tried to reinterpret "empire" to draw comparisons with European empires in Asia. For these historians, the Chinese empire was no longer seen in traditional or "historic" terms, but equated with Western empires. In their eagerness to equate Chinese history with European history, they tried to match what had happened in China with historical developments in the rest of the world. One of the consequences of this reinterpretation was to cast the tributary system in an unhistorical frame, one that tended to match tributary states with European colonies even though the Chinese had not conquered or governed any of the states outside imperial borders. Perhaps without intending to, they began to depict past Chinese empires as comparable, if not superior, to modern Western ones.

Late Qing imperial policies had begun to show this tendency, largely in order to defend the dynasty against European imperialism, especially along its borders, for example in Burma, Vietnam, and Korea. As it turned out, the efforts were ineffective and, in the end, counterproductive. In fact, occasionally they even strengthened the moral position of the European powers by allowing them to argue that their incursions had helped to liberate Burma, Laos, and Vietnam from imperialist China, an argument that continues to be used against China today. The new interpretations were certainly used to justify Japan's claim to have freed Korea from Chinese imperialism.

Consciously or not, it was the modern nationalist historians who tended to distort the function of the tributary system and the relationships it spawned. Their work continued to influence some of the histories written after 1949. Since then, of course, other developments have changed the way China's historic empire has been presented and therefore perceived by its people. One of the most important factors has been the internationalist perspective put forth by Marxism-Leninism and sinicised by Mao Tse-tung. In particular, the dominance of Soviet historiography during the 1940s and 1950s led historians to try to fit all of Chinese history into a grand Marxist framework, with the communist revolution portrayed as the inevitable end product of earlier stages of development, from primitive communism to slave society to feudal society, and then to capitalist-imperialist invasions from which the Communist Party had saved China. In addition, for the first time since the Mongol empire, China shared a long border with a huge, powerful country — the Soviet Union. The combination of these factors had profound effects on Chinese historiography from about 1930 for at least half a century. It has not been easy for the present generation of Chinese historians to free themselves from that tradition of thinking.

One consequence, however, is clear. For many decades, all Chinese history tended to be written in accordance with the existing borders with the Soviet Union. Meticulous care was taken to avoid controversy about overland boundary disputes, and this practice was extended to include all borders with countries regarded as friendly to China. This might have been done merely for the sake of diplomacy. But it did lead to important results, one of which was to strengthen the sense that the central lands of China were sacred, and that its borders were legitimately (and historically) extended to where they are today. The other was to play down the function of the tributary system altogether. The former has encouraged the practice of respecting the borders of friendly neighbours. The latter also has produced something positive and correct, namely, the reversal of nationalist claims to historic tributary states as former Chinese "colonies".

Finally, let me relate the historic question of tribute and trade to the issue of Greater China. John King Fairbank called the tributary system a key part of "the Chinese world order" in his book *The Chinese World Order*. Many readers have queried the use of "world" because China's political concerns were limited to its neighbours and the use of "order" because the tributary relationships were largely unsystematic and unenforceable, and the institution was most useful only where it helped to monitor official trading relations. Although the rhetoric in China was that various rulers and chieftains from near and far came to pay tribute to the emperor, in reality the system evolved into one that dealt with foreigners who wished to have trading or displomatic relations with China. Detailed study of these tributary relationships would show that there was really no Chinese empire outside Chinese lands, and the self-perception of historic empire is misleading, if not actually false. What is important about this kind of empire, however, is the way Chinese rulers used an essentially feudal relationship, meant to serve defense and diplomatic purposes, in order to regulate foreign trade.

Today there is no place for this kind of historic empire or such a tributary system. The Chinese scholars who know this have made it clear in the many histories written in recent years. However, this memory of the historic empire may linger in the minds of the political leaders of the region. It would be interesting to see how the current understanding of the system could overcome the deep suspicions that have been aroused in the region that China has an underlying expansionist nature. In the context of the speculations about Greater China, some of the old fears have resurfaced. These have run parallel to the earlier fears expressed about the Japanese empire, which, having failed to achieve its Greater Asian Co-Prosperity Sphere as a framework for its imperial ambitions, then used its economic power to bring it about. Is this what China might do? Is the idea of an economic Greater China another way of achieving a new economic empire in the region?

If so, it would be a new phenomenon having little to do with the historic dynastic empires of the past. The region has changed beyond recognition. So has the world. There is no return to the past. The new nations of the region may each appear relatively weak, but they have learned the most important lesson of the colonial era. When they were divided, they were easily picked off, one after another, to become bits of other countries' empires. They are unlikely to make that mistake again, and China can hardly fail to see the determination within the region to avoid doing so. Small and large regional groupings, with or without China, will intensify their efforts to bring about peaceful solutions to all potential disputes. If they are successful in ensuring that peace, the concept of empire itself should be discarded.

Chinese Civilisation

Only after 1945 did the Chinese need to think in terms of nation-building and of forming some kind of "imagined community". The return of Taiwan to Chinese rule was soon followed by division into the PRC and the ROC (Republic of China), which continues today. The appearance of China in both names reflects the heritage of the Qing borders, but the oneness of China has another source, that of a common civilisation. Chinese civilisation cannot, however, be equated with the idea of nation-state or empire. Parts of the empire in the north and west never shared in that civilisation, and parts of the civilisation spread southward and eastward beyond the confines of the empire into non-Chinese kingdoms in Korea, Japan, and Vietnam.

This leads me to another layer of self-perception, that of China as the home of a great civilisation and the Chinese as a people who share a common cultural heritage. Given the revolutionary changes that have occurred this century and the various perceptions outlined above, is this still significant? Do people really care? Even if the Chinese continue to refer to the glorious past, surely that past belongs in the museums, in displays for the tourist industry, or in the collections that antiquarians and connoisseurs cultivate at their leisure. It is true there are scholars who argue that China has always been a civilisation-state rather than a nation-state. Therefore, the fact that there is a China that people can identify with rests on the existence of that civilisation. But, if China is a modern nation, would that not contradict this residual perception of a civilisation that originated with the Chinese and still belongs to them? How would the Chinese see a civilisation that not only is shared with people of other nations, but may actually be better appreciated outside than inside the borders of the PRC?

As I have suggested above, the concept of a modern Chinese nation is imperfect and is contingent on China having a larger national culture for the Han majority and all its ethnic minorities to share and embrace. To that extent, a cultural heritage that is both modern and based on the continuous civilisation that everyone recognises as belonging to China could be the foundation of new national loyalty. Until this century, the Confucianism that supported the imperial system, together with the popular culture based on a mixture of Confucian, Buddhist, and Daoist practices, provided that heritage. But for nearly a century, nationalist and communist revolutionaries have done their utmost to relieve China of that cultural baggage. What, then, is left for those who still see China as the home of Chinese civilisation? Insofar as the Beijing government acknowledges the validity of Confucian role models and ethics in schools, and permits the revival of some Buddhist and Daoist groups around the country, the heritage is still real. To understand how important this is likely to be, we need to survey the extent of the damage done to Chinese civilisation during this century and the kinds of repair being attempted to make this heritage viable again. Is it possible for this heritage to be modernised? If so, how relevant would it be for China's position in international relations?

It would be true to say that neither the nationalists nor the communists set out to destroy their proud civilisation. When confronted by the military power of the West in the 19th century, the Chinese struggled to adapt their civilisation to the challenges and dangers from the West. On the whole, they subscribed to the view so succinctly encapsulated by Zhang Zhidong (1837–1909) in *Quanxue pien* (Exhortation to Study), published in 1898: "Zhongxue wei ti, Xixue wei yong" (Chinese learning as base, Western learning as application). Thus, this "learning", or civilisation, belonged to a deeper layer of consciousness that both nationalist and communist governments have tried, from time to time, to bring to the surface. But, as will be seen, the results were unpredictable and often contradictory. The Chinese were unable, like the Japanese, to retain the core of their values and institutions while learning what they needed from Western science and engineering. The Chinese felt they had to redefine their civilisation in order to modernise their country and their ideas. It was thought that their civilisation could be revitalised as modern and progressive if carefully selected bits of Western learning could be grafted onto it.

But it was not that simple. To begin with, for most Chinese, the great Chinese civilisation had been associated with the ruling class of mandarins who dictated artistic taste and endorsed all forms of orthodoxy, especially those pertaining to government and to religious and ethical systems. That small and privileged class was generally seen as having served the foreign Manchu rulers in the context of Confucian ideals, and, therefore, was highly suspect in the eyes of the nationalists who overthrew the Qing dynasty. Thus, when the Guomindang leaders tried to revive traditional values during the 1930s, they turned to a new generation of activists, largely radical intellectuals who found the whole exercise artificial, irrelevant, and self-seeking. The best minds among them had turned to the professions, to the study of science and technology, or to modern economics, business, and management. They were more familiar with Keynes, Mussolini, Henry Ford, Madame Curie, and Einstein and the latest artistic ideas in Europe and the United States than with the unglamorous efforts to keep traditional values alive. Already, the Great Tradition was seen by the best and brightest as more dead than alive.

Of the intellectuals who remained interested in cultural values, many had converted to anti-Confucian nationalism, to liberal ideals and capitalist practices. They were the first modern generation. But they, in turn, found themselves unacceptable to the progressive revolutionaries who regarded them as scions of the landlord and new capitalist classes, who were condemned as the exploiters of the people. They were thus two-time losers. They had lost most of their own cultural bearings as well as their credibility as cultural leaders in the eyes of their contemporaries. After the communist takeover in 1949, some of them escaped to Taiwan and served a more sympathetic government there; others found new roles as scholars and "loyalists" in the Confucian tradition. Yet others went abroad, particularly to the United States, as bearers of the civilisation, rather like the "loyalists" who went to Japan and Vietnam after the fall of the Song and Ming dynasties.

Who, then, remained on the mainland to claim the mantle of cultural heroes? Whoever they were, they would first have to make their peace with Marxism-Leninism and the Thought of Mao Tse-tung. Ironically, Mao, the romantic revolutionary, saw himself as a bearer, and an arbiter, of all that was great and worth preserving in Chinese civilisation. Thus, at the highest level, a man such as Guo Moruo (1892–1978), who was flexible enough to enjoy the personal trust of Mao Tse-tung, was able to offer some measure of protection for traditional scholarly values. Those less fortunate, such as Liang Souming (1893–1988) and Fung Youlan (1895–1990), were criticised; others were marginalised. If they managed to survive through the 1950s and early 1960s, they were then either totally ignored or brought out to serve crude propaganda purposes during the Cultural Revolution. The image of formerly famous scholars of Chinese culture being forced to support the politics of those Cultural Revolution years remains sharply etched in many minds. It was a degrading experience. Although many had to submit in order to survive, what they were put through certainly did not inspire confidence in their authority, or faith in the values they were supposed to support.

Since the 1980s, the more independent minded have taken advantage of the relative freedom to resurface and write on controversial subjects such as intellectual freedom, liberal democracy, legitimacy, the rule of law, and human rights. Understandly, most of them were more excited by the fresh ideas from the West than by any return to Chinese traditional values. However, with a loss of faith in communism, and given the tight limits on publishing and the media, there seems to be a spiritual and ideological vacuum, especially among the young. Chinese leaders are worried by the materialism and corruption in the country today and are seeking ways to bring back some of the revolutionary purity of earlier days. All the same, among them are the cultural loyalists who now find the atmosphere more congenial and openly advocate that "Chinese learning" be given back its rightful place in the curriculum before it is too late. How late it is, and how the extensive damage to China's cultural roots can be repaired, will not be known for some time. But it is impressive to see authors, editors, and publishers all around the country, and in collaboration with their counterparts in Hong Kong and Taiwan, busily producing new textbooks, literary and artistic collections, and annotated editions of the classics for students and scholars at all levels. The print and electronic media in all three parts of China have also joined in to a lesser extent, less didactically but, through entertainment and recreational activities, probably more effectively. The will to revive interest is not in question, and the number of people keen to do the work seems to be growing. It is possible to say that, at least among the Han Chinese, the glorious civilisation and the idea of a new nation can coexist.

In what way, then, is the cultural heritage generally meaningful to the Chinese people today? I have attended several conferences on such subjects as Chinese culture, Confucianism, and the interface between modern and traditional society, and have followed several controversies on historiography, archaeology, and the preservation of cultural artifacts, as well as more general issues, such as the future of the Great Tradition for the younger generation. There is undoubtedly official interest. There is also the popular conviction that the government must have a clear and strong position about the importance of the heritage. There is awareness that there are more people, including non-Chinese scholars, outside mainland China who are appreciative of traditional culture than there are within, and that the quality of the outsiders' knowledge may even be superior. But the inescapable impression is that much of the attention on the mainland is still formal and dutiful, and that, most of the time, paying lip service to tradition is all that is officially required.

At the popular level, however, there is a different picture. This is particularly true in the countryside and in small towns, both in Taiwan and on the mainland. Religions and local cults are gaining followers. Many of these are based on superstition, but they fill a void. Following the decay of Guomindang ideology and of the secular religion of Maoism that the PRC government had sponsored so vigorously for decades and that had caused so much confusion among the people for so long, it must be refreshing for the country people to find somethng different they can believe in. Unlike those in the historic cities, the temples, mosques, and less obvious places of worship in rural China are being built or restored, not in support of tourism, but for popular use.

Most notable has been the increasing desire to revive respect for family institutions everywhere. This is particularly relevant following the demise of the extended family and the introduction of the one-child policy. This can be seen not only in the new school textbooks, but also in the increasing number of primers and catechisms dedicated to *jiaxun*, or "family instructions". These have been significantly revised and modernised, but are still presented along traditional lines. They are popular not only because they embody the deepest levels of cultural consciousness among most Chinese, but also because they express a practical need when other institutions seem to be failing to sustain local communities. This is particularly true on the mainland. The new pressures toward private profit, the inadequacies of the welfare system, the trend toward insecure employment, and the growing threats of falling real incomes for the rural majority leave most people with little choice but to turn again to their families. Fortunately, the cultural heritage within the country concerning the family seems to have remained strong. Furthermore, as a common bond still appreciated by the Chinese in Taiwan and Hong Kong as well as those overseas, this can easily be reinforced through regular contacts wherever family relationships can be established.

It has been suggested that a new concept of "Cultural China" (Tu Wei-ming, "The Living Tree", in *Daedalus*, 1991), which sees China in its broadest non-political manifestation, could inspire a Chinese revival. This concept accepts that the greatest damage to traditional civilisation has been done in the PRC. Therefore, the future of that civilisation depends on whether modern intellectuals in the other two parts of China, and among the Chinese diaspora, can transmit their heritage to the younger generations who have grown up in freer environments. Unless the intellectuals outside the PRC can demonstrate that the Great Tradition is still essential to China and inspire fresh confidence among themselves and their successors, there is little chance that much of the civilisation will survive. But for many Chinese today, it will be enough if certain core values remain strong. Chief among these are respect for education and a meritocracy, including the readiness to upgrade knowledge and acquire the best in science and technology; willingness to work hard and postpone gratification (the importance of combining these first two values with the qualities of thrift and trustworthiness is well recognised in modern business and industry); and, perhaps most of all, loyalty to family networks that most Chinese people still believe is natural and profoundly central not only to the civilisation, but also to all areas of practical activity. If all of these values could bind the Chinese people together, they would play a key part in fostering a culturally united country.

In any case, the question of civilisation is primarily a matter of choice for the Chinese themselves. Whether it impinges on China's relations with the rest of the world depends on whether it has anything universal to offer to non-Chinese peoples. Sifting through the heritage and finding qualities in it that arouse more than simply pride or nostalgia is a task that the past three generations of Chinese have so far failed to undertake. Until that is done, not only to produce some defensive walls for the use of the Chinese alone (that is, to strengthen China as a modern nation-state and a great power), but also with a fresh vision of how the values of East and West can together work for all humankind, Chinese civilisation will have little to contribute to the world.

Today, the new tasks awaiting the Chinese derive largely from the need to protect the rights of all human beings as a universal principle. The principle has been thoroughly aired for decades, and is scarcely disputed among civilised peoples. The debate is about how these rights should be respected and by what means. But two problems have dogged it in recent years. One pertains to timing. Some have argued that full rights must be implemented immediately, no matter the cost. The other relates to approach. The issue of human rights has not been presented as one of civilisation and morality, but as a diplomatic, commercial, and political weapon, and has been presented confrontationally as one between East and West, between inferior Asian values and superior Western values.

This is unfortunate. If human rights and democracy still appear remote and difficult to realise, it is because the Chinese people have failed to create the political and legal structure for the new values to grow among them. On the other hand, insistence upon these values from the outside, and by foreign governments, is bound to be interpreted either as wilful ignorance of the immense problems that still exist in the country, or a reflection of the desire of these foreigners to overthrow the present regime no matter what the consequences. Such an approach has also been interpreted as interference in China's internal affairs or as an attempt by Western politicians to slow down its development. The attitude toward China's tough birth control measures best illustrates this failure, or unwillingness, to understand. If China does not control its population, it will be accused of irresponsibility, but after implementing such policies, it is accused of being draconian and inhumane. The way the one-child policy was until recently used as grounds for refugee status in the United States marks the dilemma sharply.

It appears that Chinese civilisation has bequeathed the following deep-rooted concerns: China's size gives priority to collective and public goals over individual and private goals; the necessity for immense infrastructural projects, and the continuous danger of the country's being invaded or falling apart, support the historic tradition of strong central control. However, since the ideas of democracy were introduced, there have been changes in emphasis. For almost a hundred years, democracy has been accepted and desired by the Chinese people as a civilised goal. Human rights, too, as another marker of modern civilisation, have been acknowledged as important for at least half a century. We can only hope that it will not be long before they receive the priority they deserve. But it will be surprising if the form of democracy that eventually emerges and the legal and administrative framework established for the support of human rights will be the same as those that have evolved in a Judeo-Christian and Greco-Roman cultural context. That may not, in any case, be as important as having the ideas incorporated in the Chinese way to meet the challenge of the modern civilised world.

A Global Power

I have now reached the point when we might look at the future of China as a global power. Here, I am obviously looking at China as represented now by the PRC, soon with the addition of Hong Kong, and later possibly in some special relationship with Taiwan. Many Chinese may hope that this China will soon be such a power, but I do not think that this is an important part of China's self-perception today. From what has been surveyed above, it is clear that, whichever perception China focuses on, the ingredients for being a regional power are already in place, whether in terms of a rejuvenated economic presence, a modern nation built on its historic past, or a potential model capable of challenging the Western models of the 19th and 20th centuries. But how those ingredients might contribute to China's capacity to project itself globally is harder to say.

For China's neighbours, the view is simple. China's size and location by themselves are powerful reminders of past superiority and possible future threat. China's very existence, however passive and inward-looking, has always aroused interest and concern. What would be new and alarming to the region would be a modernised China finding that it has to behave like the modern great powers of the West. For example, is it likely that China will behave like 18th- and 19th-century Britain and France in their quest for maritime empires, or like Russia in its overland drive toward the east? Or would China model itself after the intensely aggressive latecomers Germany and Japan, or aspire to some version of the American Manifest Destiny? With all those "glorious" and recent examples before them, could the Chinese resist the dynamic urges of modern competitive expansionism? Could China's neighbours be assured that future regional relations would be based on fraternal cooperation, or, at worst, merely the benign neglect of a patronising "big brother"?

This is not the place for predicting what is, or is not, likely to happen to China's growing power during the coming decade or so. As all scholars of 20th-century China know, there are many political variables at work inside inherently unstable systems, especially when so much at the centre depends on the few dominant personalities who exercise control and on the factional struggles between them. Although this has not prevented many among us from crystal-gazing, many of those who predicted confidently have already been proven wrong. What I have suggested so far is that we look not only objectively for relevant facts pertaining to China's potential power, but also for more subjective dimensions that are illustrated in past and present self-images. While this will not guarantee accurate predictions, it will aid our efforts to see larger trends and thus anticipate future developments. In the same spirit, I shall now point to five significant examples that, because of their international dimensions, and despite an apparently local and regional focus, might make a difference to China's future global ambitions.

First, the unequal relations between the PRC and the United States symbolise the global ramifications of anything China does. This includes China's participation in international organisations like the United Nations and new bodies like the Asia-Pacific Economic Cooperation (APEC) Conference. China's attempts to join the World Trade Organisation and the opposition of the United States are symptomatic of some of China's problems in becoming a player in international affairs.

The Beijing government believes that the United States, by its very nature as a superpower, will interfere globally wherever it can. The PRC is forced to deal with the United States at most forums and has to have a global strategy to keep up with U.S. plans and ambitions. It does not have the wherewithal to restrain the United States everywhere, but it can try to limit interventions in its own region, East and Southeast Asia. Indeed, it must do so if it is to have any credibility as a future power. It can do so by being active in bilateral relations, by encouraging American multinationals and financial institutions to invest in China, by opening up for more trade, by being extremely careful in northeast Asia (especially regarding the two Koreas), where U.S. interests are sensitive and unstable, and by responding as positively as possible to U.S. overtures in regions where China's own interests are minor. Since the tragedy at Tiananmen Square in 1989, the generally cooperative moves made by the PRC have been extraordinarily successful. Outside Asia, the Chinese leaders have experienced some anxiety only where U.S.-Russian relations are concerned. But as long as Russia is busy within its own borders, and more preoccupied with its future in Europe than in northern Asia, Sino-American relations need not be affected.

It is not clear how well Chinese and American policy-makers understand each other today. Neither side has any distinct advantage. It is probably true to say that more Chinese understand the West than vice versa, if only because the West is more open and the Chinese written language is so difficult to learn. But the quality of the understanding among the experts remains uncertain, and their access to power-holders seems equally limited. There have been gross misunderstandings in the past, and the results were destructive to both countries. Can the new generation of experts rise above the historical obsessions with the evils of capitalism on the one hand and communism on the other? Will they be allowed to look at present problems with open eyes?

There have certainly been major changes in perspectives. The United States is still adjusting to the fact that it is the only remaining superpower. This is happening at a time when its people are increasingly discontented with the country's politicians and critical of its financial burdens overseas. The very successes of the past decade in stimulating economic growth in East and Southeast Asia, and in trying to do the same in Eastern Europe, have led to the perception that the United States, as the leader of the West, is in relative decline. If the Chinese misread this as an opportunity for them to lead future challenges against the United States, the world will be in for troublous times.

Continued fears and suspicions of China as a communist state, however, may fail to give sufficient weight to the determination to make its form of market economy successful. The PRC has passed the stage when concentrating resources on making the country powerful while keeping the people's standard of living low was a policy considered to be both patriotic and ideologically correct. The government's commitment to economic reform is deep and far-reaching, and the people who have endured poverty for decades will not stand for a return to national self-aggrandisement at their expense. What is truly challenging for China's leaders and their advisers is to show the world that the existing structures within the country can cope with the agonies of modernisation. They have the task of convincing the world, and especially the U.S. leaders, that failure in China will harm everybody. It is no less difficult to persuade China's neighbours that its success will not endanger peaceful relations in the region and that there is no need to call for the U.S. cavalry.

There is hope that matters will improve. Detaching the Most Favoured Nation provisions from China's human rights performance was the right decision. Both sides need a greater concentration on mundane but concrete commercial issues at this stage of the economic revolution in China. However acrimonious the debate, the unflinching attack on copyright infringements in China produced results. There are genuine business problems to be solved, and solving them openly for all to see is the best way to dispel conspiracy fears. The experiences of the past decade in bilateral relations have much to teach the expert advisers on both sides. The problem is that both groups of experts remain handicapped by political and cultural environments that insist on fighting the old wars by new means.

The second issue is the treatment of Hong Kong, which will mark an early test of China's readiness to play a global role; this is one of the reasons Britain and its allies are pressing hard to ensure that Hong Kong's international position will not be constrained after 1997. It would be easy to underestimate the PRC's hostility to any suggestion that there be any British influence left in the territory, or that China's sovereignty over Hong Kong after 1997 be questioned. To the PRC, Hong Kong should have been a purely internal matter to be resolved between the PRC and the colonial power. But the city's extraordinary importance to Chinese economic reforms since 1978 has given it international clout. If not for the Tiananmen Square tragedy and the collapse of the Communist bloc in Europe, China could have expected a low-key transition, with Britain, the United States, and Japan assisting in a smooth transfer of sovereignty.

But the international dimension became a much more central issue after 1989. The Hong Kong people, who are used to a considerable amount of freedom, are understandably fearful of losing that freedom. Attention has shifted from economic matters to questions of political rights, press freedom, and the legal system. Increasingly, comparisons are being made with the lack of such protections in the PRC itself. In their efforts to preserve those protections, Hong Kong people have begun to insist on establishing the principles of universal human rights before 1997, and seek to draw international attention to their territory. Chinese officials are increasingly irritated by the widening range of foreign concerns about Hong Kong. To protect the excellent financial and business environment in Hong Kong, the PRC will have to exercise considerable diplomatic skill to persuade outside interests not to interfere. But if the transfer of sovereignty is well handled, it will enhance China's global status.

The third example concerns the independence pressures within Taiwan. This is an even more difficult test, for China will have to fiercely defend the principle that this is an entirely internal matter. The mixture of caution and blustering rhetoric has revealed the great tensions underlying this relationship. The United States has supported the leftover regime from a bitter civil war; for over 45 years, the PRC has looked on this as a U.S. thorn in its side. During the latter part of this period, Taiwan's economic success has led to political freedoms that now challenge the fundamental principle that there could be only one China, one nation, and one set of historical roots. This was the principle that gave the Guomindang its legitimacy to rule Taiwan after they left the mainland.

Now, however, among some Taiwan people, there are serious questions about the validity of sharing that one civilisation. There are calls for independence; the PRC finds this intolerable, although its actions have been surprisingly restrained so far. It probably has little choice now. But it is not clear whether the mainland government will remain calm if some excitable Taiwanese take their independence desires much further. What is clear is that if the calls develop into action, the threat of war across the straits will be great indeed.

Within the region, Taiwan is diplomatically contained, but trading relations with other countries, including the mainland itself, are growing faster than anyone expected. The biggest challenge would come if Taiwan's position were to gain sympathy as China's power rises. For the rest of the world, the efforts to isolate Taiwan globally are still continuing. It is a manageable problem, but nevertheless one that calls for the greatest vigilance. Taiwan's persistence is not allowing itself to be ignored by the rest of the world has frequently put the Beijing leaders on the defensive, and this undermines China's global position somewhat.

The issue of Tibet is the fourth example. This requires patience on all sides; it is a long-term problem that will not go away and will call for statesmanship of the highest quality. China has stood firm that this is an internal matter, and international law and U.N. practice support that position. The challenge today is really neither political nor military. The special quality of Tibet's culture and history, its unique religion, and the loyalty and faith that they arouse have produced a moral authority for Tibet that will continue to bring it considerable sympathy from the rest of the world. China's comparative wealth, its power and influence, or even its legitimacy will not help. Even if conscientious laws, good intentions, and humane administration were to be consistently applied in Tibet, China would still not easily overcome the image of having been the invader. Tibet is the only one among the various autonomous regions and districts along China's lengthy borders where normal methods of control seem to have been adequate to stop secessionist demands. It is ironic that this internal issue pertaining to a region so strategically important to China should have become such a cancer. But it highlights China's difficulty with concepts of nation and civilisation that I referred to earlier. Neither fits the Tibetan story, and the appeal to the idea of historic empire has simply not been convincing enough. As a potential global power, China here faces a real test of its patience and humanity.

The fifth example is the most immediately challenging. This is the issue of who controls the Spratly Islands in the South China Sea. It will be most difficult to prevent this political and economic issue from becoming a military one that could spill over beyond the region. The recent flare-up with the Philippines over a few reefs may well remain a purely regional affair, to be resolved between China and members of the ASEAN states. It would, of course, be best if that could be accomplished with a minimum of ill-will. In terms of China as a future global power, however, its approach to the issue will be scrutinised with great care. Which perceptions by China's neighbours will come to the fore?

The territory of a "historic empire" has been invoked; obviously it is not a matter of civilisational ambit or revolutionary socialist superiority. But this is not a traditional claim; as I have mentioned earlier, there was no concept of clearly demarcated international boundaries in the past. There is nothing in the dynastic records, not even those of the tributary system, to validate China's claim to these islands. In fact, it is a modern claim first made in answer to Western imperialist and colonial practices earlier this century. Thus, it is really a matter of national strategy or, perhaps equally, one of resources and economic interests. The Spratlys, therefore, remind us that modern great-power and nationalist politics now govern Asia just as much as appeals to history and culture, or to past practices and principles. On the road to global power, China will have to balance its various perceptions of itself and take all of these into account.

All five examples outlined above concern relations that have direct repercussions for China's leadership image in the region. From what I have discussed in these two lectures, I hope to have provided a broad base of historical background, of traditional ideals, of modern goals and ambitions, of critical self-images, and of strong commitments and residual sentiments to help examine what China may do given the major problems it faces. How the Chinese leaders deal with these issues will determine China's position in international relations and help us to understand some of the possibilities for China's development as a global power. And how they do that will depend on how they balance their various layers of self-perceptions — China as a nation, empire, or civilisation, as development model or unique socialist market economy.

For years, I have had to argue with my European friends that communist China is not the same as communist Russia, and that China is not a "normal" country, not even a "normal" communist country. Some have agreed with me by pointing out that the Chinese communists misunderstood both Marx and Lenin and did not have much of a clue regarding what communism was really about. What I have outlined above, I hope, does illustrate how China is different. The way it perceives itself shows how its rich heritage as a civilisation and empire has complicated its claims to be a modern nation; why its unique linkages with Hong Kong, Taiwan, and parts of the diaspora have eased the pains of economic reform; and how it derived socalist ideals from its checkered revolutionary history. Together, these factors have made China an entity of paradoxes. China is all of the above, and yet more than the sum of its parts. It is still divided and incomplete, but it has political weight. It is multilayered, it is large and extensive, it is modernising, but it is also inclusive and able to use traditional values and networks to reach out for new knowledge, new technology, and new investment. Finally, the transformation of China has been a most painful one, dragging on for a more than a century, but the Chinese people have never given up and still seek to be modern and global and quintessentially Chinese.

*The lectures were given at the Norwegian Nobel Institute in May 1995 and published in the Institute's Spring Lecture Series as *The Chinese Way: China's Position in International Relations*.

Can China be Governed from Beijing?

Reflections on Reform and Regionalism

Philip A. Kuhn
Harvard University

Among the many sensational writings that have been published on China recently, some have predicted that China will soon become an aggressive superpower. Others have predicted that China's internal power struggles will soon cause her to disintegrate. Taken separately, such writings would cause considerable alarm, yet some of these doomsday scenarios seem to contradict one another.

The title of this paper, "Can China be Governed from Beijing?", may be explained further by a more exact phrase, "Can the economy, society, and culture of a modernising China be managed effectively from a single centre of political power?" Nobody knows just what the appropriate format may be for governing a nation-state with more than a billion inhabitants. Until quite recently, it had never been tried; and to judge by the results of the past twenty years, there is considerable disagreement among the Chinese about whether a unitary system of government will be the most successful form for China.

Two questionable assumptions have clouded the issue. The first is that because China was ruled by a single national government over a good portion of the past two millennia, that this is somehow its natural configuration. Since the 1890s, this presumption has been immeasurably strengthened by feelings that because poor and weak Chinese central governments have been victimised by foreign powers, the solution is to build a wealthy and strong Chinese central government that can defy such victimisation. That a strong China should be linked to the idea of a strong central government has been a persuasive idea in Chinese history, and modern nationalism has added to its persuasiveness. This is entirely understandable. But it does not address the practical problem of whether, under modern conditions, the old unitary ideal can actually produce the expected results. By modern conditions, we mean an immensely larger population, a more diverse set of linkages with foreign economies and foreign ideas, and a necessary goal of rapid economic growth that requires mobilizing local energies in new ways.

The second questionable assumption is that China, having invented the world's first centralised civil-service bureaucracy, will naturally carry this great invention forward into the modern age, because centralised bureaucracy is somehow as "natural" a form for the Chinese nation-state, as it was for the old imperial state. Certainly, a modern state should have a competent and honest bureaucracy. But the idea that bureaucratic service is the only route to political power, or the only mark of social esteem, may not be suitable to modern conditions, and may even make national wealth and power more difficult to attain. Even if it could be shown that an efficient bureaucracy is necessary for China's modernisation, that would not be quite the same as showing that the bureaucracy must be controlled from a single centre.

Both these questionable assumptions, derived from historical models, are influencing Chinese (and foreign) thinkers as they assess the current debate over how to accomplish economic reform. Some differences of opinion, however, have arisen on the subject of how the central government and the regions are related to one another under the reform programmes of the past decade or so.

THE COURSE OF DECENTRALISATION

Since 1979, China's leadership has embarked on a process of economic development that stresses local initiative, transition to a market economy, and decisive moves toward opening China to foreign trade and investment.[1] Deng Xiaoping seems to have had two general aims: to stimulate growth through local initiatives and incentives; and to win provincial and municipal officials to his reforms by giving them a greater share of power.

Results have been impressive, with China achieving one of the world's fastest rates of economic growth, an economy that is attractive to investment from abroad, and rapidly rising standards of living for much of its population. Underlying all this was the marketisation of China's agriculture and the unleashing of farmers' energies to raise production for profit.

Not surprisingly, progress has not been smooth. The major problems arise from the fact that without decentralisation and incentives, there seems to be no way to achieve the economic growth that China needs. However, with local officials given their head, new investment and infrastructure spending are poured into the economy, creating inflation due to overheated growth; and inflation is considered a serious political danger. Other dangerous by-products of decentralisation are a growing gap between the rich and the poor (and between the rich areas and the poor areas), and bitter competition for control of resources among economic regions: that such difficulties should have been met in the process was only to be expected. Some of these troubles gave rise to resistance from the older conservatives, who used them to argue against the whole process of opening and marketisation. Yet Deng Xiaoping persevered, partly by enlisting the support of key provincial leaders, and partly by investing his own prestige in the process (as seen in his celebrated "southern tour" of early 1992, to boost the process of opening and local initiative).

[1]A general account of the process may be found in Jia Hao and Wang Mingxia, "Market and State: Changing Central-Local Relations in China" in Jia Hao and Lin Zhimin (eds.), *Changing Central-local Relations in China: Reform and State Capacity*. Boulder: Westview Press, 1994, pp. 35–65.

Yet the early 1990s has witnessed a rather new sort of conservative criticism. This has taken the form of dire warnings about loss of central economic control and its implications for the political stability of the state as a whole. Such warnings are rather different from the old-fashioned socialist attachment to the centralised command economy. Some of them come from Western-trained economists and political scientists who fear that the central government has lost so much power, as a result of marketisation and decentralisation, that the result must be political weakness and the ultimate breakup of China as a nation-state.

THE "STATE CAPACITY" ARGUMENT

In May, 1990, two Chinese scholars drew up a report (evidently commissioned by central authorities in Beijing) on the dangerous decline of Beijing's ability to amass revenue. One, Wang Shaoguang, is a young political scientist trained at Cornell and now teaching at Yale University. The other, Hu Angang, is a member of the National Conditions Research Group at the Chinese Academy of Social Sciences in Beijing.[2] In its pre-publication form, this analysis was apparently very encouraging to those in the central financial ministry who wanted to recoup some of Beijing's power around the time of the Plenary Central Committee meeting of 1993.[3]

[2]The report was later published in Hong Kong: Wang Shaoguang and Hu Angang, "Zhongguo zhengfu jiqu nengli de xiajiang jiqi houguo" (The decline in the extractive capacity of the Chinese government and its results), *Ershiyi shiji* (Twenty-first century). No. 21 (Feb. 1994), pp. 5–14. A revised version in English (under Wang's name alone) appeared as "The Rise of the Regions: Fiscal Reform and the Decline of Central State Capacity in China," in Andrew G. Walder (ed.), *The Waning of the Communist State: Economic Origins of Political Decline in China and Hungary*. Berkeley, CA: University of California Press, 1995.

[3](And did so, to some extent, at the Nov. 1993 plenary meeting of the Communist Party's Central Committee.) See Dali L. Yang, "Reform and the Restructuring of Central-local Relations", in David S.G. Goodman and Gerald Segal (eds.), *China Deconstructs: Politics, Trade and Regionalism*. London and New York: Routledge, 1994, pp. 59–98.

The general argument proposed that by 1990, the central government's share of national income had declined precipitously as a result of decentralisation. This decline would have serious consequences for China's "state capacity" (state power). With "extractive capacity" falling (in relation to national income), other capacities of the state would inevitably fall, too: the capacity to direct or steer the use of resources; the capacity to legitimate itself in the eyes of the people, and the capacity to force obedience. But these three last capacities really depended upon the first: the capacity of the central state to extract revenue. The authors point ominously to the breakup of Yugoslavia which, they insist, cannot be blamed on ethnic hatred, but rather on the fiscal weakness of the state. The present danger to China, we are told, is evident from the lessons of history.

> "In the late stages of the Ming and Qing dynasties ... the fiscal power of local authorities was enlarged, and they became increasingly headstrong. At first, they feigned obedience to the centre's orders but secretly opposed them. Next, they competed openly with the centre for power and wealth. Then they sought to intimidate the centre in many ways, and in the end they set up separate regimes."

With the central power so weakened, "a mere push was enough to bring the whole regime crashing down into a heap of rubble". This could happen to China now: "Anywhere in the world, if the centre is weakened to the point where it cannot control the advancing power of the regions, there is no avoiding civil war."[4] Fiscal weakness at the centre is the fatal flaw that will eventually bring any government to ruin.

Although this analysis apparently found favour in some quarters of Beijing, it was quickly attacked by commentators (some of them American-trained Chinese scholars) who seem to have perceived in it a general hostility for the reform process. They criticised it on several grounds. It was pointed out, for one thing, that the realm of government properly includes more than central government; and that if you include local

[4]Wang and Hu, pp. 13–14.

governments' share of resources under reform, then the Chinese state (broadly speaking) is not in a weakened condition at all. Furthermore, the authors are criticised for leaving out the many other capacities of the state (such as the supervision and disciplining of local officials through the Communist Party machinery) that can keep central-local relations on an even keel.[5]

This last criticism is worth exploring in some detail. A recent book by an American-trained Chinese political scientist, Huang Yasheng, makes a closely reasoned case that Beijing is not only aware of the dangers of unrestrained localism, but is doing something about it. In fact, Huang argues, the political system of the central state is amply equipped to bring local officials into line through a variety of bureaucratic carrots and sticks. The essence of the book is that control of officialdom through the personnel and auditing agencies of the state and the Communist Party are achieving successful control of local authorities, even while retaining the incentives and dynamism originally intended by the reform programme. The state is not about to fall apart. This is a cautiously optimistic book, and in many ways a persuasive one.

Nevertheless, we have some reason to doubt that Beijing has quite solved the problem of regionalism. Too much of Huang's argument rests on inferences from institutional rules rather than on actual bureaucratic behaviour. One example is the question of tenure in office. Huang shows us that rotation in office has become more frequent over the course of the reform period, which he takes as a self-evident indication that "localism" is being successfully curbed (on the assumption that the longer an official stays in a post, the more likely it is that he will become coopted by the local people and less compliant to the demands of the centre).[6] Now it has long been the practice of Chinese governments to rotate top provincial officials frequently in order to avoid their becoming too enmeshed

[5]See the critiques by Yang Dali, Cui Zhiyuan, Jao Yuqing and Xiao Geng, in the same issue of *Ershiyi Shiji*, pp. 15–26.

[6]Huang Yasheng, *Inflation and Investment Controls in China: The Political Economy of Central-local Relations during the Reform Era*. New York: Cambridge University Press, 1996, pp. 113–114.

personally in the web of local relationships, or too parochial in their policy views. But Chinese bureaucratic records suggest that, in practice, frequent rotation compelled short-term governors to rely all the more heavily on their permanent staff, local functionaries who controlled the files and knew the local ways to get things done. As a result, central directives were even less effective than they might otherwise have been. This aspect of bureaucratic behaviour makes it harder to accept conclusions based on purely procedural safeguards (such as frequent rotation of officials). Hence even if we discount the "doomsday" predictions, we can still assume that there will remain substantial tendencies toward localism in the Chinese administrative system.

There is also a certain naiveté in Huang's assumption about how provincial bureaucrats control the behaviour of their subordinates.[7] Incentives and sanctions are important, of course, but the whole dimension of patronage is missing. By patronage we mean an obvious, practical concern for the well-being of one's subordinates. In a local government agency or enterprise, for example, such patronage would take the form of practical concern for the housing, bonuses and other fringe benefits of employees. Such concern would require the retention of more funds in the locality, resulting in a "localist" approach in relations with the centre. Whether the inclination to play the role of this sort of patron is more important in China than elsewhere has never been measured; but if so, then Chinese localism may be nourished by intangible factors that cannot be measured by theories of command relationships. In sum, the best book we yet have in the optimistic vein (that is, that the centre can keep things together) leaves one less than fully convinced. Perhaps the doomsday writers are not completely without grounds for concern.

From another angle, weakness at the centre has been pictured as the cause, rather than the result, of fiscal decentralisation. One theory is that the politically insecure central Party leaders, looking forward to the succession to Deng Xiaoping, engaged in a form of pandering to provincial interests ("playing to the provinces") in return for political support. In this

[7]Huang, pp. 182–185.

case, the weakening of central finances would seem to be the price they are now paying — on the installment plan, as it were.[8] But does all this indicate that China is in serious trouble?

THE "DUKEDOMS" ARGUMENT

The "dukedoms argument" takes its name from an article in the *People's Daily* of 1989, which compared the behaviour of China's provincial regimes under reform to the petty princes (*zhuhou*) of ancient China. The term was picked up by two distinguished economists and used to exemplify what they saw as the chaos in China's economic development.[9] The dukedoms argument is not explicitly a doomsday scenario, in that it does not predict the imminent political collapse of the regime. But it does propose a scene of vast disorganisation, in which local governments follow their own paths to quick profits. The result, they warn, is economic instability and inter-regional conflict, from both of which might be inferred an unpleasant political situation for the state.

Local governments, the argument goes, have been delegated authority over economic management but have become, at the same time, interested parties in the profits of local enterprises. Administrators of cities, counties and provinces benefit in all sorts of ways from the economic growth of their regions. The result is that their managerial decisions are skewed toward super-speed growth, inefficient competition with other regions, and the inevitable short-term bottom-line.

So compelling is the competitive struggle for faster growth that local officials follow what's called the "three light" principle: "Red light means drive right ahead; yellow light means drive faster; and green light means shove forward at top speed."[10] In practical terms, such a single-minded

[8]On "playing to the provinces", see Susan L. Shirk, *The Political Logic of Economic Reform in China*, Berkeley: University of California Press, 1993.

[9]Shen Liren and Dai Yuanchen, "Woguo 'zhuhou jingji' de xingcheng jiqi biduan he genyuan", *Jingji yanjiu*, 1990.3, pp. 12–20.

[10]Shen and Dai, p. 19.

pursuit of economic expansion and profits seems to the authors a recipe for uncontrolled inflation, a widening gap between rich and poor regions, and risks of political instability.

At the outset, we can acknowledge that many of these writers' concerns are justified. Protectionism and even economic blockades among provinces, inflationary pressures due to uncontrolled investment by localities, and neglect of local services, such as education, are all unpleasant or even destructive by-products of financial decentralisation.[11] Yet there may be more to all this alarmism than meets the eye.

The Rhetorical Style of the Doomsday Scenarios

Several forms of reasoning seem to underlie these doomsday scenarios. The dominant one is what might be called the dynastic paradigm. The state capacity scenario is quite explicit in reminding us that the fall of dynastic regimes has historically been associated with declining central revenue and a consequent rise in the power of the regions. The reasoning is starkly oppositional, and based on a zero-sum principle. A constant tug-of-war between centre and periphery is perceived as the main principle of dynastic rise and fall. Division and unity alternate in the historical record, and the index of dynastic rise and fall is primarily fiscal.

In the dukedoms argument, the historical metaphor is the giveaway. The original dukedoms (*zhuhou*) in Chinese history referred to the regional nobility that arrogated power to themselves as the rule of the good-and-virtuous Zhou dynasty waned. These former vassals, history tells us, ruled illegitimately, with every duke for himself. Their disorderly and selfish contests for power were the background for the Confucian insistence on restoring legitimate and morally sound government to China.

In both scenarios, division is the evil principle and unity the good; and a finger-wagging moral tone is not far from the surface. As a result of the

[11]See, for example, the horrific results in the neglect of non-compulsory education, in Wei Houkai and Yang Dali, "Difang fenquan yu Zhongguo diqu jiaoyu chayi", *Zhongguo shehui kexue* 1, Jan. 1997, pp. 98–113.

local leadership's increased financial power, large sums have been spent on "luxury items such as cars, air conditioners, refrigerators, modern office equipment, nice office buildings, and the like". Furthermore, many such extravagances suited local tastes very well indeed: "In the 1980s, luxury hotels, state-of-the-art amusement parks, sky-high TV towers, modern overpasses, giant stadiums, and many other types of large non-productive projects sprang up like mushrooms after rain throughout China."

Thus it was easy for local leaders to build up their personal public images. Obviously, the writer implies, no national government would ever waste public funds in such a manner, and certainly not for the sake of burnishing the leadership's public image![12]

Well, how misguided is the fear of central weakness and regional strength? These conditions seem to replicate those that invited foreign aggression of modern times.[13] The sense of outraged nationalism is a pervasive background theme in the critiques of regionalism. At no time in the twentieth century have Chinese patriots considered anything more important for the survival of the Chinese people than a unified, powerful Chinese state. Nevertheless there are some problems with this equation of national survival and unified central rule: first, the illogical connection between the survival of China and the survival of a particular central regime with a particular political philosophy; and second, the place of today's regionalism in China's long-term historical development.

NATIONAL SURVIVAL AND UNIFIED CENTRAL RULE

That China's survival depends on a particular form of government, or even on a particular regime, is an assertion we have heard repeatedly in modern times. It generally comes from a regime in power, or from a political

[12]Wang Shaoguang, "Central-local Fiscal Politics in China", in Jia Hao and Lin Zhimin, *Changing Central-local Relations*, pp. 101–102.

[13]One writer even felt it necessary to point out how historically important a strong central government has been for China. Shen Yiyuan, "*Shilun zhongyang zhenquan de quanwei zai Zhongguo lishishang de zuoyong*", *Shehui kexue* (Shanghai), 1996.6, pp. 66–67.

movement in competition to achieve power. As one foreign scholar phrased it neatly, "The idea of China is implicitly identified with the ideal of the unitary state, and the unitary state itself is conflated with each successive state formation and ultimately with the particular parties which govern in its name."[14]

It is not so unheard of to link national survival with a particular regime (as it happens in the United States, for example, from time to time), but this linkage discredits alternative ways to solve national problems. Federalism, for example, was proposed in China during the 1920s as a way to achieve modernity without an oppressive central state. But the idea was quickly attacked as being a mere fig-leaf for warlordism and, therefore, virtually treasonous. Similar arguments underlie current-day attacks on regionalism. Without discounting the awkward managerial problems associated with China's reform programme, I should simply like to question the assumption that China's national survival depends on a particular balance between the centre and the regions. That national survival should be brought up at this moment of history, when the danger to China's integrity from foreign aggression seems more remote than at any time in the past century and a half, is particularly astonishing: that is, unless we take into account the long-ingrained anxiety of modern Chinese intellectuals, whose sense of mission as a national elite has historically been linked to national unity and centralisation. If businessmen were interviewed on this question, we should most likely find just as high a level of patriotism, but a lower level of anxiety on the issue of centralised power.

A Historical Perspective on China's Reforms

Although we conventionally see the twentieth-century revolutions as the beginning of a totally new stage in China's history, let us for the moment

[14]John Fitzgerald, "'Reports of my death have been greatly exaggerated': the history of the death of China", in David S.G. Goodman and Gerald Segal (eds.), *China Deconstructs*. p. 37.

look at today's China as only the most recent stage in a long historical process. First, we shall examine the relationship between business and government over the last several centuries; and second, we shall explore the role of foreign trade in stimulating regional economies.

The Interconnection of Government and Business

One message lying close to the surface of the doomsday scenarios is that it is dangerous to allow local government and private business to become intermingled. Once local government becomes a beneficiary of private business activity, the argument goes, it loses its ability to stand above the fray and allocate resources in the national interest. It loses its ability to serve as a reliable agent of the central authorities. Local investment decisions will then inevitably aim toward maximum growth, which on a national scale will produce inflation, inefficiency and regional inequality.

There is no doubt that such mixing of economic motives is going on, and that it may require a more astute macro-economic management in Beijing to prevent the dangerous by-products of decentralisation (such skilful management, in monetary policy for example, is one of the goals adopted at the Party Central Committee meeting of November, 1993). But to denounce this mingling of official and business interests as something specially produced by the reform movement is not historically accurate at all. Provincial and local governments have been enmeshed in their local economies since imperial times, and sometimes to the great benefit of local society. Regional economies under the old empire developed as a result of cooperation between officialdom and merchants.

Fujian may be cited as an example. Fujian was the province most deeply involved with foreign trade during the seventeenth and eighteenth centuries. Maritime commerce was particularly important for the Fujian people's livelihood. The court at Beijing, however, had good historical reasons for seeing the Fujian coast as a security problem (the Qing dynasty had been at war with the military regime on the island of Taiwan until the 1680s), and the Manchu rulers, like their Ming predecessors, imposed maritime bans from time to time, out of security fears. Most striking, however, is that in the face of imperial suspicions, high provincial officials there assumed the role of protectors of the province's interest. It was the recommendations of such officials that turned Beijing toward a more accommodating policy toward foreign trade in general, and the import of rice from Taiwan in particular. Thus these imperial officials protected the Fujian economy from arbitrary political interference in their maritime livelihoods.

These provincial officials became, in effect, sponsors of the merchants under their jurisdiction, rather than mere agents of the throne's commands. The record is reasonably clear in the matter of personal profit: an official, such as a provincial governor, to say nothing of his subordinates, could get substantial personal income from foreign trade, both in the form of payoffs from merchants and in opportunities for personal investments. Fees assessed unofficially on merchants must have provided a substantial part of local government revenue.

Poverty and disorder in a governor's jurisdiction were bad for his career and certainly his political position. And they were also the historically proven results of cutting off the Fujianese livelihood from the sea. Economic distress made everything harder for a governor: from collecting taxes to keeping order. The gentry elite of Fujian were also deeply immersed in local and maritime commerce, so a governor's relationship with his local elite allies depended on how well he could protect his region's economy. So a provincial governor was both an agent of the centre and a patron of the society in which he served. Obviously, both roles were indispensable to him, and each role depended on the other. Without the confidence of the Beijing court, he would be useless to Fujian; and without the confidence of the Fujianese elite and populace, he would be unable to carry out his duties. He was a man living in two cultures, harmonizing the interests of one with the other as best he could. The Fujianese case is somewhat special because of the relatively long tenures of governors there. Yet we have good reason to believe that the same considerations affected the careers of local officials elsewhere.[15]

[15]Ng Chin-Keong, *Trade and Society: The Amoy Network on the China Coast, 1683–1735*. Singapore: Singapore University Press, 1983, pp. 194–200.

The commercialisation of late imperial society involved local government as a silent partner in enterprises of all sorts. The imperial government forbade officials to engage in trade. Nevertheless, it happened not only on an individual basis, but on the basis of government offices. The need to pay local administrative expenses in the absence of an authorised local tax base made this inevitable. Seen in the light of history, the Maoist interlude (when markets of all sorts were either abolished or brought under tight central control) was an anomaly. A re-commercialised China brought local government back into the act.

Thus the idea that the only route to power and prestige was through the imperial examination system is certainly not supported by the evidence. A recent American study asserts that the blending of commercial and official roles is a sign that a regime is approaching its last gasp: "This is the overwhelmed state, the state in decline or collapse."[16]

The difficulty here is the mistaken assumption that Chinese regimes at their strongest (whether imperial dynasties or the socialist state) permit "the monolithic dominance of just one channel of real prestige".[17] That one channel would be the civil-service examination system (for the old dynasty) or the Communist Party (for the PRC). It is certainly not true, however, that real prestige was so limited in imperial days: rich merchants hobnobbed with officials, officials shared discreetly in commercial ventures, and government bodies at all levels were sustained partly by revenue from trade. It might not be going too far to say that China, since the sixteenth century, had an increasingly integrated ruling class, with both official and commercial components, particularly in areas most affected by foreign trade. This condition persisted under the Guomindang government, and evidently is reappearing today. For a Neo-Confucian moralist, or a Maoist one, this may seem repugnant. For China's economic growth, it may not be such a bad idea. In any event, it seems to be a fact.

[16]Dorothy J. Solinger, *China's Transition from Socialism: Statistic Legacies and Market Reforms, 1980–1990*. Armonk, N.Y.: M.E. Sharpe, 1993, p. 260.
[17]Solinger, p. 259.

Regional Disparities as a Result of Foreign Trade

Not only is the partial commercialisation of the governing class a historical fact, disparities of wealth among provinces is another. Ever since the arrival in Asia of the European maritime empires (that is, some four centuries ago), China's southeastern coastal provinces have taken advantage of the chance to profit from overseas trade. This trade followed an older tradition, but was greatly expanded by the growing world demand for Chinese goods, and by the European strategy of using the Chinese as middlemen in their commercial empires. The economic development of Fujian and Guangdong today, so envied elsewhere in China, is only the most recent stage of a long process.

After the mid-nineteenth century, the foreign presence became more intense as a result of the system of treaty ports that followed China's defeat in the Opium War. Shanghai, Ningbo, and ultimately the Yangtze river ports of Hangkou and Chongqing were added to the list of burgeoning trading centres whose economies were heated up by foreign trade.

Thus regional economic disparities due to foreign trade are part of a long-term historical stage, which can be called "joining the world economy." That China was a victim during the process is a generally accepted fact. That some areas of China were enriched and transformed earlier and more thoroughly than others is another fact. The rules by which today's special economic zones (SEZs) are run are, of course, determined by the Chinese, not by the foreigners. Yet, like the old treaty ports, the SEZs are enclaves in which business enterprises, both Chinese and foreign, are specially privileged; and where lots of money is being made by all concerned, including local governments and officials themselves. Here, too, the re-commercialisation of today's China can be seen as a continuation of a long experience of foreign contact and domestic transformation.

China of the 1990s, however, is not simply a continuation of late-imperial conditions. Industrialism may change China more decisively in the next three decades, than commercialisation did in the past three centuries. Nevertheless, one striking continuity is worth our attention: the political power-holding class (now closely defined by the Communist

Party hierarchy) is still forced to balance its claims to political monopoly with the realities of ruling a highly commercialised society. Dealing with businessmen (merchants as they used to be called), who hold and generate wealth, requires bargaining with them, as well as sharing power and prestige with them, and even joining them in their investment and production schemes. Joining them may be done quietly, and often corruptly; or in the form of sharing profits through taxes and *ad hoc* contributions. The result resembles the systems we have seen in Southeast Asia, particularly Indonesia, in which a Chinese businessman teams up with a member of the non-Chinese elite in a mutually beneficial arrangement, in which the Chinese manages the business and the non-Chinese patron or nominal partner provides political cover and facilities (in return for a cut of the profits).[18] For Chinese officials today, sharing power and profits is, evidently, not an option, but a necessity, if local economies are to develop. The implications for regionalism are that local territorial officials, just as in imperial days, have to live within a centralised state hierarchy — but at the same time interact with business interests in the communities to which they are posted.[19] This suggests that the tension between central and regional power is not a dysfunction, but may be a permanent feature of China's modernizing society.

The Centre and the Regions: The Issue of Sovereignty

If localised commercialisation is the dominant trend of the last four centuries, the idea of unity is also a long-term historical inheritance. How are these two aspects of China's heritage to be brought together in stable

[18]Such systems are known variously as "Ali-Baba" or "Cukong". Such arrangements all occur within societies in which Chinese businessmen are barred from membership in the political elite, but the political elite knows little about running a business. Of course, the elite partner may gain some business experience as a by-product.

[19]One term proposed for such relationships is "symbiotic clientilism". David Wank, "Bureaucratic Patronage and Private Business: Changing Networks of Power in Urban China", in Walder (ed.), *The Waning of the Communist State*, pp. 153–183.

institutions? Among scholars who have written on current political-economy, there has been some talk about a federalist solution: an establishment of rules for the sharing of power and resources between the centre and the regions.[20]

Federalism, in the sense that is familiar to Americans, is rooted in the idea of multiple sovereignties. The doctrine of reserved powers means that the central government has only those attributes of sovereignty that the constitution has specifically conferred upon it, and no more. Other aspects of sovereignty remain with the states, or with the people. In cases of disputed or contradictory sovereignties, the courts will decide. In this sense, China has no sovereignty save that of the central government. The reserved powers concept works in the reverse direction: local authorities have only those aspects of sovereignty specifically conferred on them by the central government. This fact would seem, to a culture-bound American, to make Chinese federalism rather unlikely under present conditions. Nevertheless, there is one aspect of sovereignty that seems to have taken firm root in China as a result of the post-Mao reforms: local governments are now considered economic interest groups (*liyi jituan*) or as having separate economic identities (*jingji liyi zhuti*).[21] This is the natural result of the contract system that underlies the incentives and decentralisation of Deng Xiaoping's reform programme. Some elements of this idea can be found in the early twentieth-century republic, but their legal enforcement remains weak. If such economic powers prove durable in China, this would be a new development of great import. Local control of local resources was perhaps the most important principle on which Western political systems based their representative institutions; parliaments became a solid feature of the political landscape in Europe and North America because royal governments discovered that they had to bargain with the commercial elites in order to obtain the money they needed.

But that is exactly what the doomsday writers seem to be worried about: that there is actual bargaining and competition going on between local governments and Beijing in the matter of who gets money and who spends

[20]For example, Jia and Wang, "Market and State", pp. 54–58.

[21]Huang, pp. 58, 308.

it. Such bargaining and competition would be an inevitable part of a federalist system, with representative assemblies, regulatory agencies, and courts on hand to resolve disputes. To the doomsday theorists, however, these are signs of national disintegration. In the light of comparative history, however, this sort of economic localism looks rather like at least one aspect of sovereignty in the West: the authority to dispose of local revenues as local people see fit. In the West, the process of sharing with higher levels is subject to bargaining in a legislative assembly. In China, such bargaining is currently less institutionalised and less open to public view. To the doomsday theorists, this looks like a prelude to disorder or even national break-up.[22] Certainly, economic localism is now well entrenched in the Chinese system though it is still a long way from a system of democratic institutions. In my opinion, however, it does not look like the first stages of disintegration. Perhaps it is a hopeful sign that central-local relations are entering a more sustainable balance: a balance in which the vast problems of governing China will be shared between central and local units to the ultimate benefit of the nation.

A final consideration will be what this new balance will mean for ordinary Chinese citizens. Historical records offer no reliable wisdom on this subject; dispersion of power isn't necessarily associated with democracy, or with better treatment or opportunities for the common people. In the United States, for instance, the now discredited doctrine of states' rights was once used to justify oppressive treatment of minorities. In tomorrow's China, economic development in some regions may give rise to a kind of "civil society" in which private economic interests and non-official civic action groups serve as a balance vis à vis state authorities, and are a check against abuse of official power. On the other hand, a cosy, collusive relationship between local officials and businessmen, devoted solely to their mutual enrichment, may defer civil society into an even remoter future; and leave ordinary citizens as vulnerable as ever to the ambitions of the rich and the powerful.

[22]One remedy proposed is to weaken the separate economic identity of local governments and strengthen their supervisory identity. Given what we know of the present situation, this does not seem a realistic possibility. See Shen and Dai, p. 67.

Will China Become More Democratic?

A Realistic View of China's Democratisation

ZHENG* Yongnian
East Asian Institute
National University of Singapore

A "SHORT MARCH" TO DEMOCRACY?

One major issue facing China scholars in the study of China's political development is how realistic they can be. Emotions often prevent them from reaching realistic conclusions. This is especially true in their interpretations of Chinese democracy. As Harold Issacs noted, China for Americans "is uniquely capable of arousing intense emotion" (1962: 62). Similarly, Andrew Nathan contends that Americans seem to have had a missionary impulse toward China's democracy and a special kind of concern

*Zheng Yongnian is Research Fellow of the East Asian Institute, National University of Singapore. The paper is based on the author's seminar given at the East Asian Institute on 27 June 1997. An earlier vision of this paper was presented at the conference "Elections on Both Sides of the Straits" at Harvard University on 8 and 9 May 1997. The author is grateful to all participants at both occasions for their comments on the paper. Special thanks go to Professors Wang Gungwu, John Wong, Ezra Vogel, Bill Kirby, Benjamin Schwartz, Jonathan Hecht, Ms. Joyce Ng, Dr. Qi Lou and Zeqi Qiu.

with China, "delighting when China seems to accept our values and grieving when China and America are estranged" (1990: 78).

Delight, then grieve. This fluctuation has dominated many westerners' perception of Chinese democracy. Lamenting over the government's crackdown of the 1989 democratic movement, Lucian Pye wrote,

> Why does China thwart, frustrate and even embarrass those who are only trying to help? For all who befriend China, the story is the same: high hopes, then disappointment. ... China seems to evoke in others, particularly Americans, an irresistible desire to serve as China's teachers in the ways of the modern world, and thereby presumably help China improve itself. Yet, from the time of Lord Palmerston's efforts to get the Chinese to accept the conventions of Western diplomacy, to President Bush's humiliating attempts to alter the behavior of Beijing's current rulers, China seems impelled to reject the helping hand and to act in ways that seem perversely self-damaging in the eyes of those who believe they have that country's interests at heart (1990: 56).

Many in the West believe that it is their mission to spread democracy all over the world. They also believe that they are capable of achieving this mission. When communism collapsed in Europe, Francis Fukuyama claimed that Western liberal democracy has prevailed and human history ended (1989). However, such optimism often produces illusions. Until the 1989 Tiananmen crackdown, many scholars assumed that the post-Mao reform would and should lead to China's transition to democracy, capitalism and pluralism. When student demonstrations came to Western TV screens, many saw that the Chinese were just like "us." Obviously, the June-Fourth crackdown shocked the West.

Furthermore, the West' perception about Chinese democracy affects its China policy. It has been argued that democratic states do not go to war against each other. Even before he took over the White House, President Bill Clinton argued that countries whose citizens choose their leaders are more likely than those with other forms of government to be reliable partners in trade and diplomacy, and less likely to threaten peace. An authoritarian regime with rapid economic development could become a major threat to world peace. Even though capitalism has been used to save China as a nation-state, there is no sign that China will become a liberal democracy in the near future. So, some in the West began to talk about the "China threat" and "containing China." Liberals have argued that the West should use all possible means to promote Chinese democracy. Bill Clinton did attempt to use his power to promote human rights in China in his early years in the White House. Recently, Clinton's China policy began to turn to a more *realpolitik* vision. But according to Strobe Talbot, Deputy Secretary of State, this is because the Administration believes that "continued economic and cultural engagement is the best way to induce democratisation." Talbot's logic is like this: based on the experience of political development in other East Asian nations, "promoting economic growth while monopolizing political power is an almost impossible balancing act over the long term, especially in a world increasingly linked by communications and trade. As people's incomes rise and their horizons broaden, they are more likely to demand the right to participate in government and to enjoy full protection under the rule of law" (1996: 57). In the first news conference of his second term, President Clinton said that "the impulses of the society and the nature of the economic change will work together, along with the availability of information from the outside world, to increase the spirit of liberty over time;" that China could not hold back democracy, just as eventually the Berlin Wall fell (Lee Siew Hua, 1997: 1). At the same time, many seem to have forgotten what led to the 1989 Tiananmen incident and have become optimistic again. It is argued that China will have a "Short March" and become a democracy around 2015 (H. S. Henry, 1996).

China will perhaps eventually become a democracy. Yet, the more the people become impatient about Chinese democracy, the more deeply disappointed they will feel. If Talbott's logic does not come true, or China does not go in the direction we expect, what will we feel about China? What will the West's China policy be like then? A realistic assessment of Chinese democracy is imperative to avoid another shock and to develop a "right" China policy. The West's China policy cannot be based on an illusion of Chinese democracy, but on Chinese reality.

Based on a realistic assessment of Chinese democratic development, this essay attempts to provide an overall picture of China's democracy and draw some policy implications. The prospects can be grouped under the following headings: nationalism vs democracy, liberalisation vs democratisation, capitalism vs democracy, and the rule of law vs the rule by law.

NATIONALISM VS DEMOCRACY

A brief comparison of the linkage between nationalism and democracy in the West and China will throw light on how nationalism could be a major barrier to democratic development in China. Nationalism played an essential role in the development of Western democracy. Modern Western nation-states were created by the interplay of two types of sovereignty, i.e., national sovereignty and popular sovereignty. According to Hans Morgenthau, the idea of nationalism is intimately connected with the idea of freedom. "Nationalism as a political phenomenon must be understood as the aspiration for two freedoms, one collective, the other individual: the freedom of a nation from domination by another nation and the freedom of the individual to join the nation of his choice" (1957: 481). Nationalism first meant that the nation itself was called upon to defend its freedom. But more importantly, nationalism meant the triumph of individual liberty. The rise of nationalism was not only because the absolute monarchy betrayed the nation abroad, but also because it oppressed the individual at home. "Individual freedom was taken as a precondition of national freedom and the latter, in turn, was regarded as a mere extension of the former to the international scene. The political and legal principles, originally formulated to support and guarantee the freedom of the individual, were applied to the nation" (ibid: 482). Without the rise of popular sovereignty, it is hard to understand the evolution of Western modern nation-states.

However, when Western nationalism spreads to China, national sovereignty was separated from popular sovereignty. The former became dominant, and the latter was replaced by state sovereignty. This is because

China encountered a different international environment. When China began to modernise itself, it was an age of imperialism. When China was forced to open its doors, Chinese elites saw the mighty nations of the West primarily as military powers, with strong arms, a powerful class of military leaders, and overseas bases, colonies and spheres of influence. As Akira Iriye pointed out, such perceptions made a decided impression on the elite in China (also in Japan) and they became convinced that their countries should develop similar features (1992: 8–9). Facing imperialism, China had no choice but to modernise. Nevertheless, the highest priority had to be given to national survival, rather than individual freedom or democracy. Democracy was desirable, but it had to subordinate itself to national survival.

This is the theme of Chinese nationalism proposed by Sun Yat-sen, the founder of Republic of China. For Sun, nationalism's chief concern was to ensure the survival of the Chinese nation because it had suffered from foreign aggression. According to him, the meanings of Chinese nationalism were multifold. First, nationalism was equivalent to the doctrine of the state as China had been developing a single state out of a single race even since the Qin and Han dynasties. Second, nationalism was the key to the development and survival of the Chinese nation; and third, nationalism called for equality of all human races and was the way to restore freedom and equality to China (Chou, 1996: 68). These ideas are reflected in Sun's design of three stages of Chinese political development, i.e., military government, guided democracy and constitutional democracy. This strategy of political development is followed by many newly industrialised economies in East Asia. Today, Dr. Sun is revered by the Chinese government because his "guided" democracy is similar to China's official nationalism and Sun's nationalism could fill an ideological vacuum left by a declining Marxism and Maoism.

Li Zehou, a well-respected Chinese scholar, argued that national survival priority has been in conflict with democracy in modern China. National survival required an authoritarian regime, even a dictatorship. For Chinese elites, nationalism means national freedom, rather than individual freedom, collectivism rather than individualism. Facing a hostile international environment, a strong regime only means statism (1987). Li's argument was raised in the mid 1980s and was criticised by the Chinese government. This does not mean, however, that China has resolved the contradiction between a strong state and democracy.

After Deng Xiaoping took over power, China began to seek a favorable international environment in order to give highest priority to domestic development. China was successful in improving its relations with major powers and with its neighboring countries as well. China also achieved a high rate of economic growth in the 1980s. Ironically, however, rapid economic development did not make the Chinese state stronger than before. Indeed, state power has been in decline ever since.

How could this happen? The decline of central power is a natural result of the Chinese style of reform, i.e., decentralisation. Throughout its modern history, China's modernisation encountered a dilemma. China's system was highly centralised. Yet, the national government was not able to modernise a country that has great diversities. In terms of state capacity, the center was very weak. The only strategy for modernisation was decentralisation. But decentralisation produced growing pressure at other levels of the polity for participation in the political process, and participation further limited central autonomy in decision-making. As elite involvement at the local level expanded, it was increasingly accompanied by expectations that not only local men should manage local affairs, but also that elite views should be considered by officials in formulating national policy. Local political participation made it difficult for the national government to effectively organise its resources and implement its policies (Cohen, 1988).

This is what has happened in post-Mao China. Decentralisation promoted economic growth. But the impact of economic decentralisation was far beyond economic arenas. Central revenue shrank from 34 percent of Gross Domestic Product (GDP) in 1978 to less than 13 percent in 1995. Without strong fiscal capacity, the national government was not able to coordinate development among regions. The rise of local protectionism is only one of the signs of declining central power. The World Bank has warned the Chinese government that individual Chinese provinces are tending to behave like independent countries, with an increase in external trade and a relative decline in trade flows with one another.[1]

More seriously, with its declining fiscal power, the national government was not able to balance development among regions. Income disparities have widened consistently and led to complaints among local residents and government officials in poor areas. Regional disparities give a great momentum to ethnic nationalism. During Mao's time, Chinese political elites such as Chen Yun argued that China should learn from Yugoslavia in nation-state building, i.e., decentralisation. But now many Chinese intellectuals fear that China will follow Yugoslavia, i.e., national disintegration if decentralisation continues.[2]

Even before the 1989 Tiananmen Incident, many Chinese intellectuals began to talk about neo-authoritarianism. According to its proponents, the highest priority should be given to national integration rather than to economic and political reforms. The collapse of European communism made many Chinese top leaders believe that if China goes to political liberalisation, it would be hard for the Chinese Communist Party to avoid such misfortune. On the other hand, the collapse of the Soviet Union also had a great impact on Chinese psychology toward revolutions or radical reform movements. People now overwhelmingly appreciate social stability and economic development rather than political democratisation. When Hu Yaobang and Zhao Ziyang were in power, many Chinese expressed their strong desire for radical political reform. Many regarded a totalitarian regime as a threat to the country and themselves. Hu and Zhao had to pay attention to this popular sentiment. But now they realise that a weak national government would not do any good for them and for the country; that an authoritarian government is necessary for China's continuous political stability and economic growth. This psychological condition is

[1]About local-central relations in reform China see Huang (1996), Jia and Lin, (1994), Zheng (1995), Wu and Zheng (1995), Wang and Hu (1993). A detailed discussion of the interdependence between China's provinces and the outside world see Gerald Segal (1994).

[2]This argument was raised by two Chinese scholars, Wang Shaoguang and Hu Angang (1993). Their report has been very popular among Chinese leaders.

what the new leadership wants. With this psychology, people become more indifferent to the regime's authoritarian measures against civil society. Under such circumstances, democratisation becomes more difficult (Zheng, 1996b).

Furthermore, with the rise of various anti-China theories such as "China threat" and "containing China," the Chinese now believe that China's international environment could deteriorate and domestic development could be endangered. This perception has led to the rise of popular nationalism against the West, especially the United States. For the leadership, this new nationalism can be used to justify the regime's authoritarian rule (Wu, 1995). Democratisation is regarded as a destabilizing force. As long as the Chinese dream of a strong state is not realised and nationalistic ideal is not materialised, democratisation will be unlikely.

LIBERALISATION VS DEMOCRATISATION

Many Western scholars believe that economic development will necessarily lead to liberalisation, which, in turn, will lead to political democratisation. When Singapore's Senior Minister Lee Kuan Yew contended that democracy does not necessarily lead to development, that the exuberance of democracy leads to indiscipline and disorderly conduct which are inimical to development, *The Economist* expressed its disagreement and claimed that "voting is good for you."[3] The recent transition to democracy in South Korea and Taiwan has strengthened this optimistic belief. In the long run, it may be true. However, the causal linkage between liberalisation and democratisation is rather weak in the context of Chinese political development.

The necessity of liberalisation is obvious. The state must lift its control and let individuals have freedom if it wants to promote economic development. If the national government wants local government officials

[3]The issue whether democracy promotes or hinders is very controversial among Western scholars, see *The Economist* (1994).

to make laws or regulations appropriate to local conditions, it must not impose any strict and unified laws on them from above. If economic performance becomes a foundation of the CCP's political legitimacy, liberalisation will follow. Put it in another way, individual and local autonomy is a precondition of rapid economic development. Economic reforms mean that the national government withdraws from economic affairs and decentralises economic decision-making power to individuals and local units. Without individual and local economic initiative, rapid development will be impossible.

Economic liberalisation also led to political liberalisation to some degree. Many reformist Chinese leaders, especially Deng Xiaoping, realised that a Marxist-Leninist state is incompatible with a market economy and political reforms are needed to make the system more accommodative to economic growth. China's political system has departed from the old totalitarianism. Harry Harding calls it a "consultative authoritarian regime"(1987). Institutional changes have occurred to China's political system. For example, China has carried out a local direct election system. Democracy at the grass roots level works quite impressively as Henry Rowen described (1996). The National People's Congress (NPC) has extended its functions in China's politics. Today, it has established various functional standing committees to consider and discuss state matters regularly. Many professional academic associations and research institutions are also encouraged to participate in politics through discussing political agendas, initiating or considering state policy, and providing information for the state's decision making.

However, economic and political liberalisation will not necessarily call for a western style of democracy. In other words, political democratisation is unlikely if we define "democracy" in the Schumpeterian tradition. In his pathbreaking study, *Capitalism, Socialism and Democracy*, Joseph Schumpeter provided us with a procedural definition of democracy. The "democratic method," he said, "is that institutional arrangement for arriving at political decisions in which individuals acquire the power to decide by means of a competitive struggle for the people's vote" (1947: 269). Within this tradition, Robert Dahl argued that democracy involves the two dimensions, i.e., contestation and participation. Democracy implies the existence of the civil and political freedoms to speak, publish, assemble, and organise that are necessary to political debate and the conduct of electoral campaigns (1971).

If Chinese democracy is understood in terms of this Western perception, political liberalisation apparently will not lead to democratisation in the foreseeable future. Political democracy does not necessarily facilitate economic growth and other aspects of social progress as shown in the cases of the Philippines and India. Historically, economic growth took place under different forms of government, not necessarily democratic government. This is especially in East Asia. Development requires a strong and efficient government which commits to development and is able to mobilise savings and other resources. Indeed, it has been argued that "South Korea's industrial take-off took place under a military dictatorship, Taiwan's under martial law, and Hong Kong's under colonial rule" (Wong, 1996: 15). Yes, democratisation occurred to Taiwan and South Korea recently. But social chaos also followed. What Chinese leaders have seen from their transition to democracy is that a drastic political transformation to a full democracy will bring China more chaos. Therefore, "development first, democracy later" has become a major perception among Chinese leaders for the country's modernisation.

Deng Xiaoping consistently argued that China will not follow a Western style of democracy, such as checks and balances, the separation of power and so on. Deng thus regarded all efforts that could lead to political democratisation as "bourgeois liberalisation." From the late 1970s when he took over power to the early 1990s, Deng established firmly a legacy that associated to his name. Politically, Deng transformed the Chinese Communist Party from a revolutionary party to an administrative one. Economically, Deng insisted that economic modernisation should be one of the basic principles that the CCP needs to follow. He once argued that those who do not promote economic modernisation should step down. The CCP has incorporated these principles into its constitution. Whoever wants to be Deng's heir must stick to these principles. The fall of Hu Yaobang and Zhao Ziyang was because they did not strictly follow these principles. But even their agenda of political reform is not to democratise China, but to improve government efficiency (Saich, 1991). In other words, a major aim of China's political reform in Deng's era was to consolidate and strengthen the CCP's rule. Jiang Zemin, now Deng's designated heir, has claimed that political reform will not be the Party's priority until early next century. Unlike Hu Yaobang and Zhao Ziyang, Jiang now rarely talks about political reforms. He concentrates on efforts to consolidate power, Party control and "spiritual civilisation." Only after Jiang feels that the CCP has consolidated power over society, will political reform be possible. When political liberalisation poses a political threat to the CCP's rule, the leadership becomes intolerant. As I will show later, as long as the party-state stays above the Chinese society, political liberalisation will be very limited, let alone democratisation.

Yes, China has established a rural election system. In some sense, it is a form of democracy because rural residents now are able to participate in local politics and air their voices over local decision-making. However, grass roots election is more like "local autonomy" rather than "democracy". Regime democratisation and rural political participation are two quite different things. The rural election system can be regarded as democracy from below. But it was initiated from above. Peng Zhen, the founder of the rural election system, stated clearly in 1987 that rural democracy could be used to save the CCP's rule. Without any constraints on party cadres and government officials at lower levels, the CCP's totalitarian rule could result in popular complaints, even rebellions against the CCP. Peng, Chairman of the National People's Congress then, believed that rural elections could play a role in constraining local officials' arbitrary behaviour.

The impact of the local election system on China's democratisation is mixed. On the one hand, the grass roots democracy resulted in a phenomenon that may be called "the lowering of the center's political legitimacy," that is, the lower level the government is, the higher level of political legitimacy it possesses. Because government officials at the grass roots level are elected by local residents, they can say "no" to higher authorities since their political legitimacy is no longer based on appointment or recognition from higher authorities, but on popular votes (Zheng, 1996a).

Governments at higher levels find that it is increasingly difficult to deal with lower level officials. In this sense, the local election system promotes democratisation by putting political pressure on government officials at higher levels.

However, the local election system also slows down China's democratisation. First of all, since government officials at higher levels have already felt the pressure from local officials, they feared that a rapid spread of democracy will pose a threat to the CCP's rule and to the position of individual government officials. They are therefore unwilling to extend direct elections from the village level to higher levels. China's first direct rural election occurred in 1987. A primary election was also introduced in rural areas in 1997. But there is no sign that the system will be extended to higher levels soon. Second, rural democracy did play an important role in changing local officials' "working style", constraining their corrupt behaviour and improving government efficiency at the grassroots level. Local residents apparently have benefited from this system. However, the CCP also benefits from it because it alleviates the tension between the state and society and reduces local residents' complaints. Without facing high pressure from society, the national government does not need to address political reform as its priority. We have seen in Russia and East European countries how important political pressure from below is in initiating democratisation.

CAPITALISM VS DEMOCRACY

It is widely believed in the West that capitalism and democracy are twins, that capitalism and economic wealth are conducive to democratic government, that democracy as a form of government is likely only in market or capitalist economies. This theme is reflected in works by contemporary scholars such as Charles E. Lindbloom (1977), Samuel Huntington (1991), Seymour Lipset (1959), and Barrington Moore, Jr (1966). All of these authors saw the historical and logical connections between capitalism and democracy. Remember Moore's dictum, "No bourgeois, no democracy."

So, it has been expected that China's rapid economic growth would lead to political democratisation. The 1989 Tiananmen incident naturally shocked those who were optimistic about Chinese democracy. Why did rapid economic growth liberalise politics a bit but not democratise China's political system? This essay argues that the connectedness between capitalism and democracy is unlikely to appear in China as it did in advanced western countries. The development of democracy in China cannot be understood by viewing democracy as a natural result of economic development alone. Instead, democratic development must be considered in the context of the connectedness between the state and development. The state in a developing country like China is not only an agent of political order; it is also responsible for facilitating socioeconomic development. In other words, differing from states in the West, state authorities in China have to generate capitalism and economic development. The state thus faces a dilemma between economic development and democracy. The state must attempt to establish legitimacy and order, on the one hand, and has to promote socioeconomic changes from above on the other. But the state authorities often find that these two sets of goals are in conflict. Whereas democracy tends to require that the state accommodates many competing demands, effective performance of developmental functions pushes the state to stand above society in order to act as a rational agent of change. This tension seems to be irreconcilable in China's case, at least in the short run. The state often enforces its "rational" order on society, which tries to free itself from the state.

Furthermore, democracy requires a nonpolitical, a societal sphere. Development, however, demands that the state penetrate into society. In other words, both economic growth and the creation of civil society are political tasks. The state is thus in command of socioeconomic change. State domination of society makes it difficult for democracy to develop. Democracy is thus more likely to be a gift of the political elite to the society and less likely to be a political system that significant social forces create of their own volition as the West demonstrated.[4]

[4]This summary is based on my previous studies (Zheng 1995).

Capitalism has spread all over China and gained a development momentum, especially since 1992 after Chinese paramount leaders Deng Xiaoping made a high profile tour in South China. Deng argued that capitalism not only is compatible with, but also can be used to consolidate China's political system. The Fourteenth Party Congress convened that year formally legitimated China's market economy. The Chinese Communist Party (CCP) also incorporated the development of a socialist market economy into its constitution. To promote economic development becomes a, if not *the*, major standard for the central leadership to judge government officials' political achievements. Indeed, the rise of local developmentalism, i.e., development-oriented local governments, has been the major cause of China's rapid economic growth in the past decade. Local officials become key political and economic actors and are highly entrepreneurial in promoting their local interests (Oi, 1996; Walder, 1995; Zheng, 1995).

While local developmentalism promoted rapid economic growth, it is also in conflict with democratic development in China. With the withdrawal of the national government from local affairs, the local governments stepped in and became highly interventionistic. Decentralisation will not necessarily lead to the rise of civil society. Because decentralisation is concerned with interest distribution, local governments, as interest maximisers, took over the power that the state wanted to dispense to individuals. Compared to Mao's time, decentralisation did lead to political liberalisation and an increase in local autonomy as discussed above. However, this does not mean democracy. Because local officials monopolise both political and economic power, decentralisation has produced many small local "dictatorships". These dictators make their own "laws" and regulations in order to gain social control and elicit social compliance within their territories. At the same time, they limit the reach of state power. The national government has found that it is increasingly difficult to have its policies reach the grass roots society. Some Chinese intellectuals have begun to talk about China's feudalisation (Shen and Dai, 1990). Even though in the long run, feudalisation could play a positive role in checking state power as shown in the development of European modern democracies, it is apparently undemocratic because it deprived individuals of political and economic rights.

With massive economic resources in the hand of local officials, China's democratic development at the grass-roots level is just the opposite to what Lipset found in the West. Lipset found that democracy is likely to develop and to be sustained in wealthy and economically developed societies (1959). However, in China it is found that the local election system is performed better in poor areas than in rich ones. According to the Ministry of Civil Affairs which has monitored local elections, compared to Guangdong (one of the richest area in China), local elections in Gansu (perhaps the poorest area), are more regular and fair (China Rural Villagers Self-Government Research Group, 1993). The reason is simple. Local cadres in rich areas can use their economic resources to elicit compliance from local residents and buy their votes. On the other hand, local residents fear that if they do not vote for these powerful government officials, their material life will be endangered. It is hard for them to choose between material wealth and political rights. Individual political rights frequently depend on whether a given local regime is benign or not.

Economically, entrepreneurship among local officials did play an important role in promoting economic growth. However, it also becomes a major barrier of macro-economic management. In order to promote local development, local officials have to act like entrepreneurs: developing local industries, providing coordination, finding customers, etc. Intensive competition among local governments resulted in local protectionism, which made it difficult to develop a national market system. The national government finds that it is necessary to recentralise its power frequently in order to reduce excessive power of local governments. However, the national government's measures of recentralisation often have a major impact not only on the local governments, but also on the progress of civil society. For instance, the state's recentralisation efforts after the crackdown on the 1989 democracy movement constrained the development of both local economy and new political forces.

THE RULE OF LAW VS THE RULE BY LAW

Democracy requires the rule of law. Since the reforms began in 1978, the growth rate of laws is probably higher than the economic growth rate. For instance, the National People's Congress made 7 laws from 1966 to 1978. But it made 251 laws from 1979 to 1994 (Zheng Hangsheng, 1996: 50). This development, however, does not mean that China is evolving toward democracy. China could become a country of the rule by law, but it encounters enormous difficulties in developing the rule of law.

The rule of law, according to F. A. Hayek's explanation, means that "government in all its actions is bound by rules fixed and announced beforehand — rules which make it possible to foresee with fair certainty how the authority will use its coercive powers in given circumstances and to plan one's individual affairs on the basis of this knowledge" (1994: 80). More concretely, the rule of law means, first, laws must be applicable to every individual in a given society, second, the rulers must follow the laws as the ruled do, and third, the rulers' behaviour is predictable.

The Chinese legal system has gained a development momentum since the late 1970s owing to various reasons. First, it did so because of economic necessity. The aim of the economic reform was to replace the old planned system with a market one. As the planned system faded, laws came to regulate China's economic activities. It is understandable that most of laws made since 1978 are laws on economic and commercial activities. Second, the decline of the role of the planned system made laws important to regulate people's social activities. The planned system was not only an economic system, but also a system of political control. When the planned system became ineffective, laws became important in governing people's social activities. Third, with the passing of the old generation of revolutionaries, the new generation of leadership must create a new base of political legitimacy. Old leaders could base their political legitimacy on their revolutionary experience. But this is no longer the case for the new generation of the leadership. Laws obviously could be used to consolidate and strengthen its power.

However, it is still unpredictable whether China will develop the rule of law. The government appreciates the importance of laws because Chinese leaders realised that law is an effective governmental instrument. When Deng Xiaoping transformed the CCP from a revolutionary party to an administrative one, he also emphasised that the country should be governed by law. The rule by law has become a major goal of Chinese political development. Put it in another way, laws are made for governing or regulating people's activities, but not the Party's behaviour.

Apparently, the rule by law differs greatly from the rule of law, because, as Hayek mentioned, the rule of law means that rulers have to follow laws as ordinary people do. In terms of the rule of law, China faces insurmountable difficulties.

First, the rule of law seems so remote from the Chinese tradition. Confucianism assumes that political elites should not be constrained by any institutional forces. "Popular sovereignty", as a Western concept, came to China from a Japanese translation. Chinese interpreted "democracy" as "to be master in one's own house" (*dangjia zuozhu*). But since political elites are superior to ordinary people from whatever perspective, people should be ready to give up their own decision-making power to government officials. So, for the government officials, "democracy" does not mean in any sense that people have rights to participate in decisions which will influence their daily life. Instead, "democracy" only means to make decisions for people (*weimin zuozhu*). Obviously, "to make decisions for people" is in accordance with Confucian elitism. This definition of democracy is also within the tradition of the legalist. According to the legalist, laws were made for governing people, not for checking the rulers' behaviour. So, laws must be draconian in order to form a threat to people.

This tradition is embedded in the current legal system. Constitutionally, the National People's Congress (NPC) is the highest organ of state power. But in reality, the Party has always been above the NPC. The latter is only a "rubber stamp" of the former. A recent report by the Chinese People's University stated, the NPC has the rights to revise and rescind any laws or legislations made by other state organs which are contradictory with those made by the NPC. However, up to now, the NPC has not revised and rescinded any single piece of law or legislation, because the Party or other government organs seem more powerful than the NPC and what the NPC can do is to persuade them to change and revise laws and legislations they made (Zheng Hangsheng, 1996: 57). The shadow of the CCP over the NPC makes China's legal system ineffective. Qiao Shi, Chairman of the NPC, recently came publicly to defend the role of the NPC and stressed the limits of the Chinese Communist Party in an interview with the US newspaper *The Philadelphia Inquirer*.[5] Qiao emphasised that the Party should conduct activities within the limits permitted by the constitution and the law, that Party organisations at all levels and all Party members must strictly observe the law.

As long as the Party stands above law, the Chinese legal system cannot be effective, and the rule of law cannot be realised. Top leaders are always able to initiate nationwide anti-crime campaigns at will. For instance, an anti-crime campaign in early 1996 was mobilised only because a high-rank government official was murdered. The Party-state is also using law to constrain official corruption. However, not every government official is equal before the law. The government did disclose enormous corruption cases at lower levels and punish those who committed crimes. But it has had difficulties in dealing with corruption among high rank government officials.

Another major barrier in the development of the rule of law is the personalisation of law. Differing from the old generation of leadership, the new generation has relied on laws or other institutional means for power consolidation. But in doing so, major leaders also personalised laws and institutions. In other words, laws and institutions are used for major leaders' personal interests. For instance, while Jiang Zemin, the boss of the CCP now, attempted to consolidate his power, he sent his own fellows to different government organs. Personal network is still an important means for individual leaders to strengthen their positions. The personalisation of institutions makes an effective legal system impossible, let alone the rule of law.

[5]*The Philadelphia Inquirer*, December 15, 1996. The interview was also published by *China Daily*, a Beijing based English newspaper, December 17, 1996.

A Chinese Way of Democracy

This essay neither argues that democracy is unlikely to develop in China nor does it predict that democracy will occur in the near future as many western optimists expect. Some implications can be inferred from the above analysis.

China scholars should not be too emotional about China's democracy. Instead, they need to develop a more realistic view on this issue. Yes, we may feel more comfortable about a democratic China than an authoritarian one. However, democratic development is a complicated process. Since China was forced to open its doors to the West, modern Chinese political development has related to various western concepts such as "democracy," "popular sovereignty" and so on. For better or worse, they have had an impact on the political elites' mind-set of how Chinese development needs to be directed. Without doubt, Dr. Sun Yat-sen's "republic", Taiwan's presidential election, and mainland China's rural elections, all do not originate from China's tradition. Obviously, democracy is spreading in China, but whether it will take roots depends on various factors as discussed above. In other words, democracy is not incompatible with China's development, but it needs a right time and the right environment.

Modernisation and economic wealth have had a major impact on China's political development, but it is still uncertain whether Chinese democracy will have a right external environment. As a late developing country, China's democratic development has been seriously constrained by international circumstances. Throughout its modern history, Chinese political elites aimed to build a strong and independent nation-state. Democracy was only a means to this goal. If democracy made China weaker, it would become undesirable. When nationalism revives, democratisation becomes a second priority. Mao Zedong once claimed that only democracy could save China as a nation. But when Mao felt that China was still surrounded by western imperialism, he built a totalitarian regime and made people believe that such a regime was necessary for China's survival.

Similarly, Chinese nationalism in the 1990s can be regarded as a reaction to various "anti-China" theories such as "China threat" and "containing China" in the West, especially in the US. Wu Guoguang pointed out that the "containing China" theory has resulted in China's strong nationalistic reaction and pushed the regime toward a more traditional and authoritarian direction (1995). Indeed, in the 1980s, Chinese political elites perceived a peaceful international environment and focused on domestic development. But with the rise of various anti-China theories, more and more Chinese perceive a "bad" international environment. The regime will like to use such popular perception to justify the necessity of authoritarianism. It is worthwhile to note that China was humiliated by foreign powers for more than a century. Now, when China, for the first time in its modern history, has an opportunity to be strong, the West wants to contain China, it is difficult for political elites and people not to have a nationalistic emotion and feeling.

There are enormous contradictions between democracy and Chinese tradition. But China's modernisation and economic growth are not incompatible with democracy. Since the reform policy was initiated in the late 1970s, China has shown its eagerness to learn from the West, especially in terms of economic institutions. The Chinese government has continuously turned to international organisations such as the IMF and the World Bank to solve Chinese economic problems and build a new system. On the political side, the regime has been very cautious in learning from the West. The West, based on its own conception of democracy, shows its firm support to Chinese dissenting voices and human rights, but lacks any instrumental means to materialise it. Ideological factors are still playing an important role in Western powers' China policy. Even though China has implemented the rural election system since 1987, only until recently did the media and academic circles in the West begin to pay attention to it. It is found that China is learning from western democracy and is receiving help from international organisations to improve the election system. Nevertheless, Western opinion leaders' emphasis has been on the "negative" side, i.e., how Chinese rural residents resist state power, rather than the "positive" side, i.e., how the Chinese national government makes efforts to nationalise the system and make it more effective in reducing its local officials' arbitrariness (O'Brien, 1996; Li and O'Brien, 1996, 1995). In effect, without any initiatives from above, China would not have developed rural democracy. So, any "correct" prediction of Chinese democracy requires a perception different from the one originates from the Western tradition.

Whether China will develop a democratic regime depends on its domestic development. Although external forces cannot do much about that, international circumstances do have an impact on Chinese political development. The international community, at least, can provide China with a right international environment for Chinese democracy to occur. The Chinese are optimistic people as expressed in an old Chinese proverb, "you will cross the bridge when you get to it", but they are also realistic and pragmatic as another saying shows, "it is too late to plug the leak when the boat is in midstream". China's economic reform is successful because it did not follow any existing model. Similarly, China will not follow any Western model in its democratic development. A senior Chinese government official claimed that once democracy comes, nothing can stop it. There is no reason to argue that China is not compatible with democracy. The question is: What form of democracy will China develop? Rapid modernisation requires that changes need to be introduced to the political regime. Without doubt, Chinese political elites have begun to search for a Chinese form of democracy, or as Deng Xiaoping emphasised, "a democracy with Chinese characteristics". A democratic China will be favourable to world stability and peace. Yet, how the international community can play a positive role in promoting democracy in China is an important agenda facing the world.

References

China Rural Villagers Self-Government Research Group. (1993) *Study on the Election of Villagers Committees in Rural China*, Beijing: China Society Press.

Chou, Yu-sun. (1996) "Nationalism and Patriotism in China", *Issues and Studies*, 32(11): 67–87.

Cohen, Paul A. (1988) "Post-Mao Reforms in Historical Perspective", *Journal of Asian Studies*, 47(3): 519–41.

Dahl, Robert. (1971) *Polyarchy: Participation and Opposition*, New Haven: Yale University Press.

The Economist. (1994) "Democracy and Growth: Why Voting Is Good for You", August 27th: 15–17.

Fukuyama, Francis. (1989) "The End of History?", *The National Interest*, 16: 3–18.

Harding, Harry. (1987) *China's Second Revolution: Reform After Mao*, Washington, D. C.: The Brookings Institution.

Hayek, F. A. (1994) *The Road to Serfdom*, Chicago: The University of Chicago Press.

Huang, Yasheng. (1996). *Inflation and Investment Controls in China: the Political Economy of Central-Local Relations During the Reform Era*, New York: Cambridge University Press.

Huntington, Samuel P. (1991). *The Third Wave: Democratization in the Late Twentieth Century*, Norman: University of Oklahoma Press.

Iriye, Akira. (1992) *China and Japan in the Global Setting*, Cambridge, MA.: Harvard University Press.

Isaacs, Harold R. (1962) *Images of Asia: American Views of China and India*, New York: Capricorn Books.

Jia, Hao & Lin Zhimin. eds. (1994). *Changing Central-Local Relations in China: Reform and State Capacity*, Boulder: Westview Press.

Lee, Siew Hua. (1997) "China will be 'more democratic over time'", *The Straits Times*, January 30, p. 1.

Li, Lianjiang and Kevin J. O'Brien. (1996) "Villagers and Popular Resistance in Contemporary China," *Modern China*, 22(1): 28–61.

_____ (1995) "The Politics of Lodging Complaints in Rural China", *China Quarterly*, 143: 756–83.

Li, Zehuo. (1987) *Zhongguo jindai sixiangshi lun* [History of Modern Chinese Thoughts], Beijing: Renmin chubanshe.

Lindbloom, Charles. (1977) *Politics and Markets: The World's Political-Economic System*, New York: Basic Books.

Lipset, S. M. (1961) "Some Social Requisites of Democracy: Economic Development and Political Legitimacy", *American Political Science Review*, 53: 493–514.

Moore, Barrington Jr. (1966) *Social Origins of Dictatorship and Democracy: Lord and Peasant in the Making of the Modern World*, Boston: Beacon Press.

Morgenthau, Hans J. (1957) "The Paradoxes of Nationalism", *Yale Review*, xlvi (4): 481–96.

Nathan, Andrew J. (1990) *China's Crisis: Dilemmas of Reform and Prospects for Democracy*, New York: Columbia University Press.

O'Brien, Kevin J. (1996) "Rightful Resistance", *World Politics* 49: 31–55.

Oi, Jean. (1996) *Rural China Takes Off*: Incentives for Industrialization, Berkeley: University of California Press.

Pye, Lucian W. (1990) "China: Erratic State, Frustrated Society", *Foreign Affairs*, (Fall): 56.

Rowen, Henry S. (1996) "The Short March: China's Road to Democracy", *The National Interest*, (Fall): 61–70.

Saich, Tony, "Much Ado about Nothing: Party Reform in the 1980s", in Gordon White, ed., *The Chinese State in the Era of Economic Reform*, London: Macmillan, pp. 149–74.

Schumpeter, Joseph. (1947) *Capitalism, Socialism and Democracy*, 2nd ed., New York: Harper.

Segal, Gerald. (1994) *China Changes Shape: Regionalism and Foreign Policy*, Adelphi Paper 287, Brassey's for IISS.

Shen Liren and Dai Yuanchen. (1990) "Woguo 'zhuhou jingji' de xingcheng jiqi biduan he genyuan" ["The Origins and Defects of the Economy of Dukedom in China"], *Jingji yanjiu* [Economic Studies], no. 3: 12–20.

Talbot, Strobe Talbot. (1996) "Democracy and the National Interest", *Foreign Affairs*, 75 (6): 47–63.

Walder, Andrew. (1995) "Local Governments as Industrial Firms: An Organizational Analysis of China's Transitional Economy", *American Journal of Sociology*, 101(2): 263–301.

Wang Shaoguang and Hu Angang. (1993) *Zhongguo guojia nengli baogao* [A Report of State Capacity in China], Shenyang: Liaoning renmin chubashe.

Wong, John. (1996) "China's Economy in the 21st Century: An Asian Perspective", *JETRO China Newsletter*, 120: 12–19.

Wu, Guoguang. (1996) "*Yi lixing minzuzhuyi kangheng 'weidu Zhongguo'*" ["Using Rational Nationalism to Counter the 'Containment of China'"], *Ershiyi shiji* [Twenty First Century] (Hong Kong), no. 34: 25–33.

______ (1995) "*Weidu Denghuo Zhongguo*" ["Containing Post-Deng China"], *Zhongguo shibao zhoukan* [China Time Weekly], 193: 8–9.

Wu, Guangguo and Zheng Yongnian. (1995) *Lun zhongyang difang guanxi* [On Central-Local Relations], Hong Kong: Oxford University Press.

Zheng Hangsheng (ed). (1996) *Cong chuantong dao xiandai kuaisu zhuanxing guocheng de Zhongguo shehui* [Chinese Society in the Process of Rapid Transition from Tradition to Modernity], Beijing: Zhongguo renmin daxue chubanshe.

Zheng, Yongnian. (1996a) "The Decision of the Sixth Plenum: The Chinese Communist Party's 'Spiritual Civilization'", *IEAPE Commentaries* no. 21, The Institute of East Asian Political Economy, Singapore.

______ (1996b) "*Xiangcun minzhu yu Zhongguo zhengzhi jincheng*" ["Rural Democracy and Chinese Political Development"], *Ershiyi shiji* [Twenty First Century} , no. 35: 24–33.

______ (1995) "Institutional Change, Local Developmentalism, and Economic Growth", doctoral dissertation, Department of Politics, Princeton University, USA.

______ (1994) "Development and Democracy: Are They Compatible in China?", *Political Science Quarterly*, 109(2): 235–259.

Comprehensive National Power

An Expression of China's New Nationalism

ZHENG Yongnian
East Asian Institute
National University of Singapore

Recent years have witnessed the rise of Chinese nationalism. This new nationalism can be attributed to China's success in economic reform and rapid economic growth. While many see this new nationalism to be different from China's traditional nationalism and Maoist nationalism which were characterised by their antiforeignism,[1] others believe that China is becoming increasingly assertive in international affairs.[2]

[1]For example, Allen S. Whiting, "Assertive Nationalism in Chinese Foreign Policy", *Asian Survey*, Vol. 23, No. 8 (1983), pp. 913–933; Michel Oksenberg, "China's Confident Nationalism", *Foreign Affairs*, Vol. 65, No. 3 (1987). Whiting distinguished two types of nationalism, i.e., assertive and affirmative. The former emphasises the confrontation between "us" and "them" while compromise is possible for the latter. Oksenberg argued that there have been four types of nationalism in China, i.e., self-pitying, self-righteous and aggrieved nationalism, strident, xenophobic and isolationist nationalism, militant, rigid, assertive and occasionally muscular nationalism, and confident nationalism. Nationalism in post-Mao China is in a confident mode.

[2]For example, Allen S. Whiting, "Chinese Nationalism and Foreign Policy After Deng", *China Quarterly*, No. 142 (1985), pp. 295–316; and Thomas J. Christensen, "Chinese Realpolitik", *Foreign Affairs*, Vol. 75, No. 5 (1996), pp. 37–52. Whiting changed his early view of Chinese nationalism and argued that it now tends to be characterised by aggressiveness in terms of China's foreign policy making.

Although the term "nationalism" has been used widely to indicate recent developments in China, what it means still remains unclear. While nationalism can be examined from various perspectives, this paper focuses on China's perception of "comprehensive national power" (CNP, *zonghe guoli*), which has been the core of China's new nationalism, and its impact on China's foreign policy behaviour.

The paper is divided into four sections. The first section explains the concept of CNP. The second section gives a brief description of China's strategy of lifting its CNP. The third section examines whether China has changed its perception of national interest with the end of the Cold War. The fourth section attempts to explore the impact of the perception of national interest on foreign policy making in China.

"Comprehensive National Power" as a Concept

According to an official explanation, "comprehensive national power" refers to "the totality of a country's economic, military and political power in a given period. It signals the country's comprehensive development level and its position in the international system."[3]

Chinese leaders began to use the concept "comprehensive national power" in the 1980s. Senior leaders such as Deng Xiaoping and Yang Shangkun argued that China's national power must be measured comprehensively.[4] It was in 1992 that CNP was for the first time introduced into official documents. The Fourteenth Party Congress of the Communist Party of China (CPC), convened that year, proposed a strategy called "comprehensive national power competition (*zonghe guoli jingzheng*)." Jiang

[3]Zhong Cai, ed., *zhonggong zhongyang guanyu zhiding guomin jingji he shehui fazhan "jiuwu" jihua he 2010nian yuanjing mubiao de jianyi* (*mingci shuyu jieshi*) [The Proposal of the Central Committee of the Chinese Communist Party on the Ninth Five-Year Plan of National Economy and Social Development and Long-Term Goals by 2010 (A Terminological Explanation)], Beijing: Renmin chubanshe, 1995, p. 37. The book attempts to provide an official explanation to the central document mentioned above, this article uses this definition of CNP.

[4]*Renmin Ribao* (People's Daily), 26 February 1990, p. 2.

Zemin, General Secretary of the CPC, emphasised that "the core of current international competition is comprehensive national power based on economic and political power".[5] Based on this perception of world affairs, Chinese strategists have developed a so-called "comprehensive national power competition strategy" since then. This strategy aims to set forth guidelines for China as a sovereign state to develop its national power to pursue national interests and strategic goals domestically and internationally. These goals include:

- To protect socialist China and its political system;
- To protect China's independence, sovereignty and security;
- To protect and facilitate China's continuous economic and technological development;
- To create a conducive and peaceful environment for China's socio-economic and political progress;
- To respond effectively to any external threats and challenges;
- To prevent and restrain any internal and external conflicts, and wars from happening; and,
- To maintain and raise China's international status and prestige.[6]

Even though this strategy was not formalised until recently, it has been the main guideline for China's development in the whole Deng era. In interpreting "comprehensive national power" as a political concept, it is necessary to take a brief look at the evolution of China's national strategy.

The Evolution of China's National Strategy

Since the establishment of the PRC in 1949, China's national strategies have experienced several major changes. During the Great Leap Forward

[5]The Political Department of the China News Agency, *Shisida neiwai* (Inside and Outside of the Fourteenth Party Congress), Beijing: Hualing chubanshe, 1992, p. 15.
[6]Huang Shuofeng, *Zonghe guoli lun* (A Study on Comprehensive National Power), Beijing: Zhongguo shehui kexue chubanshe, 1992, pp. 299–304.

period (1957–58), a "catching-up" strategy was carried out. Mao emphasised that China needed to catch up with advanced western countries such as Great Britain and the United States within 15 years. The strategy finally led to an economic disaster. During the Cultural Revolution, Mao Zedong regarded class struggle rather than economic development as the nation's priority. Maoist revolutionary movements led China to both political and economic chaos. In 1974, Zhou Enlai proposed the four-modernisations as the national development goal. Since Chinese leaders perceived the prevention of war as China's major national interest, anti-hegemonism was given highest priority in China's foreign policy making before the 1980s.

Because China badly needed a peaceful environment for economic development, the Third Plenum of the Eleventh Party Congress of the CPC in 1978 shifted the CPC's domestic priority from class struggle to economic development. To seek a hospitable international circumstance became its national strategic goal. To a great extent, this was due to Deng Xiaoping's perception of the linkage between domestic and international politics. Deng Xiaoping argued in the late 1970s that central to China's external and internal problems is economic construction, that economic power is the foundation of China's overall progress.

In the early 1980s, Deng again emphasised that the main goal of China's foreign policy was to seek a peaceful international environment for China to carry out its "four modernisations".[7] Deng acknowledged publicly that China's national power was very weak and the government had to pay full attention to domestic economic development, and China's foreign policy must serve domestic development needs.[8] Even though China would continue to oppose hegemonism in international politics, its main goal was to create a peaceful environment for its domestic development.

[7]*Ibid.*, p. 205.

[8]Deng made this point when he talked about Sino-American relations. Deng argued that China is still very poor and its infrastructure is backward. China's policy toward the US must be made in this context. See Deng, "Fazhan zhongmei guanxi de yuanze lichang" ("Principles in Developing Sino-American Relations") *in Shiyijie sanzhong quanhui yilai zhongyao wenxian xuandu (Selected Important Documents since the Third Plenum of the Eleventh Party Congress)*, Beijing: Renmin chubanshe, 1987, p. 265.

To cultivate a favourable international environment to serve domestic goals was the theme of China's foreign policy-making in the whole 1980s. The implementation of this strategy had been successful since 1978. China improved bilateral relations with its neighbouring countries and achieved rapid economic growth and great success in developing foreign trade.[9]

In the aftermath of the 1989 Tiananmen incident, China encountered a hostile international environment. The West, led by the US, imposed various forms of sanctions on China. The breakup of the former Soviet Union and Eastern European communist regimes left China as the only great power in the socialist camp. Deng's national development strategy therefore faced serious internal and external challenges. Nevertheless, Deng remained quite pragmatic and rational. Deng insisted that China should still give highest priority to economic development. Even though nationalist sentiments began to appear in China, Deng realised that China's national power must be based on its economic power in the later 1980s. While accusing the US of supporting the 1989 Tiananman demonstration, Deng also expressed that China was willing to improve its relations with the US.[10]

According to Deng, China has to stick to the following principles in order to concentrate on domestic priorities. First, "China must not be in a number one position in world politics."[11] Second, China's foreign policy must aim to oppose hegemonism and power politics, to protect world peace, and to establish a new international political order and economic order.[12] Third, "to facilitate rapid economic development, China needs to rely on progress in technology and education. China has to have a clear strategic

[9]See Thomas W. Robinson and David Shambaugh, eds., *Chinese Foreign Policy: Theory and Practice* (Oxford University Press, 1995); and Nicholas R. Lardy, *China in the World Economy* (Washington, D. C.: Institute for International Economy, 1994).

[10]Deng Xiaoping, "Jiesu yanjun de zhongmei guanxi, yaoyu Meiguo caiqu zhudong", ("To end a grim Sino-US relationship, the US needs to take initiatives", in Deng, *Deng Xiaoping wenxuan* (Selected Works of Deng Xiaoping), Vol. 3, Beijing: Renmin chubanshe, 1993, p. 331.

[11]Deng, "Shanyu liyong shiji jiejue fazhan wenti", ("To Catch the Opportunity to Resolve Development Problems"), in Deng, *ibid.*, 363.

[12]Deng, "Guoji xingshi he jingji wenti", in Deng, *ibid.*, 353.

goal in any major areas and once it is decided, it has to be realised. China has to occupy a position in the field of high technology."[13]

These principles were incorporated into the CPC's decision of the Fourteenth Party Congress in 1992, which accommodated a capitalist economy in China's socialism. The Decision reaffirmed the policy of reform and open-door and economic development as national priority. The strategy of "comprehensive national power competition," proposed by the Party Congress, can be regarded as a systematic expression of Deng's ideas. Even though the Decision also stressed the significance of China's involvement in world affairs and military modernisation, its underlying theme is that China needs to concentrate on domestic growth in order to be strong in international politics.

CHINA'S PERCEPTION OF THE CNP AND DEVELOPMENT PRIORITIES

According to Chinese strategists, CNP can be defined in the following aspects:

- Basic power (*jichu shili*) refers to the environment against which China as a sovereign state survives and develops, including China's geographic location, the quality and quantity of population, natural resources, and a national spirit which brings different social groups together and strengthen their national identity.
- Economic power refers to China's capacity in industry, agriculture, commerce, finance and technology.
- National defense power refers to China's capability to defend herself and to build deterrent forces including nuclear deterrence.
- Diplomatic power refers to China's influence in international affairs through its diplomatic activities.
- Organisational and coordination power refers to China's capacity to organise various power resources to serve its national goals.

[13]Deng, "Zai Wuchang, Shenzhen, Shanghai dengdi de tanhua yaodian" ("Main Points in the Speeches Made in Wuchang, Shenzhen and Shanghai," in Deng, *ibid.*, pp. 377–78.

- Rational decision-making capacity refers to China's capacity to make "right" domestic and foreign policies based on "right" information on China's internal and external affairs.
- Moral and cultural power refers to people's political attitude, belief system and national character.[14]

In order to strengthen China's CNP, the government has made and implemented a comprehensive strategy which focuses on increasing China's economic power, facilitating progress in technology, raising the educational level of its population, and strengthening military power.

Economic growth has been given the highest priority because the CPC believes that without a strong economy, the country will get nowhere. According to the Decision of the Thirteenth Party Congress in 1987, China's development goal would be achieved through three steps. The first step was to double China's gross national product (GNP) between 1980 and 1990 and to let people have enough food and clothes. The second step was to double again China's GNP by the end of this century and to let people have a relatively comfortable life or a *xiao-kang* living standard. The third step was to catch up with middle income countries by the middle of the next century.[15] According to official interpretations, the first goal

[14]The Research Group of China's Comprehensive National Power (Chinese Academy of Social Sciences), "Dui Zhongguo zonghe guoli de cedu he yiban fenxi" ("The Measurement and Analysis of China's Comprehensive National Power"), Zhongguo shehui kexue, no. 5 (1995), pp. 4–19; Li Tianran, "Guanyu zonghe guoli wenti", ("About Comprehensive National Power"), in *Guoji wenti yanjiu* (Studies of International Affairs), No. 2, 1990; Zhang Boli, "Lun zonghe guoli yaosu" ("On the Elements of Comprehensive National Power"), in *Shijie jingji yu zhengzhi* (World Economy and Politics), No. 12, 1989; Dong Xiuling, "Zonghe guoli lilun yanjiu zongshu" ("A Review of the Studies of Comprehensive National Power"), in *Xueshu yanjiu dongtai* (Academic Research Trends), No. 9, 1991; and Huang Shoufeng, *Zonghe guoli lun* (On Comprehensive National Power), Beijing: Zhongguo shehui kexue chubanshe, 1992.

[15]Zhao Ziyang, "Yanzhe you Zhongguo tese de shehui zhuyi daolu qianjin" ("Go Along with the Socialist Road with Chinese Characteristics"), in *Xinhua yuebao* (China's News Monthly), No. 517, 1987. For an interpretation of "xiao-kang" see John Wong, *Xiao-Kang: China's Concepts of Socio-Economic Development*, IEAPE Background Brief No. 101, 14 September 1996.

was achieved in 1988 and the second goal was again realised by 1995, five years earlier than the original plan.[16]

In early 1996 the Chinese National People's Congress approved a national development plan, entitled "Outline of the Ninth Five-Year Plan of National Economy and Social Development and Long-Term Goals by 2010 of People's Republic of China."[17] According to this plan, China's real per capita GNP will quadruple by the year 2000 from the 1980 level.[18] From 2000 to 2010, China will again double its per capita income so that China in 15 years from now will develop into a middle-income country.[19]

High technological development is another priority in the CPC's attempt to strengthen China's CNP. Deng emphasised that China must occupy an important position in the front of high technologies. Senior scientists such as Qian Xuesen and Zhou Guangzhao argued that the next century will be a century of high technology competition; high technology is the key to strengthen China's CNP; only after China has taken a leading position in high technology will China be able to meet various forms of external and internal challenges and become a world power.[20] In 1987, the CPC issued a plan of "Research and Development for High Technologies," which aimed to raise China's technological level in biology, space, information, energy, new materials and so on. In 1988, the CPC implemented a development strategy called the "Torch Plan" to

[16]*zhonghua renmin gongheguo guomin jingji he shehui fazhan "jiuwu" jihua he 2010nian yuanjing mubiao de gangyao* (The Outline of the Ninth Five-Year Plan of National Economy and Social Development and long-Term Goals by 2010 of People's Republic of China), Hong Kong: Ta Kung Pao, 20 March 1996, p. 8.

[17]*Ibid.*

[18]This goal was already realised in 1996.

[19]For a discussion of the Ninth Five-Year Plan see John Wong, "China's Ninth Five-Year Plan: Economic Agenda of the Fifth Party Plenum", IEAPE Commentaries No. 17, 2 October 1995.

[20]Zhou Guangzhao, "Lun chixu fazhan zhanlue" ("On Strategies of Continuous Development"), *Qiushi*, No. 12, 1995. For state policy of science and technology, see The State Commission of Science and Technology, *Zhongguo kexue jishu zhengce zhinan* (Directory of China's State Policy of Science and Technology), Vols 1–5, Beijing: Kexue jishu wenxian chubanshe, 1986, 1992.

promote the development of high technologies by establishing special development zones.[21]

The CPC has also made various efforts to modernise China's military in order to increase its CNP, especially in the 1990s. The People's Liberation Army (PLA) has attempted to shift its focus from Maoist "people's war" strategy to a high technology-centred one and to transform itself from a land power to sea power.[22] These developments have led to various forms of reaction from the international community. However, the Chinese leaders feel that they can only provide very limited economic resources to military modernisation. The military has struggled for modernisation, but it also realised that military modernisation needs enormous economic resources. There appears to be a compromise or consensus between the government and the military that China's highest priority is economic development and military modernisation has to be subordinated to this priority. Indeed, supporting national and local economic development has been one of the major duties of China's military. This in turn has had a negative impact on military professionalism.[23]

How the quality of population should be improved is also an important agenda for the CPC. The Chinese government expects to implement compulsory education at the secondary school level nationwide by the year 2000. Various policies have been carried out, including strengthening the existing compulsory system; developing occupational education; improving the existing system of high education; reforming China's educational system, and improving the quality of educators.[24]

[21]Chen Liangchao, *Dalu keji fazhan yanjiu* (A Study of the Development of Science and Technology in Mainland China), Taibei, 1993.

[22]For a discussion of the PLA's strategic shifts see Shen Mingshi, *Gaige kaifang hou de jiefangjun* (The People's Liberation Army since the Reform and Opening), Taipei: Huizong wenhua chubanshe, 1995.

[23]For example, Gerald Segal and Richard Yang, eds., *Chinese Economic Reform: The Impact on Security* (London: Routledge, 1996); and Richard Yang *et al.*, eds., *Chinese Regionalism: The Security Dimension* (Boulder: Westview Press, 1994).

[24]An introduction to the educational system in post-Mao China, see Bih-jaw Lin and Li-min Fan, eds., *Education in Mainland China: Review and Evaluation*, Taipei: Institute of International Relations, 1990.

However, it is dubious to say that the situation has been improved since the reform began in the late 1970s. Owing to the decline of its financial capacity, the government is not able to provide effective financial support for basic education, especially in the poor rural areas. The decline of state financial power also has had a very negative impact on high education, with professional educators and researchers increasingly turning their focus on profit-making in order to improve their incomes. Commercial activities became prevalent among educators. At present, there are 220 million illiterates in China, about a quarter of total illiterates in the world. Indeed, the low level of education has been a major barrier to China's economic modernisation. Moreover, because of China's limited financial and personnel resources, this situation is unlikely to be improved in a short period of time.[25] China's human resource development at present is among the weakest in the Asian Pacific region, as only 2 percent of the relevant age-group in China are receiving tertiary education, compared to 42 percent in Korea and 45 percent in Taiwan.[26] If this situation continues, China's economic growth will slow down.

Even though the CNP strategy aims to achieve a balanced development, economic growth apparently occupies top priority because the development of high technology, military modernisation and the improvement of population quality all consume enormous economic resources. The preoccupation of the Chinese government with domestic economic growth has a great impact on China's foreign policy, which is required to serve domestic priorities.

No doubt, "domestic priority" has been the cardinal principle of China's foreign policy making in the Deng era. It can also explain the consistency of China's foreign policy in this period. However, for the international community, what is important is whether China will pursue an aggressive foreign policy following the dramatic increase in its CNP. Put it in another

[25]Huang Shuofeng, "Manian xinchun huaguoli" ("Talking about National Power in the Spring of the Year of Horse"), in *People's Daily*, 26 February, 1990.
[26]See John Wong, "China's Economy in the 21st Century: An Asian Perspective", *JETRO China Newsletter*, No. 120 (Jan–Feb 1996), p. 14.

way: Is there a change in China's perception of national interests in its foreign policy making in a post-Cold War era?

National Interests in the Post-Cold War Era

Does the end of the Cold War change China's perception of national interest? How does China judge its national interest in a post-Cold War era? How should a China's resurgent nationalism be explained?

During the Cold War era, the US and USSR dominated international politics. China's national interest had to be perceived within this bipolar power structure. With the end of the Cold War and the collapse of the Soviet Union, China's national interest has to be redefined. What confronts China now is a polarised world in which China per se occupies an important position. While many previous world powers including the US are on the relative decline, China has experienced rapid economic growth for more than a decade.

An increase in economic power does have an impact on China's power ambitions. Chinese strategists have argued that any country, be it on the decline or on the rise, has to redefine the scope and content of its national interest based on its real power. In other words, a country whose comprehensive national power increases has to expand its national interest and participate in international affairs rather actively. "With its increasing national power, China feels that it is necessary to take a more firm stand to protect its national interest and dignity."[27] China's Foreign Minister Qian Qichen also argued that while China could play a more positive role in world affairs, a strong China had to be recognised by the outside world.[28]

[27]Yan Xuetong, "Guojia liyi de panduan", in *Zhanlue yu guanli*, No. 3, 1996, p. 39. Also see Gu Dexin & Huang Qi, "guojia shili de texing, pinggu yu yunyong" ("National Power: Characteristics, Judgement and Application"), *Zhanlue yu guanli* (Strategy and Management), No. 5, 1996, pp. 57–65.

[28]Qian Qichen, "1993: shijie kaishi chongxin renshi Zhongguo" ("1993: The World Re-recognised China"), *People's Daily*, 15 December 1993.

Meanwhile, nationalistic sentiments have become popular among different social groups, especially among young Chinese intellectuals.[29]

Nationalistic rhetoric, however, does not necessarily mean nationalistic perception of China's national interest. Except on the issue of sovereignty on Taiwan, the revival of nationalism did not lead to aggressive international behaviour. "Economic development" is the core of China's CNP strategy and the concept of "domestic priority as national interest" still dominates China's foreign policy behaviour.

Without continuous economic growth, China's national interest cannot be served internationally. According to the government's long-term plan issued in 1996,[30] Chinese total GNP will continue to grow at 7.4 percent per annum in the next 15 years. That will make China one of the economic superpowers in early next century. But Chinese leaders have realised that even if that is the case, China will remain poor. By the year 2010, China will have more than 1.3 billion people, with its per capita GNP far below that of developed countries. According to an estimation, China will develop into a middle-income country with a per-capita income of around US$3,500 in 15 to 20 years, and China's total GNP in nominal terms will be close to the total GNP of the United States today.[31] Chinese leaders have realised that if China wants to be real superpower, great efforts need to be made. So, "China's main strategic goal continues to aim at a peaceful international environment which will enable China to focus on domestic economic development. As long as economic construction remains the highest priority of the government, China's national security goal is to pursue a more stable international circumstance. Whether China will be able to maintain such

[29]A recent example is the publication of the book, *The China that Says No*. See "The China that Says No to the West", *The Sunday Times*, 11 August 1996. See also Wang Gungwu, *The Revival of Chinese Nationalism*, Leiden: International Institute for Asian Studies, 1996; Steven Mufson, "China's New Nationalism", *International Herald Tribune*, 20 March 1996; and Matt Forney, "Patriot Games", *Far Eastern Economic Review*, 3 October 1996.

[30]"An Outline of the Ninth Five-Year Plan of National Economy and Social Development and long-Term Goals by 2010 of People's Republic of China", Hong Kong: Ta Kung Pao, 20 March 1996.

[31]John Wong, "China's Economy in the 21st Century", *op. cit.*, p. 15.

an environment depends on whether China can avoid any form of military conflict or war."[32]

The recognition of China's current low level of the CNP has forced the Jiang Zemin-centred leadership to continue to concentrate on domestic development rather than international expansion. Like Deng Xiaoping, Jiang Zemin and other leaders also recognised that they would have to focus on lifting China's CNP and improving people's living standards in order to increase the government's political legitimacy. In order to do so, a peaceful and favourable international circumstance is vital. This consensus among China's senior leaders is consistent with China's foreign policy making in the post-Cold War Era. China has made great efforts to improve its relations with neighbouring countries. Even though China still adopts a "hard-line" policy toward the issues related to sovereignty, it has maintained low-posture and been rational as shown in the recent event on the Diaoyu (known as Senkaku in Japan) islands. China also realised that a direct confrontation with the advanced West is not in accordance with its national interest. There are enormous conflicts between China and the West, especially the US, on trade, human rights, arms sales, and other areas, and China remains nationalistic rhetorically. Nevertheless, China is also problem-solving oriented and pragmatic.

Like other major powers, the end of the Cold War brought China into an uncertain world. This dramatic change created an opportunity for China to lift its position in the international system. But how China will position itself is another matter. As Chinese strategists recognised, during the Cold War, it was easy to define the goal of China's foreign policy, i.e., to pursue national power within the US-USSR domination. The end of the Cold War makes it possible for China to expand its national interest internationally, but it is increasingly difficult to define what China's national interest is.

China has called for the establishment of a new national identity in order to reflect changes in the world system. But the leadership also

[32]Yan Xuetong, "Zhongguo anquan zhanlue de fazhan qushi" ("Trends of China's Security Strategy") in *Liaowang*, Nos. 8–9, 1996, p. 50.

emphasised that in doing so, China has to be very cautious in judging and anticipating what its national interest is and how it could be realised and promoted. Whatever external situations are, one point is clear, that is: China still has to focus on its domestic priority. A prerequisite for China to promote its national interest internationally is continuous domestic economic growth and modernisation. What Chinese leaders fear most is that major powers will use all sorts of means to disrupt China's modernisation as they did before. This is why China has made various forms of nationalistic response to the theory of "China threat" whose aim Chinese leaders believe is to constrain China's rapid development.[33]

IMPLICATIONS OF CNP ON CHINA'S FOREIGN POLICY BEHAVIOUR

How will a CNP-based perception of national interest affect China's foreign policy behaviour? Some implications can be inferred from the above analysis.

First, China is unlikely to shift its focus from economic development to international expansion. The preoccupation of the current leadership with rapid economic growth is for various reasons. Owing to a popular consensus among major leaders that political stability is a prerequisite of continuous economic development, political reform is not on the government's agenda. The leadership believes that political reform will lead to instability. However, without political reform, the government has to rely solely on economic growth to strengthen its political legitimacy. Without continuous delivery of economic goods to the public, the

[33]There has been a campaign of anti-China Threat theory in China and major leaders, especially in the military, expressed their strong opposition. For example, Xing Shizhong (Chairman of National Defensive University), "'Zhongguo weixie lun' keyi xiuyi" ("May the Theory of China Threat Come to an End"), *Qiushi*, No. 3, 1996, pp. 16–20; and Xu Xin (Present Chairman of China Association of Strategic Studies, former Deputy Chief of General Staff of the PLA), "Daodi shui weixie shui" ("Who Threats Who?"), *Liaowang*, Nos. 8–9, 1996, pp. 48–9; Jing Bo, "Bo 'Zhongguo' weixie lun," ("Refuting 'the Theory of China Threat'" in *China National Defense Newspaper*, 5 January 1996.

leadership will find it difficult to govern a vast country. The current leadership has also recognised that only after China has strengthened its CNP can it pursue and promote its national interests internationally. Based on these perceptions, China will continue to strive for a peaceful international circumstance to serve its domestic development.

Second, in terms of policy changes, continuity rather than discontinuity will be the rule. This is because, first, China has benefited from the strategy of "domestic priority" for more than a decade and increased its international prestige significantly. Both Deng Xiaoping and Jiang Zemin realised that this was the product of China's benign foreign policy and a favourable international environment. Unless there is a dramatic change in international affairs which is detrimental to China's domestic development, the current leadership is unlikely to change such a policy orientation.

More importantly, the nature of China's post-Mao development forced the government to concentrate on domestic rather than international affairs. Apparently, China's rapid economic growth has been achieved by decentralisation. Decentralisation has led to enormous domestic problems such as declining central power, increasing disparities among regions and social groups, and a growth of official corruption, and ethnic nationalism and so on. These problems more than anything else are vital to political stability.[34]

Third, China's national power in CNP term will be measured comprehensively, national development should also be balanced. This development strategy makes it unlikely for government to shift its development priority to military. Even though China is increasing its military budget in accordance with its economic growth, highest priority is unlikely to be given to military modernisation. As mentioned above, owing to China's overall backwardness, economic resources that can be used to support military modernisation are limited. Furthermore, because of the reluctance of the advanced West to transfer high technologies to

[34]The negative consequences of decentralisation, see David Goodman and Gerald Segal, eds., *China Deconstructs*, London: Routledge, 1994. Also, Segal, *China Changes Shape: Regionalism and Foreign Policy*, Adelphi Paper 287 (London: Brassey's For IISS, 1994).

China, China is not able to improve its military technology significantly in a short period of time.

Fourth, because the leadership preoccupies itself with economic interest, ideological factors no longer have a major impact on China's foreign policy making. It is recognised that "with the end of the Cold War, ideologies are no longer the key to political competition in international arenas."[35] Indeed, in principle, China has abandoned ideology as its guideline in foreign policy making since the late 1970s. Chinese leaders repeatedly emphasise that ideological factors cannot be used in dealing with international relations. However, this should not be interpreted as that ideological factors no longer affect international politics. The leadership fears that human rights and other ideological factors are increasingly utilised by the West in dealing with China. Certainly, China will not bow to such pressure. But with economic priority, the regime is willing to compromise on such issues as long as such a compromise can bring China economic benefits. This trend apparently has dominated the Sino-US relations in the 1990.

Fifth, even on territory-related issues, the government can make limited compromise if non-compromise will cost China great economic interest. With the economic interest as the core of the CNP, Chinese now believe that national interest can be measured quantitatively. "When the importance of national interest is measured, quantity must be regarded as an essential factor. In fact, the importance of national interest can be judged by quantity."[36]

This is the rationale behind the government's decision not to get embroiled too deeply in the recent Diaoyu islands dispute even though nationalistic feeling was prevalent. China also has proposed to the ASEAN countries to shelve the sovereignty dispute over South China sea and use "joint exploration" to resolve the issue. Even though China has not proposed any concrete approaches, a focus on economic interest is leading China to rationalise its foreign policy.

Sixth, with a preoccupation with economic growth, China has changed its policy over economic regionalism since it has benefited increasingly

[35] *Ibid.*, p. 43.
[36] *Ibid..*, p. 41.

from regional economic cooperation, especially in East Asia and Southeast Asia. The open-door policy has been successful in pulling overseas Chinese investment into China. But China still has enormous difficulties in attracting high technologies from the West. As mentioned above, facilitating technological progress has been one major goal of China's CNP strategy. Participating in international economic organisations no doubt is an effective way for China to achieve this goal. China has been an active member of the APEC. Even though China is able to gain similar economic benefits from bilateral trade with foreign countries, it has striven to become a member of the GATT or WTO.[37]

Finally, China is also changing its strategic thinking on international political cooperation and collective security. During the Cold War, China's policy toward the Asian-Pacific region was overwhelmingly characterised by bilateralism because "the practice of bilateralism strengthens China's hand and over the long run could help China position itself for a dominant role in Asia."[38] Chinese strategists now realised that bilateralism is no longer the most effective means to pursue China's national interest, especially security interest. "After the Cold War, that peace is the foundation of national interest has become a consensus among major powers. A given country will not be able to protect its security by relying solely on its military power. Collective security has to be established in order to protect individual countries' national interest and security."[39]

This perception of collective security was reflected in China's policy toward Asian countries. During the Cold War, China strongly opposed collective security among Asian countries. By 1993, China changed its view of collective security. A year later, China proposed five principles on collective security in Asia.[40] China's proposal to shelve the sovereignty

[37]See John Wong, "China and the GATT", IEAPE background Brief No. 38, 21 July 1992; and John Wong, "China's WTO Membership," IEAPE, 1996.

[38]Steven I. Levine, "China in Asia: The PRC as a Regional Power", in Harry Harding, ed., *China's Foreign Relations in the 1980s* (New Haven: Yale University Press, 1984), p. 118.

[39]Yan Xuetong, "Guojia liyi de panduan", *op. cit.*, p. 40.

[40]Qian Qichen's talk in the first conference of the ASEAN Forum, *People's Daily* (overseas edition), 26 July 1994.

disputes with other Asian nations aims "to promote the formation of collective security among Asian nations."[41] Although no major progress has been made, this perception no doubt helps China re-adjust its relations with its neighbouring countries.

CONCLUSION: WHAT IS THE ISSUE?

China is growing economically. What does a strong China mean for China itself and the international community? With rapid economic growth, China has lifted its position in the international hierarchy. Moreover, it is also determined to be a major actor in international affairs. For China, changes have to be made to the existing international system, or even a new international order is necessary because current international rules were set by the West and were not necessarily in accordance with Chinese interest. In this sense, China tends to be nationalistic.

However, this does not mean that China's foreign policy will be nationalistic. China's new nationalism primarily is reactive. Chinese leaders had realised that it will not be necessary for China to seek its national interests through international domination. The government has to give the highest priority to China's CNP growth. Chinese leaders are afraid that China again will be a target of foreign imperialism if China cannot raise its CNP, the very foundation of China's international status. The urgent task for China is therefore to focus on domestic development. As long as China can benefit from current international rules, China is willing to accept them. China is also willing to compromise on various matters of international affairs because the major goal of its foreign policy is to create a favourable international environment for domestic development. What China cannot accept is that the West uses these rules to constrain China's development.

On the other hand, many in the West believe that a strong China could be a major threat. With its continuous rapid economic growth, China

[41]Yan Xuetong, "Guojia liyi de panduan", *op. cit.*, p. 40.

is inevitably going to be a regional hegemon, or even a world hegemon. This perception has led to the rise of "China threat theory" in the early 1990s. How China's threat can be reduced or even eliminated becomes a major issue for the West. Various theories including "containing China" and "fragmenting China" came into being.[42] However, apparently, it is hard for the outside world to contain China's rise. Singapore's Senior Minister Lee Kuan Yew argued, if the West's seeks to block China's development, China' emergence as a major global economic player in the next two or three decades can be slowed, but cannot be stopped.[43] This is because of China's great internal dynamism. As Singapore's Prime Minister Goh Chok Tong pointed out, "I do not believe that China's growth can be stifled. The genie is already out of the bottle and cannot be put back. There is sufficient internal dynamism for China to grow robustly even without outside help."[44]

On the other hand, the West's reaction to China's development has led to strong nationalistic reaction from China. Many Chinese perceived that the West is containing China.[45] As mentioned before, the Chinese government has mounted a campaign to counter "China threat theory". Chinese leaders, especially military leaders, are irritated. At the societal level, different social and political groups also expressed their disappointment with the West, especially the US. In this sense, the rise of China's nationalism is not because of China's rapid development, but because of external stimulation. In other words, China's new nationalism is a reaction to a changing international environment.

[42]For a review of arguments viewing China as a threat see Denny Roy, "The 'China Threat' Issue", *Asian Survey*, vol. xxxvi, no. 8 (August 1996), pp. 758–771.

[43]Lee Kuan Yew, "China Has Its Role to Play", *International Business*, Issue 1 (January 1995), p. 24.

[44]Goh Chok Tong, "Global Economic Trends and Developments: The China Factor in the World Economy", Keynote address at the Asia Society International Corporate Conference in Beijing on 13 May 1995 (Press Release by Singapore's Ministry of Information and the Arts, Release no. 14/May 1995), p. 7.

[45]For example, Jiang Lingfei, "Meiguo duihua ezhi zhanlue de zhiyue yinsu he keneng zouxiang") ("US's Containing China Strategy: Constraints and Alternatives"), *Zhanlue yu guanli* (Strategy and Management), No. 5, 1996, pp. 46–50.

Up to now, the Chinese leadership remains rational. It does not want China's modernisation to be disrupted by external developments. Certainly, the government also faces increasing domestic pressures from popular nationalism. Whether or not China's nationalism will be benign depends on the interplay between China and the West. Put it in other way, whether China's nationalism will pose a threat to world stability depends on whether China will use its increasing economic clout for international territorial expansion. (This is unlikely to happen for various reasons discussed above.) It also depends on whether the West can gradually accommodate and accept China as a major power. Mr Goh Chok Tong argued that "by giving China space and time, the world will accelerate, not delay, China's ability and willingness to play global rules".[46] Indeed, what the West, especially the US, needs to do is "to encourage China to be a co-operative and constructive global player," as Mr Lee Kuan Yew pointed out.[47]

[46]Goh, "Global Economic Trends and Development", *op. cit.*, p. 9.

[47]Lee, "China Has Its Role to Play", *op. cit.*, p. 24. Samuel Huntington argued, if the US and Japan cannot accommodate China as a major player in the world politics, a hegemonic war is not impossible. See Asad Latif, "Huntington sees war if US does not accept China's rise", *The Sunday Times*, 1 September 1996.

Xiao-Kang: Deng Xiaoping's Socio-Economic Development Target for China

John WONG*
East Asian Institute
National University of Singapore

A KEY DEVELOPMENT TARGET

Ever since Deng Xiaoping made the remark on December 6, 1979 that China's Four Modernisations were aimed at realising the *xiao-kang* (小康) level of living for the Chinese people by the end of this century, this concept rapidly gained prominence in China.[1] It was incorporated in several major Party documents and adopted as the key development target by three consecutive Five-Year Plans. *Xiao-kang* has thus become a codeword for China's socio-economic development. What is the real meaning of *xiao-kang*? What does it indicate? How does China's present economic and social progress stand in the context of the Asia-Pacific region?

"*Xiao Kang*" or XK, which literally means "a relatively comfortable life", is actually a very traditional Chinese concept, steeped in profound Confucian philosophy. Originating from the *Book of Rituals*, XK denotes an ideal world of *da-tong* (great harmony) with the "whole world as one

[1]Deng made this remark to visiting Japanese Prime Minister Ohira Masayoshi. See "Realising *xiao-kang* as China's target for the present century", *Deng Xiaoping Wen-xuan* (Selected Works of Deng Xiaoping), Vol. 2, Beijing, 1994, 2nd ed., pp. 237–8.

community" (*tian-xia wei-gong*), where everybody is supposed to be comfortably off by enjoying the XK standard of living. To an ordinary Chinese, XK may vaguely convey the feeling of being "neither rich nor poor" or *bu-qiong bu-hu*. In a more concrete sense, this would imply a level of material well-being *after* his basic needs have been satisfied or *wen-bao* — literally, "enough to wear and eat".

At the 12th Party Congress in September 1982, XK was formally adopted as "an overall development target to strive for, with General Secretary Hu Yaobang speaking of "quadrupling China's gross industrial and agricultural output value by the end of this century" so that the Chinese people could enjoy the "*xiao-kang* level of material living".[2]

Similarly, at the 13th Party Congress in October 1987, Zhao Ziyang, who had now replaced Hu Yaobang as General Secretary, took up the concept of XK. According to Zhao, China's socialist economic development strategy involved three steps. Step one was to double China's 1980 level of GNP so as to satisfy the "basic needs of the people", or their *wen-bao*. But this was considered to have already been realised by 1987. Step two was to double again China's GNP by the end of the century so as to reach the XK level of living, thereby confirming that XK is one step beyond *wen-bao*. Finally, step three was for China to achieve relative affluence by the middle of the next century.[3]

XK also figured prominently in China's 8th Five-Year Plan (1991–95) and the Ten-Year Development Programme as the key development targets. In presenting this Plan to the 7th National People's Congress in April 1991, Premier Li Peng elaborated on the XK concept, linking it for the first time to a quantitative target of 3,110 billion yuan of GNP at 1990 prices. But Li Peng also went beyond GNP by associating XK with other broad areas of social development like health care, housing and culture.[4]

[2]"Opening up a New Situation for Socialist Modernisation", Report by Hu Yaobang at the 12th National Party Congress on September 1, 1982.

[3]"Marching Along the Socialist Road with Chinese Characteristics", Report by Zhao Ziyang at the 13th National Party Congress of the Chinese Communist Party, October 25, 1987.

[4]"The Outline of the 10-Year Programme and of the 8th Five-Year Plan for National Economic and Social Development", adopted on April 9, 1991 at the 4th Session of the 7th National People's Congress.

However, the 9th Five-Year Plan, 1996–2000, started to pay attention to the broader socio-economic problems beyond the pure income aspects of the XK target, because Deng Xiaoping's original objective of quadrupling the 1980 level of GNP was considered to have been achieved "five years ahead of schedule", thanks to the dynamic 11.8 percent annual growth during 1991–95.[5] Thus the 9th Plan called for the "all-round" fulfilment of the XK goals so as to "basically eliminate poverty by the year 2000".[6]

EVOLUTION OF *XIAO-KANG* AS A DEVELOPMENT CONCEPT

Economic development in any country (or "Modernisation" in the case of China) is a comprehensive process of both economic and social changes. To capture or measure these changes would involve an array of complicated socio-economic indicators. But strangely enough, despite the key role played by XK in the official development strategies since 1979, the concept was rarely discussed in public by China's media and was hardly studied by China's academics. It was not until September 1992 that the State Statistical Bureau published a small booklet to explain the XK concept in a technical manner, and this was not widely circulated. Why?

A number of obvious political and technical explanations can be offered. To begin with, China's pre-reform economic development before 1979 was called "socialist construction" which was to follow the strict ideological framework of Marxism and Maoism, with building a socialist society for China as its ultimate goal. At the peak of the Cultural Revolution (1966–75), when Mao's ideology prevailed, "socialist economic development" in China entailed preciously few economic priorities, as Mao was then obsessed with his ideological pursuit of egalitarianism. In fact, material progress (dubbed a "capitalist tail") was much frowned upon. As

[5]"Outlines of the Ninth Five-Year Plan for National Economic and Social Development and the Long-Term Target for the Year 2010", adopted on March 17, 1996 by the 4th Session of the 8th National People's Congress (*Renmin Ribao*, People's Daily, Beijing, March 20, 1996).

[6]*Ibid.*

the popular Maoist slogan of the time was "To be poor is to be glorious", any talk of XK would be accused of revisionism or capitalism.

Deng's economic reform marks an ideological liberation for China in the sense of steering its economic development process away from such non-economic pursuits as income redistribution to emphasis on economic growth and material progress. Deng denounced the idea that "socialism equates poverty". He not only legitimised material pursuits as implicit in the XK concept, but also recognised that economic development at the beginning is inherently a non-egalitarian process — not everybody and every sector can take part in and hence benefit equally from the development process, all at the same time. Accordingly, he declared that "some people will have to get rich first", which is a far-cry from Mao's past egalitarian orthodoxy.

Throughout the 1980s, Chinese officials and scholars were quite content with interpreting XK vaguely in its traditional sense of "neither rich nor poor". When Deng first used the XK concept in public in 1979, he probably expected that most Chinese people would have no difficulty in understanding the Confucian underpinning of the term XK. Even after XK was formally incorporated as an official development target in the early 1980s, no attempt had been made to officially spell out the true meaning of XK or to link it to a modern social science context.

In 1984 Deng did try to elaborate a bit his own definition of XK as "when the Chinese per-capita GNP has increased to US$800 by the end of this century".[7] It seems clear that Deng at that time had no inkling of the exact meaning of GNP nor its technical complications involved in inter-temporal and international comparison, e.g. problems of price changes and foreign exchange fluctuation. It may be pointed out that throughout the 1980s, Chinese official national income was based on the Soviet concept of "Net Material Product" (NMP) by generally excluding the service sector,

[7]Speaking to visiting President of Brazil on May 29, 1984, Deng Xiaoping said: "China is still very poor, presently with a per-capita income of US$300 . . . . China will be comfortable off by the end of the century when its per-capita income reaches US$800". "Protect World Peace and Do a Better Job in National Construction", *Deng Xiaoping Wen-xuan* (Selected Works of Deng Xiaoping), Vol. 3, Beijing, 1993, pp. 56–7.

which is considered "unproductive" in the Marxist tradition. To denote aggregate economic activity, Chinese planners often used the term "gross industrial and agricultural output value" (as Hu Yaobang did in 1982), which, because of its double counting of intermediate products, is actually not a "value added" concept adopted internationally for the computation of GNP or GDP.

Furthermore, the Chinese economy throughout most of the 1980s (at least until the second part of 1988) had experienced virtually no inflation because of price control. Therefore, neither Deng nor Hu (Yaobang), in talking about doubling or quadrupling GNP, would need to take heed of price changes or to specify if their GNP concept referred to "nominal GNP" (GNP at current prices) or "real GNP" (at constant prices of a particular base year).

By 1991, China's national income accounting practice had been adapted to the UN System of National Accounts (SNA), and China had also experienced its first bout of high inflation in November 1988. Not surprisingly, Li Peng, in defining XK, was the first to link GNP to the 1990 constant prices. At about the same time, Chinese planners started to interpret XK in accordance with internationally accepted socio-economic indicators.

Furthermore, XK was not associated only with the narrow concept of income growth, but also widened to include a broad spectrum of socio-economic progress, as commonly used in other developing countries. This culminates in the first attempt by the State Statistical Bureau to compute China's first composite socio-economic indicator as an XK Index, which was published in September 1992.[8]

A Composite *Xiao-kang* Index

Economic development was traditionally meant, especially in the 1950s and the 1960s, to be mainly a process of increasing material production

[8]State Statistical Bureau "Xiao-kang" Team, *Zhong-guo Xiao-kang Biao-zhun* (China's Xiao-kang Standard), Beijing, 1992.

through the accumulation of capital. Hence the use of growth of "real per-capita GNP" as a common economic index of development. During the 1970s, economic development came to be redefined in terms of the reduction or elimination of poverty, income inequality, and unemployment within the context of a growing economy.[9] But this concept of development was still considered to be too narrow with too much economic bias, e.g. it leaves out many non-marketed and non-price activities as well as important aspects of human welfare like quality of life. Hence some development economists conceived development as a multi-dimensional process, which can be measured only by a cluster of many socio-economic indicators.[10]

[9]This new meaning of development was originally strongly advocated by the eminent British development economist Dudley Seers, who eventually also influenced the World Bank to adopt the new development strategy of "Redistribution from Growth". See Dudley Seers, "The Meaning of Development", *Eleventh World Conference of the Society for International Development* (New Dehli, 1969).

[10]The United Nations Research Institute of Social Development (UNRSD) developed a composite social development index with 16 core indicators, including life expectancy, consumption of animal protein as well as energy and electricity consumption and percentage of GDP from manufacturing. (*Contents and Measurements of Socioeconomic Development* (Geneva, 1972), p. 63.

Adelman and Morris classified 74 developing countries according to 41 social, political and economic variables, including size of traditional agriculture, extent of dualism and social mobility, degree of competitiveness of political party system, strength of labour movement, degree of physical infrastructure, effectiveness of the tax system and financial institutions, and so on. Factor analysis was used to examine the inter-dependence of these variables and their level of economic development. (Irma Adelman and Cynthia Taft Morris, *Society, Politics, and Economic Development*, Baltimore, Johns Hopkins University Press, 1967.)

There are also studies to develop the Physical Quality of Life Index, i.e. concentrating on such indicators as life expectancy, infant mortality, and literacy, in order to measure development in terms of meeting the basic needs of the people. (Morris D. Morris, *Measuring the Conditions of the World's Poor: The Physical Quality of Life Index*, London, Frank Cass, 1979.)

For an analysis of social and economic development of ASEAN, See Habibullah Khan, *Socioeconomic Development of ASEAN: An International Perspective* (Singapore, Chopmen Publishers, 1986).

In its booklet on XK, the State Statistical Bureau constructed a general composite socio-economic development indicator as China's first "XK Index", which is supposed to retain "China's special social characteristics". The XK Index, as shown in Table 1, is actually made up of 12 rather common socio-economic indicators:

(1) *Real per-capita GNP*: For this indicator, the XK standard set for the year 2000 is, true to Deng Xiaoping's original target of quadrupling China's 1980 GNP, at 2,400 yuan based on 1990 prices. But because of dynamic economic growth during 1991–95, this XK target was already exceeded in 1995 with its real per-capita GNP reaching 2,600 yuan.[11] It may be noted that the XK per-capita GNP of 2,400 yuan works out to be only US$300 at the current exchange rate! This is because China's GNP is grossly biased downward on account of its past socialist pricing legacies and several rounds of yuan depreciation.[12]

(2) *Share of Tertiary Sector in GNP*: China likes to use the rather archaic term "tertiary industry" for the service sector. Economic development is a process typically marked by a decline in agriculture's share of GNP and a corresponding rise of manufacturing and service industries. For developed economies, the service sector, especially its "tradable activities", will continue to grow at the expense of manufacturing. In contrast, China's existing service sector is unusually small: at 20.6 percent for 1980 and 27.2 percent for 1990, with the XK standard set at only 36 percent, compared to the average share of 39 percent for the world's low-income economies in 1994 and 52 percent for the

[11]In 1995 China's GNP reached 5,760 billion yuan at current prices or 3,232 billion yuan at 1990 prices, which works out to be around 2,600 yuan per head.

[12]For further discussion of these problems, see John Wong, "What is China's Per-capita GNP?", *IEAPE Background Brief*, No. 18 (18 October 1991). For better international comparison, the World Bank therefore provides a PPP (purchasing power parity) estimate of China's per-capita GNP, which was US$2,510 at current international dollar for 1994, as against the nominal level of US$530. The PPP-based GNP is supposed to correct the downward biases. (*World Development Report 1996*.)

Table 1 China's Xiao-Kang Index

	Indicator	1980	1990	1994	Xiao-Kang Standard	Weight	Progress towards Xiao-Kang by 1990 (%)[a]	Extent of Xiao-Kang realisation in 1994 (%)[b]
A.	**Objective Economic Conditions**							
1.	Real per capita GNP (yuan)	736	1558	2600 (1995)	**2400**	15	49.4	100
2.	Share of "tertiary sector" (%)	20.6	27.2	31.8	**36**	8	42.9	88
3.	Gini Coefficient (0–1)	0.28	0.36	0.37	**0.33**	9	30.0	87
4.	Proportion of the Poor (%)	33	8	7	**5**	5	89.3	71
B.	**Quality of Life Indicators**							
5.	Average household income (yuan)	520	970	1780	**1400**	14	51.1	100
6.	Average living floor space (sq. m)	4.7	11.0	16.6	**15.5**	10	58.3	100
7.	Average daily per-capita calorie-intake (calorie)	2400	2550	2596 (1992)	**2600**	4	75.0	100
8.	Daily per-capita protein intake (grams)	50	65	67 (1992)	**75**	5	60.0	89
9.	Engel's coefficient (%)	60	54.5	—	**48**	8	45.8	90
	(For urban residents)	53	54	50	**45**	—	—	—
10.	Cultural, Educational, Recreation expenditures (%)	6	11.2	NA	**16**	5	52.0	NA
C.	**Human Resource Indicators**							
11.	Average life expectancy (years)	67	70	70	**70**	10	100	100
12.	Secondary enrolment ratio (%)	35	50	57 (1993)	**57**	6	68.2	100
	Total	—	—	—	—	**100**	**57.4**	**82.3**

Notes: (a) The value of (1990 minus 1980) divided by (Xiao-Kang minus 1980) %.
(b) The value of 1994 divided by Xiao-Kang value.

Sources: State Statistical Bureau Xiao-Kang Team: *Zhongguo Xiao-Kang Biao-Zhun* (China's Xiao-Kang Standards), Beijing, 1992; World Bank, *World Development Report 1996*; and Asian Development Bank, *Key Development Indicators of Developing Asian and Pacific Countries*, 1995.

middle-income economies — 64 percent for Singapore.[13] In future, as China completes its economic reform, the relative share of service sector is bound to rise sharply.

(3) *Gini Coefficient*: Based on the Lorenz curve, Gini coefficient is used to measure the extent of income inequality. China started off in 1980 with a high level of income equality and hence a very low Gini coefficient of 0.28 because of its socialist pattern of income distribution, mainly by controlling factor incomes and disallowing property incomes. As economic reform took hold and the market developed, inequality rose sharply with a Gini coefficient of 0.36 for 1990. Setting the Gini coefficient of 0.33 as the XK standard for the year 2000 is obviously unrealistic, as continuing economic development is likely to worsen income inequality further before greater equality will finally set in. Such a pattern of economic growth and income distribution, typically displaying an "inverted U-shaped curve", is common to many developing countries.[14]

(4) *Proportion of the Poor*: To the extent that the primary goal of economic development anywhere is manifestly to eliminate poverty, Chinese planners have rightly set the proportion of the poor in the population at 5 percent as the XK standard. In 1990, some 90 million or about 8 percent of the total population were still poverty-stricken, mainly in the rural areas. In 1995 the poverty-stricken rural population were reported to have come down to 65 million; but it still works out to be around 7 percent of the total population.[15] Future economic growth will no doubt bring down China's overall incidence of poverty further;

[13]*World Development Report 1996.*
China's service sector has been backward partly because of the historical Marxist prejudice against it for being "unproductive" and partly because of underestimation, as a whole range of services provided by the state sector has not been properly accounted for.

[14]This concept of an "inverted U-shaped curve" was first hypothesised by Simon Kuznets, a Nobel Prize laureate in economics. It is not an iron law that equality will follow development for every developing economy, though it has been true for many East Asian economies.

[15]"5 Million Less Rural Poor", *Beijing Review* (July 29–August 4, 1996).

but this indicator is fundamentally imprecise as much of it depends on how the poverty line is drawn up.

(5) *Average Household Income*: Most countries use only per-capita GNP as the main income indicator. Chinese planners additionally used "average household income" as the second income indicator probably because the concept of per-capita GNP is not well understood by the Chinese public. Thus, the XK standard of average household income is targeted to be 2,380 yuan for an urban household and 1,100 yuan for a rural household, giving a weighted average of XK household income of 1,400 yuan by the year 2000, which has been exceeded in 1994.

(6) *Average Living Floor Space*: Conceptually simple, this indicator, however, faces the formidable problem of reliable statistical estimation of disparate housing types. Thus, the XK standard requires a per-capita living floor space of 9 sq metres for urban residents and 18 sq metres for rural residents, giving the weighted average of 15.5 sq metres. Again, China claimed to have reached this XK standard in 1994.

(7) *Daily Per-capita Calorie Intake*: For this simple indicator, China set 2,380 calories as the XK standard for the year 2000, which was all but fulfilled in 1990, as China is no longer a basket case. With rural and urban incomes rapidly rising, this indicator is fast losing its development significance because of the "low income elasticity" demand (i.e. less consumption with higher income) for calorie-intensive food items, except perhaps for the small group still trapped in pockets of poverty as implied in the Indicator in (4).

(8) *Daily Per-capita Protein Intake*: Set at 75 grams as the XK standard for the year 2000, this relatively simple physical measure, much like Indicator (7), will also in time lose its development significance because of rapidly rising incomes. In China, this is manifested in the increase of per-capita annual consumption of pork, beef and mutton in the rural areas from 7.8 kg in 1980 to 11.3 kg in 1990.[16]

[16]It is interesting to note that the consumption of most food items in both rural and urban areas from 1990 remained stagnant while spending on such consumer durable like washing machines and TV sets has sharply increased. *China Statistical Yearbook 1996*.

(9) *Engel's Coefficient*: To reflect the low income elasticity of demand for all food items, this coefficient shows the decreasing proportion of household expenditure on all food items as income rises, usually about 40 percent for the middle income economies — 34 percent for the middle-income family in Singapore. But China set the XK standard at 48 percent. It may be noted that the application of this 19th-century Engel's Law to China before the completion of economic reform is apt to be inaccurate. This is because many consumption items in China from food to rental and power by urban residents are subsidised. This Law is also not suitable for measuring rural consumption because of the difficulty of imputing the farmer's total income as well as his consumption of self-grown food.

(10) *Cultural, Educational, Recreation Expenditures*: China set the XK standard for this kind of expenditures at 16 percent, which was 70 percent fulfilled by 1990. But again, this measure is also inaccurate because of the likely shift of demands and preferences at the time of rapid economic and social changes.

(11) *Average Life Expectancy*: For this rather straight-forward indicator, China set 70 years as the XK target, which was already reached in 1990.

(12) *Gross Secondary School Enrolment Ratio*: China set the XK standard for the age group enrolled in secondary schooling at 57 percent, which was almost reached in 1993 with the ratio of 55 percent.[17]

It can thus be seen that of the above 12 socio-economic indicators some are "hard" ones pertaining to simple physical data like calorie intake, and some are "soft" such as those related to income and expenditures which involve judgement in their measurement. There is also considerable redundancy among some indicators because they tend to indicate similar developments, e.g. per-capita GNP and average household income, Gini coefficient and the proportion of the poor, and daily calorie intake and Engel's coefficient.

[17]*World Development Report 1996*.

Of greater significance are the different weights ascribed to these indicators. To work out these weights, China follows the conventional techniques of first seeking the "subjective" views of experts on the selected indicators, and their views are then ranked and classified "objectively" according to their degrees of "nearness" or "natural association".[18] The resultant weights should closely reflect the average preferences of the Chinese experts as their combined version of socio-economic progress. As can be seen from Table 1, since the three items of income, housing and life expectancy take up 49 percent of the total weight and since most of the household incomes in China are spent on food and basic livelihood, the resultant XK Index is a vivid mirror image of the traditional preferences of the Chinese people, first for the basic needs of *wen-bao* and then for *chang-shou* (longevity).

Table 1 serves to show China's progress towards XK. With 1980 as the starting point, China's overall socio-economic progress by 1990 was slightly more than half-way towards its final destination, having achieved a weighted average score of 57.4. By 1994, as a result of dynamic economic growth, China has reached 82.3 percent of the overall XK target — in fact, having already over-fulfilled the income targets. Since the Chinese economy is slated to continue with its high growth for the remaining six years, China's ability to realise Deng's cherished vision of lifting the Chinese society to the XK standard by 2000 should not be in doubt.

How does China's overall socio-economic development progress stand in the context of the Asia-Pacific (AP) region? From Table 2 it is clear that China's economic performance in terms of growth and trade expansion since 1980 is virtually second to none in the AP region, even though China's current per-capita GNP is much lower than all the other AP economies except Vietnam.[19] China's high economic growth in the 1980s much resembles that of Japan in the 1950s and the 1960s, and that of the NIEs

[18]This technique of ranking and classifying observations to work out the degree of similarity is variously called "cluster analysis", "numerical taxonomy" or "factor analysis". Habibullah Khan, *op. cit.*

[19]For international comparison of the conventional GNP, the downward bias of China's GNP, as explained earlier, should be borne in mind.

Table 2 China and Other Asia Pacific Economies: Performance Indicators

	Area (Thousand of sq. km)	Population 1994 (million)	GNP per-capita 1994 (US$)	PPP estimates of GNP per-capita, 1994 (Current Int'l $)	Real GDP growth (%)						Annual Export Growth (%)		Manufacturing export as % of total exports, 1993	Export-GDP Ratio, 1993 (%)
					1960–70	1970–80	1980–90	1993	1994	1995	1980–90	1990–94		
China	9,561	1,190.9	530	2,510	5.2	5.8	9.5	13.4	11.8	10.2	11.5	16.0	89	21.6
Japan	378	125.0	34,630	21,140	10.9	5.0	4.1	0.6	0.7	0.8	4.8	4.0	97	8.6
NIEs														
S. Korea	99	44.5	8,260	10,330	8.6	9.5	9.7	5.7	8.3	8.2	12.0	10.6	93	25.0
Taiwan	36	21.1	11,604	—	9.2	9.7	7.1	6.2	6.5	6.4	—	—	93	38.5
Hong Kong	1	6.1	21,650	—	10.0	9.3	7.1	5.8	5.5	5.0	14.4	14.3	93	150.7
Singapore	1	2.9	22,010	21,900	8.8	8.5	6.4	9.8	10.1	8.2	10.0	12.3	80	134.4
ASEAN														
Brunei	6	0.3	(21,000)	—	NA	NA	NA	NA	NA	NA	NA	NA	NA	NA
Indonesia	1,905	190.4	880	3,600	3.9	7.6	5.5	7.1	7.4	7.5	2.9	10.8	53	23.3
Malaysia	330	19.7	3,480	8,440	6.5	7.8	5.2	8.7	8.5	9.2	10.9	12.9	65	73.1
Philippines	300	67.0	950	2,740	5.1	6.3	0.9	1.7	4.3	5.5	3.5	8.0	76	20.5
Thailand	513	58.0	2,410	6,970	8.4	7.2	7.6	7.8	8.5	8.8	14.0	14.6	72	29.5
Vietnam	332	72.0	200	—	—	—	—	—	—	8.5	—	—	—	—

Sources: *World Development Report* 1996 and earlier years; for Taiwan, *The Statistical Yearbook of the Republic of China 1995*; and ADB, *Asian Development Outlook 1995 and 1996*.

Table 3 China and Other Asia Pacific Economies: Social Indicators

	GNP per capita, 1994 US$	Total fertility rate, 1994 (%)	Life expectancy at birth (years) 1994	Infant mortality rate, 1994 (per 1000 births)	Population per doctor, 1993	Adult illiteracy (%) 1995	Percentage of age group male enrolled in education 1993			Human Development (1992)	
							Primary	Secondary	Tertiary	Index*	Ranking in developing world
China	530	1.9	69	30	1,060	19	120	60	4	0.644	34
Japan	34,630	1.5	79	4	609	5	102	95	30	0.929	NA
NIEs											
South Korea	8,260	1.8	71	12	950	5	100	93	48	0.859	4
Taiwan	11,604	1.5	74	5	807	8	102	95	45	—	—
Hong Kong	21,650	1.2	78	5	919	8	—	—	21	0.875	2
Singapore	22,010	1.8	75	5	720	9	—	—	20	0.836	10
ASEAN											
Brunei	21,000	—	—	—	—	—	—	—	—	—	—
Indonesia	880	2.7	63	53	4,910	16	116	48	10	0.586	41
Malaysia	3,480	3.4	71	12	2,410	17	93	56	—	0.794	17
Philippines	950	3.8	65	40	6,700	5	—	—	26	0.621	38
Thailand	2,410	2.0	69	36	4,420	6	98	38	19	0.798	16
Vietnam	200	3.1	66	42	2,300	6	—	—	2	0.514	51
Average of low-income countries	380	3.3	63	58	5,630	34	112	55	—	—	—
Average of middle-income countries	2,520	2.8	67	40	1,730	—	105	65	—	—	—

*Human Development Index combines life expectancy, educational attainment and income indicators to give a composite measure of human development.

Sources: *World Development Report 1996*; Asian Development Bank, *Key Indicators of Developing Asian and Pacific Countries 1995; Human Development Report 1994*; and *Taiwan Statistical Data Book 1995*; and national sources.

in the 1960s and the 1970s. In this context, China should hold great promises to sustain its dynamic growth for at least two or more decades, especially since China, as a large continental-size country, has much greater development potential than the other AP economies.

Most AP economies display a pretty close relationship between their economic development and social progress, as shown in Table 3. Thus, China's overall social progress lags behind Japan and the NIEs, but is ahead of several ASEAN countries, particularly in terms of demographic and human resource development indicators. This has been aptly captured in the UNDP's "human development index", which ranks China above Indonesia, the Philippines and Vietnam.[20]

FUZZY INDEX AND DELUSIVE GOAL

By the year 2000, China will have certainly fulfilled the XK goals as originally envisaged by Deng Xiaoping in 1979. But it is far from certain that Chinese people would then be satisfied with such a state of social progress. There are too many problems concerning the XK Index and its development implications.

XK is an inherently fuzzy concept, grossly imprecise. Many socio-economic indicators are similarly plagued by such conceptual and empirical difficulty, particularly when applied to a transitional economy like China, which is experiencing not just rapid economic and social change, but also a transformation of its economic and social systems. Earlier on, we have pointed out how a mixed price system can complicate the measurement of certain indicators and hence reduce their "indicating power".

Another major drawback of the XK Index is that most of its indicators in the cluster are related to the material well-being, with inadequate emphasis on the human development aspects. Is XK only a question of

[20]*Human Development Report 1994*, published by the United Nations Development Programme, (New York/Oxford, Oxford University Press, 1994). The human development index is made up of eight conventional indicators like income, health and education.

"rice bowl", related just to the past peasant mentality of "enough to eat"? Would Deng back in 1980 have anticipated China's environmental degradation, which has become a serious problem in recent years? Clearly, the XK Index should have included other indicators pertaining to the improvement of the social and physical environment, which can better reflect some of the negative social externalities created in the process of economic development. This will also provide a proper trade-off for the material progress, i.e. a more balanced picture of China's socio-economic development.

Economic and social development is basically a "normative" concept, one that is subject to value judgement. XK is such a concept. Will Deng's vision of XK be still widely acceptable in 2000 when a whole new generation of Chinese will have grown up under market reform? Chances are what constitutes XK to Deng and his generation may well be differently perceived by the new generation, who are likely to demand a different XK basket of goods and services to reflect their changing tastes and changing social priorities. The new generation, more materialistic and more individualistic in outlook, may also want greater freedom of choice for their own package of XK. After all, economic and social development is supposed to satisfy *individual* basic needs and enhance *individual* welfare.

XK is therefore also a delusive concept. Despite China's impressive GNP growth, individual Chinese by the year 2000 may well feel that their XK level of life has not yet been satisfied. Such is the continuing social challenge of economic development, for China as elsewhere. Viewed in this light, China's current ideological campaign of promoting "spiritual civilisation" as a means to counter the spread of "material culture" is unlikely to produce significant results.

Xia-Gang and Its Sociological Implications of Reducing Labour Redundancy in China's SOEs

QIU Zeqi & ZHENG Yongnian
East Asian Institute
National University of Singapore

One of the most important issues facing all former communist states in their transition to a market economy is state-owned enterprise (SOE) reform and consequent massive unemployment. In Russia and many other East European countries, unemployment resulted in civil disorder and social instability and became an insurmountable difficulty for socio-economic development. In China, due to its more than 1.2 billion population, the transition to an alleged "socialist market economy" also has led to massive unemployment. In rural areas, reforms have produced millions of flowing population (Cheng Li, 1996). In urban China, there are frequent reports about workers' unrest. Nevertheless, as a whole, China has achieved relative socio-political stability.

Central to the Chinese model of reform is "economic reform without political reform" (Shirk, 1993). Indeed, the Chinese government has used various political and administrative means to promote economic reforms and cope with enormous unexpected consequences. Government's deep involvement in economic activities, however, has overcome difficulties and resolved issues on the one hand, and carried its own burden of problems on the other hand. The costs of government involvement cannot be underestimated.

This paper attempts to explore the Chinese way of coping with massive unemployment and its impact on the state-sector reform, using the "Xia Gang" as a case study. The "Xia Gang" (literally "off-post") has become popular in urban China since the early 1990s when the Chinese government began to put much emphasis on reforming the state sector. The Chinese government has allowed state sector workers to be "off-post" from the original companies with partial payment while taking a second, even a third, job in other companies. How has the government used "Xia Gang" (XG) to deal with unemployment? What are its benefits and costs? What is the real problem for the state-sector reform and consequent unemployment? These are the central issues this paper aims to address.

"XIA GANG" AND UNEMPLOYMENT

According to the Ministry of Labour and the State Statistical Bureau, an employee (*jiuye renyuan* or *congye renyuan*)can be defined as one who has a job or a business. Statistically, one will be accounted as an employee if he/she is in a process of resigning his/her job or retiring while engaging in another job or business.

On the other hand, an unemployed is defined as one who is 16 years old and over and younger than 60 for men and 55 for women and has the capability to work but is out of work/business. Concretely, unemployment includes:

1) Those who are older than 16 and do not have a job/business or are seeking a job/business but have not found yet;
2) Those who are out of work because of bankruptcy of their original companies and are in a process of seeking a job/business but have not found yet;
3) Those who are seeking a job/business but have not found yet after his/her job is terminated by his/her employers;

4) Those who have resigned their jobs/businesses but have not found new jobs/businesses yet;
5) Those who are "legal labourers" but do not have a job.[1]

According to the definition above, in 1995, Chinese urban unemployment touched 5,196,000, about 3 percent of the total urban labour, among which 3,102,000 are youth (State Statistical Bureau 1996, p. 114). This figure, however, does not include "Xia Gang" workers.

"Xia Gang" in China does not have an official definition. Generally speaking, it can be understood as one who registers a position in a company and get partial compensation which can't afford their daily lives. It is called "off-post" by the media in China (Kahn 1995, p. 8). It includes workers who:

1) are out of work and get about 150–170 *yuan* monthly pension because of a) bankruptcy, b) stopped production, c) the rundown of their original companies;
2) have a part time job but only earn some payment that is not enough to afford their daily lives;
3) retire before the official age (60 for men and 55 for women) without annuity because of worsening performance of the original companies and are not able to afford their daily lives (Xie and Wang 1996, p. 10).

According to Zhu Jiazhen, the Deputy Minister of the Labour Ministry, jobless and part time employees will reach 216 million in the next five years (Wu, 1996). This figure includes 72 million of urban new workers, 14 million of the XG workers and 130 million of rural surplus workers. As Figure 1 shows, the total employees in urban China in 1995 was 173.5 million, among which 112.6 million were in state-owned enterprises (SOEs), 31.5 million in collectives and 29.4 million in others businesses. Figure 2 shows the trend of the employment from 1952 to 1995 by ownership.

[1]In China, "legal labourers" refer to those who are eligible for a job according to the state's labour law.

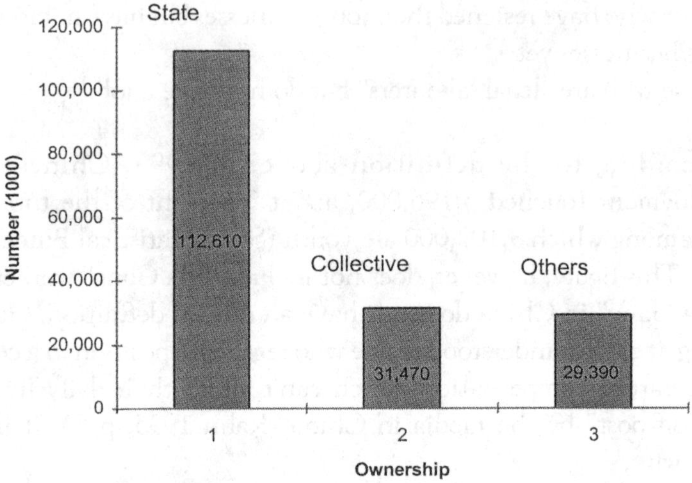

Figure 1 Urban China Employee by Ownership in 1995
Data source: *China Statistical Yearbook, 1996*, p. 90.

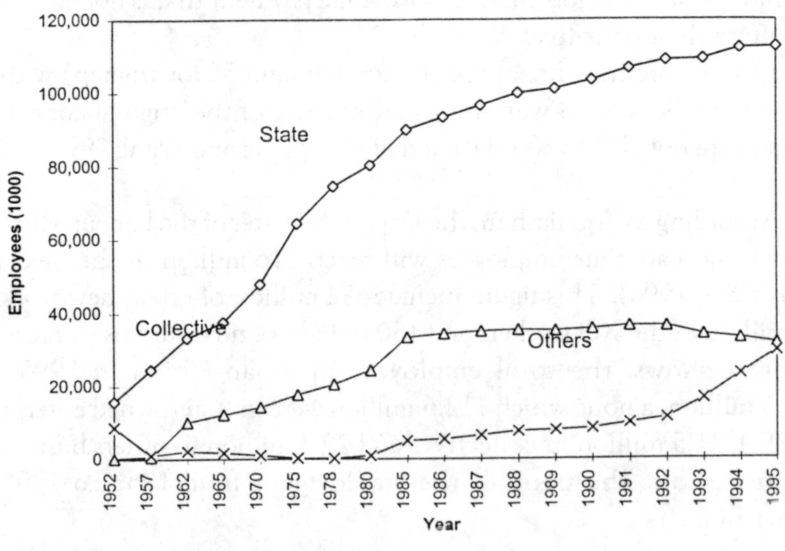

Figure 2 Trend of Urban China Employee by Ownership from 1952 to 1995
Data source: *China Statistical Yearbook, 1996*, p. 90.

It can be reasonably assumed that about 20–30 percent of the state employees are surplus labourers (*fuyu zhigong*).[2] Then XG workers would be 22.5–33.8 million among the SOEs employees in 1995 (Zhu, 1996, p. 24). In 1995, there were 173.5 million urban employees. If we add 22.5–33.8 million of the XG workers to 5.2 million officially registered unemployees (see Table 1), the unemployment rate in 1995 was about 16–22.5 percent. It was reported in early 1995 that the total unemployment and XG workers were 15–17 percent (Kahn 1995, p. 8).

Although there is no official data about the details of XG workers, various local reports and surveys reveal some further breakdown. Without

Table 1. Unemployees in Urban China

Year	Registered Number (1000)	Youth in Regist. Number (1000)	Youth in Regist. Perc. in Total Unemployees	Jobless Rate Proportion
1978	5,300	2,491	47.0	5.3
1980	5,415	3,825	70.6	4.9
1985	2,385	1,969	82.6	1.8
1986	2,644	2,093	79.2	2.0
1987	2,766	2,351	85.0	2.0
1988	2,962	2,453	82.8	2.0
1989	3,779	3,090	81.8	2.6
1990	3,832	3,127	81.6	2.5
1991	3,522	2,884	81.9	2.3
1992	3,639	2,998	83.2	2.3
1993	4,201	3,319	79.0	2.6
1994	4,764	3,010	63.2	2.8
1995	5,196	3,102	59.7	2.9

Data source: *China Statistical Yearbook*, *1996*, *p*. 114.

[2]Various Chinese sources indicate different estimations of the size of surplus labour. 1) A survey conducted in Chengdu, the capital city of Sichuan shows that about 30 percent of the employees are surplus (*China Labor Science*, No. 4, 1996, p. 3); 2) surplus laborers are about 40 percent of the total employment (*China Information*, December 16, 1996, p. 4); and 3) a survey in Tianjin shows that 18 percent of the total employment is surplus (*Economic Highlights*, February 16, 1996, p. 4).

doubt, a larger portion of the unemployment was female. For instance, in Shenyang City of North China, where the state sector dominates, this figure was 80 percent (Chen, 1995, p. 19). In Tianjin, an essential portion of the total XG workers are young mothers (Xie and Wang, 1996, p. 10). Moreover, most of the unemployed women were those who only had high- and middle-school level education (Zhou, 1995, p. 15). According to one report, 90 percent of the XG workers only had 3–9 years of education (Chen, 1995, p. 19). Table 2 and Figure 3 show that unemployees are in their middle age. According to one report, about 60 percent of the XG workers are 36 year old and over (Chen, 1995, p. 19). Table 1 also shows that the proportion of the youth in the total unemployment declined from 83 percent in 1992 to 58 percent in 1995 while the total unemployment increased from 2.3 percent to 2.9 percent during the same period.[3]

Table 2. Annual Average Wage and Index of Employees by Ownership

	Average Wage in Money (Yuan)			Index (previous year = 100)		
Year	State	Collective	Others	State	Collective	Others
1978	644	506		100.0	100.0	
1980	803	623		113.9	114.9	
1985	1,213	967	1,436	117.3	119.2	137.0
1986	1,414	1,092	1,629	116.6	112.9	113.4
1987	1,546	1,207	1,879	109.3	110.5	115.3
1988	1,853	1,426	2,382	119.9	118.1	126.8
1989	2,055	1,557	2,707	110.9	109.2	113.6
1990	2,284	1,681	2,987	111.1	108.0	110.3
1991	2,477	1,866	3,468	108.5	111.0	116.1
1992	2,878	2,109	3,966	116.2	113.0	114.1
1993	3,532	2,592	4,966	122.7	122.9	125.2
1994	4,797	3,245	6,303	135.8	125.2	126.9
1995	5,625	3,931	7,463	117.3	121.1	118.4

Data source: *China Statistical Yearbook*, 1996, p. 115.

[3]Youth unemployment in China refers to those who are searching a job for the first time in their career.

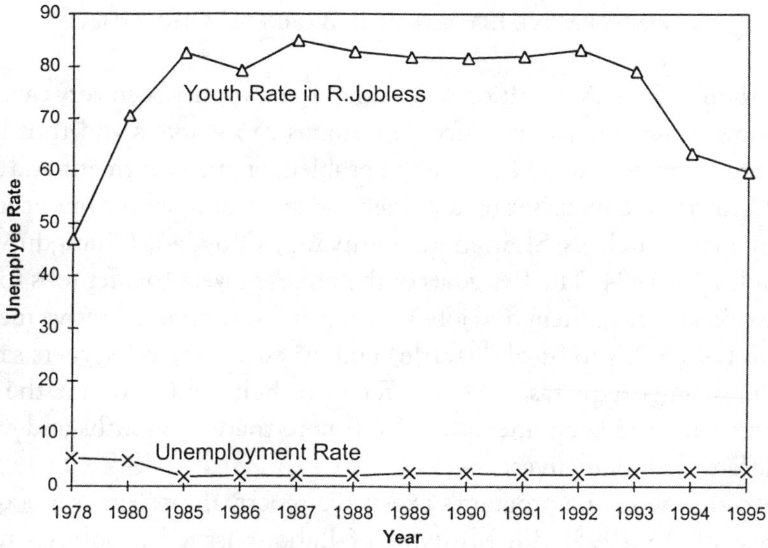

Figure 3 Unemp'mt rate and Prop. of Youth in Reg'd Jobless
Data source: *China Statistical Yearbook, 1996*, p. 90.

"Xia Gang" and unemployment have become one of the most important issues for China's next step of economic reform, an issue more serious than inflation for China's socio-political stability. It is widely believed that unemployment will have a major impact on China's social stability in the next five years due to a possibly lower rate of economic growth and a continuously increase of XG workers (Yang, 1996, p. 11; *Ming Pao*, 1996, p. 1). According to a latest report, the central government has requested that government officials of different levels pay great attention to and resolve the problems related to unemployment in order to avoid massive street strikes and demonstrations and maintain socio-political stability. If any street strike occurs, relevant officials will be punished (Jin, 1997, p. A8). The State Council also has required that the SOE reform regarding those firms with worsening performance should put priority on taking over and merging rather than bankruptcy (Jin, 1997, p. A8).

ADMINISTRATIVE EFFORTS AND WORKERS' DISCONTENT

Even though China's transition to a market economy has been very cautious and slow, it already has produced enormous XG workers and thus high pressure on government. To solve the problem of unemployment and XG, the Ministry of Labour set up a pioneer program of re-employment in 30 major cities such as Shanghai, Shenyang, Qingdao, Chengdu, and Hangzhou in 1994. The key goals of the program were to offer jobs to the XG workers or help them find jobs by using different administrative means; and to help SOEs to "*anzhi*" (settle) and evacuate surplus workers safely. The most important task was to offer to or help find a job for the XG workers who had been unemployed for more than six months and could not afford their daily lives.

According to the program's executive report, the program was quite successful. In 1995, the Ministry of Labour issued a policy on re-employment based on this experiment. In 1996, the same policy was re-issued because of its effectiveness in maintaining social stability. According to this policy, provincial or municipal governments have to issue various special policies to assist re-employment programmes and assure the programme's implementation and success (The Ministry of Labour, 1996). As a response, local governments issued relevant local policies or regulations dealing with the re-employment programme in the means of taxation, loan-issuing, registration and so on (Benkan jizhe, 1996, pp. 29–31).

This method is similar to what was used to deal with massive returned youth in the late 1970s (Qiu, 1996, pp. 91–99). The difference is that government organisations now are playing a more important role. Most recruitment fairs are organised by the regional governments especially for the XG workers.

To some extent, the XG system has been conducive to socio-political stability. The XG workers are different from unemployees because XG does not mean that workers do not have a job, but means that they want a better job with higher payment. For example, Ms. Liu, aged 26, was off-post with 170 *yuan* pension per month after she gave birth to her kid. Her husband earned 500 *yuan* per month and could not afford the daily lives for a 3-member family in Beijing. In order to help her find a new job, her original company gave her various chances. First, the company recommended her to be a telephone operator, but she declined just a few days later for the reason that the job location was too far away from her residency. Then the company asked her to be a sales clerk in a department store, which was only one block away from her home and she could earn 200 *yuan* basic wage per month, plus a bonus that could double or even triple her basic wage. But she tried for three months and then declined too. She complained that the job was too tough (Chen and Gu, 1996, p. 1).

Similar stories also happened in Wuhan, Chengdu and other major Chinese cities. In mid-1995, the Wuhan municipal government held a recruitment fair and 5,000 job-seekers attended it. But it turned out that only 820 signed draft contracts. A few months later, the municipal government organised another fair for the XG workers in the textile sector in order to recruit 450 members for securities companies. But only 48 signed their contracts. In the first quarter of 1995, Wuhan newspaper publishers tried to hire delivery workers with a monthly payment of 450 *yuan*. This effort totally failed because no one wanted to be employed (Chen and Zhao, 1996, p. 29).

In Chengdu, the municipal government organised a recruitment fair for 9,000 positions in 1996. But only 17 percent of positions were filled. Many department stores in the city expected to recruit sales clerks among over 1,000 XG workers, but only 80 of them agreed to be interviewed. In the end, twenty of them were willing to work, but asked to terminate their contracts only one month later (Zhang, 1996, p. 5). So, the problem is not that China does not have jobs for the XG workers, but that they do not want to work. Why then do the XG workers not want to work?

The Institute of "Anzhi" and Workers' Perception of Job Hierarchy

Many XG workers do not want to resign from their old posts and take a new one, even though doing so will bring them more benefits. How should this phenomenon be explained? This essay argues that this behaviour pattern is closely linked with workers' perception about socialistic job hierarchy, which was developed during the years that the planned economic system was implemented. According to the Chinese revolutionary ideology, every one should have a job if he/she is not a disabled person. In effect, after the People's Republic was established in 1949, every one was required to work. To assign a job to every one became a duty of government. This indeed became a consensus between government and labour. Workers took it for granted that they would and should be assigned a position by government. The termination of one's job would be regarded as a severe punishment.

On the other hand, if government wanted to punish someone, it would assign him/her a heavy physical job. Political movements plus ideological propaganda strengthened a classified concept of *job* based on the traditional Chinese philosophy: heavy physical jobs should be done by people in lower levels of social hierarchy while professional ones should be done by the elites with higher education and morality. *Job* either in traditional or contemporary China is not only the means to earn money. More importantly, it is a symbol of position in the social hierarchy.

It was against this background that XG workers declined their offers. XG workers believe that as urban citizens, they should have a higher position in the social hierarchy and should not accept any heavy physical jobs. For example,

> Mrs. Wang Kejun spent 15 years making radios in a state-owned factory in downtown Shanghai. At age 38, her company placed her off-post and sent her home with 40 percent of her original salary. Now she sells socks, jackets and mittens in a tiny stall between apartment blocks not far away from her old company. She rents the stall for 1,000 *yuan* (US$117) per month. "This kind of job is what the outside people should do", she complains, referring to workers who come from outside of the city. "I hate it. It's cold. Business is not so good. I don't want to be some kind of private capitalist (Kahn, 1995, p. 4).

The Chinese communist revolutionary ideology emphasises that every one has equal rights for everything. The welfare system was established at the expense of farmers' interests. Ever since the reform began, SOE employees never think that farmers should have equal rights as they do and believe that migrant workers from rural areas should serve them if they come to the city for jobs (*ibid.*, p. 4).

After more than a decade's economic reform, private capitalists are still looked down by many state sector workers. They have internalised their previous communist education that capitalism is vicious. For example. Mr. Zeng was employed by a state-owned railway construction company. The company ran out of business three years ago. That made Mr. Zeng only to be paid 120 *yuan* (US$14.4) per month, which was obviously not enough for the daily needs of his family. He was suggested to set up a small grocery or a repair shop. He knew that if he did so he would have to earn money using his own hands. He decided not to do so because he thought that this would make him lose face in front of friends or acquaintances (Li, 1996, p. 7).

The concept of job hierarchy not only refers to the differences between farmers and workers, but also to the differences between the different forms of ownership, as exemplified by what happened in Dalian City. In 1996, the Dalian First Plastic Factory was merged with the Dalian Second Plastic Factory, and as a result, 60 female workers went to XG. A local telecommunication station offered various positions for these XG workers. Most of them, however, did not even want to be interviewed. When they were asked "why?", the answer was, "the station is a collective." In effect, the monthly salary for a position in this local station was 250 *yuan* (during the probation period) and 600 *yuan* after probation. Eventually, the state was only able to hire three workers among 20 who were interviewed. But one of them withdrew her contract eventually(Benkan jizhe, 1996, p. 35).

Obviously, most of the XG workers still put their job priority on the state sector rather than the collectives and privates (Li, 1996, p. 7). How could this happen? If we read the history of ownership development, we will find that the concept of *job* hierarchy is not only a notion, but more importantly it concerns individual workers' income and welfare. Under the planned economic system, how much an individual worker could earn depended on the form of ownership he/she was in, as shown in Table 2.

The Chinese state-owned enterprises (SOEs) system, which was established after 1949, was based on confiscated officialdom capital (Qiu, 1996, pp. 53–4). As of 1957, the non-state ownership almost disappeared (see Figure 2). Almost 99 percent of the private employers and employees of manufacture industry and 85 percent of the commercial services were transferred to the state-run industries. In other words, private business was almost eliminated by the socialist movements by the middle 1950s and private business *per se* was labeled as an enemy of socialism (Qiu, 1996). The next decade embittered people's sense of non-state-run businesses. During the same time, state employees were in higher social position and had stable income sources. To be a worker in SOEs became a honor to urban residents, and for rural residents, it was only a dream.

Urban population growth, however, created a heavy burden for the regime. In the late 1950s, most of the state-run enterprises began to face the problem of surplus labourers. Most of them were spouses of formal or skilled workers. They came from the countryside and were illiterate. In order to assure family stability rather than productivity, the government created an institution called "*anzhi*" (literally "arranging") to offer surplus labourers jobs in the service sector such as road-cleaning or drink-water-boiling. Different from SOE workers, their salary usually was based on their working time. These workers were not state-employees but collective employees. So, an employment in the collective became a pronoun of disables, the weak, or labour residuals (Qiu, 1996).

In the 1970s, as a new generation grew up, job demands expanded. According to the Chinese system, young people's jobs should be arranged by the enterprises where their parents held positions. Many SOEs created a collective sector in order to absorb new labourers as required by government. But these newly created collectives were not able to afford young workers benefits as SOEs did. The employees in these collectives were paid much less than those in the state sector and were regarded as second class workers. Even within a collective enterprise, those who were registered as state-employees (used to be state enterprise employee) had a higher payment than those of the collective (Qiu, 1996, p. 291). The income gap between workers of different ownership is shown in Table 3.

In addition, collective workers were not eligible to enjoy welfare as SOE workers did, such as lower housing rent, medical insurance, allowances, etc. and their children may not have equal rights for schooling.

Table 3. Contractual Employees by Ownership in Urban China

	Contracted		State		Collective		Others	
Year	Number (1000)	Perc. in Total Employees	Number (1000)	Perc. in Total Employees	Number (1000)	Perc. in Total Employees	Number (1000)	Perc. in Total Employees
1984	2,090	1.8	1,740	2.0	320	1.0	30	8.1
1985	4,090	3.3	3,320	3.7	720	2.2	50	11.4
1986	6,240	4.9	5,240	5.6	920	2.7	80	14.5
1987	8,730	6.6	7,350	7.6	1,250	3.6	130	18.1
1988	12,340	9.1	10,080	10.1	2,060	5.8	200	20.7
1989	14,680	10.7	11,900	11.8	2,450	7.0	330	25.1
1990	17,020	12.1	13,720	13.3	2,870	8.1	430	26.3
1991	19,720	13.6	15,890	14.9	3,230	8.9	600	28.0
1992	25,410	17.2	20,580	18.9	3,990	11.0	840	29.8
1993	31,220	21.0	23,960	21.9	5,260	15.5	2,000	37.4
1994	38,390	25.9	28,530	26.2	6,450	20.1	3,410	45.6
1995	60,960	40.9	43,960	40.1	11,490	37.4	5,510	62.8

Data source: *China Statistical Yearbook*, 1996, p. 107.

It was apparent that to be a SOE employee represented a promotion. Since 1949, collective employees never attempted to give up their efforts to become SOE employees. The privileges of the SOE employees were reduced, but not eliminated by the economic reform since 1978.

To XG workers, if they take a new job in a non-state sector, they will lose their welfare they enjoyed in their original SOEs. They believe that it is a risk for the rest of their lives. Thus, they prefer to go XG, because by doing so, they are legitimate to have a second, or even a third job, to earn more money, while taking the welfare from their original SOEs.

A survey conducted in Tianjin showed that 70 percent of the XG workers had a second job while receiving pension from their original companies (Xie and Wang, 1996, p. 10). In Beijing, an interview with 40 XG workers who declined jobs offered by the re-employment programmes showed that only three of them were without a job, while the other 37 had their temporary or permanent jobs. But all of them were still registered as XG workers in their original companies (*ibid.*).

Indeed, having a second job has become a popular phenomenon among XG workers in most Chinese cities. Almost all XG workers are unwilling to terminate their contracts with the original companies. In some sense, an increase in the size of XG workers has been a major force of China's rapid development of the service sector, because most of XG workers turn to this sector for a second job. Figure 4 shows the development of the service sector after 1992. Without doubt, an essential proportion of service sector workers belongs to XG.

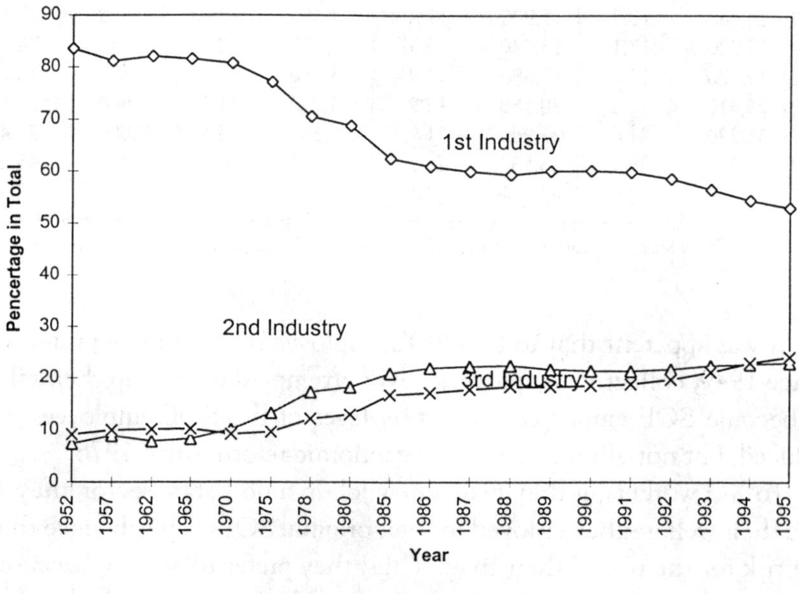

Figure 4 Employees by Industries
Data source: *China Statistical Yearbook*, 1996, p. 88.

*First industry in China refers to agriculture; second industry manufacture; and third industry services.

On the one hand, owing to their consideration of socio-political stability and pressure from governments of different levels, SOEs are not urgent to terminate the registration with XG workers even though they have a second job. Theoretically, to terminate the registration is what SOEs can do rationally. The government's "*anzhi*" system deters SOEs from making such a decision, however. In Chinese, "*an*" means poising, stabilising, settling, appeasing and arranging, while "*zhi*" means laying, putting and situating. Therefore, "*anzhi*" as a government policy, means not only job-offering, but peace-stability-keeping. Government expects to please people and gain their political support through the "*anzhi*" institution.

On the other hand, XG workers know their importance for China's socio-political stability and believe that the government would offer them better jobs rather than just kick them out. Their logic is that they had served the "*guojia*" (state) before they were out of work, and the government therefore owed them both in terms of income and motion. In some sense, government officials also think about the "*anzhi*" policy from a similar perspective. "Heavy physical and dirty jobs that make urban workers very tired should be performed by the outsider", Mr. Fang from the Labour Bureau of Shanghai told news reporters (Kahn, 1995, p. 4). In this context, it is understandable that among 30,000 XG workers in the textile sector in Wuhan, half are outsiders (Chen and Zhao, 1996, p. 29).

XG as SOEs' Vested Interest

Most of the merged or bankrupted SOE firms are small in sized and have had a bad performance. They ask their employees to go XG because they are not capable of re-settling their workers. But there has been another phenomenon, that is: big SOEs want to keep surplus labourers in order to bargain with the government. These big companies have created various forms of collective enterprises or what is called "*san chan*" enterprises in China for their surplus labourers who otherwise would go XG. By doing so, big companies could create a domain of their own. Chief Executive Officers (CEOs) of these companies have full authority over their "*san chan*" enterprises. In other words, "*san chan*" enterprises are enclaves within the state sector and are beyond state control.

"*San chan*" enterprises have become increasingly popular since the early 1990s. Big companies, such as the Wuhan Steel Mill and the Jinchuan Nonferrous Metal Mill, developed "*san chan*" enterprises rapidly and the employees of the "san chan" enterprises even reached 40 to 50 percent of the total employees of these companies.

Big companies have a strong motivation to develop "*san chan*". The reason is quite simple in terms of the relationship between SOEs and government. Extra labourers are an important bargaining chip when SOEs play the game with government. SEOs have increasingly become a vested interest with the deepening of the economic reform (Qiu, 1995). A great deal of financial resource was channelled into the development of "*san chan*" enterprises from which both entrepreneurs and SOE workers could benefit greatly (Qiu, 1996). For big companies, if they ask surplus labourers to go XG, they would be a loser in bargaining with government organisations. What they want to do is to execute high pressure on government and gain more financial resource from government.

JOB PERCEPTION AND THE DILEMMA OF SOE REFORM

A key issue facing China's SOE reforms is how workers' perception of job can be changed. The above discussion shows that XG workers have difficulty in changing their concept of job. But with the deepening of economic reforms, they are forced to change their job concept. The Chinese government has played an important role in this process. Since the reform began in 1978, two movements have provided a great dynamism for workers to change their perception of job.

The first wave was symbolised by the contract system initiated in the early 1980s. The proportion of contractual employees in the total employment increased from 1.8 percent to 40.9 percent from 1984–1995 (see Table 3). The contract system in SOEs only meant that positions would no longer be permanent. However, it still provided welfare, e.g., housing, to contracted workers.

Since the early 1990s, a second movement, i.e., "*Xia Hai*," has introduced dramatic changes into people's perception of job. "*Xia*" in Chinese not only refers to "get out of" but to "to get into." In the early 1990s, "Xia Hai" became a national tide in urban China. "*Xia Hai*" means "to get into" or "jump into" the sea. "Sea" here refers to markets. A large proportion of XG workers has jumped into the "sea". By doing so, they have tried to find an alternative way to re-define their concept of job.

For example, a XG worker in Beijing now sells vegetables during the day and works as a cart-driver in Beijing Railway Station in the evening. He earns more than 50 *yuan* daily by doing two jobs. "200 *yuan* pension (from my original company) could not support my life, how could it support my family? Now I earn over 1,500 *yuan* every months. So I need to thank '*Xia Gang*'," he told a news reporter (Li, 1995, p. 1).

In order to encourage people to transfer from "*Xia Gang*" to "*Xia Hai*,' China Central Television State made a 12-episode TV series, showing various stories about how XG workers have found a new job and how they have changed their concept of job.[4] At the same time, the media also reported enormous stories about the XG workers who became business leaders or new employees in a different sector, etc. For example, 800 XG women in the Anqiu City of Shandong Province got new jobs in private companies (Ni, 1996, p. 2). Indeed, now XG workers tend to work in private companies and change their old concept of "iron-bowl." In Shanghai, more and more XG workers are even employed by the companies owned by "outsiders" (Chen, 1996, p. 5). The transition from "Xia Gang" to "Xia Hai" has provided a dynamism of China's private and individual businesses. As shown in Figure 5, China's private and individual businesses have developed rapidly since the early 1990s.

It is clear that XG has become a second tide of the expansion of China's labour market next to "*nongmin gong*" (outsiders or farmers). Regardless of their willingness, urban workers now have to compete with "*nongmin gong*" whom they have looked down so far. On the other hand, both have created a dynamism for the development of China's labour market. In this context,

[4]The 12-episodes TV series was entitled "Autumn Stories in 1996".

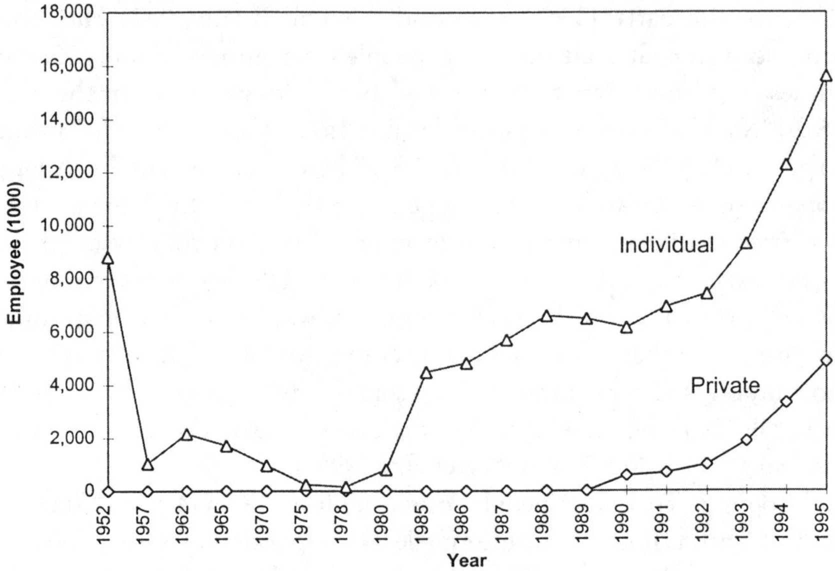

Figure 5 Individual and Private Business Development
Data source: *China Statistical Yearbook*, *1996*.

it is not advisable that government should stress the "*anzhi*" system continuously. Even though the "*anzhi*" system has been conducive to socio-political stability to an extent, it also encourages the XG workers to believe that they will be arranged ("anzhi") as long as they have the patience to wait. That means, by maintaining the "*anzhi*" system, the government *per se* has not changed its old concept of job associated with the planned economy. The government's efforts to maintain social stability are understandable. But the government also needs to change its concept of job if it wants to develop a market system.

In China, to establish a labour market is inevitable, but the government has to decide whether changes can be introduced into two other systems, i.e., household registration system and social security system. The government needs to legitimate outsiders' (farmers) participation in the urban labour market and allow them to migrate into cities as their jobs change. The competition between urban workers and rural workers will promote the development of labour markets.

Furthermore, as long as the SOE welfare system exists, workers will put their job priority on SOEs. It will be hard for a social security system to develop because the SOE welfare system is in conflict with the social security system. Take housing as an example. As long as SOE employees believe that they will have a chance to have an almost free apartment by SOEs, why should they use their own money in the housing market?

Nevertheless, an over-supply of labourers will continue for a long period of time in China. Even XG workers will be over supplied in the next few years and a high unemployment rate will exist. Both the labour and government have to face this trend. While the transition to a market economy results in massive unemployment, it also creates enormous new jobs and employment opportunities. A key issue for the government is how workers' perception of job could be changed.

References

Benkan jizhe. 1996. "Preference over regulations for the resettlement of off-post workers in provinces" (gedi shishi zaijiuye gongcheng de youhui zhengce jiqi gongzuo cuoshi), *China Labour Science* (Zhongguo Laodong Kexue), pp. 29–31.

Benkan. 1996. "Some puzzles regarding China's off-post workers" (zhongguo xiagang daiyezhe de guai xiangxiang), *Inside Information on Economic Reform* (Gaige Neican), No. 17, p. 35.

Chen, Gang. 1996. "Shanghai female off-post workers in Shanghai companies owned by outsiders" (hushao maigua), *Economic Daily* (Jingji Ribao), Septemer 4, p. 5.

Chen, Quanming and Zhao Man. 1996. "High opportunity cost of resettlement" (zai jiuye de jihui chengben gao), *Inside Information on Economic Reform* (Gaige Neicen), No. 17, p. 29.

Chen, Xing. 1995. "Unemployment in China tends to be more serious" (zhongguo jiuye xingshi yuqu yanjun), *Xin Pao* (Hong Kong), May 9, p. 19.

Chen, Zengjun & Gu Xuebin. 1996. "Hard selection" (jiannan de xuanze), *Economic Daily* (Jingji ribao), April 16, p. 1.

Jin, Yi. 1997. "Central government settles unemployment to prevent their strikes" (Zhongyang anhu shiye dajun yanfang shangjie naoshi), *Ming Pao* (Hong Kong), Jan. 9, p. A8.

Kahn, Joseph. 1995. "Unemployment soar in Chinese cities", *Asian Wall Street Journal*, Feb. 6, p. 8.

Li, Cheng. 1997. "Surplus rural laborers and internal migration in China", *Asian Survey*, vol. xxxvi, no. 11, pp. 1122–1145.

Li, Guoqin. 1995. "Unemployees do not believe in tears", (shiye bu xiangxin yanlei) *China Rural Industry News* (zhongguo xiangzhen qiye bao), August 26, p. 1.

Li, Honggang. 1996. "The image fallacy about off-post workers", (xiagang gongren de wuqu) *Economic Daily* (jinji ribao), July 17, p. 7.

Ming Pao. 1996. "The priority for the people should be put on unemployment" (zhongguo shiye lie shouyao jiejue minsheng dashi), *Ming Pao* (Hong Kong), April 17, p. 1.

Ni, Bingjun. 1996. "800 female off-post workers got their new jobs in private companies in Anqiu" (Anqiu 800 xiagang nugong jiuye siying qiye), *Economic Daily* (Jingji Ribao), October 19, p. 2.

Qiu, Zeqi. 1995. "Agent, exchange and rent-seeking" (daili, jiaohuan yu xunzu), *Chinese Social Science Quarterly* (Hong Kong), Autumn, pp. 12–36.

Qiu, Zeqi. 1996. "Construction and differentiation: the process of social structure 1949–1990", in Qiu Zeqi & Wang Mingming, eds., *Community Studies and Social Development*. Tianjin: Tianjin People's Publishing House, pp. 1541–1587.

Qiu, Zeqi. 1996. *The Development of State-Owned Enterprises in China's West Frontier*. Tianjin: Tianjin People's Publishing House.

Shirk, Susan L. 1993. *The Political Logic of Economic Reform in China*. Berkeley and Los Angeles: University of California Press.

State Statistical Bureau. 1996. *China Statistical Yearbook 1996*, Beijing: China Statistical Press.

The Ministry of Labor. 1996. "Labor policy, regulations and interpretations" (laodong zhengce ji youguan xingzheng jieshi), Supplemental Issue of *China Labour Science* (Zhongguo Laodong Kexue).

Wu, Liying. 1996. "Unemployees and semi-employees will reach 216 million in the next five years" (zhongguo shiye ji banshiye zhe wuniannei jiang da 2 yi 1600 wan), *Lianhe Zaobao*, November 14, p. 23.

Xie, Siquan & Wang Tingrui. 1996. "A statistical evaluation of the hidden unemployment in urban China" (woguo chengzhen yinxing sheye de tongyi yu guijia), *China Labor Science* (Zhongguo Laodong Kexue), no. 9, p. 10.

Yang, Yiyong. 1996. "Ten challenges for social stability in China" (yingxiang zhongguo shehui wending de shi da wenti), Lianhe Zaobao, June 12, p. 11.

Zhang, Zhongying. 1996. "Re-employment needs new concept of job" (zai jiuye, poqie xuyao zhuanbian guannian), *Economic Daily* (Jingji Ribao), July 24, p. 5.

Zhou, Wendao. 1995. "Unemployment: a new challenge of China's economic reform" (shiye: zhongguo gaige de xin kaoyan), *Xin Pao* (Hong Kong), November 13, p. 15.

Zhu, Longxiang. 1996. "Settlement for surplus laborers in SOE" (guoyou qiye fuyu zhigong de anzhi), *China Labor Science* (Zhongguo Laodong Kexue), No. 10, p. 24.

Rebuilding Their Ancestral Villages: The Moral Economy of the Singapore Chinese

KUAN Khun Eng
University of Hong Kong

INTRODUCTION

The emigrant villages, *qiaoxiang* (侨乡), of Fujian and Guangdong have been the recipient of wealth and assistance from their overseas Chinese relatives since the 1978 Reform. Indeed, it is also a policy of the central government to encourage not only remittances but contributions from overseas Chinese, *qiao-bao* (侨胞) in village infrastructure and economic reconstruction.

Among the Singapore Chinese, there has also been a revival of interests in their ancestral village. The Singapore government has been instrumental in encouraging the Singapore Chinese to invest in China. However, it has very little effect on their decision to invest or contribute to their ancestral village development. A different set of reasons, not based on economic rationalism, affects these Chinese in their contribution to help develop their ancestral village. From a culturalist viewpoint, one could argue that sentiments play a major role in pulling the Singapore Chinese back to their ancestral village.

The question of interest here is "why do the Singapore Chinese feel morally obligated to assist their ancestral home"? This paper explores the extent to which the Singapore Chinese are locked into a set of social relationships within a moral economy that constantly pushes them to assist in village rebuilding. It argues that there are two sets of factors involved in the formation of a moral economy.

WHERE IS ANXI?

This study was conducted in the PengLai district (蓬莱) in the Anxi County (安溪), in the southeastern region of Fujian. It occupies an area of 122.4 sq. km and is divided into 31 districts. It has a total population of 67,800 people (Anxi Hsien Chi, 1992, vol. 1: 139). The region is most famous for the production of two brands of Chinese tea, the *Oolong* and *Tieguanyin*, Iron Lady (Anxi Hsien Chi, 1992, vol. 1: 221–256).

During the first half of the twentieth century, about 40,000 Chinese emigrated from Anxi region to Southeast Asia and to Singapore. More crucially, during the immediate post-World War II years and Communist victory, i.e. from 1945 to 1955, some 20,000 Anxi villagers emigrated to Singapore. Today, the number of Chinese from Anxi and of Anxi ancestry is estimated at 186,000, about 10 percent of the Singapore Chinese population (1.87 million) (*ibid.*, vol. 2: 845).

Anxi County is officially listed as an important emigrant region. Here, local and regional government implemented policies and concessions that are aimed at encouraging overseas Chinese to visit and help with village reconstruction. (Singapore Anxi Association, 1994).

METHODOLOGY

Let me briefly explain the methodology that I have used in this research. This research is divided into the Singapore and Anxi sections. In Singapore, research was conducted at various levels. Participant-observation was easily conducted as the author herself is part of the Anxi community. There was much empathy and interest in my work. Non-intrusive participant-observation was conducted into the numerous communal socio-religious activities in Singapore. Conversations among the members were also recorded. Collection of these data were unstructured. This was followed by in-depth interviews with selected members, especially those actively involved in the activities in Singapore and also in the development of Anxi. The third stage involved conducting a questionnaire survey. Two sets of questionnaire were issued to a random sample of members (one set for the first generation migrants and the second set for those with Anxi ancestry) in order to provide the quantitative breadth that I wanted for this research.

Fieldwork in Anxi did not follow the conventional village study. Again, it was conducted in a manner that I thought would provide me with the most opportunities for interaction and to observe the socio-religious functions and decision-making processes. First, I usually followed the Singapore Chinese back to Anxi when there was a major event. In this case, I was able to participate and observe as a member. I also returned to Anxi on my own to conduct interviews with selected members especially those who were involved in the organising of the activities as well as some villagers. At the third stage, I again issued two sets of questionnaire, one to tap the views and attitudes of the villagers and the other to tap the views of the official cadres. The questionnaire survey was conducted with the help of four researchers from Xiamen University. I have also collected a large quantity of letter correspondences from the Singapore and village Chinese and this provided me with additional information, particularly on their livelihood during the earlier period.

The 1978 Reform and Village Reconstruction

The 1978 Reform provided a watershed in the Singapore Chinese-*qiaoxiang* relation. A more liberal political climate between China and Singapore has enabled an increasing number of Singapore Chinese making regular social visits to their ancestral villages. The Singapore Chinese have also become increasingly involved in village reconstruction. They give mostly financial assistance, but also technical support to help with village development. There are five main areas that they are involved in: (1) building of the old house, *lao-wu* (老屋); (2) building of lineage ancestral house, *zu-zhai* (祖宅) and temples; (3) development of basic infrastructure, mainly roads, bridges and power plants; (4) development of education and welfare facilities, mainly schools and hospitals; and (5) establishing petting trading and retailing.

(1) Building of the Old Home, Lao-wu

Extending a helping hand to one's ancestral village and lineage is not a new act. The early emigrants were known to have sent regular remittances to their family and home villages. Today, the number of Singapore Chinese visiting their ancestral village and financing the rebuilding of the *lao-wu* has led to a boom in the construction industry.

In my survey, I found that most villagers received some form of monetary assistance to help rebuild and renovate their old houses. Of the 203 respondents, 75 percent (152 in number) said that they or their parents received some financial assistance from their overseas kin, *qiao-qing* (侨亲), to help with the building, rebuilding or renovating of the house. In the last few years, several millions Singapore dollars have been remitted for building both the *lao-wu* and the new house, *xin-wu* (新屋).

They were helped in the following way. They would usually write to their related Singapore kin, telling them of the condition of the *lao-wu* and the state of repairs required. Upon receiving such letters, the Singapore kin, in most cases, would send some money for such purposes. Sometimes, the rebuilding process might take a few years, with bits and pieces added on to the old house. The amount sent ranges from several thousands to several tens or hundreds of thousands Singapore dollars.

How do the villagers convince their Singapore kin of the importance of rebuilding the *lao-wu*? They devised several strategies. The first strategy is to approach the visiting kin and bring them to witness the conditions of the *lao-wu*. One said, "when they are in the village, we will bring them to the *lao-wu* and let them see its poor condition. Most of our Singapore kin are sympathetic to our living condition and would give us some money to rebuild it". The second strategy is to approach only those older and immediate family members who have more empathy and greater sentiments for the ancestral village. For example, one said, "it would be easier for us to open our mouth and ask our parents or brothers or sisters to help us. But we find it embarrassing asking our grandparents or uncles as they are either too old or not so close to us". A third strategy is to stagger the demands and rebuild the old house in stages. They told me that "we realise that some of our Singapore kin are not very wealthy. They are not the fat kin, *fei-qiao* (肥侨) but are thin kin, *sou-qiao* (瘦侨). So, to lessen their financial burden and to ensure that the *lao-wu* is being rebuilt, we ask for a smaller sum each time, over a period of time. We find it easier to open our mouth this way".

Why is the *lao-wu* so important and needs to be rebuilt? What is the symbolic meaning behind it? Most villagers consider the *lao-wu* as the house of their ancestors, and this is why it should not be allowed to collapse. To the Singapore Chinese, the *lao-wu* provides them with a physical space where they can locate their cultural roots and to recollect their nostalgic feelings of village life, albeit a harsh one. It is also a way of re-establishing their filial piety towards their ancestors and to remember their source of origin, *yin-shui-si-yuan* (饮水思源) (when drinking from the fountain, one remembers its source).

At another level, it concerns the "face" and the need to preserve their feng-shui site. A villager said, "we encouraged our Singapore kin to renovate the old house. I told him that it would cost 500,000 RMB. Their father was brought up by my grandmother here and this house was originally built by their father. This is their source of origin and if they let the house goes into disrepair, they would also lose much face in the village and in Singapore if our kin know that they have deliberately allow the *lao-wu* to collapse. It would also be very bad for their and our descendants as the collapse of the *lao-wu* will bring about bad feng-shui to all the living."

Today, there are many renovated *lao-wu*. But many are left vacant with few people living in them. This is because many have moved to live in the new modernised houses. In general, most of the occupiers of *lao-wu* are elderly people who have lived in the house for several decades and do not want to move out of it. They attach great sentiment to it. They also prefer the style and the spacious central courtyard where they can sit and relax with the other elderly people during their visits.

For the wealthy households, apart from the *lao-wu*, they also build a new house, *xin-wu*. For the younger villagers, they often request their Singapore kin to build or buy them a new house. There is now a sizeable number of villagers living in luxurious three to four storey type of modern housing equipped with modern amenities. One happy 36-year-old housewife said, "our Singapore uncle sent us money to build this four storey building which cost 400,000 to 500,000 RMB. We are very happy and satisfied with it. This house is very comfortable".

Today, there are four types of housing distinguishable in the villages. The first is the *lao-wu* or traditional house with a central courtyard. They are mainly occupied by the elderly villagers. The second is the modern apartment block of three to four storeys. These buildings have modern piped water (pumped from wells), modern bathrooms and toilets and air-conditioning. The third is the modern shophouse, two to four storeys high where the ground floor is a shop and residence at the upper levels. The modern apartments and shophouses are most favoured by the younger villagers. The last type is the mud and wooden huts where the poor continue to live in.

In the village environment, having a good house is more than just for comfortable living. It is a testimony of the social status, wealth and the material comforts that an individual household enjoys. It also signals to other villagers the connection of the occupiers with their wealthy Singapore kin. It is also an important asset for marriage consideration. Having a good house is important for a good match. This is particularly so for those with grown sons who are seeking suitable brides.

The house is still considered as the single most important asset that an individual household possessed. In the villages where the paddy field and shops are communal properties, the house remains solely "individualistic". As such, the villagers look upon the house as the ultimate place where immediate family members could conduct their own individual and private affairs away from communal inspection. A related aspect is the ownership of the house. For the first time since Communism, the villagers could record their names as legal owners of the house they occupied.

The rebuilding of the *lao-wu* and *xin-wu* has transformed a rural landscape into a modernised one where instead of mud or wooden houses, stone and brick houses are now common sight. Apart from traditional style housing with a central courtyard, modern-style three- to four-storey building surrounded by paddy fields are now a ubiquitous sight.

(2) *Rebuilding the Lineage Ancestor House* (祖宅) *and Village Temples*

A second area of village development is the rebuilding of the ancestor house and temples. The lineage ancestral houses, *zu-zhai* or *zhor-chu* (H) were left in ruins during the Cultural Revolution. Since the reform years, the Singapore Chinese have spent over a million RMB on their reconstruction. Likewise, the most important temple, *Qing Shui Yan Si*, has been rebuilt.

What is the symbolic significance of the ancestral house? To begin with, it is a living ancestral house, regarded as the residence of the past ancestors. It is found on the location when the first ancestors built their first house. It is thus considered as the physical source of origin of the lineage. It was supposedly originally a communal house and with the passing of the generations, it has gradually become the present day lineage ancestral house. Its significance lies with the following factors. First, it provides the members with a physical space that helps them to relocate the physical existence of their first ancestors. Second, it allows the individual to engage in a dialogue and come to terms with the social reality of past years. Third, it provides the physical location for the present generations to interact with the events and people of the past. Fourth, it is a visible reminder of the lineage's origin and of one's membership within it. Fifth, it is a place where values and attitudes can be transmitted to the descendants and finally, it allows a group of Chinese to lay claim to their common ancestry and proclaim themselves as related kin, irrespective of historical and geographical space.

Thus, by reconstructing it and reinstating ancestor worship and its related rituals, the ancestral house has, once again, become an important focal point for two members of the same lineage to come together and become one. It has allowed them to rekindle their social relationship and to reproduce a familiar socio-religious culture.

The Singapore Chinese have also attached great significance to temple rebuilding in Anxi. The most important temple that has been reconstructed is the *Qing-Shui Yan Si* (清水岩寺) which is devoted to the deity, *Qing-Shui Zu-Shi* (清水祖师) (literally Clear Water Ancestor). A main characteristic of the deity is its black face, hence, it is also known as the *Wu-Mian-Zu-Shi-Gong* (乌面组师公) (Black-faced Clear Water Ancestor).

This deity is regarded as the guardian deity of the people of Anxi. To the villagers in PengLai and among the Singapore Chinese of Anxi ancestry, it is their ancestral deity. He is seen as a protector of the villagers from natural and human calamities. During the early migrant years, *Qing-Shui Zu-Shi* was a source of encouragement and moral support as well as a protector against banditry and the uncertain journey. In Singapore, a temple has also been built in his honour and he is being revered by the Singapore Anxi Chinese on regular occasions.

Apart from this temple, other smaller and localised temples are also being renovated by the Singapore Chinese. These smaller temples are usually funded by individuals and cater to villagers living in the vicinity.

(3) Development of Basic Infrastructure

A third area is the development of basic infrastructure. The most important are the construction of roads, bridges and power plants. Anxi is still regarded as one of the poorest regions. Despite its poverty status, funding for basic infrastructure from the central government remains miniscule. The main arterial road leading to Anxi was poor until two years ago. A poor road system hampers the movement of goods and people between interior Anxi and the regional cities and Xiamen. It is very common to hear visiting Chinese complaining about the difficulties of travelling into Anxi. The continued delay in road construction has been attributed to both the lack of governmental funding and corrupt practices which prevented the flow of funds into the region for this purpose. Visiting *qiao-bao*, have been encouraged by the county and village cadres to assist in road construction.

From 1979 to 1991, a total of 91.1 kilometres of roads have been constructed in PengLai district with overseas money (Anxi Hsien Chi, vol. 1: 361). Since 1995, the Long Men Tunnel has been constructed and is opened to traffic. The cost for building this tunnel amounted to 2 million RMB and was again fully financed by Singapore and Malaysian Chinese capital. The tunnel has effectively halved the travel time between Xiamen and PengLai from around four hours to two-and-a-half hours. It has also made travelling less hazardous, instead of through the steep winding hills.

Another important area of development is the construction of bridges. PengLai district is cut into two by the Anxi River that flows through it. In the district, seven bridges were built with *qiao-hui* (侨汇). Altogether, these bridges totalled 267 metres and cost 2.5 million RMB to build. The single longest bridge is 100 metres in length and cost 2.25 million RMB to build (*ibid.*, vol. 1: 379).

The villagers have regarded the construction of roads and bridges by the overseas Chinese as one of the most important contributions to village redevelopment. In my interviews with the villagers, all mentioned these as the most important contributions made by overseas Chinese. All were aware of these contributions. Some of the elderly men were very knowledgeable and knew the amount various wealthy individuals had made to such projects. They felt that without the contributions of overseas Chinese, these roads and bridges would never have been built and they would not be able to access the regional towns and cities as readily as at present. They also told me that it would become a gross burden on all villagers if all households had to contribute to such infrastructural projects. Without funding from the overseas Chinese, the county government would have to exact a levy of 400 RMB from each individual household to cover the construction expenses. So, it was greeted with relief that the Singapore Chinese have fully supported such construction.

In general, there are three types of attitudes adopted by the villagers in regard to contributions to infrastructural development by overseas Chinese. The first attitude, adopted by a majority of the villagers, is that the overseas Chinese have a responsibility to help them with such infrastructural projects. They argue that this is the ancestral village of the overseas Chinese. Besides, they also have the financial means to do so. The second attitude adopted by the villagers is that infrastructural development should be the responsibility of the county government. By building good infrastructure for the county and villages, the county and local governments could then encourage the overseas Chinese to invest in the region. Instead of encouraging the overseas Chinese to invest in infrastructure, such money could be better used for economic development of the region. About half of the informants subscribed to this view. A third attitude is that the overseas Chinese should contribute if they have the ability to do so but should not be coerced into contributing to such development. They argue that the Singapore Chinese should have the freedom to decide on whether, and on what, they wanted to contribute to. Furthermore, they should not be made to feel obligated to contribute. They should do so based on their own decisions. This view is held by only a small number of younger villagers.

(4) *Education and Schools*

A fourth area which the Singapore Chinese have become heavily involved in is the building of schools and expansion of education. About 90 percent of the Singapore Chinese have contributed to village education. There is lack of educational facilities and opportunities in the villages. Most schools have very old buildings and inadequate classrooms for the village children. The result is that there is a low level of literacy. Since the coming of the overseas Chinese and their contributions to school and educational development, the level of literacy has risen substantially. Anxi is now known officially as the "cultural district", *wen-hua-qu* (文化区).

A second reason for the great contribution in education by the Singapore Chinese is that they see education as a way to move out of an agrarian village environment into an urban city and hence, out of the cycle of permanent poverty. They argue that the village environment provides very little opportunities for the villagers. There are few factories and job opportunities. Without a good education, the villagers will not have the skills to compete with the urban people for jobs in cities.

A third reason is that by increasing the size of the schools and providing educational facilities, the village girls could continue their education according to their academic merits. As my findings below have shown, village girls continue to receive a lesser degree of education than the boys. In recent years, there has been a slight change in the attitude of the villagers and education for girls is beginning to be treated with some importance.

In our survey, we found that few villagers go beyond the compulsory years of education and a very small percentage of women attended schools at all. About 37 percent of the villagers had some form of primary education; 27.5 percent with secondary education; 16 percent with post-secondary education; 5.5 percent with teacher or technical education; 1.5 percent with tertiary education and 18.5 percent with no education. Of these, 67 percent of male respondents had some form of education while only 14.5 percent of female respondents had some form of education. In addition, of the 18.5 percent with no education, 15.5 percent of these were women.

In PengLai, the Singapore Chinese have contributed over several million dollars to various educational projects including new buildings for schools, teachers' residences, bursary for needy students and scholarships for those with good results. At present, they are in the process of raising one million RMB for scholarships and bursaries. It is estimated that the Chinese overseas have contributed over 53 million yuan to education in Anxi during the last 40 years. (*ibid.*, vol. 2: 974).

While the Singapore Chinese have found that contributing to schools and educational facilities is a satisfying act, the village cadres and principals of schools have also devised strategies to encourage a greater flow of contributions into their respective schools. How do they encourage contributions to schools?

One strategy adopted is to encourage each lineage to adopt a school in an unofficial capacity. In PengLai, each surname lineage adopts a school. Members of a particular surname group are encouraged to make contribution

Table 1. Sex and Distribution of Education and Literacy

	Primary	Second'y	Post-Sec	Tech	Tertiary	No Edu	Total
Male	53	38	30	11	2	6	**140**
Female	19	7	2	0	1	31	**60**
Total	**72**	**45**	**32**	**11**	**3**	**37**	**N = 200**
	37%	**27.5%**	**16%**	**5.5%**	**1.5%**	**18.5%**	**% = 100**

Table 2. Age and Education Attainment

Ages	Primary	Second'y	Post-Sec	Tech	Tertiary	No Edu	Total/%
20–29	3	14	2	0	0	2	**21(10.5)**
30–39	10	13	12	1	0	3	**39(18.5)**
40–49	19	9	6	3	1	11	**49(24.5)**
50–59	17	4	11	4	2	15	**53(26.5)**
>60	23	5	1	3	0	6	**38(18.0)**
	72	**45**	**32**	**11**	**3**	**37**	**N = 200**

to their adopted school. This *de facto* lineage school, on the other hand, will only receive contribution from members of that lineage. A *de facto* lineage school also encourages the children of that lineage to attend the school although admission is open to all surname groups. Thus, in Anxi, the major lineages such as the Ke, Lin, and Liu have adopted one school each and members of these lineages have made large contributions to their schools.

According to a school principal, there are advantages in this practice. By making the school a *de facto* lineage school, the Singapore members would feel proud and contribute more to "their school". It also creates an environment where members of the various lineages would compete with one another to build better facilities for their "lineage school". Members would feel compelled to give generous donations in order that their lineage school does not lack behind others. The school administration encourages such competition and indeed creates pressure to encourage more contribution from its members.

The Singapore Chinese also establish scholarships, rewards and bursaries for students of their "lineage school". Students with the best results for the year are given rewards, usually a sum of money and a memorabilia for their scholastic excellence. Those who make it to the university are awarded full scholarships for their studies.

Apart from this, individuals also give money to the children of their village kin who want to go for further technical and vocational studies in regional towns and cities. A popular choice for the village girls is to study secretarial courses and acquire such skills to work in offices in towns and cities. The village boys, on the other hand, go to the towns to study computing courses and other technical courses. Many hope that with such skills, they would be able to find jobs in towns and in Singapore.

It has always been a problem to retain and even more difficult to encourage good teachers in Anxi because of the interior location. To encourage teachers to perform and remain in the village, it is now a common practice to give additional salary and bonuses, better housing and living conditions to the teachers. In PengLai, a new teachers' quarters has just been completed. Married teachers are now given a two-bedroom apartment while unmarried teacher are given a one-bedroom apartment with modernised facilities. This is a great improvement in contrast to the previous arrangement where married teachers were given one-bedroom apartment while the unmarried teachers were given a room. The new teachers' quarter is funded fully by the overseas Chinese.

(5) *Public Health and Hospital*

The fifth area of redevelopment is in public health and the provision of medical facilities. PengLai Huaqiao Hospital is the only medical institution in the district. It was established in 1953, with two expansions in 1972 and 1990. From the beginning, this hospital has been funded wholly from overseas Chinese capital. In 1953, the overseas Chinese donated 124,000 yuan to the hospital. From the period of 1985 to 1992, contributions of over a million yuan was make to the hospital for equipment and medicine. Several million RMB was contributed for the building of a new wing. Today, there is no charge for medical treatment and a nominal fee is charged for the medicine.

Many Singapore Chinese felt that the lives of many villagers could be saved with little medical help and medicine. But PengLai district has been alloted with little funding from the central and provincial governments. Like the school principals, the director and his staff members have constantly engaged in raising funds for this hospital. They approached the Singapore Chinese for contributions. The Singapore Chinese, on the other hand, felt that they had to make contributions because the hospital had no independent funding except from the overseas members.

To ensure that there is a continued flow of funds for the maintenance of the hospital and service, the hospital administration has divided contributions into two funds. One fund is for buying medical equipment and other hardware. A second fund is set up for purchasing medical supplies and medicine for the patients. The Singapore Chinese are constantly asked to contribute to these two funds to ensure that the hospital has a regular supply of modern equipment and medicine. This hospital is the only one in PengLai with an X-ray machine and an ECG machine.

(6) Financing Small Businesses

The last area is to redevelop the district economically. There has been some efforts to help transform the district from an agrarian economy into a trading one. The village and county cadres have been actively encouraging the Singapore Chinese to invest in the region. Some Singapore Chinese are willing and have invested in the county town of Hsien Chen. They start factories and build shophouses. However, they are less willing to invest in their ancestral village in PengLai district. There are several reasons for this. The most important is the interior location which made siting a factory an unattractive option. The second is the relatively low level of skill for industrial production. The third is the lack of basic infrastructure including roads and power supply. In recent years, a group of Singapore Chinese together with the county government have built a hydro-electric power plant. Even then, there continues to be inadequate supply of power to the district.

Despite this, the Singapore Chinese have provided small amounts of capital to their immediate relatives to start small manufacturing and retailing businesses within the district. As in many rural counties, the villagers are opting to become self-employed and own small businesses. In my survey of the 203 households, there were 2 factory-owners, 17 shop-owners, 5 self-employed drivers, 1 photographer, 1 iron-smith, 1 carpenter and 1 artist. There were also many retailers selling a variety of goods from clothing to small hardware items. They form an increasing pool of self-employed individuals, *ge-ti-hu* (个体户) who operate within the limits of a reformed socialist market economy. Most are small retailing businesses geared towards local needs and consumption.

Today, over one hundred shops are found in the PengLai district. These shops sell a variety of goods including clothes, personal toiletries, small eletrical goods, transistor radios and cameras. A booming tyre business is found to cater to the rapidly emerging car population in the district. Service shops have become very popular. There are now several ladies' hairdressing salons and two photographic studios. Some shops have pinball machines that cater to children and for 20 cents the children could have some form of modern entertainment.

An important business called "the religious and dead industry" has sprung up and caters to the emerging religious practices found in the villages. Shops produce religious paraphenalia such as joss sticks, streamers, candles, joss papers, houses for the dead, *ling-wu* (灵屋)and fire crackers. The revival of religious activities and ancestor worship has, to a large extent, fuelled the vibrancy of this type of business. Such activities have also helped to reinstate traditional skills and handicrafts that are essential in the making of these religious items. They are extremely profitable and those who could produce them are able to make substantial profits. A religious celebration or a rite of meritorious deeds, *gong-de*, *gong-teck* (H) (功德) could amount to 5,000 RMB or more and an equivalent amount could be spent on purchasing these paraphernalia. The challenge is to attract more overseas Chinese to visit and stage communal religious fairs in the village. Because of the contribution to the village economy, religious activities have been encouraged by the villagers and tacitly approved by the village and county cadres.

For the first time since communism, there is an emergence of "the flesh industry", i.e. prostitution in PengLai. I was told by several villagers that a small number of "immoral and indecent women", *bu-zheng-jing nu-ren* (不正经女人), from other parts of China now lived in the district and catered to out of town men who came to PengLai for business and stayed overnight. A few of these women are "mistresses" of these businessmen. This kind of work is not welcomed by the villagers, especially the women. They felt that the village has been contaminated by these prostitutes and mistresses.

CREATING A MORAL ECONOMY

By contributing substantially to the above areas of activities, the Singapore Chinese have assisted substantially in village redevelopment, thereby transforming the very poor villages into economically prosperous emigrant villages that are also culturally vibrant. I will now turn to answer the question that I posed earlier on, that is, "why do the Singapore Chinese feel obligated to assist and contribute to village reconstruction?"

The main consideration that compels the Singapore Chinese to regard the redevelopment of the ancestral village as their moral responsibility lies with two main sets of forces that form the moral economy which binds these Singapore Chinese to their ancestral village. The first set of reasons lies with the attitudes of the Singapore Chinese. Here, it is their understanding of, identification and affinity to their ancestral village. This is very much shaped by three factors, namely, their collective memory, their sense of moral duty and their moral consciousness. The second set of reasons lies with how the village leaders, cadres and the villagers, through cultural concessions and moral suasion, further bind them to the moral economy.

Moral Duty and Sentiments of Singapore Chinese

The attitude of the Singapore Chinese plays a very important role in their continued interest in their ancestral village and their role in village reconstruction. Many of them continue to have strong sentiments. Their understanding of, idenfication and affinity to their ancestral village is shaped very much by the collective memory of their ancestral village.[1] Many of the first generation Singapore Chinese continue to have fond memories of their ancestral village as they recall their childhood and young adult life in the village. They also recall the extreme poverty of their ancestral village. It is this sentiment of what the village was like and the memory of poverty that is instrumental in motivating them to assist in village reconstruction whenever they are called upon to help.

A second reason that they gave is a sense of moral duty. Among this group of Singapore Chinese, they continue to be governed by a Confucian sense of moral duty to their ancestral village.[2] The Confucian notion of remembering the source when one is drinking water, *yin-shui-si-yuan*, is a phrase frequently invoked by my informants. They told me that they should not forget their ancestral home. They do not have to like it or embrace it. But they should not forget it. To many of them, this is where their parents and grandparents were from. And they have some knowledge of the place. To remember the ancestral home is also taken to mean that when they have been called upon to help with rebuilding the village, they should not

[1]For a theoretical discussion on collective memory, see Halbwach, M., 1992. Also, Fentress and Wickham, 1992.

[2]For a discussion on Confucian morality and moral cultivation, see Tu, Weiming, 1985.

turn it down. They also found it difficult and embarrassing to turn down offers to help. One common comment made was that "when the elders come to us for contributions for village projects, it is hard for us to turn it down. Somehow, it just did not seem right to say no. We usually gave whatever they asked from us. Generally, we would be asked to contribute S$500 or $1,000. Afterall, it is our ancestral village".

A third reason given is that when they returned to their home village, they are confronted with real poverty and an underdeveloped social and economic structure. For the first time, some began to understand what village life is all about and the village structure which is vastly different from an urban city. This is especially true for the Singapore born Chinese. One said, "before visiting Anxi, I imagined that the villagers were lazy and did not want to work. After visiting Anxi, I began to understand that it is not because they do not want to work, but rather that there is no work for them to do. Apart from farming, there is little they could do. We also understand that the government has very little interest in helping the region to develop. So, among some of us, we decided to help with setting up a hydro-electric power plant. We also helped our relatives to start up some small businesses to cater for local needs".

A fourth reason the Singapore Chinese gave is that of relative wealth and guilt feelings. They told me that "presently, we are relatively well off and comfortable. We also do not wish that our village kin would starve and live meagrely. They don't have to live the way we do in Singapore. But at least, we could help them to live comfortably by village standard. After paying visits to the place, we realise that many of them live in very poor conditions and have few material goods. So, we should help a little".

Finally, a fifth reason lies with the desire to maintain continuity between the two groups of Chinese. To some, the relationship between the Singapore and Anxi Chinese is likened to a thin thread. Once broken, it will be very difficult to maintain. A comment by one informant is that, "our relationship is like a thin thread. It should be maintained at all cost, so that our future generations have reference to their ancestors and their source of origin. If it is broken, then the future generations will not be able to search for their ancestral roots and they would become headless".

Cultural Concession As Cultural Capital[3]

A second set of reasons is the actions and attitudes of the Anxi village leaders, cadres and villages. By permitting and assisting the Singapore Chinese in the areas of religion and ancestor worship, these village leaders and villagers have created a set of cultural capital where they can use them effectively as bargaining chips in exchange for village redevelopment. Here, two forces, cultural concession and the extraction of cultural capital, work in favour of the villagers.

On the part of the village leaders and cadres, they are able to identify the psychological needs and provide cultural concessions to the Singapore Chinese. These village leaders told me that many of the older Singapore Chinese were interested in religious activities when they visited their ancestral village. So, within their power, they facilitated the reproduction of such cultural and communal practices. At the same time, they provided full support and assistance for the rebuilding of the ancestral house and temples.

By giving cultural concession in the form of permitting and helping the Singapore Chinese to stage large communal ancestor worship and religious celebrations and allowing the rebuilding of the ancestral house and temples, these become tangible forms of cultural capital. In so doing, they created a source of cultural capital and established good *guanxi* for themselves. These social capital and the network of *guanxi* and reciprocity serve to bind the Singapore Chinese further into the moral economy where they would be called upon to contribute and assist with various aspects of village rebuilding. Once in it, they found it difficult to extricate themselves from it.

At the more immediate level, the Anxi villagers have also actively promoted a series of moral sanctions to publicise their Singapore kin who fail to discharge their moral duty. James Scott (1985), in his study, explores the passive resistance of the peasantry towards the landowners. In this case, the moral economy involves active forms of sanctioning. In both cases, the relationship is one of patron-client.

[3]For a theoretical discussion on cultural capital, see Bourdieu, P., 1993.

i) *Labelling* — The villagers openly describe those Singapore kin who failed to help with their immediate needs or village reconstruction as having become "uncivilised", "babaised"or "detribalised", *huang* (番) (H) or *fan*. Such terms are used to label the Singapore kin as behaving like the natives of Nanyang and have no sense of propriety and kin sentiments, *qin-qing* (亲情). It is also used against those who persuade others not to contribute to their ancestral home. The villagers also commonly labelled the Singapore-born Chinese as "*huang*" because they are generally less interested and sympathetic to the rebuilding of the ancestral village and often tend to distance themselves from the villages. They also behave very differently from the older Singapore Chinese in manners and attitudes. Many of them also speak the English language and some could not speak the Fujian dialect well. In the eyes of these villagers, these Singapore-born Chinese, usually the younger generations, have betrayed their ancestral origin.

The villagers also invoke their close kinship relations as part of the moral suasion strategy to entice the Singapore Chinese to help with the reconstruction. They often invoke phrases like "we are one family", *yi-jia-ren* (一家人); "we have blood ties", *xue-yuan-guanxi* (血缘关系); "we should not forget our ancestors", *wang-ben* (忘本); "when drinking water, we should remember the source", *yin-shui-si-yuan* (饮水思源); "irrespective of wealth, one should not be divorced from the ancestor", *fu-gu-bu-li-zu* (富贵不离祖); and that "the leaves will have to return to their roots", *luo-ye-gui-gen* (落叶归根).

SOCIAL AND ECONOMIC CHANGES

By engaging in the building of the old houses, roads, bridges, schools and hospital, the Singapore Chinese have helped to redevelop and alleviate the poverty-stricken villages to prosperous ones. Such rebuilding has put into motion the wheel of economic development. It has brought about a boom in the construction industry and other related businesses. The filtering-down effect has far-reaching consequences for the village economy. During the construction boom, almost 70 percent of the able-bodied men are engaged in some form of construction work. Others are involved in retailing and service industry. Likewise, the large communal religious fairs and ancestor worship have also led to an increase in the number of people engaged in this trade. These are important economic activities that the villagers are beginning to pursue in earnest.

As the village move away from a pure agrarian economy into a mixed economy, the farms become neglected. Today, many men are involved in some kind of capitalist pursuit or have moved to the neighbouring towns and cities to work. They have left the women to work in the fields. Increasingly, it is the village women who are active farmers. Other wealthier households which have financial support from their Singapore kin also no longer worked on the farms. They either rent their farms to the poorer villagers or engage workers to work on their farms.

The rebuilding of the old houses, new houses and shophouses have also impacted on the land use pattern. Substantial farmland have been encroached upon for the building of these new buildings. As a result, there has been a shrinkage of arable land. Despite this, the villagers have adopted an optimistic outlook. Many have expressed that they no longer want to work on the farm and find that such work are both difficult and without prospect.

Under the influence of their Singapore kin, many desire to move out of the village setting and into the towns and cities. Those with wealthy Singapore kin have been able to move to the towns and cities and start small businesses. Some have also managed to go overseas, especially to Singapore for employment. In Singapore, many work in electronic factories and printing houses.

At the social level, with the ease of transportation, more Singapore Chinese are visiting their ancestral villages and participate in the communal religious fairs and ancestor worship organised by their lineage. There are now two to three communal fairs each year. Today, there are two major religious functions, namely the communal ancestor worship and a communal fair devoted to *Qing-Shui-Zu-Shi* conducted annually. In December 1996, the communal ancestor worship attracted over one hundred members from Singapore and Malaysia. Individual Singapore

Chinese also visit their ancestral village and organise small scale religious functions where only the immediate family and related village kin participate in them.

These socio-religious activities have added much "heat" and "noise" to the otherwise sedate village life. The activities have created a colourful and lively atmosphere and the villagers participate fully in them. Such activities help to break the monotony of agrarian living and allow the villagers to look forward to cultural participation. The Singapore Chinese, on the other hand, by contributing and participating in such activities, have reintroduced and revitalised the cultural and religious life of their ancestral villages.

At the same time, these Singapore Chinese, by visiting and contributing to the various developments, have become an active part of the lineage structure. By participating in communal ancestor worship, they have also acknowledged their source of origin and their affinity with their ancestral village. They have thus become insiders to their lineage and their ancestral village. In so doing, they are further expected to contribute to the development of their ancestral village and their fellow lineage members.

CONCLUSION

The rebuilding of the ancestral village and the economic prosperity that these ancestral villages experience is the result of the working of the moral economy, one that is based on collective memory and a sense of moral duty on the one hand, and the extraction of social capital through cultural concession given by the village leaders and members on the other hand.

The relationship between the Singapore Chinese and their Anxi ancestral village can be seen in the following manner. Among the Singapore Chinese, the family, *jia* (家), continues to be seen as the most important primordial social group which needs to be held together despite all adversities. The lineage, *zhong-zu* (宗族), is thus an extension of the *jia* where its primordial-ness hinges on the inter-connectedness of its people through both the collective consciousness and social conscience. Here, the moral conscience is embedded in their perception of their self-identity, their identity vis-a-vis their village kin and their identity within the Singapore nation-state. Moral conscience is couched in Confucian morality where loyalty and compassion lead them to return to their home village and help with village reconstruction.

The success or failure of ancestral village reconstruction and its transformation is also dependent on how the Anxi Chinese transform the social relations into social capital and impose it onto the Singapore kin, making it extremely uncomfortable for them not to provide any form of assistance.

In the final analysis, it is the intersection of these two sets of forces that is responsible for the creation of a moral economy that the Singapore Chinese find hard to ignore.

Romanisation

Romanisation of Chinese words is according to the Hanyu Pinyin system. However, popularly spoken terms in the Hokkien dialect are transliterated as they are spoken to ensure accurate sounding and to preserve the meaning. These romanised Hokkien words end with (H).

Selected References

Anxi Hsien Chi, 1994, Fujian, Anxi County: Xinhua Publishing House, vols. 1 and 2.

Bourdieu, P., 1993, *The Field of Cultural Production*, New York: Columbia University Press.

Chen, Kezheng (ed.), 1994, *Anxi Huaqiao Shi*, Xiamen: Xiamen University Press.

Chen, Ta, 1940, *Emigrant Communities in South China*, New York: Institute of Pacific Relations.

Fentress, J. and Wickham, C., 1992, *Social Memory*, Oxford: Blackwell.

Freedman, M., 1958, *Lineage Organisation in Southeast China*, London: LSE Monograph No. 18.

Freedman, M., 1966, *Chinese Lineage and Society: Fukien and Kwangtung*, London: LSE Monograph No. 33.
Halbwachs, M., 1992, *On Collective Memory*, Chicago: Chicago University Press.
Hicks, G.L. (ed.), *Overseas Chinese Remittances from Southeast Asia 1910–1940*, Singapore: Select Books.
Huang, Shu-min, 1989, *The Spiral Road*, Boulder: Westview Press.
Scott, J., 1985, *Weapons of the Weak*, New Haven: Yale University Press.
Singapore Ann Kway Association Yearbooks, 1982–1994, Singapore: Ann Kway Association.
Tu, Weiming, 1995, *Confucian Thought*, Albany: State University of New York Press.
Yan, Yunxiang, 1996, *The Flow of Gifts*, Stanford: Stanford University Press.
Yang, M.M.H., 1994, *Gifts, Favours and Banquets*, Ithaca: Cornell University Press.

Cities and Counties of Fujian Province

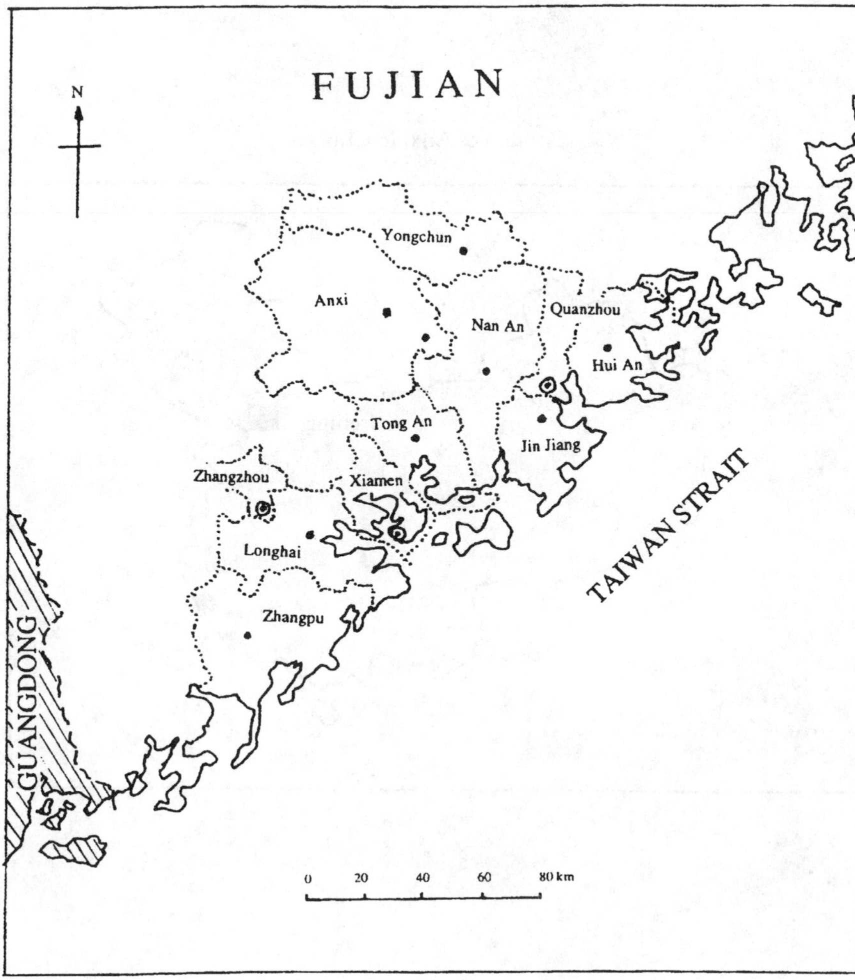

Position of Anxi in China

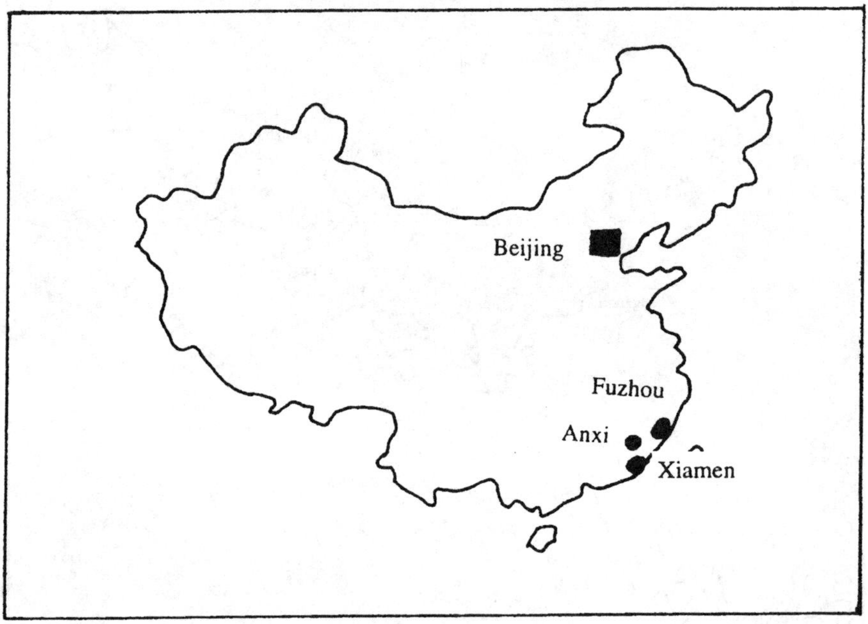

PengLai District, Anxi County, Fujian

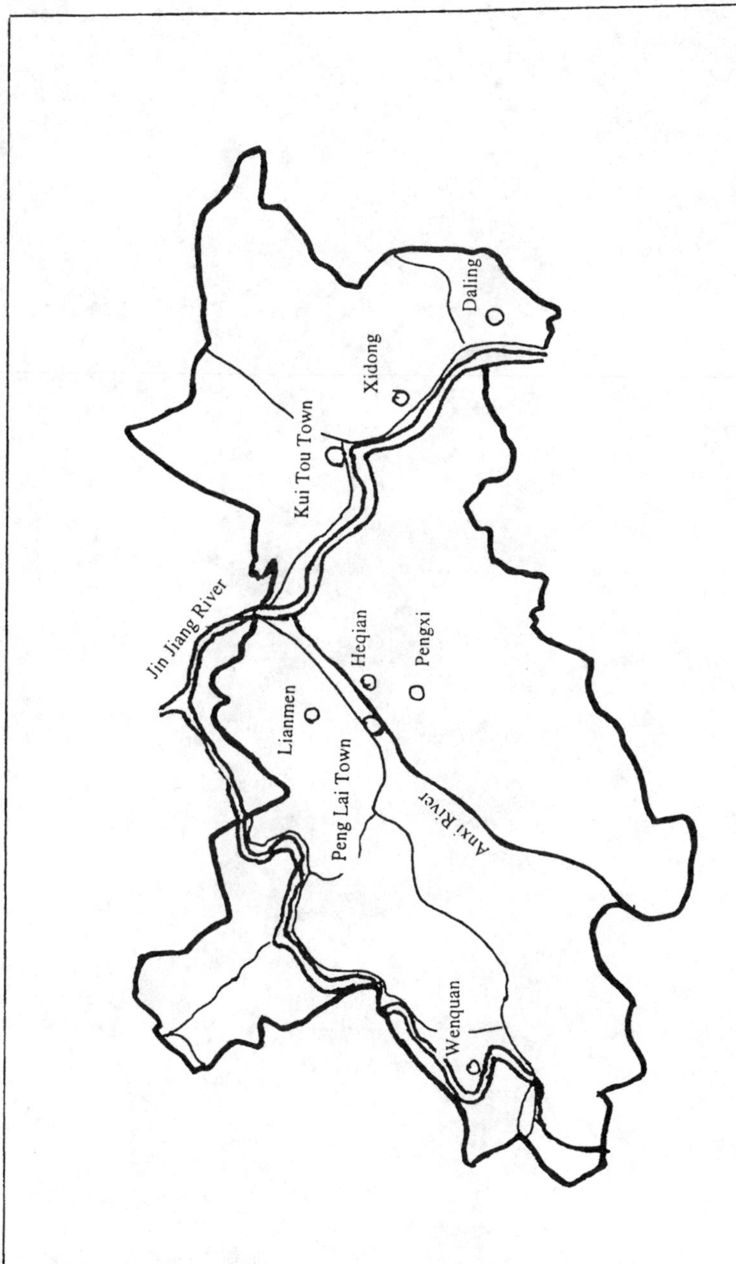

The Debate Over America's Policy Toward China, 1989–97

Harry HARDING
Dean, Elliott School of International Affairs
The George Washington University

Ever since the Tiananmen Crisis of 1989, an intense debate over America's China policy has been raging on both sides of the Pacific. Americans have been debating their national objectives toward China, and the best strategy for pursuing their goals. And the Chinese, in turn, have been debating what America's statements and actions reveal about U.S. intentions toward their country, and whether those long-term intentions are sympathetic or hostile.

This essay is divided into three sections. First, we will review the events of the late 1980s and early 1990s which produced such uncertainty about American policy toward China. Second, we will discuss the evolution of American policy toward China since Tiananmen, focusing on the various options considered or adopted by American policymakers, and describing how those options have been perceived in China. And finally, we will conclude with some speculation about the possible impact of the Clinton-Jiang summits on the future of Sino-American relations.

THE CRISIS OF 1989–91

The United States and China began exploring the prospects for a rapprochement as soon as the Nixon Administration entered office in 1969. Despite the fact that the two countries had been locked into a confrontational relationship for two decades, their relationship improved remarkably quickly. For the next twenty years, until the Tiananmen Crisis of 1989, the Sino-American relationship was essentially positive. To be sure, there were ups and downs, with periodic controversies over such issues as Taiwan, trade, and even some aspects of human rights. But in retrospect, the relationship was firmly rooted in three sets of common interests: strategic, economic, and ideological.

- Initially, the relationship was based on the most powerful common interest in international affairs: a common enemy. The Shanghai Communique of 1972, and the growing military cooperation between the two countries throughout the rest of the 1970s and early 1980s, demonstrated that the two countries shared an apprehension about the rise of Soviet power in Asia.
- Increasingly, this common strategic interest was paralleled by common economic interests. As China began its policy of "reform and opening" under Deng Xiaoping, its relationship with the United States was reinforced by the perceived complementarities between the "world's largest developed country" and the "world's largest developing country". Increasing bilateral trade, and growing American direct foreign investment in China, were concrete manifestations of this common interest.
- And, to a surprising degree, the relationship also had an ideological foundation. U.S.–China relations in the latter 1980s were supported by the American belief that China had, in effect, renounced Marxism-Leninism, and would be the first Communist country to evolve peacefully from totalitarianism and central planning to a market economy and even a democratic political system.

Unfortunately, the events of the mid-1980s and early 1990s eroded each of these three pillars. The common strategic interest was undermined first by Gorbachev's more flexible and cooperative foreign policy, then by the break-up of the Soviet empire in Eastern and Central Europe, and finally by the collapse of the Soviet Union itself. The common enemy that had once brought China and the United States together had literally disappeared.

Then, by the mid-1980s, the sense of common economic interest was also challenged by the dramatic changes in the Sino-American trade balance: from an American surplus in the early 1980s to balance in the mid-1980s to a growing deficit by the late 1980s — at least as measured by official American statistics. China was increasingly seen as another neo-mercantilist Asian economy that was eager to export but reluctant to import, and that imposed all kinds of barriers to foreign trade and investment.

Finally, the Tiananmen Crisis of 1989 shattered the optimistic American assessment that China would move smoothly and quickly toward democracy, or even toward more modest types of political reform. And the parallel collapse of communist systems in Central and Eastern Europe, and then Russia itself, meant that it was now they, not China, which were at the forefront of political change. Rather than viewed as the first Communist country to abandon Marxism-Leninism, China was now seen as an example of "market-Leninism" — as a nation that embraced economic change but rejected political liberalisation.

The First Option: Enlargement

In this setting, the previous consensus on an accommodative American policy toward China collapsed extraordinarily rapidly. Indeed, if we had full public opinion polling data, we would find that it collapsed within no more than a day — in the twenty-four hour period from June 4 to June 5, 1989.

Within a few weeks of the crackdown in Tiananmen Square, most of the American Congress, much of the press, and large segments of public opinion were pressing the Bush Administration for a new and far less cooperative policy toward China. Under this alternative policy, the promotion of human rights would become the central objective of American policy toward China. Economic sanctions, especially the revocation of China's most favoured nation status, would be a principal instrument by which human rights could be promoted. And there should be no high-level contact between the American and Chinese governments until the human rights situation improved.

Although the Bush Administration refused to adopt this new policy *in toto*, it had to bow to public and Congressional opinion to a significant degree. It tried to place human rights in what it regarded as the proper context, but with the growing trade deficit and with the collapse of the Soviet Union, it was unable to find a broader, positive rationale for Sino-American relations. It successfully resisted the revocation of China's most-favoured nation status, but had to impose other lesser economic sanctions against China, such as ceasing to vote for World Bank loans to China, and suspending the bilateral nuclear cooperation agreement with Beijing. And, although it sent National Security Advisor Brent Scrowcroft and Deputy Secretary of State Lawrence Eagleburger to China twice in 1989, it suspended all Cabinet-level contact — let alone summit meetings — until the very end of its term.

In contrast to the Bush Administration's reluctance to adopt this new China policy, the incoming Clinton Administration enthusiastically endorsed all three of its components when it first entered office in 1993. Human rights were explicitly said to be at the center of its China policy, given higher priority than either economic or security concerns. The new administration explicitly linked renewal of China's most-favoured-nation trade status with improvements in its human rights record, first during the election campaign and then when it entered office. And the U.S. eschewed high-level official contact with China for the first several months of the new administration, even though the Bush Administration had tried to facilitate such dialogue by sending the first Cabinet secretary to Beijing in its waning months.

Moreover, this new policy toward China was portrayed as an integral part of a broader American global strategy, known as "enlargement". As developed and articulated by Clinton's first National Security Advisor, Anthony Lake, "enlargement" was meant to be the overarching American strategy for the post-Cold War era, just as "containment" had been for the Cold War years. If, in the Cold War, the objective had been to contain the spread of communism, now, in the post-Cold War era, the objective would be to enlarge the sphere of democracy around the world.

The Clinton Administration gave what it regarded as a hard-nosed rationale for this new approach. Not only did democracies *ipso facto* provide better protection of political and civil rights, but it was also asserted that democracies behave better on every other dimension of international affairs: they promote more rapid and sustained economic growth, they make better trading partners, they do not make war on each other, they do not engage in proliferation of weapons of mass destruction, nor do they practice state-sponsored terrorism. Thus, by promoting democracy in China and around the world, the United States would be advancing virtually all of its vital international interests.

How did the Chinese perceive this new American policy toward their country — both the milder form reluctantly adopted by the Bush Administration, and the fuller version enthusiastically embraced in the early Clinton years? From the very beginning, the Chinese government attacked America's preoccupation with human rights as an illegitimate intervention in China's internal affairs, and as a strategy of encouraging China's "peaceful evolution" from socialism to capitalism. But Beijing also understood that George Bush was trying to defend U.S.–China relations against the critics of the previous American policy, and appreciated his efforts. Moreover, many ordinary Chinese, especially urban intellectuals, welcomed America's outrage at the events of June 1989 and the subsequent American pressure on human rights.

But Chinese attitudes, both public and private, turned in a much more critical direction in 1993, shortly after Bill Clinton took office. Certain specific American actions were viewed with suspicion and resentment in China, among them the Clinton Administration's decisions to link China's human rights record to its most-favoured-nation trading status, to oppose Beijing's bid to host the Olympic Games in the year 2000, and to order the U.S. Navy to search a Chinese merchant ship allegedly carrying precursors for chemical weapons to the Middle East. At the same time, the Chinese became more confident of their own country's ability to achieve rapid economic growth and political stability despite the trauma of 1989.

As Chinese analysts tried to place these seemingly hostile American actions in perspective, they looked to ongoing developments elsewhere in the former Communist bloc. Many of them concluded that the U.S. demands for political liberalisation were aimed at producing, in China, the same degree of economic decline and social disorder that was being experienced in the former Soviet Union and Eastern Europe. They therefore concluded that American policy was not a well-motivated effort to advance human rights in China, but rather an ill-intentioned effort to block China's rise and to keep it weak.

THE SECOND OPTION: ENGAGEMENT

The Clinton Administration soon began to doubt the efficacy of the policy of enlargement, at least as applied to China. There was no sign that the Chinese would make even the modest concessions on human rights that Washington had confidently predicted. At the same time, the Clinton Administration realised that the actual revocation of MFN would be counterproductive. Thus, in the late summer of 1993, it announced a policy of "engagement", which differed from its previous policy of "enlargement" in the following ways:

- First, it entailed the restoration of higher official contact with China, at the Cabinet level.
- Second, it sought to move beyond human rights to identify a broader set of issues for bilateral discussion, including some areas in which the two countries could cooperate.
- And third, the new policy involved the decoupling of the renewal of China's most-favoured-nation status from Beijing's record on human

rights, even though Beijing had not met the conditions for renewal that the Clinton Administration had laid out in the spring of 1993.

This rather dramatic change of course was not perceived as positively in China as the Administration might have hoped. For one thing, the overall meaning of the "engagement" policy was never explained clearly to Beijing. The term itself is extremely difficult to translate into Chinese, since it has so many meanings in English — ranging from an agreement to marry to a military skirmish. And the meaning that was intended by the Clinton Administration — a process of continuous bilateral dialogue with China — denoted merely a tactic or process, rather than a strategy with a clear objective. (To their credit, China's best America-watchers translated the term appropriately, but their translation retained the ambiguities of the original English.)

Nor did the first several years of bilateral dialogue clarify matters. The high-level official contact that was conducted under the engagement policy involved sending a large number of American Cabinet missions to China. But collectively they had very different agendas — some (such as the Department of Commerce and the Department of Defense) relatively accommodative, and others (such as the U.S. Trade Representative and the human rights desk of the State Department) more confrontational. Even as engagement proceeded, the guiding objectives of American policy toward China remained obscure.

The Taiwan policy review revealed by the Clinton Administration in the early fall of 1994 further complicated matters. This was the first major statement on U.S. policy toward Taiwan in some seven years, since Secretary of State George Shultz had said that the U.S. supported the expansion of cultural and economic relations between Taiwan as part of a "continuing, evolutionary process toward peaceful resolution of the Taiwan question". But the Clinton Administration's policy review did not clarify long-term U.S. intentions toward the island, particularly on the sensitive issue of Washington's posture toward the rising demands for independence on Taiwan. Instead, it focused on a secondary issue: the rules governing contact between U.S. and Taiwan officials. And one of the most important of these new rules — that high Taiwanese officials would be allowed to enter the United States only in transit to some other country — was soon violated when the Clinton Administration bowed to intense Congressional pressure and allowed Taiwan's popularly-elected president, Lee Teng-hui, to make a major speech at Cornell University in the late spring of 1995.

Faced with the ambiguities of "engagement" and with the sudden reversal of American policy on visas for Taiwanese officials, many Chinese concluded that "engagement" was simply a euphemism for what they called "soft containment". As they saw it, the true American policy toward China had three components: the use of human rights policy to subvert China, support for separatist movements in Taiwan and Tibet to fragment China, and enhanced relations with Vietnam and Japan to contain China. Thus, at the end of the day, Chinese analysts did not regard "engagement" as a significant improvement over "enlargement".

Although the Clinton Administration perceived these Chinese suspicions, it initially could do little to alleviate them. The public skepticism about China in the U.S. remained strong. Not only could the Clinton Administration offer few comprehensive reassurances to China, but it also had to expend its scarce political capital to fight against proposed legislation that would have imposed lesser economic sanctions against Beijing for human rights violations. It also had to overcome continued domestic opposition to high-level contacts with Beijing in the absence of progress on human rights. Sino-American relations continued their downward drift.

THE THIRD OPTION: INTEGRATION

Ironically, the Taiwan Strait crisis of 1995–96, in which mainland China fired missiles and deployed its fleet off the coast of Taiwan to demonstrate its displeasure with the advocates of Taiwanese independence, had a relatively salutary effect on U.S.–China relations. The prospect of a military confrontation between China and the U.S. forced the Clinton Administration to reassess its policy toward Beijing once again. Soon after the crisis subsided, U.S. policy entered a new stage — one that I call "integration".

In essence, "integration" was an extension of the policy of "engagement". The difference was that the policy of "integration" specified the sense of purpose — the overall direction — that the policy of "engagement" had lacked. The Clinton Administration announced that its strategic objective was to complete the integration of China into the international community, with all the privileges and responsibilities of a major power. That is, China would deserve an important seat in all the fora and institutions in which the rules of international conduct are being written or revised. In turn, China would have the obligation to honour those rules in its own behaviour. This strategy, the Clinton Administration hoped, would provide a positive and effective way of addressing perhaps the most difficult challenge in international affairs: how the international system can absorb a new rising power without losing its stability.

This redefinition of the purpose of engagement was intended to reassure Beijing about America's intentions. The policy of "integration" would not be an attempt either to block the rise of China or to contain the expansion of Chinese influence. Instead, its aim would be to welcome China into the international community as a respected but responsible major power. This suggested, in turn, that the United States did not see its core national interests as conflicting with China's, but rather envisioned an essentially cooperative relationship over the longer term.

In keeping with this new formulation of its strategic vision of U.S.–China relations, the Clinton Administration indicated its willingness to resume official bilateral contact at the very highest level. It dispatched Vice President Al Gore to China in the spring of 1997, and scheduled an exchange of visits between the presidents of the two countries, with President Jiang Zemin to visit the United States in October 1997, and President Clinton to visit China at some unspecified time in the following year. Although the presidents of the two countries had met in several multilateral settings since the Tiananmen Crisis, such as the United Nations and APEC, this was the first exchange of state visits since then-Premier Zhao Ziyang visited the U.S. in 1984, and since then-President George Bush visited China in 1989.

The Chinese might well have reacted quite negatively to the concept of integration. Historically, China had resisted the concept that international relations should be governed by international regimes. In part, this was because of the Chinese commitment to the principle of absolute state sovereignty; in part, because of China's belief that most international regimes reflected the interests of wealthier Western powers and slighted the interests of poorer developing countries. And, indeed, many Chinese regarded the new American concept of "integration" as a way of enmeshing China in institutions it did not create, and restricting its autonomy through rules it did not write.

But the official reaction of the Chinese government to the new American policy was much more positive than might have been predicted. Beijing actually welcomed the concept of integration, once Washington made clear that the United States acknowledged China's status as a major power, with the right to revise old rules and help write new ones. The American statements that it hoped to build a cooperative relationship with Beijing, and Washington's willingness to restore summit meetings with China, offered some of the reassurances about long-term American intentions that China had been seeking.

At home, the public reaction to the new American policy toward China was also positive — at least initially. Press commentary on the concept of "integration" was largely affirmative. The annual renewal of China's most-favoured-nation status passed through Congress surprisingly easily in 1996. And, despite the fact that the Clinton Administration's decision to abandon the linkage of MFN and human rights could be interpreted as a major foreign policy failure, Senator Robert Dole did not make China policy a major issue in his unsuccessful presidential election campaign in 1996. At the end of the year, the *New York Times* columnist Thomas Friedman wrote a widely-cited opinion essay in which he forecast that a "new consensus" was emerging on America's China policy for the first time since the Tiananmen Crisis of 1989.

THE FOURTH OPTION: CONTAINMENT

Developments in the spring of 1997, however, demonstrated how shallow and fragile that apparent consensus was. Within a few months after

Friedman had proclaimed that the debate over China policy had ended, critics launched the harshest attack on an accommodative American posture toward China since the Clinton Administration entered office in 1993. Three factors fueled this assault: partisan politics, interest group politics, and more ominous forecasts of China's capabilities and intentions in international affairs.

First, frustrated by their defeat in the Presidential elections of 1996 — especially in contrast to their ability to retain control of both houses of Congress — Republicans were looking for issues that could embarrass the Clinton Administration. With the country at peace and with the economy strong, a scandal involving the President was one of the few issues that might prove damaging to the Democrats. The charges that the Chinese government had attempted to influence American policy by making illegal contributions to the Democratic Party constituted one potentially ruinous scandal. But the impact of those charges would be enhanced the more that China was seen as a hostile power whose interests fundamentally conflicted with those of the United States.

Second, several powerful interest groups — on both ends of the political spectrum — also found benefit in attacking China. Some groups, such as human rights organisations and the non-proliferation lobbies, appeared to have specific concerns about objectionable Chinese activity at home and abroad. Other groups, however, found criticism of China to be a way of dramatising problems closer to home: as an extreme version of abortion abuses and religious repression, and as a cause of the inequalities and uncertainties allegedly produced by globalisation.

Finally, a new theme entered analytical discussions of the future of China. For several years after the Tiananmen Crisis, the conventional wisdom in the United States was that China was on the verge of some kind of domestic political upheaval — either geographic fragmentation, political decay, or democratic revolution. Now, eight years of essential stability and sustained economic growth gave rise to a very different image. Not only was China seen as an emerging economic and military power, but it was also viewed as a threat to American interests because of its authoritarian system, its strategic ambitions, and its neo-mercantilist economic strategy. Analysts in this camp variously described China as a new Soviet Union, the next Japan, or a new fascist state. Although some elements of this analysis had been discussed publicly for several years, Richard Bernstein and Ross Munro's best-selling book, *The Coming Conflict with China*, published in the spring of 1997, represented the first time this line of argument had been presented in book-length form.

The alternative approach to China proposed by the critics, although normally called "containment", also included elements of the earlier policy of enlargement.* On the one hand, they advocated that the United States contain the expansion of Chinese power in Asia, by maintaining (and possibly increasing) the forward deployments of American forces, enhancing the American alliance with Japan, bolstering the American commitment to the security of Taiwan, and providing both Taiwan and Japan with theater missile defense.

At the same time, many critics also wanted to declare the collapse of Communism to be the principal American objective in China. This was an even more ambitious and aggressive definition of American policy than the Clinton Administration's concept of enlargement, which sought more generally to enhance human rights and to promote democratisation, but did not specifically aim at the overthrow of the Chinese Communist Party.

Predictably, the Chinese expressed extreme concern about this proposed policy of containment and enlargement. And they claimed to find signs that the Clinton Administration, despite its protestations to the contrary, was in fact adopting many of its elements. In particular, Beijing criticised the new guidelines for security cooperation being negotiated between the U.S., denounced the American military presence in Asia, and described the American alliance structure in the region as an outmoded and unacceptable relic of the Cold War.

As of this writing, however, the domestic attack on the Clinton Administration's prior policy of "engagement" and "integration" has not been successful. In part, this is because the investigations of the campaign finance scandal have not produced compelling evidence of Chinese

*To be fair, Bernstein and Munro explicitly rejected a policy of containment in *The Coming Conflict* of China in favor of a tougher form of engagement with China.

involvement. In addition, relatively few Americans seem to want a confrontational relationship with China. Thus, although the annual Congressional resolution to revoke China's most-favoured-nation status did receive somewhat more votes in 1997 than it had in 1996, in the end Congress decided to allow the renewal of MFN more readily than had anticipated.

Equally importantly, preparations for the first Sino-American summit — the visit by Jiang Zemin in October — were not interrupted. Whatever their remaining suspicions about American intentions, the Chinese indicated that they hoped the summits could help stabilise U.S.–China relations.

Prospects

The future of Sino-American relations will depend to a great extent on the outcome of the twin summits in 1997–98. In essence, there are two possible scenarios:

- In the first scenario, both sides approach the summits with ambitious objectives, and with a willingness to invest political capital in rebuilding their bilateral relationship. As a result, they provide each other with effective reassurances about their long-term intentions, and reach agreement on a strategic framework for Sino-American relations. On that basis, they identify common interests, narrow their differences on major problems, and make concrete progress on concrete issues.
- In the second scenario, the two sides approach the summit with more modest ambitions. Neither leader is willing to invest much political capital into Sino-American relations, out of fear of criticism by hard-liners back home. As a result, neither is willing to make the gestures necessary to evoke similar concessions by the other. The summits are therefore essentially ceremonial, and producing a few photo opportunities and bland communiques, but few concrete accomplishments nor a lasting feeling of goodwill.

Although the first scenario would not produce a second honeymoon between China and the United States, but it might lead to a significant stabilisation of Sino-American relations. By providing a strategic framework for the ties between the two countries, it would enable Beijing and Washington to work together to advance common interests and narrow their differences.

In contrast, the second scenario would be extremely dangerous. If together the twin summits fail to achieve concrete results, such a development will reinforce the argument of American critics who charge that "engagement" means little more than "appeasement", and who propose a tougher policy of containment and enlargement. The resumption of that line of argument in the United States, in turn, would convince many Chinese analysts that Washington was committing itself to a hostile policy toward China. While the result might not be military confrontation between the two countries, the prospect of another Cold War between China and the United States would be significantly enhanced.

The Xiamen Experience in Introducing Foreign Direct Investment[1]

Luo Qi
East Asian Institute
National University of Singapore

The Xiamen Municipality (厦门市) is situated on the southeastern coastal area of Fujian Province. It consists of the Xiamen Island, the Gulangyu Islet (darkened area in Map 1), the coastal part of the northern bank of the Jiulongjiang River in the mainland (grey area in the map), and Tong'an County, with a total area of 1,516 square kilometres and a population of 1.2 million (at the end of 1995). The 2.2-kilometre Gaoji Causeway built in 1955 and the Xiamen Bridge completed in 1991 connect the Island with the Chinese mainland.

When China launched the reform and open-door policy in the late 1970s, Xiamen was already a medium/small-sized industrial city within the country's old, command economic structure. It possessed an outmoded but all-embracing industrial system, encompassing 33 of the 40 major industrial

[1]An earlier version of this paper was published in *Issues & Studies* Vol. 33, No. 7 (July 1997). I would like to thank Professor John Wong and Dr. Zheng Yongnian of EAI for their comments and suggestions in relation to the revision of this paper. Of course, any remaining deficiencies are mine alone.

Map 1. The Sketch Map of the Xiamen SEZ.

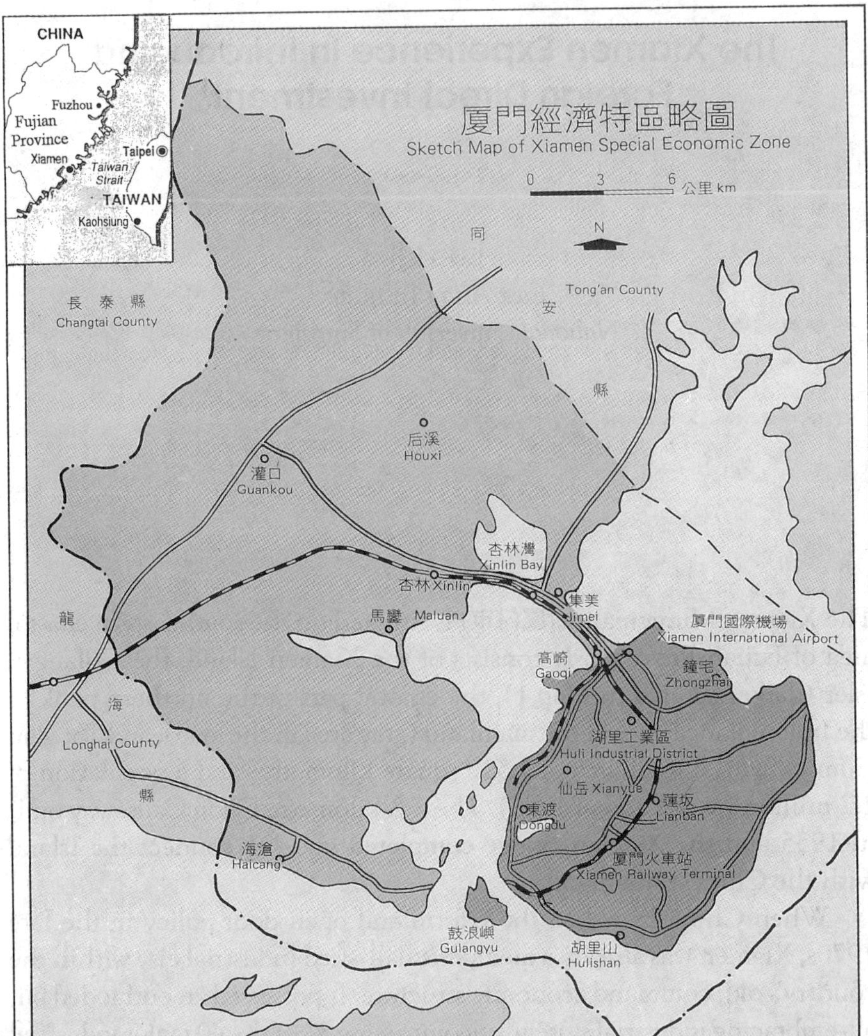

Source: The Xiamen SEZ Government.

sectors identified in China.[2] By the early 1980s, six of them, food-processing, chemicals and pharmaceuticals, machinery, textiles, paper and stationery, and building materials, had emerged as key sectors. With some 500 enterprises and an 110,000-strong workforce, Xiamen's industry generated about 60 percent of the city's GDP and 12.5 percent of Fujian's total gross value of industrial output (GVIO) in 1985.[3]

In July 1980, the State Council approved the proposal presented by the Fujian Provincial Government to open up an area of 2.5 square kilometres in the Huli (湖里) District, northwest of the Xiamen Island, as the Xiamen Special Economic Zone (SEZ).[4] In March 1984, after Deng Xiaoping made a high-profile visit to Xiamen the central government decided to expand the Xiamen SEZ into the whole Xiamen Island, including the Gulangyu Islet (i.e. the darkened area in the map). It covers a total area of 131 square kilometres and, at the end of 1995, had a population of 437,939, representing 8.6 and 36.1 percent of the Xiamen Municipality's totals, respectively.[5]

In order to make its economy more open and competitive, the SEZ government has taken a series of measures to restructure the local industry. A salient feature of Xiamen's industrial restructuring is the authorities' strategy of using foreign direct investment (FDI) to facilitate the transformation of local, old enterprises. Experiences in many developing countries show that FDI tends to be very effective in creating employment opportunities and increasing export earnings for the host economy but less so in transferring technology and management expertise, to say nothing of facilitating local industrial restructuring.

So, what impact has FDI created on the Xiamen economy? And can Xiamen fulfil its goal of using FDI to promote local industrial restructuring?

[2]Editorial Board, (1989), *Xiamen jingji shehui fazhang zhanlue 1985–2000* (The Strategy of Socio-Economic Development in Xiamen 1985–2000). Xiamen: Lujiang Publishing House, p. 124.

[3]*Xiamen Jingji Tequ Nianjian 1986* (Almanac of the Xiamen SEZ 1986), pp. 113, 131; and *Fujian Jingji Nianjian 1985* (Almanac of the Fujian Economy 1985), p. 486.

[4]However, the formal construction of the SEZ did not start until October 1981.

[5]*Xiamen Jingji Tequ Nianjian 1996*, pp. 297, 302.

This paper seeks to investigate these two crucial issues. After providing an overview of the economic development in Xiamen since 1980, the paper will start to explore the impact of FDI on the local economy, examine the performance of the foreign-invested enterprises (FIEs), and analyse the problems Xiamen has encountered in the process of utilizing FDI. This study will conclude with a critical assessment of the role of FDI in Xiamen.

OVERVIEW OF THE XIAMEN ECONOMY

After 16 years of development as a SEZ, the Xiamen economy has experienced spectacular growth. As can be seen from Table 1, its GDP in 1995 was 13 times bigger than that of 1980 while its exports expanded by an astonishing 23.8 times, with the average annual growth rates hitting 19.3 and 23.9 percent respectively. These two rates compare favourably with 10.2 and 14.6 percent for the country as a whole over the same period, and with 12.9 and 16.9 percent for Xiamen's own record over the pre-SEZ period of 1950–79.[6] Compared with Shenzhen, China's most developed SEZ, Xiamen had a lower growth in GDP because the bulk of its economy consisted of old industrial enterprises, but it enjoyed a higher growth in exports due to the massive influx of foreign-invested export-oriented companies since the early 1980s. For example, between 1990 and 1995 the average annual growth rates for Xiamen's GDP and exports were 23.8 and 34.8 percent respectively, in contrast with Shenzhen's 30.4 and 32.4 percent.[7]

At the same time, Xiamen's economic structure has also been upgraded significantly, with agriculture's share in GDP dropping from 21.6 percent

[6]For the national figures, *Jingrong Shibao* (Financial News) (Beijing), 29/02/96, p. 1; *Lianhe Zaobao* (United Morning Newspaper) (Singapore), 4/3/96, p. 14; and *Zhongguo Nianjian 1995* (People's Republic of China Yearbook 1995), pp. 150, 152; and for Xiamen's pre-SEZ figures, *Xiamen Jingji Tequ Nianjian 1986*, pp. 110–23.

[7]See Table 1 and *Shenzhen Jingji Tequ Nianjian 1996* (Almanac of the Shenzhen SEZ 1996), p. 66.

Table 1. Growth of Xiamen's GDP and Exports, 1980–1995.

	GDP (RMB million, at 1980 prices)	Change over previous year (%)	Exports (US$ million)	Change over previous year (%)
1980	647.6	—	40.3	—
1981	707.1	9.2	141.1	0.7
1982	822.3	16.3	132.0	–6.4
1983	860.4	4.6	128.3	–3.0
1984	1,061.4	23.4	145.9	14.1
1985	1,374.5	29.5	165.3	13.0
1986	1,495.4	8.8	163.7	–0.6
1987	1,823.9	22.0	261.1	59.2
1988	2,343.9	28.5	576.1	120.7
1989	2,764.3	17.9	646.8	12.3
1990	3,144.1	13.7	781.5	20.7
1991	3,732.0	18.7	1,150.6	47.4
1992	4,456.0	19.4	1,765.7	53.4
1993	5,668.1	27.2	2,355.3	33.4
1994	7,323.1	29.2	3,390.9	44.0
1995	9,132.0	24.7	3,481.8	2.7
Average annual growth rate(%)	—	19.3	—	23.9

Sources: *Xiamen Tongji Nianjian 1991* (Xiamen Statistical Yearbook 1991), pp. 9, 15; and *Xiamen Jingji Tequ Nianjian 1991*, pp. 227, 236; *1992*, pp. 246, 255; *1993*, pp. 219, 229; *1994*, pp. 246, 254; *1995*, pp. 289, 299; and *China Economic Review*, July 1996, p. 32.

in 1980 to 6.9 percent in 1994 and manufacturing's from 57.8 to 48.7 percent; in contrast, the services sector's rising from 20.6 to 44.4 percent.[8]

As a result, Xiamen's profile in the country has also been raised. Its GDP per capita in 1994 (15,662 yuan) rose to 13th place among 188 major Chinese cities, despite the fact that the size of its economy ranked beyond

[8]*Xiamen Jingji Tequ Nianjian 1991*, p. 248; and *1995*, p. 283.

40th in the country.[9] In 1995, its export volume (US$3.48 billion) was the fourth largest among all the Chinese cities, behind Shenzhen, Shanghai and Guangzhou.[10] Before the opening of the SEZ, Xiamen's seaport was very small and could not accommodate large vessels of over 8,000 tons. Today, its seaport, with a handling capacity of 13.1 million tons a year (in 1995), is classified as Class-I large port (大型一类港口) in the country, ranking sixth in terms of volume of containers handled and eleventh of foreign trade goods handled. Linked with over 60 ports in more than 40 countries and regions, the seaport now has 65 berth, of which 11 are capable of serving large ships of over 10,000 tons.[11] Xiamen's international airport, on the other hand, is currently used by 26 airlines providing flights to 53 domestic and overseas destinations. All these indicate that the establishment of the SEZ and especially the implementation of the "Special Policy" have created a greater economic prosperity in Xiamen, making it one of the strong economic growth centres in southern China.

THE IMPACT OF FDI ON THE LOCAL ECONOMY

The inflow of FDI into Xiamen started as soon as it was designated as a SEZ in 1980. By the end of 1995, as shown in Table 2, Xiamen had concluded 3,450 contracts covering the major forms of FDI — Equity Joint Ventures (EJVs), Contractual Management Enterprises (CMEs), and Wholly Foreign-Owned Enterprises (WFOEs). These contracts committed foreign investors to make investments in cash (usually foreign currencies), equipment, machinery and technology totalling US$10.3 billion. Of this amount, US$4.7 billion had already been delivered.

From a provincial perspective, although taking only 18.5 percent of 2,729 contracts signed by Fujian with foreign investors in 1995, Xiamen

[9] *Xiamen Jingji Tequ Nianjian 1993*, p. 4; and *1995*, p. 499.

[10] Lu Yonghui, "On Xiamen's role in the southwestern Fujian economy", *Tequ Jingji* (The SEZ Economy) (Shenzhen), June 1996, p. 26.

[11] *Xiamen Jingji Tequ Nianjian* 1995, pp. 56–57; and *1996*, p. 132.

Table 2. Growth of FDI in Xiamen, 1983–1995.

	No. of contracts signed	Change over previous year (%)	FDI pledged (US$ m.)	Change over previous year (%)	FDI realized (US$ m.)	Change over previous year (%)
1983	24	—	37.2	—	7.8	—
1984	86	258.3	149.7	302.9	40.4	421.8
1985	105	22.1	242.0	61.7	73.3	81.2
1986	34	−67.6	27.6	−88.6	33.9	−53.7
1987	50	47.1	56.7	105.6	17.5	−48.3
1988	180	260.0	155.6	174.5	48.0	173.6
1989	201	11.7	514.5	230.6	129.8	170.6
1990	262	30.4	485.6	−5.6	72.7	−44.0
1991	213	−18.7	519.8	7.0	132.6	82.3
1992	443	108.0	1,697.0	192.7	563.0	324.7
1993	655	47.9	2,404.0	41.7	1,037.0	84.2
1994	692	5.7	1,864.9	−22.4	1,241.0	19.7
1995	505	−27.0	2,062.4	10.6	1,321.6	6.5
Total	3,449	28.9*	10,261.7	39.8*	4,721.3	53.5*

*Average annual growth rate between 1983 and 1995.
Sources: *Xiamen Jingji Tequ Nianjian 1986*, p. 92; *1990*, p. 327; *1991*, p. 50; *1992*, p. 40; *1993*, pp. 37–38; *1994*, p. 55; *1995*, p. 66; and *1996*, p. 472.

successfully attracted 23.2 percent of the total foreign commitment (US$8.9 billion) and 32.7 percent of the actually invested amount (US$4 billion) in the province within that year. Thus, the average capitalisation of the FDI projects in Xiamen (US$4.08 million per project) was 24.9 percent higher than Fujian's level (US$3.26 million) and 65.3 percent higher than the national level (US$2.47 million).[12]

[12]*China Economic News* (Beijing), 17/6/96, No. 22, pp. 22–23. For more information and analyses of FDI development in Fujian Province, see Luo Qi and R. Ash (1996), "The Economic Challenge", in *Fujian: Gateway to Taiwan*, edited by Brian Hook. Hong Kong: Oxford University Press, pp. 123–52.

In terms of the source of FDI, most of the investors came from the Asia-Pacific region, with Hong Kong (and Macau) and Taiwan taking the lead. In 1995, for example, the Hong Kong investment accounted for 53.5 percent of the total FDI in the SEZ, Taiwan 16.7 percent, USA 5.7 percent, Great Britain 5.4 percent, Japan 3.9 percent, Singapore 2.6 percent, and Malaysia 2.4 percent.[13]

As a result of this infusion of foreign capital and, above all, the dynamism associated with it, at least four noticeable structural changes can be observed in Xiamen's economy. Firstly, as illustrated in Table 3, in terms of sectoral structure, the electronics sector, which was non-existent in 1981, has emerged as the largest industrial sector in Xiamen, accounting for nearly 21 percent of the SEZ's GVIO in 1994, whereas the food-

Table 3. Composition of Xiamen's Industry by Major Sector, 1981 & 1994.

	1981		1994	
	GVIO (RMB million, at 1980 prices)	Share (%)	GVIO (RMB million, at 1990 prices)	Share (%)
Electronics	—*	—*	468.1	20.8
Machinery	19.8	18.2	446.6	19.8
Food-processing	26.5	25.5	245.2	10.9
Textiles	12.9	12.4	240.7	10.7
Chemicals & pharmaceuticals	19.8	19.1	158.9	7.0
Paper & stationery	4.5	4.3	129.7	5.8
Building materials	3.7	3.6	—	—
Sub-total	86.2	83.1	1,689.1	74.9
Others	17.5	16.9	566.3	25.1
Total	103.7	100.0	2,255.4	100.0

*Non-existent.

Sources: *Xiamen Jingji Tequ Nianjian 1995*, pp. 334–35; and *1986*, p. 72.

[13] *Xiamen Jingji Tequ Nianjian 1996*, p. 473.

processing sector, which was the largest until mid-1980s, has been relegated to the third place, with its share plunging from 25.5 percent in 1981 to 10.9 percent in 1994. The other two major sectors, machinery and textiles, only experienced a small change, with the former's share increasing from 18.2 to 19.8 percent while the latter's dropping from 12.4 to 10.7 percent. The share for the chemical and pharmaceutical sector, on the other hand, shrank sharply because the category of "rubber" was no longer included in this sector. Thus, it appears that Xiamen's overall industrial structure has been improved markedly.

Table 4, showing different growth rates among different products, confirms the above significant structural change. Between 1985 and 1995,

Table 4. Quantity of Major Industrial Products in Xiamen, 1985 and 1995.

	1985	1995	Change over 1985
Tinned Food (10,000 tons)	2.33	3.48	49.4%
Sugar (10,000 tons)	3.12	0.91	–70.8%
Fabric (10,000 metres)	2,607	3,137	20.3%
Caustic Soda (ton)	7,134	9,084	27.3%
Light Bulb (10,000 units)	2,087	2,447[a]	17.3%
Synthetic (ton)	618	91,367	146.8 times
Telephone (10,000 sets)	20	489	23.5 times
TV (10,000 sets)	15	63	3.2 times
Electronic Components (10,000 pieces)	20,860	393,517	17.9 times
Semiconductor IC (10,000 pieces)	114[b]	784	5.8 times

Notes: a: the 1992 figure; and b: the 1990 figures.

Sources: *Xiamen Jingji Tequ Nianjian 1986*, pp. 73–74; *1996*, pp. 428–29: *Xiamen Tongji Nianjian 1993*, p. 106; *1994*, p. 89.

the production of five major traditional products in Xiamen either grew slowly or experienced sharp drop (ranging from 50 percent to negative 70 percent), whereas that of new five major products, which are largely technology/capital-intensive, expanded rapidly, ranging from 3.2 to 147 times.

Secondly, in terms of ownership structure, the FIE sector has replaced the SOE sector to become the largest manufacturing force in Xiamen's economy. As illustrated in Table 5, the FIE sector generated over 75 percent of the SEZ's GVIO, transforming the industry from one dominated by inefficient state-owned enterprises (SOEs) to one dominated by dynamic FIEs.

Thirdly, the FIE sector has also been a dominant exporting force in Xiamen, contributing 40 percent of the SEZ's total export.

And finally, Table 5 also tells us that foreign capital has played an important role in supplementing domestic investment capital, forming 22 percent of the SEZ's total investment in social fixed assets in 1995.

Table 5. Contribution by Foreign Investment to the Xiamen Economy, 1990–95.

(%)

	1990	1991	1992	1993	1994	1995
Percentage of foreign investment in Xiamen's total fixed-asset investment	13.3	13.5	17.8	15.2	20.9	22.3
Percentage of FIEs' GVIO in Xiamen's total GVIO	54.8	53.8	57.1	60.0	70.5	75.6
Percentage of FIEs' exports in Xiamen's total exports	30.2	26.1	29.2	43.0	38.8	40.2

Sources: *Xiamen Tongji Nianjian 1991*, pp. 178, 303; *1992*, pp. 148, 267; *1993*, pp. 160, 274; *1994*, pp. 148, 309; *1995*, pp. 48, 309; *1996*, pp. 54, 279; *Xiamen Jingji Tequ Nianjian 1991*, p. 51; *1992*, p. 43; *1993*, p. 39; *1994*, p. 56; *1995*, p. 67; *1996*, p. 85.

The Performance of the FIEs

The rapid expansion of FIEs in Xiamen has been phenomenal, as indicated in Table 6. By 1995, a total of 1,204 FIEs had gone into operation, accounting for 60 percent of the total number of local enterprises practising independent accounting (实行独力核算的企业). The FIE sector as a whole employed more workers (63 percent of the total) and paid more tax (46 percent) than any of the local sectors. More profoundly, it generated over three quarters of the SEZ's total GVIO, playing a decisive role in the local economic development. In fact, all these spectacular achievements have, as can be seen from Table 6, been made mainly at the expense of the two public sectors, the state and collective sectors.

Concealed in Table 6, however, is the economic efficiency of the FIE sector's performance, which is more important in measuring its real impact on the local economy. Derived from the absolute indicators in Table 6, the three relative indicators listed in Table 7 reflect the economic efficiency of all the six economic sectors in Xiamen in 1995. As shown in Table 7, the FIE sector had the second highest labour productivity — RMB158,100 per labour, which is 68 and 171 percent higher than that of the SOE sector and the collective sector respectively. Perhaps this explains why the FIE sector has been able to expand its production so rapidly. On the other hand, the FIE sector was the second least efficient in terms of tax payment as it only paid RMB410 of tax for every RMB10,000 of GVIO it generated. This is in sharp contrast with the RMB1,830 paid by the SOE sector, RMB1,620 by the joint-stock sector, and RMB980 by the mixed sector. The SOE sector, in particular, contributed as much as 40 percent of the local government's total tax revenue although it only generated 14.7 percent of the total GVIO. So in relative terms, the FIEs have in fact paid less tax than the local enterprises, despite the fact that the FIE sector as a whole has paid more tax than the other local sectors (see Table 6).

Of course, various tax concessions offered by the local government to the FIEs may, to a large extent, explain why they have been able to pay less tax than their local counterparts. But it is also well known that many FIEs in developing countries try to avoid corporate taxation by sustaining a book loss (or accounting loss), that can easily be realised through,

Table 6. Major Indicators for All Industrial Enterprises Practising Independent Accounting in Xiamen, 1985 and 1995.

		No. of enterprises (A)		No. of employees (B)		GVIO (C)		Taxes/profits delivered[a] (D)		Total financial loss (E)	
						(RMB10,000, at current prices)					
		No.	As %	No.	As %	No.	As %	No.	As %	No.	As %
State	1985	187	30.4	61,002	58.5	130,646	61.4	21,594	96.3	52	19.6
	1995	179	8.9	52,085	20.6	489,999	14.7	89,634	39.7	3,388	3.6
Collective	1985	381	61.9	38,382	36.8	36,526	17.2	738	3.3	155	58.5
	1995	541	26.8	30,433	12.0	177,329	5.3	12,790	5.7	3,117	3.4
Private	1985	4	0.7	233	0.2	353	0.2	0	0	29	10.9
	1995	12	0.6	400	0.2	2,602	0.1	–149	–0.1	192	0.2
Mixed	1985	30	4.9	3,708	3.6	35,070	16.5	80	0.4	4	1.5
	1995	75	3.7	6,843	2.7	57,620	1.7	5,662	2.5	1,093	1.2
Joint Stock	1985	0	0	0	0	0	0	0	0	0	0
	1995	5	0.3	4,147	1.6	85,893	2.6	13,892	6.2	0	0
FIE	1985	14	2.3	1,012	1.0	10,291	4.8	2	0	25	9.43
	1995	1,204	59.7	159,075	62.9	2,514,775	75.6	104,079	46.1	85,329	91.6
Total	1985	616	100.2	104.337	100.1	212,886	100.1	22,414	100.0	265	99.9
	1995	2.016	100.0	252,983	100.0	3,328,218	100.0	225,908	100.1	93,118	100.0

Notes: a: In general, SOEs, especially profitable ones, have to hand over a part of their profits to the local government in addition to all taxes due to them; whereas enterprises of other sectors only have to pay the tax/taxes due to them.

b: The sum should equal 100.0, but slight inaccuracy is due to rounding error.

Sources: *Xiamen Tongji Nianjian 1986*, pp. 39–40, 53, 65, 69, 85, 97; *Xiamen Jingji Tequ Nianjian 1996*, pp. 396–97, 400–401.

Table 7. Economic Efficiency of All Industrial Enterprises Practising Independent Accounting in Xiamen, 1995.

	Labour productivity (RMB10,000/per labour) (C/B)	Ratio of taxes/profits delivered to GVIO (%) (D/C)	Ratio of total loss to GVIO (%) (E/C)
State	9.41	18.3	0.7
Collective	5.83	7.2	1.8
Private	6.51	–5.7	7.4
Mixed	8.42	9.8	1.9
Joint stock	20.71	16.2	0
FIE	15.81	4.1	3.4
Average level	13.16	6.8	2.8

Source: Table 6.

e.g. transfer pricing. Thus, it is not accidental that the FIE sector in Xiamen sustained a huge " financial loss" of RMB853 million in 1995, accounting for 92 percent of the total loss incurred by all the enterprises in Xiamen (see Table 6). Indeed, the FIE sector had the second highest loss ratio — 3.4 percent, in sharp contrast with 0.7 and 1.8 percent for the SOE sector and the collective sector respectively (see Table 7).

PROBLEMS IN UTILISING FDI

Unlike the Shenzhen SEZ, which was built on the basis of a little fishing village, the Xiamen SEZ was converted wholesale from the old city. The enlargement of the SEZ in 1984, therefore, has not only increased its territory from 2.5 to 131 square kilometres but, more significantly, embedded the 588 existing enterprises situated in the old city area, in addition to the 180 already established in Huli District since 1981. As a result, it became clear that the performance of the mainstay of the SEZ's economy, i.e. the 588 old enterprises, was crucial to the success of the SEZ. This meant that the restructuring of the old enterprises should become the priority of Xiamen's industrial reform and development.

Accordingly, soon after the expansion the Xiamen authorities started to readjust the SEZ's industrial restructuring policy. The new policy included the following ambitious goals:

> " ... to rationalise the industrial structure and upgrade technology in the enterprises through introducing foreign direct investment. As a SEZ, Xiamen should make maximum use of FDI to import as much as possible advanced foreign technology and management expertise into local industrial enterprises. ... From the strategic point of view, the electronics industry should be chosen as the leading industry because it not only represents modern advanced technology but also has a great bearing on technological transformation of other industries".[14]

[14]*Xiamen jingji shehui fazhang zhanlue 1985–2000*, p. 139.

Clearly, the Xiamen authorities tried to use FDI to promote the restructuring of local, old enterprises. This strategy, especially to develop electronics as the leading sector, may be very appealing to developing countries, particularly those with a heavy presence of obsolete industry in their economies, but it will inevitably conflict with the objectives of foreign investors. In the case of Xiamen, most of the investors want to make use of local cheap but relatively skilful workforce to produce labour-intensive products for export, while a few intend to use Xiamen as their stepping-stone to enter China's vast domestic market. Clearly, these objectives bear little congruence with Xiamen's goal of utilising FDI. As a result, Xiamen has encountered the following four major problems in the process of using FDI to restructure the local enterprises.

The first has been the lack of linkage between the electronics sector and other industrial sectors. Table 8, showing the change in the composition of the electronics sector's GVIO by major product group from 1987 to 1994, tells us that consumer goods, mainly composed of coloured TV sets, radio cassettes, video recorders, and camcorders, still took the lion's share in 1994 (43 percent) while simple telecommunication equipment, largely

Table 8. Composition of the Electronics Industry in Xiamen by Major Product Group, 1987–1994.

	1987		1990		1994	
	GVIO	%	GVIO	%	GVIO	%
	(RMB million, at 1980 prices)				(at 1990 prices)	
Consumer goods	543.9	63.1	1,423.5	68.4	2,014.8	43.0
Simple telecommunication equipment	256.4	29.8	246.4	11.8	839.7	17.9
Components and parts	57.7	6.7	303.7	14.6	1,238.8	26.5
Computers	0.22	0.1	36.5	1.8	54.1	1.2
Others	3.1	0.3	70.5	3.4	533.5	11.4
Total	861.3	100.0	2,080.8	100.0	4,680.9	100.0

Sources: *Xiamen Tongji Nianjian 1988*, p. 39; *1991*, p. 43; and *1995*, p. 192.

made up of telephones and walkie talkies, accounted for nearly 18 percent. Computer manufacturing, on the other hand, only played a minor role in the sector, contributing a mere 1.2 percent in 1994. This left components and parts and other unspecified products to take the rest of the share (nearly 38 percent).

Experience in other Export Processing Zones (EPZs) suggests that the electronics industry tends to have a low propensity to use local inputs.[15] This was not exceptional in Xiamen, where most of the electronics products were made of imported components and parts and, once assembled or processed, re-exported to their overseas markets. In 1994, for example, the electronics sector imported about 93 percent of its input and exported nearly 83 percent of its output.[16] In other words, the producers, most of which were FIEs, were in fact engaged in enclave-typed export-processing activities. Obviously, an industry like this can hardly play the role of so-called "leading industry", i.e. to stimulate the technological transformation of other industries through linkage effect, as originally envisaged by the Xiamen authorities.

The second problem has been the lack of linkage between the FIEs and the local enterprises. This was due largely to the domination of WFOEs in the FIE sector. Table 9 shows that the share of WFOEs in the total number of the FIEs in Xiamen rose steadily from 5.7 percent in the period of 1981–85 to the peak of 78.6 percent in 1990. By 1994, it still hovered around 60 percent. To some extent, this large swing from EJVs to WFOEs, rare in the history of FDI within developing countries, was caused by the large-scale influx of Taiwanese capital, which accounted for 40–50 percent of the total FDI in Xiamen during the late 1980s and early 1990s.[17]

Compared with other foreign investors in Xiamen, the Taiwanese preferred wholly owned ventures to other forms of investment and, in many

[15]See, e.g. Basile and Germidis (1984), *Investing in Free Export Processing Zone.* Paris: OECD, pp. 48–49.

[16]Chen Qilin, "The industrial structure in China's SEZs", *Fujian Xuekan* (The Fujian Academic Journal) (Fuzhou), Jan. 1995, p. 46.

[17]*Xiamen Jingji Tequ Nianjian 1990*, p. 329; *1991*, p. 51; and *1992*, p. 315.

Table 9. Composition of the FIEs in Xiamen by Type of Contract, 1981–1994.

	1981–85		1986		1987		1988		1989		1990		1991		1992		1993		1994	
	No.	%	No.	%	No.	%	No.	%	No.	%	No.	%	No.	%	No.	%	No.	%	No.	%
Wholly foreign-owned enterprises	12	5.7	5	14.7	13	26.0	79	43.9	136	67.7	195	78.6	125	58.7	254	57.4	345	52.7	413	59.7
Equity joint ventures	134	63.5	26	76.5	31	62.0	87	48.3	55	27.4	36	14.5	54	25.3	126	28.4	219	33.4	215	31.1
Contractual management enterprises	65	30.8	3	8.8	6	12.0	14	7.8	10	5.0	17	6.9	34	16.0	63	14.2	91	13.9	64	9.2
Total	211	100.0	34	100.0	50	100.0	180	100.0	201	100.0	248	100.0	213	100.0	443	100.0	655	100.0	692	100.0

Sources: *Xiamen Jingji Tequ Nianjian 1990*, p. 328; *1991*, p. 290; *1992*, p. 314; *1993*, p. 303; *1994*, p. 321; and *1995*, p. 376.

cases, emphasised their independence by supplying their own raw materials and export markets.[18] For example, in 1990 more than three-quarters of all the raw materials, components and parts needed by the Taiwanese firms in Xiamen were imported from Taiwan and about 85 percent of the finished products exported to their existing overseas markets.[19] Some midstream factories even invested with upstream and/or downstream factories and formed a self-sufficient and self-sustained operational system, almost wholly independent of the local economy.[20]

Obviously, as most WFOEs tend to be vertically integrated into their parent corporations abroad, their concern is to maintain their own international production network rather than to set up links with the local economy. Thus, it may be unrealistic to expect the WFOEs in Xiamen to develop economic and technological links with the local Chinese companies.

The third problem has been the preponderance of small-sized projects in FDI. In spite of the enormous effort made by the Xiamen authorities to attract large-sized FDI projects, especially those from Western multinationals, small-sized projects still accounted for 97.7 percent of the total FDI projects in operation in 1994 while medium-sized constituted 1.9 percent. Only three firms could be classified as large-sized projects.[21] Without doubt, the small size of most of the FIEs has considerably restricted their impact on the local industrial restructuring. As can be seen from

[18]For more information and analyses about Taiwanese investment in Xiamen, see Luo Qi and C. Howe, "Direct investment and economic integration in the Asia Pacific: the case of Taiwanese investment in Xiamen", *China Quarterly*, Dec. 1993, pp. 746–69.

[19]Qin Xuezhen, "An analysis of wholly foreign-owned enterprises in the Xiamen SEZ", *Xiamen Tequ Yanjiu* (Studies of the Xiamen SEZ) (Xiamen), No. 4, 1992, p. 37.

[20]*Xiamen Tequ Yanjiu*, No. 3, 1991, pp. 17–18; and Kong Zhang, "Assessment of Taiwanese investment in Xiamen", *Gang'ao Jingji* (Hong Kong and Macau Economies) (Guangzhou), June, 1991, p. 34.

[21]*Xiamen Jingji Tequ Nianjian 1995*, p. 330.

In China, the size of industrial enterprises is normally classified on the basis of their production capacities. In this case, however, the FDI projects are divided according to the number of employees, with those having 100 employees or below to be classified as small-sized firms, those between 101 and 500 as medium-sized, and those 501 or above as large-sized.

Table 10, from 1986 to 1994 the overall enterprise structure in Xiamen experienced only a small change, with the proportion of small-sized enterprises remaining uncomfortably large — 96.3 percent. This will inevitably hinder the enterprises from exploiting economies of scale in the wider export market, crucial to the success of export-led industrialisation.

Table 10. Composition of Industrial Enterprises in Xiamen by Size, 1986–1994.

	1986			1994		
	No.	% of total no.	% of GVIO	No.	% of total no.	% of GVIO
Large	4	0.2	3.8	9	0.6	15.7
Medium	12	0.7	22.4	47	3.1	21.0
Small	1,677	99.1	63.8	1,472	96.3	63.3
Total	1,693	100.0	100.0	1,528	100.0	100.0

Sources: *Xiamen Tongji Nianjian 1986*, pp. 37–38; and *Xiamen Jingji Tequ Nianjian 1995*, pp. 320–21.

The final main problem has been limited technology transfer from the FIEs to the local enterprises. Apart from the afore-mentioned three problems, generally high labour-intensity of the FIEs was also a key reason for this problem. Most of the FIEs in Xiamen were engaged in the production of light industrial/consumer goods destined for their existing overseas markets, and hence tended to apply simple and standardised technology and equipment, which require little skill to operate. A survey shows that about 75 percent of the FIEs used simple and, in some cases, second-hand machines imported from abroad, manufacturing such goods as footwear, clothing, toys, umbrellas, handicrafts, luggage, and sporting equipment. Indeed, some Taiwanese firms even used less capital per unit of labour than the local Chinese SOEs.[22] Needless to say, it is quite difficult, if not impossible, to use these FIEs to promote the technological transformation of the local enterprises.

[22] *Xiamen Tongji Yanjiu* (Xiamen Statistical Studies) (Xiamen), 1990 issue, p. 25.

CONCLUSION

This paper has sought to assess the performance of FDI in Xiamen and the local authorities' strategy of utilizing FDI over the period of 1980–95. It shows that the inflow of foreign capital has injected dynamism into the local economy, stimulating the improvement of the overall industrial structure. The FIE sector in Xiamen has expanded rapidly and now dominated the local economy. However, like in many developing countries it has had a poor financial performance, which is clearly incompatible with its rapidly growing size of production in Xiamen. Perhaps it is high time now for the local authorities to reconsider various tax concessions they have offered to the FIEs and take firm and effective actions to minimise transfer pricing.

This study also shows that Xiamen was still far away from fulfilling its goal of using FDI to facilitate the restructuring of local, old enterprises. There were three reasons for this. First, although the newly established electronics sector has emerged as the largest industry in the local economy, it was by and large a foreign-transplanted, labour-intensive industry and had limited forward and/or backward linkage with other industries. Naturally, it could not function as a "leading industry" to stimulate the technological transformation of other industries through linkage effect, as expected by the authorities.

Second, although the FIE sector has become a dominant manufacturing and exporting force in the local economy, a considerable part of it was still not integrated into the local economy yet and thus to a large degree did not interact with the local enterprises. As many FIEs were engaged in enclave-type export-processing operations, it was hard for them to transfer technology and/or management expertise to the local enterprises.

And third, the small size and relatively high labour intensity of most of the FIEs have further restricted their impact on the local industrial restructuring.

Thus, the Xiamen experiment highlights the importance of a basic issue — having a more realistic expectation on the role of FDI projects in developing countries. FDI may be used to create jobs, increase foreign exchange earnings, and indeed promote the prosperity of local economy, but there are difficulties in using it to facilitate the restructuring of local, old industry because it will inevitably conflict with the objectives of FDI in developing countries. In other words, the Xiamen experience has proved that the strategy of using FDI to facilitate the restructuring of local, old enterprises is, at least for the time being, an unduly high expectation on the role of FDI.

How China Views Korea

A Balanced Act Tilting toward the South

ZHAO Quansheng
School of International Service
American University

It took 35 days for the People's Republic of China (PRC) to handle the defection of Hwang Jang Yop, a top North Korean Communist Party theorist and philosopher. On February 12, 1997, Hwang walked into the South Korean Embassy in Beijing,[1] and stayed there for five weeks. On March 18, Hwang was transferred to the Philippines, where he was required by the Chinese to stay at least for one month before transferring to South Korea.[2] On April 20, Hwang arrived in Seoul escorted by South Korean fighters.[3] On July 10, 1997, Hwang made his first press conference since arriving in Seoul, warning "that the North will stage an 'all-out' war" against the South.[4]

[1]See Shim Jae hoon, "Man in the Middle", *Far Eastern Economic Review* (February 27, 1997): 14–15.

[2]Kevin Sullivan, "N. Korean Defector Leaves Beijing for Philippines", *The Washington Post* (March 19, 1997): A24.

[3]Kevin Sullivan, "Defector Warns 2nd Korean War 'Dangerously Close'", *The Washington Post* (April 21, 1997): A12.

[4]"Defector 'Sure' North Korean Will Launch War", *The Straits Times* (July 11, 1997): 2.

To work out a solution for the case of Hwang Jang Yop, there were extensive negotiations in Beijing among and between diplomats from China, North Korea, and South Korea. There was a treaty between Beijing and Pyongyang that the Chinese government should return defectors to North Korea.[5] Indeed, there was quite a tension between China and North Korea during Hwang's month-long stay in Beijing that North Korean agents lurked in parked cars just outside the South Korean Embassy, prompting the Chinese to ring the building with soldiers. There were even worries that the North Koreans might try to shoot down the planes that carried Hwang from China to the Philippines, and then to South Korea.[6]

Beijing initially attempted to avoid choosing sides in a dispute between an old communist ally and a new commercial partner. Chinese Foreign Ministry spokesman Guo Chongli indicated several days after the defection that the negotiations may "take a very long time", citing examples of the standoff in Lima, Peru, where Tupac Amaru guerrillas had been holding diplomats and other officials hostage in the Japanese ambassador's residence for two months.[7] A month later, Chinese Premier Li Peng reiterated the issue, "China will exercise caution, and we will handle the issue by proceeding from the maintenance of peace on the Korean peninsula".[8] The turn of Hwang from China to South Korea (via the Philippines), therefore, was regarded by Seoul as a "victory" for South Korea in the competition between the two Koreas "in terms of economy, in terms of ideology and in terms of morality".[9] It will be fascinating for policy-makers and scholars in the region to watch the changing dynamics of this triangle

[5]Mary Jordan, "Fearing Deluge, Political Fallout, China Spurns fleeing N. Koreans", *The Washington Post* (April 14, 1997): A14.
[6]Kevin Sullivan, "Defector Warns 2nd Korean War 'Dangerously Close'", *The Washington Post* (April 21, 1997): A12.
[7]Steven Mufson, "China Steps Back From Diplomatic Row", *The Washington Post* (February 16, 1997): A35.
[8]Steven Mufson, "Premier Li Smooths Over Divisive Issues with U.S. as China's Congress Winds Up", *The Washington Post* (March 15, 1997): A24.
[9]Kevin Sullivan, "Defector Warns 2nd Korean War 'Dangerously Close'", *The Washington Post* (April 21, 1997): A12.

relationship among Beijing, Seoul and Pyongyang when approaching the 21st century and beyond.

The case of Hwang not only presented a drama in the dynamics of North-South relations in the Korean Peninsula, but also highlighted the diplomatic dilemma China has faced. China has always been regarded as a wild card in any analysis of North Korea's future. Beijing's dilemma began in the 1980s when China started the process of normalising relations with South Korea, while attempting to keep working relations with the North. Although Beijing showed extreme cautiousness toward this highly sensitive incident, the relative smooth transfer of Hwang from Beijing to Seoul has demonstrated the completion of the transitional process of China's Korea policy — from a pro-North polity to a balanced policy tilting toward the South. It took more than a decade for Beijing to complete this transition; and this change has profound significance not only to Chinese foreign policy, but also to international relations in the Asia-Pacific region.

To fully understand the shift of China's Korea policy, we need to look at least the following six factors:

- Changing priorities in Chinese foreign policy
- Balance of power in the region
- Economic modernisation
- Strategic stability
- Top leaders personal attachment
- Frustrations with the North

Changing Priorities in Chinese Foreign Policy

The most important factor behind the shift of Chinese foreign policy is the profound changes from the era of Mao Zedong to the era of Deng Xiaoping and the post-Deng era. This change of leadership marked the beginning of a new period in contemporary Chinese history. The era of Mao, which lasted from 1949 to 1976, was a radical revolutionary period highlighted by the Cultural Revolution, which caused what the Chinese Communist Party (CCP) itself has described as "the most severe setback and the heaviest losses ... since the founding of the People's Republic". The era of Deng (1978–1997), a period of pragmatism, has led to a "new situation in all fields of socialist modernisation".[10]

The Deng era (and the post-Deng era) can be regarded as a post-revolutionary era, clearly different from the Mao era in its national priorities and behaviour toward the rest of the world community. A revolutionary state conducts a 'continuous revolution' internally and externally, whereas a post-revolutionary state sets economic development as its first priority, thereby introducing 'a more mass-regarding political climate'.[11] A revolutionary state regards itself as an outsider trying to change the status quo within the international community, whereas a post-revolutionary state acts like an insider seeking maximum opportunities for its development from within the existing order. And a revolutionary state emphasises ideological considerations, whereas a post-revolutionary state believes that pragmatism better serves its national interests.

The transition of the Chinese leadership's interpretations and perceptions of China's internal and external environments has brought considerable changes in Beijing's foreign policy priorities. Such changes of world views frequently form the basis for determining priorities, or at least for determining how such enduring priorities as regime survival and the promotion of national interests can be best advanced.

China experienced a fundamental change from the era of revolution to the era of modernisation. Under Mao, the regime emphasised revolutionary objectives: dramatic and sweeping social reform in the domestic arena and survival as a communist nation in the international environment. This period was characterised by an emphasis on revolutionary ideology, a lack of respect for the prevailing international norms and extreme sensitivity to outside threats. This perception of external threats to the new Communist regime often led the Beijing leadership under Mao to meet perceived threats to security with military means.

[10]See Central Committee of the Communist Party of China, *Resolution on CPC History (1949–81)*, Beijing: Foreign Languages Press, 1981, p. 32.

[11]Brantly Womack, "The Party and the People: Revolutionary and Postrevolutionary Politics in China and Vietnam", *World Politics* 39, No. 4 (July 1987): 479–507.

In the post-revolutionary era, or the era of modernisation, China has moved beyond a single-minded preoccupation with world revolution. As the world becomes increasingly interdependent, particularly in terms of economic integration, the Beijing leadership has gradually recognised that the concept of regime survival has broader meanings. National security today is not only related to political and strategic issues, but also to economic development. Beijing, of course, recognised the importance of the economic aspect previously, but felt that economic security and development could be achieved in self-sufficient, classless, socialist fashion. Now the leadership has realised that economic development by necessity in this age also means 'economic interdependence' which requires less antagonistic world behaviour than Maoist ideology would prescribe. Deng Xiaoping has warned on several occasions that China may face the danger of losing its *qiuji* (global citizenship) if its economy fails to catch up with that of the rest of the world. The PRC leadership now has multiple goals for national development and places particular emphasis on economic development and modernisation.[12]

Deng's idea is that "by the middle of the next century", China should "have basically realised modernisation", and then it can be said that China "has succeeded".[13] The changing priorities in Chinese foreign policy in the Deng and post-Deng era has inevitably produced profound impact on Beijing's policy toward the two Koreas.

Balance of Power in the Region

In the early 1950s the PRC, inspired by its perceived threat of the invasion of Western imperialism, provided substantial military support to

[12]For detailed analyses of the changing priorities of Chinese foreign policy, see Chapter 3 of Quansheng Zhao, *Interpreting Chinese Foreign Policy*, Hong Kong and New York: Oxford University Press, 1996.

[13]See Deng Xiaoping, "With Stable Policies of Reform and Opening to the Outside World, China Can Have Great Hopes for the Future", September 4, 1989, in Deng Xiaoping, *Selected Works of Deng Xiaoping, Vol. 3 (1982–1992)*, Beijing: Foreign Languages Press, 1994, pp. 305–311.

the North Korean in its war with the South. The Korean War brought direct military confrontations between China and the United States. It is no doubt that strategic and political calculations dominated China's Korea policy. Beijing has also learned lessons from the war — in terms of casualties and political implications for Chinese foreign policy and the evolution of East Asian international relations, the war proved very costly for China.

With the changing international and domestic environments Beijing made substantial adjustment in its Korea policy. Despite its openly stated alignment with Pyongyang, China long ago ceased to support a North Korean military attack on the South since the complete withdrawal of its military forces from the North in 1958. Since the death of Mao, China has consistently expressed a particular interest in the creation and maintenance of a peaceful and stable situation in the Korean Peninsula, leading to the peaceful unification of North and South Korea.[14] Beijing, for example, hailed the talks that took place in September 1990 between North Korean Prime Minister Yon Hyoung Muk and South Korean Premier Kang Yong Hun as "a good beginning" that "will help alleviate tensions and promote the process of Korean reunification".[15] Beijing has also encouraged both Pyongyang and Seoul to create a nuclear-free Korean Peninsula,[16] considering the move would be in line with China's national interests.

While improving its relations with South Korea, the PRC nevertheless managed to maintain a workable relationship with the North. High-level bilateral visits took place virtually every year since the beginning of the Deng era. Political unrest in China and Eastern Europe in the late 1980s brought Beijing and Pyongyang closer together. Kim Il Sung was one of the few world leaders who openly supported Deng Xiaoping's military suppression of student demonstrations in 1989.

[14]Some scholars believe that from the security perspective, China would not want to see a united Korea. Chalmers Johnson, for example, argues that Beijing "prefers a structurally divided Korea that is unable to play its full role as a buffer between China, Russia, and Japan, thereby giving China a determining influence on the peninsula". See C. Johnson, "Korea and Our Asia Policy", *The National Interest*, No. 41 (Fall 1995), p. 67.

[15]"Korea's First High-Level Talks", *Beijing Review* 33, No. 39 (September 24–30, 1990): 15.

[16]Xu Baokang, "A Good Foundation for Solving the Nuclear Problem in the Korean Peninsula", *Renmin Ribao*, December 2, 1991, 6.

From the 1960s to the mid-1980s, Pyongyang was able to play the "Beijing card" against the "Moscow card", effectively preventing China from moving closer to Seoul. As the international situation changed, especially after the Soviet Union and Eastern European countries established diplomatic relations with South Korea, the PRC gained more freedom and confidence in expanding its relations with South Korea. Several events that took place in the year of 1990 were described in a *Beijing Review* article as indicative of South Korea shedding "the cloak of the Cold War". These events were the establishment of diplomatic relations between South Korea and the Soviet Union; three meetings of the prime ministers of North and South Korea; and the decision reached by China and South Korea to set up nongovernmental trade offices in each other's capitals. These developments are seen as part of the "realignment of relations among Asian nations".[17]

In fact, in the post-Cold War era beginning with the late 1980s Beijing has had strong incentives to develop relations with Seoul, because a closer relationship might increase China's leverage in dealing with the Korean problem and with East Asia as a whole. As one U.S. official in Washington suggests, "Having good relations with both [Koreas] puts China in the best possible situation" in world politics as well as regional affairs.[18]

Economic Modernisation

In the shift of Chinese foreign policy toward the two Koreans, modernisation as a major theme has played a leading role. China had long changed its priorities from political campaigning to economic modernisation. Economic development was one of Beijing's primary incentives for normalising relations with South Korea. China's modernisation programmes cannot be realised without extensive external

[17]Hu Xueze and Bing Jinhu, "World Situation Unstable Despite Detente", *Beijing Review* 34, No. 2 (January 14–20, 1991): 27–31.

[18]Nayan Chanda, "Chinese Welcome North Korea's Kim, But Relations are Subtly Changing", *The Asian Wall Street Journal Weekly*, October 21, 1991, 24 and 26.

support and exchanges from industrialised countries that can provide advanced technology, capital, markets, and managerial skills. South Korea was apparently a nearby supplier of these resources, in addition to Japan and Western powers, making China's suppliers more diversified.

Table 1. China's Trade with South Korea and North Korea (1980–1995).

(US$ millions)

Year	South Korea	North Korea
1980	188	678
1981	280	531
1982	139	585
1983	120	528
1984	434	498
1985	1161	488
1986	1289	510
1987	1679	513
1988	3087	579
1989	3143	563
1990	3821	483
1991	5812	610
1992	8218	697
1993	9078	890
1994	11660	624
1995	17000	550

Source: Compiled from Chae-Jin Lee, *China and Korea*, Stanford, CA: Hoover Institution, 1996, pp. 140 & 146; and Yu Meihua, "Chaoxian bandao xingshi ji zhongguo zhengce fenxi" [The Situation in the Korean Peninsula and China's Korea Policy], *Contemporary International Relations* (October 1996): p. 38.

Table 1 shows that South Korea has become increasingly important as a trading partner for China. In 1995, for example, China s trade with South Korean reached US$17 billion, 30 times more than its trade with North Korea of US$550 million.

In his November 1995 state visit to South Korea, President Jiang Zemin re-emphasised the importance of China's ties with South Korea.[19] As a newly industrialised country and a close neighbour, South Korea can also provide China with valuable experience and lessons in terms of economic development strategy, especially in "export-led" industrialisation. South Korean businessmen began to conduct direct investment and joint ventures in China. The actual investment in China increased quickly, from, for example, US$48.3 million in 1990 to US$474.6 million in 1993 (see Table 2).

The geographic distribution of South Korean investment in China has indicated that the South Korean investment are primarily concentrated in the Bohai Sea area, most notably in Shandong Province, and the Northeast region, totally accounted for 85.9 percent by the end of 1993 (see Table 3).

Table 2. South Korean Investment in China.

(1988–1993)

Item \ Year	1988–89	1990	1991	1992	1993	Total
Number of cases approved	11	35	107	260	630	1,043
Amounts approved (in millions of US dollars)	13.8	50.0	121.9	220.9	570.3	976.9
Actual investment (in million of US dollars)	12.8	48.3	91.0	168.6	153.9	474.6

Source: Chungguk Pyonram (China almanac) (1994), p.634. Quoted from Chae-Jin Lee, *China and Korea*, p. 156.

[19]*Renmin Ribao*, November 16, 1995, p. 1.

Table 3. Geographic Distribution of South Korean Investment In China.

(By the end of 1993)

	Number of cases approved	Percentage	Total amount (in thousands of US dollars)	Percentage
Bohai Sea area				
Shandong	293	28.1	374,331	38.3
Tianjin	109	10.5	131,053	13.4
Beijing	69	6.6	62,362	6.4
Hebei	27	2.6	23,553	2.4
Subtotal	498	47.7	591,299	60.5
Northeast region				
Liaoning	221	21.2	125,155	12.8
Jilin	99	9.5	46,186	4.7
Heilongjiang	79	7.6	76,990	7.9
Subtotal	399	38.3	248,241	25.4
Central China				
Jiangsu	44	4.2	45,897	4.7
Shanghai	19	1.8	18,612	1.9
Zhejiang	11	1.1	6,676	0.7
Subtotal	74	7.1	71,186	7.3
South China				
Guangdong	40	3.8	42,609	4.4
Fujian	10	1.0	16,195	1.7
Hainan	2	0.2	800	—
Subtotal	52	5.0	59,604	6.1
Other regions				
TOTAL	1,043	100.0	976,923	100.0

Source: Chungguk Pyonram (China almanac) (1994), p. 635; Quoted from Chae-Jin Lee, *China and Korea*, p. 161.

The first official step to enhance bilateral relations was the agreement to set up trade offices in each capital in October 1990. South Korea quickly appointed a former assistant foreign minister as the head representative of its trade office, and both offices formally opened in the spring of 1991, leading to the next year's normalisation of relationship between the two countries.

Strategic Stability

Since the opening of the Deng era, Beijing has consistently expressed interest in avoiding another major military conflict and, therefore, has a keen interest in the maintenance of a peaceful and stable environment in the Korea Peninsula. China has to make balanced actions between the two Koreas. To maintain warm relationship with both North and South Korea can strengthen China's leverage in international affairs.

It is believed that Beijing does have certain degree of influence on Pyongyang in terms its policy toward Seoul. In May 1991, for example, North Korea announced a dramatic reversal of its "one Korea" policy, saying that it would seek separate United Nations membership, which had been demanded by South Korea. Beijing is reportedly to have played a key role in Pyongyang's sudden shift, engaging in much behind-the-scenes maneuvre.[20] In late 1990, Beijing made it clear to Pyongyang that China would no longer commit itself next year to meeting North Korea's demand for a veto of any South Korean application to join the United Nations.[21] This is not only a reflection of China's difficult position in facing pressures from the international community, but also a de facto and effective ultimatum to press North Korea to change its position. In April and May of the following year, frequent consultations were held between Beijing and Pyongyang on the UN membership issue, including a visit by Chinese

[20]Damon Darlin, "North Korea Reverses Position on U.N., Seeks Admission Separately From South", *The Asian Wall Street Journal Weekly*, June 3, 1991, 18 and 23.

[21]Ted Morello, "Veto Vanishes: Thaw Clears Way to (United Nations) Membership for Koreas", *Far Eastern Economic Review* (December 5, 1990): 15.

Premier Li Peng to North Korea in early May.[22] Immediately after North Korea's announcement to seek separate UN membership, Li Peng commented that this move was "an interim measure before the unification", and would be "welcomed by the international community, including China".[23] The two Koreas now have separate UN memberships, a major step toward peaceful settlement in the Korea Peninsula.[24]

China's balanced act in the Korean Peninsula is also reflected in the controversial issue of nuclear development in North Korea. In the spring of 1994, the International Atomic Energy Agency (IAEA) under the United Nations unearthed fresh evidence of North Korea's clandestine nuclear programme; and IAEA director Hans Blix called the Yongbyon facility, which Pyongyang described as a radiochemical laboratory, "the most proliferation-sensitive facility" of North Korea's seven nuclear installations. Since then, Pyongyang was under tremendous pressure from Washington and Seoul, including possible economic sanctions from the international community, to further open its nuclear installations for international inspection.[25] While admitting that China did not have accurate information regarding North Korea's nuclear weapons development program,[26] Beijing would oppose an economic sanctions on Pyongyang. In meeting with South Korean President Kim Young Sam and Foreign Minister Han Sung Joo during their March 26–30 visit to Beijing, Chinese leaders made clear that it would oppose any economic sanctions on North Korea, and even be reluctant to go along with a resolution from the United Nations Security Council. Rather, Beijing would like to have more time to "work its persuasion on Pyongyang before any UN sanctions

[22]*World Journal*, April 12, 1991, 1.

[23]"Li Peng on Domestic and World Issues", *Beijing Review* 34, No. 26 (July 1–7, 1991): 24–29.

[24]It is interesting to note that the PRC has been firm in opposing Taiwan's UN membership, for fearing of the creation of "two Chinas".

[25]Nayan Chanda, "Seal of Disapproval", *Far Eastern Economic Review* (March 31, 1994): 14–15.

[26]"South Korea: Information Gap", *Far Eastern Economic Review* (April 21, 1994): 13.

are imposed". The PRC demanded that the Security Council should downgrade its plea for inspections of the North's nuclear installations from a resolution to a non-binding "statement". A vote on a resolution would require China to go on record with either a veto or an abstention. A statement requires no vote.[27]

On the other hand, Beijing, Washington, Tokyo, and Moscow have already reached a consensus on prohibiting the development of nuclear weapons in the Korean peninsula, particularly in North Korea. Such cooperation serves not only China's security interests, but also its economic interests.

The death of Kim Il Sung in July 1994 and his replacement by his son Kim Jong Il did not change China's policy toward the Korean peninsula. In his October–November 1994 visit to Seoul, Chinese Premier Li Peng assured South Korean President Kim Young Sam that China was positive toward the Geneva nuclear accord signed between North Korea and the United States in September.[28] Soon after, Chinese President Jiang Zemin also expressed "strong support" for the nuclear deal to U.S. President Bill Clinton when the two met at the APEC summit in Jakarta.[29] At the same time, Beijing indicated that it supported replacing the Panmunjom armistice with a permanent peace treaty — a position strongly supported by Pyongyang, but not Seoul at that time. These actions further demonstrated that China was "playing both sides of the Korean equation", and Beijing was "in favour of resolving the North's nuclear issue but without hurting its interests in the North".[30]

[27]"Making Haste Slowly: Seoul, Tokyo, Play up to Beijing on North Korean issue", *Far Eastern Economic Review* (April 7, 1994): 16. For a detailed analysis of China's assessment of North Korea, see Banning Garrett and Bonnie Glaser, "Looking Across the Yalu: Chinese Assessments of North Korea", *Asian Survey* 35, No. 6 (June 1995): 528–545.

[28]Shim Jae Hoon, "Sitting on the Fence", *Far Eastern Economic Review* (November 10, 1994): 15.

[29]"Beijing Backs North Korea Pact", *South China Morning Post* (November 15, 1994): p. 1.

[30]Shim Jae Hoon, "Sitting on the Fence", *Far Eastern Economic Review* (November 10, 1994): 15.

TOP LEADER'S PERSONAL ATTACHMENT

The changes in Beijing's top leadership have also played a significant role in the evolution of China's policy toward Korea, a policy that was significantly altered in September 1992, when China finally agreed to establish official diplomatic relations with South Korea. It had taken more than two years for Beijing to follow Moscow's lead in establishing relations with Seoul. In fact, both Pyongyang and Seoul have adopted a "dual-recognition" policy since mid-1950s. Up to the end of 1995, for example, there are 182 countries have diplomatic relations with South Korea, and 132 countries with the North; among which 127 countries have diplomatic ties with both North and South.[31] A major difficulty in establishing relations with South Korea was Beijing's old leadership's attachment to the North.

Historically, China and Korea shared complex and intimate relations, which was symbolised by a hierarchical tributary system. As Chae-Jin Lee points out, "Korea's tributary relations with China began as early as the fifth century, were regularised during the Koryo dynasty (918–1392), and became fully institutionalised during the Yi dynasty (1392–1910).[32] There were many significant interactions between the two countries during the past centuries.

In Korea's early history, for example, the Peninsula was divided into three kingdoms: Silla, Koguryo, and Paekche. In the seventh century, Silla, the kingdom located in the south, entered into a political and military alliance with China's Tang Dynasty, and in 668 A.D. unified the Korean Peninsula into a single country. During the unification process, the Chinese and the Silla state also repulsed a Japanese expedition sent to aid Paekche. From that time on, Korea remained a unified country, with only occasional and relatively brief periods of political division. The tributary relations

[31]Yu Meihua, "*Chaoxian bandao xingshi ji zhongguo zhengce fenxi*" [The Situation in the Korean Peninsula and China's Korea Policy], *Contemporary International Relations* (October 1996): p. 38.

[32]Chae-Jin Lee, *China and Korea: Dynamic Relations*, Stanford, CA: Hoover Institution, 1996, p. 1.

between China and Korea came to an end when China was defeated in the Sino-Japanese war of 1894–95, and was forced to sign the treaty of Shimonoseki with Japan. In 1910 Korea became a colony of Japan, which lasted until 1945 when Japan was defeated in World War II. In 1945 the Peninsula was once again divided, as a result of the beginning of the Cold War primarily between the two super-powers, the United States and the Soviet Union.

In the postwar era China did not get involved in the Korea affairs until October 1950, when the new Chinese Communist leadership made the momentous decision to cross the Yalu River and enter the Korean War, thereby placing itself in direct military confrontation with the United States. This conflict was to end in a military stalemate three years later. The casualties for both sides, the estimations for which vary, were tremendous with different estimations. According to Chinese statistics, the U.S. casualties reached 390,000, whereas the Chinese casualties were 366,000 with 115,000 dead and 221,000 wounded.[33] One other account claimed that the number of dead on the Chinese side alone reached about 400,000.[34] China's decision to enter the Korean War[35] had other lasting consequences for the Asia-Pacific region. It prompted President Harry Truman to order the U.S. Seventh Fleet into the Taiwan Straits to guarantee Taiwanese security, thereby internationalising the issue of Taiwan and making it a focus of future conflict between Beijing and Washington. The War also left the Korean Peninsula with the long-term legacy of North-South division.

[33]Deng Lifeng, *Jianguo hou junshi xingdong quanlu* [The complete records of China's military actions since 1949], Taiyuan: Shaanxi renmin chubanshe, 1994, pp. 312–313.

[34]Jonathan Adelman and Chih-yu Shih, *Symbolic War: The Chinese Use of Force, 1840–1980*. Taipei: Institute of International Relations, National Chengchi University, 1993, p. 189.

[35]There are many studies analyzing the Korean War. One may see, for example, Allen Whiting, *China Crosses the Yalu: The Decision to Enter the Korean War*, New York: The Macmillian Company, 1960; Bruce Cumings, The Origins of the Korean War (two volumes), Princeton: Princeton University Press, 1981 & 1990; Sergei Goncharov, John W. Lewis, and Xue Litai, *Uncertain Partners: Stalin, Mao, and the Korean War*, Stanford: Stanford University Press, 1993; and Jian Chen, *China's Road to the Korean War*, New York: Columbia University Press, 1994.

The intimate relations between Beijing and Pyongyang during and after the Korea War translated into personal ties at the micro level, which had considerable influence in the era of Deng, long time after the death of Mao. The Chinese attachment to North Korea throughout the 1980s was underpinned by personal ties and sympathies. Leaders such as Deng Xiaoping, Chen Yun, Yang Shangkun, Li Xiannian, Peng Zhen, Wang Zhen, and Bo Yibo held leading positions during the 1950s, and were personally involved to varying degrees in the Korean War. Their contemporaries in North Korea, headed by Kim Il Sung, also retained power. This decades-long-friendship was sustained and enhanced through frequent, mutual public or private visits.

After the Tiananmen Incident of 1989, the Chinese leadership under Deng Xiaoping felt strongly a need for Pyongyang's support for the survival of the Beijing communist regime. China and North Korea were isolated at that time both from the other remaining socialist countries and from the international community at large, and rely on each other for moral support. The collapse of Soviet Communism and the development of political democratisation and pluralisation in the former Soviet Union and Eastern Europe caused alarm in Beijing. In some countries, local Communist parties formally relinquished their monopoly of political power; in others, their power simply collapsed. Beijing's leaders were pleased to announce to the Chinese people that Kim Il Sung firmly supported the 1989 military crackdown against the student demonstrations that was ordered by Deng Xiaoping. When Kim Il Sung paid his 29th visit to China in October 1991,[36] this political and moral support was highlighted.

In the aftermath of the Tiananmen incident, the struggle for succession to political authority from the aging leadership became the predominant concern of the Chinese Communist Party. This struggle had a profoundly deadening effect on all aspects of Chinese domestic and foreign policy, rendering the formulation of new initiatives and imaginative policy virtually impossible. It was much more difficult for the Beijing leadership at that

[36]Lincoln Kaye, "Friend in Need", *Far Eastern Economic Review* (October 17, 1991): 14–15.

time to break or downplay its ties with North Korea than it was for Gorbachev, who shared with Kim Il Sung neither age nor personal ties. This could explain why Beijing was relatively slow in developing official relations with Seoul.

Since the beginning of the 1990s the influence of the elders in Chinese politics has gradually phased out. When key members of old revolutionaries, such as Deng Xiaoping, Chen Yun, Li Xiannian, Peng Zhen, and Wang Zhen, passed away, personal attachment at the highest levels between Beijing and Pyongyang became much less important. It is not surprising that Chinese foreign policy toward North Korea has now become more "business-like", rather than the old fashion of "comrades plus brothers".

Frustrations with the North

Although in general China maintained close relations with North Korea, there were sporadic quarrels between Beijing and Pyongyang during the past several decades — its nadir was in 1969 (the peak of the chaotic period of China's Cultural Revolution), when Chinese and North Korea forces clashed along their border. The relations were restored in the 1970s.

Since the 1980s, Beijing has long pushed for economic reform in North Korea, and it has long been rebuffed.[37] The China initiated Tumen River project, which was supported by UNDP, was to bring international players, such as Russia, North and South Korea, and Japan, to develop this strategically important area. In this way, the North Korean economy may be, at least partially, opened up, which will lead to further economic reform. But the response from Pyongyang has been cool.[38]

Beijing's frustration with Pyongyang was in line with the increasingly negative image of North Korea among the Chinese people. Many Chinese,

[37]Nayan Chanda, Shim Jae Hoon, and Peter Landers, "On Borrowed Time", *Far Eastern Economic Review* (June 26, 1997): 22–28.

[38]Observation based on the author's field trip to Hunchun City and the Tumen River area in China's Yanbian Korean Minority Autonomous Region, summer of 1995.

intellectuals and commoners alike, regarded today's North Korea as yesterday's China during the Cultural Revolution (1966–76). In contrast, public opinion toward South Korea became much more favourable since the 1980s. Pyongyang was unhappy with the changing attitude of Beijing. With Beijing further strengthening its ties with Seoul, there were signs in the mid-1990s that the Beijing-Pyongyang relationship appeared to become cool. In July 1995, for example, a North Korean official told an American group, members of a delegation of the New York-based Council on Foreign Relations who were visiting Pyongyang, "If you need to balance China's growing power, you should establish relations with us."[39] This comment could remind people of the balancing game played by North Korea between China and the Soviet Union during the 1970s and 1980s.

In 1995, South Korea suggested a four-power peace conference including the United States, China, and the two Koreas to work out a new peace agreement replacing the armistice, thereby bring a formal end to the 47-year-old Korean War. Initially, Pyongyang did not want the Chinese participation.[40] After prolonged negotiations with the United States and South Korea in New York in July 1997, North Korea finally agreed to hold the four-power conference on August 5, 1997.[41]

The biggest problem for North Korea since the beginning of the 1990s is its collapsing economy and serious food shortages. North Korea's economy since 1990 has been in negative growth for seven straight years, and its food shortages have reached tragic proportions (see Table 4). There is widespread famine in North Korea today: North Koreans exist on a daily ration of just 100 grams of corn a day, one-fifth the minimum daily requirement.[42]

Although China has become virtually the only external source of food and energy for North Korea since the Soviet Union fell in 1989, bilateral

[39]Nayan Chanda, "Lesser Evil", *Far Eastern Economic Review* (December 21, 1995): 17–18.
[40]Selig Harrison, "Promoting a Soft Landing in Korea", *Foreign Policy*, No. 106 (Spring 1997).
[41]"Pyongyang Accepts Framework for Peace Talks", *The Straits Times*, July 2, 1997, p. 21.
[42]Nayan Chanda, Shim Jae Hoon, and Peter Landers, "On Borrowed Time", *Far Eastern Economic Review* (June 26, 1997): 22–28.

Table 4. The Decline of the North Korean Economy (1990–96)

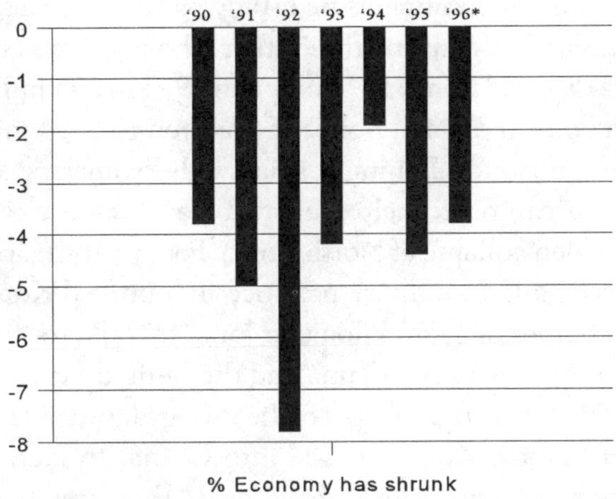

*Estimate by Korea Institute for National Unification
Source: Bank of Korea

North Korea's Food Shortage (1991–96)

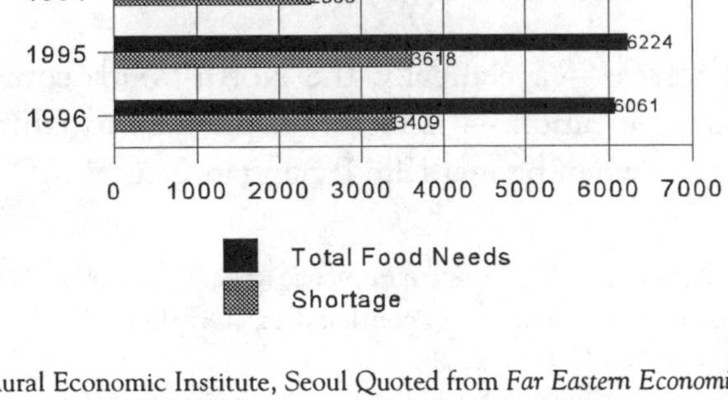

Source: Korea Rural Economic Institute, Seoul Quoted from *Far Eastern Economic Review*, June 26, 1997, p. 26.

economic exchanges between China and North Korea has nevertheless reduced. According to an unpublished study by the American Enterprise Institute's Nicholas Eberstadt and three other scholars, China's food exports to North Korea dropped from $149 million in 1993 to $55 million in 1994, and its coal and oil exports fell from $264 million to $194 million.[43]

Despite the frustration Beijing has had with Pyongyang and the limit that the Chinese can do to help North Koreas, China clearly does not want to see a sudden collapse of North Korea. For one thing, Beijing would adamantly oppose a U.S. military presence in a unified Korea along the China-Korean border of 1,400 kilometer long. It could set the stage for a serious confrontation between China and the United States.[44]

One other fear is that the collapse of the Pyongyang regime will certainly bring a flood of North Koran refugee into China. In fact, hundreds of North Koreans were reportedly to have made their way over the Sino-Korean border either by swimming or walking over the mountains. The flow of refugees was so great that South Korean consulates in Beijing and Hong Kong were swamped with requests for asylum. And many more refugees were caught by the Chinese and returned to North Korea, where severe punishment was awaiting. To prepare for the worse, China in spring 1997 built temporary shelters for about 100,000 people in Jilin Province; but worried that millions may flee into China from famine-stricken North Korea.[45]

FUTURE DIRECTIONS

The future of Korea — specifically, the North-South conflict and the issue of Korean unification — is closely connected to China. As Jiang Zemin emphasised when he met Kim Il Sung in October 1991: "China is

[43]Nayan Chanda, "Lesser Evil", *Far Eastern Economic Review* (December 21, 1995): 17–18.
[44]Nayan Chanda, Shim Jae Hoon, and Peter Landers, "On Borrowed Time", *Far Eastern Economic Review* (June 26, 1997): 22–28.
[45]Mary Jordan, "Fearing Deluge, Political Fallout, China Spurns Fleeing N. Koreans", *The Washington Post* (April 14, 1997): A14.

concerned about the situation on the Korean Peninsula, since detente and stability in this region has a direct bearing on the overall situation in northeast Asia."[46] With regard to the future directions of Chinese foreign policy toward the two Koreas, the following additional points need to be addressed.

Links between China and Korea

Chinese interest in the Korean Peninsula has been based on the combined factors of the consideration of national interest and the historical connections. Although the Korea of today is substantially different from the Korea of the past, both domestically and internationally, there are clear links between China and Korea.

The Korea problem has always remained an important consideration in Chinese foreign policy in both strategic and economic dimensions, and vice versa. Indeed, China has been actively involved in the conflicts related to Korea, the most notable of these, as discussed earlier, being the Korean War of 1950–53. It is clear that China and the United States are the two leading powers today that have maintained significant influence over the Korean conflict.

In addition, the historical ties between China and Korea may provide a ground for cooperation. Each side, for instance, may regard the other as a counterweight to the increasing economic and military strength of Japan. This possibility was confirmed by the fact that Japan's past experience of militarism was jointly condemned by China's Jiang Zemin and South Korea's Kim Young Sam, during Jiang's state visit to Seoul in November 1995.[47]

One other link is that both the Chinese and the Koreans have always had a strong sense of political continuity and a keen desire for national

[46]"North Korea Leader Pays 39th China Visit", *Beijing Review* 34, No. 41 (October 14–20, 1991): 7.

[47]"*Zhonghan tongsheng ling riben shise*" [Both China and South Korea criticised Japan], *Yazhou Zhoukan* [The international Chinese newsweekly], November 26, 1995, p. 24.

unification; therefore, the unification issue in both countries has always occupied central positions in both countries' domestic politics and foreign policy. In this regard, we need to consider the Taiwan factor in Sino-Korean relations.

It is known that the PRC has always adhered to certain principles regarding its own unification policy towards Taiwan. Since its establishment in 1949, the Beijing government has insisted that whenever the PRC establishes diplomatic relations with another nation, that nation must explicitly recognise that there is only one China, that Taiwan is a part of China, and that Beijing is the sole representative of China. When the PRC opens diplomatic relations with another country, that country must cut off relations with Taiwan. Conversely, when Taiwan sets up relations with another country, Beijing severs its relations with that country to avoid a "two Chinas" situation. This principle has been consistently upheld because it is crucial to regime legitimacy in both the international community and domestically. When South Korea established its diplomatic relations with PRC in 1992, it had to cut off official relations with Taiwan.

While actively promoting relations and contacts with Taipei, Beijing is extremely sensitive about the "Taiwan independent" movement, which has increased its influence within and outside of the Taiwan Island in recent years. Any move toward strengthening relations with Taipei from either Seoul or Pyongyang will jeopardise its relations with Beijing. This concern has been demonstrated by the unhappiness of the PRC toward a controversial plan between Taiwan and North Korea to ship Taiwan's nuclear waste for storage in North Korea in early 1997. As some experienced Asia watchers put it, "North Korea knows all too well that its most important patron can be extremely testy when it comes to any fancy Taiwanese maneuvers."[48] Although it is unlikely that North Korea will develop close ties with Taiwan under current conditions, it is not unimaginable that Pyongyang may use its relations with Taiwan as a card to play when it feels necessary.

[48]Charles Lee and Julian Baum, "Radioactive Ruckus, Nuclear-waste Plan Comes Between Taipei and Seoul", *Far Eastern Economic Review* (February 6, 1997): 16.

The Involvement of Other Powers

China's keen interest in the development of the two Koreas is also accentuated by the involvement of other three powers in the Asia-Pacific region, namely the United States, Japan, and Russia. According to a Chinese assessment, in the foreseeable future the United States, with its 37,000 troops in South Korea, will continue to play a major role in the Korean Peninsula. Japan will be a close follower of the United States, and will actively pursue its own interests, particularly in the security and economic dimensions. Russia has developed close ties with South Korea and attempted to restore its warm relations with the North. But since Russia itself is still in the recovery process, it is unlikely that Russia will play a major role in this region in the near future.[49]

China's main concern is the United States. In Washington there has been advocates of a "soft landing" in Korea — a gradual process of unification in which neither side is swallowed up by the other and the United States helps North Korea to achieve a China-style economic reform.[50] Beijing has had deep suspicion toward the role played by the United States. It does not believe that the U. S. would really want to solve the Korean problem.[51] As discussed earlier, China would not want to see a U.S. military presence in a unified Korea along the China-Korean border. As such, it is necessary for the two countries to further develop confidence-building measures, and to coordinate routing consultations between Beijing and Washington over the issue of Korea. These mechanisms are extremely important to both China and the United States, as well as to the interests of the two Koreas.

[49] Yu Meihua, "*Xin shiqi mei ri er dui chaoxian bandao zhengce tedian jiqi zoushi*" [The Korea Policies of the United States, Japan, and Russia in the New Era and Future Directions], *Contemporary International Relations* (January 1997): 32–35

[50] Selig Harrison, "Promoting a Soft Landing in Korea", *Foreign Policy*, No. 106 (Spring 1997).

[51] Yu Meihua, "*Xin shiqi mei ri er dui chaoxian bandao zhengce tedian jiqi zoushi*" [The Korea Policies of the United States, Japan, and Russia in the New Era and Future Directions], *Contemporary International Relations* (January 1997): 33.

THE KOREAN MINORITIES IN CHINA AND THE BORDER ISSUE

Although Sino-South Korean relations have developed rapidly, there are also problems between the two countries. Their differing political systems and levels of economic development, as well as historical legacies, are sure to contribute to the friction. Let us look at the Korean minorities in China and potential territorial disputes along the China-Korean border as two examples.

There are about two million Korean minorities in China, most of whom live in the bordering Jilin Province. The most well-known Chinese-Korean community area is the Yanbian Korean Minority Autonomous Region. In general, this large number of Korean minorities have played positive roles in facilitating Sino-South Korean relations. But as the bilateral relations further developed in the past years, some problems have emerged. A sizable Chinese-Koreans have been "recruited" to South Korea to work as a way of making quick money. By the end of 1996, there were more than 77,000 Chinese working in South Korea, more than half of whom were illegal residents. Furthermore, a few South Korean swindlers went to the Korean-Chinese communities in Yanji, Changchun, and Harbin to "recruit" labours or to "make investment" there. These "recruiters" or "investors" disappeared as soon as they collected fees and funds from the local Chinese-Koreans. The total losses of the Chinese-Korean community is estimated to be as high as RMB 280 million (about US$30 million).[52]

One alarming development is that a few South Korean visitors even openly advocated that these Korean-Chinese regions were actually parts of Korean territory. Some South Koreans have indicated that the issue of the China-Korean border will be opened up once Korea achieves its national unification.[53] These problems prompted Chinese Premier Li Peng to ask South Korean government to exercise more "self-control", when he

[52]"*Nanhan pianzi pian chaoxian tongbao*" [South Korean swindlers cheat minority Koreans in China], *Yazhou Zhoukan* [The international Chinese newsweekly], November 25–December 1, 1996, pp. 50–51.

[53]The author's field trip to South Korea, summer 1994.

met the visiting South Korean Prime Minister Lee Hongkoo in Beijing in 1995.[54]

In fact, Beijing and Seoul have already begun to work on drawing a border between their countries across the Yellow Sea. Up to the summer of 1997, China and South Korea have held negotiations on an agreement on the water border, because the Yellow Sea between them is as narrow as 200 miles; U. N. Convention gives countries exclusive rights to marine resources within 230 miles of their shores. There have been different claims over the water border between the two countries.[55]

In conclusion, with the changing international and domestic environments, the PRC has changed its Korea policy substantially. China's Korea policy has gradually moved from a pro-North position to balanced actions between the two Koreas, tilting toward the South. The shift of China's Korea policy has profound implications to international relations in the Asia-Pacific area. China today has continued to be a leading external player (along with the United States) in the Korean Peninsula. Since its Korea policy is a balanced one, China has been regarded as a wild card in Korea's uncertain future. It is believed that there is still a danger of military confrontation between China and the United States if the issue of Korea (the sudden collapse of North Korea, for example) were not handled well. It is, therefore, in the interests of Beijing and Washington to maintain and enhance the communication channels between the two countries. On the other hand, since China's policy is leaning toward the South, China, as a Pentagon Korea observer in his analysis of war scenarios argues, "would not directly support the North unless Seoul was clearly the aggressor".[56]

[54]"*Nanhan pianzi pian chaoxian tongbao*" [South Korean swindlers cheat minority Koreans in China], *Yazhou Zhoukan* [The international Chinese newsweekly], November 25–December 1, 1996, pp. 50–51.

[55]"South Korea, China to Hold Talks", The Associated Press, June 23, 1997.

[56]Lonnie Henley, "A War Scenario, Korean Cataclysm", *The Washington Post* (May 4, 1997): C1 & C4.

Is China a Threat to the Asia-Pacific Region?

SHEE Poon Kim
Visiting Professor, Institute of International and Area Studies, Seoul National University

In March 1996, when China launched a military exercise along its southern coast, firing missiles over the Straits of Taiwan, questions about China's future militaristic behaviour as a result of its impressive economic growth and growing military capabilities were raised. Many western analysts predict that China will emerge as an economic superpower in the 21st century.[1] Given China's rising power, it is legitimate to ask whether China is going to emerge as a hegemon and pose a threat to the countries in the Asia-Pacific region.

There are two schools of thought appearing in the literature of international relations on China's increasingly important role in international politics. The first is the realist[2] school of thought which argues

[1]William Overholt, *China: The Next Economic Superpower* (London: Weidenfeld and Nicolson, 1993).

[2]Some of the threat proponents (realists) are as follows: Denny Roy, 'Hegemon on the Horizon?: China's Threat to East Asian Security', *International Security*, Vol. 19, No. 1 (Summer 1994); Nicholas D. Kristof, 'China's Rise', *Foreign Affairs*, Vol. 72, No. 5 (November/December 1993); Richard Bernstein and Ross H. Munro, 'The Coming Conflict

that China is a threat and will be a future hegemon in the Asia-Pacific region. The neo-liberals, on the other hand, argue that China is not a threat and has no hegemonic ambitions. The focus of this essay is to analyse the meaning and the bases of the so-called 'China threat', by examining the arguments of both the threat and the non-threat proponents.[3] The pertinent questions to be asked are: what is the meaning and nature of the so-called 'China threat'? What are the bases of the arguments by both the threat and the non-threat proponents regarding the 'China threat'? Are these arguments valid?

DEFINING THE CHARACTERISTICS OF THE 'CHINA THREAT'

What exactly constitutes a threat? A threat can be defined as a declaration of intention of an individual to punish, hurt or cause trouble or danger to others. At the state level for example, state A is considered to pose a threat to state B if the former contemplates to use coercive measures or acts to undermine the basic national interests of state B.

How do the states in the Asia-Pacific region regard China as a threat? One can approach this question from three perspectives, i.e. cognitive, affective and evaluative.[4]

with America', *Foreign Affairs* (March 1997); Michael Yahuda, *The China Threat* (Malaysia: Institute of Strategic and International Studies, 1986); Gerald Segal, 'East Asia and the Constrainment of China', *International Security*, Vol. 20, No. 4 (Spring 1996).

Some of the non-threat proponents (neo-liberals) are as follows: Michael G. Gallagher, 'China's Illusory Threat to the South China Sea', *International Security*, Vol. 19, No. 1, Summer 1994; Robert S. Ross, 'Beijing As a Conservative Power', *Foreign Affairs*, March 1997; Joseph S. Nye, 'Wise For Us to Engage China as a Responsible Power', *The Straits Times* (Singapore) 16 September 1997, p. 44; Tom Plate, 'Sino-Summit Should Aim for Concrete Results', *The Straits Times*, 13 September 1997.

[3]Lee Francis, A., *China Superpower: Requisites for High Growth* (New York: MacMillan, St. Martin Press, 1997).

[4]For the concept of cognition, affection and evaluation, see G.A. Almond and S. Verba, *The Civil Culture* (Boston: Little Brown, 1965), pp. 1–44.

Cognitive Perspective

The cognitive perspective refers to the understanding, knowledge and perception of China's intention and behaviour by those who perceive China as a threat. Perception is the basis of a behavioural response. However, what is being perceived may not necessarily transform into concrete or systematic responsive behaviour (such as policy outputs) because there is invariably a gap between cognition and behavioural responses. At any rate, perceptions of a threat can vary from state to state, i.e., what is perceived to be a threat for state A, e.g. Vietnam, may not be a threat for state B, e.g. Thailand. The logic of this reasoning leads us to conclude that the perception of a threat can be subjective and is conditioned by memories of history or prejudice. In other words, cognitive perspectives may consist of rationality or irrationality, depending on the particular individual or state.

Affective Perspective

The affective dimension refers to the extent of the action taken by one state against another. Thus, the responses from those who are affected vary, depending on the nature of the relationship. For example, countries which are further away from China due to geographical distance, such as Brunei, may be less threatened by China as compared to Vietnam which is closer to China. Thus, because of the geographical proximity, the impact of the so-called 'China threat' for Vietnam can be stronger compared to Brunei or Indonesia. However, the perception of a threat may not necessarily be shaped by geographical proximity alone because the policy adopted by a distant superpower may adversely affect the basic national interests of a distant weaker power. The insistence on human rights practices by the US against the State Law and Order Restoration Council (SLORC) of the Myanmar military government can be perceived as a threat to the military regime in Myanmar.

EVALUATIVE PERSPECTIVE

Evaluative perspective refers to the judgement of the decision-makers who shape the foreign policy outputs of states. Ultimately, the state concerned has to make a decision whether China is really a threat or not. The evaluative perspective is the cumulative effect of both the cognitive and the affective perspective. In other words, cognition and affection are bases of evaluation.

It is pertinent to note that the so-called 'China threat' can be divided into six categories, i.e. ideological, political, economic, military-cum security, ethnic and cultural.

Firstly, ideology can be a threat due to conflicts of ideas or beliefs and the imposition of ideology by one state against others. Maoist communism, for example, was perceived as a threat to all of the anti-communist ASEAN states in the 1960's. Mao's promotion of communist revolutionary ideology during the period of the Cultural Revolution (1966–1976) and the CCP's support of the communist insurgencies in Southeast Asia were viewed by the ASEAN states as serious ideological and security threats to Southeast Asia.[5]

In the post-cold war era, however, the ideology of nationalism and Chinese irredentist thinking appear to have replaced Chinese communism as the dominant ideology in China. Does nationalism as a form of ideology pose a threat to neighbouring states? Nationalism can be a double-edged sword because extreme nationalism can lead to fascism and expansionism as was the case in the 1930's with Japan and Germany. However, nationalism can also be a positive ideology as it can strengthen national feelings of unity among its people. It can also be used as a driving force for economic growth, as was the case with Japan after World War Two. Nationalism was used by the Japanese political elites to mobilise political concensus for its economic reconstruction and development.

Secondly, a political threat can be defined as an attempt by a state to arbitrarily intervene in the internal affairs of another state so as to seek

[5]See Shee Poon Kim, 'Insurgency in Southeast Asia', *Problems of Communism*, May–June 1983, pp. 45–55.

political influence and domination against the will of another state. China's efforts to influence Vietnam's occupation of Cambodia from 1979 to 1989 was perceived as a political threat by Hanoi.

Thirdly, an economic threat is the utilisation of economic resources by a state with the intention to compete, manipulate and exploit the economic resources of another state at the expense of its economy. It can be argued that the so-called 'China threat' looks more like an economic rather than a military threat to the NIEs and industrialised economies because China has a huge number of low-wage earning workers and cheap exports which can undermine the jobs of workers and living standards of other states.[6]

Fourthly, a military-cum-security threat can be defined as an attempt by a state to influence, dominate or undermine the security and independence of another state through the use of force or via the possession of force capabilities. China's military exercise in the Fujian province in March 1996 which was aimed at Taiwan, was perceived as a serious military threat by Taiwan's President, Lee Teng Hui.

Fifthly, the ethnic threat can be defined as the challenge or domination of an ethnic group who is in the majority over an ethnic group who is in the minority. Due to the huge size of China's population of more than 1.2 billion, there is a potential fear of the 'yellow peril' threat, namely should there be a major collapse in the country's economic development, or colossal natural catastrophes, there could be a possible massive mass exodus.[7]

Last, a cultural threat can be defined as the imposition of one's cultural values (including religious values) upon others. Is Huntington correct in asserting that the clash of civilisations is due to deep irreconcilable cultural differences between the East and the West? Is Chinese culture a threat to the Asia-Pacific region?

[6]See Reginald Dale, 'China's Rise as a New Great Power Looking Positive', *The Straits Times*, 20 September 1997.

[7]Thousands of illegal migrants to Japan for example, have given rise to the concern of undermining the country's homogeneous social fabric. Thus Japan is concerned that China might pose a potential 'human threat'.

BASES OF CHINA'S THREAT

What are the bases of those threat proponents who argue that China is a threat and will be a rising regional hegemon in the 21st century?

Economic Bases of the 'China Threat'

The threat proponents argue that there is a positive correlation between growing economic power and a more assertive militaristic behaviour. The logic of the argument is that growing economic power[8] would in turn fuel greater efforts towards strengthening military power. Thus a militarily strong China would not hesitate to dictate regional order and would be less inclined to cooperate with other actors in the region because it has the military prowess and economic clout to lay down the terms and conditions for inter-state relations. They also point out to the historical example of Imperial China's hegemony during the Ming period[9] (1405–1433) as an argument to support the 'China threat' theory, notwithstanding the official assurance that 'China does not seek hegemony now nor will it do so in the future, even when it is economically developed'.[10]

Secondly, the threat proponents argue that China is also prone to use force in the region. This proneness for armed struggle mentality can be seen from China's 1979 limited war with Vietnam and the naval armed skirmishes over the Paracels in 1974 and the Spratlys in March 1988. Indeed, since 1949, the PLA has not hesitated from time to time to use force to attain its political objectives as it did recently when firing missiles

[8]See Denny Roy, *op. cit.*, p. 160.

[9]For China's supremacy over the sea, see Louise Levathes, *China Ruled the Seas: The Treasure Fleet of the Dragon Throne 1405–1433*, (New York: Simon and Schuster, 1994); see also Jane K. Leonard, *Wei Yuan and China's Rediscovery of the Maritime World*, (Cambridge: Harvard University Press, 1984).

[10]This statement was made by Chinese Foreign Minister Qian Qichen in Michael Richardson, 'China Said to Court Asians as a Buffer Against US', *International Herald Tribune*, 24–25 July 1993.

over the Taiwan Straits in February/March, 1996. Thus the 'threat' proponents conclude that 'China has shown its willingness to use force to settle disputes even when its own territory is not under attack.[11] Besides the 'war-proneness' mentality of the PLA, the 'threat' proponents argued that China has an advantage in its military buildup efforts because it has relatively few constraints hampering its build up of military power.[12] Japan's military buildup inescapably will incur suspicion, apprehension and fear, while China's military buildup has been tolerated by the international community.[13] The net outcome then would be a growing imbalance of power between Japan and China not only in military terms, but also in economic terms. Furthermore, China has one great advantage, i.e. its 'overseas Chinese connection', with more than fifty million people living abroad, whereas Japan does not have this advantage. This connection will lead to an increase of Chinese economic power in the Asia-Pacific region which may heighten the possible fear of the 'yellow peril' from the neighbouring states.

Thirdly, the threat proponents argue that an authoritarian political system has a propensity to be more aggressive. China's domestic characteristics make it comparatively likely to use force to achieve its political goals.[14] In other words, China's authoritarian political system is unlikely to promote a long term peaceful foreign policy. The logic of this argument is that a democratic state has a better chance to produce a peaceful foreign policy than an authoritarian one. From the threat proponents' perspective, economic liberalism does not necessarily result in political liberalism, as could be seen from the 1989 Tiananmen incident. Furthermore, the threat proponents argue that an authoritarian style of political leadership is potentially unstable, and this is even more so in the case of China as the Chinese political system is ruled by men and not by political institutons, and political succession can therefore be potentially problematic. David Shambaugh argues that China 'may become more

[11]Denny Roy, *op. cit.*, p. 156.
[12]Denny Roy, *ibid.*, p. 156.
[13]Denny Roy, *ibid.*, p. 155.
[14]Denny Roy, *ibid.*, p. 150.

confrontational if it becomes more fragmented internally.[15] China has no internal constraints to use force, whereas Japan is hampered by domestic impediments, such as article 9 of the Constitution.

Ideologically, the Chinese leaders are communists whose core values are based on the notion of 'struggle', besides, they are embedded with growing nationalistic feelings and irredentist thinkings. Hence on the issue of protecting its sovereignty, as is the case regarding the unification of Taiwan, China has repeatedly threatened to use force as a means to achieve its political objective; especially in matters involving territorial disputes and national pride and prestige, where scarce resources, such as oil in the South-China Sea, are concerned.

The temptation to use force to achieve its foreign policy objectives would be even more desirable if China is becoming economically more affluent and militarily more powerful.

The 'threat' proponents argue that China is a dissatisfied power as it has been historically humiliated since 1840. A frustrated state is therefore more likely to challenge the status quo of the international order, like Germany did in the 1930's.[16] Thus China is a potentially destabilising actor in international relations. China is different from Japan as the latter has enjoyed the fruits of economic success and a relatively stable democratic order. Further, the threat proponents argue that China is more likely than Japan to be a regional threat to East Asian security.[17] In short, since the collapse of the Sino-centric world in the mid-19th century, China has been a frustrated power for more than one hundred and fifty years, and it is thus hoping to change the existing international order in its favour, if necessary by using threats and if necessary force or coercive diplomacy.

To sum up, the 'threat' proponents conclude that since states are still concerned about their relative gains in international competitions, they

[15]David Shambaugh, 'China's Security Policy in the Post-Cold War Era', *Survival*, Vol. 34, No. 2 (Summer 1992), p. 89. See also Denny Roy, *op. cit.*, p. 161.

[16]John Garver, "Will China Be Another Germany?" (Pennsylvania: Carlisle Barracks, US Army War College National Strategy Institute, 1996).

[17]Denny Roy, *op. cit.*, p. 149.

advocate that a potential threat to the regional order by China cannot be simply dismissed.

Bases of the Non-Threat Arguments

The 'non-threat' proponents argue that China does not pose a threat to the regional order in the Asia-Pacific region. This argument is based on the following premises:

Deficiency in Military Capability

The 'non-threat' proponents argue that China does not have the military capability to project itself as an aggressive hegemon because of its deficient military capability. At the moment, only the US has the military capability to shape the regional order in the Asia-Pacific region. It is doubtful, for example, that China has the naval capability to control the South China Sea in the foreseeable future since both the US and Japan insist on 'innocent passage' and freedom of navigation through the South China Sea. Thus China does not have adequate military power to deter or block the strategic presence of the major powers in Southeast Asia in general, and the South China Sea in particular. In any case, China will not behave like an irresponsible hegemon since it is willing to abide by the principles of the International Law of the Sea. Thus the advocation of China being a potential threat from the military power perspective is not convincing.

A Strong and Prosperous China is a Peaceful and Stable China

The non-threat proponents argue that a strong and prosperous China is likely to be a peaceful and stable rather than a threatening power. This argument is based on the assumption of the dynamics of economic interdependence. The more China integrates into the international economic system, the less likely is China to become an aggressive hegemon because an aggressive hegemonistic China will bring about a loss in huge foreign investments and markets thus undermining its own economic interests, especially its goals of economic modernisation. As long as China recognises the importance of interdependence, it will not indulge in hegemonistic and harmful behaviour towards its neighbours.

Internal Rather than External Considerations Direct the Day

The third 'non-threat' argument is based on the assumption that the most important priority of China's policies is propelled by internal rather than by external considerations. China's foreign policy, especially its external security policy is primarily internally — rather than externally-driven, concentrating mainly on internal economic modernisation. Foreign policy is an offshoot of its internal imperatives. Thus, it is in China's paramount interest to preserve an external stable regional environment rather than embarking upon aggressive hegemonistic behaviour and destabilising the regional order.

International Constraints: The US Factor

The 'non-threat' proponents such as Michael Gallagher argue that the US factor is important, as it affects the overall regional dynamics in the East Asia region.[18] Although the US has shifted from a policy of containment in the 1960's to a policy of engagement in the post-cold war era, one of the objectives of the US foreign policy is to deny the rise of any regional hegemon in East Asia. One can argue that the US motivation in seeking a military alliance with Japan has been to ensure that both China and Japan will not emerge as regional hegemons in the Asia-Pacific region,

[18]Michael Gallagher, 'China's Illusory Threat to the South China Sea', *International Security*, Vol. 19, No. 1 (Summer 1994), pp. 169–194.

challenging its supremacy in East Asia. Although the US has publicly declared that the 1954 Manila Pact does not legally oblige the US to render military assistance to the Philippines in case of a Chinese attack in the South China Sea, it would be a mistake for China not to take into consideration a possible strong US response. In any case, China has of late shown flexibility in resolving the South China Sea disputes, as it has even shown willingness to shelve the sovereignty disputes and to stress on joint cooperation instead.

The fallacy of the 'threat' proponents' argument is that they have not taken into consideration China's self-imposed constraints. Joseph Nye has a point in arguing that 'given the priority Beijing attaches to economic modernisation and reliance of the Chinese economy on external markets and resources, China faces a constraints of its own making.[19] Thus the 'threat' proponents have not taken into consideration that China has been facing massive domestic constraints, so much so that one can make a strong case against China using force as an instrument in resolving inter-state disputes. Furthermore, for China to launch an aggressive militaristic policy towards its neighbours may lead to intense internal debates within the Chinese Communist Party (CCP) which could bring about a split in the leadership. It is questionable whether Jiang Zemin is in a strong position to seek the necessary political consensus to mount an aggressive foreign policy such as Deng did in February 1979 by 'teaching Vietnam a lesson'. Thus it can be argued that the 'China threat' theory is based on a misconception about China's priorities, military capability as well as defence spending.

An Illusionary Threat

Finally, the 'non-threat' proponents argue that the so-called 'China threat' is more apparent than real. It is a psychological illusion aimed at fuelling a self-fulfilling prophecy. It is true that China was aggressive in some

[19]Joseph Nye, *op. cit.*, p. 44.

instances, but this should not necessarily lead to the conclusion that China will emerge as an aggressive hegemon destabilising the regional order. The 'threat' proponents' argument is self-fulfilling in the sense that it may inadvertently provoke China to be an aggressive hegemon because it may be forced into a situation whereby it has no choice but to be aggressive. Thus the outcome could create a new serious problem which did not exist in the first place. Hence, the anti-China hardline policy adopted by the West may result in China becoming a reluctant aggressive hegemon. In any case, the non-threat proponents argue that the 'China threat' is nothing but an illusion.[20]

ASSESSMENT: THE LOGIC OF ARGUMENTS

The perception whether China is posing a threat or is going to pose a threat to its neighbouring states can be subjective, relative and according to changing circumstances. A threat can be subjective in the sense that it can be a psychological spin-off from past negative historical experiences. What is perceived to be a threat for state A, may not be necessarily one for state B. For example, despite China's efforts to normalise diplomatic relations since Vietnam's withdrawal of its troops from Cambodia in 1989, Vietnam still perceives China's growing military and economic power as a threat to its national security. Vietnam's anxiety, apprehension and perception of China as a rising hegemon, is partly shaped by historical negative images, as it was colonialised by China for more than one thousand years, and partly because of its geographical proximity so much so that at times, it feels threatened to be a neighbour of China.

On the other hand, Singapore does not perceive China as a hegemon posing a threat to the island Republic's security and least not as a threat to Singapore's survival. On the contrary, it perceives China as a great trading partner, providing golden opportunities to do business. China has proved to be an important partner for joint development projects, such as the Suzhou Industrial Park.

[20]Michael Gallagher, *op. cit.*, p. 169.

Indonesia, being the natural leader of Southeast Asia, by virtue of its size and population, especially in the maritime area of Southeast Asia, perceives China's growing assertiveness towards the South China Sea, not only as taking on the role of a 'trespasser'[21] but also as challenging Indonesia's leadership in the archipelago. Although Indonesia under President Suharto's leadership has changed its perception of the China threat in the 1960's to that of a non-threat perception in the post-cold war era, Indonesia nevertheless perceives China's rising power with growing concern, especially its long-term ambition to become a maritime superpower. Malaysia is another example, where the argument holds true, that the threat perception by the same decision-maker changed over time. Prime Minister Mahathir for example perceived China as a threat in 1981 when he assumed power, yet the same leader changed his perception towards China drastically in the 1990's. ASEAN too, which was suspicious of China in the 1960's, has now accepted China which is presently an important dialogue partner in the ASEAN Regional Forum.

A distinction can be made between a threat and a force. A threat can be applied in various forms and different ways without resorting to violence. Furthermore a larger state may not necessarily pose a direct threat to the smaller neighbouring state unless the former has the superior military capability to use force. Thus a state is not a threat to others without having the necessary capability to exercise force. Furthermore, the so-called 'China threat' has to be qualified in the first place to ascertain whether the state has the real intention to use force. To argue that a hegemon will pose a threat to others will not be a sufficient argument unless one is certain of its intention to do so. For example, one can ask the following questions: firstly, does China have the intention to be a hegemon? Secondly, does China have the will to be a hegemon even if it has the intention? Thirdly, does China have effective means to be a hegemon? Fourthly, would the threat against other states achieve its desirable objective? Finally, a valid question to be asked is: does the international community view China as a hegemon? Will they allow China to get away with it should it use force? What are the

[21]Michael Yahuda, *op. cit.*, pp. 9–15.

implications of China's relations with other major powers if China poses a threat to other states? Threats carry costs. How far is China willing to bear the costs if its threats transform to real military operations?

The arguments of the threat proponents have a valid point, namely that China's political power is likely to expand because China's economy and military capabilities are growing and expanding. However, they overemphasize or overplay the China threat because China's most important priority since 1978 and in the foreseeable future, is and will be on internal economic modernisation rather than on expanding China's power abroad. In fact, one of the major problems for China today is how to feed and satisfy the rising expectation of its growing population of about 1.2 billion people.[22] Thus, it is premature to conclude that an economically powerful China will pose a threat to others.

The argument that China is a hegemon which poses a direct threat to other states, loses ground when its military capability is brought to light since it is inferior to other major powers, such as Japan and not to mention the US. Furthermore, it is not clear whether the Chinese leaders and the people want to make China a military superpower at the expense of economic modernisation. This is because the desire to succeed in its economic modernisation makes it necessary to give the lowest priority to the allocation of resources for military modernisation in its overall policy decisions. The Chinese people are now enjoying the fruits of economic growth, why should they sacrifice their hard earned wealth for the sake of military adventurism. Given the limited resources available, China would not want to use them to propel itself into the superpower league and least of all, not the maritime superpower category, to compete with other major powers for global leadership role or hegemony. Given the fact that China is still a developing economy, the possibility of China posing a threat to the region is low.

It is questionable whether China can be a regional hegemon in the South China Sea since its naval capability is still inferior to that of Japan and the US. China's efforts to modernise its navy is primarily for defense

[22]The number is expected to reach 1.5 billions by the year 2040.

purposes to safeguard its national interests, but not to aim at becoming a maritime 'policeman' in the South China Sea. If China wants to be a hegemon, it must have the political will, the military capability and the economic might and last but not least a hegemon as such must be proven, recognised and be accepted by the international community. This was and is the case for the US which has been accepted as being the only world hegemon in the post-cold war era.

Is China really a threat? From the US' perspective, China will be a threat because the US believes that in the long term, Beijing will challenge its predominance in the Asia-Pacific region. The US knows very well that in the post-cold war era, China's reemergence as a superpower means that it is the only power in the Asia-Pacific region which has the potential to challenge the US' dominant leadership.

Two main hypotheses presented by the threat proponents are worth considering. The first hypothesis is the argument that growing economic power will lead to militarism. The weakness of this argument is that the threat proponents assume that there is a casual relationship between economic power and militarism. Such an argument tends to be deterministic, unilinear and simplistic. The rising of China's power argument is a 'catch 22' phrase because it may or may not lead to militarism. A rising hegemon may not necessarily threaten the regional order. In fact, a hegemon may provide a stable regional order rather than destabilising the region. The US is a good example of a benign hegemon which has brought stability to the East-Asian region. So far, there is not enough historical evidence to substantiate the thesis that a modern powerful China will lead to the emergence of an aggressive hegemon which can pose a serious threat to others. China's support of the communist insurgencies in Southeast Asia was more a function to counter the US threat rather than to promote such threats in Southeast Asia. No one can predict with certainty how China will behave in the international relations in the Asia-Pacific region in the 21st century.

A short-term analysis of China's strategic thinking and security policy would tend to show that China is neither a hegemon nor a threat to the Asia-Pacific region. At most, China's rising power may pose certain problems due to the size of its huge population, which is the largest in the world, as well as its inherent problems.

If one defines hegemonism as an act of expansionism on a regional or a global scale, then by this definition, China does not qualify as a hegemon because the 'threat' proponents cannot point to any historical precedent since the 15th century which could highlight hegemonistic tendencies on the part of China. One important motivation of a hegemon is the intention to dominate others, such as, for example to occupy other states' territories by force. Although the PLA has from time to time used force as was the case during the Korean, the Sino-Indian, and the Sino-Vietnamese wars, these armed conflicts were never motivated by an act of imperialism and the intention to occupy other states' territories. The thesis of the 'China threat' proponents underlines the assumption that China is a rising 'Ba-Chun' (hegemon). From the Chinese perspective, a 'Ba-Chun' is a big bully who is using its superior physical power against the will of its adversary. Hence, hegemonism connotes an element of injustice and is morally unacceptable and therefore should be resisted or condemned. If China is going to behave like a big bully, how will it justify its behaviour when it condemns the idea of 'Ba-Chun'?

The second hypothesis of the threat proponents' argument that China is a threat because of its authoritarian political system, is problematic. The underlying assumption of this argument is that a democratic political system has a better chance to promote a peaceful foreign policy rather than an authoritarian political system like China. But there seems to be no causal relationship between threats and the nature of political systems. Britain and France were two great democracies in the 19th century, and yet, the threat to the European order was the result of competition to seek colonies and promote spheres of influence between major European powers, including both Britain and France. Furthermore, the threat proponents argue that there is a correlation between frustration, dissatisfaction and threats. It is difficult to accept the argument that a dissatisfied frustrated China will behave aggressively and threaten others. One of the foreign policy objectives of China since 1949 was and is to ensure that it will not be humiliated again by the stronger major powers as was the case in the

19th century. Thus, China's growing assertive role in world politics does not necessarily need to lead to the conclusion that it will bring about the destruction of regional order.

Though some of the threat proponents' arguments may not appear convincing, nevertheless both the threat proponents and the 'non-threat' proponents have their valid points of arguments, in the sense that the former stress more on the long-term threats by China, whereas the latter emphasise China's short-term foreign policy priorities. The writer tends to veer closer to the non-threat school of thought, as China is not posing a real threat to the Asia-Pacific region in the short-term because the Chinese are pragmatists whose utmost priority is to promote internal economic development. Robert S. Ross has a valid point in arguing that China behaves like a conservative rather than an aggressive power.[23] I would argue that the so-called 'China threat' is more apparent than real because China does not want to jeopardise its amicable relationship with its neighbours. A stable and secure regional environment is vital for China's modernisation programme. Moreover, the US factor is still a potent force and China must take into consideration potential losses of its fruits of modernisation and its military capabilities. The US has stated unambiguously that it would never want to allow a rising Chinese hegemon, challenging its strategic interests in the Asia-Pacific region, as for example in the South China Sea which straddles strategically important sea-lanes and is crucial to both the US' and Japan's life-lines. Thus, the South China Sea will remain as 'American lake' rather than a 'Chinese lake' well into the 21st century.[24] In any case, for China's modernisation to succeed, it has to depend to some extent on both the US and Japan for trade, investment, capital and technology. There is no reason for Beijing to strain any further the US-China relations which have been plagued by irritants such as the human rights, arms supply and the trade issues.

[23]Robert S. Ross, 'Beijing As a Conservative Power', *Foreign Affairs*, Vol. 76, No. 2, March/April 1997, pp. 33–44.
[24]Robert S. Ross, *op. cit.*, p. 38.

TOWARDS A 'POSITIVE CS' PARADIGM TO UNDERSTAND CHINA'S BEHAVIOUR

The thesis of the 'China threat' is based on the misconception and misunderstandings from the perspective of a combination of either ideological bias, cultural arrogance, historical distortion, racial prejudice (the 'yellow peril') or self-fulfilling prophecy. Thus the concepts of the 'negative Cs', such as confrontation, contradiction, conflict, containment, circlement, 'constraintment',[25] clash of civilisation, conspiracy, etc. commonly appear in the literature of international relations on China. The frequency with which these 'negative Cs' appear in Western scholarly journals of international relations is clearly a sign of how popular it is now, especially in the West, in the post-cold war era after the collapse of the Soviet Union to depict China as the number one threat or potential threat to the international order in the Asia-Pacific region. Thus, China misperceives that there is a long-term 'conspiracy' on the part of the West to undermine its political system, especially the legitimacy of the political leadership of the Communist Party of China to rule the country.

As an alternative to the 'China threat' proponent's paradigm, I propose a 'positive Cs' paradigm can be useful in understanding the inter-state interactions, especially as far as the thinking and perception of China's external behaviour in the post-cold war era is concerned. These 'positive Cs' concept such as the Javanese concept of 'Musyawarah' (consultation), 'Mufakat' (consensus), compromise, coordination, cooperation, communitarianism, and coexistence, can be useful concepts to serve as the basis of an Asian approach in studying China's rising power in the Asia-Pacific region. A multi-lateral security mechanism such as the ASEAN Regional Forum can be a very useful security mechanism for engaging China through constructive and cooperative security dialogues[26] so that

[25]For the concept of 'constrainment', see Gerald Segal, *op. cit.*, pp. 107–135. See also David Shambaugh, *op. cit.*, p. 185.

[26]For the conceptual discussion of 'cooperative security', see Craig A. Synder, 'Multilateral Security in the South China Sea', *Asian Perspective*, Vol. 21, No. 1, Spring/Summer 1997.

misperceptions and misunderstandings of each others' intentions can be avoided.

The ASEAN style of diplomacy based on consultation, compromise and reaching consensus, for example, has proven to be an important Asian way of efforts to resolve conflicts through preventive diplomacy, confidence-building and conflict resolution. If China can be absorbed through a multilateral cooperative security arrangement, such as the ARF, then by means of contacts, dialogues and consultations, the misconception of the 'China threat' can be removed. Hence a common, comprehensive and cooperative ASEAN security arrangement among the disputing states is not an impossible task to be achieved, although sovereignty disputes in the South China Sea appear to be unresolvable in the foreseeable future.

Adopting the 'positive Cs paradigm' is better than the 'negative Cs paradigm' in minimising misunderstandings in inter-state relations because the former is based on a win-win premise whereas the latter is based on a zero-sum game. The intellectual foundation of the realists' thesis of the 'China threat' theory is primarily based on the western notion of a classical concept of 'power' since the Westphalia Treaty of 1648. Since then, the historical experience of power-politics in Europe is based on the concept of power which is zero-sum. But the concept of 'power' alone as an intellectual tool in explaining international relations is not satisfactory as it mainly explains the conflict dimensions of inter-state relations. The argument of the 'China threat' which is based on the assumption that China is a rising 'power' is not an adequate variable in explaining the way how and why China behaves in international politics since the birth of the PRC in October, 1949. If one takes the historical perspective, one can argue that since 1840, China has felt that the international order was unjust and humiliating as it was denied its 'place in the sun'.[27] China therefore was determined to restore its rightful place in the international order. China is an old society with an ancient civilisation deeply rooted in Confucianism which is based on the philosophy of harmony. Furthermore, historical

[27]See, B. Emmott, K. Watanabe, and P. Wolfwitz, *Managing the International System Over the Next Ten Years* (New York: The Trilateral Commission, 1997), p. 48.

records show that even though China was a supreme maritime power during the Ming dynasty (15th century) it did not behave aggressively towards its neighbouring states, which would give reason for guarded optimism that China is not likely to be a threat to the Asia-Pacific region. What China wants in contemporary international relations since 1949 is to be treated with respect and equality. Thus it is unwise to overemphasize the 'China threat' issue unduly. The most urgent task is to engage China constructively in the Asia-Pacific region, and not to adopt a policy of soft containment or constraint towards China. Constructively engaging China, for example, by the ASEAN regional grouping through the ARF would not only help to clarify China's intention towards the Asia-Pacific region but certainly in the long term, it would contribute to create a more predictable and stable regional order in the Asia-Pacific region as a whole. Such a stance would especially help in the foreseeable future to minimise the flashpoints in the South China Sea between China and other disputants.

Power Shift in Post-1997 Hong Kong

Friedrich WU*
Chief Economist
Development Bank of Singapore

Beijing's resumption of Chinese sovereignty over Hong Kong on July 1, 1997 will bring a wave of changes to the territory in both the political and business arenas. While the China-Hong Kong relationship is supposed to be governed by the "one country, two systems" principle as enshrined in the Basic Law (the mini-constitution for post-1997 Hong Kong), the new sovereign's dominance over the territory's affairs is bound to spread. Under the former colonial system, the British governor, together with his appointed Executive Council and only partially elected Legislative Council, represented the authoritative final decision-makers on local matters with

*A former Hong Kong resident, the author is chief economist for the Development Bank of Singapore, the island-republic's largest financial institution. He received his PhD from the University of Washington with a dissertation on the political economy of China's "open-door" policy. His publications on China and Hong Kong have appeared in *Asian Wall Street Journal*, *China Business Review*, *Columbia Journal of World Business*, *Far Eastern Economic Review*, *Journal of Asian Business*, *JETRO China Newsletter*, *Modern China*, *The World Economy*, among others. Views in this article represent his personal opinions only.

little interference from London. Drawn almost exclusively from the territory's business and professional elite, these councillors shared homogenous views on public policies. In the post-1997 era, however, the autonomy of the Hong Kong Special Administrative Region (HKSAR) government is likely to be more circumscribed by the continuous presence of, and the rise of new, influential players with intimate connections to powerful institutions in China.

NEW CHINA (XINHUA) NEWS AGENCY

Hitherto, the Xinhua News Agency Hong Kong Branch has remained the umbrella organisation for the Chinese Communist Party (CCP) to conduct and coordinate its political activities in Hong Kong [Exhibit 1]. Since the mid-1950s, the branch's principal role has been to act as a "smokescreen" for the Hong Kong & Macau Work Committee (HKMWC) of the CCP — an underground body whose existence was nonetheless known to, and tacitly accepted by, the former colonial government [Exhibit 2]. In the early years, the body was mainly charged with championing CCP doctrines and ideas, spreading propaganda and gathering support from overseas Chinese in Southeast Asia. However, with the 1997 issue coming to the surface in the early 1980s, the HKMWC was upgraded to provincial-level status in 1982 as part of Beijing's strategy to restructure and empower its institutions for handling Hong Kong affairs, including Xinhua and its nominal superior, the Hong Kong & Macau Affairs Office of the State Council. In subsequent years, the branch had assumed a high profile in the 1997 transitional matters, as seen in its role in the appointment of Hong Kong Affairs Advisers for Beijing as well as its aggressive stance in dealing with the territory's democrats. Today, with its director serving concurrently as the secretary-general of the HKMWC, the branch is openly recognised as China's "de facto embassy" in Hong Kong.

With an estimated local membership of over 30,000, the extent of the CCP's influence in the territory is far deeper than it seems on the surface. The HKMWC, with its vast network of direct and indirect affiliations

Exhibit 1
Organisation Structure of
Xinhua News Agency Hong Kong Branch

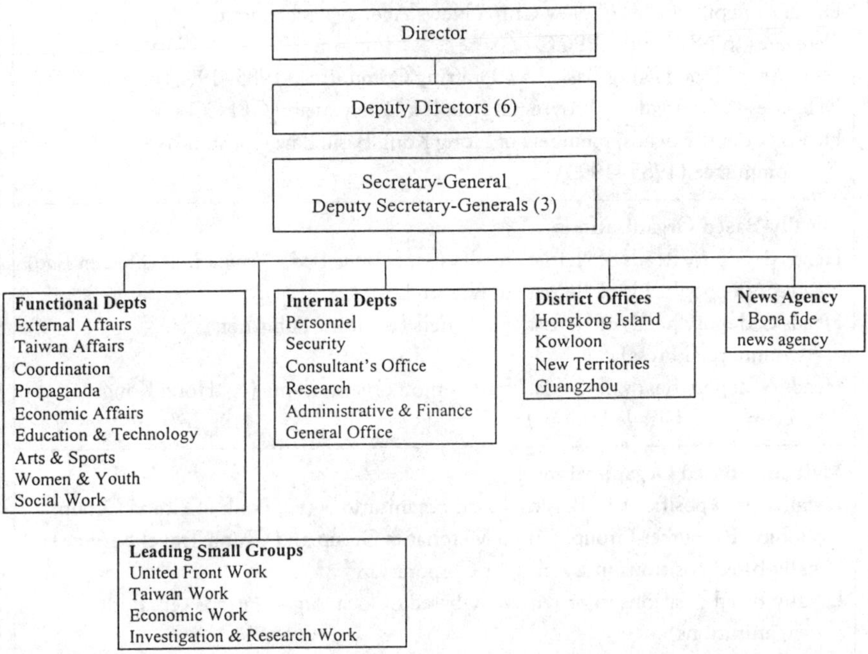

Source: Compiled from various Hong Kong and Taiwan newspapers.

Exhibit 2
The Hong Kong & Macau Work Committee
(Hong Kong Portion)

Party/State and Legislative Positions
Heads & deputy heads of New China News Agency departments
Delegates to NPC and CPPCC
Members of Hong Kong Basic Law Drafting Committee (1985–1990)
Delegates to Guangdong Provincial People's Congress and CPPCC
Heads & deputy heads, members of Hong Kong Basic Law Consultative Committee (1985–1990)

Locally-Based Organisations
Heads & deputy heads of "leftist" media (eg, *Dagong Bao*, *Wenhui Bao*, *Xinwan Bao*)
Heads & deputy heads of "leftist" movie studios
Heads & deputy heads of "leftist" publishers (eg, Joint Publishers, Commercial Press)
Heads & deputy heads of "leftist" trade union organisations (eg, Hong Kong Federation of Trade Unions)

Mainland-Based Organisations
Locally-hired positions in Beijing-based organisations (eg, Bank of China Group, China Resources Group, China Merchants Group and China Travel Service)
Locally-hired positions in Everbright Corporation
Locally-hired positions in provincially-based or local organisations (eg, trade organisations)

Source: John Burns, "The Structure of Communist Party Control in Hong Kong," *Asian Survey*, 30 (August 1990), p. 760.

with mainland-based economic entities (such as the Bank of China Group and the Hong Kong subsidiaries of the China Merchants Group, China Resources Group and China Travel Service), is believed to have stepped up its presence in recent years in preparation for the July 1997 transfer of sovereignty. Besides the news agency itself, the HKMWC has also gained control of a network of Hong Kong propaganda agencies, including "leftist" media, movie studios, publishing companies and trade unions, and has the power to "hire and fire" as well as influence business decisions in the Hong Kong offices of various mainland Chinese enterprises and financial institutions. These include the Bank of China Hong Kong Branch, China Resources Corp, China Merchants Group and China Travel Service — all of which have their heads serving as ordinary members of the HKMWC. In particular, the Bank of China Group, which collects nearly 30 percent of the territory's total deposits and is one of the three currency-issuing institutions (the other two being Hong Kong Bank and Standard Chartered Bank), falls directly under the joint supervision of Xinhua's Economic Department and the bank's Hong Kong & Macau Management Division (HKMMD). The head of HKMMD also serves as a member of the HKMWC's Standing Committee. In addition, the HKMWC is believed to play a partial role in the management of other China-linked corporations and watches over the hiring of employees in Hong Kong.

The sovereignty change on July 1, 1997 has given rise to confusions and fears over the post-1997 status of Xinhua in Hong Kong. At the present stage, Beijing still seems undecided on what role the branch and its 600 staff should play in the future. While there have been mixed signals from Beijing that it may want to downgrade the role of Xinhua, no concrete action has been taken as of todate.

Needless to say, a continuous high-profile Xinhua presence after 1997 would most likely be perceived as a rival political base set up by some conservative factions in Beijing to "spy" on the HKSAR government. It is feared that, in performing this "political-commissar" role, Xinhua may even interfere in local policy-making by attempting to "supervise" the HKSAR administration in the future. This likelihood is underpinned by the fact that the HKMWC is a provincial-level party committee and such committees in China have executive powers over provincial governments, including the right to make personnel changes. Accordingly, while a governor or mayor formally ranks as the head of a province or municipality, he is not the real boss — the party secretary, who is normally a member of the CCP Central Committee, is. The latter, along with his party committee, is empowered to "supervise" the workings of government bureaucrats by setting up various functional departments to oversee the corresponding government departments. Given the primacy of the CCP over the Chinese government, therefore, the HKMWC could in theory be given the mandate to "supervise" the HKSAR government in the future as none of the latter's senior officials is a CCP member. Consequently, unless its role is pared down considerably after the transition, a power-sharing arrangement could eventually erode the authority and autonomy of the HKSAR government.

MINISTRY OF FOREIGN AFFAIRS

Likewise, the post-1997 era could witness the emergence of the Ministry of Foreign Affairs (MFA) as yet another political heavyweight in the territory's power equation. In operation after July 1, 1997, the Hong Kong office of the MFA has a staff of around 400. While the establishment of the MFA office in Hong Kong is guaranteed by the Basic Law, many are still perplexed about its exact role. According to the Basic Law, the office would be solely responsible for the territory's "foreign affairs" — a domain out of the jurisdiction of the HKSAR government. This rather nebulous definition has aroused anxieties among HKSAR officials as well as the international diplomatic community, since the term could possibly cover a vast range of areas such as vetting visa applications, handling visits of foreign diplomats/dignitaries, processing the migration of Hong Kong citizens, dealing with international organisations on sensitive political issues such as human rights in Hong Kong, and so on. Also at issue is whether the MFA would have the power to intervene in contacts between HKSAR officials and foreign envoys/representatives stationed in the territory. In that eventuality, this could adversely affect the HKSAR's external relations when conflicts erupt between China and other countries. With the head of the MFA office in Hong Kong — Commissioner Ma Yuzhen (former Chinese Ambassador to London) — holding vice-ministerial rank, he should command substantial political clout in the territory. It remains to be seen whether this new institution would work to facilitate or impede the territory's myriad international linkages.

People's Liberation Army (PLA)

Another new player coming into the limelight in the near future will be the PLA. Although the 10,000-strong Hong Kong garrison is barred from directly engaging in commercial activities, the PLA high command in the mainland has nevertheless built up a thriving business empire there with a labyrinthine network of some 30,000 companies employing over one million workers operating in such lucrative and "civilian" sectors including telecommunications, real estate, health care and tourism [Exhibit 3]. Such commercial ventures have generated massive financial gains for the Chinese armed forces with estimated revenues reaching around US$4.0 billion in 1993 [Exhibit 4]. Bolstered by its commercial success domestically as well as its desire to earn foreign exchange and acquire technology, PLA Inc. has begun to push into overseas markets including Hong Kong. Powerful military conglomerates such as the Poly Group, China Carrie Group and 999 Enterprise Group have led the way in globalising their business operations by forging close links with leading civilian corporations which have enabled them to "hide" their army affiliations while doing business abroad. For example, both the Poly Group and CITIC (China's most diversified and powerful conglomerate) are chaired by Wang Jun (son of the late Vice President Wang Zhen), and the two corporations have joint interests in two Hong Kong-listed firms, namely Continental Mariner Investments and Poly Investments Holdings. In addition, Poly has an 8 percent stake in SHK Industries, the industrial investment arm of Hong Kong's property giant Sun Hung Kai & Co. Besides the Poly Group, the China Carrie Group is the other military-owned conglomerate (owned by

Exhibit 3
PLA INC: Chain of Command

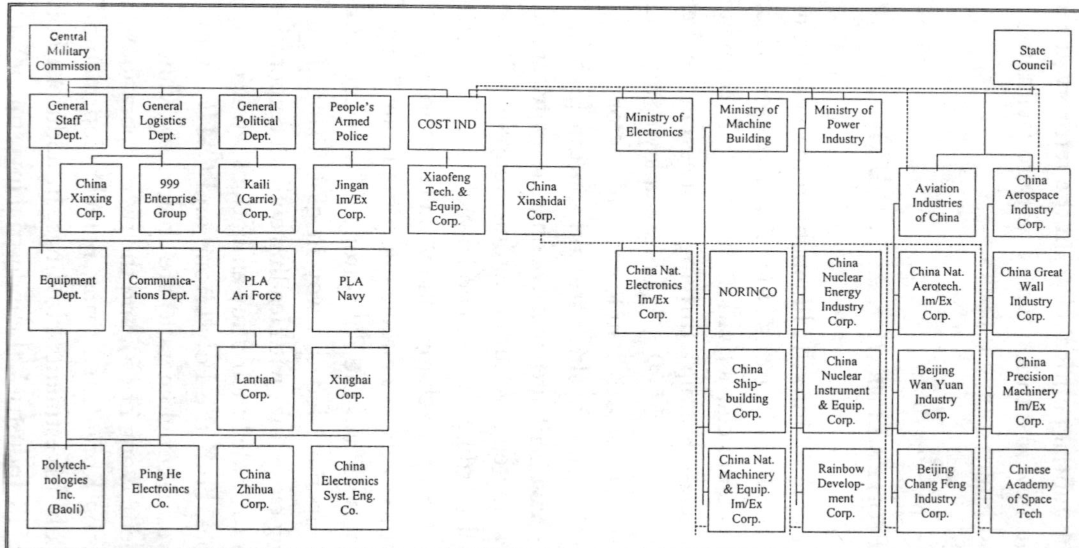

Direct Control ——— Guidance and Coordination --------

Note: China Aerospace Industry Corporation is also known as the State Aerospace Bureau.
COST IND stands for Committee for Science, Technology & Industry for National Defense.

Source: Thomas J Bickford "The Chinese Military and its Business Operations", *Asian Survey*, 34 (May 1994) p. 465.

Exhibit 4
Sectoral Breakdown of PLA Commercial Revenues, 1993*

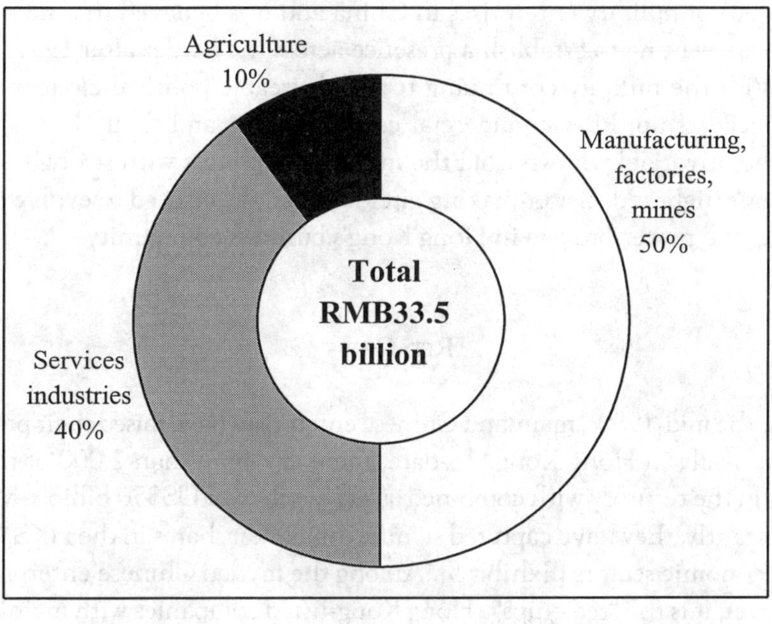

*latest available

Source: *Institutional Investor* (July 1996).

the PLA's General Political Department) presently with a Hong Kong-listed vehicle, namely Hong Kong Macau Holdings. It is a small property and mineral mining firm with real estate ventures in the neighboring Shenzhen Special Economic Zone and Guangdong province. Such back-door acquisitions of small dormant firms in Hong Kong by PLA enterprises could become a norm after 1997. Indeed, the change in sovereignty could bring about a new influx of PLA-backed companies to Hong Kong. Guangdong province already boasts the highest concentration (estimated at 5,000) of military enterprises in China and it is believed that many of these are waiting to establish a presence across the border after 1997.

With the military continuing to wield sizeable political clout in the CCP leadership, PLA commercial establishments and their "bosses" — who are invariably drawn from the military's top brass with strong ties to Beijing's highest decision-making circles — are anticipated to evolve into influential power-brokers in Hong Kong's business community.

RED CHIPS

Since the mid-1980s, mainland Chinese enterprises have raised their profile dramatically in Hong Kong. To-date, there are more than 2,000 of these firms in the territory with combined assets worth over US$50 billion. More importantly, they have captured significant market shares in the HKSAR's key economic sectors [Exhibit 5]. Among the myriad Chinese enterprises, however, it is the "red chips" (Hong Kong-listed companies with mainland parents) that are set to emerge as the next batch of Hong Kong's corporate giants after 1997. Because of their powerful connections to high offices in Beijing, the July 1997 changeover will boost the status of "red-chip" companies in Hong Kong to unprecedented heights. For example, "red-chip" parents under the direct control of the State Council include CITIC, China Everbright Group, China Non-ferrous Metals Industry Corporation (CNNC), and China Travel Service. Most other "red chips" are linked to some ministries as in the case of the China National Cereals, Oils & Foodstuffs Import & Export Corp (COFCO) and China Resources Group, which are both under the Ministry of Foreign Trade & Economic Cooperation (MOFTEC). The COSCO Group and China Merchants Group are linked to the Ministry of Communications, while others are linked to powerful provincial governments. Examples of the latter include the Guangdong Provincial Government's "window" company Guangdong Enterprises in Hong Kong, the Guangzhou Municipal Government's Yue Xiu Enterprises and the Shanghai Municipal Government's overseas investment arm Shanghai Industrial Investment (Holdings) [Exhibit 6].

Given their powerful connections, which would be an indispensable tool for doing business in Hong Kong after 1997, prominent "red-chip" companies are poised to increase their penetration into the "strategic" sectors of the Hong Kong economy, such as in telecommunications, airlines, property, banking and utilities. While the combined market capitalisation of "red-chip" companies on the Hong Kong stock exchange is currently at about 15 percent of the total, one can expect this ratio to rise in view of the long "queue" of China-affiliated listing candidates waiting to join the ranks of the big players. Furthermore, it is believed that around 300 more mainland Chinese companies are looking to tap into the territory's stock market in the longer run. Meanwhile, many other "red-chip" parents have announced plans to inject assets into their Hong Kong subsidiaries to boost their market capitalisation. These include the China Everbright Group, China Merchants Group, COSCO, China Resources and Guangdong Enterprises, and so on [Exhibit 7]. As this trend is certainly to continue, "red-chip" companies will eventually emerge as the new "movers and shakers" of the Hong Kong stock market, and be able to tip the territory's business playing field in their favour. In that eventuality, the real concern is whether the takeover of Hong Kong Inc. by China Inc. would leave the territory's highly transparent framework of doing business still intact. The highly publicised convictions of senior executives of Hong Kong-listed Shougang Holdings and China Everbright Technology for bribery and corruption in 1995 and 1996 respectively do not inspire confidence that "red-chip" companies would abide by the territory's existing rules of doing business, which have been based on Western paradigms.

Exhibit 5
Estimated Market Shares of Chinese Enterprises in Hong Kong's Economic Sectors

TOTAL NUMBER OF ENTERPRISES	**>2,000**
TOTAL ASSETS	**>US$50 billion**
TOTAL INVESTMENTS	**US$30 billion**
China-related travel & tourist services	>60%
Property transactions	25–30%
Cargo transportation & handling	>25%
Banking (deposits)	28–30%
Insurance (premium income)	>20%
Construction contracts	>15%
Imports & exports	>25%
List companies (market capitalisation)	15%

Sources: Various Hong Kong newspapers and trade magazines.

Exhibit 6
Major Hong Kong Red Chips and Their Mainland Parents

Parent Companies	Hong Kong-Listed Red Chip(s)
China Everbright Holdings — Under State Council	China Everbright IHD-Pacific China Everbright International China Everbright Technology
CITIC — Under State Council	CITIC Pacific Continental Mariner Poly Investments
China Merchants — Under Ministry of Communications	China Merchants Hai Hong
COFCO — Under Ministry of Foreign Trade & Economic Cooperation (Moftec)	Top Glory China Foods
China Non-Ferrous Metals Holdings (HK) — Under State Council	Silver Grant Onfem Holdings Oriental Metals
COSCO (HK) Group — Under Ministry of Communications	COSCO Pacific Shun Shing Holdings
China Resources (Holdings) — Under Ministry of Foreign Trade & Economic Cooperation (Moftec)	China Resources Enterprises Ng Fung Hong China Resources Beijing Land
China Travel Service (Holdings) Hong Kong — Under Overseas Chinese Affairs Office	China Travel International Investment
Guangdong Enterprises — Under Guangdong Municipal Government	Guangdong Investment Guangnan Holdings Guangdong Tannery
Shanghai Industrial Investment (Holdings) — Under Shanghai Municipal Government	Shanghai Industrial Holdings
Yue Xiu Enterprises (Holdings) — Under Guangzhou Municipal Government	Guangzhou Investment GZI Transport Denway Investment

Source: Credit Lyonnais Securities Asia (March 1997).

Exhibit 7
Recent Asset Injections by Red Chip Parents

Parent Company	Date
China Everbright Holdings	
National Mutual Asia (5%) to China Everbright IHD-Pacific	23 Jan 97
International Bank of Asia (20%) to China Everbright IHD-Pacific	23 Jan 97
Everbright Timber (55%) to China Everbright International	3 Feb 97
CITIC	
Inner Mongolia power plant (48%) joint investment with CITIC Pacific	10 Oct 96
CNNC (HK)	
Magnetic materials manufacturer (33%) to Onfem Holdings	7 Jan 96
COSCO (HK)	
Container-related services company to COSCO Pacific	3 Dec 96
China Resources (Holdings)	
HIT (10%) to China Resources Enterprises	3 Dec 96
Ice cream business (51%) to Ng Fung Hong	16 Dec 96
CRC supermarkets (60%) to Ng Fung Hong	16 Dec 96
Lishui refrigerated foods (28%) to Ng Fung Hong	16 Dec 96
China Travel Hong Kong	
Shenzhen World Miniature Park (51%) to China Travel Int Inv	Jan 96
Metropole Hotel to China Travel Int Inv	9 Sept 96
Wiehe Power Station (51%) joint investment with China Travel Int Inv	25 Sept 96
Tianjin section of Beijing-Shanghai expressway (31%) joint investment with China Travel Int Inv	14 Feb 97
Guangdong Enterprises	
Hengchang feed mill (30%) to Guangnan	27 Mar 96
Seaweed (51%) and canned foods (30%) businesses to Guangnan	Aug 96
Guangdong Mountain Building to Guangdong Investment	7 Sept 96
New World-Guangdong Highway (50%) to Guangdong Investment	7 Sept 96
Shanghai Industrial Investment	
Huizhong Auto (50%) to Shanghai Industrial Holdings	25 Nov 96
Yanan Elevated Road (W) (50.2%) to Shanghai Industrial Holdings	25 Nov 96
Shanghai Transport Electric (30%) to Shanghai Industrial Holdings	25 Nov 96
Shanghai Bright Dairy (50%) to Shanghai Industrial Holdings	25 Nov 96
Orient Shopping Centre (51%) to Shanghai Industrial Holdings	25 Nov 96
Yue Xiu Enterprises	
Xin Feng toll roads (55%) to Guangzhou Investment	Apr 96
Injection of roads as part of GZI Transport listing	30 Jan 97
Hotels to Guangzhou Invesment	28 Feb 97

Source: Credit Lyonnais Securities Asia (March 1997).

Conclusion

In short, despite the Basic Law's guarantee of "one country, two systems" for Hong Kong's post-1997 status, the emergence of several mainland-connected powerful institutions could significantly alter the territory's commercial and political landscapes. As these new actors espouse different agendas, some of which could be in direct conflict with the policies of the HKSAR government, the latter would need the firmest support from Beijing to assert its authority and preserve its autonomy. In view of the strong sectoral interests behind these new power centres, it would be an uphill struggle in the years ahead.